✠ ✠ ✠

ENGLISH THEN & NOW

READINGS AND EXERCISES

ENGLISH
THEN & NOW

READINGS
AND EXERCISES

Alan M. Markman
University of Pittsburgh

Erwin R. Steinberg
Carnegie-Mellon University

Random House   New York

For Laurel

and Bev

PREFACE

One of the conspicuous failures of American education has been in teaching the average student, or even the better than average, something about his own language. There are many reasons for this. For many of our students, the native language tradition is but a thin surface coating, going back no more than one or two generations at most. The way in which the English language has traditionally been presented emphasizes a superficial correctness rather than an understanding of the way in which language functions as a medium of communication and of its role in a society like ours. Our reluctance to spend enough time in the study of even one foreign language really to master it has carried over to the study of the native tongue. For the vast majority of our pupils, and even their teachers, Browning's grammarian would seem to have given his life over to the exploration of the inconsequential. It is language study rather than political economy which they would characterize as the dismal science.

Part of the difficulty, though not all, lies with the way in which the subject has been presented. Here we have made a number of pedagogical blunders. We have talked *about* the language far too much and have failed to encourage the student to examine it for himself and to learn from this examination. We have tended to overlook the intimate connection between a language and the culture of the people who speak it, presenting it instead as a hermetically sealed mechanism. We have focused attention upon detail rather than upon an underlying system and rationale.

It is these defects in presentation which the authors of this volume have sought to overcome. First of all, they have given us an anthology rather than an attempt to cover the subject in their own words, and it is fair to ask what advantages they derive from doing so. The answer is clear. As the etymology of the word implies, an anthology can be a selection of the best. The word comes from the Greek roots for "to gather" and "flowers." Not every plant has blooms of equal beauty, but it may have one which is superb. Not every book on language has chapters of equal relevance to the current state of English, but it may have one which, though written years ago, is wholly modern in its tone and germane to the overall purpose of this volume. The authors have chosen wisely. Essays such as those by Sapir on drift and by John Livingston Lowes on the art of Geoffrey Chaucer have become classics of linguistic and literary scholarship.

Another important consideration is that of range. Not only is the period from Old to Modern English included within the limits of this anthology, but the ancestry and the future of the language are dealt with as well. All of this is presented in the light of an initial chapter which considers the function of language and the various ways in which it has been and is now studied. This gives the student a sense of proportion and extent, which he cannot always derive from the somewhat more circumscribed conventional approach, in terms of merely Old, Middle, and Modern English.

The intimate connection between language and the cultural heritage of its speakers has already been alluded to. In the sections devoted to the successive stages in the development of English, attention is given not merely to the state of the language at that time but to its use by one or two outstanding individuals, to the intellectual currents of the era, and to the prevailing points of view about the English language. All of these are essential ingredients of the discipline of language study considered in its most humane terms. In recent years we have often dwelt too much upon the mechanics and technology of linguistic study at the expense of these broader aspects—the art and philosophy as well as the science.

Anyone who has taught a foreign language or who has learned one knows that mastery is achieved not through talking about it but through practice and experience in its use. Skill comes as a result of manipulation. The same principle applies to the historical study of language. It is not enough to speak in abstract terms about the state of the noun declensions or verb conjugations, of the sound system or the word-order patterns of tenth or twelfth or sixteenth-century English. Such abstractions can be forgotten in a fortnight. But the student who has painstakingly analyzed an Old English homily or a Middle English lyric, to the point of creating for himself an aural image, who has struggled with its possible ambiguities in structure, who has considered its vocabulary from the point of view of the resources available to the author, comes away from such an exercise not merely with a keen sense of the linguistic components of the one selection he has worked with, but with an approach which will continue to serve him at other times and on other occasions when a sensitivity to language and a skill in its analysis is called for. Thus, part of the language-teaching process must consist in carefully devising opportunities of every kind for discovery procedures. These principles apply not merely to the mastery of one or another stage in the development of English but to the formulation of broad ideas about language structure and development as well.

In the exercises which conclude this volume, the authors have made every effort to provide the kind of inductive experience essential to a firm, soundly based understanding of the development of the English language and to a judicious assessment of its present state. Devised with remarkable skill, these exercises avoid the dangers of confusion because of massed heterogeneous detail on the one hand, and easy generalization based upon insufficient evidence on the other. It is here that their long and successful experience as teachers of contemporary English and of its forerunners shows to remarkable advantage. Pedagogically resourceful and theoretically sound, this book provides an engaging adventure not only in learning the English language in its successive stages, but in acquiring a firm grasp of the nature of language itself.

Albert H. Marckwardt
Princeton University

ACKNOWLEDGMENTS

In preparing a book, authors invariably incur debts which they must acknowledge. Our earliest debt is probably to our students, from whom we learned the need for such a book as this and with whom we first tried many of the materials included here.

As this book took shape, Albert H. Marckwardt and Edmond L. Volpe were generous with suggestions for improvement. We must affirm, however, that final responsibility for what appears in the following pages is ours and not theirs.

The physical preparation of the manuscript and the obtaining of permissions rested heavily with Lee Martin, who performed calmly and capably amidst frequent chaos. At the end, Virginia Schenck provided similar competent assistance.

A.M.M.
E.R.S.

CONTENTS

PART ONE

LANGUAGE
AND LANGUAGE STUDY

✠

INTRODUCTION

"Language," says the *Encyclopaedia Britannica,* "is a system of conventional spoken or written symbols by means of which human beings, members of a social group and participants in its culture, communicate." A very succinct definition. It is probably too succinct for the nonspecialist, however. For as the *Britannica* goes on to warn, "Each term in this definition should be examined."

Some of that examination from the *Britannica* is provided in the opening selection in this section. The passage on language from the *Oxford English Dictionary*, which follows it, provides the derivation of the word, its meanings, and examples of its use from Middle English to the end of the nineteenth century. These two selections, read together, demonstrate many of the principles and raise many of the problems discussed more fully in later sections.

The next selection, from Bloomfield and Newmark, opens with an extended definition of language which supplements the one from the *Britannica,* and then goes on to examine in some detail various important aspects of language—such matters as the arbitrariness of language, the relation of language to thought, the relation of oral to written language, the emotional and ritualistic aspects of language, and the relation of language to race. The concluding paragraphs, which explain why one should study the history of a language, function as a bridge to the Waterman selections that follow.

Since most of what appears in later sections of this book is by modern students of language, it seemed useful to give the reader some idea of what its study was like in earlier times. The two selections by Waterman serve that purpose by providing a summary of recorded language study through the eighteenth century.

This section, then, presents the nature of language and raises some of the problems one meets in the study of language. It is a beginning.

✠ ✠ ✠

LANGUAGE

ENCYCLOPAEDIA BRITANNICA

1. 11TH ED. (1911) VOL. XVI, 179.

LANGUAGE (adopted from the Fr. *langage*, from *langue*, tongue, Lat. *lingua*), the whole body of words and combinations of words as used in common by a nation, people, or race, for the purpose of expressing or communicating their thoughts; also, more widely, the power of expressing thought by verbal utterance. See generally under PHILOLOGY, PHONETICS, VOICE, WRITING, GRAMMAR, &c.; and the articles on the various languages, or under headings of countries and races.

2. 1965 PRINTING. VOL. 13, 697–704.

(Half a century after the 11th Ed. of 1911, in an article signed by George L. Trager and Joshua Whatmough, the statement runs through thirteen columns. Here just the first three paragraphs are reproduced, with an outline of the remaining parts of the article. The whole of it is very much worth reading.)

LANGUAGE is a system of conventional spoken or written symbols by means of which human beings, members of a social group and participants in its culture, communicate.

Each term in this definition should be examined. By "conventional" is meant that there is no necessary relation between any linguistic item and what it symbolizes. In English a certain animal is called "horse," in French *cheval*, in Russian *loshad'*, and no one of these words is more adequate or appropriate than any other to the reality of the animal. Even onomatapoetic words turn out to be in part conventional, since they are always made up of ordinary sounds of the language. The English verb "purr" and the French *ronronner* can both be said to imitate the sound a cat makes, but note how different they are. It is apparent that language is a "system." A baby babbles unsystematically, but when it learns to talk only certain of the possible noises are used, and they are arranged in orderly ways. "Spoken" means that it is specifically speech which is being defined. Other communication systems exist, and will be mentioned below. Writing is a systematic, conventional system dependent on speech. "Symbols" are tokens of things, rather than the things themselves. The word "book" is not a book, and the word "democracy" refers to a system of behaviour that requires many pages to describe. Human beings live in social groups and learn and participate in the behaviour patterns of their societies and cultures. The behaviour consists of interaction of human beings with their environment, which includes language. The interaction is largely involved with the communication of information from one individual to another.

The science of linguistics (*q.v.*) is the systematic study of language, as distinct from the study of languages for the purpose of being able to speak, read, and write them.

The rest of this article has this outline:
LANGUAGE IN CULTURE
Cultural Systems
Communication
Origin of Language
THE STRUCTURE OF LANGUAGE
Words and Grammatical Forms
Sounds
Text
Meaning
Language Typology
Linguistic Analysis
HISTORICAL DEVELOPMENT OF LANGUAGES
Principal Language Families

☩ ☩ ☩

LANGUAGE

OXFORD ENGLISH DICTIONARY

Language (lǽ·ŋgwèdʒ), *sb.*[1] Forms: 3–6 langage, (3 langag, 4 longage, langwag, 5 langwache, langegage), 3, 5– language. [a. F. *langage* (recorded from 12th c.) = Pr. *leng(u)atge, lengage,* Sp. *lenguaje,* Pg. *linguage (m,* It.) *linguaggio* :—pop. L. type **linguāticum,* f. *lingua* tongue, language (F. *langue*: see LANGUE).

The form with *u,* due to assimilation with the F. *langue,* occurs in AF. writings of the 12th c., and in Eng. from about 1300.]

1. The whole body of words and of methods of combination of words used by a nation, people, or race; a 'tongue'. *Dead language*: a language no longer in vernacular use.

c **1290** *S. E. Leg.* I. 108/55 With men þat onder-stoden hire langage. **1297** R.

GLOUC. (Rolls) 1569 Vor in þe langage of rome rane a frogge is. *a* **1300** *Cursor M.* 247 (Gött.) Seldom was for ani chance Englis tong preched in france, Gif we þaim ilkan þair language [*MS. Cott.* langage], And þan do we na vtetrage. *Ibid.,* 6384 (Gött.) Þis mete.. Þai called it in þair langag man .**1387** TREVISA *Higden* (Rolls) II. 157 Walsche men and Scottes, þat beeþ nouȝt i-medled wiþ oþer nacions, holdeþ wel nyh hir firste longage and speche. *c* **1400** *Apol. Loll.* 32 In a langwag vnknowun ilk man and womman mai rede. *c* **1449** PECOCK *Repr.* 1. xii. 66 Thei..han vsid the hool Bible..in her modris langage. *c* **1450** *Mirour Saluacioun* 3650 Wymmen spak these diuerse langegages. **1588** SHAKS. *L. L. L.* v. i. 40 They haue beene at a great feast of Languages, and stolne

Reprinted from the *Oxford English Dictionary,* Volume VI, pages 56–57, by permission of The Clarendon Press, Oxford.

the scraps. **1589** PUTTENHAM *Eng. Poesie* III. iv. (Arb.) 156 After a speach is fully fashioned to the common vnderstanding, and accepted by consent of a whole countrey and nation, it is called a language. **1699** BENTLEY *Phal.* xiii. 392 Every living Language..is in perpetual motion and alteration. **1769** *De Foe's Tour Gt. Brit.* (ed. 7) IV. 303 It is called in the Irish Language, I-colm-kill; some call it Iona. **1779–81** JOHNSON *L. P., Addison* Wks. III. 44 A dead language, in which nothing is mean because nothing is familiar. **1823** DE QUINCEY *Lett. Yng. Man* Wks. 1860 XIV. 37 On this Babel of an earth..there are said to be about three thousand languages and jargons. **1845** M. PATTISON *Ess.* (1889) I. 13 In fact, Bede is writing in a dead language, Gregory in a living. **1875** STUBBS *Const. Hist.* II. 414 The use of the English language in the Courts of law was ordered in 1362. *fig.* **1720** GAY *Prol. Dione* 4 Love, devoid of art, Spoke the consenting language of the heart. **1812** W. C. BRYANT *Thanatopsis* 3 To him who in the love of Nature holds Communion with her visible forms, she speaks A various language.

b. *transf.* Applied to methods of expressing the thoughts, feelings, wants, etc., otherwise than by words. *Finger language* = DACTYLOLOGY. *Language of flowers*: a method of expressing sentiments by means of flowers.

1606 SHAKS. *Tr. & Cr.* IV. v. 55 Ther's a language in her eye, her cheeke, her lip. **1697** COLLIER *Ess. Mor. Subj.* II. 120 As the language of the Face is universal so 'tis very comprehensive. **1711** STEELE. *Spect.* No. 66 ¶ 2 She is utterly a Foreigner to the Language of Looks and Glances. **1827** WHATELY *Logic* (1850) Introd. § 6 A Deaf-mute, before he has been taught a Language, either the Finger-language, or Reading, cannot carry on a train of Reasoning. **1837** *Penny Cycl.* VIII. 282/2 Dactylology must not be confounded with the natural language of the deaf and dumb, which is purely a language of mimic signs. **1876** MOZLEY *Univ. Serm.* VI.134 All action is..besides being action, language. **1880** *Times* 23 June 9/5. Teaching the deaf by signs and by finger language. **1894** H. DRUMMOND *Ascent Man* 212 A sign Language is of no use when one savage is at one end of a wood and his wife at the other.

c. *transf.* Applied to the inarticulate sounds used by the lower animals, birds, etc.

1601 SHAKS. *All's Well* IV. i. 22 Choughs language, gabble enough, and good enough. **1667** MILTON *P. L.* VIII. 373 Is not the Earth With various living creatures, and the Aire Replenisht,.. know'st thou not Thir language and thir wayes? **1797** BEWICK *Brit. Birds* (1847) I. p. xxvii, The notes, or as it may with more propriety be called, the language of birds.

2. In generalized sense: Words and the methods of combining them for the expression of thought.

1599 SHAKS. *Much Ado* IV. i. 98 There is not chastitie enough in language, Without offence to vtter them. **1644** MILTON *Educ.* Wks. (1847) 98/2 Language is but the instrument conveying to us things useful to be known. **1781** COWPER *Conversat.* 15 So language in the mouths of the adult,..Too often proves an implement of play. **1841** TRENCH *Parables* ii. (1877) 25 Language is ever needing to be recalled, minted and issued anew. **1862** J. MARTINEAU *Ess.* (1891) IV. 104 Language, that wonderful crystallization of the very flow and spray of thought. **1892** WESTCOTT *Gospel of Life* 186 Language must be to the last inadequate to express the results of perfect observation.

b. Power or faculty of speech; ability to speak a foreign tongue. Now *rare*.

1526 WOLSEY *Let. to Tayler* in Strype *Eccl. Mem.* I. v. 66 A gentleman

..who had knowledge of the country and good language to pass. **1601** SHAKS. *All's Well* IV. i. 77, I shall loose my life for want of language. If there be heere German or Dane, Low Dutch, Italian, or French, let him speake to me. **1610** —*Temp.* II. ii. 86 Here is that which will giue language to you Cat; open your mouth. **1790** COWPER *Receipt Mother's Pict.* 1 Oh that those lips had language!

3. The form of words in which a person expresses himself; manner or style of expression. *Bad language*: coarse or vulgar expressions. *Strong language*: expressions indicative of violent or excited feeling.

a **1300** *Cursor M.* 3743 Iacob..Þat es to sai wit right langage, Supplanter als of heritage. *c* **1384** CHAUCER *H. Fame* II. 353 With-outen any subtilite Of speche ..For harde langage and hard matere Is encombrouse for to here Attones. *c* **1425** LYDG. *Assembly Gods* 368 In eloquence of langage he passyd all the pak. **1430–40** — *Bochas* II. xiii. (1554) 53 a, Though some folke wer large of their langage Amisse to expoune by report. *c* **1489** CAXTON *Blanchardyn* i. 14 For it is sayde in comyn langage, that the goode byrde affeyteth hirself. *a* **1533** LD. BERNERS *Huon* lxix. 236 Come to yᵉ poynt, and vse no more such langage nor suche serymonyes. **1593** SHAKS. *2 Hen. VI,* IV. ix. 45 Be not to rough in termes, For he is fierce, and cannot brooke hard Language. **1611** BIBLE *Ecclus.* vi. 5 Sweet language will multiply friends. **1643** SIR T. BROWNE *Relig. Med.* 1. § 5 By his sentence I stand excommunicated: Heretick is the best language he affords me. **1694** PENN *Pref. to G. Fox's Jrnl.* (1827) I. 15 They also used the plain language of Thou and Thee. **1770** *Junius Lett.* 187 They suggest to him a language full of severity and reproach. **1809–10** COLERIDGE *Friend* (1865) 135 These pretended constitutionalists recurred to the language of insult. **1849** MACAULAY *Hist. Eng.* vi. II. 118 He lived

and died, in the significant language of one of his countrymen, a bad Christian, but a good Protestant. **1855** MOTLEY *Dutch Rep.* II. ii. (1856) 155 In all these interviews he had uniformly used one language: his future wife was to 'live as a Catholic'. **1875** JOWETT *Plato* (ed. 2) V. 348 The language used to a servant ought always to be that of a command.

b. The phraseology or terms of a science, art, profession, etc., or of a class of persons.

1502 *Ord. Crysten Men* (W. de W. 1506) Prol. 4 The swete and fayre langage of theyr phylosophy. **1596** SHAKS. *1 Hen. IV,* II. iv. 21, I can drinke with any Tinker in his owne Language. **1611** — *Cymb.* III. iii. 74 This is not Hunters Language. **1651** HOBBES *Leviath.* III. xxxiv. 207 The words Body, and Spirit, which in the language of the Schools are termed Substances, Corporeall and Incorporeall. **1747** SPENCE *Polymetis* VIII. xv. 243 Those attributes of the Sword, Victory, and Globe, say very plainly (in the language of the statuaries) that [etc.]. **1841** J. R. YOUNG *Math. Dissert.* i. 10 Thus can be expressed in the language of algebra, not only distance but position. **1891** *Speaker* 2 May 532/1 In it metaphysics have again condescended to speak the language of polite letters.

c. The style (of a literary composition); also, the wording (of a document, statute, etc.).

1712 ADDISON *Spect.* No. 285 ¶ 6 It is not therefore sufficient that the Language of an Epic Poem be Perspicuous, unless it be also Sublime. **1781** COWPER *Conversat.* 236 A tale should be judicious, clear, succinct, The language plain. **1886** SIR J. STIRLING in *Law Times Rep.* LV. 283/2 There are two remarks which I desire to make on the language of the Act.

d. *Long language*: † (a) verbosity (tr. Gr. μακρολογια); (b) language composed of words written in full, as opposed to cipher.

1589 PUTTENHAM *Eng. Poesie* III. xxii. (Arb.) 264 *Macrologia*, or long language, when we vse large clauses or sentences more than is requisite to the matter. **1823** J. BADCOCK *Dom. Amusem.* 34 Those Greeks did not use cypher, but the long language of the country.

e. *vulgar.* Short for *bad language* (see above).

1886 BESANT *Childr. Gibeon* II. xxv, That rude eloquence which is known in Ivy Lane as 'language'. **1893** SELOUS *Trav. S. E. Africa* 3 The sailor..had never ceased to pour out a continuous flood of 'language' all the time.

† 4. The act of speaking or talking; the use of speech. *By language*: so to speak. *In language with*: in conversation with. *Without language*: not to make many words. *Obs.*

a **1400** *Cov. Myst.* iv. *Noah's Flood* ii, Afftyr Adam withoutyn langage, The secunde fadyr am I [Noe] in fay. *a* **1450** *Knt. de la Tour* (1868) 18 My fader sette me in langage with her. **1461** *Paston Lett.* No. 393 II. 17, I said I dwelled uppon the cost of the see here, and be langage hit were more necessare to with hold men here than take from hit. **1477** EARL RIVERS (Caxton) *Dictes* 57 One was surer in keping his tunge, than in moche speking, for in moche langage one may lightly erre. **1490** CAXTON *Eneydos* xxviii. 107 Wythout eny more langage dydo..seased thenne the swerde. **1514** BARCLAY *Cyt. & Uplondyshm.* (Percy Soc.) p. xviii, To morowe of court we may have more language.

† b. That which is said, words, talk, report; *esp.* words expressive of censure or opprobrium. Also *pl.* reports, sayings. *To say language against*: to talk against, speak opprobriously of. *Obs.*

a **1450** *Knt. de la Tour* (1868) 2 And so thei dede bothe deseiue ladies and gentilwomen, and bere forthe diuerse langages on hem. **1465** MARG. PASTON

in *P. Lett.* No. 502 II. 188, I hyre moch langage of the demenyng betwene you and herre. **1467** *Mann. & Househ. Exp.* (Roxb.) 172 ʒe haue mekel on setenge langwache aʒenste me, were of I mervel gretely for I have ʒeffen ʒowe no schwsche kawse. **1470–85** MALORY *Arthur* II, xl, Euery daye syre Palomydes brauled and sayd langage ageynst syr Tristram. **1485** CAXTON *Chas. Gt.* 225 Feragus said in this manere...The valyaunt Rolland was contente ryght wel, & accepted hys langage. **1636** SIR H. BLUNT *Voy. Levant* 33 A Turke.. gave such a Language of our Nation, and threatening to all whom they should light upon, as made me upon all demands professe my selfe a Scotchman.

5. A community of people having the same form of speech, a nation. *arch.* [A literalism of translation.]

1388 WYCLIF *Dan.* v. 19 Alle puplis, lynagis, and langagis [**1382** tungis]. **1611** BIBLE *Ibid.* **1653** URQUHART *Rabelais* I. x, All people, and all languages and nations.

b. A national division or branch of a religious and military Order, *e.g.* of the Hospitallers.

1727–52 CHAMBERS *Cycl., Language* is also used, in the order of Malta, for *nation.* **1728** MORGAN *Algiers* I. v. 314 Don Raimond Perellos de Roccapoul, of the Language of Aragon,..was elected Grand Master. **1885** *Catholic Dict.* (ed. 3) 413/2 The order [of Hospitallers]..was divided into eight 'languages', Provence, Auvergne, France, Aragon, Castile, England, Germany, and Italy.

6. *attrib.* and *Comb.* a. simple attributive, as *language-capacity*, *-family*, *-history*, *-turn*; b. objective, as *language-maker*, *-teacher*; language-master, a teacher of language or languages.

1875 WHITNEY *Life Lang.* xiv. 281 Every division of the human race has been long enough in existence for its *language-capacities to work themselves out. **1891** *Tablet* 29 Aug. 331 The rank it holds among the *language-families of the world. **1875** WHITNEY *Life Lang.* Pref. 5 Scholars..versed in the facts of *language-history. **1607** BREWER *Lingua* III. v. F 2, These same *language makers haue the very quality of colde in their wit, that freezeth all Heterogeneall languages together. **1712** ADDISON *Spect.* No. 305 ¶ 11 The Third is a sort of *Language-Master, who is to instruct them in the Style proper for a Foreign Minister in his ordinary Discourse. **1831** T. MOORE *Mem.* (1854) VI. 190 It turned out that what his friend, the language-master, had..been teaching him was Bas-Breton! **1826** PUSEY *Let. to Lloyd* in *Life* (1893) I. v. 97 A *language-teacher gives me lectures.. five times a week. **1803** SOUTHEY *Let. to C. W. W. Wynn* 9 June, In all these modern ballads there is a modernism of thought and *language-turns to me very perceptible.

Language (læ·ŋgwėdȝ), *v.* [f. LANGUAGE *sb.*] *trans.* To express in language, put into words.

1636 ABP. WILLIAMS *Holy Table* (1637) 95 Learn, Doctour, learn to language this Sacrament from a Prelate of this Church. *a* **1652** J. SMITH *Sel. Disc.* VI. xiii. (1821) 294 The style and manner of languaging all pieces of prophecy. **1655** FULLER *Ch. Hist.* VI. v. False Miracles § 11 Predictions..were languaged in such doubtfull Expressions, that they bare a double sense. **1667** WATERHOUSE *Fire Lond.* 185 Seneca has languaged this appositely to us.

b. *transf.* To express (by gesture).

1824 *New Monthly Mag.* X. 196 'Twas languaged by the tell-tale eye.

Hence La·nguaging *vbl. sb.* In quot. *attrib.*

1875 LOWELL in *N. Amer. Rev.* CXX. 395 It is very likely that Daniel had only the thinking and languaging parts of a poet's outfit.

✠ ✠ ✠

LANGUAGE AND THE
HISTORY OF LANGUAGE

MORTON W. BLOOMFIELD AND
LEONARD NEWMARK

Language is fundamentally the means by which men communicate with each other and with themselves, and by which they express themselves. All societies of human beings use language; there are no known exceptions. A person's linguistic destiny is determined by his birth and early circumstances, and the individual conforms and becomes a speaker and hearer of the language or languages thrust on him. The existence of a usable language gives human beings a potential social, historical, and intellectual dimension, linking them to each other, to the past, and to the world.

Language is a product of human culture, and speech is an aspect, a very important aspect, of human behavior. In all cultures, "there occur, among others, certain events known as utterances, or single instances of speech produced at given times and places by individual speakers."[1] In order to perform their social function, the noises people make must somehow be grouped into shared samenesses, or what are taken to be samenesses in the conventions of the language, so that recognition of meaning in each other's speech may take place. Without this recognition, any speech utterance would be a mere jumble of noise.

We are deeply attuned to the samenesses we hear or see in the use of language, so much so that when we unexpectedly hear a foreign language, whose rules are different from those which operate in our own language, we try to force it into our own language pattern. Everyone has had this experience, an experience which testifies to the strong hold our own language has on us. When we speak a foreign language, if we are not complete masters of it, we also tend to force the language into the pattern and rules with which we are familiar. We find it difficult to hear distinctions which are of importance in the foreign language but are not in our own, and to ignore distinctions which are of significance only in our own. We find it difficult to pronounce sounds of a foreign language with which we are not familiar.

A Frenchman trying to speak English will have difficulty with our *th* in *the*, because that sound does not occur in his language. He may say *ze* instead of *the* because *z* is familiar to him. An American speaking French will have much difficulty with the French word *rue* "street," because in English we have neither a uvular *r* or a front rounded vowel, as in *ue*. In English we do not use *thou* except in prayers; when we speak French, German, or Italian we find it difficult to remember that some of our *you's* should be *thou's* in the acceptable forms of the language being used.

All this proves how important the rules of language are in practice. Rules are the fundamental principles by which we can both use and understand our noise signs; without them we should not be understood nor should we understand others. When we know a language we know its rules thoroughly, though obviously not consciously, and indeed try to impose them, even without knowingly intending to do so, on other languages.

The samenesses of speech must lie in some kind of regularity in the sounds or combinations of sounds, in the orderly pattern of utterances. The existence of meaningful utterances, utterances with samenesses that can be interpreted, presupposes orderliness and pattern—in short, a *system* that we call a language. A language in this sense is that interpretative system which enables its users to make understandable utterances and to interpret properly utterances made by other speakers. The utterances we call speech; the interpretative system, language.

The importance of the distinction between language and speech was first insisted on by the great Swiss linguist Ferdinand de Saussure. In the field of linguistic activity, he distinguished between what he called *parole* (the speech utterance) and *langue* (the system by which *parole* is carried on). In this sense, the proper subject of linguistics is not speech as such, but language, although we may investigate a language only through its individual speech acts or utterances.

We may, of course, study a language purely as a system operating at a given time, thus disregarding the ways in which the system has changed through time and continues to change through use. In doing so, we abstract the language from its history and life and study it as a system of correspondences, arrangements, and potentialities. We call this kind of study synchronic linguistics. If, on the other hand, we concentrate on change and development in language, we call the study diachronic linguistics. To achieve a total understanding of a language, we must consider not only its anatomy and physiology, its form and function, but also its phylogeny and ontogeny, its history and development.

The utterances by which language lives (or, if the language is dead, the documents of the language which survive) are the physical means through which we arrive at the language system. Utterances as such are ephemeral unless they are recorded in some way, and these records of whatever sort are speech utterances at one remove. Until recently visual representation (writing) was the only available method of making these records, but today, of course we have additional ways at our disposal—phonograph records, for example, and magnetic tapes—which are certain to play important roles in future speech and language study.

Language is a subject of great complexity. It is a connecting medium: it connects men with other men, men with the world, men with themselves, parts of the world with other parts of it, and, in terms of time, the present with the past and the future. It forms a complex series of intricate relationships. We must even use language in our analysis of language. In order for us to see it as a whole satisfactorily, we must regard a language from a variety of perspectives. In both its oral and written forms, it is an aspect of human behavior; a biological and sociological phenomenon with a survival role in evolution; the basis for all education in the broadest sense of the word; a consistent structure with dynamic possibilities; a key to the intellectual structure of various cultures; an esthetic and magical phenomenon. It is a process, a structure, and a preserving medium all at once. It is no wonder that the word "language" is full of ambiguities and that scholars attempt to resolve them by distinguishing terms such as speech, language, tongue, discourse, utterance, and so forth.

Language is not only a creature of society, but like other social institutions, it is also a creator of society: sharing a language is a necessary result and a necessary condition of people living together. But a language is also of the most intimate importance for individuality as such. The acquisition of language in the life of an individual is closely bound up with his mental development and growth. His sense of the world, for example, depends to a great extent on the language he uses. Language enables man both to express himself and to orient himself to the world and society. Because the structure of an individual's personality is so intimately bound up both genetically and systematically with the language he speaks, it is very difficult for people to be objective about their own language. We are so conditioned to these conventionally accepted noises that it is hard for us even to think of them as noises. Thus, to become linguistically aware requires a special concentration on language as an object, which, for humans, who tend to regard the vagaries and accidents of their own language as having an inherent universal and permanent validity, is difficult and perhaps even shocking. We should remind ourselves that linguistics, the objective study of language, can serve not only its own proper function of adding to our general knowledge about language, but can also serve to liberate us from the tyranny, in its subtlest form, of the word. In the course of his life each human being discovers his language, and comes to think of it as a given natural object, rather than as the product of human behavior that it is. One of the reasons we find it difficult to look at our own language objectively arises from the way by which we come to know it. A horse is really a "horse" because our experience tells us it is a "horse."

As Julian Marias writes, "Language is something which each of us encounters; we have not made it ourselves; no one in particular has made it; it is 'there,' with its precise phonetic laws, with a phonemic system, with a vocabulary and a syntax; it is a *social* reality and it serves us precisely for that reason: a language is understood because it is apart from the individuality of each one of its speakers, because it is valid for all, and therefore recourse to it is automatically effective . . . There is, then, a linguistic ambit which is prior to individuals, in which the latter find themselves immersed, just as they do in the physical world or in the system of beliefs and customs."[2]

The great contribution of modern linguistics has been its stress on the structural aspect of language—the synchronic "systematicness" of language design. Language has a structure of its own right; it is not merely a formless, changing phenomenon. Although the development of English as seen at different periods and from different perspectives is to be the main subject of this book, much attention will be paid to its internal organization. In the nineteenth century, before the recent revolution in linguistic studies, language was studied largely in terms of individual psychology and historical development. The nineteenth century liberated linguistics from too close a dependence on logic, but came to depend, in its study of language, too much on psychology and history.

In this century, new developments in linguistics, especially in America, have been chiefly concerned with structure, and all over the world we find an increasing interest in the structural rather than the historical analysis of language. Today this interest is beginning to lead us once again into some aspects of logic. But we shall probably not fall again into the logical trap. The greater danger today is that we may neglect the importance of the history and psychology of language.

Modern linguistics has developed new concepts which enable us to analyze a language at any given stage of its history in a more systematic and exact way than was previously possible. We have discovered kinds of contrasting and complementary elements (differences and samenesses) within a language that were only suspected before, and kinds of patterning in languages that can now be more precisely identified and specified. A language is not a static structure; it is a structure with potentialities for change. The changes

confusing the picture with the depicted if we were to identify directly these devices as language, rather than as reflections, representations, or records of speech or potential speech. Just as the arts of painting and photography have introduced immense new possibilities of presentation in what they depict, so writing, the visual representation of language, introduces immense potentialities of expression and communication in language. You may learn much about nature by studying pictures and photographs and much about languages by studying written records, but no serious student of nature should be satisfied until he has studied nature directly, and no serious student of language should be content until he has studied language in its oral form, if it is at all possible. Otherwise, one's insights into language would be dimmed; one's grasp on reality would be unreliable; one's confusion of the representation with what was represented would be inevitable.

Let us now take up some of these points in greater detail.

In the common, though perhaps incorrect, interpretation of the *Cratylus*, it is said that Plato argued that there was some logical connection between the sounds used to symbolize events or objects and what is symbolized by them. Today no serious linguist or linguistic philosopher would maintain this proposition, except perhaps in the case of a few onomatopoeic words. The sounds used for linguistic symbolism are logically arbitrary, although if we have enough material and can start at a certain point in the past, we can explain how it came to be that we pronounce a word as we do or how it came to mean what it does mean. It is perfectly easy to explain, if we start at a certain point in history—say the Old English period—how it comes about that we pronounce *knight* as *nite* or even how it came to have its present meaning. But there is no explanation as to why this combination of sounds should designate what it does designate. It is not more natural to say it this way than to use the corresponding words *Ritter*, *chevalier*, or *caballero*, in German, French, and Spanish.

It used to be thought, however, that the structure or grammar of language (its system), as opposed to its vocabulary, was based on logic, the permanent and universal categories of the human mind. The great growth of our knowledge, in the past hundred years, of languages other than those classified as Indo-European and Semitic (the only families of languages well known in the West before) has cast considerable doubt on this belief. Newly studied languages have revealed linguistic categories and structures so different from those with which we had been familiar that many linguists have given up trying to establish any categories that would be general to all languages. Certain linguistic categories, such as *adjective* and *tense*, for instance, which seemed completely natural and logical to earlier students of language, are simply irrelevant in some languages.

However, it is possible that some general statements can be made about linguistic categories and that some relations between language and the world are not so completely arbitrary as the relations between things and the sounds that designate them. As John Carroll puts it, "Language universals, phenomena found in all languages, would be of as much interest psychologically as language differences. Is it true that all languages have subject-predicate construction in sentences? Do all languages have some type of noun-verb contrast? What features of verb-tense system are common to all languages? Answers to such questions would assist in the development of a generalized psychology of cognitive functions."[4] It will take some time before such answers can be given, if indeed they ever can be.

The patterning that a language imposes on thought is a fascinating subject; in recent years it has been the subject of considerable discussion in the United States, as a result of the work of Benjamin Lee Whorf, following the lead of the great American anthropological linguist Edward Sapir. If language is ultimately responsible, as some philosophers think, for many if not all of our philosophical confusions, it may also be responsible for all our thinking in a much more fundamental sense. It may occupy a very special place in the determination of culture, fundamental not only in being the *sine qua non* of all culture but in the sense of creating the very preoccupations and mode of thinking characteristic of any culture. Whorf has made just this claim. He argues that the very language we use, and especially its over-all grammatical categories, controls the way in which we see the world and influences the basic concepts of our culture.

Speakers of English organize their utterances in the form of subjects and predicates. We say, to take an example from Whorf's writings, "*a light flashes*," with a division of the "thing" from the "action," although the light and the flashing are obviously the same. In Hopi, a North American Indian language, the same point is made by a simple word equivalent to *flash*. Hopi does not typically put its utterances into an agent-action pattern as we typically do. Our agent-action pattern determines, in some measure, how we think about and look at the world.

The differences in fundamental world view between the various languages of western civilization—what Whorf calls SAE (Standard Average European) —are not, he claims, very significant. The grammatical categories of these languages correspond very closely, and the chief differences lie in vocabulary and idiosyncratic idiom; but when we come to some of the more exotic —the so-called primitive—languages, we have to do with a very different matter. In these languages we often find radically different grammatical concepts from those current in SAE. In them we can recognize a completely different way of looking at the world, of dividing it up into categories. No longer do we find the classification of matters which speakers of SAE automatically take for granted—singularity and plurality of substances, even substances themselves, measurable time, certain spatial relations, and so forth; but matters which we think to be of secondary or occasional importance—such as the degree of validity of the statement made, the shape of the object handled, the extent of persistence of the event—may in these languages have to be designated in almost every sentence.

If, as he has sometimes been interpreted, Whorf would claim the complete sovereignty of his principle, that is, that intellectual activity within a culture is linguistically determined, it would be easy enough to refute it. If there were no area of intercultural truth, then the principle itself would be impugned. Also if it were true, translation would be impossible, and we would not be able to follow his argument when Whorf tells us what it is like to think in Hopi. As Hockett says, "An effective speaker—for example, Whorf —will have the skill to force his native language to express meanings for which he may believe some other language (say Hopi) is better adapted."[5] We are forced then to the conclusion that "intercultural communication, however wide the difference between cultures may be, is not impossible. It is simply more or less difficult, depending on the degree of difference between the cultures concerned."[6]

Whorf probably overemphasized his insight and underestimated the fact that a language can express matters of any sort in some way, as he himself demonstrated by describing Hopi. One can get out of one's language pattern, though sometimes only with difficulty, and this fact alone refutes the complete relativity of language categories. But there is now good evidence that the language one speaks, especially the vocabulary it offers to its speakers— the kinds of things, events, sensations, for which there are unitary, individual words—has a definite influence on the thinking one does.

Let us turn to another aspect of historical languages: the relation between the oral and written aspects of language.

Historically and ontogenetically speaking, it is clear that the spoken aspect of language is prior to its written aspect. Probably from the beginnings of human society (estimates run from 250,000 to 1,000,000 years ago) language has existed in its oral form. Then, in the Near East about 5000 years ago, it was discovered that a more enduring set of visual symbols, carved in stone or made on papyrus, could be used to symbolize the existing sound signs. The speech utterance could be preserved and made into an object, an artifact, by writing or carving. Anthropologists and archaeologists attribute the rise of civilization to two factors—the creation of cities and the invention of writing. The latter, for the first time, made possible the preservation of records and ritual in a form more objective and reliable than human memory could give them. The invention of writing took a great burden off the human memory and transformed the evanescent sounds of human speech into artifacts which could be moved about and preserved at will.[7]

Languages constantly change, but there are certain conservative forces which obscure the process. Among them the influence of writing is perhaps the most important; written forms remain stable long after the spoken forms they represent have changed. If one considers the great gap between English speech and English spelling, for example, one can get a good idea of the conservatism of writing. In spite of the historical priority of speech, educated people who speak a language with a written form tend to think of the written form as prior to and more fundamental than their speech. Instead of reforming spelling to conform with speech, men have occasionally done the opposite and made pronunciation conform to spelling. From this attitude we get phenomena which linguists call spelling pronunciations. The "w" in *Greenwich* used to be pronounced in a way reflected by the spelling. After a time the pronunciation changed so that a more accurate spelling would have been *Grennitch*. Now, hundreds of years later, many people influenced by the traditional spelling pronounce the name as if it were a combination of *green* and *witch*.

Although there is actually a very long history of interest in language of a general or descriptive sort, in the early days of linguistics, beginning in the late eighteenth century, the emphasis was put on languages with a literary tradition. This study had to be based on documents and led perhaps to an undervaluation of the oral aspect of language. With the rise of the science of phonetics in the late nineteenth century and the coeval development of anthropology with its interest in preliterate societies, the oral aspects of language began to be emphasized. The influence of anthropology on modern linguistics has been great, and this may have led to an unjustifiable neglect of the written aspect of language. Both speech and writing may be used for the study of languages, and neither one nor the other should be condemned or neglected. We may admit a kind of fundamental priority to speech without at the same time minimizing the importance and role of writing.

This book, because it is a book, presents language by means of fixed printed marks on pieces of paper. But we should try to remember that these marks reflect some actual speech reality. The marks on paper or parchment are conventional signs of the conventional sound forms which compose numerous speech acts or possible speech acts. Once writing has been invented, it is of course possible to use language, yet bypass the oral aspect of speech. In writing this chapter we pass from thought to writing and do not have to speak out the lines we write. When you read these words you understand them without converting them into speech, unless you are such a poor reader that you must frame the words aloud to understand them. Writing becomes a system in itself, and it introduces a new factor into language behavior, a factor of great complexity and importance.

It is widely recognized that communication is a fundamental function of language. When language exists, people may communicate with each other in carrying on the work and amusements of society. Without any form of communication, no social effort would be possible; in deaf-mute societies, artificial gesture systems based on natural languages perform the necessary functions of language. If all the papers and records—all language surrogates— were destroyed, things would get seriously entangled, but without speech, organized life as we know it would be impossible.

The role that expression plays in language is less widely recognized, but is certainly no less important, than the role of substantive communication. Much speech is not uttered for the purpose of communication in an ordinary sense at all. It reassures people, affords emotional release, and gives ego satisfaction. When a man stubs his toe and says "damn it!" he is not communicating at all. It is true that such a remark does tell bystanders what the injured man feels, but his purpose is not communication. We all know people who cannot help talking, and much of their talk, although in the form of communication, is not seriously meant to convey information but is merely intended to be friendly or to externalize internal tensions. Of course, much of the value of language as expression does depend on the fact that it also exists to communicate. Human beings are not, however, completely rational beings who talk only to convey wishes and information to other human beings.

In many of the uses of language the information which seems to be conveyed is of no great importance in itself. Language may be used to exercise power over other human beings. It may satisfy a need to dominate or control others. Language can serve ritualistically to solemnize and even legalize occasions, as when the preacher says, "I pronounce you man and wife." This sentence is not merely a communication of a fact, but is also the establishment of that fact. John Austin has called these types of sentences performatives.[8] And language may also be used to comfort other human beings.

Thinking and language are intimately connected. We think to ourselves in language. During the course of a day most people think in words more than they utter them. This internal dialogue with oneself is an extremely important function of language. It enables one to communicate with oneself. Much, if not all, thinking is the internal use of words: if we had no language, we could not really think, although we might well have mental or emotional experiences of other sorts. Thus, although communication with others is the essential characteristic of language, it is not its only function.

Language is not an innate characteristic as, for example, walking or one's blood group is. If such a concept as race has any validity, it certainly has none with respect to language. Now it is true that part of what makes Frenchmen French is the French language and part of what makes Americans American is American English, but there is no innate connection between a language and a people; there is merely an historical one. We can say that no known historical or natural language is more advanced *per se* than any other; this fact is irrelevant in an argument as to whether certain peoples are more advanced than other peoples. Hottentot has no vocabulary to deal with physics whereas English has. This does not mean that Hottentot is less advanced as a language than English, but merely that speakers of Hottentot have not used their language for physics whereas English speakers have.

These comments would perhaps not be necessary if it were not for the fact that in the past century and even in this one, crude racial and evolutionary concepts were applied to language development, largely, though not always consciously, for the purpose of supporting certain prejudices in social thinking. Superior races implied superior languages. This idea dies hard, in spite of its having been totally discredited in linguistics, especially since linguists have become aware of the variety and complexity of languages.

Leaving our general discussion of language, let us turn to the question of why we should study the history of a language.

First of all, we should study the history of our language for the same reason that we should study the history of our country and of Europe. The man who does not know some history is a man who loses one of the major dimensions of his humanity. History has made man what he is today, and to understand him one must know something of his past.

A person is not born with his language; as we have already said, he learns it. And he learns it from other people who in turn learned it from others, and so on back in time, and back into unrecorded history. Thus the language of a given person is in some sense the creation, or at least the product, of the whole society and of that society's historical antecedents. Since historical events and conditions have a way of being reflected in language—for instance, in the names of technical achievements (such as the telephone), in words borrowed from societies with superiority in a given area (Italian musical terms in English), even in individual sounds which are influenced by sounds in a language felt to belong to a superior culture (the final sound in some people's pronunciations of the words *garage* and *rouge*, which English has adopted under the influence of French)—there is a very valid sense in which we can say that a person's language contains within itself the history of the societies in which that language was developed. A man who has no knowledge of the history of his language lacks a sure foundation for the study of the history of his nation or people.

A second reason is that in order to read properly—in the original—the great written monuments of his civilization, a man must know something about the history of his language. To know Shakespeare, one must know something about Elizabethan English; to read the Declaration of Independence intelligently one must know something about eighteenth-century English. Not everyone can be a specialist in Old English or Middle English, but anyone can increase his appreciation of the great written achievements of the past by increasing his knowledge of the language in which they were written.

Third, one studies the history of the language to be liberated from a narrow view of his present language. One learns that language changes and that the "rules" of grammar are not fixed like the "laws" of nature or the rules of artificial languages. One learns that what is now often considered a heinous solecism was not considered such a long time ago. Although one must follow certain grammatical norms in order to be considered educated, one should realize that much that has gone into the making of English is due to the replacing of some norms by others. The "errors" of the past have made present-day English for us. A language which is alive will change its rules and what is considered correct at one time may only be a current fad. This, of course, is not to say that "anything goes," but it should suggest tolerance and understanding in linguistic matters.

Fourth we study the history of a language to understand many of its apparent irrationalities. Why do we, for instance, say *men* rather than *mans* for the plural of *man*? The history of English will give us a very satisfying explanation of this irregularity. Although we do not know why *book* has the plural *books* when from OE we would expect *beek*, we can easily show many historical parallels for the change and for the resultant analogical construction. We cannot explain a language by laws of logic, but we can account for much of what seems illogical in a language by referring to historical periods in which the present anomaly fitted into a regular, systematic structure.

Fifth, the study of language at various stages in its past can provide us with an opportunity for studying language objectively and can introduce us to linguistic methods through materials which are important in their own right and fascinating to boot.

NOTES

1. Ralph L. Beals and Harry Hoijer: *An Introduction to Anthropology* (New York: The Macmillan Co.; 1953), 507.

2. *Reason and Life, The Introduction to Philosophy.* Trans. from the Spanish by K. S. Reid and E. Sarmiento (New Haven: Yale University Press; 1956), 267.

3. For a recent résumé and exposition of a new theory, see G. Révész: *The Origins and Pre-history of Language.* Trans. J. Butler (New York: Philosophical Library; 1956).

4. In his introduction to Benjamin Lee Whorf: *Language, Thought and Reality, Selected Writings* (New York and London: Technology Press of Massachusetts; 1956), 30–31.

5. In a review in *Language* XXXII (1956), 467.

6. J. Greenberg in *Language in Culture; Conference on the Interrelations of Language and Other Aspects of Culture.* Ed. Harry Hoijer (Chicago: University of Chicago Press; 1954), 94.

7. For recent studies of the history of writing, see David Diringer: *Writing, Its Origins and Early History* (London: Thames and Hudson; 1962), I. Gelb: *A Study of Writing, The Foundations of Grammatology* (Chicago: The University of Chicago Press; 1952), and David Diringer: *The Alphabet, A Key to the History of Mankind.* Second Edition (New York: Philosophical Library; 1951). For a good popular study of the history of the decipherment of many ancient scripts, see Ernst Doblhofer *Voices in Stone, The Decipherment of Ancient Scripts and Writings.* Trans. M. Saville (New York: The Viking Press; 1961).

8. See his *Philosophical Papers.* Ed. Urmson and Warnock (Oxford: Clarendon Press; 1961), Chapters 3 and 10.

✠ ✠ ✠

THE STUDY OF LANGUAGE
IN ANCIENT TIMES

JOHN T. WATERMAN

The most ancient expressions of linguistic interest generally known to the Western world are recorded in the second and eleventh chapters of the Book of Genesis in the Old Testament. The first reference is to the naming of the animals (Gen. 2:19–20):

And out of the ground the Lord God formed every beast of the field, and every fowl of the air; and brought them unto Adam to see what he would call them: and whatsoever Adam called every living creature, that was the name thereof. And Adam gave names to all cattle, and to the fowl of the air, and to every beast of the field. . . .

In chapter II of Genesis, verses 1–19, is recorded the account of the Tower of Babel:

And the whole earth was of one language, and of one speech. And it came to pass, as they journeyed from the east, that they found a plain in the land of Shinar; and they dwelt there. And they said one to another, Go to, let us make brick, and burn them thoroughly. And they had brick for stone, and slime had they for morter. And they said, Go to, let us build us a city and a tower, whose top may reach unto heaven; and let us make us a name, lest we be scattered abroad upon the face of the whole earth. And the Lord came down to see the city and the tower, which the children of men builded. And the Lord said, Behold, the people is one, and they have all one language; and this they begin to do: and now nothing will be restrained from them, which they have imagined to do. Go to, let us go down, and there confound their language, that they may not understand one another's speech. So the Lord scattered them abroad from thence upon the face of all the earth: and they left off to build the city. Therefore is the name of it called Babel; because the Lord did there confound the language of all the earth: and from thence did the Lord scatter them abroad upon the face of all the earth.

Most civilizations and cultures—in their sacred writings, in their oral traditions, in their folklore—have some reference to the origin and occasionally to the dispersion of speech. Only rarely (at least in the records that have come down to us) did the ancients try to learn something about speech phenomena by observation or experimentation. The Greek historian Herodotus (fifth century B.C.) records one such incident: an Egyptian king named Psammetichos wished to determine which of the world's languages was oldest. To gain this information he decided to isolate two newborn infants until such time as they should begin to speak; the assumption being that, lacking any pattern to imitate, they would therefore instinctively employ the most primitive of natural languages. In the course of time the children were heard to utter something that was recorded as *bekos*—which turned out to be phonetically similar to the Phrygian word for "bread." Therefore, Phrygian (once spoken in Asia Minor) was held to be the first language of mankind, at least by King Psammetichos and— we may presume—by his court.

Linguistic investigation in the conventional sense of the word, however, could not begin until philosophy and the analytic study of language had been developed. And this goal was not realized until the Greeks and the Indians applied their peculiar genius toward investigating the nature of language. Although they had certain goals in common—such as the clarification of the already obsolescent idiom of the Homeric poems and of the Vedic hymns— their respective approaches to the study of language were fundamentally different. By and large the Greeks speculated about language, whereas the Indians described it.

The earliest Indian literature is religious in theme, consisting of ritualistic hymns composed in a language called Vedic Sanskrit, to distinguish it from the later Classical Sanskrit. Although not recorded until approximately 800 B.C., the language of the oldest of these hymns is held to be considerably older. With the passage of time this ancient form of Indic, as well as the somewhat later variety known as Classical Sanskrit or simply Sanskrit (the border-line between Vedic and Classical Sanskrit is not sharply drawn), became less and less accessible; a situation that posed special problems for the Hindu priests and scholars, since they believed that the efficacy of certain religious ceremonies depended not only upon the faithfulness of the received text to the original language of the hymns, but also upon an oral rendition accurately reflecting the original pronunciation. Although educational practices coupled with religious zeal had preserved and handed down a most detailed corpus of grammatical and phonetic information, a knowledge of the older language would in time surely have perished, had it not eventually been written down.

This feat was accomplished by the most famous of Indian grammarians, Pānini, writing toward the end of the fourth century B.C. His grammar, the first of which we have any knowledge, remains to this day the most marvelously succinct and definitive statement of Sanskrit ever written. It is not a grammar in the conventional sense of the term—indeed, one must be an accomplished Sanskritist even to "read" it!—but rather an algebra-like condensation of the structure of the language, consisting of some four thousand *Sūtras* ("string") or aphorisms. Obviously, one "reads" Pānini's grammar in the same way we "read" the Periodic Table or the structural formulas of chemistry. In both cases we need a great deal of background. As a matter of fact—with respect to Pānini's work—Indian linguistics is little more than one grand, protracted effort to elucidate and elaborate his grammar, an effort culminating in the *Great Commentary* (*Mahābhāsya*) of Patañjali (second half of second century B.C.). Later treatises are essentially "commentaries on the commentaries."

The Sanskrit word for grammar is *Vyākarana*, which means "separation, analysis." True to this sense, Indian grammar is almost wholly analytic and descriptive. As pointed out earlier, the practical goal of linguistic study was to establish the morphology and phonology of an archaic and obsolescent language. In this the Indian grammarians were singularly successful, due in part to their objective approach, but no doubt due also to the structure of the language itself, for it is an idiom in which the affixing of grammatical elements to a root, and the joining together of simple words to form compounds, is beautifully formalized and obvious. Not so obvious at first blush, of course, since one must first learn how to resolve the phonetic "mergings" that have taken place between roots, affixes, and even larger phrasal elements, for written Sanskrit is roughly analogous to a phonetic transcription. It reflects quite accurately the desired pronunciation, and leaves to the reader the task of resolving the phonetic combinations into discrete lexical units— much as if we were to write something like *Jeetawredi*? and rely upon the reader to convert this into "Did you eat already?" However, once the external and internal phonetic combinations (called *sandhi*) have been accounted for, the neat structure of the language becomes apparent. At this stage of analysis, the student works his way back from some larger grammatical unit to a root, listing and identifying each element that has been affixed in some manner to the root; somewhat analogous to taking a word like *ungentlemanly* and breaking it down into *un-gentle-man-ly*, accompanying each step in the analysis with a statement as to the function and meaning of the unit under discussion. A Sanskrit dictionary, incidentally, consists principally of roots, not "words" as we normally use them.

The Indian grammarians scarcely mention what we customarily refer to as "syntax"—the grammar of the sentence. Of course, one can argue that the borderline between "phrase" and "sentence" is at best tenuous; however, it is equally true that the linking together of phrases in Sanskrit is not nearly so complicated a procedure as, say, in Latin or Greek.

Although they frequently tried their hand at etymologies, the Indians accomplished little of enduring value in this area. Much of their prose is given over to interpretations of their poetic works, in a manner reminiscent of our Bible commentaries, and although a detailed word-study is characteristic of this sort of exegesis, the results are sometimes fanciful and scientifically unreliable.

It is interesting to speculate about what direction Western grammar might have taken had it derived from the carefully descriptive studies of the Indians rather than from the speculative flights of Greek philosophy. Be that as it may, it was the Greeks, in grammar as in so many other things, who gave to the Western world an approach to the analysis of language that has endured almost unchanged even unto the present day—for better or for worse.

The earliest extant document in Greek dealing with the subject of language is one of Plato's (425–348/47 B.C.) dialogues, the *Cratylus*. Not only is this the earliest recorded instance of Greek linguistic expression; it is also one of the most important, for in it is presented the philosophical doctrine that language arose "by nature" (*physis:* "nature, inborn quality"). Although the meaning of the text is sometimes quite obscure, Plato apparently believed that there was an ontologically valid and compelling connection between a thing and its name, for he taught (or, more accurately, he accepted and developed the doctrine) that the only enduring reality is an intellectual reality existing essentially in the world of ideas. "Things" are but lower-level physical extensions or counterparts of these idealistic prototypes. Language, therefore—and by "language" Plato means "vocabulary"—probably arose by *necessity*: words *had* to have a certain predetermined meaning, because they could only reflect the immutable and eternal nature of the Idea. A corollary of this doctrine, of course, is that language can only be logical and reasonable, even though in practice we may not always be able to establish the relationship between the shadowy things of the sense world and the intelligible realities of Ideas.

As erudite as his philosophy may sound, Plato's attempt to clarify it by examples—as he does in the *Cratylus*—results in some incredibly naive etymologizing. In fact, some scholars cannot believe that he was serious; they feel he must have been joking. However, professional philosophers are not noted for their published humor, and I rather suspect that Plato meant most of what he wrote about the history and meaning of words.

As an example of his method, at one place in the dialogue he has Socrates explaining to his young friends Hermogenes and Cratylus why the Greek word for "air" is *aēr*. He quotes a verbal form, *airei*, which may be translated "it raises," and, after noting its phonetic similarity to the word *aēr*, concludes that "air" is so called because it is capable of "raising" things like leaves and smoke from the ground. In this case, however, he is not absolutely sure of his etymology, since he quotes another possibility, the phrase *aei rhei*, "always flows," which might also he thinks be the philosophical justification for the term *aēr*. Unfortunately, modern etymologists can demonstrate quite conclusively that the phonetic similarities between *aēr*, *airei*, and *aei rhei* are entirely fortuitous, and that none of the words is related to any of the others.

Plato's most distinguished pupil, Aristotle (384–322/21 B.C.), differed with his master as to the origin and nature of language. Aristotle, the father of grammar in the Occidental world, believed and taught (see his essay entitled *On Interpretation*) that language was arrived at by convention or agreement. To describe this process he uses the Greek words *thesis* and *synthēkē*, meaning "arrangement" and "convention," respectively. He opposed what he considered to be the Platonic doctrine that real being belongs only to the Ideas or Universals, whose existence is independent of the objects that imperfectly manifest them. Aristotle believed that every object in the world is a union of two ultimate principles: matter and form (or essence), the latter force yielding the potential or power to determine the structure of matter. In things linguistic, therefore, he did not feel compelled to search for the rationale behind every name or utterance, since to him the fact that language presented to the observer something formed and structured was, in itself, philosophical proof of its reality. The particular form that a given word assumed was merely one of an infinite number of possible material embodiments. He did not, therefore, do much etymologizing, since the problem of "original meaning" was of little importance to him. At some time or another a word had come into being because two or more people had agreed to symbolize a certain thing by reference to a given linguistic configuration. Whatever reasons may have entered into this process of selection, they were quite arbitrary; any of a dozen reasons might have served equally well.

This is a view adopted by most linguists today. Language is arbitrary. A Spaniard says *caballo* because his ancestors at one time said *caballus*, not because there is anything about the term *caballo* (or *caballus*) that suggests a four-legged domesticated animal known to speakers of English as a horse. This viewpoint does not, by the way, disclaim the validity of sound-symbolism: onomatopoetic derivation. Linguists do not deny the obvious force of onomatopoeia in language formation; what *is* denied is that there is any *necessity* attached to this naming. Otherwise, of course, all languages would use the same imitative words—which they certainly do not.

From its very beginnings Greek linguistics was closely aligned with philosophy. The notions of language origins held by both Plato and Aristotle were predicated upon philosophical doctrines concerning the nature of reality and knowledge, and in no important sense were they derived from an inspection of linguistic data; although Aristotle, in addition to his philosophical speculating, did make some empirically based observations about the Greek language. He investigated the parts of speech, for instance, distinguishing nouns, verbs, and a third catch-all class he called "conjunctions."

True to its origins, the study of language among the Greeks remained the special province of the philosophers, and all the important "schools" contributed something. The Stoics (founded 308 B.C. in Athens by Zeno), for example, formulated much of our traditional grammar. Continuing the study of case-relationships begun by Aristotle, they devised the names of the cases that have come down to us in Latin translation.

The very word "case" derives via French from the Latin *casus*, itself a translation of Greek *ptōsis*, meaning "fall." The Stoics held that all the cases had "fallen away" from the original case, the nominative—the case of the *nomen* or "name." Unfortunately, the Greek terminology did not always fare so well in translation. The accusative case, as an example, was called by the Greeks *aitiatikē*, that is, "the thing caused by the verb." But *aitia* means both "cause" and "accusation," and certain of the Latin grammarians later called it the "accusing" case rather than the "causing". Today we should really refer to the "causative case," but tradition has frozen the mistranslation into our terminology, and it will probably stay there forever.

In many ways the Alexandrian Age of literature (roughly 300–150 B.C.) may be considered the high point of Greek linguistic studies. This was the age of Aristarchus, especially noted for his analysis of the language of the Homeric poems; of Apollonios Dyskolos, writer on syntax and student of the literary dialects of Greek; Dionysios Thrax, who wrote the first formal grammar of Greek: a book of less than four hundred lines, yet acknowledged to be the prototype for all subsequent conventional grammars of both Greek and Latin.

Oddly enough, the Greeks, whose intellectual curiosity was well-nigh insatiable, showed almost no interest in any language other than their own. This fact is all the more remarkable when we remember that the armies of Alexander the Great roamed the then-known world as far to the east as India, and from the shores of the seas called Black and Caspian in the north to the waters of the Persian Gulf and the Arabian Sea in the south. And yet not a word about the speech of the peoples occupying those vast stretches! The ships of all nations dropped anchor in Hellas' ports-of-call, and Greek merchants sold their wares in Egypt, Babylonia, and Italy, conversing much of the time no doubt in the local tongues. But, of course, the foreigners were all barbarians—all "babblers"—and, too, the gods on Mount Olympus spoke Greek. Only one language other than their own ever merited even passing consideration: We know of two works—since vanished—that dealt with Latin; and one of these had as its theme the proposition that Latin was derived from Greek. Centuries later, to be sure (fifth century A.D.), Hesychios compiled a dictionary in which he listed words not only from

Greek and Latin, but also from many other languages, most of them located in Asia and Asia Minor. This lexicon is especially treasured because of its multilingual word-lists, and also because certain of these languages are otherwise most skimpily preserved. But a dictionary tells us very little about the structure of a language. And—this is true certainly of Hesychios' lexicon—we have few hints as to pronunciation, a drawback attending most older dictionaries. The Greeks, incidentally, tell us next to nothing about how their language was pronounced.

In summary, the Greeks approached language by way of metaphysics, bequeathing to the world a form of linguistic analysis which has come to be known as "philosophical grammar." The term is used here without reproach, for theirs was an intellectual achievement of awesome proportions. Not only did they succeed in describing in a highly satisfactory manner their own intricate language, but they gave to posterity an intellectual discipline and a tool that may still one day be reckoned superior to certain of our twentieth-century linguistic "-isms."

As in so many other areas of learning and culture, the Romans were content to accept the legacy of Greece. Their dictionaries and grammars are all cast in traditional Grecian mold.

The first Latin grammar of consequence was compiled by Varro (116–27 B.C.) and bears the straightforward title *De lingua Latina*. Consisting originally of twenty-six books, only numbers five through ten have come down to us. Mention should also be made of Quintilian's (ca. A.D. 35–90) *Institutio oratoria*, although, as the title indicates, it is devoted mainly to rhetoric. Aside from these, about the only other grammatical work of enduring significance is the *Ars minor* of Aelius Donatus, who taught in Rome around the middle of the fourth century A.D. His grammar was widely used for elementary instruction well into the Middle Ages. As evidence of its influence and popularity, it was the first book to be printed by means of wooden type.

With the slow disintegration and collapse of the empire during the fourth and fifth centuries, Rome could no longer maintain a climate conducive to intellectual pursuits, and many of her scholars and men of letters found refuge in the new capital on the Bosporus, Constantinople. It was here that Priscian (512–60) wrote his elaborate *Grammatical Categories,* the standard Latin grammar of the Middle Ages, consisting of eighteen books devoted to the parts of speech (*Priscianus maior*) and two books to syntax (*Priscianus minor*).

Likewise in the field of etymology the Romans did not get beyond their Greek models. The outstanding accomplishment in Latin is the etymological dictionary of St. Isidore of Seville (ca. 570–639), *Origines sive etymologiae*. But just as Plato in the *Cratylus*, so the Latin authors in their writings gave free rein to the imagination when searching for reasons *why* a word had a given meaning. The word *vulpēs* "fox," for example, was explained as being derived from *volō* "I fly" plus *pēs* "foot," thus meaning "flyfoot"; or *lepus* "hare" was supposedly compounded from *levis* "light" and *pēs* "foot."

As is obvious from the examples, no proof of linguistic relationship or of regular phonetic correspondences valid throughout the language was required. The wildest guesses were not only admissible but entirely in order, even the notion that things could be named from opposing qualities. In line with this reverse logic, *bellum* "war" was explained as coming from the adjective *bellus* "beautiful" because war is not beautiful! Latin etymological works contain many such bizarre derivations.

Obviously, this survey touches only the most prominent and enduring monuments of linguistic activity among the Ancients—and certainly not even all of these, as a glance at one of the larger specialized handbooks will reveal. However, as far as grammatical theory and practice are concerned, the Western world followed faithfully the paths marked out by the Greeks. Although we must mention briefly certain achievements of the late Middle Ages and Early Modern period, we shall find little actually new in the study of language until we reach the eighteenth, or even indeed, the nineteenth century.

✠ ✠ ✠

MEDIEVAL AND
EARLY MODERN PERIODS

JOHN T. WATERMAN

The spread of Christianity had as one of its secular benefits a vast widening of linguistic horizons. In accordance with Christ's commission to the Apostles to go into all the world and preach the Gospel to every creature, missionaries ventured far beyond the boundaries of the Greco-Roman world. Translating the Scriptures into the vernaculars became a principal task for Christian scholars, with the result that we can date many of the great Bible translations from these centuries: the Armenian (fifth century), the Gothic (fourth century), the Old Church Slavonic (ninth century). From these centuries, too, are dated many of the collections of words known as "glosses"—originally marginal translations or paraphrasings into some vernacular of Latin words and expressions intended to help the reader, presumably a priest, in his preaching and catechizing. Indeed, glossaries such as these occasionally constitute some of our oldest records of certain languages; German is such an instance.

Training the clergy involved, of course, the teaching of Latin, for which Priscian was the principal authority, although a textbook written in 1199 by

Alexander de Villa Dei entitled *Doctrinale puerorum* became the standard school grammar of the Middle Ages. Above and beyond the practical goal of becoming literate, however, Latin grammar was studied in its relation to philosophy, constituting as it did one of the branches (along with logic and rhetoric) of the *trivium*: the basic curriculum established by the Scholastics.

Although a practical knowledge of diverse linguistic types gradually became available to medieval scholars, this information could not become generally accessible until the introduction of printing with movable type. It is the sixteenth century, therefore, that deserves to be called Early Modern in things linguistic, for not until then was anything like a comprehensive survey of language possible. Almost overnight there appeared a spate of grammars and dictionaries, most of them dealing with the vernaculars rather than the classical languages. Since this was also the age of geographical discoveries, it is not surprising to find among these early linguistic treatises accounts of faraway tongues, usually limited, however, to word-lists and phrases. Some of these descriptions—meager though they be—are extremely valuable. Our sole direct knowledge of Gothic as it lived on in the Crimea, for example, is limited to a word-list compiled by a Flemish nobleman, Ogier Ghiselin van Busbecq, who, on a diplomatic mission to Constantinople in the years 1560–62, recorded and subsequently published a list of words and phrases, dictated presumably by a native speaker of the last living dialect of an East Germanic language.

From this era are also dated the early attempts to survey all the then-known languages, such as C. Gesner's *Mithridates* (Zurich, 1555) and Hieronymus Megiser's *Specimens of Forty Languages* (Frankfort, 1592). This sort of activity reached its zenith later on in the eighteenth century, culminating in such works as *A Comparative Vocabulary of the World's Languages* (1786–89) by the German traveler and natural scientist, P. S. Pallas, and a similar work dealing with more than eight hundred languages by the Spanish Jesuit, Lorenzo Hervas y Panduro in 1800–1805. The last and perhaps best known work of this kind is the *Mithridates* of Johann Christoph Adelung, which contains the Lord's Prayer in over five hundred languages and dialects. This monumental enterprise was published in four parts over the years 1806–17, after Adelung's death.

Of works dealing with the general nature of language, probably the most important is the famous "Port Royal Grammar" of 1660. The title itself achieves a certain grandeur: *Grammaire générale et raisonnée contenant les fondamens de l'art de parler, expliqués d'une manière claire et naturelle. Les raisons de ce qui est commun à toutes les langues et des principales différences qui s'y rencontrent; et plusieurs remarques nouvelles sur la langue françoise.* This was one of several more or less contemporary attempts to give "reasonable explanations" for the facts of language: philosophical grammar in the grand tradition.

Etymology was no better off than it had been under the Greeks and Romans. Scholars assumed as an article of faith that Hebrew had been man's first language, and most etymological studies monotonously attempt to skew the facts to fit the theory—even as did James IV of Scotland (1488–1513), who, like King Psammetichos, is said to have interned two children in order to discover which was mankind's first language. He is reported to have determined that the children "spak very guid Ebrew." In the same, even if somewhat more learned, spirit, is the work of the Frenchman E. Guichard, who in 1606 compiled an etymological dictionary of Hebrew, Chaldaic, Syriac, Greek, Latin, French, Italian, Spanish, German, Flemish, and English. He maintained that words could be traced from language to language by adding, subtracting, inverting, and transposing letters, "the which is not hard to believe when we consider that the Hebrews write from right to left, and the Greeks and others from left to right." Other scholars, more patriotically inclined, proposed their own language as the original one. Probably the most celebrated linguistic chauvinist is the Dutchman, Goropius Becanus (1518–72). A close runner-up, however, is the Swede, Andreas Kemke, who maintained that in the Garden of Eden God spoke Swedish, Adam Danish, and the serpent French.

The Medieval and Early Modern eras—that is, until about the end of the eighteenth century—witnessed a tremendous increase in the *amount of information* about language. Significantly, however, the *methods of analysis and interpretation* were still those of the Ancients. A scientific approach had to wait until the nineteenth century, although of course there were those whom we may appropriately call precursors. Three of these—Gottfried Wilhelm von Leibniz, Johann Gottfried von Herder, and Sir William Jones—we shall now discuss.

Although Leibniz (1646–1716) is known to the world primarily as a philosopher and mathematician, he was in fact what the Germans call a *Universalgenie*, a scholar who commanded all the formal knowledge of his time. His background and interest in linguistics were scarcely more than that of an extremely able and gifted dilettante, yet he stands at the beginning of the modern era, pointing the way toward a true science of language.

He was especially interested in studying the relationship of languages and establishing a linguistic genealogy. In order to achieve anything substantial in these areas, Leibniz realized that scholars would have to abandon their sterile practice of trying to relate all languages to biblical Hebrew. Instead, he encouraged his contemporaries to examine and describe extant languages, and, on the basis of mutually shared features, seek to establish valid genealogies. He himself attempted just such a genealogy, although it must be admitted that he, too, was not always guided by the facts. For example, he suggests a very broad grouping of the "Eurasian" languages that derives more from intuition than from observation. Nevertheless, he is the first known scholar to propose that all these languages were derived from a common, prehistorical ancestor. This thesis, in a modified form, has become the cardinal tenet of comparative linguistics. Leibniz' classification of the languages of Europe, Asia, and Egypt was printed in 1710 in the memoirs of the Berlin Academy (*Miscellanea Berolinensia*).

Another area of concern to him was the collecting and describing of living languages. As one of the leading intellectuals of his age, Leibniz had a circle of acquaintances that was influential as well as cosmopolitan. For instance, he persuaded the tsarina of Russia, Catherine II, to subsidize P. S. Pallas' collection of specimens of two hundred languages and dialects, and he urged the tsar, Peter the Great, to have studies made of all the languages of the Russian Empire, to have them reduced to writing, and to have dictionaries and grammars prepared.

Leibniz, incidentally, was one of the earliest to champion the use of the vernacular languages as vehicles of instruction and literature. He was especially desirous that his fellow Germans take pride in their tongue, study it, and cultivate it as a medium of polite and learned discourse. In what must be considered a revolutionary step for his time, he went so far as to publish several essays in German rather than in Latin or French, the only two academically acceptable languages of the day.

Johann Gottfried von Herder (1744–1803) is another eighteenth-century figure who did much to usher in the era of scientific linguistics. In 1772 he wrote a prize essay entitled *Concerning the Origin of Language* (*Über den Ursprung der Sprache*). In this essay the German clergyman attacked the orthodox view of his age that speech is the direct gift of God. Herder rejected this belief, maintaining that language would be more logical if it were from God. Neither did he adopt the premise that man had invented language, but he held rather that the genesis of language was due to an impulse like that "of the mature embryo pressing to be born." Man, he concludes, is the only creature who has the ability to single out sensations: he alone is capable of conscious linguistic reflection. While accepting the belief that Hebrew was the original language, he believed that it developed of necessity from man's innermost nature. The speech impulse itself, he concedes, is from God, but man has worked out his own linguistic destiny from that point on.

Not nearly so well known as Leibniz or Herder, but with more immediate and direct influence on nineteenth-century linguistics than either, was the Englishman, Sir William Jones (1746–94). Like the other two precursors we have discussed, Jones was not a professional philologist. Educated in the law, he served from 1783 until his death as a jurist on the bench of the British court of Calcutta in India. Throughout the last nine years of his brief life, Sir William studied Sanskrit, acquiring in the course of time not only a remarkable command of the language, but also—and of greater importance —a profound insight into its relationship to certain other languages. It is in fact customary to date the beginnings of modern comparative grammar in a general way from a statement contained in a speech which Jones delivered before the "Asiatick" Society on February 2, 1786. Like so many momentous utterances, this one too is neither superficially spectacular nor obviously significant, and yet it is usually accepted as the first known printed statement of the fundamental postulate of comparative linguistics:

The *Sanscrit* language, whatever be its antiquity, is of a wonderful structure; more perfect than the *Greek*, more copious than the *Latin*, and more exquisitely refined than either, yet bearing to both of them a stronger affinity, both in the roots of verbs and in the forms of grammar, than could possibly have been produced by accident; *so strong indeed, that no philologer could examine them all three, without believing them to have sprung from some common source, which, perhaps, no longer exists* [italics mine]: there is a similar reason, though not quite so forcible, for supposing that both the *Gothick* and the *Celtick*, though blended with a very different idiom, had the same origin with the *Sanscrit*; and the old *Persian* might be added to the same family.

Scholars before Jones had of course noticed the similarities between these various languages, but to the best of our knowledge no one prior to him had reached the conclusion—arrived at not by intuition but by inspection of the data—that these resemblances must be due to a common descent from a hypothetical earlier language "which, perhaps, no longer exists."

Once the authority of religion and tradition had been successfully challenged, the way was clear to approach the study of language in this new perspective. Scholars came to understand that language was in a state of constant flux, that it had a history, and that its genesis and development could be studied from the historical point of view. This—the notion of history applied to things other than wars and dynasties—was not generally appreciated until the late eighteenth and early nineteenth centuries. Applied to language it meant that scholars were now interested in tracing the records of speech as far back as possible, explaining language growth and change in the same manner as other historical phenomena, namely, by establishing a causal relationship between events bound together in time and space. From 1800 on, therefore, we may speak of the scientific study of language, or, to use the term in its narrower sense, "linguistics."

PART TWO

THE ANCESTRY OF ENGLISH
AND SOME PRINCIPLES
OF LINGUISTIC CHANGE

✠

INTRODUCTION

English, of course, is just one language among many and part of a family of languages which is also one among many. The selection from Schlauch examines those families, their interrelationships, and the interrelationships of the languages within them. Schlauch describes not only Indo-European, which is the ancestor of the Germanic languages (including English), the Romance languages, and the Slavic languages, but also such families as the Semitic, the Sudanese and Bantu, the Sino-Tibetan, the Malay-Polynesian, and the American Indian. Like other writers in this book, she circles warily the problem of a possible single source for all languages, and, like her colleagues, pronounces that aspect of our linguistic past probably irretrievable.

The selection from Robertson and Cassidy offers more information about Indo-European, which the authors call our "hypothetical speech ancestor," and then gives us four important characteristics of the Germanic sub-group of that family. This selection demonstrates as one of its major points, as earlier selections have also indicated, that language is constantly developing. It may be difficult to predict how a language will change, but how it has changed can be described accurately when adequate records are available.

The last two selections in this section describe other such changes. Fisher traces the development of the English alphabet: its heavy dependence on the Latin alphabet, the temporary influences from runic, the effect on sound and spelling of the Norman scribes. He shows how the alphabet used for English changed from the period of Old English through that of Middle English to that of Modern English. Sapir tells us that "Language moves down time in a current of its own making. It has a drift." He examines the reasons for dialects; and then, employing the contemporary problem of when to use 'who' and when 'whom,' he shows in general how that drift operates to change languages over the years and in particular how an increasingly fixed word order has affected English.

After having read this section, then, the reader should understand what the antecedents of English were and some of the dynamic of change in language in general and in English in particular. Knowing something of the roots of English and its dynamic characteristics, he will be better able to understand the actual history of the language, which follows in the later sections.

✠ ✠ ✠

FAMILY RELATIONSHIPS AMONG LANGUAGES

MARGARET SCHLAUCH

FAMILIES OF LANGUAGES

In happier times, it was possible to cross the length and breadth of Europe by train in so few days that the journey could still be conveniently measured by hours. Paris to Berlin, fifteen hours; Berlin to Moscow, forty hours; Berlin to Milan, twenty hours. In certain parts of that complex and explosive continent, it was necessary to change one's official language three or four times in the course of a pilgrimage which in the United States would appear to be, in length, a mere uneventful hop. You could cross the English Channel and find yourself greeted within a couple of hours by the slow even courtesy of a Dutch immigration officer; a few more hours and a Belgian would appear at the door of your compartment and, in French idiom sounding somehow un-French, make the same routine demands with a courtesy of a different tang. Then eastwards, you could encounter the clipped precision of German officialdom, followed by softer accents emanating from the speakers of a series of Western Slavonic national languages. And to the south there lay, also easily accessible, the varied music of Mediterranean Romance languages, maintaining a certain insidious charm even as spoken by the stampers of passports and openers of trunks. The landscape might not change perceptibly at the political borders, but there would be a stir in your compartment, a coming and going of people, new phrases to be caught on the wing as travelers passed by in the corridor; and as you sat in your corner eagerly experiencing the linguistic kaleidoscope of the continent, you would strain to catch the first sounds of the new idiom as fresh companions settled themselves about you. The Dutch commercial travelers condoling or congratulating with one another in measured tones on the current market would give place to a group of French *permissionaires* exchanging rapid chaff on the exploits of their leave, in an esoteric professional jargon of considerable gayety; their still-warm places might be occupied by a domestic group on the German border, *Vati*, and *Mutti* complete with *Bruderlein* and *Schwesterlein* who were sure to be the silent, well-behaved recipients of a series of solicitous imperatives. Cries from the station platforms might echo in your mind in rich polyglot confusion at the end of such a long journey eastwards: "*Cigarren! Cigaretten!*"—"*Paris-Soir! Figaro!*"—"*Abfahrt!*"—"*Het is al tien uur.*"—"*A la aduana ...*" "*Auga mineral, chocolade ...*" "*Priidjite, pozháluista!*"

Certainly these differences in tongue would be bewildering in the extreme to any traveler, until instruction and experience could bring order out of the chaos of aural impressions. But an enthusiast who set out to acquire some smattering of the languages in a series of countries to be so traversed would soon begin to observe some curious parallelisms in the words learnt to designate the same object. For two or even more languages he would find repeated similarities, remote but still perceptible, not only in individual words but in the manner in which these words were put together in sentences. Naive observers explain these similarities by talking of a vague "mixture" or "corruption." When they come across a sentence in Dutch like "*Ik heb het voor mijnen zoon gekocht*" they are pleased and surprised to observe how much it resembles English "*I have bought it for my son*" or German "*Ich habe es fur meinen Sohn gekauft.*" And so they inform you gleefully, with all the assurance of a non-linguist: "Dutch is a funny language; it's a mixture of English and corrupt German."

A Hollander would of course protest vehemently that Dutch is no more corrupt, funny, or mixed than any other national speech in Europe, and he would be quite right. There is another way of explaining its gratifying resemblance to things we already know.

Let us take a single sentence and follow its land-changes, its mutations, over a fairly wide territory—as territories are reckoned in Europe.

Suppose you begin a trip in Sweden, and you find yourself seated with a mother who is anxiously supervising the box lunch of several small children. She turns solicitously to one of them and says, "Did you get any cookies (or apples, or candies)?" And the child replies: "Yes, Mother, I have three."

In Swedish that would be, "*Ja, moder, jag har tre.*" In Norway, to the west, or Denmark, to the south, it would be almost the same: "*Já, mor, jeg har tre.*"

The slight differences in vowel sound and in sentence melody do not disguise the fact that we are listening to the same words. A moment's reflection will suggest the right explanation. We are not confronted by a borrowing or "mixture" in any case. The three Scandinavian languages mentioned are equally ancient. At one time they were identical, for all practical purposes. A traveler in olden times (let us say the ninth century) could traverse the whole length of Norway or Sweden and pass to the southern extremity of Denmark without any change in his speech. Everywhere he would hear children say: "*Já, módir, ek hefi þrjá.*" (The last word was pronounced [θrja:].) The changes and differences developed during centuries, rather rapidly in Denmark, more slowly in Sweden. As a result, we now have diversity where once there was unity. Three national languages, equally venerable, have replaced Old Scandinavian. They are extremely close relatives, but none could claim parental precedence over the others. If any branch of Scandinavian could exact respect on the grounds of conservatism (that is, fidelity to the parent, the Old Scandinavian) it would be modern Icelandic, spoken in the distant island which Norwegians settled in the ninth century. Here children still say: "*Já, módir, ek hefi þrjá.*" The values of the vowels have changed slightly; that is all.

When the train crosses from Denmark into Germany, a greater change becomes apparent. Here the maternal inquiry elicits the answer, "*Ja, Mutter, ich habe drei.*" In Holland or the Flemish-speaking parts of Belgium tow-headed lads murmur, "*Ja, moeder* (or *moer*) *ik heb er drie.*" The cleavage is greater, but the separate words still look distinctly familiar. We can even group the versions of our little sentence to show where two or more languages show particular likeness:

ICELANDIC:	*Já, módir, ek hefi þrjá.*
SWEDISH:	*Ja, moder, jag har tre.*
DANISH:	*Ja, mor, jeg har tre.*
NORWEGIAN:	*Ja, mor, jeg har tre.*
GERMAN:	*Ja, Mutter, ich habe drei.*
DUTCH:	*Ja, moeder, ik heb drie.*
FLEMISH:	*Ja, moeder, ik heb drie.*
ENGLISH:	*Yes, mother, I have three.*

German stands somewhat apart because its consonants show certain peculiarities: it alone has a [t] between vowels (that is, intervocalic) in the word for mother. Still, it is clear that we are dealing with variations on the same theme.

Just as the Scandinavian examples revealed close kinship among themselves, so all of those in the extended list show some degree of relationship with one another. Sentences betraying the close linguistic ties within this same group could be multiplied indefinitely. Such being the case, we are justified in speaking of a "family" of languages, borrowing a metaphor from the realm of human relations.

PARENT GERMANIC

Detailed comparisons of this sort indicate that all members of this Germanic group go back to a single parent language, now lost, spoken as a unity somewhere between the first century B.C. and the first A.D. We call this lost parent language Primitive Germanic. Its modern descendants are grouped into what is known as the Germanic family of European languages. English is one of them. The precise geographical location of Primitive Germanic is not known. We can surmise the nature of its sounds (*phonology*) and inflections (*morphology*) with what is probably fair accuracy, however, because of some early literature and inscriptions dating back to a time when the separate descendants had as yet separated very little from one another. The runic inscription on the Gallebus horn belongs to this early period. It was Old Scandinavian, but it might almost have been composed in an early form of any of the others mentioned.

By comparative study it has been established which sounds in the quoted words are most faithful to the original language. We know that English has preserved the initial consonant of the word "three" [θ] as spoken in Primitive Germanic; but that Icelandic, Flemish, and Dutch have kept the consonant at the end of the first person pronoun singular (*ik*), which has been lost in English and transformed in the others. Back of the multiplicity of extant forms we can feel our way to the existence of the single speech called parent Germanic.

ROMANCE LANGUAGES

But now let us continue the journey south. In Belgium our anxious Flemish mother may be replaced by a fellow-countrywoman who speaks French. Her child will say something strikingly different from anything heard so far. "*Oui, mère* (or *maman*), *j'en ai trois.*" As the train goes southwards towards that fertile cradle of cultures, the Mediterranean basin, it may be routed towards the Pyrenees, or across the Alps into Italy. If it should cross the Iberian peninsula you would hear in Spain: "*Si, madre,* (*yo*) *tengo tres*; and in Portugal: "*Sim, mãe, tenho tres.*" But if it should take you across the barrier which Hannibal—even Hannibal—found all but impassable, down the steep slopes to the smiling Lombard plains, you would hear: "*Si, madre, ce n'ho tre.*" And even across the Adriatic, on the far side of the Balkan peninsula, hardy descendants of the Roman army and Roman colonists will be saying in Rumanian: "*Da, mama mea, eu am trei.*"

The similarities are apparent:

FRENCH: *Oui, mère, j'en ai trois.*
SPANISH: *Si, madre, (yo) tengo tres.*
PORTUGUESE: *Sim, mãe, tenho tres.*
ITALIAN: *Si, madre, ce n'ho tre.*
RUMANIAN: *Da, mama mea, eu am trei.*

The situation is comparable to the one which diverted and probably mystified you in Germanic territory. You have been traversing lands where the people communicate with one another in tongues clearly descended from a single parent. This time the parent language was a form of Latin: not the solemn speech, stilted and formal, which was reserved for polite literature and speeches in the forum, but the popular or "vulgar" Latin spoken by common people throughout the length and breadth of the Roman territory. Plain soldiers, tavern keepers, itinerant merchants, freedmen, small traders, naturalized citizens of all the polyglot Roman provinces, must have used this form of discourse as an international *lingua franca*. In this idiom they bought and sold, exchanged jokes, flirted, lamented, and consoled with one another. We know from late written documents and inscriptions (especially those on the humbler tombstones of poor folk) just how ungrammatical, rapid, informal, and even slangy this Latin was, compared with the intricate and highly mannered periods of a Cicero. People had become impatient with the many case endings required in classical Latin, and were reducing them to two or three. Even these were treated with playful carelessness. The verb was handled in a different way—a more vivid one—to show changes in tense; and the word order was simplified. Moreover, slang words triumphed completely over traditional ones in some provinces. Ordinary people in Gaul (perhaps emulating the jargon of the army) stopped referring to the human head as *caput*, and substituted *testa* or "pot" from which comes the modern French *tête*. It is as if all persons speaking English should have fallen into the way of saying "my bean" for the same object, so that it became the accepted word, while "head" was lost entirely.

The popular Roman speech differed from one province to another because popular locutions do tend always to be regional, and because the Romans came in contact with widely differing types of native speech. Thus the pronunciation and even the grammar were affected by the underlying populations. In one place the Latin word *habere* continued to be used for "to have"; in the Spanish peninsula, however, it so happened that *tenere*, meaning "to hold," came to be used in its place in the more general sense of "to have." That is why our imaginary Spanish child says *tengo* instead of any form of the classical *habere*. The number "three" on the other hand, varies only slightly in the series of Romance sentences quoted. The numbers have remained fairly stable in the various daughter languages perpetuated from vulgar Latin. One of the factors tending to preserve a similarity in them throughout the ages has been their similar experience in developing a strong

stress accent during the transition to the Middle Ages. This new accentuation caused similar losses in unaccented syllables in a given word in all Mediterranean areas. There were differences, of course, in the forms that emerged; but certainly not enough to make the results unrecognizably alien to one another.

The neo-Latin languages (if the expression may be permitted) give us another example, therefore, of a family which bears its signs of consanguinity very legibly on the external aspect of each of its members. In Roman times, Latin itself could claim cousins (in the ancient *Italic* group) which have since been lost.

THE SLAVIC FAMILY

And here is one further example of language relationship which may metaphorically be called close consanguinity. In eastern Europe a sharp-eared traveler on an international train will also have an opportunity to detect fundamental similarity behind the changing visages of national speech. A farflung territory is occupied by peoples speaking *Slavic* languages and dialects. It would be possible to pursue the transformation of our key sentence addressed to an imaginary Slavic mother to the east as follows:

CZECHISH: *Ano, matko, mam tři.*
POLISH: *Tak, matko, mam trzy.*
RUSSIAN: *Da, mat^j, u men^{j}á tri.*

When our international train crosses into the Soviet Union, it will pass through various sections of Russia showing distinct dialect colorings. Ukrainian, for instance, shows enough differentiation to be dignified as a national language, with an official spelling of its own. Even an untutored eye, however, can see how close it is to the official language of Great Russia, the classical medium of literature known to the world as "Russian." In the Balkan states, South Slavic languages show these perceptible nuances of our chosen theme. For instance, the Bulgarian version of it would be: "*Da, maika, imom tri.*"

Once again, we are justified in assuming that centuries ago there was a single language from which these cousins descended. About the seventh century it was probably still fairly unified. In the ninth century a southern dialect of this early Slavic (Old Bulgarian) was written down in a translation of the Bible made by Saints Cyril and Methodius. The text helps us to get quite a clear picture of parent Slavic, just as runic inscriptions bring us close to Primitive Germanic, and unofficial documents of the Roman Empire tell us much about Vulgar Latin.

INDO-EUROPEAN, PARENT OF PARENTS

Slavic, Romance, and Germanic represent three families of languages spoken in Europe today. But surely it must be clear that similarities link these families to one another besides linking the smaller subdivisions within each given

family. In *all* the national languages surveyed so far, it will be noticed, the word for "mother" began with the labial nasal [m]; in a considerable number a dental [t], [đ], or [d] appeared in the middle of the word after the first vowel. Likewise in *all* of the languages listed, "three" began with a dental [t], [d], or [θ], followed by an [r]. Why is this?

Clearly, at a still earlier period than the days of early (prehistoric) Germanic and Slavonic, and of Vulgar Latin, there must have been a more ancient and inclusive unity which embraced all three.

The same procedure, if pursued farther, would have revealed to us other major families belonging to the same larger embracing unity in Europe and parts of Asia. These are:

Celtic, including Irish, Highland Scottish, Welsh, and Breton. (In modern Irish, "mother" is *mathair* and "three" is *tri*.)

Baltic, including Lettish, Lithuanian, and an extinct dialect once spoken in the territory of modern Prussia (Old Prussian). The word for "mother" is *motina*, not closely related to the cognates already cited. *Tris* for "three" is, on the other hand, an obvious cognate.

Hellenic, including modern Greek dialects, some of which go back to very ancient times. (An ancient Greek dialect, Attic, spoken in the city of Athens, produced a body of literature of enduring splendor. Its word for "mother" was *matèr* and for "three," *treîs*. This is the classical language studied in school.)

Albanian, the national language of Albania, with no close relatives outside its own borders. Here "three" is *tre*; but the word for "mother" is not related to the forms in the above languages. A new form, *nona*, has replaced the Indo-European term preserved elsewhere.

Armenian, spoken in Armenia (between Europe and Asia Minor), is, like Albanian, a language with many diverse elements borrowed from outside, but it has an independent history traceable back to the fifth or sixth century A.D. Its word for "mother," *mair*, is easily recognizable as a cognate of the others given; not so, however, is *erek* for "three."

Even in Asia there are languages with venerable histories and rich literary heritage which can be recognized as members of the same linguistic clan:

Indian, including Hindustani, Bengali, Marathi, and Hindi. These dialects are descended from Old Indian, preserved to us in a classical literary form (Sanskrit) which dates back to the fifteenth century B.C. or even several hundred years earlier. Sanskrit, despite its great antiquity, still shows close generic resemblance to its modern European cousins. Its word for "mother" was *mātṛ* and for "three," *tri*.

Iranian, very closely related to Sanskrit, was spoken in the Persian highlands while Indian was spreading over the interior of India. It produced an early literature in the form of Zoroastrian hymns. Since those ancient times Persian has been subjected to large foreign infiltration, notably Arabic, but its structure still reveals its kinship with the other groups listed.

Hittite, a language spoken by people frequently mentioned in the Bible,

is now extinct. Cuneiform inscriptions give us enough material to reveal its fundamental character. Some sort of relationship it surely must have had with the members of the broad family of families now being surveyed, but the precise nature of that relationship is still under discussion.

Tocharian, now extinct, is represented by some fragmentary texts (probably antedating the tenth century), which were discovered in eastern Turkestan in a Buddhist monastery. The material is too scanty to permit of definitive analysis, but it shows relationship to the above subsidiary groups.

Our railroad trip beginning with Germanic territory has taken us far afield, even to the shores of the Indus River in Asia. Even so, and despite the most baffling diversities, skilled comparison of key words has been able to establish that the miniature families surveyed do undoubtedly belong to the same large, inclusive family already postulated to account for likenesses observed among Germanic, Slavonic, and Romance (from Old Italic).

Back of the smaller families lay a single family; attached to this single family it is almost certain there must have been a single language. We call the whole family by the name "Indo-European," a term generally preferred today to "Indo-Germanic" or "Aryan," both of which could easily be misunderstood. That is to say, every language mentioned so far is an Indo-European language, no matter what smaller group it may belong to.

HOMELAND OF INDO-EUROPEAN

But if they are all related thus, we must assume that a single definite language, parent Indo-European, gave rise to all of them. This is probably true. Some time before 2000 B.C., in some part of the world, a group which was essentially a single community spoke this single parent language. Later, dialect forms of this tribal language were carried into many different countries, from Iceland to India—by emigration, by conquest, by peaceful transfer. We do not know how this occurred in every case, but the expansion had already begun in earliest historical times.

Where the parent language was spoken, and by whom, is something of a mystery. By studying words that are common to a number of the family groups listed above we can, to be sure, get some idea of the culture these people had before their divisions, migrations, or conquests of a half-dozen millennia ago. We can surmise that they probably lived in a temperate climate because a number of the descended languages have similar words for spring, summer, autumn, and winter. There are common words indicating a developed (though still simple) agriculture: terms having to do with the plow, spade, sickle, and mill; with carting, sowing, and mowing. For instance, the word for plow is *arðr* in Icelandic, *áratron* in Greek, *arātrum* in Latin, *arathar* in Irish, *árklas* in Lithuanian, *araur* in Armenian. The names of certain plants and animals are supposed to offer some guidance. Parent Indo-European had terms for dogs, cows, sheep, bulls, goats, pigs, and horses; also for wild animals such as the bear, the wolf, and the fox. Hermann Hirt,

author of an elaborate discussion of the subject, considers the common words for "eel" in several languages as very important. If the original speakers of Indo-European knew this fish, they could not have lived originally near the Black Sea, where it is not found. Another important word is the old term for the beech tree in the various languages. The words *Buche* in German, *fagus* in Latin, *Bachenis* Forest in a Celtic place-name, and *Phegós* (φηγός) in Greek (where it had been transferred, however, to the oak tree), indicate that the beech was a tree known at the time of the parent language. The forms just quoted could all have come from a single root. Now the eastern boundary for the presence of this European tree is a line drawn roughly from Konigsberg to the Crimea. Therefore Hirt argues that the parent language must have developed to the west of such a line.

North central Germany, Lithuania, the Danube Valley, and Southern Russia (near the Black Sea) have been suggested in turn as the original homeland of the parent language. India, once regarded as the cradle of our general Indo-European speech, has been relinquished in favor of European territories answering to the geographical clues of the joint vocabularies. Of these it may be said that probability favors those districts in which there are many physical traces of early mankind, such as burial mounds, skeletons, fragments of pottery, signs of human habitation. The Danube Valley is particularly rich in these, and also Germany and Southern Russia. Lithuania can boast an extraordinarily archaic language, similar in many ways to ancient Sanskrit, but its territory is poor in archaeological remains, those mute witnesses to the daily living of people like ourselves who "flourished" (if that is the proper word) in prehistoric times. Lithuania may have been settled early in the age that saw the spread of Indo-European, but it is less likely than other districts to have seen its first development.

No matter where Indo-European developed out of still earlier linguistic stages now hopelessly lost, it is important to remember that we know absolutely nothing about the physical appearance of its first speakers. They have long since been leveled with the dust; we cannot say whether their skin was light or dark, their vanished hair shadowy or bright. Among the broad-skulled and long-skulled and medium-skulled remains of prehistoric man, we cannot tell which—if any—moved their bony jaws in olden times to the sounds and rhythms of the Indo-European parent language. Although most of the contemporary peoples of Europe may be descendants, in part, of members of our postulated Indo-European community, still it is not safe to assume that this community was itself racially homogeneous.

In any event we cannot be sure about what happened in those early ages. It is instructive to think of the mutations of history in the era since writing began. Whole peoples have suffered extinction as nations in past centuries, yet they may perpetuate and hand on the language of the conquerors when the latter in their turn are destroyed or absorbed. A West Indian Negro today can often be found speaking with the faultless accents and intonation of choice classical English; if you closed your eyes you would think he had been nurtured on the playing fields of Eton or by the Cam. He speaks standard English *as his native tongue*; he is aware of nothing alien about it as it leaves his lips; there is no psychological strain involved in employing this particular instrument merely because his ancestors in Africa used a very different one long ago. No doubt flawless Latin was spoken in the streets of Rome by naturalized provincials of many races, showing wide variety in the hues of their epidermises. In somewhat the same way all of us, for that matter, may be using variations of a borrowed instrument. So completely separate are the questions of language and race.

Most scholars would, to be sure, look to one or another of the contemporary peoples of Europe or India or even Persia to find lineal descendants of those who first spoke Indo-European. Yet two well-known authorities, Sigmund Feist (a German) and Vendryès (a Frenchman), have argued that even the Germans of today—who usually claim that honor—do not have the blood of the parent tribe in their veins even though they speak an Indo-European language (which they now choose to call "Aryan"). Feist and Vendryès point out that German (like Dutch, English, and Scandinavian) shows a very great change from the parent speech which lies back of the other Indo-European offshoots. The Germanic family has changed many of the supposed original sounds. Where Latin had *piscis*, Germanic substituted a form like *fisk* (English "fish"); where Latin and Greek had *patēr*, Germanic showed something like English "father." Thus this one particular group looks quite different from its Romance, Slavonic, Hellenic and other cousins because of an unusually complete shift of consonants. According to Feist and Vendryès, the reason is that the Primitive Germanic tribesmen were an alien race trying to learn to pronounce an Indo-European or "aryan" language. They had trouble with sounds like [p] and [t], and so distorted them to [f] and [θ]. If this theory is sound, the Germans of today would be a non-"Aryan" race (granting that the phrase means anything), speaking an "aryan" language imposed upon them by conquerors in prehistoric times! The whole question is very speculative. It may be pointed out that if Germanic tribesmen had trouble with [p] and [t] in primitive times, at least their descendants soon made good the loss by developing new [p] and [t] sounds out of Indo-European [b] and [d].

At the moment, however, what interests us most is the evidence of underlying unity, not of divergence, in the Indo-European family. As we shall see, the divergences turn out to be fairly regular when they are closely examined. Because they are more or less predictable by an advanced student, they do not disturb seriously his impressions of the underlying unity which justifies him in regarding the whole majestic array of tongues as a close-knit family. The more acutely one observes the principles of correspondence and divergence, the easier it becomes to learn a new member within the widely scattered group.

Cursory as this review has been, it has probably indicated the approach and even something of the methods used in the study of comparative linguistics.

Comparisons of a similar sort have established family relationships for the rest of the world. For the languages less familiar to us speakers of English a briefer survey will suffice.

THE FINNO-UGRIC FAMILY

Within Europe itself there are several languages which are completely alien to those of the Indo-European confraternity. A visitor in Finland, for instance, will look at posters and newspapers and remark with a puzzled air: "How strange! Not a word looks or sounds familiar! Why, in most countries you can guess something here and there, at least phrases—but not this, it's *outlandish*." The same remark will be heard from tourists in Hungary, Estonia, and (on rare occasions, I suppose) from visitors among the Laplanders in the far north of western Russia and Scandinavia. The term "outlandish" is here justified in its literal sense. The languages here spoken did come from an "outer land" centuries ago. They reached Europe by migration from the Volga and the slopes of the Ural Mountains, both from the Asiatic and the hither side. The Magyar (Hungarian) speech was transferred in a series of incursions lasting down into the Middle Ages, which were fraught with considerable terror for the turbulent inhabitants already more or less established on the fringes of the Roman Empire.

Finnish, Estonian, Lappish, and Magyar are members of the *Finno-Ugric* family. It also includes minor languages and dialects spoken in restricted areas, such as Carelian, Mordvian, Cheremiss, and the Permian languages (Zyrian and Votiak) which were carried to the northern Urals from the Volga region. Mordvian and Cheremiss are still spoken in scattered communities of the Volga basin. It is thought that Lappish is a Finno-Ugric language imposed by conquest on a people who originally spoke a quite different tongue. The Lapps, indeed, may be the physical survivors of one of the primeval races inhabiting Europe long before history began.

FINNO-UGRIC, NENETS, AND PARENT URALIC

In north central Siberia a number of small scattered tribes speak variations of a language referred to in most textbooks as Samoyedic. The term is an unflattering one, and did not originate with the tribesmen themselves. It is a Russian word used in Tsarist times and seems to mean "self-eaters" or cannibals. (It comes apparently from two common Indo-European roots: *samo*-cognate with English "same," and *jed*, cognate with English "edible," from Latin *edere*, meaning "to eat.") According to the *Soviet Encyclopedia* these people refer to their own nation and language as Nenets—a term preferable, therefore to the contemptuous epithet hitherto current.

Finno-Ugric and Nenets ("Samoyed") together form a super-group showing remote but still perceptible similarities among themselves. There is one trait of sound patterns common to almost all, which in particular impresses even a beginner in Finno-Ugric linguistics. It is known by the pretty term "vowel harmony." To Finno-Ugric ears, the vowels of single words are like notes in a musical chord. To combine front, back, and mid-tongue vowels in the same word indiscriminately is as bad as striking a group of notes on the piano by bringing down the flat of your hand forcefully on the white keys. In constructing a word, when the first syllable happens to contain a front vowel (*e, i, ä, ö, ü*),[1] then all following syllables must also contain front ones; and if the first syllable contains a back vowel (*a, o, u*) then all suffixed syllables must likewise contain one. You can have words like *äpä, küsöb, vesi, mato*, and *muna*, but not *veso*. Vowel harmony existed, apparently, in early Finno-Ugric, but Magyar shows exceptions and the Permian group and Lappish no longer observe it. A very practical result of this craving for vocalic similarity is the necessity to vary vowels in regular suffixes (inflectional endings). There must be two forms to choose from, according to the root vowel of the word. In Magyar, for instance, *marad-unk* means "we remain," but *el-ünk* means "we live." The vowel of the suffix alternates between [u] (after a back vowel) and [y], written *ü* (after a front one).

Here again we are justified in assuming a single parent language, a common ancestor of Nenets and Finno-Ugric, which we may call parent Uralic. This broad term may be used for all the ramified descendants, just as Indo-European was applied to all the languages descended from it. The geographical location of this lost ancestral Uralic speech is not known. Some of its characteristics can be deduced by reasoning back from extant dialects, as in the case of Indo-European. It has been claimed that a still more ancient kinship existed between Uralic and Altaic (a group centered in the region of the Altai Mountains in Central Asia) and even Japanese, but most specialists regard these speculations as unconvincing.

BASQUE

One more language of an "outlandish" character remains in Europe: Basque, which is spoken by a small but closely knit group in the French and Spanish Pyrenees. The vocabulary and grammatical structure are as alien to Indo-European as can be imagined. Hence the legends (current about Finnish too, by the way) to the effect that the devil himself was foiled in an attempt to learn this language, and his tutor (unlike Faust) emerged safe from the bargain to teach it, with his soul still his own. According to some writers, it is possible that Basque represents the sole surviving fragment of a common speech spoken by Neolithic tribesmen scattered over Europe, long before Indo-European or Finno-Ugric had entered the continent by migration or conquest. Possibly the same type of speech extended into the British Isles and across the Spanish peninsula into Northern Africa in these prehistoric times. The arguments in support of this possibility have to do with similarities in culture and physique among the prehistoric peoples concerned. They are not based primarily on linguistic evidence.

SEMITIC LANGUAGES

This brings us to another linguistic family which has had cultural contacts with Indo-European at various points in its history: namely, the semitic group. The name for it is taken from Genesis 1:10, in which the names of the three sons of Noah are given as Sem (or Shem), Cham (or Ham), and Japheth. It was believed that the numerous folk speaking Semitic languages owed their physical existence to the first son, to whom descendants of remarkable fecundity would appear to have been attributed. In ancient historical times, branches of Semitic were spoken in the city-states of Babylonia and Assyria in Mesopotamia. (An earlier language, Sumerian, was superseded by this spread of East Semitic.) To the West, Phoenician and Hebrew and Aramaic (including Syriac) occupied territory in Asia Minor which extended to the eastern shores of the Mediterranean. Hebrew was destined to play a memorable part, long after the end of political independence for Palestine, because of the incalculable influence of its Biblical literature. South of Palestine, and extending far west across the north of Africa, at one time even including Spain, there lay an imposing concatenation of peoples using Arabic, which with the rise of Islam became a world language of prime importance. It is still one of the first claimants for the attention of students desiring to broaden their studies beyond the more proximate Indo-European subgroups. Finally, the dialects of Ethiopian in Abyssinia, though close to Arabic in many features, constitute a separate division in the group of southwest Semitic languages.

One striking feature in grammatical structure is common to all the semitic languages, and that is a marked preference for verbal roots using three consonant sounds. These consonants remain clearly recognizable no matter what vowels appear or disappear between them, or what prefixes and suffixes may be added. The characteristic core of the word, stripped of its mutations, is called the "triliteral root." A student learns, for example, that variations of the idea "to kill" cluster around the unpronounceable abstraction [qtl],[2] which has no independent existence but which can be detected in these related forms meaning "they killed:"

	Hebrew	Aramaic	Arabic	Ethiopian
Imperfect	yiqtəlū	yiqtəlūn	yaqtulu	yəqattəlū
Perfect	qātəlu	qətal(ū)	qatalū	qatalu

Nouns related to verbs show the same three-pillared structure of consonants. In Hebrew the present-tense root form meaning "reigning as king" is [moːleːχ]; "to be or become king" is [mɔːlaχ]; "to make one king" is [mɔlaχ]; "a king" is [meleχ], plural [məlɔχiːm]; and "kingdom" is [maləχuːs].

The consonantal abstraction of the root is [mlχ].[3] These examples are sufficient to clarify a persistent and very easily recognized trait in Semitic.

HAMITIC LANGUAGES

Contiguous with parts of Semitic territory and rather similar to Semitic in structure are the languages of the Hamitic group. They were named from the second son of that early navigator, Noah. Ancient Egyptian (known historically since 4000 B.C.) belonged to it, and produced in turn the Coptic or neo-Egyptian language which continued to be spoken down to the seventeenth century of our era. This Hamitic tongue has one of the longest careers so far as records are concerned. Akin to it are surviving dialects of Berber, spoken in scattered communities across the north of Africa as far as the Canary Islands, and also the Cushite languages bordering the Red Sea: Bedja, Somali, Saho, and Afar.

There is good reason to suppose that Hamitic and Semitic are themselves differentiations of an original linguistic unity called Hamito-Semitic by specialists. For one thing, Old Egyptian shows a marked preference for triliteral consonant roots, as a glance at its grammar will show, even though biliteral consonant roots are also common. Moreover, there are a few phonological traits common to the combined group, and one or two grammatical usages which appear to come from a common source. The peoples concerned have been neighbors from time immemorial. It is not unlikely that the idioms now spoken by them had a single origin. There has been quite enough time during and before recorded history for the multiple ramifications to occur.

SUDANESE AND BANTU GROUPS

The rest of Africa is occupied almost entirely by two large groups, somewhat loosely defined: the Sudanese (generally southwest of the Hamitic belt) and Bantu (south of Sudanese). Though the field of African Negro languages has been comparatively neglected, the study of these two major groups has already revealed evidence of common origin from a single language before the cleavage into these two major divisions. Research is hampered, of course, by an almost complete absence of written texts before modern times. (The study of Indo-European reveals clearly how illuminating and decisive an ancient text can be in determining family relationships among languages.) Even today, however, Bantu and Sudanese agree in classifying nouns grammatically according to the class of objects they represent, each class being marked off by an affixed syllable to designate it. Parent Bantu, for instance, probably had a prefix *mu-*, usually reserved for human beings. An example is *mu-na* ("child") in the Duzala dialect. Other prefixes were *ba-*, *gu-*, *mi-*. Sudanese uses such class prefixes for nouns too. Bantu and Sudanese also inflect their verbs to show *aspects* of action rather than the time relations which we consider so very important. A Bantu verb shows completeness, negation, emphasis, continuity, and other relations, but not very many temporal ones.

Na-pula means "I desire" in Duala, and *na-puli*, "I desired"; other inflexions are: *na-si-pula*, "I desire not"; *na-pulise*, "I cause to desire"; *na-pulana*, "I desire because of something." Phonology and vocabulary mark off Bantu as distinct from its northern neighbor in Sudan, but it may well be that underlying similarities will be increasingly revealed in this domain too.

ALTAIC LANGUAGES

Returning to the Balkans and the Near East we find another huge family of languages represented by one, Turkish, spoken within the very portals of Europe. The broad term for Turkish and its relatives is Altaic. It includes three main divisions: Turkic, Mongol, and Tunguz. These extend from the southeast of Europe (Istanbul) through the Volga district and Turkey, through Azerbaijan, Anatolia, and the Caucasian districts, to Mongolia and the Tunguz-Manchu region around the Yenisei River. Among the Turkic sub-divisions are the groups in the east or Altai region (including Yakut); the Central Asian groups; the western ones (including Tatar in the Volga district and Kirghiz); and the southern (Turcoman, Anatolian, Caucasian Turkic dialects, etc.).

The Mongolian subdivision centers in Mongolia, showing little diffusion outside the political boundaries of the country. Tunguz is spoken east of the Yenisei River, while Manchu, a close relative, is limited to the valleys of the Khurkha and Sungari rivers. It is being replaced by Chinese.

A common trait which links these widely sundered languages is the principle of vowel harmony, which also marks Finno-Ugric, as we have seen. There are other characters of a general phonological nature which can be found in all of them. An example of the vowel harmony is a pair of compounds from the Osmanli dialect (spoken in the Balkans):

öl-dür-mä-yälim, "*let us not kill.*"
otur-ma-yaḷïm, "*let us not stay seated.*"

Notice that in the first word, the first syllable began with a front vowel, so that all the following vowels—including those of the first person plural suffix—had to be fronted. In some, this front quality is indicated by two dots over the vowel. The second group began with [o], a back vowel, and as a consequence the following syllables also show lowered vowels. Even the [i] is lowered to [ï], and the [l] preceding it is lowered from its front position. (The sign [ł] represents an *l*-sound made with the back of the tongue instead of the tip.) These subtle gradations of sound within the phrasal unit are practiced automatically by the vast numbers of people who speak Turkic-Mongolian-Tunguz as well as those who employ Finno-Ugric, making a very imposing total in all.

SINO-TIBETAN LANGUAGES

In the Far East there is another inclusive group employed by an imposing section of humanity, namely the Sino-Tibetan languages. The subdivisions are Chinese, Tai, and Tibeto-Burman, covering a belt from China on the east

to the Tibetan highlands of India, and dipping down into Siam. The characteristic word-form in all these languages is an uninflected monosyllable
which shows its role in the sentence by position only. Yet there are traces of
dissyllabic roots and inflectional forms which must have been common in
the parent language. To a very limited degree English may be compared to
Sino-Tibetan languages, since we too depend on word order to show relationships in the sentence; but of course we use many other devices as
well.

Musical pitch is an important feature of all these languages. It may change
the meaning of a word, since many syllables otherwise complete homonyms
(that is, identical) are distinguished by high or low pitch alone. It is as if we
distinguished between "sea" and "see" by giving one a high and the other
a low tone. There is evidence that originally high pitch accompanied syllables
beginning with a voiceless consonant, so that *tai* would necessarily be spoken
—or, rather, intoned—higher than *dai*; but many intricate sound changes
throughout the centuries have obscured this neat correlation.

MALAY-POLYNESIAN GROUPS

The Malay-Polynesian belt, including peoples in the Dutch East Indies,
Philippines, Malay Peninsula, Madagascar, Hawaii, and small Pacific archi-
pelagos, reveals the close connection of its members with one another to
the most casual observation. They make use of roots of two syllables and
employ a variety of prefixes, suffixes, and infixes; yet their nouns are innocent of inflection to show gender and number. In Hawaiian, original consonants have been slurred away in so many positions that the language has
become a tissue of vowels held together by a minimum of consonants in
initial and intervocalic positions.

AMERICAN INDIAN FAMILIES

Across the Pacific we come once more to the two American continents where
a pair of Indo-European languages, English and Spanish (together with
Portuguese) dominate official life. They have displaced but not yet eliminated
completely an enormously diversified series of Indian languages, extending
from the Arctic to the Antarctic. Some families of these have been carefully
studied, but the variety is so great that we are in no position to make hypoth-
eses concerning underlying unities. Specialists differ widely in their estimates of the numbers of groups showing so little similarity at present as to
appear to be independent. Emigration, conquest, cultural interpenetration,
and merging have done much to confuse the picture. The reader will recognize
the names of some of the larger groups in North America, such as the
Algonquian, Iroquoian, Muskogean, Siouan, and Uto-Aztecan. Eskimo,
which is spoken in the north of Canada, is now considered to be a relative of
Nenets (Samoyedic) in the Uralic group which includes Finno-Ugric.

AUSTRALIAN, CAUCASIAN, AND DRAVIDIAN FAMILIES. KOREAN AND JAPANESE

In this rapid encirclement of the globe several important linguistic territories have been omitted, either because they have been too little charted for even the most summary description, or because they were too unified or too limited to illustrate ramified family relationships. The native languages of Australia are, for instance, a treasure-house of unexplored mystery. The region of the Caucasus mountains presents a bewildering complexity of diversified tongues spoken by fairly small groups, neighbors to one another, many of which are mutually unintelligible. Of these, one, Georgian, achieved literary expression at a comparatively early date (fourth century A.D.), but others have remained practically unknown outside their own territory. (Now that they are being recorded in print there will be a basis for comparative study.) In India, the Dravidian dialects represent a large but shrinking language group which antedated the conquering Indo-European Sanskrit in the Indus valley, and has retreated before it. India, the Malay peninsula, and the Siamese territory include linguistic patches or "islands" designated as Austro-Asiatic, grouped together on the basis of parallelisms in vocabulary and word-formation.[4] Korean and Japanese, both languages associated with high cultures, resemble each other in vocabulary and general grammatical forms, but the relations of the two are not entirely clarified despite arguments to prove their kinship. Both have impersonal verbs and uninflected nouns; both depend largely on word order to indicate relationships within the sentence.

There is much work still to be done in charting the unknown or little known territories of human speech. If we can judge from experience in the past, we may expect that further relationships may be discovered by the comparative method, and that groups hitherto thought to be isolated will have relatives discovered for them, sometimes in lands quite far away. Indo-European linguistics was launched on its triumphant way by the discovery of a most distant émigré member of the family in India. The agreeable experience of perceiving unity beneath diversity has rewarded linguists so often that they have some justification for expecting it to be repeated in the future.

SINGLE OR MULTIPLE ORIGIN OF SPEECH?

Already the question has often been asked: "Do we know enough to decide whether all languages, the world over, had a single origin? Is *every* language related to every other?"

It is a fascinating question. The mere possibility of unified origin for all human speech appeals strongly to the imagination. Here indeed would be a most gratifying satisfaction for our natural desire to simplify our understanding of the universe around us by reducing the number of categories under which we conceive of it. There is also something aesthetically grandiose about the thought that the vast symphony of all languages and dialects was elaborated, so to speak, from a single theme.

In the early days of linguistic science, the presuppositions were naturally in favor of monogenesis of speech, because the story of the Garden of Eden, whether understood literally or not, exerted a strong influence on investigators. Then under the spell of Darwinism there was a reaction to a belief in polygenesis, likewise often expressed in dogmatic terms. Analogies were drawn and misapplied in linguistic science, for which Darwin himself should not be blamed. The chief exponent of linguistic polygenesis was Friedrich Muller, who assumed that the "speech" of animals must have developed gradually into human speech, so gradually indeed that man must have been a diversified type long before the evolution was completed, "and, herewith," he argued, "we may be said to have an *a priori* postulate, from the point of view of the history of evolution, of the derivation of human speech (as an ideational and conceptional language based on sounds) from several mutually independent sources."

Today most authors are extemely cautious when they touch upon the unrecoverable epoch when speech originated. They usually avoid committing themselves on the question as to whether this happened once or several times in various parts of the world. In any case, they say, the answer is unimportant, even irrelevant, for the solution of problems significant for us today.

Nevertheless a few individual writers are willing to commit themselves. Alfredo Trombetti, for instance, has presented a lengthy, ambitious argument for monogenesis, fortified with many concrete illustrations. On the basis of extremely wide and detailed study, Trombetti builds up a scheme including wider and wider groups and families of languages, making use of surviving similarities in numerals, pronominal forms, and the like. Such structural words are apt to be conservative of their form, and they are not readily borrowed from one language by another in most cases. He records similarities between the numerals in Sudanese-Bantu and Munda-Khmer of the Austro-Asiatic group; between pronouns in Hamitic-Semitic, Dravidian, Munda, and Polynesian; between numerals in Indo-Chinese and Uralic (he says "Ural-Altaic"); between verbs in Dakọta (American Indian) and Georgian (in the Caucasian territory). He observes that the greatest similarities are to be found between groups most widely separated on the periphery of a huge circle having its center in India. Therefore he deduces that India was the home and the starting point for all races as well as all languages. It is true that Trombetti produces some astonishing parallelisms. But one becomes suspicious of them when one reflects upon the great mobility of language: its proneness to change and transformation. After observing the behavior of vowels and consonants over the very short span of recorded history, one begins to suspect that two words that look alike now are probably unrelated for that very reason—unless they belong to two subgroups in demonstrably close generic relation, and also mean approximately the same thing. English "book" and German *Buch* are indeed cognates, but it is quite accidental that Quiche *buj* or *vuj* (also pronounced [buχ], but with a loose *b*) means the same thing. We know too little about the early history of the languages outside of Indo-European and Hamito-Semitic to commit ourselves too far on the matter of ultimate relationships. For one thing, change operates very slowly in some groups and with almost dizzying rapidity in others. We must allow for this in estimating the value of Trombetti's parallels. The question about a single origin for the diverse tongues of mankind must be tabled until we know more of their earlier forms; and that may be—forever.

NOTES

1. ä = [ɛ]; ö = [ɛ'], a sound formed by rounding the lips while pronouncing [ɛ]; ü = [y]. For [ɛ] see chapter 2, p. 13, *The Gift of Tongues*; ö and ü are familiar to students of German.

2. The phonetic symbol [q] stands for a consonant resembling [k], but spoken much deeper in the throat.

3. It may be noticed in passing that in certain of the Semitic languages a consonant is modified in pronunciation if it comes after a vowel. In Hebrew and Aramaic, for instance, an older [k] became [χ] in such a position. An earlier form of the verbal root [m¹ₓ] appears in the word [malka̱:], "queen."

4. Father Wilhelm Schmidt has tried to prove their generic relation to Malay-Polynesian. This hypothesis is described by Przyluski as "grandiose—but fragile."

✠ ✠ ✠

THE ANCESTRY OF ENGLISH

STUART ROBERTSON AND
FREDERIC G. CASSIDY

We do not at present know whether human languages spring from a single common starting point or from more than one. Nevertheless, we can demonstrate today that of the hundreds of languages and dialects spoken in the world, many fall into historically related groups, usually called "families." Most of the languages now spoken in Europe, for example, and in parts of the world colonized by Europeans, are agreed by students of language to be members of a single family and to have descended from one hypothetical speech ancestor—Indo-European, otherwise known as Indo-Germanic and sometimes as Aryan.[1] This ancestor language is no longer spoken—indeed, no actual records of it remain and what we know has had to be laboriously reconstructed from the features preserved in its offspring.

Because English is one of its members, the Indo-European family is at the center of our present interest, but there are many non-Indo-European families of languages in the world. Those that have been most directly in contact with Indo-European include the following: Finno-Ugrian, comprising Finnish, Lappish, Hungarian (Magyar), and others; Altaic, including Turkish, Mongolian, and Manchu; Hamitic, made up of certain African

Reprinted from *The Development of Modern English,* Second Edition, by Stuart Robertson and Frederic G. Cassidy, © 1954, by permission of Prentice-Hall, Inc., Englewood Cliffs, New Jersey.

languages, among them Egyptian; and Semitic,[2] the best-known members of which are Hebrew and Arabic. There are many more-distant families—for example, the Sino-Tibetan (or Indo-Chinese), whose members are found in Tibet, Burma, Thailand, and China. The total number of families of languages is in the hundreds, but the majority of these are limited dialects, spoken chiefly in Africa and the Americas, whose relationship to any of the larger groups has not yet been shown. The number of native American Indian language-families alone is thus estimated at over one hundred and twenty. If more evidence were available as to earlier forms, it would doubtless be possible to reduce this number greatly; it is even conceivable that, with fuller knowledge, all the families now recognized might be grouped together as branches of a common unit. But a great many languages have never been studied adequately, many are totally unknown, and though there is vigorous activity in the field of language study today, a very great deal of work lies ahead before linguists can begin to demonstrate such broader relationships, if ever they can. In any consideration of the ancestry of English, therefore, we must be satisfied at present with the conception of an Indo-European starting point.

Before beginning with the Indo-European theory, however, it may be well to inquire into the factors that account for the splitting up of a language into subdivisions and new groupings. We have used the metaphor of a "family," of "ancestor" and "descendants," because it is convenient, though not literally accurate. Languages are not organisms living by generations and having individual offspring. This much truth there is in the metaphor, however: that though in the course of time the elements of a language are constantly subject to natural change, they do not change altogether or all of a sudden. Thus, as one may recognize the features and traits of parents in their children, a historical study of language shows some features preserved where others have changed; and if several languages exhibit common characteristics, they must have come by them either through coincidence, or by borrowing, or through derivation from a common source. The chief labor of the historical linguist goes into solving such questions and explaining observed similarities and differences.

Languages split up for at least three reasons, which may work separately or together: *natural change, geographic division*, and *contact with other languages*. The first depends on the fact that language is normally learned by imitation—by hearing and repeating. But since this imitation is never exact—and indeed need not be so, for a fairly close imitation will usually get the same result as a precise one—in the course of a few generations a language may easily come to sound quite different in many respects. Spelling alone could show us, for example, if there were no other evidence, that Shakespeare, at the end of the sixteenth century, said many things quite differently from Chaucer, at the end of the fourteenth. Add to this the changes in vocabulary that come from altered conditions of life, new inventions, and our individual differences of expression, and it is easy to see why we do not speak like our grandparents. In the most conservative societies such changes are reduced to a minimum, and a cultural and educational tradition may (as with us) hold them in check to some extent; but change is a fundamental, unavoidable fact of language.

Secondly, geographic division may foster language division by inhibiting communication. Two groups, let us say, migrate from a common point, but settle on opposite sides of a mountain or river. At the time of parting they spoke alike; but they lose touch, and the rate and type of the natural changes in their speech do not correspond. One group, perhaps, takes to farming, the other to seafaring; or one develops a static society, the other a dynamic. Inevitably such differences will be reflected in speech. The separated groups will speak different dialects, and in time perhaps different languages. But this situation itself will not necessarily last indefinitely. After the original separation and subsequent changes, lines of communication may be established despite the geographic obstruction, and a whole new phase of development may begin. The science of linguistic geography (of which more shall be said later) furnishes countless examples of such developments. One need only glance at the map of Europe to see that natural barriers—the Alps or the Pyrenees—are often also the frontiers of language. On a smaller scale, the separation of Old English (Anglo-Saxon) into dialects, though it began on the continent before the tribes migrated, is emphasized by the fact that the boundaries are rivers: the region of the Northumbrian dialect was from the Humber to the Forth; of the Mercian from the Thames to the Humber: and of the West Saxon, most of the country south of the Thames.

Thirdly, languages change because of contact with other languages. This may come about in various ways, but commerce and conquest furnish the most striking examples. An alien tongue has often been imposed upon a conquered people. Or it may work the other way: the Normans afford the remarkable instance of conquerors twice giving up their own language for that of a conquered people; for they first exchanged their Scandinavian language for the Romance tongue of Normandy, and eventually they gave up the French dialect thus acquired and accepted the Germanic speech of conquered Britain. Commerce involves travel and exploration, and the introduction of things from other lands. Though less sudden than conquest, it is thus an important means of increasing changes in language. From the earliest times we know of, English has been so influenced by other tongues; many of the brave new words that the Elizabethans spouted with such delight had come from brave new worlds that were opening yearly before them.

Let us return, then, to the Indo-European hypothesis. This holds that in the Later Stone Age there lived a people or peoples speaking a tongue that was the common ancestor of the greater number of cultivated languages now existing in the world. This does not imply either that the original Indo-Europeans were racially a unit or that their speech descendants are racially akin. It does, however, assume that the hypothetical language which we call Indo-European was the speech of a people inhabiting a comparatively limited geographical area, and that from this focal point have radiated all the subdivisions of the Indo-European family of languages.[3] What was the focal area from which these languages spread? During the last half-century there have been a number of investigations into the problems of the Indo-European "home" and of the classification of language that the Indo-European theory implies. Partly anthropological and archeological but chiefly linguistic, these investigations have altered the old belief that the home of the Indo-Europeans was in Asia, and most probably in the fabled region of the Garden of Eden, between the Tigris and the Euphrates. It is now generally held that the Indo-European home was in central or southeastern Europe, though some scholars contend that it was farther to the north. Some of the methods used in attacking the problem may be of interest.

The evidence of language is fairly clear as to the climate, the animals, and the plants of the region that the original Indo-Europeans inhabited. Everything points to the temperate zone, and in all probability not to the southern part of that zone. For in many Indo-European languages we find the same words (not, of course, words identical in form, but words strongly alike in both form and meaning, and therefore recognizable as variants of the same original) for such phenomena as snow, winter, and spring; for such animals as the dog, the horse, the cow, the sheep, the bear; but *not* the camel, the lion, the elephant, or the tiger; for such trees as the beech, the oak, the pine, the willow, but not the palm or the banyan.[4] It is urged, further, that the country could not have had access to the sea: there is apparently no common word for "ocean."[5] If it was on the continent of Europe, it is unlikely, for other reasons, that it was near the seacoast: the pre-Hellenic inhabitants of Greece, for example, were not Indo-European, nor were the Etruscans in Italy, the pre-Celtic peoples who inhabited Britain, or the Basques in Spain and southern France; and over the greater part of northern and eastern Europe were the Finno-Ugrians.

A single argument may be given in greater detail to illustrate the way in which the problem of the Indo-European home has recently been approached. Professor Bender[6] observes that almost every Indo-European language shares with its fellow a common word for honey or for an intoxicating drink made from honey. The first stem is Indo-European *melit*,[7] the second *medhu*. The former appears, for example, in Greek *méli* (honey) and *mélissa* (bee), Latin *mel* (honey), and Old English *milisc* (honey-sweet) and *mildēaw* (mildew—literally, "honey-dew"). The latter appears, among many other places, in Sanskrit *madhu* (honey, mead), Greek *méthu* (intoxicating drink), Dutch *mede* (mead), and Old English *medu* (mead). The inference is that the original home of the Indo-Europeans was a land where the honey-bee abounded; and none of the Asiatic sites that have been seriously considered by linguists falls within the bee-belt. In ways like this, though with full recognition that one or another single argument may be fallacious, the weight of the evidence favors the theory of a central or southeastern European site. Professor Bender argues for Lithuania as the specific region, pointing out that "Lithuanian . . . has preserved into modern living speech more of the

Indo-European past than any other language on earth," and that "the Lithuanian stock has dwelt in its present location for at least five thousand years, the duration of the Indo-European period, so far as it is known."[8]

Accepting, then, the concept of an Indo-European starting point, we may proceed to examine the classification of language that follows from this theory. There are nine divisions, groups, or branches recognized today as composing the Indo-European family.[9] These are further divided, according to the sound of the initial consonant that appears (in the various languages) in such words as the Latin *centum* and the Avestan *satem*, the word for "hundred," into the *centum* group (Tokharian, Hellenic, Italic, Celtic, and Germanic) and the *satem* group (Indo-Iranian, Armenian, Balto-Slavic, and Albanian). Upon what cause this observed difference depends is unknown, and it may be doubted whether it betokens important early differences between the languages; but if, as is possible, the *s* represents a palatalization[10] of the *k*, it may suggest something about the sequence of the migrations.

. . .

The common features by means of which scholars have classified the Indo-European languages as a family, setting them apart from non-Indo-European languages are chiefly two: they are all *inflectional* in structure[13] and they have a *common word-stock*. The term *inflectional* means that such syntactic distinctions as gender, number, case, mood, tense,[14] and so forth, are usually indicated by varying the form of a single word or word-base. Thus, in English inflection, we add -*s* to a noun base to differentiate the plural from the singular, or -*ed* to a verb base to indicate past tense. English inflection uses endings almost entirely, though (as we shall see) inflection may come also at the beginning of words or within them.

The *inflectional* structure is only one type; languages outside the Indo-European system that are inflectional may be: *isolating*, like Chinese, in which invariable word-forms, mostly monosyllabic, are used, and in which the relation between words is indicated by their relative position ("word-order") or occasionally by variation in tonal patterns; *agglutinative*, like Turkish or Hungarian, in which formal affixes are attached to independent and invariable bases in such a way that base and affix are always distinct; or *incorporating* or *polysynthetic* like the language of Greenland (Eskimo), in which a single word may express not only subject and verb, but also such other concepts as direct and indirect object; hence, what would be, in an isolating language, a sentence of five or six words, may be "incorporated" as a single word.[15] Still other types of structure are to be found.

As to the second criterion of the Indo-European languages, the possession of a common word-stock, it will strike even the novice that, for example, Greek *nuktos*,[16] Latin *noctis*, German *Nacht*, French *nuit*, Spanish *noche*, Italian *notte*, and English *night* have a similarity of form and meaning that seems too striking to be accidental. Unless some of these had been borrowed or loaned from one language to another, such similarity must imply a common origin. Further examples of *cognates* (as such words are called) appearing in different Indo-European languages are:[17]

English	Dutch	German	Gothic	Lithuanian
three	drie	drei	thri	tri
seven	zeven	sieben	sibun	septyni
me	mij	mich	mik	manen
mother	moeder	mutter	——	moter
brother	broeder	bruder	brothar	brolis

Celtic	Latin	Greek	Persian	Sanskrit
tri	tres	treis	thri	tri
secht	septem	hepta	hapta	sapta
me	me	me	me	me
mathair	mater	meter	matar	matar
brathair	frater	phrater	——	bhratar

These are not isolated examples; there are hundreds of other such words preserved in the various branch languages, which gives the classification a sound basis.

Coming closer to English we may ask what special characteristics the Germanic languages have in common that serve to differentiate Germanic, as a branch, from the other divisions of Indo-European. The four principal ones are:[18]

1. A simpler conjugation of verbs (only two tenses), including a twofold classification (strong and weak);
2. A twofold classification of adjectives (strong and weak);
3. A fixed stress-accent;
4. A regular shifting of the stopped (or explosive) consonants.

Each of these points requires fuller explanation.

As to the first: even a slight acquaintance with Latin or Greek makes it apparent that their conjugation of verbs is far more complex than is that of German or English. The terminology sometimes used should not be allowed to obscure this contrast. The fact that in a grammar-book the phrase *I had loved* or *ich hatte geliebt* may be labeled as a "pluperfect tense" does not mean that in structure it really parallels *amaveram*, which is similarly labeled. The English and German examples show "analytical" structure—that is, the three words, though they function as a single group, are still separate units in combination; but the Latin equivalent shows "synthetic" structure—that is, the word is made up of inseparable parts that cannot stand by themselves.[19]

Latin verbs have a very elaborate series of such synthetic forms to differentiate various concepts of voice, mood, tense, person, and number; Greek, being still nearer the complexity of the Indo-European verb, has at least one more complication in almost every category: there are not only the two numbers of Latin, singular and plural, but also a third, the dual, there are not only the two voices, active and passive, but also a third, the middle: there are additional moods, like the optative, and additional tenses, like the aorist. In sharp contrast to this is the system of Germanic, characterized by having only two tenses, one to express past time, the other to express present and future. The inflected passive voice of Germanic, likewise, was early lost; it is represented in Old English by only a single form, *hātte* (was called), a related form of which survives as the poetic relic *hight*; elsewhere the passive voice was expressed as in Modern English by an analytic combination of an auxiliary verb with the past participle of the main verb (as in the example *I had loved* just mentioned).

The most distinctive feature of the Germanic verb, however, is its development of a new way of indicating the preterit and past participle by means of a dental suffix[20] the *-ed* of English and the *-te* and *-t* of German. The pattern inherited from Indo-European in the verb, then, is called "strong" and the new pattern is called "weak." Both types last into Modern English: the weak (less accurately called "regular") verbs are those with the dental preterit, as *walk, walked*; the strong (or "irregular") are those with internal vowel change, such as *sing, sang, sung*. The latter group corresponds historically to the verbs of other languages, but the former is distinctively Germanic. Because more verbs belong to the weak conjugation, we have come to feel, as the term "regular" suggests, that it is not only the simpler but the normal pattern. When we borrow or create new verbs, they are made to conform to it.

The second distinguishing characteristic of the Germanic languages is the twofold classification of the adjective that developed: it was declined according to one system ("strong") when it stood alone before the noun or was used in the predicate relation, and according to another system ("weak") when used substantively or when it was preceded by a defining element, such as an article or a demonstrative. Since Modern English has lost all declension of the adjective, this distinction between the strong and weak forms cannot be illustrated with contemporary examples. It lasted, however, into Old English, and is still to be found in German. Thus, in Modern English we used the identical form *good* in the expressions *good men* and *these good men*. In Old English, however, the corresponding phrases would be *gōde menn* and *þās gōdan menn*—as in German the corresponding phrases are *gute Männer* and *diese guten Männer*. As with the verbs, it is the weak inflection that is distinctively Germanic, the strong forms corresponding more or less to adjective declension in other Indo-European languages. The loss of the distinction in Modern English need hardly be mourned—it is difficult to see any gain in expressiveness that would justify this peculiar inflectional complexity! Nevertheless, its former presence in English and its retention in German are significant in marking these languages unmistakably as members of the Germanic branch.

The third characteristic of the Germanic languages is their accent, fixed rather than free or variable, and a matter of stress rather than of pitch. To English-speaking people it may seem at first sight that accent in any language must necessarily be fixed—that is, that it must come on a particular syllable of a word. But it is clear to linguists that the original Indo-European and the primitive Germanic accent was variable; for example, it might shift, in the inflection of a word, from the base syllable to a syllable of the inflectional ending. Greek and Latin partially preserve this, as when the Greek *poûs* (foot) is declined *podós, podí, póda*; the accent, that is to say, shifts in the genitive and dative from the base to the inflectional ending, and comes back, in the accusative, to the base. Latin also exhibits this freer accent (in contrast to the Germanic) as, for example, in the conjugation of the present indicative of *amō*, where we find *ámō, ámās, ámat, amámus, amátis, ámant*. Or note how in the inflection of *gubernátor* the accent is shifted from the nominative *gubernátor* to the genetive *gubernatóris*. We should be doing something equivalent in English if we spoke of the *góvernor*, and then proceeded to speak of *the govérnor's house*. But this, of course, or anything remotely like it[21] we never do: our tendency is to stress strongly the first syllable of a word (excluding prefixes that are felt as such). The Germanic branch, then, during the primitive period when it was becoming separated from the Indo-European parent language, shifted its accent back to the base syllable, where it became fixed; it is therefore called the *recessive* stress-accent, and this is inherited in Modern English.

The other aspect of the Germanic accent is even more important: many other Indo-European languages retain something of the original "musical" or pitch accent; in the Germanic languages, by contrast, accent has become to all intents a matter of stress. The implications of this distinction are considerable. The accentuation of English and German is utterly unlike that of French, which in words of two syllables has more nearly a hovering or distributed accent than a firm stress on one syllable. Such pronunciations as *wéekènd, bóokcàse, sáucepàn*, with stress on both syllables, are the exception in English; in most cases we have come to overemphasize, as compared even with German, the accented syllable, and to underemphasize the unaccented.[22] Perhaps this is the chief reason why French as pronounced by an English-speaking person, who can scarcely help carrying over his usual habits of accentuation, so often sounds curiously unreal. The versification of Germanic languages likewise depends upon this distinction between the stressed and unstressed syllable, and its effect is utterly different from that achieved by the quantitative system of the classical languages and its partial retention in the Romance languages.

Finally, perhaps the most important effect that the heavy Germanic stress-accent has had upon the development of English has been that of slurring and frequently altogether dropping unstressed vowels. Because the accent usually falls on the first syllable of the word and because English inflections are chiefly in the final syllables, it has been easy for inflectional endings to become weakened, obscured, and lost—and consequently to simplify the whole system of inflection. Here is the chief reason, too, for the largely monosyllabic quality of the native English word-stock.

The fourth distinctive mark of the Germanic languages is their almost regular shifting of the Indo-European stopped consonants.[23] That is to say, the original Indo-European sounds remained in general unchanged in all branches except the Germanic; but there their articulation shifted, a new set of sounds being substituted for them. The evidence for this shift was discovered by comparing hundreds of words whose meaning was very close, but whose forms differed as between the Germanic and the non-Germanic branches, whereupon it was seen that these differences were not haphazard but clearly followed a pattern. The regularity of these changes was first stated by the Danish linguist Rasmus Rask, in 1814; but their later formulation by Jacob Grimm in 1822 has given the principles the designation "Grimm's Law." It is now more often called the *first Germanic consonant shift*.[24] A full statement of it and of its subsequent modifications would be out of place here. It may, however, be broadly stated as follows:

Voiced aspirated stops	Voiced stops	Voiceless stops[25]
bh dh gh	b d g	p t k
v v v	v v v	v v v
b d g	p t k	f th h
Indo-European voiced aspirated stops lost aspiration and became Germanic voiced stops.	Indo-European voiced stops lost voice and became Germanic voiceless stops.	Indo-European voiceless stops lost their stopped quality and became Germanic voiceless spirants.[26]
(Stage 3)	(Stage 2)	(Stage 1)

It is to be understood, of course, that each original set of consonants changed only once; for example, the *b, d, g* that resulted from the shift of *bh, dh, gh* did not shift further. Indeed, had they done so, the words formerly distinguished by these sounds would have fallen together as homophones, losing distinction and producing much confusion. The whole process is understood to have taken place in three stages; after *p, t* and *k* had shifted, it was possible for *b, d,* and *g* to shift without producing homophones.

Illustrations of the situation "before" may be drawn generally from the non-Germanic languages (Greek, Latin, Sanskrit, Old Irish, and so on), and the situation "after" from any Germanic language (Old Norse, Old High German, Old English, Old Saxon, and so on), the only difficulty being that in some cases further simplifications took place in individual languages, which somewhat obscured the earlier shift. For instance, in Greek the Indo-European *bh* became *ph*, and in Latin it became *f*; thus Greek *phrater* and Latin *frater* represent Indo-European **bhratar*, the shift being seen in English *brother*. Similarly, Indo-European *dh* and *gh* were reduced initially in Latin to *f* and *h*, therefore we find such correspondences as Latin *facere*, English *do*, and Latin *hostis*, English *guest*. The changes of the third stage, then, cannot be simply illustrated; the others, however, may be seen in the following tabulation:[27]

Change: *b* > *p*
Lithuanian *troba* (house)—Old Norse *thorp* (village)
Old Bulgarian *slabu* (slack, weak)—English *sleep*
Lithuanian *dubus*—English *deep*

Change: *d* > *t*
Latin *dentem*—English *tooth*
Greek *édein*—English *eat*
Russian *dva*—Old English *twā* (two)

Change: *g* > *k*
Sanskrit *yuga*—English *yoke*
Greek (*gi*)*gnŏ* (*skein*)—English *know*
Latin *genu*—German *Knie* (knee)

Change: *p* > *f*
Greek *plōtós* (floating)—English *flood*
Latin *nepos*—Old English *nefa* (nephew)
Persian *pidar*—English *father*

Change: *t* > *th*
Polish *tarn*—English *thorn*
Latin *tū*—English *thou*
Old Latin *tongēre* (know)—English *think*

Change: *k* > *h*
Greek *deka*—Gothic *taíhun* (ten)
Latin *canem*—German *Hund* (dog)
Irish *cridhe*—English *heart*

Later philologists than Grimm found it necessary to modify his statement of the consonant-shift. Chief of these modifications, called Verner's Law, bears the name of the Danish linguist who first showed (in 1875) how the seeming exceptions to Grimm's Law, if once understood according to the principle of accent, turned out to be regular, not erratic. His postulate was that when the first consonant-shift began it found the early Germanic stress on the same syllables as in Indo-European, and that it was this stress on many medial and final syllables that accounted for the presence of voiced consonants instead of the voiceless consonants which might otherwise have been expected. Thus the primitive Indo-European *voiceless stops* (*p, t, k*), no matter in what position in a word they happened to be, changed to *voiceless spirants* (*f, þ, h*) in early-primitive-Germanic. In later-primitive-Germanic, however, a split developed: those which came in initial position in a word, or immediately after a stressed vowel, changed no further—but those which came in any other position changed to *voiced spirants*; thus, *f, þ, h,* (and *s*) became respectively *b, ð, ʒ,* and *z*.[28] Verner argued that it was the difference in the pattern of stress that was responsible for this change of internal consonant sounds, and that when the Germanic stress shifted back, soon after, to the base syllable of all words, the cause of the consonant-split became obscured.

The English verb *to be* furnishes a good illustration of Verner's Law, since in the forms *was* and *were* we find an *s* in correspondence with an *r*. The difference is explained thus: in early-primitive-Germanic the singular and plural forms had both had *s* (**wǽs, *wǣsún*); in later-primitive-Germanic the *s* became *z* unless it was initial or just after a stressed vowel (*wǽs, *wǣzún*); then the stress shifted to the base syllable (**wǽs, wǽzun*). Further changes took place in the West Germanic stage of development, and when we come to Old English we find that the four voiced spirants, *b, ð, ʒ,* and *z,* have become respectively *f, d, ʒ,* and *r*. Thus the forms of *to be* appear as *wæs* and *wæron*. One may follow the process further in English by mining in the *Oxford Dictionary* (or any other which has good etymologies) under such words as *seethe, sodden; freeze, frore; rear* (the verb), and *raise*.

A few broader illustrations may also be given. Germanic, in the situation described, has *d* when *th* would be expected as the simple shift from Indo-European *t*; thus English *old* (Old English *eald*) is cognate with Latin *altus*,[29] English *yard* (Old English *geard*) with Latin *hortus*, English *sad*[30] with Latin *satis*. Likewise Indo-European *p* and *k*, instead of appearing as *f* and *h*, become *b* and *g* respectively under the conditions of Verner's Law.[31] Verner's brilliant discovery showed all the more clearly that the greatest progress was made in the solution of problems when investigators proceeded on the assumption of basic regularity ("laws"), the exceptions to which were themselves to be explained by the assumption of regular processes of development and change. Linguistic geography has since shown that qualifications must be made to this, but as a broad working hypothesis it marked a great advance over the less rigorous methods which preceded it.

Of the four distinguishing Germanic characteristics that have been reviewed, it is probably accurate to suggest that the accent contributed most to make Germanic words distinctive and to give the modern Germanic languages a unique place among European languages. The stress-shift that took place, as Verner's Law implies, after the first consonant-shift had begun, was even more important than the other process in changing the character of Germanic words.[32] The result of the stress-shift was that, in general, the Germanic accent was fixed on the base syllable of the word, except that in nouns and adjectives, and in verbs derived from these, it rested on the first syllable, whether prefix or base. As a result of both consonant-shift and stress-shift, the Germanic branch emerged as a highly individualized and easily identifiable member of the Indo-European family of languages.

In order to understand the specific position of English, we must now return and consider the subdivisions of the Germanic branch. To the eastern group belongs Gothic; to the northern belong Old Norse and the modern Scandinavian languages; the western became divided into the high and low groups (according to their geographic distribution in southern uplands or northern lowlands), the former being chiefly represented by modern standard German, the latter by Low German ("Plattdeutsch"), Dutch, Frisian, and English. In all these divisions of Germanic there are remains from early centuries. The accompanying diagram shows schematically the relations of the various branches of Indo-European,[33] and the subdivisions of the Germanic branch. English, as we see, is a member of the Low German subdivision, and is therefore contrasted with modern German, which belongs to the High German subdivision; yet both are West Germanic languages, and in that respect contrast with Swedish or Norwegian, which are North Germanic.

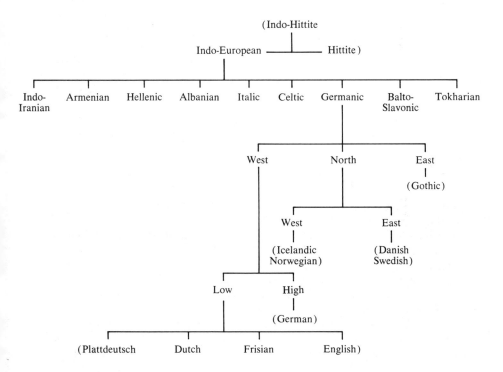

This diagram shows:
a. *The nine main branches of the Indo-European family of languages;*
b. *The position of Hittite (above, in parentheses) according to the Indo-Hittite theory (unless Hittite is considered the tenth branch, on a par with the other nine);*
c. *The subdivisions of the Germanic branch, with the position of English in relation to the other sub-members.*
  The diagram shows only lines of descent; if it also showed the many interrelations through borrowing, it would include numerous lateral lines—e.g., between members of the Italic and the Germanic branches.

To point out that English is genetically a Germanic language does not, however, by any means tell the whole story. For English, compared with modern German—or with its own earliest stage, Old English—has clearly undergone vast alterations in the course of a few centuries. High German, relatively isolated within the continent, has been conservative; the Low German dialects have been open to more influences that might bring change. And English, particularly, with a population that had migrated, with conquest by Danes and Normans, with its surrounding seas opening it early and always to maritime and mercantile activity, with early Christianization and an eager reception of much of Roman culture, has developed more rapidly and much farther away from old patterns than any other Germanic language —so much so that it is now considerably mixed.

REFERENCES FOR FURTHER READING

Baugh, Albert C., *A History of the English Language,* New York (Appleton-Century), 1935.

Bender, H. H., *The Home of the Indo-Europeans,* Princeton (Princeton University Press), 1922.

Brugmann, Karl, and Delbrück, B., *Grundriss der Vergleichenden Grammatik der Indogermanischen Sprachen,* Strassburg (Trübner), 1886–1900, 3 vols. Also translated.

Bryant, Margaret M., *Modern English and Its Heritage,* New York (Macmillan), 1948.

Emerson, O. F., *History of the English Language,* New York (Macmillan), 1894.

Hirt, Hermann, *Handbuch des Urgermanischen,* Heidelberg (Winter), 1931.

———, *Indogermanische Grammatik,* Heidelberg (Winter), 1927.

Jespersen, Otto, *Growth and Structure of the English Language,* Leipzig (Teubner), 8th ed., 1935.

Jóhannesson, Alexander, "Um frumtungu Indógermana og frumheimkynni," Fylgir Arbók Háskóla Islands (1940–1), Reykjavík (Gutenberg), 1949.

Meillet, A., *Introduction à l'étude comparative des langues indo-européennes* (Hachette), 7th ed., 1934.

Schmidt, P. W., *Sprachfamilien und Sprachenkreise der Erde,* Heidelberg (Winter), 1926.

Wright, Joseph and Elizabeth M., *Old English Grammar,* Oxford (Oxford University Press), 3rd ed., 1925.

Whitney, W. D., *Language and the Study of Language,* New York (Scribner), 1867.

NOTES

1. "Aryan" is best avoided; it is ambiguous, having been used as a synonym of Indo-Iranian as well as of Indo-European. Furthermore, it has been used as a racial designation, which gives the false implication of a connection between race and language.

2. The terms *Semitic* and *Hamitic* reflect the old belief that from the different languages spoken by the sons of Noah sprang the great groups of languages later spoken in the world. In line with this belief, the Indo-European was once called the *Japhetic*.

3. The migrations from this center are thought to have begun during the third millennium B.C. On the basis of common words for copper that remain in the various branches, Prof. Gray argues (*Foundations of Language,* p. 307), "it seems safe to infer that Indo-European unity came to an end after copper had become known, but before the Bronze Age ... The use of bronze was established in Europe by 1700 B.C."—which sets the start of migration as probably before 2000 B.C.

4. It must be recognized that, singly, these words would offer inadequate proof; the names of trees, for example, are likely to apply to entirely different species in different times and places: the ancient Greek word corresponding to English *beech* meant *oak*, and sometimes *chestnut*.

5. This, however, is sometimes asserted with more confidence than is warranted; cf. Hirt, *Indogermanische Grammatik,* Vol. I, pp. 77–78.

6. *The Home of the Indo-Europeans,* pp. 19–20.

7. An asterisk (*) prefixed to any word indicates that it is a linguistic reconstruction, not a form attested historically.

8. The question, however, is not settled—at least, so far as the specific region is concerned. See, for example, the new arguments made by Professor Jóhannesson, *Um frumtungu Indógermana og frumheimkynni,* 1941.

9. This number would be increased to ten if Hittite were considered to be on a par with the other members; but according to the Indo-Hittite hypothesis of Prof. E. H. Sturtevant it is not.

10. Palatalization means that a sound (such as that of *k*) which is articulated in the back of the mouth cavity, changes, becoming articulated in the area of the hard palate farther toward the front of the mouth, and therefore also changes its quality.

. . .

13. Not all inflectional languages are Indo-European, however.

14. If the student is not familiar with these and other common grammatical terms, he had better look them up at once in a good dictionary or grammar.

15. Cf. Pedersen, *Linguistic Science in the Nineteenth Century,* pp. 99–100.

16. This form, the next, and others later on are given as usual in oblique cases, in order to show the full bases. (Bases were often reduced in the nominative case.)

17. From Whitney, *Language and the Study of Language,* p. 196.

18. It should perhaps be added that the four chief changes from Indo-European to Germanic give a very incomplete picture of the whole process. Cf. Hirt, *Handbuch des Urgermanischen.*

19. If we break up the Latin word we find that *am-* means love, *-av-* indicates past time (like *-ed* in *loved*), *-er-* indicates completed action (like *had*), and *-am* has the same function as *I*.

20. That is, one including the sound *d* or *t*, which are produced in the dental area of the mouth, behind the upper teeth.

21. It may be objected that we have shifting accent, in Modern English, in pairs of words like *pérfume* (n.), *perfúme* (v.), or in classical derivatives like *phótograph* and *photógrapher*. But this is clearly different from an accent which shifts in the inflection of a single part of speech.

22. For this reason it is frequently said that in the pronunciation of Modern English only those vowels that are protected by the stress have their full quality, all others tending to be neutralized. Only the most recent of dictionaries make this clear; it has been customary for dictionaries to use different characters for the unstressed vowels of such words as *tuba, camel, robin, carrot, circus,* even though the vowels are not sounded *a, e, i, o, u,* but almost identically, with the sound whose phonetic symbol is [ə].

23. A stopped consonant is one produced by stopping the breath stream momentarily, which stoppage, when released, makes an audible explosion.

24. The second Germanic consonant shift took place only in High German dialects, and therefore does not affect English.

25. Sounds are *voiced* when the vocal cords are vibrating during their production, *voiceless* when the vocal cords are not vibrating. *Aspiration* is the quality of a sound produced by puffing the breath out, with a slight constriction of the oral or throat passage.

26. A *spirant* (or *fricative*) is a sound made by forcing the breath, without actually stopping it, through a narrowed outlet in the oral or throat passage.

27. Initial consonants regularly illustrate this shift, as do most medial and final consonants; the exceptions to the latter will be dealt with under "Verner's Law," a discussion of which follows.

28. These four symbols represent respectively a bilabial, an interdental, or labiodental, a velar, and an alveolar—all voiced spirants. For further light on these terms see Robertson and Cassidy, *The Development of Modern English,* Ch. 4.

29. Representing an Indo-European *alt-ós.*

30. Originally meaning "sated"; cf. German *satt.*

31. An excellent, detailed treatment of these two laws may be found in Wright, *Old English Grammar,* sections 229–239.

32. For a discussion of the relative significance of these two processes, see Jespersen, *Growth and Structure of the English Language,* Leipzig (Teubner), 1935, pp. 22–28.

33. For a short exposition of the Indo-Hittite hypothesis, see Sturtevant, *An Introduction to Linguistic Science,* New Haven (Yale University, 1947), secs. 229–235 and Fig. 8.

☦ ✠ ☦

THE ANCESTRY OF
THE ENGLISH ALPHABET

JOHN HURT FISHER

English grammar is wonderfully direct, economical, expressive. English spelling is five centuries out of date, illogical, and misleading—a crazy-quilt of conflicting principles which has evolved from the practice of semi-literate mechanics like scribes and printers. For at least three hundred years English spelling has been a source of consternation to scholars who knew something of the French or Latin from which over sixty percent of our vocabulary is taken and the changes in pronunciation that have taken place since Chaucer's day, but there has been little that they could do about it.

The situation was once much better. The earliest writing in the English language, dating from before 800 A.D., was done by scribes who had previously been trained to read and write Latin. They wrote English on exactly the same principle that the missionary uses when he writes an African dialect with the English alphabet. They matched the sounds of English as carefully as they could with the sounds represented by the letters in the Latin alphabet, leaving out the letters for which English had no need, and borrowing from the runic alphabet letters needed for sounds not represented in the Latin alphabet.

Reprinted from *Archaeology*, Volume 4, number 4, copyright, 1951, Archaeological Institute of America, by permission of the publisher.

So far as we know, these early English scribes were starting almost from scratch. There is little evidence that the Teutonic tribes which conquered England between 450 and 600 A.D.—Angles, Saxons, and Jutes, the Venerable Bede designated them—had had any experience with writing. Their own manuscripts and inscriptions all date from some time after St. Augustine and his forty monks landed in Kent in 597 A.D. They may have brought with them some knowledge of the runic alphabet in which the earliest inscriptions in northern Europe (dating from about 300 A.D.) are preserved, but even here the evidence is not clear. As we shall see, their earliest vernacular records made little use of the "thorn" þ and "wen" ƿ borrowed from the runic. However, the earliest runic inscriptions are contemporary with the oldest manuscripts, and the special developments in the English runic alphabet likewise suggest that the Angles and Saxons had been familiar with that alphabet for some time.

The runic alphabet, which may have stemmed originally from the ancient Greek alphabet, was apparently used more for symbolic purposes than for writing in any real sense. The Old Norse word *rún* meant 'secret' as well as 'letter,' and the characters were originally used for inscription on stone or wood or metal more for their religious or magical significance than to convey information. In their wanderings the Vikings disseminated runic inscriptions very widely—perhaps from Minnesota to Antioch—but the alphabet was never used extensively except in Iceland and the Scandinavian countries. Although it was in some ways better adapted to the sounds of English than the Latin alphabet, and persisted in England along with the latter for some time, it had no lasting influence upon the development of our present alphabet.

From the Latin and runic alphabets the writers of Old English devised a fairly satisfactory phonetic alphabet. But the English language has been fated to undergo, at the hands of conquering invaders, many more profound changes than any of the other European languages. In the ninth and tenth centuries came the Danes. They spoke a dialect very nearly like Old English in its vocabulary, but different in pronunciation and grammar. Their influence probably had much to do with the disappearance of inflectional endings which makes the chief difference between modern German and English.

A hundred years later, the Norman Conquest put English into the hands of scribes who had been trained to write French, and to assign French instead of English sounds to the letters in the Latin alphabet. They practically, but not completely, respelled English to conform with French orthography. Furthermore, hundreds of French words were brought into the language by the French-speaking scribes and nobility, and many kept their French spelling even after they had been Anglicized in pronunciation.

Finally, between the time of Chaucer and Shakespeare, the English language underwent great changes in pronunciation. As fate would have it, printing with its attendant standardizing effects was introduced just in the middle of this period (1476)—when both spelling and pronunciation were least stable.

As a result, the early printers were constantly bedeviled by whether to follow the spellings in their manuscripts, usually representing the old pronunciation, or to alter the spellings to indicate the new pronunciation. As the Norman scribes had done before them, they did a little of both, and English spelling emerged into the sunlight of the Elizabethan age a palimpsest historically fascinating, but practically maddening.

THE CONSONANTS

Our consonant letters have come fairly directly from Latin through Old English: b, d, l, m, n, p, r, and t show little change.

c, k, q*

But the early English monks realized that c, k (used infrequently in the Latin they knew), and q were redundant. Hence they used c for the *k* sound, which produced spelling such as *cing* for *king* and *cwic* for *quick*. In French c had already begun in certain positions to have the sound of *s*, as in *cent* and *cité*; so Norman scribes introduced k to prevent confusion. Likewise in both Latin and Old French, the *cw* sound was spelled qu (it has since been reduced to the *k* sound in French), and Norman scribes introduced this spelling into English, changing *cwen* to *queen* for example, and *cwacian* to *quake*.

The spelling ck for the *k* sound in the middle and at the end of words occurred only occasionally in Middle English, and then usually as a variant for kk as in *licke* beside *likke, packe* beside *pakke*, and *locke* beside *lokke*. Otherwise the spelling was simply k, as in *quik* and *reken*. By the sixteenth century the medial and final *k* sound had almost always come to be spelled ck, and in the eighteenth Dr. Johnson, believing that ck represented an etymological spelling, insisted on spelling *logick, rhetorick, politick,* and *cholerick* with their "Saxon k." The ck has remained in the middle of words and at the end of words of one syllable. But at the end of most words of more than one syllable the final k has dropped off since the eighteenth century, partly through Noah Webster's efforts to simplify spelling.

ch

Apparently Old English at first had no sound *ch* as in *church*, since no spelling was devised to indicate it. We believe that this sound developed during the Old English period at least by the beginning of the tenth century. When Norman scribes began to write English, they recognized it as a sound that had long existed in French and been spelled ch in French manuscripts since the eighth century. So when *ceap* becomes *cheap* and *cild* becomes *child*

*Except when they are used as rubrics for section headings, individual letters standing for themselves are *not* italicized, but individual letters standing for sounds are. [Editors]

between 1100 and 1200, we must suppose not that the sound represented by the symbol c was itself changing, but that a distinctive symbol had been adopted for a sound already established.

f, v

The early English scribes recognized no more difference in writing between sounds of f and v than we do between the f in *roof* and *of* which we represent by the same letter, or the *v* in *have* and colloquial *have-to*. They used only the letter f, which automatically had the sound of v in *have* when it came between voiced sounds. Thus we find *lufode* for *loved* and *ofer* for *over* where the f in Old English certainly had the sound of *v*. However, Old French did have the *f* sound intervocalically, in words like *afermer*, so the Norman scribes could not follow English usage. Instead they used the v as in French and Latin, interchangeable with u in shape, but always followed by a vowel. Since u was seldom followed by a vowel, there was little confusion. Thus was established the tradition, to which we still adhere, of never ending a word with v: have, solve, slave (Slav is a modern abbreviation of *Slavonian*—cognate with *slave*). The silent -e, as we shall see, was not silent at the time these spellings were introduced.

g, h, gh

The letters g and h at the beginnings of words usually represent the sounds that they did in Latin and Old English. In words like *gnaw* and *gnat*, however, the initial g disappeared from pronunciation in Middle English, although it was retained in the spelling. The simplification of consonant clusters which produced this change likewise accounts for the disappearance of the initial *k* sound from words like *knowledge* and *knight*. On the other hand, initial h had ceased to be pronounced in French, and was not pronounced in Middle English in words taken over from the French, such as *history, hospital,* and *human*. In these examples, the h was reintroduced into the pronunciation through the influence of the spelling and of the Latin pronunciation. But in several words it has never been pronounced, for instance, *honor, herb,* and *heir*, and the archaic *eremite*. These and other words from French beginning with a silent h have fallen in with native English words beginning with vowels as being preceded by *an* rather than *a—an honor, an heir*. This fact has produced one of those errors of the semi-literate rather than the illiterate —*an hundred, an habitation*, and the like. Actually, when the h is pronounced, the article *a* has been used since early Middle English.

G's and h's in the middle or at the ends of words have either disappeared or survive as vowels or diphthongs. A g in either of these positions is generally evidence that a word is borrowed, like *big* and *egg* from Danish, or *beg* and *fig* from Old French—but it is dangerous to generalize, for *dog* and *stag* are good native English. In Old English medial and final h and g (except before i and e) had the guttural sound heard in German *ach* and *sagen*. The Norman scribes were not familiar with this sound, though they were used to the ordinary g and h. To represent the unfamiliar guttural sound, they devised the digraph gh and spelled Old English *bog, bough; thurh, through;* and *niht, night*. During Middle English the guttural sound disappeared from pronunciation, and from the spelling of some words, such as *bow* for Old English *bugan*, and *draw* which is the same word as *drag* save that the latter preserved the g; but in other words, the *gh* spelling has persisted to the present time. In a few words the guttural sound became *f* instead of a vowel or diphthong: *enough* which has the archaic variant *enow, cough* which once had the plural *couwen*, and *draft* which has the variant spelling *draught* and is really just the past tense of *draw* and *drag*.

G before i and e in late Old English already had the sound of consonantal y; the g of Old English *gear* was pronounced like the y in *year*, and that of *ge* as in *ye*. The Old English scribes had used the y (redundant in Latin and seldom used) for rounded *u* as in French *lune*, to distinguish it from the unrounded *u* of *dune*. When the rounded *u* disappeared in Middle English, scribes began using the *y* as we do today, both as a consonant—*year, you, yes* —and a vowel, equivalent to *i*—*by*, Old English *bi*; *tyrant*, Old French *tiran*.

j, dg

The sound represented in Modern English by *j* and *dg* almost never occurred at the beginnings of words in Old English—and not at all in Latin. When it came in the middle or at the end of words in Old English, scribes spelled it *cg*—*hecg* for *hedge* and *brycg* for bridge. The cg probably originally represented a sound nearer to hard *g* than to *j*, but it softened as time went along. Middle English scribes changed the spelling to *dg* which better represented the palatalized sound, as they did the g in a few French words—*judge* from *juger* and *pledge* from *plege*—but not in *rage, large, sergeant*, and many others.

The hard *dg* sound of *large* and *sergeant* represents the pronunciation of Norman French from which most of our early borrowings come. The sound palatalized further in Central (Parisian) French, to the g in French *large* today. Words which we have borrowed from French since the Anglo-Norman time tend to have the soft g sound—*rouge* and *garage*—though even in these the French g tends to be attracted by analogy to the *dg* sound.

Almost all words with initial j come from French (*gem* with g is found in Old English). In Latin, i was used like y in Modern English, both as a vowel and a glide consonant. When it was a consonant at the beginning of a word in Old French it came to be palatalized to a *j* sound. However, the letters i and j were used interchangeably in French and Middle English up into the sixteenth century, with only the content determining the pronunciation. In Middle English, then, the first letters in *iuge* and *jn* were pronounced as they are today, in spite of their spelling.

s, z

The letter s was used by scribes of Old English to represent the sounds of *s* and *z*, as we use it today in many cases. For instance, although we spell it s, plurals and possessives end in the *z* sound whenever they follow voiced sounds: *boys, dogs, fishes,* as compared with *hats, caps, racks.* Actually, this s is another archaic spelling, dating from Middle English when these inflections were always voiceless. In the oldest French texts of the eighth and ninth centuries, z was already used to distinguish the voiced sound, and the Norman scribes introduced it into such words as *freeze,* Old English *freose,* and *dizzy,* Old English *dysig,* where the intervocalic *s* was already pronounced *z.* They also introduced two other ways of indicating the soft *s:* doubling the *s* as in *vessel* or the feminine suffix *-ess, mistress, poetess*; and spelling it *c* as in *twice,* originally *twies,* and *dice,* Chaucer's *dys.*

sh

The sound represented by sh in *shin* probably did not exist in Oldest English. The spelling sc in Old English (*scip, ship,* and *fisc, fish*) probably at first represented the *sk* sound of *skin.* By the time of the Danish conquest sc had already developed the sound of *sh,* however, although the spelling had not changed. In Danish this change in pronunciation had not taken place. As a result, we have in English many doublets, pairs of words distinguished by this difference: *shirt* and *skirt, shoot* and *scoot, shuttle* and *scuttle, shrub* and *scrub* (oak), and many more. Old French had neither the sound nor the spelling sh, and Norman and Middle English scribes simply invented the spelling, probably on the analogy of ch, to distinguish the sound from the hard sc in many words from French: for example *scout, scorn,* and *scale.*

The voiced *sh* sound of *vision* has developed in English where s comes before i or u. In words like *illusion* or *measure* the original (French) pronunciation of the intervocalic s was *z,* but the raised position of the tongue in pronouncing *i* and *u* has palatalized the *z* to its present voiced *sh* sound. The sound represented by ch of *chew* in Parisian French changed to the *sh* of *shoe* after the Anglo-Norman period, and some words which we have taken into the language since Middle English preserve this later French pronunciation— *chateau, chagrin, chaise.*

th

There were two sounds in Old English that were not clearly distinguished either in the Latin of the Old English scribes or the French of the Normans. These were *th* and *w.* The th digraph was, however, found in Latin, although we are not sure how it was pronounced. In the oldest English manuscripts (before 900 A.D.) this digraph was usually used for the *th* sound at the *beginning* of words; in the middle or at the end, where the sound in English was frequently voiced, it was spelled d or ð, supposedly in imitation of contemporary Latin pronunciation. The ð (called the "eth" or "thed") is not a runic symbol, but simply a d with a stroke through the stem to indicate that it is aspirated. Originally, it may have been pronounced somewhat like the uncultivated pronunciation of *this* and *that*: "*d^his*" and "*d^hat.*"

After 900 the symbol þ, borrowed from the runic alphabet, replaced th at the beginning of words and was used interchangeably with ð elsewhere. Norman scribes, who were not familiar with the Old English alphabet and did not have the sound in their own language, began a movement toward restoring the Latin digraph. The ð disappeared by the end of the thirteenth century, but þ lasted until the beginning of printing.

The earliest fonts of type, imported into England from the Continent, did not, in fact, have the þ. In an effort to supply this lack, and also because in the handwriting of the sixteenth century þ and y were made nearly alike, and perhaps, too, because of the form that the capital þ sometimes took, printers —and sign painters—came to use the y for þ. In *Ye* [famous] *Olde Tea Shoppe* the first letter represented *th*, and the word was always pronounced *the*. In the few words with th brought in from French, the th was simply pronounced *t*, as it still is in French. In Middle English manuscripts we find *trone* for *throne* and *teme* for *theme*. The *th* pronunciation was reintroduced in the sixteenth century from the spelling and the Greek originals. But in some words, like *thyme* and *Thomas*, th still shows the Middle English pronunciation taken from French.

w

The sound represented by the w in *well* gave the Old English and Norman scribes almost as much trouble as *th*. The sound was clearly distinguished in Old and Middle English, as it is today, but not in either Latin or French. In Oldest English the scribes experimented with u and uu, but by about 800 they had adopted the runic symbol þ. The Norman scribes had already met the sound in Teutonic words in Northern French and had adopted the same uu that the English scribes had first experimented with. Hence, the Anglo-Normans discarded þ in favor of their own letter which can be considered either a double u (the English name) or a double v (the French name). The sound in Central French was at first pronounced *gw* and spelled gu as in *Guillaume* for *William*, *guerre* for *war*, and *guêpe* (the accent indicating the lost s) for *wasp*. Eventually, as with qu, the *u* was lost in pronunciation, and the sound became a simple *g*. But we in English have several doublets, one representing the Teutonic form from Old English or Anglo-Norman and the other the French: for instance *ward, guard,* and *wile, guile.*

In Old English, an initial w before a consonant was pronounced, and it persisted in spelling sometimes even when the consonant cluster was simplified in Middle English (like g and k in *gnat* and *know*): for instance, *wrestle, wring,* and *wright.*

hw

The sound spelled wh in Modern English was in Old English spelled hw: *hwæl* for *whale, hwæt* for *what*, and *hwy* for *why*. The letters were reversed by the Middle English scribes, partly, perhaps, because there came to be less of a stress on the *h*—the aspiration. This aspiration has grown milder and milder since Middle English until today the "*wich*" and "*wy*" pronunciations are accepted in standard British, and used a good deal in colloquial American. On the other hand, in *who* and its derivative (*whose, whom*) the *w* part of the combination has been lost in pronunciation, although it has been retained in the spelling. This has given rise to several analogical spellings for words which have never had a *w* in their pronunciation: *whole* from Old English *hal*, cognate with *hale*; *whoop* from Old French *houper*; and *whore* from Old English *hora*.

x

The sound of *x* occurred much less frequently in Old English than it does today because the Greek borrowings had not yet arrived and because the plurals of the many words ending in *k* (*c*) were still two syllables: *rockës* for *rocks* and *backës* for *backs*. But where the sound did occur in Old English, it was usually spelled x—*fox* was *fox* and *wax, weax*.

THE VOWELS

The spelling of the vowels in Modern English is not nearly as close to that of their Old English and Latin ancestors as the spelling of the consonants, but their real confusion dates only from the fifteenth century. In Old and Middle English, the vowels a, e, i, o, and u represented virtually the sounds that they did in Latin and do still in all the European languages, and they had the same distinctions in length without change in quality that they had in Latin. What changes there are in spellings of vowels between Old and Middle English usually represent actual changes in pronunciation. Like the consonant changes we noted above, they had been underway in Old English, but had not been recorded in the spelling. When the words were respelled by the Norman scribes, they used the vowel letters that represented contemporary pronunciation.

Throughout the Middle English period when Latin and French were the official written languages, everyone who wrote English tended to write it as the missionary writes African, making the spelling indicate his own pronunciation. Hence, in Middle English there was the great diversity in the spelling of English in various parts of England, diversity which represented diversity in sound. When a northern man spelled *home, ham*, and a southwestern man spelled *sin, sunne*, it was not because the symbols had different phonetic values in different districts but because they pronounced these words differently.

Two Old English vowel letters need to be mentioned especially. One æ, represented a sound still found in English, the *a* in *hat*. The other, y, represented a sound that has been lost, the rounded *u* of French *lune*, mentioned above. Both the letters æ and y were taken from the Latin alphabet, but they represented adaptations rather than matching of the sounds. The Latin æ apparently had a sound somewhere between Modern English long *i* (*ice*) and a flat *a* (*hat*). French did not have the long *i* diphthong, and it spelled the flat *a* sound *ai: main* and *plain* in Old and Modern French, which came into English with the same spelling (though the pronunciation changed in the Great Vowel Shift, as we shall see below) and by analogy produced the spellings of the native English *rain* and *maid*. French, therefore, had no need for the æ digraph, and Norman scribes did not use it in their transcription of English. This has led to much discussion of the actual pronunciation of words like *and* and *that* in Middle English. They had been spelled with æ in Old English, but the Middle English scribes did not spell them ai. Hence, some believe that they were pronounced with flat *a* in Old English, became broad *a* (the Boston *a* in *grass*) in Middle English, and changed back to the Old English pronunciation in Modern English. However, it is obvious that the flat *a* or flattish *a* was spelled simply a in French words like *dame* and *fame*.

As we said before, y was found only in foreign words in Latin, where it was derived from the capital form of the Greek upsilon. In Greek, upsilon could have the sound of either the rounded *u* (French *lune*) or the unrounded *u* (English *dune*), and Old English scribes, probably with some knowledge of Greek—it could hardly have been by chance—adapted the y for the rounded sound and u for the unrounded. French, like Latin, had only one *u* sound, but it was the rounded *u* instead of the unrounded *u* of Latin. So the Old English y represented the sound that the Norman scribes were in the habit of spelling u. The history of the rounded *u* sound in Middle English is complicated, but it does seem that early in the period the Anglo-Normans tended to use plain u for the rounded sound in all words from the French (naturally) and in English words where it persisted. In the Northern dialect, from which standard Modern English pronunciation developed, the rounded *u* (y) developed into i, as in *kin*, Old English *cynn*, or *pit*, Old English *pytt*. The unrounded *u* of Old English the Middle English scribes tended to spell ou. Thus the spelling which we associate with the diphthong in *house* and *mouse* did not originally indicate a diphthong at all, but rather the Middle English pronunciation "*hoose*" and "*moose*." There was never any real uniformity in this distinction between the u and ou spellings, however, as there has been none in the change of the ou to ow which seems to have begun when the unrounded *u* began to diphthongize in the Great Vowel Shift.

At the end of the Middle English period, between about 1400 and 1550 (the dates are subject to hot debate still), the quality of all the long vowels in English played musical chairs in the change that has been called the Great Vowel Shift and which has produced most of the chaos in the spelling of our vowels today—especially in the eyes of Europeans in whose languages this change did not take place.

There were seven long vowels in Middle English: the *a* of *alms* which in the Great Vowel Shift became the *a* of *name*; the close *e* of *they* which became the *e* of *he*; the open *e* of *ere* which became the close *e* (spelled ea) in Shakespeare's time, and later the *e* of *sea*; the close *o* of *home* which became the *oo* of *spoon*; the open *o* sound of *awe* which became the close *o*; the *i* of *machine* which became the diphthong *ou* of *down*.

As a matter of fact, there was already confusion in the spelling of vowels in Middle English, a confusion inherent in the fact that all of the European vernaculars had or developed more vowel sounds than the five simple vowels of the Roman alphabet provided for. Various languages have solved the problem by means of accents and digraphs. In Middle English there were two serious confusions: the open and close sounds for long *e* (*sell* and *sail*) indicated by the same spelling, and the open and close sounds for long *o* (*awe* and *owe*) frequently spelled the same. These distinctions had not been recognized in Old English spelling, besides which Old English had had the long *æ* which approached (and developed into) the open *e* sound. But in Middle English Chaucer could not rime *sweete* (rimes with *mate*) and *heete* (rimes with *met*) or *tree* (rimes with *say*) and *see* (modern *sea*, rimes with *eh*), in spite of their identical spellings. In Shakespeare's time these sounds still did not rime. The close *e* of *sweet* had become what it is today, but the open *e* had simply become the close *e* (*great*), a sound which it still retains to some extent in Irish pronunciation. The ea spelling was confined in the sixteenth and seventeenth centuries (it had existed in Middle English) to the close *e* sound. Pope still distinguished the two sounds, for instance in the famous lines from *The Rape of the Lock* about Hampton Court:

Here thou, great Anna! whom three realms obey
Dost sometimes counsel take—and sometimes tea.

But the sounds fell in together during the eighteenth century. Some confusion in spelling still arises from the fact that occasionally Middle English short *e*'s (as in *let*) were spelled ea and also that a good many long open *e*'s have come down with their sounds unchanged. For instance we have *dead*, with the Elizabethan pronunciation "*daid*" still alive in the colloquial vulgate; and Noah Webster ardently supported the regularly shifted pronunciation "*deef*" for *deaf*. There are a few words in standard English, like *great* and *steak* which preserve the Elizabethan pronunciation. In addition, there is the archaic spelling of the past tense of *read* (rimes with *red*) which might be expected to be spelled with a short e like *led*, since their shortening in the past tense in Middle English by analogy with verbs like *creep-crept* and *sweep-swept* (where the pt caused shortening) is identical.

The open and close *o* sounds had produced identical spellings in Middle English for words like *rote* and *mone* (modern *root* and *moon*) and *hope* and *note* (which then had the vowel sound of modern *nought*). On the whole, however, this confusion has been reduced in Modern English by confining the simple o to the sound in *note*, and using the double oo for the shifted o of *moon* (which is really the unrounded *u* sound). Thus we have few cases like *shoe* and *sloe* in which there is genuine confusion.

When the written language began to be standardized around the writing of the court and the government in the London of Chaucer's day (before 1400), the Great Vowel Shift had not greatly affected spelling or pronunciation. Caxton and his successors, when they began to print (about 1476), set type from manuscripts written with this fourteenth and early fifteenth century spelling, and based their own spelling upon it. Caxton was aware of the confusion in spelling and pronunciation in his own day, but he was, after all, a practical printer who wanted to please his public, not a language reformer. He and his successors did some adapting, like regularizing the use of the ea and oo as mentioned above, but for the most part they set in type and passed on to us the spelling of the fourteenth and fifteenth centuries.

The most important adaptation that the printers and writers at the beginning of the sixteenth century made was to use the final e as a means of indicating the pronunciation of vowels that had undergone the Great Vowel Shift. As late as Chaucer's time, the final e was still a rudimentary inflectional ending left over from Old English when the language had been fully inflected and pronounced like the final *a* of *sofa*. But it was already beginning to be slurred off in pronunciation, as Chaucer's prosody and the carelessness of scribes in using it prove. Hence, in the manuscripts which Caxton used, a great many words had final e's which by his time were never pronounced. These e's were, therefore, used to indicate the new, shifted long vowels—to show that the vowels of *sit* and *site, hat* and *hate*, and *met* and *mete* did not simply differ in quantity, but that they were completely different.

✠ ✠ ✠

LANGUAGE AS A
HISTORICAL PRODUCT: DRIFT

EDWARD SAPIR

Everyone knows that language is variable. Two individuals of the same generation and locality, speaking precisely the same dialect and moving in the same social circles, are never absolutely at one in their speech habits. A minute investigation of the speech of each individual would reveal countless differences of detail—in choice of words, in sentence structure, in the relative frequency with which particular forms or combinations of words are used, in the pronunciation of particular vowels and consonants and of combinations of vowels and consonants, in all those features, such as speed, stress, and tone, that give life to spoken language. In a sense they speak slightly divergent dialects of the same language rather than identically the same language.

There is an important difference, however, between individual and dialectic variations. If we take two closely related dialects, say English as spoken by the "middle classes" of London and English as spoken by the average New Yorker, we observe that, however much the individual speakers in each city differ from each other, the body of Londoners forms a compact, relatively unified group in contrast to the body of New Yorkers. The individual variations are swamped in or absorbed by certain major agreements—say of pronunciation and vocabulary—which stand out very strongly when the language of the group as a whole is contrasted with that of the other group. This means that there is something like an ideal linguistic entity dominating the speech habits of the members of each group, that the sense of almost unlimited freedom which each individual feels in the use of his language is held in leash by a tacitly directing norm. One individual plays on the norm in a way peculiar to himself, the next individual is nearer the dead average in that particular respect in which the first speaker most characteristically departs from it but in turn diverges from the average in a way peculiar to himself, and so on. What keeps the individual's variations from rising to dialectic importance is not merely the fact that they are in any event of small moment —there are well-marked dialectic variations that are of no greater magnitude than individual variations within a dialect—it is chiefly that they are silently "corrected" or canceled by the consensus of usage. If all the speakers of a given dialect were arranged in order in accordance with the degree of their conformity to average usage, there is little doubt that they would constitute a very finely intergrading series clustered about a well-defined center or norm. The differences between any two neighboring speakers of the series[1] would be negligible for any but the most microscopic linguistic research. The differences between the outermost members of the series are sure to be considerable, in all likelihood considerable enough to measure up to a true dialectic variation. What prevents us from saying that these untypical individuals speak distinct dialects is that their peculiarities, as a unified whole, are not referable to another norm than the norm of their own series.

If the speech of any member of the series could actually be made to fit into another dialect series,[2] we should have no true barriers between dialects (and languages) at all. We should merely have a continuous series of individual variations extending over the whole range of a historically unified linguistic area, and the cutting up of this large area (in some cases embracing parts of several continents) into distinct dialects and languages would be an essentially arbitrary proceeding with no warrant save that of practical convenience. But such a conception of the nature of dialectic variation does not correspond to the facts as we know them. Isolated individuals may be found who speak a compromise between two dialects of a language, and if their number and importance increases they may even end up creating a new dialectic norm of their own, a dialect in which the extreme peculiarities of the parent dialects are ironed out. In course of time the compromise dialect may absorb the parents, though more frequently these will tend to linger indefinitely as marginal forms of the enlarged dialect area. But such phenomena—and they are common enough in the history of language—are evidently quite secondary. They are closely linked with such social developments as the rise of nationality, the formation of literatures that aim to have more than a local appeal, the movement of rural populations into the cities, and all those other tendencies that break up the intense localism that unsophisticated man has always found natural.

The explanation of primary dialectic differences is still to seek. It is evidently not enough to say that if a dialect or language is spoken in two distinct localities or by two distinct social strata it naturally takes on distinctive forms, which in time come to be divergent enough to deserve the name of dialects. This is certainly true as far as it goes. Dialects do belong, in the first instance, to very definitely circumscribed social groups, homogeneous enough to secure the common feeling and purpose needed to create a norm. But the embarrassing question immediately arises: If all the individual variations within a dialect are being constantly leveled out to the dialectic norm, if there is no appreciable tendency for the individual's peculiarities to initiate a dialectic schism, why should we have dialectic variations at all? Ought not the norm, wherever and whenever threatened, automatically to reassert itself? Ought not the individual variations of each locality, even in the absence of intercourse between them, to cancel out to the same accepted speech average?

If individual variations "on a flat" were the only kind of variability in language, I believe we should be at a loss to explain why and how dialects arise, why it is that a linguistic prototype gradually breaks up into a number of mutually unintelligible languages. But language is not merely something that is spread out in space, as it were—a series of reflections in individual minds of one and the same timeless picture. Language moves down time in a current of its own making. It has a drift. If there were no breaking up of a language into dialects, if each language continued as a firm, self-contained unity, it would still be constantly moving away from any assignable norm, developing new features unceasingly and gradually transforming itself into a language so different from its starting point as to be in effect a new language. Now dialects arise not because of the mere fact of individual variation but because two or more groups of individuals have become sufficiently disconnected to drift apart, or independently, instead of together. So long as they keep strictly together, no amount of individual variation would lead to the formation of dialects. In practice, of course, no language can be spread over a vast territory or even over a considerable area without showing dialectic variations, for it is impossible to keep a large population from segregating itself into local groups, the language of each of which tends to drift independently. Under cultural conditions such as apparently prevail today, conditions that fight localism at every turn, the tendency to dialectic cleavage is being constantly counteracted and in part "corrected" by the uniformizing factors already referred to. Yet even in so young a country as America the dialectic differences are not inconsiderable.

Under primitive conditions the political groups are small, the tendency to localism exceedingly strong. It is natural, therefore, that the languages of primitive folk or of non-urban populations in general are differentiated into a great number of dialects. There are parts of the globe where almost every village has its own dialect. The life of the geographically limited community is narrow and intense; its speech is correspondingly peculiar to itself. It is exceedingly doubtful if a language will ever be spoken over a wide area without multiplying itself dialectically. No sooner are the old dialects ironed out by compromises or ousted by the spread and influence of the one dialect which is culturally predominant when a new crop of dialects arises to undo the leveling work of the past. This is precisely what happened in Greece, for instance. In classical antiquity there were spoken a large number of local dialects, several of which are represented in the literature. As the cultural supremacy of Athens grew, its dialect, the Attic, spread at the expense of the rest, until, in the so-called Hellenistic period following the Macedonian conquest, the Attic dialect, in the vulgarized form known as the "Koine," became the standard speech of all Greece. But this linguistic uniformity[3] did not long continue. During the two millennia that separate the Greek of today from its classical prototype the Koine gradually split up into a number of dialects. Now Greece is as richly diversified in speech as in the time of Homer, though the present local dialects, aside from those of Attica itself, are not the lineal descendants of the old dialects of pre-Alexandrian days.[4] The experience of Greece is not exceptional. Old dialects are being continually wiped out only to make room for new ones. Languages can change at so many points of phonetics, morphology, and vocabulary that it is not surprising that once the linguistic community is broken it should slip off in different directions. It would be too much to expect a locally diversified language to develop along strictly parallel lines. If once the speech of a locality has begun to drift on its own account, it is practically certain to move further and further away from its linguistic fellows. Failing the retarding effect of dialectic interinfluences, which I have already touched upon, a group of dialects is bound to diverge on the whole, each from all of the others.

In course of time each dialect itself splits up into subdialects, which gradually take on the dignity of dialects proper while the primary dialects develop into mutually unintelligible languages. And so the budding process continues, until the divergences become so great that none but a linguistic student, armed with his documentary evidence and with his comparative or reconstructive method, would infer that the languages in question were genealogically related, represented independent lines of development, in other words, from a remote and common starting point. Yet it is as certain as any historical fact can be that languages so little resembling each other as Modern Irish, English, Italian, Greek, Russian, Armenian, Persian, and Bengali are but end-points in the present of drifts that converge to a meeting-point in the dim past. There is naturally no reason to believe that this earliest "Indo-European" (or "Aryan") prototype which we can in part reconstruct, in part but dimly guess at, is itself other than a single "dialect" of a group that has either become largely extinct or is now further represented by languages too divergent for us, with our limited means, to recognize as clear kin.[5]

All languages that are known to be genetically related, i.e., to be divergent forms of a single prototype, may be considered as constituting a "linguistic stock." There is nothing final about a linguistic stock. When we set it up, we merely say, in effect, that thus far we can go and no farther. At any point in the progress of our researches an unexpected ray of light may reveal the "stock" as but a "dialect" of a larger group. The terms dialect, language, branch, stock—it goes without saying—are purely relative terms. They are convertible as our perspective widens or contracts.[6] It would be vain to speculate as to whether or not we shall ever be able to demonstrate that all languages stem from a common source. Of late years linguists have been able to make larger historical syntheses than were at one time deemed feasible, just as students of culture have been able to show historical connections between culture areas or institutions that were at one time believed to be totally isolated from each other. The human world is contracting not only prospectively but to the backward-probing eye of culture-history. Nevertheless we are as yet far from able to reduce the riot of spoken languages to a small number of "stocks." We must still operate with a quite considerable number of these stocks. Some of them, like Indo-European or Indo-Chinese, are spoken over tremendous reaches; others, like Basque,[7] have a curiously restricted range and are in all likelihood but dwindling remnants of groups that were at one time more widely distributed. As for the single or multiple origin of speech, it is likely enough that language as a human institution (or, if one prefers, as a human "faculty") developed but once in the history of the race, that all complex history of language is a unique cultural event. Such a theory constructed "on general principles" is of no real interest, however, to linguistic science. What lies beyond the demonstrable must be left to the philosopher or the romancer.

We must return to the conception of "drift" in language. If the historical changes that take place in a language, if the vast accumulation of minute modifications which in time results in the complete remodeling of the language, are not in essence identical with the individual variations that we note on every hand about us, if these variations are born only to die without a trace, while the equally minute, or even minuter, changes that make up the drift are forever imprinted on the history of the language, are we not imputing to this history a certain mystical quality? Are we not giving language a power to change of its own accord over and above the involuntary tendency of individuals to vary the norm? And if this drift of language is not merely the familiar set of individual variations seen in vertical perspective, that is historically, instead of horizontally, that is in daily experience, what is it? Language exists only in so far as it is actually used—spoken and heard, written and read. What significant changes take place in it must exist, to begin with, as individual variations. This is perfectly true, and yet it by no means follows that the general drift of language can be understood[8] from an exhaustive descriptive study of these variations alone. They themselves are random phenomena,[9] like the waves of the sea, moving backward and forward in purposeless flux. The linguistic drift has direction. In other words, only those individual variations embody it or carry it which move in a certain direction, just as only certain wave movements in the bay outline the tide. The drift of a language is constituted by the unconscious selection on the part of its speakers of those individual variations that are cumulative in some special direction. This direction may be inferred, in the main, from the past history of the language. In the long run any new feature of the drift becomes part and parcel of the common, accepted speech, but for a long time it may exist as a mere tendency in the speech of a few, perhaps of a despised few. As we look about us and observe current usage, it is not likely to occur to us that our language has a "slope," that the changes of the next few centuries are in a sense prefigured in certain obscure tendencies of the present and that these changes, when consummated, will be seen to be but continuations of changes that have been already effected. We feel rather that our language is practically a fixed system ànd that what slight changes are destined to take place in it are as likely to move in one direction as another. The feeling is fallacious. Our very uncertainty as to the impending details of change makes the eventual consistency of their direction all the more impressive.

Sometimes we feel where the drift is taking us even while we struggle against it. Probably the majority of those who read these words feel that it is quite "incorrect" to say "Who did you see?" We readers of many books are still very careful to say "Whom did you see?" but we feel a little uncomfortable (uncomfortably proud, it may be) in the process. We are likely to avoid the locution altogether and to say "Who was it you saw?" conserving literary tradition (the "whom") with the dignity of silence.[10] The folk makes no apology. "Whom did you see?" might do for an epitaph, but "Who did you see?" is the natural form for an eager inquiry. It is of course the uncontrolled speech of the folk to which we must look for advance information as to the general linguistic movement. It is safe to prophesy that within a couple of hundred years from to-day not even the most learned jurist will be saying "Whom did you see?" By that time the "whom" will be as delightfully archaic as the Elizabethan "his" for "its."[11] No logical or historical argument will avail to save this hapless "whom." The demonstration "I:me = he:him = who:whom" will be convincing in theory and will go unheeded in practice.

Even now we may go so far as to say that the majority of us are secretly wishing they could say "Who did you see?" It would be a weight off their unconscious minds if some divine authority, overruling the lifted finger of the pedagogue, gave them *carte blanche*. But we cannot too frankly anticipate the drift and maintain caste. We must affect ignorance of whither we are going and rest content with our mental conflict—uncomfortable conscious acceptance of the "whom," unconscious desire for the "who."[12] Meanwhile we indulge our sneaking desire for the forbidden locution by the use of "who" in certain twilight cases in which we can cover up our fault by a bit of unconscious special pleading. Imagine that some one drops the remark when you are not listening attentively, "John Smith is coming to-night." You have not caught the name and ask, not "Whom did you say?" but "Who did you say?" There is likely to be a little hesitation in the choice of the form, but the precedent of usages like "Whom did you see?" will probably not seem quite strong enough to induce a "Whom did you say?" Not quite relevant enough, the grammarian may remark, for a sentence like "Who did you say?" is not strictly analogous to "Whom did you see?" or "Whom did you mean?" It is rather an abbreviated form of some such sentence as "Who, did you say, is coming to-night?" This is the special pleading that I have referred to, and it has a certain logic on its side. Yet the case is more hollow than the grammarian thinks it to be, for in reply to such a query as "You're a good hand at bridge, John, aren't you?" John, a little taken aback, might mutter "Did you say me?" hardly "Did you say I?" Yet the logic for the latter ("Did you say I was a good hand at bridge?") is evident. The real point is that there is not enough vitality in the "whom" to carry it over such little difficulties as a "me" can compass without a thought. The proportion "I:me = he:him = who:whom" is logically and historically sound, but psychologically shaky. "Whom did you see?" is correct, but there is something false about its correctness.

It is worth looking into the reason for our curious reluctance to use locutions involving the word "whom," particularly in its interrogative sense. The only distinctively objective forms which we still possess in English are *me, him, her* (a little blurred because of its identity with the possessive *her*), *us, them*, and *whom*. In all other cases the objective has come to be identical with the subjective—that is, in outer form, for we are not now taking account of position in the sentence. We observe immediately in looking through the list of objective forms that *whom* is psychologically isolated. *Me, him, her, us,* and *them* form a solid, well-integrated group of objective personal pronouns parallel to the subjective series *I, he, she, we, they.* The forms *who* and *whom* are technically "pronouns" but they are not felt to be in the same box as the personal pronouns. *Whom* has clearly a weak position, an exposed flank, for words of a feather tend to flock together, and if one strays behind, it is likely to incur danger of life. Now the other interrogative and relative pronouns (*which, what, that*), with which *whom* should properly flock, do not distinguish the subjective and objective forms. It is psychologically unsound to draw the line of form cleavage between *whom* and the personal pronoun on the one side, the remaining interrogative and relative pronouns on the other. The form groups should be symmetrically related to, if not identical with, the function groups. Had *which, what,* and *that* objective forms parallel to *whom*, the position of this last would be more secure. As it is, there is something unesthetic about the word. It suggests a form pattern which is not filled out by its fellows. The only way to remedy the irregularity of form distribution is to abandon the *whom* altogether, for we have lost the power to create new objective forms and cannot remodel our *which-what-that* group so as to make it parallel with the smaller group *who-whom*. Once this is done, *who* joins its flock and our unconscious desire to form symmetry is satisfied. We do not secretly chafe at "Whom did you see?" without reason.[13]

But the drift away from *whom* has still other determinants. The words *who* and *whom* in their interrogative sense are psychologically related not merely to the pronouns *which* and *what*, but to a group of interrogative adverbs— *where, when, how*—all of which are invariable and generally emphatic. I believe it is safe to infer that there is a rather strong feeling in English that the interrogative pronoun or adverb, typically an emphatic element in the sentence, should be invariable. The inflective *-m* of *whom* is felt as a drag upon the rhetorical effectiveness of the word. It needs to be eliminated if the inter- rogative pronoun is to receive all its latent power. There is still a third, and a very powerful, reason for the avoidance of *whom*. The contrast between the subjective and objective series of personal pronouns (*I, he, she, we, they: me, him, her, us, them*) is in English associated with a difference of position. We say *I see the man* but *the man sees me; he told him,* never *him he told* or *him told me.* Such usages as the last two are distinctly poetic and archaic: they are opposed to the present drift of the language. Even in the interroga- tive one does not say *Him did you see?* It is only in sentences of the type *Whom did you see?* that an inflected objective before the verb is now used at all. On the other hand, the order in *Whom did you see?* is imperative because of its interrogative form; the interrogative pronoun or adverb normally comes first in the sentence (*What are you doing? When did he go? Where are you from?*). In the "whom" of *Whom did you see?* there is concealed, therefore, a conflict between the order proper to a sentence containing an inflected objective and the order natural to a sentence with an interrogative pronoun or adverb. The solution *Did you see whom?* or *You saw whom?*[14] is too contrary to the idiomatic drift of our language to receive acceptance. The more radical solution *Who did you see?* is the one the language is gradually making for.

These three conflicts—on the score of form grouping, of rhetorical empha- sis, and of order—are supplemented by a fourth difficulty. The emphatic *whom,* with its heavy build (half-long vowel followed by labial consonant), should contrast with a lightly tripping syllable immediately following. In *whom did,* however, we have an involuntary retardation that makes the locution sound "clumsy." This clumsiness is a phonetic verdict, quite apart from the dissatisfaction due to the grammatical factors which we have ana- lyzed. The same prosodic objection does not apply to such parallel locutions as *what did* and *when did.* The vowels of *what* and *when* are shorter and their final consonants melt easily into the following d, which is pronounced in the same tongue position as *t* and *n.* Our instinct for appropriate rhythms makes it as difficult for us to feel content with *whom did* as for a poet to use words like *dreamed* and *hummed* in a rapid line. Neither common feeling nor the poet's choice need be at all conscious. It may be that not all are equally sensi- tive to the rhythmic flow of speech, but it is probable that rhythm is an uncon- scious linguistic determinant even with those who set little store by its artistic use. In any event the poet's rhythms can only be a more sensitive and styli- cized application of rhythmic tendencies that are characteristic of the daily speech of his people.

We have discovered no less than four factors which enter into our subtle disinclination to say "Whom did you see?" The uneducated folk that says "Who did you see?" with no twinge of conscience has a more acute flair for the genuine drift of the language than its students. Naturally the four restraining factors do not operate independently. Their separate energies, if we may make bold to use a mechanical concept, are "canalized" into a single force. This force or minute embodiment of the general drift of the language is psychologically registered as a slight hesitation in using the word *whom*. The hesitation is likely to be quite unconscious, though it may be readily acknowledged when attention is called to it. The analysis is certain to be unconscious, or rather unknown to the normal speaker.[15] How, then, can we be certain in such an analysis as we have undertaken that all of the assigned determinants are really operative and not merely some one of them? Certainly they are not equally powerful in all cases. Their values are variable, rising and falling according to the individual and the locution.[16] But that they really exist, each in its own right, may sometimes be tested by the method of elimination. If one or other of the factors is missing and we observe a slight diminution in the corresponding psychological reaction ("hesitation" in our case), we may conclude that the factor is in other uses genuinely positive. The second of our four factors applies only to the interrogative use of *whom*, the fourth factor applies with more force to the interrogative than to the relative. We can therefore understand why a sentence like *Is he the man whom you referred to?* though not as idiomatic as *Is he the man (that) you referred to* (remember that it sins against counts one and three), is still not as difficult to reconcile with our innate feeling for English expression as *Whom did you see?* If we eliminate the fourth factor from the interrogative usage,[17] say in *Whom are you looking at?* where the vowel following *whom* relieves this word of its phonetic weight, we can observe, if I am not mistaken, a lesser reluctance to use the *whom. Who are you looking at?* might even sound slightly offensive to ears that welcome *Who did you see?*

We may set up a scale of "hesitation values" somewhat after this fashion:

Value 1: factors 1, 3.   "The man whom I referred to."
Value 2: factors 1, 3, 4.   "The man whom they referred to."
Value 3: factors 1, 2, 3.   "Whom are you looking at?"
Value 4: factors 1, 2, 3, 4. "Whom did you see?"

We may venture to surmise that while *whom* will ultimately disappear from English speech, locutions of the type *Whom did you see?* will be obsolete when phrases like *The man whom I referred to* are still in lingering use. It is impossible to be certain, however, for we can never tell if we have isolated all the determinants of a drift. In our particular case we have ignored what may well prove to be a controlling factor in the history of *who* and *whom* in the relative sense. This is the unconscious desire to leave these words to their interrogative function and to concentrate on *that* or mere word order as expressions of the relative (e.g., *The man that I referred to* or *The man I referred to*). This drift, which does not directly concern the use of *whom* as such (merely of *whom* as a form of *who*), may have made the relative *who* obsolete before the other factors affecting relative *whom* have run their course. A consideration like this is instructive because it indicates that knowledge of the general drift of a language is insufficient to enable us to see clearly what the drift is heading for. We need to know something of the relative potencies and speeds of the components of the drift.

It is hardly necessary to say that the particular drifts involved in the use of *whom* are of interest to us not for their own sake but as symptoms of larger tendencies at work in the language. At least three drifts of major importance are discernable. Each of these has operated for centuries, each is at work in other parts of our linguistic mechanism, each is almost certain to continue for centuries, possibly millennia. The first is the familiar tendency to level the distinction between the subjective and the objective, itself but a late chapter in the steady reduction of the old Indo-European system of syntactic cases. This system, which is at present best preserved in Lithuanian,[18] was already considerably reduced in the old Germanic language of which English, Dutch, German, Danish, and Swedish are modern dialectic forms. The seven Indo-European cases (nominative, genitive, dative, accusative, ablative, locative, instrumental) had been already reduced to four (nominative, genitive, dative, accusative). We know this from a careful comparison of and reconstruction based on the oldest Germanic dialects of which we still have records (Gothic, Old Icelandic, Old High German, Anglo-Saxon). In the group of West German dialects, for the study of which Old High German, Anglo-Saxon, Old Frisian, and Old Saxon are our oldest and most valuable sources, we still have these four cases, but the phonetic form of the case syllables is already greatly reduced and in certain paradigms particular cases have coalesced. The case system is practically intact but it is evidently moving towards further disintegration. Within the Anglo-Saxon and early Middle English period there took place further changes in the same direction. The phonetic form of the case syllables became still further reduced and the distinction between the accusative and the dative finally disappeared. The new "objective" is really an amalgam of old accusative and dative forms; thus *him*, the old dative (we still say *I give him the book*, not "abbreviated" from *I give to him*; compare Gothic *imma*, Modern German *ihm*), took over the functions of the old accusative (Anglo-Saxon *hine*; compare Gothic *ina*, Modern German *ihn*) and dative. The distinction between the nominative and accusative was nibbled away by phonetic processes and morphological levelings until only certain pronouns retained distinctive subjective and objective forms.

In later medieval and in modern times there have been comparatively few apparent changes in our case system apart from the gradual replacement of *thou—thee* (singular) and subjective *ye*—objective *you* (plural) by a single undifferentiated form *you*. All the while, however, the case system, such as it is (subjective-objective, really absolutive, and possessive in nouns; subjective, objective, and possessive in certain pronouns) has been steadily weakening in psychological respects. At present it is more seriously undermined than most of us realize. The possessive has little vitality except in the pronoun and in animate nouns. Theoretically we can still say *the moon's phases* or *a newspaper's vogue*; practically we limit ourselves pretty much to analytic locutions like *the phases of the moon* and *the vogue of a newspaper*. The drift is clearly toward the limitation of possessive forms to animate nouns. All the possessive pronominal forms except *its* and, in part, *theirs* and *their,* are also animate. It is significant that *theirs* is hardly ever used in reference to inanimate nouns, that there is some reluctance to so use *their*, and that *its* also is beginning to give way to *of it*. *The appearance of it* or *the looks of it* is more in the current of the language than *its appearance*. It is curiously significant that *its young* (referring to an animal's cubs) is idiomatically preferable to *the young of it*. The form is only ostensibly neuter, in feeling it is animate; psychologically it belongs with *his children*, not with *the pieces of it*. Can it be that so common a word as *its* is actually beginning to be difficult? Is it too doomed to disappear? It would be rash to say that it shows signs of approaching obsolescence, but that it is steadily weakening is fairly clear.[19] In any event, it is not too much to say that there is a strong drift towards the restriction of the inflected possessive forms to animate nouns and pronouns.

How is it with the alternation of subjective and objective in the pronoun? Granted that *whom* is a weak sister, that the two cases have been leveled in *you* (in *it, that,* and *what* they were never distinct, so far as we can tell[20]), and that *her* as an objective is a trifle weak because of its formal identity with the possessive *her*, is there any reason to doubt the vitality of such alternations as *I see the man* and *the man sees me*? Surely, the distinction between subjective *I* and objective *me*, between subjective *he* and objective *him*, and correspondingly for other personal pronouns, belongs to the very core of the language. We can throw *whom* to the dogs, somehow make shift to do without an *its*, but to level *I* and *me* to a single case—would that not be to un-English our language beyond recognition? There is no drift toward such horrors as *Me see him* or *I see he*. True, the phonetic disparity between *I* and *me, he* and *him, we* and *us*, has been too great for any serious possibility of form leveling. It does not follow that the case distinction as such is still vital. One of the most insidious peculiarities of a linguistic drift is that where it cannot destroy what lies in its way it renders it innocuous by washing the old significance out of it. It turns its very enemies to its own uses. This brings us to the second of the major drifts, the tendency to fixed position in the sentence, determined by the syntactic relation of the word.

We need not go into the history of this all-important drift. It is enough to know that as the inflected forms of English became scantier, as the syntactic relations were more and more inadequately expressed by the forms of the words themselves, position in the sentence gradually took over functions originally foreign to it. *The man* in *the man sees the dog* is subjective; in *the dog sees the man,* objective. Strictly parallel to these sentences are *he sees the dog* and *the dog sees him.* Are the subjective value of *he* and the objective value of *him* entirely, or even mainly, dependent on the difference of form? I doubt it. We could hold to such a view if it were possible to say *the dog sees he* or *him sees the dog.* It was once possible to say such things, but we have lost the power. In other words, at least part of the case feeling in *he* and *him* is to be credited to their position before or after the verb. May it not be, then, that *he* and *him, we* and *us,* are not so much subjective and objective forms as pre-verbal and post-verbal[21] forms, very much as *my* and *mine* are now pre-nominal and post-nominal forms of the possessive (*my father* but *father mine; it is my book* but *the book is mine*)? That this interpretation corresponds to the actual drift of the English language is again indicated by the language of the folk. The folk says *it is me,* not *it is I,* which is "correct" but just as falsely so as the *whom did you see?* that we have analyzed. *I'm the one, it's me; we're the ones, it's us that will win out*—such are the live parallelisms in English today. There is little doubt that *it is I* will one day be as impossible in English as *c'est je,* for *c'est moi,* is now in French.

How different our *I: me* feels than in Chaucer's day is shown by the Chaucerian *it am I.* Here the distinctively subjective aspect of the *I* was enough to influence the form of the preceding verb in spite of the introductory *it*; Chaucer's locution clearly felt more like a Latin *sum ego* than a modern *it is I* or colloquial *it is me.* We have a curious bit of further evidence to prove that the English personal pronouns have lost some share of their original syntactic force. Were *he* and *she* subjective forms pure and simple, were they not striving, so to speak, to become caseless absolutives, like *man* or any other noun, we should not have been able to coin such compounds as *he-goat* and *she-goat,* words that are psychologically analogous to *bull-moose* and *mother-bear.* Again, in inquiring about a new-born baby, we ask *Is it a he or a she?* quite as though he and she were the equivalents of *male* and *female* or *boy* and *girl.* All in all, we may conclude that our English case system is weaker than it looks and that, in one way or another, it is destined to get itself reduced to an absolute (caseless) form for all nouns and pronouns but those that are animate. Animate nouns and pronouns are sure to have distinctive possessive forms for an indefinitely long period.

Meanwhile observe that the old alignment of case forms is being invaded by two new categories—a positional category (pre-verbal, post-verbal) and a classificatory category (animate, inanimate). The facts that in the possessive animate nouns and pronouns are destined to be more and more sharply distinguished from inanimate nouns and pronouns (*the man's,* but *of the house; his* but *of it*) and that, on the whole, it is only animate pronouns that distinguish pre-verbal and post-verbal forms[22] are of the greatest theoretical interest. They show that, however the language strives for a more and more analytic form, it is by no means manifesting a drift toward the expression of "pure" relational concepts in the Indo-Chinese manner. The insistence on the concreteness of the relational concepts is clearly stronger than the destructive power of the most sweeping and persistent drifts that we know of in the history and prehistory of our language.

The drift toward the abolition of most case distinctions and the correlative drift toward position as an all-important grammatical method are accompanied, in a sense dominated, by the last of the three major drifts that I have referred to. This is the drift toward the invariable word. In analyzing the "whom" sentence I pointed out that the rhetorical emphasis natural to an interrogative pronoun lost something by its form variability (*who, whose, whom*). This striving for a simple, unnuanced correspondence between idea and word, as invariable as may be, is very strong in English. It accounts for a number of tendencies which at first sight seem unconnected. Certain well-established forms, like the present third person singular *-s* of *works* or the plural *-s* of *books*, have resisted the drift to invariable words, possibly because they symbolize certain stronger form cravings that we do not yet fully understand. It is interesting to note that derivations that get away sufficiently from the concrete notion of the radical word to exist as independent conceptual centers are not affected by this elusive drift. As soon as the derivation runs danger of being felt as a mere nuancing of, a finicky play on, the primary concept, it tends to be absorbed by the radical word, to disappear as such. English words crave open spaces between them, they do not like to huddle in clusters of slightly divergent centers of meaning, each edging a little away from the rest. *Goodness*, a noun of quality, almost a noun of relation, that takes its cue from the concrete idea of "good" without necessarily predicating that quality (e.g., *I do not think much of his goodness*) is sufficiently spaced from good itself not to need fear absorption. Similarly, *unable* can hold its own against *able* because it destroys the latter's sphere of influence; *unable* is psychologically as distinct from *able* as is *blundering* or *stupid*. It is different with adverbs in *-ly*. These lean too heavily on their adjectives to have the kind of vitality that English demands of its words. *Do it quickly!* drags psychologically. The nuance expressed by *quickly* is too close to that of *quick*, their circles of concreteness are too nearly the same, for the two words to feel comfortable together. The adverbs in *-ly* are likely to go to the wall in the not too distant future for this very reason and in face of their obvious usefulness. Another instance of the sacrifice of highly useful forms to this impatience of nuancing is the group *whence, whither, hence, hither, thence, thither*. They could not persist in live usage because they impinged too solidly upon the circles of meaning represented by the words *where, here* and *there*. In saying *whither* we feel too keenly that we repeat all of *where*. That we add to *where* an important nuance of direction irritates rather than satisfies. We prefer to merge the static and the directive (*Where do you live?* like *Where are you going?*) or, if need be, to overdo a little the concept of direction (*Where are you running to?*).

Now it is highly symptomatic of the nature of the drift away from word clusters that we do not object to nuances as such, we object to having the nuances formally earmarked for us. As a matter of fact our vocabulary is rich in near-synonyms and in groups of words that are psychologically near relatives, but these near-synonyms and these groups do not hang together by reason of etymology. We are satisfied with *believe* and *credible* just because they keep aloof from each other. *Good* and *well* go better together than *quick* and *quickly*. The English vocabulary is a rich medley because each English word wants its own castle. Has English long been peculiarly receptive to foreign words because it craves the staking out of as many word areas as possible, or, conversely, has the mechanical imposition of a flood of French and Latin loan-words, unrooted in our earlier tradition, so dulled our feeling for the possibilities of our native resources that we are allowing these to shrink by default? I suspect that both propositions are true. Each feeds on the other. I do not think it likely, however, that the borrowings in English have been as mechanical and external a process as they are generally represented to have been. There was something about the English drift as early as the period following the Norman Conquest that welcomed the new words. They were a compensation for something that was weakening within.

NOTES

1. In so far as they do not fall out of the normal speech group by reason of a marked speech defect or because they are isolated foreigners that have acquired the language late in life.

2. Observe that we are speaking of an individual's speech as a whole. It is not a question of isolating some particular peculiarity of pronunciation or usage and noting its resemblance to or identity with a feature in another dialect.

3. It is doubtful if we have the right to speak of linguistic uniformity even during the predominance of the Koine. It is hardly conceivable that when the various groups of non-Attic Greeks took on the Koine they did not at once tinge it with dialectic peculiarities induced by their previous speech habits.

4. The Zaconic dialect of Lacedaemon is the sole exception. It is not derived from the Koine, but stems directly from the Doric dialect of Sparta.

5. Though indications are not lacking of what these remoter kin of the Indo-European languages may be. This is disputed ground, however, and hardly fit subject for a purely general study of speech.

6. "Dialect" in contrast to an accepted literary norm is a use of the term that we are not considering.

7. Spoken in France and Spain in the region of the Pyrenees.

8. Or rather apprehended, for we do not, in sober fact, entirely understand it as yet.

9. Not ultimately random, of course, only relatively so.

10. In relative clauses too we tend to avoid the objective form of "who." Instead of "The man whom I saw" we are likely to say "The man that I saw" or "The man I saw."

11. "Its" was at one time as impertinent a departure as the "who" of "Who did you see?" It forced itself into English because the old cleavage between masculine,

feminine, and neuter was being slowly and powerfully supplemented by a new one between thing-class and animate-class. The latter classification proved too vital to allow usage to couple males and things ("his") as against females ("her"). The form "its" had to be created on the analogy of words like "man's," to satisfy the growing form feeling. The drift was strong enough to sanction a grammatical blunder.

12. Psychoanalysts will recognize the mechanism. The mechanisms of "repression of impulse" and of its symptomatic symbolization can be illustrated in the most unexpected corners of individual and group psychology. A more general psychology than Freud's will eventually prove them to be as applicable to the groping for abstract form, the logical or esthetic ordering of experience, as to the life of the fundamental instincts.

13. Note that it is different with *whose*. This has not the support of analogous possessive forms in its own functional group, but the analogical power of the great body of possessives of nouns *(man's, boy's)* as well as of certain personal pronouns *(his, its;* as predicated possessive also *hers, yours, theirs)* is sufficient to give it vitality.

14. Aside from certain idiomatic usages, as when *You saw whom?* is equivalent to *You saw so and so and that so and so is who?* In such sentences *whom* is pronounced high and lingeringly to emphasize the fact that the person just referred to by the listener is not known or recognized.

15. Students of language cannot be entirely normal in their attitude towards their own speech. Perhaps it would be better to say "naive" than "normal."

16. It is probably this *variability* of value in the significant compounds of a general linguistic drift that is responsible for the rise of dialectic variations. Each dialect continues the general drift of the common parent, but has not been able to hold fast to constant values for each component of the drift. Deviations as to the drift itself, at first slight, later cumulative, are therefore unavoidable.

17. Most sentences beginning with interrogative *whom* are likely to be followed by *did* or *does, do.* Yet not all.

18. Better, indeed, than in our oldest Latin and Greek records. The old Indo-Iranian languages alone (Sanskrit, Avetan) show an equally or more archaic status of the Indo-European parent tongue as regards case forms.

19. Should *its* eventually drop out, it will have had a curious history. It will have played the role of a stop-gap between *his* in its non-personal use (see footnote 11) and the later analytic *of it.*

20. Except in so far as *that* has absorbed other functions than such as originally belonged to it. It was only a nominative-accusative neuter to begin with.

21. Aside from the interrogative: *am I? is he?* Emphasis counts for something. There is a strong tendency for the old "objective" forms to bear a stronger stress than the "subjective" forms. This is why the stress in locutions like *He didn't go, did he?* and *isn't he?* is thrown back on the verb; it is not a matter of logical emphasis.

22. *They: them* as an inanimate group may be looked upon as a kind of borrowing from the animate, to which, in feeling, it more properly belongs.

PART THREE

OLD ENGLISH

✠

INTRODUCTION

The pattern of this section and the two sections following is the same: a selection which discusses the language of the period; a selection which portrays the society at the time, including something about education and the use of language; a selection which describes the impact of other literatures and languages on the English literature at the time and thus, indirectly at least, on the English language; and selections which provide examples of the writings in England of the time.

The chapter from Baugh covers the development of language in England from the time of the Celts (about whom relatively little is known) through the Old English period. Baugh discusses the use of Latin in England under the Romans, the impact of the many invasions from the continent, and the various dialects of the time. He then goes on to describe Old English (i.e., the language of the Anglo-Saxons) in some detail.

From the selection by Duckett one obtains a picture of an English court when King Alfred was a boy, including something of the education available and the politics of the time. Whitelock offers another view of education and describes the uses of Latin writings in the society, uses which affected not only the society, but the English language of the time as well. The translation (from the Latin) of Ælfric's "Colloquy" gives the reader still another view of education and the society of the period, this time a view of the laborer and the tradesman.

In his Preface to *The Pastoral Care* (presented here in a very literal translation), Alfred speaks vigorously of the serious damage caused in his kingdom by the Danish invaders and the deterioration which resulted in the early years of his rule. He also sets out some of the details for his plan to rehabilitate the kingdom.

The selection from Alfred is presented here in translation, but elsewhere in this book examples of Old English are available in the original. The selection from Baugh contains an Old English version of the Lord's Prayer and of a portion of Bede's *Ecclesiastical History* (with interlinear translation in modern English); and the exercises at the back of the book contain the first eighty-two lines of "The Legend of St. Andrew" and the first fifty lines of Ælfric's "The Assumption of St. John the Apostle," both in Old English.

From this point on, the reader should undertake the exercises appropriate to the section he is reading. The introductory statements to the various sections there will tell him more about the state of the language in the various periods, the texts employed will provide examples of the language of those periods, and the exercises based on those texts will provide a better understanding of the language of the time than the readings can by themselves.

In this section, as this short discussion has shown, we are concerned, therefore, with what might be called the beginnings and early development of English as a separate language. From roughly 450, when the Teutonic invasions began, to 1154, the year of the last entry in *The Anglo-Saxon Chronicle*, Old English developed into a language quite distinct from the other Teutonic languages, a language which developed in response to the needs and nature of the Anglo-Saxon community which spoke it.

✠ ✠ ✠

OLD ENGLISH

ALBERT C. BAUGH

THE LANGUAGES IN ENGLAND BEFORE ENGLISH

. . .

The first people in England about whose language we have definite knowledge are the Celts. It used to be assumed that the coming of the Celts to England coincided with the introduction of bronze into the island. But the use of bronze probably preceded the Celts by several centuries. . . . Celtic was the first Indo-European tongue to be spoken in England and is still spoken by a considerable number of people. One other language, Latin, was spoken rather extensively for a period of about four centuries before the coming of English. Latin was introduced when Britain became a province of the Roman Empire. Since this was an event that has left a certain mark upon later history, it will be well to consider it separately.

THE ROMANS IN BRITAIN

In the summer of 55 B.C. Julius Caesar, having completed the conquest of Gaul, decided upon an invasion of England. What the object of his enterprise was is not certainly known. It is unlikely that he contemplated the

Reprinted from *A History of the English Language,* Second Edition, by Albert C. Baugh, copyright © 1957 by Meredith Corporation, by permission of Appleton-Century-Crofts.

conquest of the island; probably his chief purpose was to discourage the Celts of Britain from coming to the assistance of their kinsmen in Gaul, should the latter attempt to throw off the Roman yoke.[1] The expedition this year almost ended disastrously, and his return the following year was not a great success. In crossing the Channel some of his transports encountered a storm which deprived him of the support of his cavalry. The resistance of the natives was unexpectedly spirited. It was with difficulty that he effected a landing, and he made little headway. Since the season was far advanced, he soon returned to Gaul. The expedition had resulted in no material gain and some loss of prestige. Accordingly the following summer he again invaded the island, after much more elaborate preparations. This time he succeeded in establishing himself in the southeast. But after a few encounters with the natives, in which he was moderately successful, he exacted tribute from them (which was never paid) and again returned to Gaul. He had perhaps succeeded in his purpose, but he had by no means struck terror into the hearts of the Celts, and Britain was not again troubled by the Roman arms for nearly a hundred years.

THE ROMAN CONQUEST

It was in A.D. 43 that the Emperor Claudius decided to undertake the actual conquest of the island. With the knowledge of Caesar's experience behind him he did not underestimate the difficulty of the task. Accordingly an army of 40,000 men was sent to Britain and within three years had subjugated the tribes of the central and southeastern regions. Subsequent campaigns soon brought almost all of what is now England under Roman rule. The progress of Roman control was not uninterrupted. A serious uprising of the natives occurred in A.D. 61 under Boudicca (Boadicea), the widow of one of the native chiefs, and 70,000 Romans and Romanized Britons are said to have been massacred. Under the Roman Governor Agricola (78–85) the northern frontier was advanced to the Solway and the Tyne and the conquest may be said to have been completed. The Romans never penetrated far into the mountains of Wales and Scotland. Eventually they protected the northern boundary by a stone wall stretching across England at approximately the limits of Agricola's permanent conquest. The district south of this line was under Roman rule for more than three hundred years.

ROMANIZATION OF THE ISLAND

It was inevitable that the military conquest of Britain should have been followed by the Romanization of the province. Where the Romans lived and ruled, there Roman ways were found. Four great highways soon spread fanlike from London to the north, the northwest, the west, and the southwest, while a fifth cut across the island from Lincoln to the Severn. Numerous lesser roads connected important military or civil centers or branched off as spurs from the main highways. A score of small cities and more than a hundred towns, with their Roman houses and baths, temples and occasional theaters, testify to the introduction of Roman habits of life. The houses were equipped with heating apparatus and water supply, their floors were paved in mosaic, and their walls were of painted stucco—all as in their Italian counterparts. Roman dress, Roman ornaments and utensils, and Roman pottery and glassware seem to have been in general use. By the third century Christianity had made some progress in the island, and in 314 bishops from London and York attended a church council in Gaul. Under the relatively peaceful conditions that existed everywhere except along the frontiers, where the hostile penetration of the unconquered natives was always to be feared, there is every reason to think that Romanization had proceeded very much as it had done in the other provinces of the empire. The difference is that in Britain the process was cut short in the fifth century.

THE LATIN LANGUAGE IN BRITAIN

Among the other evidences of Romanization must be included the use of the Latin language. A great number of inscriptions have been found, all of them in Latin. The majority of these proceed no doubt from the military and official class and, being in the nature of public records, were therefore in the official language. They do not in themselves indicate a widespread use of Latin by the native population. Latin did not replace the Celtic language in Britain as it did in Gaul. Its use by native Britons was probably confined to members of the upper classes and the inhabitants of the cities and towns. Occasional *graffiti* scratched on a tile or piece of pottery, apparently by the workman who made it, suggest that in some localities Latin was familiar to the artisan class. Outside the cities there were many fine country houses, some of which were probably occupied by well-to-do natives. The occupants of these also probably spoke Latin. Tacitus tells us that in the time of Agricola the Britons, who had hitherto shown only hostility to the language of their conquerors, now became eager to speak it. At about the same time a Greek teacher from Asia Minor was teaching in Britain and by A.D. 96 the poet Martial was able to boast, possibly with some exaggeration, that his works were read even in this far-off island. On the whole, there were certainly many people in Roman Britain who habitually spoke Latin or upon occasion could use it. But its use was not sufficiently widespread to cause it to survive, as the Celtic language survived, the upheaval of the Teutonic invasions. Its use probably began to decline after 410,[2] the approximate date at which the last of the Roman troops were officially withdrawn from the island. The few traces which it has left in the language of the Teutonic invaders and that can still be seen in the English language today will occupy us later.

THE TEUTONIC CONQUEST

About the year 449 an event occurred which profoundly affected the course of history. In that year, as commonly stated, began the invasion of Britain by certain Teutonic tribes, the founders of the English nation. For more than a hundred years bands of conquerors and settlers migrated from their continental homes in the region of Denmark and the Low Countries and established themselves in the south and east of the island, gradually extending the area which they occupied until it included all but the highlands in the west and north. The events of these years are wrapped in much obscurity. While we can form a general idea of their course, we are still in doubt about some of the tribes that took part in the movement, their exact location on the continent, and the dates of their respective migrations.

The traditional account of the Teutonic invasions goes back to Bede and the Anglo-Saxon Chronicle. Bede in his *Ecclesiastical History of the English People*, completed in 731, tells us that the Teutonic tribes which conquered England were the Jutes, Saxons, and Angles. From what he says and from other indications it seems altogether most likely that the Jutes and the Angles had their home in the Danish peninsula, the Jutes in the northern half (hence the name Jutland) and the Angles in the South, in Schleswig-Holstein, and perhaps a small area at the base. The Saxons were settled to the south and west of the Angles, roughly between the Elbe and the Ems, possibly as far as the Rhine. A fourth tribe, the Frisians, some of whom almost certainly came to England, occupied a narrow strip along the coast from the Weser to the Rhine together with the island opposite. But by the time of the invasions the Jutes had apparently moved down to the coastal area near the mouth of the Weser, and possibly also around the Zuyder Zee and the lower Rhine, thus being in contact with both the Frisians and Saxons.

Britain had been exposed to attacks by the Saxons from as early as the fourth century. Even while the island was under Roman rule these attacks had become sufficiently serious to necessitate the appointment of an officer known as the Count of the Saxon Shore, whose duty it was to police the southeastern coast. At the same time the unconquered Picts and Scots in the north were kept out only at the price of constant vigilance. Against both of these sources of attack the Roman organization seems to have proved adequate. But the Celts had come to depend on Roman arms for this protection. They had, moreover, under Roman influence settled down to a more peaceful mode of life and had lost some of their barbaric power in war. Consequently when the Romans withdrew in 410 the Celts found themselves at a disadvantage. They were no longer able to keep out the warlike Picts and Scots. Several times they called upon Rome for aid, but finally the Romans, fully occupied in defending their own territory at home, were forced to refuse assistance. It was on this occasion that Vortigern, one of the Celtic leaders, is reported to have entered into an agreement with the Jutes whereby they were to assist the Celts in driving out the Picts and Scots and to receive as their reward the isle of Thanet.

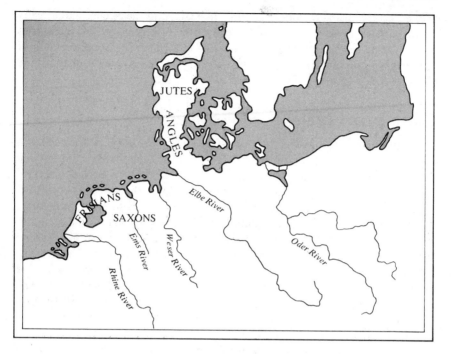

The Home of the English

Note.—The location of the Teutonic tribes that invaded England is still a matter of dispute. The above map presents the traditional view, based upon the rather late testimony (eighth century) of Bede. An alternative opinion places the Angles on the middle Elbe and the Jutes near the Frisians.

The Jutes, who had not been softened by contact with Roman civilization, were fully a match for the Picts and Scots. But Vortigern and the Celts soon found that they had in these temporary allies something more serious to reckon with than their northern enemies. The Jutes, having recognized the superiority of England over their continental home, decided to stay in the island and began making a forcible settlement in the southeast, in Kent.[3] The settlement of the Jutes was a very different thing from the conquest of the island by the Romans. The Romans had come to rule the native population, not to dispossess it. The Jutes came in numbers and settled on the lands of the Celts. They met the resistance of the Celts by driving them out. Moreover the example of the Jutes was soon followed by the migration of other continental tribes. According to the Anglo-Saxon Chronicle some of the Saxons came in 477, landed on the south coast, and established themselves in Sussex. In 495 further bands of Saxons settled a little to the west, in Wessex.[4] Finally in the middle of the next century the Angles occupied the east coast and in 547 established an Anglian kingdom north of the Humber. Too much credence, of course, cannot be put in these statements or dates. There were Saxons north of the Thames as the names Essex and Middlesex (the districts of the East Saxons and Middle Saxons) indicate, and the Angles had already begun to settle in East Anglia by the end of the fifth century. But the entries in the Chronicle may be taken as indicating in a general way a succession of settlements extending over more than a century which completely changed the character of England.

ANGLO-SAXON CIVILIZATION

It is difficult to speak with surety about the relations of the newcomers and the native population. In some districts where the inhabitants were few the Teutons probably settled down beside the Celts in more or less peaceful contact. In others, as in the West Saxon territory, the invaders met with stubborn resistance and succeeded in establishing themselves only after much fighting. Many of the Celts undoubtedly were driven into the west and sought refuge in Wales and Cornwall. In any case such civilization as had been attained under Roman influence was largely destroyed. The Roman towns were burnt and abandoned. Town life did not attract a population used to life in the open and finding its occupation in hunting and agriculture. The organization of society was by families and clans with a sharp distinction between *eorls*, a kind of hereditary aristocracy, and the *ceorls* or simple freemen. The business of the community was transacted in local assemblies or moots, and justice was administered through a series of fines—the were-gild—which varied according to the nature of the crime and the rank of the injured party. Guilt was generally determined by ordeal or by compurgation. In time various tribes combined either for greater strength or under the influence of a powerful leader to produce small kingdoms. Seven of these are eventually recognized, Northumbria, Mercia, East Anglia, Kent, Essex, Sussex, and Wessex, and are spoken of as the Anglo-Saxon Heptarchy. But the grouping was not very permanent, sometimes two or more being united under one king, at other times kingdoms being divided under separate rulers. In the early part of the seventh century Northumbria gained political supremacy over a number of the other kingdoms and held an undoubted leadership in literature and learning as well. In the eighth century this leadership passed to Mercia. Finally, in the ninth century, Wessex under the guidance of Egbert (802–39) began to extend its influence until in 830 all England, including the chieftains of Wales, acknowledged Egbert's overlordship. The result can hardly be called a united nation, but West Saxon kings were able to maintain the claim to be kings of all the English, and under Alfred (871–99) Wessex attained a high degree of prosperity and considerable enlightenment.

THE NAMES "ENGLAND" AND "ENGLISH"

The Celts called their Teutonic conquerors Saxons indiscriminately, probably because they had had their first contact with the Teutons through the Saxon raids on the coast.[5] Early Latin writers, following Celtic usage, generally call the Teutons in England *Saxones* and the land *Saxonia*. But soon the terms *Angli* and *Anglia* occur beside *Saxones* and refer not to the Angles individually but to the Teutons generally. Aethelbert, king of Kent, is styled *rex Anglorum* by Pope Gregory in 601, and a century later Bede called his history the *Historia Ecclesiastica Gentis Anglorum*. In time *Angli* and *Anglia* become the usual terms in Latin texts. From the beginning, however, writers in the vernacular never call their language anything but *Englisc* (*English*). The word is derived from the name of the Angles (O.E. *Engle*) but is used without distinction for the language of all the invading tribes. In like manner the land and its people are early called *Angelcynn* (Angle-kin or race of the Angles), and this is the common name until after the Danish period. From about the year 1000 *Englaland* (land of the Angles) begins to take its place. The name *English* is thus older than the name *England*.[6] It is not easy to say why England should have taken its name from the Angles. Possibly a desire to avoid confusion with the Saxons who remained on the continent and the early supremacy of the Anglian kingdoms were the predominant factors in determining usage.[7]

THE ORIGIN AND POSITION OF ENGLISH

The English language of today is the language which has resulted from the fusion of the dialects spoken by the Teutonic tribes who came to England in the manner described. It is impossible to say how much the speech of the Angles differed from that of the Saxons or that of the Jutes. The differences were certainly slight. Even after these dialects had been subjected to several centuries of geographical and political separation in England the differences were not great. As we have seen above English belongs to the Low West Teutonic branch of the Indo-European family. This means in the first place that it shares certain characteristics common to all the Teutonic languages. For example it shows the shifting of certain consonants described above under the head of Grimm's Law. It possesses a 'weak' as well as a 'strong' declension of the adjective and a distinctive type of conjugation of the verb—the so-called weak or regular verbs such as *fill, filled, filled*, which form their past tense and past participle by adding *-ed* or some analogous sound to the stem of the present. And it shows the adoption of a strong stress accent on the first or the root syllable of most words,[8] a feature of great importance in all the Teutonic languages, since it is chiefly responsible for the progressive decay of inflections in these languages. In the second place it means that English belongs with German and certain other languages because of features which it has in common with them and which enable us to distinguish a West Teutonic group as contrasted with the Scandinavian languages (North Teutonic) and Gothic (East Teutonic). These features have to do mostly with certain phonetic changes, especially the gemination or doubling of consonants under special conditions, matters which we do not need to enter upon here. And it means, finally, that English along with the other languages of northern Germany and the Low Countries did not participate in the further modification of certain consonants, known as the Second or High German Sound-Shift.[9] In other words it belongs with the dialects of the lowlands in the West Teutonic area.

THE PERIODS IN THE HISTORY OF ENGLISH

The evolution of English in the fifteen hundred years of its existence in England has been an unbroken one. Within this development, however, it is possible to recognize three main periods. Like all divisions in history the periods of the English language are matters of convenience and the dividing lines between them purely arbitrary. There is no break in the process of continuous transition. But within each of the periods it is possible to recognize certain broad characteristics and certain special developments that take place. The period from 450 to 1150 is known as Old English. It is sometimes described as the period of full inflections, since during most of this period the endings of the noun, the adjective, and the verb are preserved more or less unimpaired. From 1150 to 1500 the language is known as Middle English.[10] During this period the inflections, which had begun to break down towards the end of the Old English period, become greatly reduced, and it is consequently known as the period of level inflections. The language since 1500 is called Modern English. By the time we reach this stage in the development a large part of the original inflectional system has disappeared entirely and we therefore speak of it as the period of lost inflections. The progressive decay of inflections is only one of the developments which mark the evolution of English in its various stages. We shall discuss the other features which are characteristic of Old English, Middle English, and Modern English in their proper place.

THE DIALECTS OF OLD ENGLISH

Old English was not an entirely uniform language. Not only are there differences between the language of the earliest written records (about A.D. 700) and that of the later literary texts, but the language differed somewhat from one locality to another. We can distinguish four dialects in Old English times: Northumbrian, Mercian, West Saxon, and Kentish. Of these Northumbrian and Mercian are found in the region north of the Thames settled by the Angles. They possess certain features in common and are sometimes known collectively as Anglian. But Northumbrian, spoken north of the Humber River, and Mercian, between the Humber and the Thames, likewise possess each certain distinctive features. Unfortunately we know less about them than we should like since they are preserved mainly in charters, runic inscriptions, a few brief fragments of verse, and some interlinear translations of portions of the Bible. Kentish is known from still scantier remains and is the dialect of the Jutes in the southeast. The only dialect in which there is

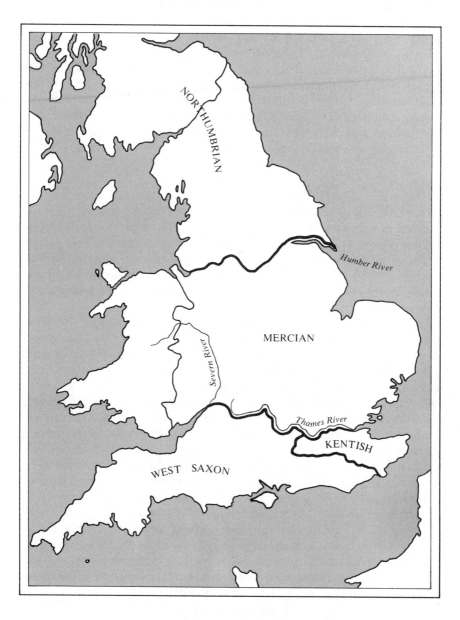

The Dialects of Old English

an extensive collection of texts is West Saxon. It was the dialect of the West Saxon kingdom in the southwest. Nearly all of Old English literature is preserved in manuscripts trasncribed in this region. With the ascendancy of the West Saxon kingdom the West Saxon dialect attained something of the position of a literary standard, and both for this reason and because of the abundance of the materials it is made the basis of the study of Old English. Such a start as it had made toward becoming the standard speech of England was cut short by the Norman Conquest which, as we shall see, reduced all dialects to a common level of unimportance. And when in the Middle English period a standard English once more began to arise it was on the basis of a different dialect.

SOME CHARACTERISTICS OF OLD ENGLISH

The English language has undergone such change in the course of time that one cannot read Old English without special study. In fact a page of Old English is likely at first to present a look of greater strangeness than a page of French or Italian because of the employment of certain characters that no longer form a part of our alphabet. In general the differences which one notices between Old and Modern English concern spelling and pronunciation, the vocabulary, and the grammar.

The pronunciation of Old English words commonly differs somewhat from that of their modern equivalents. The long vowels in particular have undergone considerable modification. Thus the Old English sord *stān* is the same word as Modern English stone, but the vowel is different. A similar correspondence is apparent in *hālig—holy, gān—go, bān—bone, rāp—rope, hlāf—loaf, bāt—boat*. Other vowels have likewise undergone changes in *fōt* (foot), *cēne* (keen), *metan* (mete), *fȳr* (fire), *riht* (right), *hū* (how), *hlūd* (loud), but the identity of these words with their modern descendants is still readily apparent. Words like *hēafod* (head), *faeger* (fair), or *sāwol* (soul) show forms which have been contracted in later English. All of these cases represent genuine differences of pronunciation. However, some of the first look of strangeness which Old English has to the modern reader is due simply to differences of spelling. Old English made use of two characters to represent the sound of *th*: þ and ð, as in the word *wiþ* (with) or *ðā* (then), which we no longer employ. It also expressed the sound of *a* in *hat* by a digraph *æ* and since the sound is of very frequent occurrence, the character contributes not a little to the unfamiliar appearance of the page. Likewise Old English represented the sound of *sh* by *sc*, as in *scēap* (sheep) or *scēotan* (shoot), and the sound of *k* by *c*, as in *cynn* (kin) or *nacod* (naked). Consequently a number of words which were in all probability pronounced by King Alfred almost as they are by us present a strange appearance in the written or printed text. Such words as *folc* (folk), *scip* (ship), *bæc* (back), *þorn* (thorn), *bæð* (bath), *þæt* (that) are examples in point. It should be noted that the differences of spelling and pronunciation that figure so prominently in one's first impression of Old English are really not very fundamental. Those of spelling are often apparent rather than real, since they represent no difference in the spoken language, and those of pronunciation obey certain laws as a result of which we soon learn to recognize the Old and Modern English equivalents.

A second feature of Old English which would become quickly apparent to a modern reader is the absence of those words derived from Latin and French which form so large a part of our present vocabulary. Such words make up more than half of the words now in common use. They are so essential to the expression of our ideas, seem so familiar and natural to us, that we miss them in the earlier stage of the language. The vocabulary of Old English is almost purely Teutonic. A large part of this vocabulary moreover has disappeared from the language. When the Norman Conquest brought French into England as the language of the higher classes much of the Old English vocabulary appropriate to literature and learning died out and was replaced later by words borrowed from French and Latin. An examination of the words in an Old English dictionary shows that about 85 per cent of them are no longer in use. Those that survive, to be sure, are basic elements of our vocabulary, and by the frequency with which they recur make up a large part of any English sentence. Apart from pronouns, prepositions, conjunctions, auxiliary verbs, and the like, they express fundamental concepts like *mann* (man), *wīf* (wife), *cild* (child), *hūs* (house), *benc* (bench), *mete* (meat, food), *gœrs* (grass), *lēaf* (leaf), *fugol* (fowl, bird), *gōd* (good), *heah* (high), *strang* (strong), *etan* (eat), *drincan* (drink), *slœpan* (sleep), *libban* (live), *feohtan* (fight). But the fact remains that a considerable part of the vocabulary of Old English is unfamiliar to the modern reader.

The third and most fundamental feature that distinguishes Old English from the language of today is its grammar.[11] Inflectional languages fall into two classes: synthetic and analytic. A *synthetic* language is one which indicates the relation of words in a sentence largely by means of inflections. In the case of Indo-European languages these most commonly take the forms of endings of the noun and pronoun, the adjective and the verb. Thus in Latin the nominative *murus* (wall) is distinguished from the genitive *muri* (of the wall), dative *muro* (to the wall), accusative *murum*, etc. A single verb form like *laudaverunt* (they have praised) conveys the idea of person, number, and tense along with the meaning of the root, a conception which we require three words for in English. The Latin sentence *Nero interfecit Agrippinam* means 'Nero killed Agrippina.' It would mean the same thing if the words were arranged in any other order, such as *Agrippinam interfecit Nero*, because *Nero* is the form of the nominative case and the ending *-am* of *Agrippinam* marks the noun as accusative no matter where it stands. In Modern English, however, the subject and the object do not have distinctive forms, nor do we have, except in the possessive case, inflectional endings to indicate the other relations marked by case endings in Latin. Instead we make use of a fixed order of words. It makes a great deal of difference in English whether we say *Nero killed Agrippina* or *Agrippina killed Nero*. Languages which make extensive use of prepositions and auxiliary verbs and depend upon word order to show other relationships are known as *analytic* languages. Modern English is an analytic, Old English is a synthetic language. In its grammar Old English resembles modern German. Theoretically the noun and adjective are inflected for four cases in the singular and four in the plural, although the forms are not always distinctive, and in addition the adjective has separate forms for each of the three genders. The inflection of the verb is less elaborate than that of the Latin verb, but there are distinctive endings for the different persons, numbers, tenses, and moods. We shall illustrate the nature of the Old English inflections in the following paragraphs.

The Noun. The inflection of the Old English noun indicates distinctions of number (singular and plural) and case. The case system is somewhat simpler than that of Latin and some of the other Indo-European languages. There is no ablative, and generally no locative or instrumental case, these having been merged with the dative. In the same way the vocative of direct address is generally identical with the nominative form. Thus the Old English noun has only four cases. The endings of these cases vary with different nouns, but they fall into certain broad categories or declensions. There is a vowel declension and a consonant declension, also called the strong and weak declensions, according to whether the stem ended in Germanic in a vowel or a consonant, and within each of these types there are certain subdivisions. The stems of nouns belonging to the vowel declension ended in one of four vowels: *a, o, i,* or *u,* and the inflection varies accordingly. It is impossible here to present the inflections of the Old English noun in detail. Their nature may be gathered from two examples of the strong declension and one of the weak: *stān* (stone), a masculine *a*-stem; *giefu* (gift), a feminine *o*-stem; and *hunta* (hunter), a masculine consonant-stem:

Sing.	N	stān	gief-u	hunt-a
	G	stān-es	gief-e	hunt-an
	D	stān-e	gief-e	hunt-an
	A	stān	gief-e	hunt-an
Plur.	N	stān-as	gief-a	hunt-a n
	G	stān-a	gief-a	hunt-e na
	D	stān-um	gief-um	hunt-u m
	A	stān-as	gief-a	hunt-an

It is apparent from these examples that the inflection of the noun was much more elaborate in Old English than it is today. Even these few paradigms illustrate clearly the marked synthetic character of English in its earliest stage.

Grammatical Gender. As in Indo-European languages generally the gender of Old English nouns is not dependent upon considerations of sex. While nouns designating males are generally masculine and females feminine, those indicating neuter objects are not necessarily neuter. *Stān* (stone) is masculine, *mōna* (moon) is masculine, but *sunne* (sun) is feminine, as in German. In French the corresponding words have just the opposite genders: *pierre* (stone) and *lune* (moon) are feminine while *soleil* (sun) is masculine. Often the gender of Old English nouns is quite illogical. Words like *mægden* (girl), *wīf* (wife), *bearn* and *cild* (child), which we should expect to be feminine or masculine, are in fact neuter, while *wīfmann* (woman) is masculine because the second element of the compound is masculine. The simplicity of Modern English gender has already been pointed out as one of the chief assets of the language. How so desirable a change was brought about will be shown later.

The Adjective. An important feature of the Teutonic languages is the development of a twofold declension of the adjective, one, the strong declension, used with nouns when not accompanied by a definite article or similar word (such as a demonstrative or possessive pronoun), the other, the weak declension, used when the noun is preceded by such a word. Thus we have in Old English *gōd mann* (good man) but *sē gōda mann* (the good man). The forms are those of the nominative singular masculine in the strong and weak declensions respectively, illustrated below:

		Strong Declension			Weak Declension		
		Masc.	*Fem.*	*Neut.*	*Masc.*	*Fem.*	*Neut.*
Sing.	N	gōd	gōd[12]	gōd	gōd-a	gōd-e	gōd-e
	G	gōd-es	gōd-re	gōd-es	gōd-an	gōd-an	gōd-an
	D	gōd-um	gōd-re	gōd-um	gōd-an	gōd-an	gōd-an
	A	gōd-ne	gōd-e	gōd	gōd-an	gōd-an	gōd-e
	I	gōd-e		gōd-e			
Plur.	N	gōd-e	gōd-a	gōd	gōd-an		
	G	gōd-ra	gōd-ra	gōd-ra	gōd-ena *or* gōd-ra		
	D	gōd-um	gōd-um	gōd-um	gōd-um		
	A	gōd-e	gōd-a	gōd	gōd-an		

This elaboration of inflection in the Old English adjective contrasts in the most striking way with the complete absence of inflection from the adjective in Modern English. Such complexity is quite unnecessary, as the English language demonstrates every day by getting along without it. Its elimination has resulted in a second great advantage which English possesses over most other languages.

The Definite Article. Like its sister language of today, German, Old English possessed a fully inflected definite article. How complete the declension of this word was can be seen from the following forms:

		Masc.	*Fem.*	*Neut.*	*All Genders*	
Sing.	N	sē	sēo	ðæt	Plur.	ðā
	G	ðæs	ðǣre	ðæs		ðāra
	D	ðǣm	ðǣre	ðǣm		ðǣm
	A	ðone	ðā	ðæt		ðā
	I	ðȳ, ðon		ðȳ, ðon		

While the ordinary meaning of *sē*, *sēo*, *oæt*, is 'the,' the word is really a demonstrative pronoun and survives in the Modern English demonstrative *that*. Its pronominal character appears also in its not infrequent use as a relative pronoun (= who, which, that) and as a personal pronoun (= he, she, it). The regular personal pronoun, however, is shown in the next paragraph.

The Personal Pronoun. From the frequency of its use and the necessity for specific reference when used, the personal pronoun in all languages is likely to preserve a fairly complete system of inflections. Old English shows this tendency not only in having distinctive forms for practically all genders, persons, and cases, but also in preserving in addition to the ordinary two numbers, singular and plural, a set of forms for two people or two things— the dual number. Indo-European had separate forms for the dual number in the verb as well, and these appear in Greek and to a certain extent in Gothic. They are not found, however, in Old English. The distinction between the dual and the plural is an unnecessary complication in language and was disappearing from the pronoun in Old English. The dual forms are shown, however, in the following table of the Old English personal pronoun:

Sing.	N	ic		ðū		hē	*(he)*	hēo	*(she)*	hit	*(it)*
	G	mīn		ðīn		his		hiere		his	
	D	mē		ðē		him		hiere		him	
	A	mē	(mec)	ðē	(ðec)	hine		hīe		hit	
Dual	N	wit	*(we two)*	git	*(ye two)*						
	G	uncer		incer							
	D	unc		inc							
	A	unc		inc							
Plur.	N	wē		gē				hīe			
	G	ūser	(ūre)	ēower				hiera			
	D	ūs		ēow				him			
	A	ūs	(ūsic)	ēow	(ēowic)			hīe			

The Verb. The inflection of the verb in the Germanic languages is much simpler than it was in Indo-European times. A comparison of the Old English verb with the verbal inflection of Greek or Latin will show how much has been lost. Old English distinguished only two simple tenses by inflection, a present and a past, and, except for one word, it had no inflectional forms for the passive as in Latin or Greek. It recognized the indicative, subjunctive, and imperative moods, and had the usual two numbers, and three persons.

A peculiar feature of the Germanic languages was the division of the verb into two great classes, the weak and the strong, often known in Modern English as regular and irregular verbs. These terms, which are so commonly employed in modern grammars, are rather unfortunate since they suggest an irregularity in the strong verbs which is more apparent than real. The strong verbs, like *sing, sang, sung,* which represent the basic Indo-European types, are so called because they have the power of indicating change of tense by a modification of their root vowel. In the weak verbs, such as *walk, walked,*

walked, this change is effected by the addition of a dental, sometimes of an extra syllable.

The apparent irregularity of the strong verbs is due to the fact that verbs of this type are much less numerous than weak verbs. In Old English, if we exclude compounds, there were only a few over three hundred of them, and even this small number falls into several classes. Within these classes, however, a perfectly regular sequence can be observed in the vowel changes of the root. Nowadays these verbs, generally speaking, have different vowels in the present tense, the past tense, and the past participle. In some verbs the vowels of the past tense and past participle are identical, as in *break, broke, broken,* and in some all three forms have become alike in modern times (*bid, bid, bid*). In Old English the vowel of the past tense often differs in the singular and the plural; or, to be more accurate, the first and third person singular have one vowel while the second person singular and all persons of the plural have another. In the principal parts of Old English strong verbs, therefore, we have four forms, the infinitive, the preterite singular (first and third person), the preterite plural, and the past participle. In Old English the strong verbs can be grouped in six general classes, to which may be added a seventh, the reduplicating verbs. While there are variations within each class, they may be illustrated by the following seven verbs:

I.	drīfan	*(drive)*	drāf	drifon	(ge)	drifen
II.	cēosan	*(choose)*	cēas	curon[13]		coren
III.	helpan	*(help)*	healp	hulpon		holpen
IV.	beran	*(bear)*	bær	bǣron		boren
V.	sprecan	*(speak)*	spræc	sprǣcon		sprecen
VI.	faran	*(fare, go)*	fōr	fōron		faren
VII.	feallan	*(fall)*	fēoll	fēollon		feallen[14]

The origin of the dental suffixes by which weak verbs form their past tense and past participle is not known. It was formerly customary to explain these as part of the verb *do*, as though *I worked* was originally *I work-did* (i.e., *I did work*). More recently an attempt has been made to trace these forms to a type of verb which formed its stem by adding *-to-* to the root. The origin of so important a feature of the Germanic languages as the weak conjugation is naturally a question to which we should like very much to find the answer. Fortunately it is not of prime importance to our present purpose of describing the structure of Old English. Here it is sufficient to note that a large and important group of verbs in Old English formed their past tense by adding *-ede, -ode,* or *-de* to the present stem, and their past participles by adding *-ed, -od,* or *-d*. Thus *fremman* (to perform) has a preterite *fremede* and a past participle *gefremed*; *lufian* (to love) has *lufode* and *gelufod*; *libban* (to live) has *lifde* and *gelifd*. The personal endings except in the preterite singular are similar to those of the strong verbs and need not be repeated. It is to be noted, however, that the weak conjugation has come to be the dominant one in our language. Many strong verbs have passed over to this conjugation, and practically all new verbs added to our language are inflected in accordance with it.

THE LANGUAGE ILLUSTRATED

We have spoken of the inflections of Old English in some detail primarily with the object of making more concrete what is meant when we call the language in this stage synthetic. In the later chapters of this book we shall have occasion to trace the process by which English lost a great part of this inflectional system and became an analytic language, so that the paradigms which we have given here will also prove useful as a point of departure for that discussion. The use of these inflections as well as the other characteristics of the language so far pointed out may be seen in the following specimens. The first is the Lord's Prayer, the clauses of which can easily be followed through the modern form which is familiar to us from the King James version of the Bible.

> Fæder ūre,
> þū þe eart on heofonum,
> sī þīn name gehālgod.
> Tōbecume þīn rīce.
> Gewurþe ðīn willa on eorðan swā swā on heofonum.
> Ūrne gedæghwāmlīcan hlāf syle ūs tō dæg.
> And forgyf ūs ūre gyltas, swā swā wē forgyfað ūrum gyltendum.
> And ne gelæd þū ūs on costnunge,
> ac ālȳs ūs of yfele. Sōþlīce.

The second specimen is from the Old English translation of Bede's *Ecclesiastical History* and tells the story of the coming of the missionaries to England under St. Augustine in 597:

Ðā wæs on þā tīd Æþelbeorht cyning hāten on Centrīce, and
Then (there) was in that time a king named Æthelberht in Kent, and (a)

mihtig: hē hæfde rīce   oð   gemæru   Humbre strēames,
mighty (one): he had   dominion up to (the) confines of the Humber   river,

sē   tōscādeþ   sūðfolc   Angelþēode   and   norðfolc.   Þonne
which separates the south folk   of the English   and the north folk.   Now

is on ēasteweardre Cent micel ēaland, Tenet, þæt is siex hund
there is   in eastward   Kent a large island Thanet, that is six hundred

hīda micel æfter Angelcynnes eahte. . . .   On þyssum ēalande
hides large after the reckoning of the English. . . . On this   island   5

cōm ūp sē Godes þēow Augustinus and his gefēran;   wæs hē
came up the servant of God, Augustine and his companions; he was

fēowertiga sum. Nāmon hīe ēac swelce him wealhstodas of
one of forty. Took they likewise with them interpreters from

Franclande mid, swā him Sanctus Gregorious bebēad. And þā
Frank-land, as them Saint Gregory bade. And then (Augustine)

sende to Æþelbeorhte ǣrendwrecan and onbēad þæt hē of Rōme
sent to Æthelberht a messenger and announced that he from Rome

cōme and þæt betste ǣrende lǣdde; and sē þe him hīersum
had come and the best message brought (led); and he who (if any) would   10

bēon wolde, būton twēon hē gehēt ēcne gefēan on heofenum
be obedient to him, without doubt he promised eternal happiness in heaven

and tōweard rīce būton ende mid þone sōþan God and þone
and a future kingdom without end with the true God and the

lifigendan. Ðā hē þā sē cyning þās word gehīerde, þā hēt hē hīe
living (God). When the king heard these words, then bade he them

bīdan on þǣm ēalande þe hīe ūp cōmon; and him þider hiera þearfe
to bide on the island that they had come upon; and them thither their need

forgēaf, oð þæt hē gesāwe hwæt hē him dōn wolde. Swelce ēac ǣr
provided, until that he saw what he would do with them. Likewise ere   15

þǣm becōm hlīsa tō him þǣre crīstenan ǣfæstnesse, forþon hē
that had come to him the fame of the Christian religion, since he

crīsten wīf hæfde, him gegiefen of Francena cyningcynne,
had a Christian wife, given him from the royal family of the Franks,

Beorhte wæs hāten. Þæt wīf hē onfēng fram hiere ieldrum
(who) was named Bertha. That wife he received from her parents (elders)

þǣre ārǣdnesse þæt hēo his lēafnesse hæfde þæt hēo þone þēaw
on the condition that she should have his permission that she the practice

þæs crīstenan gelēafan and hiere ǣfæstnesse ungewemmedne healdan
of the Christian faith and her religion unimpaired might   20

mōste mid þȳ biscope, þone þe hīe hiere tō fultume þæs gelēafan
hold with the bishop whom they to her for the help of the (her) faith

sealdon, þæs nama wæs Lēodheard.
had given, whose name was Leodheard.

Ðā wæs æfter manigum dagum þæt sē cyning cōm tō þǣm ēalande,
Then it was after many days that the king came to the island

and hēt him ūte setl gewyrcean; and hēt
and commanded (them) to make him a seat in the open air; and he bade

Augustinum mid his gefērum þider tō his sprǣce cuman.
Augustine with his companions to come thither to a (his) consultation.   25

Warnode hē him þȳ lǣs hīe on hwelc hūs tō him inēoden;
He guarded himself lest they in the same house with him should enter;

brēac ealdre hēalsunga, gif hīe hwelcne drȳcræft hæfden
he employed an old precaution in case they any sorcery had with

þæt hīe hine oferswīðan and beswīcan sceolden. . . . Þā
which they should overcome and get the better of him. . . . Then

hēt sē cyning hīe sittan, and hīe swā dydon; and hīe sōna him
the king bade them to sit, and they did so; and they soon to him

līfes word ætgædere mid eallum his gefērum þe þǣr æt wǣron,
the word of life together with all his companions that thereat were, 30

bodedon and lǣrdon. Þā andswarode sē cyning and þus cwæð:
preached and taught. Then answered the king and thus quoth:

"Fæger word þis sindon and gehāt þe gē brōhton and ūs secgað. Ac
"Fair words these are and promises that ye have brought and say to us. But

forðon hīe nīwe sindon and uncūðe, ne magon wē nū gēn þæt þafian
since they new are and unknown, we may not yet consent to this

þæt wē forlǣten þā wīsan þe wē langre tīde mid ealle Angelþēode hēoldon.
that we give up the ways that we longtime with all the English have held.

Ac forðon þe gē hider feorran elþēodige cōmon and, þæs þe
But since ye hither from afar as strangers have come and, as it 35

mē geþūht is and gesewen, þā þing, ðā ðe [gē] sōð and betst gelīefdon,
seems to me and appears, the things that ye believed true and best

þæt ēac swelce wilnodon ūs þā gemǣnsumian, nellað wē forðon ēow
that likewise (ye) wished to impart them to us, we will not therefore on you

hefige bēon. Ac wē willað ēow ēac fremsumlīce on giestlīðnesse onfōn and
be heavy. But we will you also kindly in hospitality receive and

ēow andleofne sellan and ēowre þearfe forgiefan. Ne wē ēow beweriað þæt
give you food and your needs provide for. Nor do we you forbid that

gē ealle, ðā þe gē mægen, þurh ēowre lāre tō ēowres gelēafan æfæstnesse
ye all those that ye may through your teaching to of your faith (the) religion 40

geðīeden and gecierren."*
may join and convert."

THE RESOURCEFULNESS OF THE OLD ENGLISH VOCABULARY

To one unfamiliar with Old English it might seem that a language which
lacked the large number of words borrowed from Latin and French which
now form so important a part of our vocabulary would be somewhat limited
in resources, and that while possessing adequate means of expression for
the affairs of simple everyday life would find itself embarrassed when it
came to making the nice distinctions which a literary language is called upon

*The original is here somewhat normalized.

to express. In other words, an Anglo-Saxon would be like a man today who is learning to speak a foreign language and who can manage in a limited way to convey his meaning without having a sufficient command of the vocabulary to express those subtler shades of thought and feeling, the nuances of meaning, which he is able to suggest in his mother tongue. This, however, is not so. In language, as in other things, necessity is the mother of invention, and when our means are limited we often develop unusual resourcefulness in utilizing those means to the full. Such resourcefulness is characteristic of Old English. The language in this stage shows great flexibility, a capacity for bending old words to new uses. By means of prefixes and suffixes a single root is made to yield a variety of derivatives, and the range of these is greatly extended by the ease with which compounds were formed. The method can be made clear by an illustration. The word *mōd*, which is our word *mood* (a mental state), meant in Old English 'heart,' 'mind,' 'spirit,' and hence 'boldness' or 'courage,' sometimes 'pride' or 'haughtiness.' From it, by the addition of a common adjective ending, was formed the adjective *mōdig* with a similar range of meanings (spirited, bold, high-minded, arrogant, stiff-necked), and by means of further endings the adjective *mōdiglīc* magnanimous, the adverb *mōdiglīce* boldly, proudly, and the noun *mōdignes* magnanimity, pride. Another ending converted *mōdig* into a verb *mōdigian*, meaning to bear oneself proudly or exultantly, or sometimes, to be indignant, to rage. Other forms conveyed meanings whose relation to the root is easily perceived, *gemōdod* disposed, minded, *mōdfull* haughty, *mōdlēas* spiritless. By combining the root with other words meaning 'mind' or 'thought' the idea of the word is intensified, and we get *mōdsefa, mōdgepanc, mōdgeþoht, mōdgehygd, mōdgemynd, mōdhord* (*hord* = treasure), all meaning 'mind,' 'thought,' 'understanding.' Some sharpening of the concept is obtained in *mōdcræft* intelligence, and *mōdcræftig* intelligent. But the root lent itself naturally to combination with other words to indicate various mental states, such as *glædmōdnes* kindness, *mōdlufu* affection (*lufu* = love), *unmōd* despondency, *mōdcaru* sorrow (*caru* = care), *mōdlēast* want of courage, *mādmōd* folly, *ofermōd* and *ofermōdigung* pride, *ofermōdig* proud, *hēahmōd* proud, noble, *mōdhete* hate (*hete* = hate). It will be seen that Old English did not lack synonyms for some of the ideas in this list. By a similar process of combination a number of adjectives were formed: *micelmōd* magnanimous, *swīþmōd* great of soul (*swīþ* = strong), *stīþmōd* resolute, obstinate (*stīþ* = stiff, strong), *guþmōd* warlike (*guþ* = war, battle), *torhtmōd* glorious (*torht* = bright), *mōdlēof* beloved (*lēof* = dear). The examples given are sufficient to illustrate the point, but they are far from telling the whole story. From the same root more than a hundred words were formed. If we had space to list them, they would clearly show the remarkable capacity of Old English for derivation and word-formation, and what variety and flexibility of expression it possessed. It was more resourceful in utilizing its native material than Modern English, which has come to rely to a large extent on its facility in borrowing and assimilating elements from other languages.

SELF-EXPLAINING COMPOUNDS

In the list of words given in the preceding paragraph there is a considerable number which we call self-explaining compounds. These are compounds of two or more native words whose meaning in combination is either self-evident or has been rendered clear by association and usage. In Modern English *steamboat, railroad, electric light, sewing machine, one-way street*, are examples of such words. Words of this character are found in most languages, but the type is particularly prevalent in Old English, as it is in modern German. Where in English today we often have a borrowed word or a word made up of elements derived from Latin and Greek, German still prefers self-explaining compounds. Thus for hydrogen German says *Wasserstoff* (water-stuff), for telephone *Fernsprecher* (far-speaker), and for fire insurance company *Feuer│ versicherungs│gessellschaft*. So in Old English many words are formed on this pattern. Thus we have *leohtfæt* lamp (*leoht* light +*fæt* vessel), *medu-heall* mead-hall, *dægred* dawn (day-red), *ealohūs* alehouse, *ealoscop* minstrel, *ēarhring* earring, *eorþcræft* geometry, *fiscdēag* purple (lit. fish-dye), *fōtādl* gout (foot-disease), *gimmwyrhta* jeweler (gem-worker), *fielleséocnes* epilepsy (falling-sickness; cf. Shakespeare's use of this expression in *Julius Caesar*), *frumweorc* creation (*fruma* beginning + work), and many more. The capacity of English nowadays to make similar words, though a little less frequently employed than formerly, is an inheritance of the Old English tradition, when the method was well-nigh universal. As a result of this capacity Old English seems never to have been at a loss for a word to express even the abstractions of science, theology, and metaphysics, which it came to know through contact with the church and Latin culture.

PREFIXES AND SUFFIXES

As previously mentioned, a part of the flexibility of the Old English vocabulary comes from the generous use made of prefixes and suffixes to form new words from old words or to modify or extend the root idea. In this respect it also resembles modern German. Among the words mentioned in the preceding paragraphs there are several which are formed with the suffixes *-ig, -full, -lēas, -līce, -nes,* and *-ung.* Others frequently employed include the adjective suffixes *-sum* (*wynsum*) and *-wīs* (*rihtwīs*), the noun suffixes *-dōm* (*cyningdōm, eorldōm*), *-end*, and *-ere* denoting the agent, *-hād* (*cildhād*), *-ing* in patronymics, *-ung* (*dagung* dawn), *-scipe* (*frēondscipe*), and many more. In like manner the use of prefixes was a fertile resource in word-building. It is particularly a feature in the formation of verbs. There are about a dozen prefixes that occur with great frequency, such as *ā-, be-, for-, fore-, ge-, mis-, of-, ofer-, on-, tō-, un-, under-,* and *wiþ-.* Thus, with the help of these, Old English could make out of a simple verb like *settan* (to set) new verbs like *āssetan* place, *besettan* appoint, *forsettan* obstruct, *foresettan* place before, *gesettan* people, garrison, *ofsettan* afflict, *onsettan* oppress, *tōsettan* dispose, *unsettan* put down, and *wiþsettan* resist. The prefix *wiþ-* enters into more than fifty

Old English verbs, where it has the force of *against* or *away*. Such, for example, are *wiþcēosan* reject (*cēosan* = choose), *wiþcweþan* deny (*cweþan* = say), *wiþdrīfan* repel, *wiþsprecan* contradict, and *wiþstandan*. Of these fifty verbs *withstand* is the only one still in use, although in Middle English two new verbs, *withdraw* and *withhold* were formed on the same model. The prefix *ofer-* occurs in over a hundred Old English verbs. By such means the resources of the English verb were increased almost tenfold, and enough such verbs survive to give us a realization of their employment in the Old English vocabulary.

In general one is surprised at the apparent ease with which Old English expressed difficult ideas adequately and often with variety. *Companionship* is literally rendered by *gefērascipe, hospitality* by *giestlīþnes* (*giest* stranger, *līþe* gracious), *gītsung* covetousness (*gītsian* = to be greedy). *Godcundlic* divine, *indryhten* aristocratic (*dryhten* = prince), *giefolnes* liberality (*giefu* = gift), *gaderscipe* matrimony (*gadrian* = to gather), *lǣcecrǣft* medicine (*lǣce* = physician) illustrate, so to speak, the method of approach. Often several words to express the same idea result. An astronomer or astrologer may be a *tunglere* (*tungol* = star), *tungolcrǣftiga, tungolwītega,* a *tīdymbwlātend* (*tīd* = time, *ymb* = about, *wlātian* = to gaze) or a *tīdscēawere* (*scēawian* = see, scrutinize). In poetry the vocabulary attains a remarkable flexibility through the wealth of synonyms for words like war, warrior, shield, sword, battle, sea, ship—sometimes as many as thirty for one of these ideas—and through the bold use of metaphors. The king is the leader of hosts, the giver of rings, the protector of eorls, the victory-lord, the heroes' treasure-keeper. A sword is the product of files, the play of swords a battle, the battle-seat a saddle, the shield-bearer a warrior. Warriors in their woven war-shirts, carrying battle-brand or war-shaft, form the iron-clad throng. A boat is the sea-wood, the wave-courser, the broad-bosomed, the curved-stem, or the foamy-necked ship, and it travels over the whale-road, the sea-surge, the rolling of waves, or simply the water's back. Synonyms never fail the Beowulf poet. Grendel is the grim spirit, the prowler on the wasteland, the lonely wanderer, the loathed one, the creature of evil, the fiend in Hell, the grim monster, the dark death-shadow, the worker of hate, the mad ravisher, the fell spoiler, and the incarnation of a dozen other attributes characteristic of his enmity toward mankind. No one can long remain in doubt about the rich and colorful character of the Old English vocabulary.

OLD ENGLISH LITERATURE

The language of a past time is known by the quality of its literature. Charters and records yield their secrets to the philologist and contribute their quota of words and inflections to our dictionaries and grammars. But it is in literature that a language displays its full power, its ability to convey in vivid and memorable form the thoughts and emotions of a people. The literature of the Anglo-Saxons is fortunately one of the richest and most significant of any preserved among the early Teutons. Since it is the language mobilized, the language in action, we must say a word about it.

Generally speaking, this literature is of two sorts. Some of it was undoubtedly brought to England by the Germanic conquerors from their continental homes and preserved for a time in oral tradition. All of it owes its preservation, however, and not a little its inspiration to the introduction of Christianity into the island at the end of the sixth century. . . . Two streams thus mingle in Old English literature, the pagan and the Christian, and they are never quite distinct. The poetry of pagan origin is constantly overlaid with Christian sentiment, while even those poems which treat of purely Christian themes contain every now and again traces of an earlier philosophy not wholly forgotten. We can indicate only in the briefest way the scope and content of this literature, and we shall begin with that which embodies the native traditions of the race.

The greatest single work of Old English literature is the *Beowulf*. It is a poem of some 3000 lines belonging to the type known as the folk epic, that is to say, a poem which, whatever it may owe to the individual poet who gave it final form, embodies material long current among the people. It is a narrative of heroic adventure relating how a young warrior, Beowulf, fought the monster Grendel, which was ravaging the land of King Hrothgar, slew it and its dam, and years later met his death while ridding his own country of an equally destructive foe, a fire-breathing dragon. The theme seems somewhat fanciful to a modern reader, but the character of the hero, the social conditions pictured, and the portrayal of the motives and ideals which animated men in early Teutonic times make the poem one of the most vivid records we have of life in the heroic age. It is not an easy life. It is a life that calls for physical endurance, unflinching courage, and a fine sense of duty, loyalty, and honor. No better expression of the heroic ideal exists than the words which Beowulf addresses to Hrothgar before going to his dangerous encounter with Grendel's dam: "Sorrow not. . . . Better is it for every man that he avenge his friend than that he mourn greatly. Each of us must abide the end of this world's life; let him who may, work mighty deeds ere he die, for afterwards, when he lies lifeless, that is best for the warrior."

Outside of the *Beowulf* Old English poetry of native tradition is represented by a number of shorter pieces. Anglo-Saxon poets sang of the things that entered most deeply into their experience—of war and of exile, of the sea with its hardships and its fascination, of ruined cities, and of minstrel life. One of the earliest products of Teutonic tradition is a short poem called *Widsith* in which a scop or minstrel pretends to give an account of his wanderings and the many famous kings and princes before whom he has exercised his craft. *Deor,* another poem about a minstrel, is the lament of a scop who for years has been in the service of his lord, and now finds himself thrust out by a younger man. But he is no whiner. Life is like that. Age will be displaced by youth. *He* has his day. Peace, my heart! *Deor* is one of the most human of Old English poems. The *Wanderer* is a tragedy in the medieval sense, the story of a man who once enjoyed a high place and has fallen upon evil times. His lord is dead and he has become a wanderer in strange courts, without friends. Where are the snows of yesteryear? The *Seafarer* is a monologue in which the speaker alternately describes the perils and hardships of the sea and the eager desire to dare again its dangers. In *The Ruin* the poet reflects on a ruined city, once prosperous and imposing with its towers and halls, its stone courts and baths, now but the tragic shadow of what it once was. Two great war poems, the *Battle of Brunanburh* and the *Battle of Maldon* celebrate with patriotic fervor stirring encounters of the English, equally heroic in victory and defeat. In its shorter poems, no less than in *Beowulf*, Old English literature reveals at wide intervals of time the outlook and temper of the Teutonic mind.

More than half of Anglo-Saxon poetry is concerned with Christian subjects. Translations and paraphrases of books of the Old and New Testament, legends of saints, and devotional and didactic pieces constitute the bulk of this verse. The most important of this poetry had its origin in Northumbria and Mercia in the seventh and eighth centuries. The earliest English poet whose name we know was Cædmon, a lay brother in the monastery at Whitby. The story of how the gift of song came to him in a dream and how he subsequently turned various parts of the Scriptures into beautiful English verse comes to us in the pages of Bede. Although we do not have his poems on Genesis, Exodus, Daniel, and the like, the poems on these subjects which we do have were most likely inspired by his example. About 800 an Anglian poet named Cynewulf wrote at least four poems on religious subjects, into which he ingeniously wove his name by means of runes. Two of these, *Juliana* and *Elene*, tell well-known legends of saints. A third, *Christ*, deals with Advent, the Ascension, and the Last Judgment. The fourth, *The Fates of the Apostles*, touches briefly on where and how the various apostles died. There are other religious poems besides those mentioned, such as the *Andreas* and *Guthlac*, a portion of a fine poem on the story of *Judith* in the Apocrypha, *The Phoenix* in which the bird is taken as a symbol of the Christian life, and *Christ and Satan* which treats the expulsion of Satan from Paradise together with the Harrowing of Hell and Satan's tempting of Christ. All of these poems have their counterparts in other literatures of the Middle Ages. They show England in its cultural contact with Rome and being drawn into the general current of ideas on the continent, no longer simply Teutonic, but cosmopolitan.

In the development of literature prose generally comes late. Verse is more effective for oral delivery and more easily retained in the memory. It is therefore a rather remarkable fact, and one well worthy of note, that English possessed a considerable body of prose literature in the ninth century, at a time when most other modern languages in Europe had scarcely developed a literature in verse. This unusual accomplishment was due to the inspiration of one man, the Anglo-Saxon king who is justly called Alfred the Great (871–99). Alfred's greatness rests not only in his capacity as a military leader and statesman but on his realization that greatness in a nation is no merely physical thing. When he came to the throne he found the learning which in the eighth century, in the days of Bede and Alcuin, had placed England in the forefront of Europe, had greatly decayed. In an effort to restore England to something like its former state he undertook to provide for his people certain books in English, books which he deemed most essential to their welfare. With this object in view he undertook in mature life to learn Latin and either translated these books himself or caused others to translate them for him. First as a guide for the clergy he translated the *Pastoral Care* of Pope Gregory, and then, in order that his people might know something of their own past, inspired and may well have arranged for a translation of Bede's *Ecclesiastical History of the English People*. A history of the rest of the world also seemed desirable and was not so easily to be had. But in the fifth century when so many calamities were befalling the Roman Empire and these misfortunes were being attributed to the abandonment of the pagan deities in favor of Christianity, a Spanish priest named Orosius had undertaken to refute this idea. His method was to trace the rise of other empires to positions of great power and their subsequent collapse, a collapse in which obviously Christianity had had no part. The result was a book which, when its polemical aim had ceased to have any significance, was still widely read as a compendium of historical knowledge. This Alfred translated with omissions and some additions of his own. A fourth book which he turned into English was *The Consolation of Philosophy* by Boethius, one of the most famous books of the Middle Ages. Alfred also caused a record to be compiled of the important events of English history, past and present, and this as continued for more than two centuries after his death is the well-known Anglo-Saxon Chronicle. King Alfred was the founder of English prose, but there were others who carried on the tradition. Among these is Ælfric, the author of two books of homilies and numerous other works, and Wulfstan, whose *Sermon to the English* is an impassioned plea for moral and political reform.

So large and varied a body of literature, in verse and prose, gives ample testimony to the universal competence, at times to the power and beauty, of the Old English Language.

BIBLIOGRAPHY

For the early races of Europe there is an abundant literature. In spite of its unconventional classification R. B. Dixon's *The Racial History of Man* (New York, 1923) is on the whole the most satisfactory statement of what we know about the subject. H. F. Osborn's *Men of the Old Stone Age* (2nd ed., New York, 1916) is a fuller treatment of the oldest period. More recent discoveries and speculations are embodied in the early chapters of Carleton S. Coon's *The Story of Man* (New York, 1954). Robert Munro, *Prehistoric Britain* (London, 1913) and Norman Ault, *Life in Ancient Britain* (London, 1920) are excellent accounts of conditions in England, while T. Rice Holmes' *Ancient Britain and the Invasions of Julius Caesar* (Oxford,

1936) is invaluable for the advanced student. For the Roman occupation of England the work of E. Haverfield is authoritative, especially *The Romanization of Roman Britain* (London, 1905) and *The Roman Occupation of Britain* (Oxford, 1924). R. G. Collingwood's *Roman Britain* (New York, 1932) is an admirable brief survey, and B. C. A. Windle's *The Romans in Britain* (London, 1923) is a readable account. For detailed studies of both the Roman occupation and the Teutonic invasions, the best treatments are R. G. Collingwood and J. N. L. Myres, *Roman Britain and the English Settlements* (2nd ed., Oxford, 1936) and F. M. Stenton, *Anglo-Saxon England* (2nd ed., Oxford, 1947), both of them in the *Oxford History of England,* to which may be added R. H. Hodgkin, *A History of the Anglo-Saxons* (3rd ed., Oxford, 1953) and the Kenneth Jackson, *Language and History in Early Britain* (Edinburgh, 1953). For divergent views the advanced student may consult A. Erdmann, *Über die Heimat und den Narmen der Angeln* (Uppsala, 1890); H. M. Chadwick, *The Origin of the English Nation* (Cambridge, 1907); E. Thurlow Leeds, *The Archaeology of the Anglo-Saxon Settlements* (Oxford, 1913); E. Wadstein, *On the Origin of the English* (Uppsala, 1927) and *An Historical Geography of England before A.D. 1800: Fourteen Studies,* edited by H. C. Darby (Cambridge, 1936). On early Teutonic civilization F. B. Gummere's *Germanic Origins* (New York, 1892) is classic. It is now available with supplementary notes by F. P. Magoun, Jr., under the title *Founders of England* (New York, 1930). For the character of Old English the best source is the grammars mentioned in footnote 11.

NOTES

1. In the opinion of R. G. Collingwood, Caesar's intention was to conquer the whole island. See R. G. Collingwood and J. N. L. Myres, *Roman Britain and the English Settlements* (2nd ed., Oxford, 1936), p. 34.

2. Cf. J. Loth. *Les mots latins dans les langues brittoniques* (Paris, 1892).

3. On the basis of archaeological evidence it has been maintained that the bulk of those who settled in Kent were Franks from the lower Rhine area, and it is suggested that with the Frisians they joined leaders who were Jutes, possibly from Jutland. See C. F. C. Hawkes, "The Jutes of Kent," in *Dark-Age Britain: Studies Presented to E. T. Leeds* (London, 1956), pp. 91–111. We must remember, however, that the possession of an ornament does not establish its maker or place of manufacture. See the remarks of T. C. Lethbridge in the same volume, p. 114.

4. It will be recalled that the King Arthur of romance is thought by some to represent a military leader of the Celts, possibly a Roman or Romanized Celt, who led his people, at the beginning of the sixth century, in their resistance to the Teutons, and who enjoyed an unusual, if temporary, success.

5. The Teutons, on the other hand, called the Celts *Wealas* ("foreigners"), from which the word *Welsh* is derived.

6. The spelling *England* no longer represents the pronunciation of the word. Under the influence of the nasal *-ng* the *e* has undergone the regular change to *i* (cf. O. E. *streng > string;* M.E. *weng > wing*). The spelling *Ingland* occurs in Middle English, and the vowel is accurately represented in the Spanish *Inglaterra* and Italian *Inghilterra*.

7. The term *Anglo-Saxon* is occasionally found in Old English times and is often employed today to designate the earliest period of English. It went out of use after

the Norman Conquest until revived in the sixteenth century by the antiquarian William Camden. While amply justified by usage, it is logically less defensible than the term *Old English,* which has the advantage of suggesting the unbroken continuity of English throughout its existence, but it is too convenient a synonym to be wholly discarded.

8. This is obscured somewhat in Modern English by the large number of words borrowed from Latin.

9. The effect of this shifting may be seen by comparing the English and the German words in the following pairs: English *open*—German *offen*; English *water*—German *wasser*; English *pound*—German *pfund*; English *tongue*—German *zunge.*

10. Some of the developments which distinguish Middle English begin as early as the tenth century, but a consideration of the matter as a whole justifies the date 1150 as the general line of demarcation.

11. The principal Old English grammars, in the order of their publication, are F. A. March, *A Comparative Grammar of the Anglo-Saxon Language* (New York, 1870), still of value; P. J. Cosijn, *Altwestscähsische Grammatik* (Haeg, 1883–6); E. Sievers, *An Old English Grammar,* trans. A. S. Cook (3rd ed., Boston, 1903); K. D. Bülbring, *Altenglisches Elementarbuch* (Heidelberg, 1902); Joseph and Elizabeth M. Wright, *Old English Grammar* (2nd ed., Oxford, 1914); and the same authors' *An Elementary Old English Grammar* (Oxford, 1923); Karl Brunner, *Altenglishe Grammatick* (Halle, 1942), based on Sievers; and Randolph Quirk and C. L. Wrenn, *An Old English Grammar* (London, 1955).

12. When the stem is short the adjective ends in -u in the nominative singular of the feminine and the nominative and accusative plural of the neuter.

13. The change of *s* to *r* is due to the fact that the accent was originally on the final syllable in the preterite plural and the past participle. It is known as Grammatical Change or Verner's Law for the scholar who first explained it. In Modern English the *s* has been restored in the past participle *(chosen)* by analogy with the other forms. The initial sound has been leveled in the same way.

14. The personal endings may be illustrated by the conjugation of the first verb in the above list, *drīfan:*

	Indicative		*Subjunctive*
	Present		*Present*
ic	drīf-e	ic	drīf-e
ðū	drīf-st (-est)	ðū	drīf-e
hē	drīf-ð (-eð)	hē	drīf-e
wē	drīf-að	wē	drīf-en
gē	drīf-að	gē	drīf-en
hīe	drīf-að	hīe	drīf-en
	Past		*Past*
ic	drāf	ic	drif-e
ðū	drif-e	ðū	drif-e
hē	drāf	hē	drif-e
wē	drif-on	wē	drif-en
gē	drif-on	gē	drif-en
hīe	drif-on	hīe	drif-en

In addition to these forms the imperative was *drīf* (sing.) and *drīfað* (plur.), the present participle *drīfende,* and the gerund (i.e., the infinitive used as a verbal noun) *tō drīfanne.*

✠ ✠ ✠

THE WORLD OF
ALFRED'S BOYHOOD, 849-865

ELEANOR SHIPLEY DUCKETT

In the reign of Ethelwulf, Berkshire had at last become permanently part of Wessex. Here, at Wantage, in 849 Alfred was born, on a royal manor of his father's holding, a family estate which long afterward he himself was to leave in legacy to his wife. Beyond it to the north lay the Vale of the White Horse, of fertile meadowland and harvest, and south of it were the Lambourn Downs, the home of wandering sheep. This manor of Lambourn also lay in Alfred's possession when he was king. Nearby ran the ancient Icknield Way, along which men were already traveling a thousand years before Christ, by which perhaps Saxon invaders had first come into Berkshire from their landing on England's east coast, moving on across the Fens of Cambridgeshire and the Chilterns to the Berkshire Downs.

Alfred was the youngest of five children, four sons and a daughter, born to Ethelwulf by his wife Osburh. From her they inherited a strain of Jutish blood through her father, Oslac, who as seneschal presided over the hospitality of King Ethelwulf's banquet hall. His descent, and therefore hers, is of twofold interest. It connected her herself with her husband's royal House of Wessex, since Oslac, it would appear, counted among his ancestors that Cerdic who founded the line of West Saxon kings. And, second, among Oslac's forebears is seen at least one of the Jutish nobles who came, probably from Kent, during the sixth century to settle in Hampshire and the Isle of Wight.

Around Alfred as a little child men and women talked constantly of the Viking invaders. He was hardly two years old when word came that King Ethelwulf's eldest son, Athelstan, who seems to have been born of a union previous to the marriage with Osburh and now ruling under his father the four regions of Kent, Essex, Sussex, and Surrey, had won a great victory at sea over the Danes off Sandwich in Kent, had killed very many of their men, had captured nine of their ships and put the rest to flight. About the same time not fewer than three hundred and fifty Viking ships had appeared at the mouth of the Thames. These ships had not yet reached the awesome size and array which they were to assume later on. But even now the ships of the leaders surely struck terror into southeastern England by their high sterns ending in a dragon's or in a serpent's head, their four-square sails gaily striped in bright colors, the shields, painted black and yellow, hanging along their sides, their prows, beaked and crested like a bird. And, in any case, the rapid ten-fold increase from thirty-five to three hundred and fifty ships, each with from thirteen to twenty benches of rowers on either side, and the sight of these rowers striking the water in regular measure as they came toward the river must have brought the men of Thames-side breathless to the shore.

The Danes landed in Kent and wrought ruin on Canterbury and London. London, as we have seen, was a Mercian city and already had been assaulted with great loss of life nine years before. Wiglaf's successor as king of Mercia, Beorthwulf, marched promptly to its defense; but he could do nothing, and fled, leaving the invaders to cross the river into Surrey. Somewhere south of the Thames, at an unknown place called "Aclea," their march was stopped. King Ethelwulf, with his second son, Ethelbald, and all his army, fought them long and fiercely and, as the old record puts it, "made there the greatest slaughter in a heathen host of which we have heard tell unto this present day, and took the victory."

Such tidings made good hearing to those at home. But their joy was more than offset by the fact that the Vikings now, for the first time, had remained all the winter just past, of 850–51, in Kent upon the Isle of Thanet. Men realized now that this menace, after fifteen years of scattered raiding, had at last come to stay.

Two years afterward Mercia's king and his counselors appealed for aid to Ethelwulf against another foe. The Welsh had crossed the border and were ravaging lands of England in return for English assaults of earlier days.

The history of Wales in the ninth century has its own place in our story. Its land was then divided into four great regions: Gwynedd in the northwest, including Anglesey and the wild solitudes of the mountains of Snowdonia; Powys, the central part; Deheubarth, in the south, extending over Ceredigion,

Dyfed, Ystrad Tywi, and Brycheiniog; and fourth, Morgannwg, running down to the southern coast and the Bristol Channel. These years saw much political change in Wales, especially in Gwynedd. In the year 825 its royal line of kings had come to an end through the death of its ruler Hywel. Promptly one Merfyn Frych, Merfyn the Freckled, a noble of slender right in descent but of personal power and ambition, not only won its crown but proceeded further to strengthen his stand by taking as wife Nest, sister of Cyngen, king of Powys. hus The held his power intact for nineteen years. At his death in 844, five years before the birth of Alfred, it had come to an heir who was to be far more renowned. This was Merfyn's son, Rhodri Mawr, Rhodri the Great, destined to reign until 878 and to rule a kingdom far wider than that which he had inherited.

North Wales was not left unmolested by the Vikings. Its annals tell that in 850 one Cyngen was slain by them; that three years later Anglesey was laid waste by the same "Black Gentiles."

Now, in this year of 853, King Ethelwulf listened to the plea of Mercia, led his army through its land into Wales, wrung promise of tribute from the Welsh, and after Easter sealed his alliance with Mercia by giving his only daughter, Alfred's sister Ethelswith, to Burhred, its king since the preceding year, in a splendid ceremony at his royal manor of Chippenham in Wiltshire. She was only a mere child, for in this royal family she was born next to the youngest, Alfred himself, in line.

Perhaps Alfred was present at his little sister's wedding. He was four years old. Perhaps, child though he was, he was even then thinking, half-thrilled, half-afraid, of the summer that lay before him. His father, the king, who by now had long despaired of getting to Rome in the present state of things, decided to send there this youngest son of his that he at least might receive the blessing of the Holy Father.

We are not told exactly what led Ethelwulf to this resolve. We do know that Pope Hadrian the First, at Easter, 781, had blessed and anointed two little sons of Charles the Great: Pepin as king of Italy and Louis as king of Aquitaine. Pepin was four and Louis was three. The pope, too, had made himself godfather to Pepin and regularly afterward addressed Charles as *compater* in his letters. In England itself, Offa, the great ruler of Mercia, had seen his young son, Egfrith, anointed in solemn rite by the church as sharer with himself in Mercia's kingship. Perhaps, with such precedents before him, Ethelwulf desired the same honors for his son.

Yet, at the age of four, Alfred's succession to a crown, in the place of his father or under his father during Ethelwulf's life, rested on nothing but a dream, with three older brothers and their sons in view or in prospect. We know, however, that Alfred was especially dear to his father, and this affection, to a king as devoted to Rome as Ethelwulf, might well have seemed sufficient reason for his son's reception at the hands of the pope.

News spread very slowly in those times. Men's ears were not smitten hourly by reports of death, disaster, and destruction. Moreover, sickness, injury, death itself, were accepted as necessary, inevitable, as the normal lot of man, whether he journeyed forth or stayed at home. Ethelwulf, apparently, would not have hesitated to send this little boy across a channel infested by pirates, past cities destroyed by fire and still burning, to a land terrified by invasion, even had he been clearly aware of perils on the Continent. Three years before, Rorik the Dane, brother of that Harold the Second who had submitted to baptism under Louis the Pious in return for his aid, had scoured the land of Frisia and the banks of the Rhine and the Lek. The Emperor Lothar could do nothing to stop him and was forced to offer him alliance and to seal it with the gift of Duursted, a busy and much-frequented Frisian port. But the devastation in Frisia and along the Rhine went on. The monastery of St. Bavo in Ghent was ruined; Beauvais went up in flames; and on Christmas Day, 852, the Emperor Lothar and his brother, Charles the Bald, sat encamped on the Seine, looking across the river to the enemy's massed strength. Nothing, once more, could be done here by the two Frankish rulers. Their men would not rally for battle; instead, they soon drifted away in ignominious retreat. The year of Alfred's journey to Rome, 853, was to find the Vikings also in the region of the Loire, burning Nantes, Angers, Poitiers, and—a sacrilege which horrified all the Christian world—"like a savage hurricane" destroying and plundering in Tours the treasures of the two monasteries of St. Martin, one within the city, the other outside it, at Marmoutier, where one hundred and twenty-six monks were killed.

We do not know by what route Alfred and his large escort "of men, noble and simple," crossed the Channel. Perhaps they traveled by way of Quentavic, near Etaples, on the estuary of the river Canche in the Pas-de-Calais. This was the regular port for travelers from England, but it had been badly damaged by Viking raids in 842 and 844. And, when at last the company reached Rome, they found that Holy City beset by troubles of its own.

Much had been happening in Rome of late, and there was much, not only old but new, for Alfred to hear and to see. The pope at this time was Leo the Fourth, who left behind him at his death a notable record of unceasing effort for the care of his city and its Cathedral of St. Peter. Seven years before, during the rule of his predecessor, Sergius the Second, Saracen pirates from Africa and Spain had sailed up to the mouth of the Tiber, had landed, and had marched upon Rome. Outside its walls they had fallen upon the Basilica of St. Peter to rob and ransack as they would. Sergius had died before plans for its defense could be realized; but Leo had worked hard and long.

When the boy Alfred arrived, he could see around St. Peter's and its precincts a great wall newly raised, reinforced with strong towers. The Emperor Lothar himself had aided the work; from all sides money had poured in for its making; during four years it had slowly risen. Only the year before, in 852, Pope Leo had dedicated it, and no doubt the royal pilgrims from Wessex now heard all that had been done.

Escorted by his bishops and priests and lesser clergy, Leo had walked in procession around the great church, now, as all hoped, safe from assault, all of them barefooted, with ashes on their heads, singing litanies and psalms. Three times the procession had stopped, the third time at the Postern Gate which looked toward the quarter known as the "School of the Anglo-Saxons." This lay not far from the Tiber and held inns for pilgrims and the "Church of the Blessed Virgin Mary, where the Divine Mysteries were celebrated for the English who came to Rome and where an Englishman who died there might find burial." Here, as the procession halted, the pope had prayed the Lord that "this City, which I, Thy servant, Leo the Fourth, Bishop, have dedicated in new building through Thine aid, which from my name is now called Leonine, may ever remain unharmed and secure." It was the twenty-seventh of June, two days before the Feast of St. Peter and St. Paul. After the procession the pope had sung Mass in his Cathedral and had given gifts to all in the city, whether Roman or stranger. For so he had vowed he would do, if God allowed his intent.

But Alfred had come to Rome that he might be received by the head of his church. Leo the Fourth was no idle dreamer and did not anoint the little boy as one who was to be king. What he did he told in a letter which he now wrote to King Ethelwulf: "Your son Alfred, whom you have sent at this time to the *limina* of the Holy Apostles, I have gladly received, and as my spiritual son I have girded him with the honor and the outward array of nobility after the manner of consuls at Rome, because he has given himself into my hands."

Doubtless this ceremony lingered in Alfred's imagination as he crossed the Channel homeward. Many years afterward he must have had it in mind when he knighted his young grandson, Athelstan, arrayed him in scarlet cloak and jeweled baldric, and hung from his side a Saxon sword sheathed in gold.

Meanwhile Alfred's royal father, Ethelwulf, was at home in Wessex, planning, praying, listening. Soon he had other news from Rome. Cyngen, that king of Powys in north-central Wales, who was uncle of Rhodri the Great, king of Gwynedd, had left his kingdom to seek in the Holy City solace from the vexation of invaders and aggressors, and there in 854 he died. His realm of Powys was at once captured by this nephew, Rhodri, who added its lands to his own of Gwynedd. The men of Powys raised no revolt. No doubt at this moment they were glad to have a strong ruler who might defend them from English assault.

News, and disheartening news, came also this year from Viking quarters. King Horik the Dane, who had befriended St. Anskar in his missionary work and had done much to keep Danish jarls from raiding the Channel coasts, was dead, murdered with all his heirs, except one boy, in a rebellion raised by his nephew, Guthrum. Henceforth the Danish menace, Ethelwulf knew well, would surely not lessen its energy; in all probability it would instead rapidly increase.

The year 855 brought word of two more deaths. July the seventeenth saw that of young Alfred's lately won Father in God, Pope Leo the Fourth, presently enrolled as saint of the church. At the end of September the monastery of Prum, near Trier in the modern Rhineland of Germany, was chanting requiem for the departed soul of the Frankish emperor, Lothar the First. Sick in body and weary at heart of family quarrels and pirate visitations, he had renounced his crown, divided his realms among his three sons, and retreated to spend his last days in religion. Within a few weeks his body lay in its coffin, tonsured and girded with monastic habit. His eldest son, Louis the Second, now became emperor of the Franks. To the middle son, Lothar the Second, came those lands between France and Germany, the lands of the Rhine, the Moselle, and the Meuse. Now under him and in his name they were made into a newborn entity, destined to play an important part amid medieval intrigue as the state of Lotharingia.

Meanwhile the Danes were still keeping men awake at night on the English coast. All the winter of 854–55 they had remained encamped on the Isle of Sheppey, Kent. Whether King Ethelwulf, like the Emperor Lothar, lost strength for the struggle, or whether he judged that prayer and pilgrimage and consultation with the pope were his best resource in this hour of emergency, we do not know. At all events, sometime during this year of 855 he decided to make his own way to Rome and to take with him on yet a second visit his son Alfred, now six years old.

Perhaps, too, the loss by death of Alfred's mother, Osburh, had strengthened in Ethelwulf's mind the desire for this pilgrimage. Little is told us about this wife of his. But there is one scene in our sources, described to us by Alfred's friend and bishop, Asser, which shows her in a pleasant light. Her youngest son, Alfred, from his earliest years loved to listen to his mother's reading of the old stories told in verse in that Anglo-Saxon which he used every day as his own familiar tongue. Long afterward when he was a man, he was bitterly vexed that, as he said, he did not himself learn to read until his twelfth year, and he blamed his parents and those who had charge of him for this careless neglect. He added, however, that there were no good teachers in the whole of Wessex when he was growing up, and this we may understand as true of the south of England. Learning and the art of script were still flourishing in the north during the ninth century in spite of Viking battles and siege. In the south, on the other hand, the storming of Canterbury, the constant raids upon the coast, and the permanent presence of Vikings at Thanet and Sheppey were taking their toll of men's energy and of their leisure for books.

But Queen Osburh read the Anglo-Saxon poems in her family. And one day, Asser tells us, she held out to Alfred and his brothers the book in her hands and said, "Whichever of you shall learn to read this book first shall have it for his own." Alfred eagerly asked whether she really meant it. When she answered with a smile and a nod that indeed she did, he took the book from her and went with it to his teacher, such as he was. Apparently the teacher read all its poems to him again and again, until the little boy, five or six years old, knew them by heart. Then he returned to recite them to his mother and triumphantly to carry off his prize.

This story does throw some light upon the lack of education of even royal children at this time and of the absence of educated men even at the Wessex court. Ethelwulf, it is true, held for some while in his service a Frankish secretary, named Felix, versed in Latin and in Saxon language and script. But from him we learn only of his royal master's zeal and generosity toward his church.

This zeal was now proved. Before the king left England for Rome, he gave over, apparently to various individual officers and nobles of his household and administration, estates amounting to one-tenth of his land, estates which in his careful and deliberate planning were eventually to pass into ecclesiastical and monastic ownership, free from all obligation of tax except the three usual contributions to public funds for the support of the national army and for the building of fortresses and of bridges over streams and rivers.

On his way to Rome the king of Wessex was welcomed in France with all royal honor by Charles the Bald, king of the Franks in the west, who discussed with him matters of deep interest for their future friendship and gave him escort to the frontier. Ethelwulf lingered nearly a year in the Holy City, asking counsel of the pope, visiting many shrines, and offering to the Church of St. Peter magnificent gifts of Saxon workmanship which he had brought from England. These are duly described in the *Book of the Popes*; a crown, two basins and two little statues, all of the purest gold, a sword, bound with gold; four hanging disks of silver, covered with gold, to be used as support for sanctuary lights; a silk dalmatic, with stripe woven in gold thread; an alb of white silk, embroidered in gold; two curtains of texture rich and shining. The king also gave presents of money of gold and silver to bishops, priests, deacons, lesser clerics, and secular nobles of Rome. Lastly, he scattered small pieces of silver among its people in general, at the desire of the pope.

The pope was now Benedict the Third. Very possibly Ethelwulf and his son Alfred were already in the Holy City at the time of the troubles which followed Benedict's election in the summer of 855. A conspiracy had risen to oppose this candidate. High dignities, including envoys of the Emperor Louis, clamored for the well-known cardinal-priest Anastasius, who under Leo the Fourth had been excommunicated as traitor to the Holy See. For three days tumult raged in Rome, where, it was said, "things were done which no Saracen would think of doing." Probably matters in tradition were to appear worse than the reality. We read, however, of images broken in St. Peter's, of the pope-elect Benedict, stripped of his vestments, beaten, and imprisoned. Finally, order was restored. A multitude of Rome's people, crowding into the Lateran, called for Benedict as pope, a triduum of fast and prayer was held, the rebels submitted, and Benedict was consecrated, either on the last Sunday in September or the first in October.

The winter of 855–56 was severe, and plague carried off many in Europe. Ethelwulf and his son, in the spring or early summer of 856, came to stay a second time in France, on their way home, as guests of its king. There was once again plenty of matter for discussion. Charles the Bald, like Ethelwulf, was passionately devoted to his church and as keen on theological argument as his grandfather, Charles the Great, had been. Political troubles, however, were harassing him more and more. For years Brittany had been a source of trouble, fighting to maintain its independence. Aquitaine, which had sworn loyalty seven years before, had since then been constantly in revolt and now in 856 was asking aid of Louis, ruler of Germany; only delay on Germany's part drove the men of Aquitaine to make peace with Charles and accept his will. In the middle of August the Viking Danes were once more on the Seine, burning monasteries and castles on either bank and preparing to remain for the winter. The Saracens had worked ruin in Naples. The church of France was rent by ecclesiastical turmoil and by theological strife. And everywhere men were talking about Charles the Bald's nephew, the young Lothar who held that new kingdom of Lotharingia.

Lothar had been forced by his father and the nobles of France into a marriage which he hated and now was longing to break. For years he had been devoted to a mistress named Waldrada; and he was trying to induce church and state to allow him to repudiate his wife, Theutberga, and to make Waldrada his lawful queen. The storm raised by this struggle was to last fourteen years and end only upon Lothar's death: "the source of ruin," as a Frankish record described it, "not only of himself but of all his realm."

In these circumstances it was natural that Charles the Bald, king of France, should be glad to ally himself firmly with the king of Wessex in England and that both rulers should be united in facing the common threatening of pirate raids. Accordingly, it was announced in July that Ethelwulf, whose wife Osburh had died, we do not know when, was to marry the daughter of Charles, Judith by name. No reason other than that of political expediency is suggested for this union of a devout king, a ruler now for seventeen years and the father of six children, with a young girl, little more than a child. The nuptials were solemnly celebrated on the first of October, 856, in the royal castle at Verberie-sur-Oise, near the Forest of Compiegne, by the leading prelate of France, Hincmar, archbishop of Reims.

The choice of officiant for the ceremony was natural. It was Hincmar who constantly upheld the cause of Charles the Bald; who was to crown him in 869 as king of Lotharingia, after the death of that unhappy nephew Lothar; who was to denounce in words which rang throughout France Lothar's faith-lessness to his marriage vows; who was holding captive in his own diocese the young Gottschalk, condemned by the church for heresy; who fought the long and bitter theological battle raging in France against predestination, both to good and to evil; who upheld with zeal the priestly character of a king and, with still greater zeal, the duty of a king to obey in humility and faithfulness the head of God's church on earth.

It was he, then, who now not only blessed young Judith as a wedded wife but anointed and crowned her as a queen, in her own dignity as consort to King Ethelwulf of Wessex—a crowning at that time not of tradition or of usage for a king's consort even in Judith's own France. We still have in its original wording the Latin ritual chanted over her at Verberie by the arch-bishop. He was now about fifty years old, and Ethelwulf was, more or less, of the same age.

The Lord crown thee with glory and honour and place upon thy head the precious
stones of the Spirit; that whatsoever is here of token in the sheen of gold and the varied
sparkling of jewels, may ever shine forth in thee and in thy doings: Which thing may He
Himself vouchsafe to grant, to Whom is honour and glory for all ages to come, Amen.
Bless, O Lord, this Thy servant: Thou Who from all time dost rule the realms of
Kings. Amen.

One would like to have seen young Alfred, at the age of six, watching and listening—as presumably he did—during this splendid ceremony which gave him in place of Queen Osburh a stepmother thirteen years old.

The marriage was to bear unwelcome harvest. When Ethelwulf at last, in 856, after a year's absence returned home to Wessex, many men of his land received him with joy. His nobles, indeed, were surprised to see Judith, crowned in France, sitting at his side as queen, contrary to Wessex custom. Men of Wessex had not forgotten the story of their King Beorhtric's death at the hands of Eadburh, his Mercian wife. Yet this was not the worst. Either before or during Ethelwulf's stay on the Continent, his eldest son, Athelstan, had died. To the next son in age, Ethelbald, had doubtless fallen the fulfilling of many royal functions in Wessex. Now the king's long absence, together with outraged feeling against this new and strange marriage of his, and, we may suppose, with ambition, also, on the part of Ethelbald, was moving this son to aim at permanent possession of his father's crown.

Ethelbald was a man of very different character from his father. He was determined and unscrupulous; but he, too, had friends. He was supported by a following under two Wessex leaders: the warlike Ealhstan, bishop of Sherborne, and Eanwulf, ealdorman of Somersetshire. These men had at first plotted to keep Ethelwulf from even setting foot again in his kingdom; but they were foiled in this by the loyalty of Wessex lords and officials at large.

Matters, however, became daily more serious. Soon civil war was threatening. The people, hurrying to the support of their king, were ready to rise and drive Ethelbald and his party into exile. Then Ethelwulf, to save his country, yielded his right. He gave over to Ethelbald the rule of Wessex proper and retired to govern as underking the four regions formerly administered by his eldest son, Athelstan: Kent, Essex, Sussex, and Surrey. It was an act in keeping with his character; and here his wife Judith was freely accorded the honor due to a queen.

Some two years later Ethelwulf was dead. These years in the southeast of England were darkened by news from the Frankish kingdom of his father-in-law, Charles the Bald. There the Viking pirates on the Seine under Bjorn Ironside, held in tradition as another son of Ragnar Lothbrok, once more set Paris on fire and worked havoc among its churches, one after another. Only four were said to have remained unharmed. Paschasius Radbert, the learned monk of Corbie, near Amiens, turned from his study of the *Lamentations* of Jeremiah to write lament for his own world in words which recall Alcuin's horror over ruined Lindisfarne:

The kings of the earth, and all the inhabitants of the world, would not have believed that the adversary and the enemy should have entered into the gates of Jerusalem:

"Who would believe," Paschasius wrote, "which among us could have imagined, that that could happen which we have seen and wept, that the enemy should enter our own Paris and burn the churches of Christ on its river's shore?"

In 858, the year of Ethelwulf's death, Charles, driven by necessity, marched to besiege Viking headquarters on the Isle of Oissel in the Seine, near Mantes; but he was forced to abandon the blockade when his brother, Louis the German, seized this opportune moment to attack him. It was Hincmar who rallied the bishops of France to the cause of their King Charles and turned the evil tide.

Ethelwulf was buried at Winchester. In his will he directed that one poor man, native or stranger, should be given allowance, of food and clothing, for every ten hides of the royal estates that were not barren land and that this direction should stand in permanence. To Rome he left an annual revenue of three hundred mancuses, gold coins, each equal in value to thirty silver pennies, or somewhat more than the current price of an ox. Of these three hundred mancuses, two hundred were to be used in buying oil for lamps in honor of St. Peter and St. Paul at Rome, and one hundred were left to the pope to use every year at his discretion. A ring of gold, bearing Ethelwulf's name and the heraldic device of two birds, and also one inscribed with the name of Alfred's sister Ethelswith, wife of King Burhred of Mercia, are still to be seen in the British Museum.

Ethelbald, Alfred's eldest surviving brother, was now, in 858, ruler of Wessex in full right. The rule of the four regions of the southeast passed to the next brother, Ethelbert. Ethelbald's reign was brief; but it was marked by an event described in record of this ninth century as "contrary to the law of God and the honor of Christendom, nay, contrary to all *heathen* use." The king took as wife his, and Alfred's, own stepmother, the young widow, Judith, even now only fifteen years of age. All men in England, we are told, were horrified.

The marriage lasted only two years or a little more. In 860 Ethelbald died and was buried at Sherborne, in Dorset. Then Alfred's third brother, Ethelbert, as king united under his rule all the lands of Wessex, both in the west and in the southeast. Judith, twice a widow at eighteen, sold all her possessions in England and returned to France, where her father kept her under close guard in his castle at Senlis, hoping that she might soon be decently and honorably settled in marriage. He had other matters to think about. The

Vikings were still on the Seine, and he was pondering all means in his power to drive them thence.

Her father's troubles did not worry young Judith overmuch. She was finding consolation for her long dull hours at Senlis in visits from the handsome and energetic Baldwin "Iron-Arm," destined to be the first count of Flanders. Her brother Louis the Stammerer, secretly gave her aid; and soon all France was scandalized by the news that Baldwin and this princess and former queen had eloped. In his rage King Charles incited the bishops of France to excommunicate his daughter's lover. Had not Gregory the Great declared that he who steals a widow for wife is anathema? And was not he himself, the king of France, at this very moment uniting with his archbishop, Hincmar of Reims, in defense of a marriage sealed by the church, in defense of the unhappy Theutberga, the wife of that immoral nephew of his, Lothar of Lotharingia? And had not the guilty couple, his daughter and her paramour, fled for refuge to this very Lothar himself?

But Baldwin fled also to an abler source of help. He went to Rome and laid his cause before the pope, now the great Nicholas the First. Nicholas listened with sympathy. He wrote to the wrathful Charles that these two young people sincerely loved each other and that it would be an act of mercy to forgive them. An act of wisdom, as well. It would not do, the pope pointed out, to drive young Baldwin by this wrath into alliance with those enemies of all good, the Viking robbers.

Letter after letter followed, to Charles, to his queen, Ermentrude, to the bishops of France, and at last Hincmar, however unwilling, was able to write to the pope that his wish had been in some part fulfilled: "When, Your Holiness, I had received with all reverence your letter and had read it to my fellow-bishops, we pleaded for Judith with her father and her mother and told them of your prayers. And so our Lord King Charles allowed the two to be married at Auxerre according to civil law, and he honored Baldwin, as you had asked of him. But he would not attend the ceremony."

In the meantime Danish Vikings were still busy in France, both on the river Seine and, under a leader named Weland, on the river Somme. Charles, still trying in vain to drive them out, resorted to bribery, in the hope of dividing one camp against the other. He offered to the Danes on the Somme three thousand pounds of silver, carefully weighed, which he proposed to exact from the revenues of the church and the pockets of his people, if these Danes would attack the encampment on the Seine. The amount, however, proved to be greater than Charles could raise, press and drive as he might. The Vikings on the Somme grew weary of waiting, withdrew the hostages through whom they had pledged their bargain, and went off across the Channel to plunder England. Early in this reign of Ethelbert they fell upon Winchester in force, but they were driven off after sharp fighting by the ealdormen of Hampshire and Berkshire.

For some years there now was peace, until in the summer of 865 Thanet was again occupied by Danes who gave no sign of retreating. At length the men of Kent bargained with them for safe living in return for money payments; and the invaders accepted the promise of money. Then, protected by this agreement, when all had settled down in quiet, they sallied out by night and laid waste all eastern Kent.

During these years of Ethelbert's reign, five in all, Alfred was growing from a boy of eleven into a lad of sixteen. He was spending his days in the royal manors of Wessex, at Wantage and Chippenham, at Wilton and Winchester. He was visiting, we may suppose, his sister, Queen Ethelswith, in Mercia, riding along the old Roman roads. With other boys he ran and wrestled. He delighted in the mornings when the king, his brother, and the nobles of the court hunted in Selwood Forest the deer, the wolf, and the wild boar. As he grew older, he joined them in their sport and, we are told, loved it. On the royal lands he saw men plowing, sowing, reaping, tending the gardens where grew the herbs for the healing of the sick, for the savoring of food; he talked with the bailiffs and seneschals; in the women's bower he watched curiously the maids who spun and wove. He wore day by day a short belted tunic and carried, like all boys, a knife for many needs; on high days of holiday he put on a cloak of red or purple or blue, fastened by a brooch made of gold or silver and inset with enamel and jewels in the beautiful Frankish and Anglo-Saxon work of early medieval days. In the afternoons he sat at dinner in the king's great hall, where the log fire leaped on the hearth and the torches and candles threw shadows on the walls, and watched the king's nobles and warriors drinking mead and ale from their horns and on feast days wine from the wassail bowl. He heard them talk of pirate raids, of plague and murder, of the darkening of the sun and the moon, of storms and rushing floods. Now and then he listened eagerly to stories of heathen gods, of dragons and witches, of giants and elves, of brave soldiers and their deeds in battle. Sometimes wandering minstrels would arrive and would sing to the harp their tales of heroes of an older land.

He learned, too, his lessons, and now he could himself read his books in Anglo-Saxon. He knew very little Latin at this time; but now and again in curiosity he would pore over the illuminated Latin texts which visitors to the court brought from Canterbury, from the north of England, from Irish monasteries. Something he knew of his family's royal standing. On coins he saw the names of his family and brothers; envoys were always arriving; now and then, when he was old enough, he was called to give his witness to a royal deed of grant, written on parchment by the king's scribe.

Above all, he was taught the meaning of his Christian faith. Day after day he heard Mass in the royal chapel and often, probably, listened to its Offices of the Day. He knew the splendor of great feasts, spiritual and social rejoicing, as at Yuletide and Easter, and felt, too, the strait living of Lent, when high feasting gave way to meager fare of herrings and eels. Sometimes, no doubt, he listened to the ritual of the church at Sherborne and saw its bishop, Ealhstan, who was always talking with the king on the business of war. Sometimes he must have talked with Swithhun, who was his father's counselor in the ways of religion, had taught his father, Ethelwulf, as a boy, and was bishop of Winchester from the time that Alfred was three years old. It was he, men believed, who had inspired Ethelwulf to give the tenth of his land to God.

Many familiar stories were told of Swithhun's humility and of the power of his prayer with heaven. Once, men said, he was standing on a bridge in Winchester when his eye fell upon a woman crossing it on her way to market. She had on her arm a basket of eggs, and, as he looked, she stumbled, her eggs rolled out, and every one of them was broken. Immediately he went up to her and saw that she was old and miserably clad and that tears were running down her face. He lifted his hand, so the story went, made the sign of the cross, and lo! the eggs lay on the street whole, in their unbroken shells once more. Like holy Aidan long before him, this bishop Swithhun would not ride on horseback about his great diocese but went on foot, and did it at night lest men should mock or taunt him for his humility. Solitude and simple living were alike dear to his heart. He died when Alfred was twelve or thirteen, and left word that he be buried outside his cathedral, "beneath the feet of passers-by and the rain dripping from the eaves."

The quiet which marked much of Ethelbert's reign was the quiet before the breaking of the storm. In 865 he, too, died' and was buried beside his brother Ethelbald at Sherborne. Then Alfred's last remaining brother, Ethelred, came to the throne of Wessex; and Alfred at the age of sixteen turned to face with him years of assault and battle such as they had never known or dreamed could come in their time upon their land.

✠ ✠ ✠

EDUCATION AND
LATIN SCHOLARSHIP

DOROTHY WHITELOCK

Since under the Roman system a bishop was bound to have at his see a school for educating suitable persons for the ministry, Augustine at Canterbury and his suffragan at Rochester would establish such schools. Afterwards, when East Anglia was converted, King Sigerberht, who had been converted in Gaul and 'was eager to imitate the things which he saw well ordered there,' set up a school in his own land. 'Bishop Felix helping him and furnishing him with masters and teachers according to the custom of the people of Kent.' These early schools probably attracted pupils from beyond the frontiers of the kingdom in which they were situated; already before the middle of the seventh century men of Anglo-Saxon race were equipped to become bishops, and two of them, Deusdedit the West Saxon who was made archbishop in 654, and Damian the South Saxon who became a bishop in the next year, were from areas where no education was obtainable at that early date. Similarly, the Irish missionaries at once commenced the education of a native clergy. Aidan was given twelve boys to train for this purpose, and one of them, Eata, was abbot of Melrose by 651. About the middle of the century, education could also be acquired from the Irish community settled at Malmesbury, and it was here that Aldhelm was introduced to learning.

In these early schools attention was first concentrated on the knowledge essential for the priestly office—the Latin language, the Scriptures, the computation of the Church seasons, the music necessary for the services. How far beyond this studies went before the days of Theodore and Hadrian is uncertain, but Ogilvy has drawn attention to the citation of Rufinus's Latin translation of the Greek *Ecclesiastical History* of Eusebius at the synod of Whitby in 663, and to the familiarity with Latin authors revealed by Aldhelm very early in his literary career.

Northumbrians flocked to the monasteries of Ireland in the second half of the seventh century. Aldfrith, later king of Northumbria, went 'to acquire celestial wisdom,' and Cynefrith, brother of Abbot Ceolfrith, 'to study the Scriptures.' Theology held first place in the curriculum, but as the Irish schools had lain far from the path of the barbarian invasions, they had not shared in the general decline, and continued to study grammar and rhetoric, which included some attention to secular Latin literature. By the end of the century Aldhelm is claiming that as good an education is obtainable in England, though many unnecessarily go to Ireland. We have already seen that before this several young Northumbrians looked towards Canterbury and the Continent, even as far as Rome, and a new era set in for scholarship in England with the arrival of Archbishop Theodore, whom Bede calls 'a man deep in all secular and ecclesiastical learning, whether Greek or Latin,' and Abbot Hadrian, a man of similar attainments. Benedict Biscop stayed two years with them in Canterbury, and his foundations of Monkwearmouth and Jarrow doubtless benefited by their teaching.

Bede, who spent his life in these foundations, and his older contemporary Aldhelm, who was educated at Malmesbury and then at Canterbury and who became bishop of Sherborne in 705, were both men of great erudition and must have had access to libraries well equipped with the works of Latin authors. They were, of course, familiar with the Bible and the writings of the Christian Fathers, and with the Christian poets, Juvencus, Prudentius, Sedulius, Prosper, Fortunatus, Lactantius and Arator. Bede makes use of a number of historical writings, of Josephus, Eusebius (in Latin translation from the Greek), Orosius, Cassiodorus, Gregory of Tours, etc., and of saints' lives such as Paulinus's *Life of Ambrose*, Possidius's *Life of Augustine*, Constantius's *Life of Germanus*. Of classical authors, both Bede and Aldhelm knew Virgil and Pliny at first hand, and Aldhelm used Lucan, Ovid, Cicero and Sallust. Citations of other authors occur, but could have been taken from the works of Isidore of Seville, or from the Latin grammarians, of whom a really remarkable number were available in England already in the seventh century. Some very rare works had already found their way to England, and one, the grammar of Julian of Toledo, owes its preservation to this circumstance, for all surviving manuscripts go back to an English copy. The apocryphal literature of the early Church also was known in England, and works like *The Gospel of Nicodemus, The Vision of St Paul*, various legends of the Apostles, and rarer works like *The Pseudo-gospel of St Matthew*, and the legend of Jamnes and Mambres, influenced both Anglo-Latin and vernacular literature.

Books must have been imported in great numbers soon after the conversion for such learning to have been possible. King Alfred believed that Augustine's equipment included Pope Gregory's *Pastoral Care*, which is probable enough. Theodore and Hadrian may have come provided with some Greek books as well as Latin works, for Bede testifies to the proficiency of their disciples in the Greek language, but it is difficult to discover direct influence of Greek writings in Anglo-Saxon authors, though some Greek influence on liturgical manuscripts can be demonstrated. We read also of the book-collecting activities of Benedict Biscop, Acca, and Bishop Cuthwine of Dunwich (716–31), who collected illuminated manuscripts, and of the dispatch to England of many books from a monastery in Gaul in the seventh century. William of Malmesbury has preserved a tradition of Aldhelm looking among the merchandise landed at Dover for valuable books, and it is likely enough that traders were quick to realize that there was a market for books in England.

The books that were introduced were not left to lie fallow. They were industriously copied in the scriptoria of English monasteries. Already by 678 Wilfrid ordered for his church of Ripon the four Gospels 'in letters of purest gold on purpled parchment and illuminated'; the first abbot of Jarrow, Ceolfrith, ordered three whole bibles, of the 'new' translation by Jerome, to be transcribed in his monastery. One which he had meant to present to the Pope, if death had not overtaken him on his way to Rome, still survives to witness to the skill of this recently founded house, and fragments of another are in the British Museum and Durham. The famous Lindisfarne Gospels were produced about this time. Other biblical manuscripts and copies of other works were produced in England in considerable number in the eighth century. The missionaries on the Continent frequently write home to ask for books to be written, both elaborate, impressive copies of the Scriptures for ceremonial use, and also plainer texts, and it is of interest to note that women practised this art, not men alone. Boniface asked the Abbess Eadburh to copy the Epistles of St Peter in gold. Meanwhile the import of books from abroad did not cease and by the time of Alcuin York had an excellent library, of which he gives some account in his poem on the saints of York, and for which he sighed after he left England in 782 to help Charles the Great in his educational schemes. As late as the mid ninth century, an abbot of Ferrières applies to it for the loan of some rare books. Well could Alfred say in about 890: 'I remembered how I saw, before everything was ravaged and burnt, that the churches throughout all England were filled with treasures and books.'

It was not very long after the conversion to Christianity that the English were producing original works for themselves, in the Latin language. Aldhelm's major works, his poem and prose treatise on virginity, are alien to

modern taste both in subject and style, but the number of surviving manuscripts witnesses to their great popularity in the Middle Ages. His style was
ornate and artificial, fond of rare words and elaborate similies, and full of
alliteration. It was admired in his own day, and imitated by many later
writers, though fortunately others preferred the simple straightforward
style of Bede. Aldhelm's letters and shorter poems have more interest for us;
he describes in dɩ ail a contemporary church, and tells us something of
Theodore's teaching at Canterbury; a long letter addressed to King Aldfrith
of Northumbria includes a hundred metrical riddles, the first examples in
this country of a type of intellectual activity that proved popular among men
of scholarship in their lighter moments. It had classical authority in the
work of the fifth-century poet Symphosius, and the example was followed
by Hwætberht, abbot of Monkwearmouth in succession to Ceolfrith, and by
Tatwine, archbishop of Canterbury from 731 to 734. Boniface and his fellows
also amused themselves with riddles and acrostics, and the metrical riddle
was adopted by vernacular poets. While the riddles vary greatly in literary
quality, they often show the authors' acute observation of the things around
them, and are of assistance to the historian who desires a picture of everyday things. As far as we know, Aldhelm was the first Englishman to compose
Latin verse.

Meanwhile Northumbria was producing a crop of biographies. Prior to
the work of Bede are anonymous lives of St Cuthbert and Ceolfrith, abbot
of Jarrow, the life of St Gregory by an anonymous monk of Whitby, and
Eddius's interesting life of St Wilfrid. These were all known and used by
Bede, who also had access to a lost life of St Æthelburh of Barking, the
nunnery for which Aldhelm wrote his prose work on virginity; the writing
of saints' lives was therefore not confined to Northumbria. Bede was in
communication with learned men from all over the country. It was Albinus,
abbot of the monastery of St Peter and St Paul at Canterbury, who encouraged him to write his *Ecclesiastical History*, and supplied him with
material from Kent and Nothhelm, a priest of London, searched the papal
archives in Rome to find for Bede the letters relating to the English mission.
Bishop Daniel of Winchester, the writer later on of shrewd advice to Boniface on the conversion of the heathen, corresponded with Bede about the
history of the conversion of Wessex and Sussex, and an East Anglian abbot
Esius and Cynerberht, bishop of Lindsey, were consulted on matters in their
provinces. We have seen that Aldhelm was in correspondence with the
learned king, Aldfrith of Northumbria, and Bede speaks with appreciation of
Tobias, bishop of Rochester and Tatwine, who was a Mercian. It is clear
that political boundaries formed no obstacle to scholarly intercourse. Aldhelm
was also in correspondence with a continental abbot, Cellan of Péronne.

Bede was not, first and foremost, a historian in contemporary eyes, and his
most famous work, his *Ecclesiastical History of the English Nation*, belongs
to the end of his literary career, which began with the writing of textbooks,
on metrics, orthography, science and chronology. In connexion with the

latter subject, he included a short chronicle of world history, and his verse
Life of St Cathbert was written early in his career, but between these works
and his major historical works must be placed volume after volume of commentaries on various books of the Bible, and it was as a theologian rather than
a historian that the Middle Ages honoured him most. Some time after 716
he wrote his *Lives of the Abbots*, followed in two or three years by the prose
Life of St Cuthbert. His longer chronicle can be dated 725, and he finished his
Ecclesiastical History in 731. Between this and his death in 735 can be placed
a commentary on the Acts, and a long letter on Church organization addressed
to his pupil Egbert, archbishop of York, and there survive also a number of
theological treatises, homilies, hymns, etc., whose date is uncertain. In
contrast to the writings of Aldhelm, there has never been a period in which
Bede's work was entirely neglected; manuscripts were multiplied throughout
the Middle Ages, and it has always formed the basis of modern historical
studies of the early Saxon period. One cannot sum up better the reason for
this than to quote Sir Frank Stenton's words: 'But the quality which makes his
work great is not his scholarship, nor the faculty of narrative which he shared
with many contemporaries, but his astonishing power of co-ordinating the
fragments of information which came to him through tradition, the relation
of friends, or documentary evidence. In an age when little was attempted
beyond the registration of fact, he had reached the conception of history.'

During Bede's lifetime a work of a different kind was compiled by a man who
called himself 'a disciple of the Humbrians.' It consists of a collection of the
answers and decisions given by Archbishop Theodore on matters of penance
and canon law, and goes under the name of *Theodore's Penitential*. Bede's
pupil Cuthbert wrote an account of the last days of his master, and to the
pen of another pupil, Archbishop Egbert, there is ascribed a penitential and
a dialogue concerning ecclesiastical government. This last work illustrates
the system of teaching used in the school of York, a school which under
Egbert and his kinsman Ethelbert became one of the most famous centres of
learning in Europe. It was here that Alcuin was educated, and he speaks with
great reverence of his master Ethelbert, the founder of the great library there,
and Egbert's successor in the see. From the work of Alcuin and his biographer
we find that pupils were instructed both by exposition and by disputation,
and the purpose of the dialogue was to give practice in discourse in the Latin
tongue, and at the same time impart necessary information on an important
subject. Alcuin carried the method with him to the Continent, and some of
his own work is couched in dialogue form. He had himself succeeded Ethelbert as master of the school of York, and acquired a reputation that brought
foreigners to study there, before he was invited to take charge of Charles the
Great's palace school, and left Northumbria in 782 to spend most of the rest
of his life abroad, assisting the revival of learning in the Carolingian empire.
Latin poems, sent to him by his students at York, on the miracles of St Ninian,
are extant, and much work from his own pen, treatises, letters, poems, etc.
He saw himself divinely called to the Continent to combat the Adoptionist

heresy, and much of his writing is on religious polemic. Of greater general interest are his poem on York, and his *Life of the Anglo-Saxon missionary St Willibrord*. He was not an original scholar, but his work was influential out of all proportion to its literary merits, and Dr Levinson has pointed out that his methods opened the way for later thinkers of greater independence. His work as a liturgical and biblical scholar had very far-reaching results, and he left behind a number of men, some of them of English nationality, to carry on his work in the ninth-century Frankish empire. He lived to see and be overwhelmed with grief by the first of the Viking raids, the sack of Lindisfarne in 793, but not to know that this was but the beginning of a catastrophe destined within a century totally to destroy Northumbrian scholarship. It was on the Continent, not at home, that his work had permanent results.

From the lands south of the Humber few original works have been preserved, though the letters of St Boniface reveal a powerful intellect that might have been productive of distinguished literary work if the writer's energies had not been so completely occupied in other affairs. As it is, there are only these letters and a grammar from his pen. There were many men and women throughout England of adequate education to write good Latin letters to him and his successor Lul, and an English nun at Heidenheim, one of the monasteries founded in Germany by the missionaries, by name Hygeburh, has left us a most interesting work, the *Lives of St Wilibald and St Wynnebald*, in the third quarter of the eighth century. It includes a fascinating account of a pilgrimage undertaken by Willibald to the Holy Land, written from his recollections. From the Midlands a generation earlier comes Felix's *Life of St Guthlac of Crowland*, a work which throws some welcome light on a period and locality for which evidence is hard to come by. In spite of scanty evidence, one gets the impression that in almost all parts of England during the eighth century there were centres where a liberal education could be obtained, and it was not confined to the male sex. Aldhelm's writings for the nuns of Barking and Rudolf's *Life of St Leofgyth*, Boniface's helper in his missionary work, who was educated at Minster and at Wimborne, show that women, like men, studied the Scriptures and their fourfold interpretation the works of the Fathers, chronography, grammar and metrics.

Already Bede's *Ecclesiastical History* includes several examples of a type of literature that attained a great vogue, the accounts of visions of heaven and hell revealed to various individuals to whom it is permitted to return to earth to relate what they have seen for the benefit of others. The visions of the Irish hermit Fursey and of the Northumbrian Dryhthelm became particularly renowned, and often survive as separate extracts in our manuscripts. One of Boniface's letters describes at length a similar vision seen by a man at the abbey of Wenlock, in which he saw prophetically King Ceolred of Mercia among the damned, and this letter was later translated into English. The terror of the Danish invasions in the ninth century caused men to see more visions, and in 839 envoys sent by King Æthelwulf of Wessex to the Emperor

Louis warned him of the vision revealed to a certain religious priest, which threatened famine and pagan attack if men did not amend their ways and, in particular, keep religiously the proper observance of Sunday. This seems like a reference to the work of a priest Pehtred, who wrote in the province of York (though not in that diocese or that of Lindisfarne) before 837 a book which has been lost, but whose contents are known in part from the horror its heresy roused in the breasts of the archbishop and of his suffragan at Lindisfarne. It told of a deacon Nial who came to life after being dead for seven weeks, and never partook of food afterwards; of a letter of gold written by the hand of God, dealing with the due observance of Sunday, and found on St Peter's altar in the days of Pope Florentius. This tale had been condemned by a Frankish capitulary already in the eighth century, and the bishop of Lindisfarne is urgent that effective steps be taken to suppress this heresy. With a historical sense proper to a countryman of Bede he had consulted lists of popes and failed to find any trace of a Pope Florentius. Yet the fact that no fewer than six vernacular homilies are to be found in tenth- and eleventh-century manuscripts which accept the authenticity of this letter from heaven indicates how unsuccessful were the efforts of the saner element of the population to prevent the spread of such wild tales.

However, Northumbria was not only producing heresy in the ninth century. A certain Æthilwulf wrote a long Latin poem on the abbots of an unidentified Northumbrian monastery, as well as a work on the English saints which has not survived; and the monks of Lindisfarne wrote in letters of silver and gold their 'Book of Life,' containing the names of those for whom they were bound to pray. York was still in touch with at least one continental monastery. Wessex, too, had its continental connexions: King Æthelwulf at one time employed a Frankish secretary, and was a benefactor to continental houses. The knowledge shown of the lives of Frankish saints in the ninth-century Old English *Martyrology* is further evidence of intercourse across the Channel. Book-production had not entirely ceased. Yet already Alcuin had complained of a decline in the zeal for study in England, and this can only have been hastened by the constant threat of Viking raids. King Alfred's impression was that before the monasteries were destroyed by these raids the monks in them did not know Latin and could make no use of their richly equipped libraries.

Alfred's educational reforms, which he found time to put into force during the latter part of his reign, aimed at spreading the ability to read English and at supplying suitable books in English. . . . Men destined for the Church are, however, to study Latin, and it is clear that Alfred regrets that the decay of Latin scholarship should have made translation necessary. The half-century following his death is not prolific in signs of intellectual activity, and it may well be that men's energies were largely absorbed in the re-conquest and re-conversion of the areas ceded to the Danes; yet it was not as utterly devoid of such signs as the mid tenth-century reformers and their pupils were ready to believe. Oda, who became archbishop of Canterbury in 940, and who is the author of a short series of Latin canons, had been able to obtain an education in a thane's household. King Athelstan was generous in gifts of books to religious houses, obtaining some from abroad. The copy of Bede's *Life of St Cuthbert*, in prose and verse, which he gave to the church of that saint at Chester-le-Street, was however an English production, probably from Glastonbury; and there survive manuscripts of works of Bede and Aldhelm which are assigned to this period. The influence of Aldhelm's style is visible in the highly flamboyant Latinity of the charters of this period. There is evidence of the production in England of a version of the *History of the Britons* of Nennius during the reign of King Edmund (939–46), and a Latin poem on the life of St Wilfrid by a certain Frithegod was dedicated to Archbishop Oda. Parts of a Latin verse panegyric on King Athelstan are quoted by William of Malmesbury. Manuscripts of vernacular prose were being copied. Nevertheless the best minds of the time thought that in scholarship as in monastic usage England was behind the Continent, and the reform movement drew its inspiration from abroad.

The monastic reformers devoted great care to the teaching of Latin in their monasteries. Works meant solely for use there are in Latin. Athelwold translated the Benedictine Rule into English, but there is a possibility that he did so for the use of communities of women. At any rate, it was at the special request of the king and queen that he undertook this task, receiving an estate in recompense. His own compilation for securing uniformity of observance in the monasteries of England, the *Regularis Concordia*, he wrote in Latin, and similarly his pupil Ælfric, master of Old English prose though he was, used Latin for his letter to his monks at Eynsham which is based on this *Concordia*, and for the Life of St Athelwold which he meant for monastic reading. This life contains a brief comment on Athelwold as a teacher:

It was always a pleasure to him to teach young men and boys, and to explain books to them in English, and with kindly exhortations to encourage them to better things.

Archbishop Oswald brought over from Fleury a distinguished continental scholar, Abbo, to teach his monks at Ramsey, and Abbo wrote a grammar for their use and a Latin *Life of St Edmund*. It was a monk of Ramsey who wrote a Latin biography of St Oswald. When Ælfric and Byrhtferth of Ramsey write works in English, they are thinking of a wider public than those trained in monasteries. Byrhtferth shows his belief that the education of the average priest would be below that obtainable in the cloister, when he says:

But because we know that these things seem complex enough to clerks and rustic priests, we will now address our words to the young monks who have occupied their childhood with scientific books. I mention a few such, out of many: they have investigated Sergius and Priscian, and gone slowly through the *Distichs* of the bald fellow Cato, and the narratives of Bede, the venerable scholar.

To assist in the teaching of Latin, Ælfric wrote a Latin grammar, a Latin-English glossary, and a colloquy to exercise his pupils in Latin conversation. The characters are a master, a novice, and representatives of the various crafts. . . .

It is clear both from extant manuscripts and also from the knowledge revealed by writers of the period, chiefly by Ælfric and Wulfstan, that the monastic revival led to the introduction into England of many Latin works of the Carolingian revival and later, especially canonistic writings, some of which were translated into English. Scholars of this age knew, in addition to the works of the Fathers and classical writers, those of the more recent authors Alcuin, Hrabanus Maurus, Amalarius of Metz, Atto of Vercelli, Smaragdus, Haymo of Halberstadt, and so on. And Abbo was not the only foreigner to write in England; one of the earliest lives of St Dunstan was the work of a foreigner, and an account of the miracles of St Swithin was written at Winchester by someone whom Ælfric calls 'Landferth, the man from across the sea.' Winchester possessed also a writer of Latin verse, an Englishman called Wulfstan the precentor, whose poem on St Swithin is extant, and to whom William of Malmesbury attributes a life of St Athelwold.

One Latin work is written by a layman, Ealdorman Æthelweard, a patron of Ælfric. He was a descendant of King Alfred's elder brother, and he wrote, for the benefit of his kinswoman, Matilda, abbess of Essen, a descendant of Alfred, a Latin chronicle, based in general on the Anglo-Saxon Chronicle, of which he seems to have possessed a manuscript better in some respects than any that have survived. If the printed text of his work, which, except for a few badly scorched and illegible fragments of the burnt manuscript, is all that we possess, fairly represents him, he wrote a strange and at times incomprehensible Latin; but it is remarkable that a layman should attempt such a task at all.

Another result of the revival was an enormous activity in manuscript production, which continued for the rest of the Saxon period. There poured out elaborate illuminated manuscripts and plainer utilitarian ones; manuscripts in Latin and in English; gospels, psalters, service books of all kinds; works of earlier Latin writers, including the English scholars Aldhelm and Bede, Felix's Life of St Guthlac, and the Life of King Alfred by the Welshman Asser; collections of canons; books of extracts from various sources; calendars, almanacs, etc. Before 1066 the libraries must have again become as full as ever they were in the days before the Viking ravages.

⊹ ✠ ⊹

PREFACE TO
THE PASTORAL CARE

ALFRED

Translation by Alan M. Markman*

With his words King Alfred orders Bishop Wærferth to be greeted warmly
and in a friendly fashion; and bid be made known to you that it has very
often come to my mind what kind of scholars formerly were throughout
England, both of holy positions and secular positions; and how happy times
then were throughout England; and how those kings who had control of the
people in those days obeyed God and His ministers; and how they maintained both their peace and their customs and their control at home, and also
enlarged their territory outside; and for them it then succeeded both in war
and in wisdom; and also the Divine Ranks, how eager they were about both
teaching and learning, and all those services which they should do for God;
and how one in other lands sought wisdom and learning in (this) land, and
how we now should have to obtain it abroad, if we should have it. It was so
completely fallen off in England that exceedingly few were there on this side
of the Humber who were able to understand their services in English or even
translate a single writing from Latin into English; and I believe there were

*The words in parentheses were added by the translator to clarify difficult passages.

not many beyond the Humber. So few of them were there that I cannot think of even a single one south of the Thames, when I succeeded to the throne. Thanks be to God Almighty that we now have any supply of teachers. And therefore I bid you that you do as I believe you will, that you free yourself from the things of this world as often as you are able to, so that there where you might apply the wisdom which God gave you, apply it. Think what miseries befell us then for our concern with this world, when we neither loved it (Christian virtues) ourselves nor even permitted it to other men; we had only the name that we were Christians, and very few of the customs.

When I remembered all this, then I remembered also how I saw, before it all had been completely destroyed and burned, how the churches throughout all England stood filled with treasures and books, and also a very large number of servants of God; and those had very little use from the books, because they were not able to understand one bit of them, for they were not written in their own language. Thus they might have said: 'Our elders, those who formerly held these places, they loved wisdom, and through that they acquired and left riches to us. Here one may still see their path, but we are unable to follow along it, and because we now have forsaken both the riches and the wisdom, because we would not incline our mind to that path.'

When I then remembered all this, then I wondered a great deal about those scholars who formerly were throughout England, and who had fully mastered all those books, that they then wished not at all to translate them into their own language. But then I at once answered myself, and said: 'They did not think that men should ever become so careless and that scholarship would so decline; for that reason they abandoned it (translation), and hoped that here there would be greater learning where, in this land, we know more languages.'

Then I remembered how the Law (Old Testament) was first encountered in the Hebrew language, and later, when the Greeks learned it, then they translated it all into their own language, and also all the other books (the whole of the Old Testament?). And later Latin-speaking people likewise, after they learned it, they translated them all through learned translators into their own language. And also all other Christian peoples translated a certain part of them into their own language. Therefore it seems better to me, if it seems so to you, that we, also, certain books, those which may be most necessary for all men to know, that we translate them into that language that we all can understand, and let us do it, as, with God's help, we very easily can, if we have peace and quiet, so that all the youth of free men which is now in England, of those who have the means that they might devote to it (i.e., free men who can afford to allow their children to be set to it), be set to studying as long as they are not fit for any other occupation, until such time as they know how to read an English document well. One might teach further in the Latin language those whom one wishes to teach more and place in a higher office.

When I then remembered how before this time instruction in the Latin language had decayed throughout England—and yet many could read an

English document—then, among the other various and manifold duties of this kingdom, I translated into English the book which in Latin is called *Pastoralis*, and in English *Herder-Book*, sometimes word for word, sometimes sentence for sentence, as I learned it from Plegmund, my Archbishop, and from Asser, my Bishop, and from Grimbald, my mass-priest, and from Iohannes, my mass-priest. And after I had then learned it, so that I understood it, and so that I might interpret it most reasonably, I translated it into English.

And to each bishopric in my kingdom I will send one (copy); and in each will be a bookmark, which will be worth fifty mancuses.* And I command in the name of God that no one take the bookmark from the book, nor the book from the cathedral. It is not known how long such learned bishops will be there as now, thanks to God, nearly everywhere there are. Therefore I wish it always to be in that place, unless the bishop wishes to have it with him, or it is somewhere on loan, or someone is making a copy from it.

---

*A mancuse equals one eighth of a pound, and the pound then was worth fifty pounds today. Therefore, each bookmark would be valued today at approximately $875.00.

✠ ✠ ✠

A COLLOQUY
ON THE OCCUPATIONS

ÆLFRIC

Translation by George K. Anderson

1

PUPIL: We children pray thee, O teacher, that thou teach us to speak aright, for we are untutored and speak corruptly.

MASTER: What would ye talk about?

PUPIL: What care we what we talk about, provided it be right and fitting, not idle or wicked?

MASTER: Would ye be chastised in your learning?

PUPIL: We had liefer be chastised for the sake of learning than not to know; but we know thee to be kind, loath to inflict a flogging unless thou art forced to do so by our stupidity.

MASTER: I ask thee, what sort of stuff art thou saying? What occupation hast thou?

PUPIL: I am a confessed monk, and I sing each day seven times[1] with my brothers, and I am busied with reading and singing; but nevertheless I should like to learn to speak in Latin.

Reprinted from *The Literature of England*, Volume I, by Woods, Watt, and Anderson, copyright 1936, © 1963 by Scott, Foresman and Company, by permission of the publishers.

MASTER: What do these thy companions know?

PUPIL: Some are farmers, some shepherds, some cowherds; some indeed are hunters, some fishers, some fowlers, some merchants, some cobblers, salt-workers, bakers.

2

MASTER: What sayest thou, farmer, how goest thou about thy work?

FARMER: Alas, dear master, I am sorely in need; I go out at dawn, forcing my oxen to the field, and I yoke them to the plow; there is no winter so severe that I dare lounge about my home for fear of my lord;[2] but with yoked oxen and affixed plowshare and coulter with the plow, every day I must cultivate a full acre or more.

MASTER: Hast thou any companions?

FARMER: I have a boy who urges on the oxen with his goad, who is now hoarse from cold and bawling.

MASTER: What more dost thou in a day?

FARMER: Well, I certainly do more. I must fill the bin of the oxen with hay, and water them, and carry out their dung.

MASTER: Hey! Hey![3] That is a lot of labor.

FARMER: Yea, master, it is a great labor, for I am not free.

3

MASTER: Well, cowherd, what kind of work dost thou do?

COWHERD: Alas, my lord, I labor very hard: when the farmer unhitches the oxen, I lead them to pasture, and all night I stand watching over them against thieves, and then in the early morning I give them back to the farmer well filled and watered.

MASTER: Is this one of thy companions?

COWHERD: Yea, he is.

4

MASTER: Knowest thou anything?

HUNTER: I know a trade.

MASTER: Which one?

HUNTER: I am a hunter.

MASTER: Whose?

HUNTER: The king's.

MASTER: How dost thou go about thy business?

HUNTER: I take my nets, and set them in all sorts of places, and I urge on my hounds, that they harry the wild beasts until they come in unforeseen fashion into the nets, so that they are trapped; then I kill them off in the nets.

MASTER: Canst thou not hunt except with nets?

HUNTER: Yea, I can hunt without nets.

MASTER: How?

HUNTER: With swift hounds I ensnare the wild beasts.

MASTER: What kind of wild animals dost thou most often catch?

HUNTER: I catch harts and bears and stags and roes, and sometimes hares.

MASTER: Wert thou hunting today?

HUNTER: I was not, for today is Sunday, but yesterday I was hunting.

MASTER: What didst thou catch?

HUNTER: Two harts and a bear.

MASTER: How didst thou catch them?

HUNTER: The harts I caught in the nets, and the bear I killed myself.

MASTER: How wert thou so bold as to stab the bear?

HUNTER: The hounds drove him towards me, and I there, standing up to him, suddenly stabbed him to death.

MASTER: Truly thou wert very brave.

HUNTER: No hunter can be fearful, because various wild beasts live in the woods.

MASTER: What dost thou do about thy kill?

HUNTER: I give to the king whatsoever I catch, because I am his hunter.

MASTER: What does he give to thee?

HUNTER: He clothes me well and feeds me, and sometimes he gives me a horse or ring,[4] that I may the more joyfully go about my trade.

5

MASTER: Which trade dost thou know?

FISHER: I am a fisher.

MASTER: What dost thou derive from thy trade?

FISHER: Sustenance and clothing and cattle.

MASTER: How dost thou catch fish?

FISHER: I get in my ship, and cast my nets in the sea, and I throw my fishhook and basket, and whatsoever they bring up, I take it.

MASTER: What if it be unclean fishes?[5]

FISHER: I throw the unclean ones out, and keep the clean for food.

MASTER: Where dost thou sell thy fish?

FISHER: In the town.

MASTER: Who buy them?

FISHER: The townsfolk. I can never catch as many as I could sell.

MASTER: What kind of fish dost thou catch?

FISHER: Eels and pikes, minnows and eelpouts, trout and lampreys, and whatsoever swims in the water.

MASTER: Why dost thou never fish in the ocean?

FISHER: Sometimes I do, but seldom, because it is hard rowing for me to go to the ocean.

MASTER: What dost thou catch in the ocean?

FISHER: Herring and salmon, porpoises and sturgeons, oysters and crabs, mussels, periwinkles, cockles, plaices and flounders, and lobsters, and many other such.

MASTER: Wouldst thou catch a whale?

FISHER: Not I.

MASTER: Why not?

FISHER: Because it is a dangerous matter to catch a whale. Safer it is for me to go to the ocean with my ships, than to go with many ships hunting after whales.

MASTER: Why so?

FISHER: Because I had liefer catch a fish which I could slay, than one that with one blow could sink and drown not only myself but my companions too.

MASTER: And yet many catch whales, and escape the dangers, and get a great deal of money for it.

FISHER: Thou sayest the truth, but I dare not, out of the ignorance of my mind.

6

MASTER: What sayest thou, fowler? How dost thou trap birds?

FOWLER: In many ways I ensnare birds; sometimes with nets, sometimes with nooses, sometimes with birdlime, sometimes by whistling, sometimes with hawks, sometimes with traps.

MASTER: Hast thou a hawk?

FOWLER: I have.

MASTER: Dost thou know how to tame it?

FOWLER: Yea, I know how. What good would they do me, if I did not know how to tame them?

MASTER: How dost thou feed thy hawk?

FOWLER: They feed both themselves and me in the winter, and in the spring I let them fly away to the wood, and catch my birds in the autumn, and tame them.

MASTER: And why dost thou let the tamed ones fly away from thee?

FOWLER: Because I am not willing to feed them in summer, because they eat excessively.

MASTER: And yet many feed the tame hawks through the summer, so that they may have them all ready in the autumn.

FOWLER: Yea, so they do, but I am not willing to worry over one of them, because I can catch others, not that one, and many more if I need.

7

MASTER: Well, merchant, what sayest thou?

MERCHANT: I say that I am necessary to the king, and to the nobles and the wealthy, and to all people.

MASTER: And why?

MERCHANT: I get in my ship with my cargoes, and I row over the watery wastes, and I sell my goods and buy valuable goods in return, which are unknown in this land, and I bring them[6] hither to you with great risk over the sea, and sometimes I suffer shipwreck with the loss of all my goods, myself barely escaping alive.

MASTER: What sort of things dost thou bring us?

MERCHANT: Robes of pall[7] and silk, precious jewels and gold; strange booty, and spices, wine, and oil, ivory and brass, bronze, and tin, sulphur, and glass, and many other such things.

MASTER: Wilt thou sell thy goods here, for the same price as thou didst buy them there?

MERCHANT: I will not. What profit would there be for me from my labors? But I will sell them here at a greater price than that for which I bought them there, that I may get some advantage from it, when I can feed myself and my wife and son.

8

MASTER: What sayest thou, wise man?[8] Which trade, as it seems to thee, is the more important among all these people? Which, as it seems to thee, holds sovereignty among all the trades of the world?

COUNCILOR: Tilling of the earth, because the farmer feeds us all.

SMITH: Whence does the farmer get his plowshare or his coulter, who does not even have a goad except from my trade? Whence does the fisher get his fishhook, or the cobbler his awl, or the tailor his needle? Is it not from my works?

COUNCILOR: Truly thou speakest rightly: but we had all liefer live with the farmer than with thee; because the farmer gives us bread and drink; thou —what dost thou give us in thy smithy, except iron sparks and the resounding of beating sledges and blowing bellows?

CARPENTER: Which one of you has no need of my trade? I make thy house and many a vessel and ships for all of you.

SMITH: O carpenter, why dost thou speak so, when not even one hole couldst thou make in thy business without the fruit of my labor?

9

COUNCILOR: O companions and good laboring men: let us leave immediately this controversy, and let there be peace and harmony among us, and let each do for the other according to his trade, and agree with the farmer, whence we have food for ourselves and fodder for our horses. And this thought I give to all workers, that each one of you go about his business with pleasure, because he who abandons his profession is abandoned by that profession. Whosoever thou may be, mass-priest, monk, churl, warrior, observe this rule for thyself: be what thou art, for it is a great shame and abasement for a man not to be what he is and what he ought to be.

10

MASTER: Thou, boy, what didst thou today?

PUPIL: I did many things. In the night, when I heard the bell, I arose from my bed and went to church and sang matins with the brothers; after that we sang about all the saints and the daily lauds;[9] after that we sang prime-service and seven psalms with the litany and early morning mass; after that we sang mid-day-mass and ate and drank and slept, and again we arose and sang nones;[10] and now we are here before thee ready to hear what thou hast to tell us.

MASTER: When will you sing evensong or compline?[11]

PUPIL: When it is time.

MASTER: Wert thou scourged today?

PUPIL: I was not, for I behaved circumspectly.

MASTER: And how about thy companions?

PUPIL: Why dost thou ask me about them? I dare not disclose to thee our secrets. Each one knows whether he was scourged or not.

MASTER: What eatest thou by day?

PUPIL: I still enjoy meat, because I am a child leading my life under the rod.

MASTER: What more dost thou eat?

PUPIL: Roots and eggs, fish and cheese, butter and beans, and all clean things I eat with much gratitude.

MASTER: Thou must be very eager to grow, when thou eatest all things that are put before thee.

PUPIL: I am not so big a glutton[12] that I can eat all kinds of food at one meal.

MASTER: How then?

PUPIL: I enjoy sometimes this dish and sometimes that dish in moderation, as befits a monk, not with greed, because I am not a glutton.

MASTER: And what dost thou drink?

PUPIL: Ale, if I have any; or water, if I have no ale.

MASTER: Dost thou not drink wine?

PUPIL: I am not so well-to-do that I can buy wine for myself; and wine is not a drink for children or foolish people, but for the old and wise.

MASTER: Where dost thou sleep?

PUPIL: In the dormitory with the brothers.

MASTER: Who wakens thee for matins?

PUPIL: Sometimes I hear the sound of the bell and arise; sometimes my master wakens me sternly with the rod.

MASTER: O all ye good children and delightful pupils, your master admonishes you that you obey the laws of God, and keep yourselves excellent wherever you may be. Go with devotion when you hear the churchbell, and go into the church and bow yourselves humbly before the holy altar, and stand with devotion and sing whole-heartedly and pray for your sins, and depart without foolishness to the cloister or to study.

NOTES

1. seven times. The seven Divine Offices are mentioned later, in section 10: matins, lauds, prime-mass, midday-mass, nones, vespers, and compline. See note 9, below.

2. fear of my lord. The farmer, as he tells us, is not a freeman; he is still the churl bound to the land of the earl (his lord). In Anglo-Saxon times, long, hard service by the churl and great generosity on the part of the lord were necessary to enable the churl to amass enough riches to buy his way out of bondage and become a freeman.

3. Hey! Hey! "Ha! Ha!" the sound of laughing. There is a deliberate pun in the Old English text; the word for "hay" and the "ha! ha!" are both expressed by the word *hig*.

4. gives . . . ring. The reward of the hunter is comparable to that of the warrior.

5. unclean fishes. The adjective "unclean" is applied to anything not edible.

6. bring them . . . risk . . . sea; cf. *The Seafarer*.

7. pall, a rich purple cloth.

8. wise man, apparently a member of the *Witenegemot* (assembly of wise men).

9. lauds, the seven psalms of praise sung after matins. prime-service, or simple "prime," the Divine Office at the hour of prime, originally six o'clock in the morning.

10. nones, the Divine Office at the ninth hour—three o'clock in the afternoon.

11. compline, the last service of the day, held after supper.

12. glutton. Gluttony or over-indulgence in food and drink, is one of the Seven Deadly Sins; see *Piers Plowman*.

PART FOUR

MIDDLE ENGLISH

✠

INTRODUCTION

The chapter from Bryant analyzes for the reader the effect on the English language of the Norman invasion of England in 1066. By the middle of the twelfth century, the change in the language was quite apparent. Bryant discusses the relationship between the Anglo-Saxons and their Norman conquerors, the ascendancy of French over Old English; the decline in quality of Old English, the growing interest of the nobility in things English as a result of their loss of Normandy, and the shift, obvious by the fourteenth century, to English—an English by this time, however, much different from the English the Normans found when they arrived in 1066. She then describes that English, which we now call Middle English, and which we date roughly from 1150 to 1500.

The two chapters from Scott's *Ivanhoe* bring to life the nature of the relationship between Anglo-Saxons and Normans alluded to by Bryant and give the reader some feeling as well for the structure of the social class system of the period. In addition, the first chapter contains a well-known passage on the use of Old English words for an animal on the hoof and the use of French words for the dressed meat, a distinction which holds even today: 'swine,' 'pork'; 'calf,' 'veal'; etc.

In his discussion of Chaucer's reading and travels Lowes shows the continental models for many of Chaucer's writings. From this selection it is easy to see one way in which languages can influence one another and in particular how English was influenced through literature by Latin, French, and Italian.

The final selection, Caxton's "Prologue" to his translation of Eneydos, not only provides a sample of late Middle English (1490), but also gives some examples of the problems of a language in a period of transition. Caxton comments that the language spoken at the time he was writing the "Prologue" differs noticeably from that spoken when he was born, about sixty years before.

Bryant also provides samples of Middle English, of course. The exercises at the back of the book provide several more: the *Ancrene Wisse*—an example of early Middle English from about the year 1200; three passages from Chaucer—one from 1370 and two from 1385; and the *Polychronicon*—

a late Middle English revision by Caxton (in 1482) of a translation done almost a hundred years before.

The Middle English period, therefore, sees English transformed from a language which, in Caxton's words, looks "more lyke to dutsche than englysshe" to one which most of us today can read with not too great an effort. It is thus a period of major change.

✠ ✠ ✠

MIDDLE ENGLISH HERITAGE

MARGARET M. BRYANT

Continuous Process Although linguistic changes are a continuous process and all dates are a mere approximation, for the sake of convenience the four centuries from 1100 to 1500 are generally regarded as the Middle English period.[1] Certain it is that within that span of years the language developed a pattern that was distinctly different from that of Old English and was the precursor of Modern English. The one factor of overwhelming significance in that period was of course the Norman Conquest at its outset. Without the invasion of William the Conqueror and his cohorts English presumably would have grown along Germanic lines to become even more closely linked to Modern Dutch and Modern German than it is. And if, three centuries after the conquest, the Normans had not lost their land holdings in France, Norman French might have remained in the ascendancy and the dominant language of the British Isles today would be a variation of French. So much for the "ifs" of history and linguistics.

The Conquering Hero It was in September 1066 that William and some 60,000 Normans landed on English soil, but their language had actually preceded them. Edward the Confessor, next to the last of the old Saxon kings, had a Norman mother and had been reared on the Continent when the

Saxon princes were exiled from Britain during the reign of the Danish usurpers. Proclaimed king and crowned at the cathedral in Winchester in 1042, Edward was almost a stranger to the land and the language of his forefathers. He had brought with him a small group of Normans, and more kept coming over each year of his reign, so that the Norman tongue even banished from the palace the Anglo-Saxon, which had become an object of ridicule to the foreign courtiers, and no flattering discourse was any longer addressed to the king except in Norman French.

Infiltration Tactics This infiltration of Norman French had gone on, therefore, over a period of nearly twenty-five years before the arrival of Duke William to wrest the English crown from Edward's successor, King Harold. If the Normans had been defeated at the battle of Hastings and hurled back to France, the vogue of the new tongue doubtless would have died out quickly at the English court, but William's victory naturally made it possible for Norman French to consolidate its position. Nevertheless, the Norman Conquest was not a national migration, and the modification of English law, language, and social custom through French influence was a very gradual process.

English Not Banned William did not despise the old language or forbid its use in private affairs and around the family fireside. He even took pains to acquire some knowledge of English, and the *Anglo-Saxon Chronicle* continued to be written in it for almost another hundred years—until 1154. Nevertheless, the Venerable Wulfstan, Bishop of Worcester, was deposed from his See in 1095 as "an idiot who did not know French."[2] Wulfstan was only a conspicuous example of a process that went on throughout England as members of the native clergy were forced to give up their duties and benefices to make way for Norman priests, the result being that French became the language of the churches and monasteries for all secular business. Harsh treatment this undoubtedly was, but from practically contemporary accounts, notably that of Odericus Vitalis, it would seem that a portion at least of the English clergy had become illiterate, even in their own tongue. It is to the credit of William the Conqueror that he brought to England the zest for intellectual affairs that swept over the Continent after its first contacts with the lore of the Arabs and the Far East, a zest that was the precursor of the full-blown Renaissance a few centuries later. "The Conqueror himself patronized and loved letters . . . Many of the Norman prelates, preferred in England by the Conqueror, were polite scholars," remarks the preface to Warton's *History of English Poetry*.[3]

Effect of Architecture The invaders also brought with them their delight and skill in erecting imposing buildings in what came to be known as the Norman style of architecture. Doubtless it was English laborers and craftsmen who did most of the manual work on the construction of the imposing cathedrals, monasteries, and manor houses, and in the course of their work they were bound to pick up many words of the new tongue, as did shopkeepers in the towns who had business with the newcomers.

"Uplandish" Folk   The farmers, herdsmen, and other "uplandish" folk, as the rural dwellers were sometimes called—corresponding to our modern "hillbillies"—clung to the old language, just as the mountaineers of the southeastern United States have held on to some of the Shakespearian English of more than three hundred years ago that their ancestors brought over with them. In more thickly settled regions of England the new Norman culture was superimposed on the old, but even there did not drive out the Anglo-Saxon completely, in the way that the Anglo-Saxons had all but obliterated the Britons. In the stratification of society after the Norman Conquest, the Normans were the "high men" and the English, even though called "uplandish" on some accounts, were the "low men," to use the terms employed by Robert of Gloucester in his *Chronicle,* written in 1300. As the chronicler put it,

> . . . The folc of Normandie,
> Among us woneth [dwelleth] yet, and schulleth ever mo. . . .
> Of the Normannes beth thys hey men that beth of thys lond
> And the lowe men of Saxons.

Ascendancy of French   As was to be expected, it was the language of the "high men" that prevailed, not only because an inferior culture would imitate a superior one, but also because the use of French was enforced by law in public business, in court trials, and, most importantly, in the schools. Robert Holcot, writing in the early part of the fourteenth century, observed that there was no instruction of children in the old English, that the first language they learned was French, through which they were later introduced to Latin, and he added that this practice had been established immediately after the conquest. Or, to quote Robert of Gloucester's *Chronicle* again:

> þe Normans ne couþe speke þo, bote hor owe speche,
> speke French as hii dude at om   hor children dude also teche.
> So þat heiemen of þis lond, þat of hor blod come,
> Holdeth alle þulke speche that hii of hom nome.
> Vor bote a man conne Frenss, me telþ of him lute.

Students who have not acquired a knowledge of Middle English will need to have this translated in some such fashion as the following: "And the Normans could not then speak any speech but their own; and they spoke French as they did at home, and had their children taught the same. So that the high men of this land, that came of their blood, all retain the same speech that they brought from their home. For unless a man know French, people think little of him."

Forced on English   This learning of French was compulsory for those children of the English who attended school. This situation brought a complaint from Ranulf Hygden in his *Polychronicon.* A passage, as translated into Middle English by Trevisa, deplores "this apayringe [impairing] of the birthe tonge" resulting in part from the fact that "children in scole, aghenes [against] the usage and maner of alle other naciouns, beth [be] compelled for to leve her [their] owne langage, and for to constrewe her [their] lessouns and her [their] thingis a Frensche. . . ."

Decline in Quality So, not only was the English language losing quantitatively; it was also felt to be slipping in quality. For one thing, with no formal instructions in the schools and no new literature being created, the language was becoming so diversified in form and utterance—since used only by the "low men"—as to be hardly understood from one district to another. Even at the time of the conquest, the number of Englishmen who could read and write their own language was not large, relatively, and when that generation died out the language, ceasing to be read and written, lost almost all its bookish words, three centuries of misery and national degradation having stripped the native tongue of fully half its vocabulary and left the remainder in utter confusion. Under such circumstances, English must have possessed amazing vitality to survive at all, even if it did become interlarded with French borrowings to replace part of its forgotten vocabulary and to express new concepts that the old vocabulary could not have coped with.

Impact of History Even linguistic vitality, however, does not go far toward explaining the ascendancy that English finally achieved over Norman French. Recourse must be had to the general history of the times, in its military and political aspects and also in its social and economic trends. A detailed analysis of these factors lies outside the scope of this work, but some general conclusions can be set forth, bearing on the subject at hand.

Territory Lost For nearly one hundred forty years after the conquest of England, the Normans expanded territorially as well as linguistically, not only in Britain but also on the Continent. Their influence, if not actual control, extended over two-thirds of France as a result of the weakness of the nominal monarchs of that country and of the valor and ability of William of Normandy and his five immediate successors. But the seventh in this Norman line, King John, was a "trifler and a coward," asserts the brilliant if biased historian, Macaulay, and "just at this conjuncture, France, for the first time since the death of Charlemagne, was governed by a prince of great firmness and ability."[4] King John was driven from Normandy in 1204, and the holdings that the rulers of England retained in the south of France were inconsequential. "The Norman nobles were compelled to make their election between the island and the continent," Macaulay adds. "Shut up by the sea with the people whom they had hitherto oppressed and despised, they gradually came to regard England as their country, and the English as their countrymen."[5]

The Melting Pot To quote this nineteenth-century historian further, "The stages of the process by which the hostile elements were melted down into one homogeneous mass are not accurately known to us. But it is certain that, when John became king, the distinction between Saxons and Normans was strongly marked, and that before the end of the reign of his grandson, it had almost disappeared."[6] Actually, the inhabitants of England, whether of high or low rank in the social scale and whether of Norman or Saxon stock, began to cultivate an interest in all things English that centuries later developed into the insular patriotism that made the modern British the butt of the world's jibes—and envy. The rivalries with France that turned into open and protracted warfare hastened this process. The Hundred Years' War (1337–1453) and the notable victories of English arms at Crécy (1346) and Poitiers (1356) provided new incentives for abandoning the language of the enemy.

War and Plague   Social and economic forces were meanwhile at work toward the same end. As the bitterness of the years immediately after the conquest receded, intermarriage between the Normans and Saxons became frequent, especially in the more isolated sections of the realm, so that more and more Norman courtiers and their descendants acquired a knowledge of the English language. Then, in the middle of the fourteenth century, there came upon the land a great catastrophe, the Black Death, a plague that swept through the length and breadth of the land with awful thoroughness. As usual in such calamities, the fatalities were far larger, both absolutely and relatively, among the lower classes than among the nobles and the wealthy burghers who could get away from pestilential spots. The loss in population was so great that an acute labor shortage developed, wages shot upward, and the working man—and his language, which was English—achieved a new importance in the community. This new importance of the old English stock was enhanced further a century later when the Wars of the Roses (1453–1485) between the rival royal houses of York and Lancaster so decimated the ranks of the nobles that they had to turn to the once despised Saxon underlings to recruit their respective forces for continued hostilities.

Poetry as Clue   But even before the Black Death gave the Saxon artisans an enhanced economic and social status, one of the odd poetical customs of the early fourteenth century provides an inkling of the shape of things to come. It became the custom to write verses in bilingual form, with first a couple of lines of French and then a couple of lines of English, the latter not translating the French but continuing the story or sentiment. Thus, a political song of 1311 "On the King's Breaking His Confirmation of the Magna Charta" even maintains a rhyme scheme between French and English sections, as the following lines indicate, the first two in French and the other two in English:

> Nostre prince de Engleterre,
> Par le consail de sa gent
> At Westminster after the feire
> Made a gret parlement . . .

Shift to English   But this sort of linguistic and poetic duality could not be maintained indefinitely, in view of the growing trend of the times toward English. In 1356 the Mayor and aldermen of London ordered that proceedings in the Sheriff's Court of that city and Middlesex should be English,[7] and six years later the Chancellor opened Parliament for the first time in English. In 1362 a statute was enacted to require all cases before the King's Courts to be pleaded in English instead of in French, and entered and enrolled in Latin. Nevertheless, for another hundred years or more, the laws themselves continued to be drawn up in French, and the first bill of the House of Commons that was written in English bears the date 1485; the House of Lords apparently retained the language of the conquest a few years longer, and some law reports were written in French as late as 1600.

Reconversion in Schools Above were quoted the remarks of Ranulf Hygden on the compulsory teaching of French in the schools in the middle of the fourteenth century. Trevisa's translation was made some thirty years after Hygden wrote, so by way of bringing the situation up to date, as of 1385, the translator added:

"This maner [that is, of instruction solely in French] was myche yused tofore the first moreyn [that is, before the plague of 1349] and is sith the som dele [somewhat] yechaungide. For John Cornwaile, a maister of gramer, chaungide the lore [learning] in gramer scole and construction of [from] Frensch into Englisch, and Richard Pencriche lerncd that maner teching of him, and other men of Pencriche. So that now, the yere of owre Lord a thousand thre hundred foure score and fyve, of the secunde Kind Richard after the Conquest nyne, in alle the gramer scoles of England children leveth Frensch, and construeth and lerneth an [in] Englisch, and haveth thereby avauntage in oon [one] side and desavauntage in another. Her [their] avauntage is, that thei lerneth her [their] gramer in lasse tyme than children were wont to do; desavauntage is, that now children of gramer scole kunneth [know] no more Frensch than can her lifte heele [knows their left heel]; and that is harm for hem [them], and if they schul passe the see [sea] and travaile in strange londes, and in many places also. Also gentilmen haveth now mych ylefte for to teche her [their] children Frensch."

A Different French As a matter of fact, even the English who did go abroad to strange lands found that Norman French, which once had set the standard for the language, had undergone so many changes, due in part to the influence of English on it (especially the tendency to accent the first syllable and slur over the others), that it was not always easy for the traveler from England to understand or be understood by speakers of Continental French. Chaucer's famous pen portrait of the prioress in the *Prologue* to *The Canterbury Tales* bears witness to this fact:

> And Frensh she spak ful faire and fetisly,
> After the scole of Stratford atte Bowe,
> For Frensh of Paris was to hir unknowe.

That being the case, French had no longer had any inherent claim to preference as the language of Englishmen, and this was another factor in accelerating the reestablishment of English as the dominant tongue. But the English that came again into its own was not the language of four centuries earlier.

A Different English   William Caxton, born in Kent about 1415 and famous as the man who introduced printing to England, saw a tremendous change in the language even in his lifetime. In the preface to his *Eneydos*, translated from the French in 1490, he remarked how some gentlemen had complained that his translations used curious terms which could not be understood by the common people "and desired me to vse olde and homely termes," to which Caxton adds;

"And fayn wolde I satysfye euery man / and so to doo, toke an olde boke and redde therein / and certaynly the englysshe was so rude and brood that I coude not wele vnderstande it. And also my lorde abbot of westmynster ded do shewe to me late certayn euidences wryton in olde englysshe, for to reduce it into our englysshe now vsid / and certaynly it was wreton in such wyse that it was more lyke to dutche than englysshe; I coude not reduce ne brynge it to be vnderstonden / And certaynly our langage now vsed varyeth ferre from that whiche was vsed and spoken whan I was borne / For we englysshe men / ben borne vnder the domynacyon of the mone, which is neuer stedfaste / but euer wauerynge / wexynge one season / and waneth & dyscreaseth another season."[8]

Changes Fundamental   If one were to ask in what way the language was altered, the answer must be: "In almost every way." The Normans found English a synthetic, highly inflected language like Greek, Latin, and Modern German, but after a few centuries had passed it had become an analytic language,[9] with rapidly disappearing inflections, like Modern French. Grammatical gender and transposed word order were succeeded by natural gender[10] and the normal word order of present-day English. Grammar was only one aspect of change. The pronunciation shifted, and the alteration in vocabulary was particularly farreaching, with thousands of French and Latin terms added to the word stock. The whole pattern of the language was modified. The conquest did not account for all these changes, but for many of them.

Causes of Loss of Inflections   One of the chief reasons for the leveling of inflectional endings in the Middle English period was undoubtedly a change in the method of accenting words. In Old English, although the stress was generally on the root syllable, unstressed vowels were so pronounced as to retain their individual quality, but in Middle English the stress began to be stronger on the first syllables of words, as it is in Modern English, thus making weaker the syllables following. As a result the unstressed *a, e, o,* and *u* in inflectional endings became neutral in sound, the so-called "indeterminate vowel," or *schwa,*[11] usually written as *e.* Also the unstressed distinct endings *-a, -u, -e, -an, -um* were leveled under the vowel *-e,* losing at the same time grammatical distinctions formerly expressed.[12] The first ending to be weakened, beginning in Old English, was *-um* of the dative plural in nouns and adjectives, gradually appearing as *-un, -on, -en,* and *-an,* the last becoming predominant by the end of the Old English period.

Noun   It has been previously mentioned that there was a leveling of the various Old English vowel endings under the vowel *-e.* The declensions of

the few nouns given [earlier] illustrate this change. In the declension of
fisc, the eight forms of the singular and plural were reduced to three: *fisc*,
fisces, and *fisce*. The various declensions of Old English, based on the
difference in vowel ending, had largely been abandoned. The endings of Old
English shown leveled off in the beginning as follows:[13]

	Singular	Plural
Nom.	_, -e.	_, -e, -es, -en.
Gen.	-e, -es, -en.	-e, -ene.
Dat.	_, -e, -en.	-en.
Acc.	_, -e, -en.	_, -e, -es, -en.

Two classes of nouns remained: the strong and the weak. The strong nouns
formed their genitive singular and nominative and accusative plurals in *-es*
whereas the weak nouns had the ending *-en* for these and other forms. With
the inflections leveling under *-e, -es, -en*, the means of distinguishing grammatical gender passed and words began to be used as in Modern English.
The inflections below show a typical strong noun in Middle English (*fisc*) and
a typical weak noun (*oxe*):[14]

	Singular	Plural
Nom.	fisc	fisces
Gen.	fisces	fisce, fisces
Dat.	fisc(e)[15]	fisc(en)e, fisces
Acc.	fisc	fisces

Nom.	oxe	oxen
Gen.	oxe(n)	ox(en)e
Dat.	oxe(n)	oxen
Acc.	oxe(n)	oxen

All nouns tended to fall into these two groups, the strong nouns being much
more numerous. If a strong noun ended in an unstressed *-e* in the nominative and accusative singular, as in *ende, helpe*, and *soule*, the plural and the
genitive singular were formed by adding *s* only. Thus in early Middle English
there were two main ways of designating the plural: the *-s* or *-es* in the
strong declension and the *-en* in the weak. Until the thirteenth century the
plural in *-en* was used to a great extent in the South. It was even added to
nouns not originally weak.

Trend in Plurals In other parts of England, however, the *-s* for the plural
and genitive singular, derived from the first declension masculine nouns with
the plural in *-as*, was employed much more extensively and became widespread. Even in Old English in the North many nouns originally from other
declensions had gone over to this declension. Thus, by the middle of the
thirteenth century, *-s* was the usual plural ending for nouns in the North and
in the Midlands, and during the fourteenth century this method of forming

the plural was accepted as the standard one throughout England. The number of nouns ending in -*en* decreased throughout the Middle English period, so that at the end only a few like *oxen, brethren*, and *children* were left to appear in Modern English.

The Adjective As has been stated, the noun lost grammatical gender along with the loss of inflections. With the loss of grammatical gender in the noun went the loss of agreement, so far as gender is concerned, in inflection between the noun and its adjective. At the same time the inflectional endings in the adjective leveled off as they had done in the noun. In both the strong and weak declensions, the nominative singular was extended to all cases in the singular and the nominative plural to all cases in the plural. Thus *wīs*, "wise," would be declined in Middle English as follows:[16]

	Strong	*Weak*
Sing.	wīs (all cases and genders)	wīse (all cases and genders)
Plur.	wīse (all cases and genders)	wīse (all cases and genders)

In the weak declension there was no difference in the singular and plural, both ending in -*e* (*wīsa* became *wīse* and *wīsan* became *wīse*). This was also true of adjectives of the strong declension, ending in -*e*. Thus by about the middle of the thirteenth century there was no distinction between the singular and plural in the strong declension except with a number of monosyllabic adjectives ending in a consonant, as *mad* (sing.), *made* (plur.). In the fourteenth century, the final *e* was no longer pronounced, surviving only in the spelling, and by the end of the Middle English period, the adjective had lost all inflections.

The Definite Article Since the majority of the forms of the definite article began with þ (*th*), by analogy þ was substituted for *s* of *sē* and *sēo*, giving in the nominative singular þē, þēo, þæt. The vowel of þēo became the same as that of þē by a regular phonetic development, and with the discarding of grammatical gender in the noun, the neuter form þæt was no longer used as an article but the one form þē was employed for all three genders, the form þæt remaining as a demonstrative with a changed value. Analogy extended even further in that þē became the one form for all numbers, genders, and cases of the article after the loss of inflections in the noun. Thus one form, giving Modern English *the*, forced out the many forms of the Old English article.

Personal Pronouns The great loss of inflections found in the noun and adjective did not take place in the personal pronouns. Only they preserved throughout the Middle English period and even in Modern English most of the distinctions existing in Old English. The dual number, however, although generally confined to poetic texts, had entirely disappeared by the thirteenth century. Also the dative and accusative cases were merged generally under the form of the dative: *him, her, (t)hem*. It should be pointed out that this merging had already taken place in the first and second persons during the Old English period: *mē, þē*. In the third person neuter, however, since the dative *him* would have been confused with the masculine, the accusative (*h*)*it* survived, becoming the general objective case, no doubt by analogy with the nominative which had the same form. The forms of the third person plural through normal development should be *hi* (*he*), *here, him* (*hem*) instead of *they, their, them*, but the Scandinavian influence was strong enough in the North to crowd out the Old English forms. The Scandinavian form *þei* first replaced the nominative *hi*, as can be seen from Chaucer who generally used *thei, here, hem*. After *they* was accepted, by analogy the other forms *their* and *them* were adopted so that at the end of the Middle English period the forms *they, their,* and *them* were well established. One other different form is the nominative feminine *she* which had the form *hēo* in Old English. It is thought by some that *hēo* must have been influenced by the nominative feminine *sēo* of the definite article, originally a demonstrative, in order to give *she*.

Verb   The division of the verb into strong and weak, or irregular and regular, continued in the Middle English period, but there was a tendency for the strong verbs to become weak, as in the case of *climb, help, flow, weep*. This tendency has continued on into the Modern English period, no doubt, because the weak verbs exemplify the human preference for regularity and simplicity of form. Occasionally by analogy with strong verbs, a strong past tense or past participle was formed, as in Modern English *dive*. This verb has recently developed in the United States a past tense *dove,* by analogy, no doubt with *drive, drove*. All new verbs in Middle English formed from adjectives and nouns or brought in from other languages were conjugated as weak verbs and still are in Modern English. Thus the number of strong verbs is small in comparison with the ever-increasing stock of weak verbs.

Strong Verbs Disappear   In the early Middle English period nearly a third of the Old English strong verbs died out and today more than half of them have disappeared. The dropping out of the strong forms was a gradual one. The strong forms continued to be employed while the weak ones were coming into use. For instance, *climb*, a strong verb of the third class, appeared as a weak verb in the thirteenth century, but the strong past tense *clomb* continued in use and can be found in Chaucer, Spenser, and Dryden. The strong forms, surviving from Old English, can even be heard today in illiterate speech. Subtracting the verbs that have been lost and those that have become weak, only sixty-six of the Old English strong verbs are still used.[17] Some of the past participles of strong verbs which developed weak forms have survived, oftentimes used as adjectives, as *molten, shaven, swollen*. While the fluctuation was going on between the strong and weak verbs in the Middle English period, the leveling or changing of the various inflectional vowels to the vowel *-e* was also taking place. The endings *-að* and *-iað* of the present plural merged with the *-eð* of the third singular.[18] In the imperative the endings, *-e, -a* and *-að, -iað* became *-e* and *-eð* respectively and in the infinitive the *-an* and *-ian* became *-en*. The gerund ending in *-anne* became *-enne* and the preterite plural endings *-on* and *-don* became *-en* and *-den*. With the present participle ending in *-ende* a different change occurred. The present participle tended to fall in with nouns naming actions that ended in *-ung* or *-ing*, such as *blētsung*, "blessing," so that the participal ending was given up and the noun and present participle both used the ending *-ing*.

Another Simplification One other simplification of the verb took place in the preterite tenses. In Old English the preterite plural stem of strong verbs often differed from the preterite singular and the past participle frequently was different from both. In giving principal parts of a strong verb in Old English, one therefore gave four forms, as *findan, fand, fundon, funden,* which became in Middle English *finde, found, found.*[19] This simplification did not take place in all strong verbs, for we have a number in Modern English which still have three separate forms, as *write, wrote, written,* and *ride, rode, ridden.* It should also be mentioned here that the past tense of surviving strong verbs may be derived from the past tense singular of Old English, as in *rode,*[20] or from the past tense plural, as in *bit.*[21]

Additions to Vocabulary The conditions following the Norman Conquest were favorable not only to great inflectional and grammatical changes in the language but also to great vocabulary changes.[22] When two languages exist side by side for a long time, as did French and English in England, many words are transferred from one language to the other, especially to the one in the inferior position. So it was with English, which borrowed an incredibly large number of words from the French, enough to change the general character of the language from unilingual to bilingual.

French as Model English thus began to be influenced by Romance languages as well as by Teutonic, becoming a language made up of two merging strains. Never before or since has English taken in so many words. French, in addition to being the language of the ruling class in England, was also generally regarded as the polite language of Europe. In it was written a great literature which was influencing other nations, especially England. The University of Paris was visited by all the scholars of Europe. Paris itself was considered to be the center of learning and refinement. Parisian French had taken the place of Norman French in the hearts of the English. The admiration for everything French reached its height in the fourteenth century. In attempting to make English as nearly like French as possible, words, phrases, and idioms were borrowed. Many of these took the place of English words, bringing about the obsolescence of the latter. French pronunciations and spellings came in at this time too. For instance, the introduction of *u* after *g* to indicate the hard *g* accounts for Modern English *tongue* from Old English *tunge*, which should give *tung*, like *lung*; it also accounts for spellings like *guest, guilt, guild,* and *language.*

Types of French Words Borrowed During the whole Middle English period words of all types, of all parts of speech, and from every sphere of life, came into English, some from Norman and some from Parisian French. In many instances the English word was preserved along with the French, but often on a somewhat less dignified plane, as English *work* but French *labor*, English *town* but French *city*. Many words that were introduced had to do with the table, preparation of food, and eating, such as *dinner, taste, appetite, supper, napkin, pastry, roast, broil,* and *boil*. To these should be added terms dealing with fashions, dress, and social life, including *apparel, gown, veil, cloak, coat, embroidery, kerchief, mitten, taffeta, satin, jewel, ornament, sapphire, diamond, dance, melody, conversation, tournament, palfrey, falcon, checkers, chess*. As a result of the influence of French life and civilization the English people had a much fuller and more varied life in the fourteenth century than previously, and with it went words of French origin. One would naturally expect many words connected with the court, government, and legal procedures. To mention only a few, among them are *government, reign, court, parliament, tax, revenue, exchequer, traitor, treason, liberty, mayor, treasurer, coroner, duke, duchess, nobility, peer, squire, justice, attorney, plaintiff, jury, verdict, sentence, plead, indict, acquit, assault, libel, fraud*. The church likewise added its share: *prayer, clergy, cardinal, friar, religion, faith, mystery, preach, devotion*, and many others. But many simple, commonplace words were also introduced, such as *fruit, flower, chair*, and *age*. Since war also played a great part in the Middle Ages, many French military terms were introduced, such as *battle, combat, soldier, guard, captain, sergeant, lieutenant, vanquish*, and *besiege*. The arts and formal learning donated their share. There were words connected with architecture, literature, and science, particularly medicine. Among these words are *painting, sculpture, figure, beauty, cathedral, palace, ceiling, chimney, tower, porch, pillar, poet, romance, story, tragedy, prologue, preface, paper, pen, treatise, geometry, grammar, copy, compile, physician, surgeon, malady, anatomy, sulphur, alkali, arsenic, pestilence*. From these lists one can get some idea of the breadth and universality of French influence in the Middle Ages. It contributed words to every walk of life.

Changes in Words As has been pointed out, Old English combined native elements into self-explaining compounds and made use of prefixes and suffixes in meeting new needs of vocabulary, but with the influx of thousands of French words—easily acquired new words—the English habits of word formation were weakened. If both the English and French words survived, the meanings were usually differentiated as may be seen from *doom* and *judgment, house* and *mansion, ask* and *demand*. Many of the Old English prefixes gradually fell into disuse. Take, for example, *for-*, employed in Old English to stress the meaning of a verb or to suggest the idea of destructiveness or prejudice. It survived the Middle English, being added even to a few French words, but it died out completely as a formative prefix. In Modern English only a few of the verbs remain, among them *forbear, forbid, forget, forgive*, and *forsake*, all originating in Old English. The prefix *with-*, meaning against, made possible *withdraw* and *withhold* in Middle English, which survive in Modern English along with Old English *withstand*, but the prefix *to-* has disappeared entirely. *Over-* and *under-*, greatly weakened in the Middle English period, have, on the other hand, been revived in Modern English. Most of the compounds including these two prefixes belong either to the Old English or to the Modern English period. The prefix *on-* (now *un-*) kept more of its vitality than most prefixes, giving *unfasten, uncover, unwrap* among the Middle English words employed often in Modern English to show the negative. Prefixes of Latin origin, such as *dis-, re-,* and *trans-,* came in to crowd out the Old English ones. With the suffixes, some few remained, among them the noun suffix *-ness* and the adjective endings *-full, -less, -some,* and *-ish,* but most have been lost. A few words were formed in Middle English employing *-dom,* as *dukedom; -hood,* as *manhood, womanhood, likelihood.* The suffix *-hood* has completely died out along with *-ship,* as in *hardship.* The ending *-dom,* on the other hand, has recently been revived. Consider *fandom, filmdom, sportsdom,* and many others, not at all nonce-words. The self-explaining compounds, however, have not suffered the same fate as many words. We speak of a *gateleg table,* a *tablecloth,* a *gingersnap, sugar beet, sugar cane, sugar maple,* and a host of others.

Latin Words Borrowed in Middle English   The Latin influence actually increased with the inflow of French words and ideas. During the Middle English period words continued to be borrowed directly from Latin, some from the spoken language of the ecclesiastics and men of learning, but most from the written language. One of the important sources of Latin words which became everyday terms was Wycliffe's translation of the Bible. Many words relating to science, literature, theology, law, and medicine were introduced, the vast majority in the fourteenth and fifteenth centuries. A few may be mentioned: *allegory, legal, mechanical, nervous, prosody, pulpit, rosary, scripture, secular, testify, testimony, ulcer, zephyr.* Among the formative suffixes which became common and still are active are *-able, -al, -ent, -ible, -ive,* and *-ous.* In addition poets and writers of prose, chiefly in the fifteenth century, affected a style in which they consciously brought in unusual Latin words, known as "aureate terms."[23] Not a great number but a few of these also dropped into current use. Chaucer in the fourteenth century used some of these words which became common, such as *laureate* and *oriental.* As a result of the French and Latin borrowings, English became a richer language with innumerable synonyms. For instance, one finds *ask* (Old English), *inquire* (French), and *interrogate* (Latin); *bold* (Old English), *valiant* (French), and *consecrated* (Latin). English has profited greatly by this variety of vocabulary, which enables a person to use a simple, popular style or a more learned, elevated one as the occasion demands.

Flemish, Dutch, and Low German Borrowings in Middle English   Although there was a predominance of Latin and French borrowings in Middle English, one must not disregard the constant intercourse between England and the people of Holland, Flanders, and northern Germany, beginning in the time of William the Conqueror, who married a Flemish wife. During this period many persons from the Low Countries came to settle in England, principally in connection with the trade carried on with the Low Countries. Wool was exported from England to these areas; their expert weavers were urged to come to England and many did. Much travel also went on between these countries and England. As a result of the contacts and intercommunication a number of words were borrowed, among them *deck, dock, freighter, lighter, nap* (of cloth), *furlough, dollar, easel, etching*, and *landscape*. At times it is difficult to tell whether a word has been borrowed or is of native origin because of the similarity of these languages.

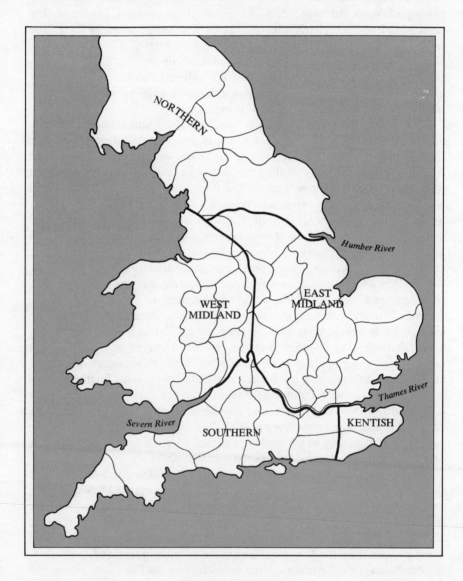

Middle English Dialects

Dialects in Middle English Roughly, Middle English is divided into four main dialects: the Northern, spoken north of the Humber River; the West Midland and the East Midland, used in the district between the Humber and the Thames; and the Southern, employed in the Kentish and West Saxon areas of Old English, the region south of the Thames along with Gloucestershire and portions of Hereford and Worcestershire Counties.[24] Kentish was a separate dialect of Southern English in the Middle English period.

Traits of the Dialects A few outstanding traits may be cited here to give an idea of the difference in dialects. In the third person plural the Old English vowel followed by *ð* leveled off to *eð*, retained in the Southern dialect. In the Northern dialect the *-eð* was changed to *-es* and in the Midlands to *-en*, probably taken .over by analogy to the corresponding forms of the preterite and the subjunctive or of the preterite-present verbs and the verb *to be*.[25] Thus we find, for example, in the South *serveth*, in the North *serves*, and in the Midlands *serven*. The present participle also had a separate form in each dialect before the ending *-ing* was adopted universally: *servinde* in the South, *servande* in the North, and *servende* in the Midlands. The Midlands and the South accepted the ending *-ing* before the North. As has been pointed out, the Scandinavian forms of the pronouns *they, their,* and *them* were current in the North while the South still used *hi, here* (*hire*), *hem*. There were likewise differences in pronunciation. For instance, *f* and *s* in initial positions were often voiced in the South, giving *v* and *z*, as in Southern *vox, vals, vaste, verst, volk, vorð* for *fox, false, fast, first, folk, forth.* In Modern English one observes the dialectal distinction in *fox* and *vixen.* Another difference is the retaining of the Old English *a* in the North which developed into *o* in the South in such words as *stone* and *home.* Scotland still has *stane* and *hame.* Often too where there was *ch* in the South, the North had *k* as in *kirk* for *church.* With the introduction of printing at the end of the Middle English period these differences were more readily wiped out and certain forms were adopted as standard.[26]

Standard English Near the close of the fourteenth century a written language developed which was accepted generally in the fifteenth century and became the standard speech. This speech developed in the East Midland district, the most highly populated area, the seat of the capital, London, the metropolitan center of England, important politically, commercially, socially, and intellectually. Into London came the various dialects, finally mingling and merging with the local dialect there to form a standard speech. The Midland dialect, not so conservative as the Southern and not so far advanced as the Northern, held a middle course between the two and developed into the speech which Chaucer used and which was to become the parent of the English we speak today.

NOTES

1. Middle English was, undoubtedly, being spoken much earlier. See Kemp Malone, "When Did Middle English Begin?" *Curme Volume of Linguistic Studies, Language Monograph No. 7* (Baltimore, Waverly Press, 1930), pp. 110–117.

2. "Quasi homo idiota, qui linguam Gallicanum non noverat . . . " Matthias Paris, ad ann., quoted by Jean Roemer, *Origins of the English People and of the English Language* (London, Kegan Paul, Trench & Co., 1888), p. 296.

3. Thomas Warton, *History of English Poetry* (London, Thomas Tegg, 1824), Vol. I.

4. Thomas B. Macaulay, *History of England,* Vol. I, p. 12, in *The Works of Lord Macaulay,* edited by his sister, Lady Trevelyan (London, Longmans, Green and Co., 1871).

5. *Ibid.*

6. *Ibid.,* p. 13.

7. R. R. Sharpe, *Calendar of Letter-Books . . . of the City of London,* Letter-Book G (London, 1905), p. 73.

8. The crossbar, used in the passage, is found in manuscripts and early printed books as a punctuation mark standing for either a period or a comma.

9. C. C. Fries, "On the Development of the Structural Use of Word-Order in Modern English," *Language* (Vol. XVI, 1940), pp. 199–208, shows statistically that the change was complete by 1500.

10. See Samuel Moore, "Grammatical and Natural Gender in Middle English," *Publications of the Modern Language Association* (Vol. 36, March, 1921), pp. 79–103.

11. Discussed on pages 69–70.

12. For the chronology of the changes, see Samuel Moore's two articles: "Loss of Final *n* in Inflectional Syllables of Middle English," *Language* (Vol. III, 1927), pp. 232–259; "Earliest Morphological Changes in Middle English," *Language* (Vol. IV, 1928), pp. 238–266.

13. Compare Old English endings on page 118.

14. Compare Old English declensions on page 118.

15. Letters in parentheses were sometimes used, but not always.

16. Compare with declension in Old English on page 119.

17. Charles C. Fries, *American English Grammar* (New York, D. Appleton-Century Company, for *The National Council of Teachers of English,* 1940), pp. 60–61.

18. See conjugation of Old English verb on pages 120–121.

19. See David W. Reed, *The History of Inflectional "n" in English Verbs Before 1500 (University of California Publications in English,* Vol. 7, No. 4), Berkeley and Los Angeles, University of California Press, 1950.

20. The principal parts in Old English are: *rīdan, rād, ridon, riden.*

21. The principal parts in Old English are: *bītan, bāt, biton, biten.*

22. See Hereward T. Price, "Foreign Influences on Middle English," *University of Michigan Contributions in Modern Philology,* No. 10 (Ann Arbor, April, 1947).

23. G. H. McKnight, *Modern English in the Making* (New York, D. Appleton and Company, 1930), pp. 38–55. See also the standard treatment of the subject by John C. Mendenhall, *Aureate Terms* (Lancaster, Pa., Wickersham Printing Company, 1919).

24. See Samuel Moore, Sanford B. Meech, and Harold Whitehall, "Middle English Dialect Characteristics and Dialect Boundaries," *Essays in Studies in*

English and Comparative Literature (Ann Arbor, University of Michigan Press, 1935), pp. 1–60; also Mary S. Serjeanston, "The Dialects of the West Midlands in Middle English," I, II, III, *Review of English Studies* (Vol. III, January, April, July, 1927), pp. 54–68, 186–204, 319–332.

25. W. F. Bryan, "The Midland Present Plural Indicative Ending *-e(n)*," *Modern Philology* (Vol. XVIII, January, 1921), pp. 457–473. See also Gösta Forsström, *The Verb "to be" in Middle English (Lund Studies in English)*, Vol. 15, Lund, C. W. K. Gleerup, 1948 (an exhaustive survey of the forms of the verb *be* in some ninety-four Middle English texts representative of the major chronological and dialect areas in England from c. 1150 to c. 1450).

26. McKnight, *op. cit.,* pp. 56–59.

✠ ✠ ✠

IVANHOE

WALTER SCOTT

CHAPTER I

> "Thus communed these; while to their lowly dome,
> The full-fed swine returned with evening home;
> Compell'd, reluctant, to the several sties,
> With din obstreperous, and ungrateful cries." *Pope's Odyssey.*

In that pleasant district of merry England which is watered by the river Don there extended in ancient times a large forest, covering the greater part of the beautiful hills and valleys which lie between Sheffield and the pleasant town of Doncaster. The remains of this extensive wood are still to be seen at the noble seats of Wentworth, of Wharncliffe Park, and around Rotherham. Here haunted of yore the fabulous Dragon of Wantley; here were fought many of the most desperate battles during the Civil Wars of the Roses; and here also flourished in ancient times those bands of gallant outlaws whose deeds have been rendered so popular in English song.

Such being our chief scene, the date of our story refers to a period toward the end of the reign of Richard I, when his return from his long captivity had become an event rather wished than hoped for by his despairing subjects, who were in the meantime subjected to every species of subordinate oppression. The nobles, whose power had become exorbitant during the reign of

Stephen, and whom the prudence of Henry the Second had scarce reduced into some degree of subjection to the crown, had now resumed their ancient license in its utmost extent; despising the feeble interference of the English Council of State, fortifying their castles, increasing the number of their dependents, reducing all around them to a state of vassalage, and striving, by every means in their power, to place themselves each at the head of such forces as might enable him to make a figure in the national convulsions which appeared to be impending.

The situation of the inferior gentry, or Franklins, as they were called, who by the law and spirit of the English constitution were entitled to hold themselves independent of feudal tyranny, became now unusually precarious. If, as was most generally the case, they placed themselves under the protection of any of the petty kings in their vicinity, accepted of feudal offices in his household, or bound themselves, by mutual treaties of alliance and protection to support him in his enterprises, they might indeed purchase temporary repose; but it must be with the sacrifice of that independence which was so dear to every English bosom, and at the certain hazard of being involved as a party in whatever rash expedition the ambition of their protector might lead him to undertake. On the other hand, such and so multiplied were the means of vexation and oppression possessed by the great Barons, that they never wanted the pretext, and seldom the will, to harass and pursue, even to the very edge of destruction, any of their less powerful neighbors who attempted to separate themselves from their authority, and to trust for their protection, during the dangers of the times, to their own inoffensive conduct, and to the laws of the land.

A circumstance which greatly tended to enhance the tyranny of the nobility, and the sufferings of the inferior classes, arose from the consequences of the Conquest by Duke William of Normandy. Four generations had not sufficed to blend the hostile blood of the Normans and Anglo-Saxons, or to unite, by common language and mutual interests, two hostile races, one of which still felt the elation of triumph, while the other groaned under all the consequences of defeat. The power had been completely placed in the hands of the Norman nobility by the event of the battle of Hastings, and it had been used, as our histories assure us, with no moderate hand. The whole race of Saxon princes and nobles had been extirpated or disinherited, with few or no exceptions; nor were the numbers great who possessed land in the country of their fathers, even as proprietors of the second, or of yet inferior classes. The royal policy had long been to weaken, by every means, legal or illegal, the strength of a part of the population which was justly considered as nourishing the most inveterate antipathy to their victor. All the monarchs of the Norman race had shown the most marked predilection for their Norman subjects; the laws of the chase, and many others equally unknown to the milder and more free spirit of the Saxon constitution, had been fixed upon the necks of the subjugated inhabitants, to add weight, as it were, to the feudal chains with which they were loaded. At court, and in the castles of the great nobles, where the pomp and state of court was emulated, Norman-French was the only language employed; in courts of law, the pleadings and judgments were delivered in the same tongue. In short, French was the language of honor, of chivalry, and even of justice, while the far more manly and expressive Anglo-Saxon was abandoned to the use of rustics and hinds, who knew no other. Still, however, the necessary intercourse between the lords of the soil, and those oppressed inferior beings by whom the soil was cultivated, occasioned the gradual formation of a dialect, compounded betwixt the French and the Anglo-Saxon, in which they could render themselves mutually intelligible to each other; and from this necessity arose by degrees the structure of our present English language, in which the speech of the victors and the vanquished have been so happily blended together; and which has since been so richly improved by importations from the classical languages, and from those spoken by the southern nations of Europe.

This state of things I have thought it necessary to premise for the information of the general reader, who might be apt to forget, that, although no great historical events, such as war or insurrection, mark the existence of the Anglo-Saxons as a separate people subsequent to the reign of William the Second; yet the great national distinctions between them and their conquerors, the recollection of what they had formerly been, and to what they were now reduced, continued, down to the reign of Edward the Third, to keep open the wounds which the Conquest had inflicted, and to maintain a line of separation between the descendants of the victor Normans and the vanquished Saxons.

The sun was setting upon one of the rich grassy glades of that forest which we have mentioned in the beginning of the chapter. Hundreds of broad-headed, short-stemmed, wide-branched oaks, which had witnessed, perhaps, the stately march of the Roman soldiery, flung their gnarled arms over a thick carpet of the most delicious greensward; in some places they were intermingled with beeches, hollies, and copsewood of various descriptions, so closely as totally to intercept the level beams of the sinking sun; in others they receded from each other, forming those long, sweeping vistas, in the intricacy of which the eye delights to lose itself, while imagination considers them as the paths to yet wilder scenes of sylvan solitude. Here the red rays of the sun shot a broken and discolored light that partially hung upon the shattered boughs and mossy trunks of the trees, and there they illuminated in brilliant patches the portions of turf to which they made their way. A considerable open space, in the midst of this glade, seemed formerly to have been dedicated to the rites of Druidical superstition; for, on the summit of a hillock, so regular as to seem artificial, there still remained part of a circle of rough unhewn stones, of large dimensions. Seven stood upright; the rest had been dislodged from their places, probably by the zeal of some convert to Christianity, and lay, some prostrate near their former site, and others on the side of the hill. One large stone only had found its way to the bottom, and in stopping the course of a small brook, which glided smoothly round the foot of the eminence, gave, by its opposition, a feeble voice of murmur to the placid and elsewhere silent streamlet.

The human figures which completed this landscape were in number two, partaking, in their dress and appearance, of that wild and rustic character which belonged to the woodlands of the West Riding of Yorkshire at that early period. The eldest of these men had a stern, savage and wild aspect. His garment was of the simplest form imaginable, being a close jacket with sleeves, composed of the tanned skin of some animal, on which the hair had been originally left, but which had been worn off in so many places, that it would have been difficult to distinguish, from the patches that remained, to what creature the fur had belonged. This primeval vestment reached from the throat to the knees, and served at once all the usual purposes of body-clothing; there was no wider opening at the collar than was necessary to admit the passage of the head, from which it may be inferred that it was put on by slipping it over the head and shoulders, in the manner of a modern shirt, or ancient hauberk. Sandals, bound with thongs made of boars' hide, protected the feet, and a roll of thin leather was twined artificially around the legs, and, ascending above the calf, left the knees bare, like those of a Scottish Highlander. To make the jacket sit yet more close to the body, it was gathered at the middle by a broad leathern belt, secured by a brass buckle; to one side of which was attached a sort of scrip, and to the other a ram's horn, accoutered with a mouth-piece, for the purpose of blowing. In the same belt was stuck one of those long, broad, sharp-pointed, and two-edged knives, with a buck's-horn handle, which were fabricated in the neighborhood, and bore even at this early period the name of Sheffield whittle. The man had no covering upon his head, which was only defended by his own thick hair, matted and twisted together, and scorched by the influence of the sun into a rusty dark-red color, forming a contrast with the overgrown beard upon his cheeks, which was rather of a yellow or amber hue. One part of his dress only remains, but it is too remarkable to be suppressed; it was a brass ring, resembling a dog's collar, but without any opening, and soldered fast around his neck, so loose as to form no impediment to his breathing, yet so tight as to be incapable of being removed, excepting by the use of the file. On this singular gorget was engraved, in Saxon characters, an inscription of the following purport: "Gurth, the son of Beowulph, is the born thrall of Cedric of Rotherwood."

Beside the swineherd, for such was Gurth's occupation, was seated, upon one of the fallen Druidical monuments, a person about ten years younger in appearance, and whose dress, though resembling his companion's in form, was of better materials, and of a more fantastic appearance. His jacket had been stained of a bright purple hue, upon which there had been some attempt to paint grotesque ornaments in different colors. To the jacket he added a short cloak, which scarcely reached half-way down his thigh; it was of crimson cloth, though a good deal soiled, lined with bright yellow; and as he could transfer it from one shoulder to the other, or at his pleasure draw it all around him, its width, contrasted with its want of longitude, formed a fantastic piece of drapery. He had thin silver bracelets upon his arms, and on his neck a collar of the same metal, bearing the inscription: "Wamba, the son of Witless, is the thrall of Cedric of Rotherwood." This personage had the same sort of sandals with his companion, but instead of the roll of leather thong, his legs were cased in a sort of gaiters, of which one was red and the other yellow. He was provided also with a cap, having around it more than one bell, about the size of those attached to hawks, which jingled as he turned his head to one side or other; and as he seldom remained a minute in the same posture, the sound might be considered as incessant. Around the edge of his cap was a stiff bandeau of leather, cut at the top into open work, resembling a coronet, while a prolonged bag arose from within it, and fell down on one shoulder like an old-fashioned nightcap, or a jelly-bag, or the headgear of a modern hussar. It was to this part of the cap that the bells were attached; which circumstance, as well as the shape of his head-dress, and his own half-crazed, half-cunning expression of countenance, sufficiently pointed him out as belonging to the race of domestic clowns or jesters, maintained in the houses of the wealthy, to help away the tedium of those lingering hours which they were obliged to spend within doors. He bore, like his companion, a scrip, attached to his belt, but had neither horn nor knife, being probably considered as belonging to a class whom it is esteemed dangerous to intrust with edge-tools. In place of these he was equipped with a sword of lath, resembling that with which Harlequin operates his wonders upon the modern stage.

The outward appearance of these two men formed scarce a stronger contrast than their look and demeanor. That of the serf, or bondsman, was sad and sullen; his aspect was bent on the ground with an appearance of deep dejection which might be almost construed into apathy had not the fire which occasionally sparkled in his red eye manifested that there slumbered, under the appearance of sullen despondency, a sense of oppression, and a disposition to resistance. The looks of Wamba, on the other hand, indicated, as usual with his class, a sort of vacant curiosity, and fidgety impatience of any posture of repose, together with the utmost self-satisfaction respecting his own situation, and the appearance which he made. The dialogue which they maintained between them was carried on in Anglo-Saxon, which, as we said before, was universally spoken by the inferior classes, excepting the Norman soldiers, and the immediate personal dependents of the great feudal nobles. But to give their conversation in the original would convey but little information to the modern reader, for whose benefit we beg to offer the following translation:

"The curse of St. Withold upon these infernal porkers!" said the swineherd, after blowing his horn obstreperously, to collect together the scattered herd of swine, which, answering his call with notes equally melodious, made, however, no haste to remove themselves from the luxurious banquet of beech-mast and acorns on which they had fattened, or to forsake the marshy banks of the rivulet, where several of them, half-plunged in mud, lay stretched at their ease, altogether regardless of the voice of their keeper. "The curse of St. Withold upon them and upon me!" said Gurth; "if the two-legged wolf snap not up some of them ere nightfall, I am no true man. Here, Fangs! Fangs!" he ejaculated at the top of his voice, to a ragged wolfish-looking dog, a sort of lurcher, half mastiff, half greyhound, which ran limping about as if with the purpose of seconding his master in collecting the refractory grunters; but which, in fact, from misapprehension of the swineherd's signals, ignorance of his own duty, or malice prepense, only drove them hither and thither, and increased the evil which he seemed to design to remedy. "A devil draw the teeth of him," said Gurth, "and the mother of mischief confound the Ranger of the Forest, that cuts the fore-claws off our dogs, and makes them unfit for their trade! Wamba, up and help me and thou be'st a man; take a turn round the back o' the hill to gain the wind on them; and when thou'st got the weather-gage, thou mayst drive them before thee as gently as so many innocent lambs."

"Truly," said Wamba, without stirring from the spot, "I have consulted my legs upon this matter, and they are altogether of opinion, that to carry my gay garment through these sloughs, would be an act of unfriendship to my sovereign person and royal wardrobe; wherefore, Gurth, I advise thee to call off Fangs, and leave the herd to their destiny, which, whether they meet with bands of traveling soldiers, or of outlaws, or of wandering pilgrims, can be little else than to be converted into Normans before morning, to thy no small ease and comfort."

"The swine turned Normans to my comfort!" quoth Gurth; "expound that to me, Wamba, for my brain is too dull, and my mind too vexed, to read riddles."

"Why, how call you those grunting brutes running about on their four legs?" demanded Wamba.

"Swine, fool, swine," said the herd; "every fool knows that."

"And swine is good Saxon," said the jester; "but how call you the sow when she is flayed, and drawn, and quartered, and hung up by the heels, like a traitor?"

"Pork," answered the swineherd.

"I am very glad every fool knows that too," said Wamba, "and pork, I think, is good Norman-French; and so when the brute lives, and is in the charge of a Saxon slave, she goes by her Saxon name; but becomes a Norman, and is called pork, when she is called to the Castle-hall to feast among the nobles; what dost thou think of this, friend Gurth, ha?"

"It is but too true doctrine, friend Wamba, however it got into thy fool's pate."

"Nay, I can tell you more," said Wamba, in the same tone; "there is old Alderman Ox continues to hold his Saxon epithet, while he is under the charge of serfs and bondsmen such as thou, but becomes Beef, a fiery French gallant, when he arrives before the worshipful jaws that are destined to consume him. Mynheer Calf, too, becomes Monsieur de Veau in the like manner; he is Saxon when he requires tendance, and takes a Norman name when he becomes matter of enjoyment."

"By St. Dunstan," answered Gurth, "thou speakest but sad truths; little is left to us but the air we breathe, and that appears to have been reserved with much hesitation, solely for the purpose of enabling us to endure the tasks they lay upon our shoulders. The finest and the fattest is for their board; the loveliest is for their couch; the best and bravest supply their foreign masters with soldiers, and whiten distant lands with their bones, leaving few here who have either will or the power to protect the unfortunate Saxon. God's blessing on our master Cedric, he hath done the work of a man in standing in the gap; but Reginald Front-de-Boeuf is coming down to this country in person, and we shall soon see how little Cedric's trouble will avail him. Here, here," he exclaimed again, raising his voice, "So ho! so ho! well done, Fangs! thou hast them all before thee now, and bring'st them on bravely, lad."

"Gurth," said the Jester, "I know thou thinkest me a fool, or thou wouldst not be so rash in putting thy head into my mouth. One word to Reginald Front-de-Boeuf, or Philip de Malvoisin, that thou hast spoken treason against the Norman—and thou art but a castaway swineherd—thou wouldst waver on one of these trees as a terror to all evil speakers against dignities."

"Dog, thou wouldst not betray me," said Gurth, "after having led me on to speak so much at disadvantage?"

"Betray thee!" answered the Jester; "no, that were the trick of a wise man; a fool cannot half so well help himself—but soft, whom have we here?" he said, listening to the tramping of several horses which became then audible.

"Never mind whom," answered Gurth, who had now got his herd before him, and, with the aid of Fangs, was driving them down one of the long dim vistas which we have endeavored to describe.

"Nay, but I must see the riders," answered Wamba; "perhaps they are come from Fairy-land with a message from King Oberon."

"A murrain take thee," rejoined the swineherd, "wilt thou talk of such things while a terrible storm of thunder and lightning is raging within a few miles of us? Hark, how the thunder rumbles! and for summer rain, I never saw such broad, downright flat drops fall out of the clouds; the oaks, too, notwithstanding the calm weather, sob and creak with their great boughs as if announcing a tempest. Thou canst play the rational if thou wilt; credit me for once, and let us home ere the storm begins to rage, for the night will be fearful."

Wamba seemed to feel the force of this appeal, and accompanied his companion, who began his journey, after catching up a long quarter-staff which lay upon the grass beside him. This second Eumæus strode hastily down the forest glade, driving before him, with the assistance of Fangs, the whole herd of his inharmonious charge.

CHAPTER XIV

"In rough magnificence array'd,
When ancient Chivalry display'd
The pomp of her heroic games,
And crested chiefs and tissued dames
Assembled, at the clarion's call,
In some proud castle's high arch'd hall."   *Warton.*

Prince John held his high festival in the Castle of Ashby. This was not the same building of which the stately ruins still interest the traveler, and which was erected at a later period by Lord Hastings, High Chamberlain of England, one of the first victims of the tyranny of Richard the Third, and yet better known as one of Shakespeare's characters than by his historical fame. The castle and town of Ashby, at this time, belonged to Roger de Quincy, Earl of Winchester, who, during the period of our history, was absent in the Holy Land. Prince John, in the meanwhile, occupied his castle, and disposed of his domains without scruple; and seeking at present to dazzle men's eyes by his hospitality and magnificence, had given orders for great preparations, in order to render the banquet as splendid as possible.

The purveyors of the Prince, who exercised on this and other occasions the full authority of royalty, had swept the country of all that could be collected which was esteemed fit for their master's table. Guests also were invited in great numbers; and in the necessity in which he then found himself of courting popularity, Prince John had extended his invitation to a few distinguished Saxon and Danish families, as well as to the Norman nobility and gentry of the neighborhood. However despised and degraded on ordinary occasions, the great number of the Anglo-Saxons must necessarily render them formidable in the civil commotions which seemed approaching, and it was an obvious point of policy to secure popularity with their leaders.

It was accordingly the Prince's intention, which he for some time maintained, to treat these unwonted guests with a courtesy to which they had been little accustomed. But although no man with less scruple made his ordinary habits and feelings bend to his interest, it was the misfortune of this Prince, that his levity and petulance were perpetually breaking out, and undoing all that had been gained by his previous dissimulation.

Of this fickle temper he gave a memorable example in Ireland, when sent thither by his father, Henry the Second, with the purpose of buying golden opinions of the inhabitants of that new and important acquisition to the English crown. Upon this occasion the Irish chieftains contended which should first offer to the young Prince their loyal homage and the kiss of peace.

But, instead of receiving their salutations with courtesy, John and his petulant attendants could not resist the temptation of pulling the long beards of the Irish chieftains; a conduct which, as might have been expected, was highly resented by these insulted dignitaries and produced fatal consequences to the English denomination in Ireland. It is necessary to keep these inconsistencies of John's character in view that the reader may understand his conduct during the present evening.

In execution of the resolution which he had formed during his cooler moments, Prince John received Cedric and Athelstane with distinguished courtesy, and expressed his disappointment, without resentment, when the indisposition of Rowena was alleged by the former as a reason for her not attending upon his gracious summons. Cedric and Athelstane were both dressed in the ancient Saxon garb, which, although not unhandsome in itself, and in the present instance composed of costly materials, was so remote in shape and appearance from that of the other guests that Prince John took great credit to himself with Waldemar Fitzurse for refraining from laughter at a sight which the fashion of the day rendered ridiculous. Yet, in the eye of sober judgment, the short close tunic and long mantle of the Saxons was a more graceful, as well as a more convenient dress, than the garb of the Normans, whose under garment was a long doublet, so loose as to resemble a shirt or waggoner's frock, covered by a cloak of scanty dimensions, neither fit to defend the wearer from cold or from rain, and the only purpose of which appeared to be to display as much fur, embroidery and jewelry work, as the ingenuity of the tailor could contrive to lay upon it. The Emperor Charlemagne, in whose reign they were first introduced, seems to have been very sensible of the inconveniences arising from the fashion of this garment. "In Heaven's name," said he, "to what purpose serve these abridged cloaks? If we are in bed they are no cover, on horseback they are no protection from the wind and rain, and when seated, they do not guard our legs from the damp or frost."

Nevertheless, spite of this imperial objurgation, the short cloaks continued in fashion down to the time of which we treat, and particularly among the princes of the House of Anjou. They were, therefore, in universal use among Prince John's courtiers; and the long mantle, which formed the upper garment of the Saxons, was held in proportional derision.

The guests were seated at a table which groaned under the quantity of good cheer. The numerous cooks who attended on the Prince's progress, having exerted all their art in varying the forms in which the ordinary provisions were served up, had succeeded almost as well as the modern professors of the culinary art in rendering them perfectly unlike their natural appearance. Besides these dishes of domestic origin, there were various delicacies brought from foreign parts, and a quantity of rich pastry, as well as of the simnel bread and wastel cakes, which were only used at the tables of the highest nobility. The banquet was crowned with the richest wines, both foreign and domestic.

But though luxurious, the Norman nobles were not, generally speaking, an intemperate race. While indulging themselves in the pleasures of the table, they aimed at delicacy, but avoided excess, and were apt to attribute gluttony and drunkenness to the vanquished Saxons, as vices peculiar to their inferior station. Prince John, indeed, and those who courted his pleasure by imitating his foibles, were apt to indulge to excess in the pleasures of the trencher and the goblet; and indeed it is well known that his death was occasioned by a surfeit upon peaches and new ale. His conduct, however, was an exception to the general manners of his countrymen.

With sly gravity, interrupted only by private signs to each other, the Norman knights and nobles beheld the ruder demeanor of Athelstane and Cedric at a banquet to the form and fashion of which they were unaccustomed. And while their manners were thus the subject of sarcastic observation, the untaught Saxons unwittingly transgressed several of the arbitrary rules established for the regulation of society. Now, it is well known, that a man may with more impunity be guilty of an actual breach either of real good breeding or of good morals, than appear ignorant of the most minute point of fashionable etiquette. Thus, Cedric, who dried his hands with a towel, instead of suffering the moisture to exhale by waving them gracefully in the air, incurred more ridicule than his companion Athelstane when he swallowed to his own single share the whole of a large pasty, composed of the most exquisite foreign delicacies, and termed at that time a *Karum-pie*. When, however, it was discovered by a serious cross-examination, that the Thane of Coningsburgh (or Franklin, as the Normans termed him) had no idea what he had been devouring, and that he had taken the contents of the Karum-pie for larks and pigeons, whereas they were in fact beccaficoes and nightingales, his ignorance brought him in for an ample share of the ridicule which would have been more justly bestowed on his gluttony.

The long feast had at length its end; and while the goblet circulated freely, men talked of the feats of the preceding tournament—of the unknown victor in the archery games—of the Black Knight, whose self-denial had induced him to withdraw from the honors he had won—and of the gallant Ivanhoe, who had so dearly bought the honors of the day. The topics were treated with military frankness, and the jest and laugh went round the hall. The brow of Prince John alone was overclouded during these discussions; some overpowering care seemed agitating his mind, and it was only when he received occasional hints from his attendants that he seemed to take interest in what was passing around him. On such occasions he would start up, quaff a cup of wine, as if to raise his spirits, and then mingle in the conversation by some observation made abruptly or at random.

"We drink this beaker," said he, "to the health of Wilfred of Ivanhoe, champion of this Passage of Arms, and grieve that his wound renders him absent from our board. Let all fill to the pledge, and especially Cedric of Rotherwood, the worthy father of a son so promising."

"No, my lord," replied Cedric, standing up, and placing on the table his untasted cup, "I yield not the name of son to the disobedient youth, who at once despises my commands, and relinquishes the manners and customs of his fathers."

"'Tis impossible," cried Prince John, with well-feigned astonishment, "that so gallant a knight should be an unworthy or disobedient son!"

"Yet, my lord," answered Cedric, "so it is with this Wilfred. He left my homely dwelling to mingle with the gay nobility of your brother's court, where he learned to do those tricks of horsemanship which you prize so highly. He left it contrary to my wish and command; and in the days of Alfred that would have been termed disobedience—ay, and a crime severely punishable."

"Alas!" replied Prince John, with a deep sigh of affected sympathy, "since your son was a follower of my unhappy brother, it need not be inquired where or from whom he learned the lesson of filial disobedience."

Thus spake Prince John, wilfully forgetting that of all the sons of Henry the Second, though no one was free from the charge, he himself had been most distinguished for rebellion and ingratitude to his father.

"I think," said he, after a moment's pause, "that my brother proposed to confer upon his favorite the rich manor of Ivanhoe."

"He did endow him with it," answered Cedric, "nor is it my least quarrel with my son that he stooped to hold as a feudal vassal the very domains which his fathers possessed in free and independent right."

"We shall then have your willing sanction, good Cedric," said Prince John, "to confer this fief upon a person whose dignity will not be diminished by holding land of the British crown. Sir Reginald Front-de-Boeuf," he said, turning toward the Baron, "I trust you will so keep the goodly Barony of Ivanhoe that Sir Wilfred shall not incur his father's displeasure by again entering upon that fief."

"By St. Anthony!" answered the black-browed giant, "I will consent that your Highness shall hold me a Saxon, if either Cedric, or Wilfred, or the best that ever bore English blood, shall wrench from me the gift with which your Highness has faced me."

"Whoever shall call thee Saxon, Sir Baron," replied Cedric, offended at a mode of expression by which the Normans frequently expressed their habitual contempt of the English, "will do thee an honor as great as it is undeserved."

Front-de-Boeuf would have replied, but Prince John's petulance and levity got the start.

"Assuredly," said he, "my lords, the noble Cedric speaks truth; and his race may claim precedence over us as much in the length of their pedigrees as in the longitude of their cloaks."

"They go before us indeed in the field—as deer before dogs," said Malvoisin.

"And with good right may they go before us—forget not," said Prior Aymer, "the superior decency and decorum of their manners."

"Their singular abstemiousness and temperance," said De Bracy, forgetting the plan which promised him a Saxon bride.

"Together with the courage and conduct," said Brian de Bois Guilbert, "by which they distinguished themselves at Hastings and elsewhere."

While with smooth and smiling cheek, the courtiers, each in turn, followed their Prince's example, and aimed a shaft of ridicule at Cedric, the face of the Saxon became inflamed with passion, and he glanced his eyes fiercely from one to another, as if the quick succession of so many injuries had prevented his replying to them in turn; or, like a baited bull, who surrounded by his tormentors, is at a loss to choose from among them the immediate object of his revenge. At length he spoke, in a voice half-choked with passion; and addressing himself to Prince John, as the head and front of the offense which he had received, "Whatever," he said, "have been the follies and vices of our race, a Saxon would have been held *nidering* (the most emphatic term for abject worthlessness), who should, in his own hall, and while his own wine-cup passed, have treated, or suffered to be treated, an unoffending guest, as your Highness has this day beheld me used; and whatever was the misfortune of our fathers on the field of Hastings, those may at least be silent," here he looked at Front-de-Boeuf and the Templar, "who have within these few hours once and again lost saddle and stirrup before the lance of a Saxon."

"By my faith, a biting jest!" said Prince John. "How like you it, sirs? Our Saxon subjects rise in spirit and courage; become shrewd in wit, and bold in bearing, in these unsettled times—What say ye, my lords? By this good light, I hold it best to take our galleys, and return to Normandy in time."

"For fear of the Saxons!" said De Bracy, laughing; "We should need no weapons but our hunting spears to bring these boars to bay."

"A truce with your raillery, Sir Knights," said Fitzurse—"and it were well," he added, addressing the Prince, "that your Highness should assure the worthy Cedric there is no insult intended him by jests which must sound but harshly in the ear of a stranger."

"Insult!" answered Prince John, resuming his courtesy of demeanor; "I trust it will not be thought that I could mean, or permit any to be offered in my presence. Here! I fill my cup to Cedric himself, since he refuses to pledge his son's health."

The cup went round amid the well-dissembled applause of the courtiers, which, however, failed to make the impression on the mind of the Saxon that had been designed. He was not naturally acute of perception, but those too much undervalued his understanding who deemed that this flattering compliment would obliterate the sense of the prior insult. He was silent, however, when the royal pledge again passed round. "To Sir Athelstane of Coningsburgh."

The knight made his obeisance, and showed his sense of the honor by draining a huge goblet in answer to it.

"And now sirs," said Prince John, who began to be warmed with the wine which he had drank, "having done justice to our Saxon guests, we will pray of them some requital to our courtesy. Worthy Thane," he continued, addressing Cedric, "may we pray you to name to us some Norman whose mention may least sully your mouth, and to wash down with a goblet of wine all bitterness which the sound may leave behind it?"

Fitzurse arose while Prince John spoke, and gliding behind the seat of the Saxon, whispered to him not to omit the opportunity of putting an end to unkindness betwixt the two races, by naming Prince John. The Saxon replied not to this politic insinuation, but rising up, and filling his cup to the brim, he addressed Prince John in these words: "Your Highness has required that I should name a Norman deserving to be remembered at our banquet. This, perchance, is a hard task, since it calls on the slave to sing the praises of the master—upon the vanquished, while pressed by all the evils of conquest, to sing the praises of the conqueror. Yet I *will* name a Norman—the first in arms and in place—the best and the noblest of his race. And the lips that shall refuse to pledge me to his well-earned fame, I term false and dishonored, and will so maintain them with my life—I quaff this goblet to the health of Richard the Lion-hearted!"

Prince John, who had expected that his own name would have closed the Saxon's speech, started when that of his injured brother was so unexpectedly introduced. He raised mechanically the wine-cup to his lips, then instantly set it down to view the demeanor of the company at this unexpected proposal, which many of them felt it as unsafe to oppose as to comply with. Some of them, ancient and experienced courtiers, closely imitated the example of the Prince himself, raising the goblet to their lips, and again replacing it before them. There were many who, with a more generous feeling, exclaimed, "Long live King Richard! and may he be speedily restored to us!" And some few, among whom were Front-de-Boeuf and the Templar, in sullen disdain suffered their goblets to stand untasted before them. But no man ventured directly to gainsay a pledge filled to the health of the reigning monarch.

Having enjoyed his triumph for about a minute, Cedric said to his companion: "Up, noble Athelstane! we have remained here long enough, since we have requited the hospitable courtesy of Prince John's banquet. Those who wish to know further of our rude Saxon manners must henceforth seek us in the homes of our fathers, since we have seen enough of royal banquets, and enough of Norman courtesy."

So saying, he arose and left the banqueting room, followed by Athelstane, and by several other guests, who, partaking of the Saxon lineage, held themselves insulted by the sarcasms of Prince John and his courtiers.

"By the bones of St. Thomas," said Prince John, as they retreated, "the Saxon churls have borne off the best of the day, and have retreated with triumph."

"They are breaking up," said the Prince, in a whisper to Fitzurse; "their fears anticipate the event, and the coward Prior is the first to shrink from me."

"Fear not, my lord," said Waldemar; "I will shew him such reasons as shall induce him to join us when we hold our meeting at York. Sir Prior," he said, "I must speak with you in private before you mount your palfrey."

The other guests were now fast dispersing, with the exception of those immediately attached to Prince John's faction, and his retinue.

"This, then, is the result of your advice," said the Prince, turning an angry countenance upon Fitzurse; "that I should be bearded at my own board by a drunken Saxon churl, and that, on the mere sound of my brother's name, men should fall off from me as if I had the leprosy?"

"Have patience, sir," replied his counselor; "I might retort your accusation, and blame the inconsiderate levity which foiled my design, and misled your own better judgment. But this is no time for recrimination. De Bracy and I will instantly go among these shuffling cowards, and convince them they have gone too far to recede."

"It will be in vain," said Prince John, pacing the apartment with disordered steps, and expressing himself with an agitation to which the wine he had drank partly contributed. "It will be in vain; they have seen the handwriting on the wall; they have marked the paw of the lion in the sand; they have heard his approaching roar shake the wood; nothing will reanimate their courage."

"Would to God," said Fitzurse to De Bracy, "that aught could reanimate his own! His brother's very name is an ague to him. Unhappy are the counselors of a Prince who wants fortitude and perseverance alike in good and in evil!"

✠ ✠ ✠

THE ART OF GEOFFREY CHAUCER

JOHN LIVINGSTON LOWES

The range of Chaucer's reading is as extraordinary as the scope of his activities. He read in three languages besides English—French, Latin, and Italian. French he probably both knew and spoke from his childhood. Latin with little doubt he learned at school. It has hitherto been assumed that he picked up Italian in Italy, during his first visit in 1372–73. It is possible, though not yet proven, that he may have known it earlier. But in either case, the bulk of his known reading, until the great Italians swam into his ken, was French, with a good deal of Latin besides. And French he never abandoned, and Latin he read copiously to the end. The French and Italian works which he knew may best for our purpose be considered later. His wide and diversified reading of Latin, however, is both typical of his varied interests and important for its contributions, and I shall rapidly summarize it here.

Of the classics he knew in the original Ovid, especially the *Metamorphoses* (his 'owne book,' as he called it), and the *Heroides*. Virgil he knew, but apparently only the *Aeneid*; the *Thebaid* of Statius; Claudian; and either in Latin or French or both, the *Pharsalia*. Cicero's *Somnium Scipionis* he read in a copy of the commentary of Macrobius which he or somebody else had thumbed to pieces—'myn olde book to-torn,' as he refers to it. Horace he quotes half a dozen times, but I doubt whether he knew either Horace or Juvenal at first hand. Dante, or John of Salisbury, or the *florilegia* may well have been intermediaries. But for Virgil, Statius, and Lucan, and also for Ovid, he had two strings to his bow. For the Middle Ages seized upon the Latin epics and made them over into their own likeness as romances. And so there was, for the *Aeneid*, the *Roman d'Eneas*, in which both Dido and (especially) Lavinia sigh, wake, and 'walwe,' like Chaucer's own Dido in the *Legend*, in the throes of heroic love. For the *Thebaid*, too, there was the *Roman de Thèbes*, and for the *Pharsalia* the *Roman de Julius Cesar*. And the Homeric story of the Trojan War passed by devious ways into the *Roman de Troie* of Benoit de St^e-Maure, and thence to Guido delle Colonne. The *Metamorphoses* were transmogrified into the interminable and portentous triple allegory of the *Ovide moralisé*, on which Machaut had freely drawn for his classical lore. They are all, as I can testify, diverting documents, after their fantastic fashion, even yet, and Chaucer, who probably in his salad days read French more readily than Latin, and who also would be apt to read what his fellow pages and squires at Court were reading, certainly knew and freely used the *Roman de Troie*, and drew, on occasion, upon the *Ovide moralisé*. He also read—I feel sure myself on grounds which have no place here—the *Roman d'Eneas* and the *Roman de Julius Cesar*. And there is evidence that he knew the mythographers, and was not unfamiliar with the mass of misinformation accumulated in the medieval commentaries on the classics. It was, in fact, more than once Servius or Lactantius or Junius Philargerius who either directly or indirectly first made for him his mistakes. For few things about Chaucer are more important to remember than the fact that even the classical authors whom he read in the original were deeply coloured in his mind through the various medieval metamorphoses which they had undergone.

His reading in the medieval Latin authors was far too extensive for enumeration here. But nothing in his dealings with them is more characteristic than his trick of suffusing with his own inalienable humour his borrowings from the dullest and most arid documents. He knew well both the *Anticlaudianus* and the *De Planctu Naturae* of Alanus de Insulis, and especially remembered, as he would, the concrete bits, and enriched them, as he also would, with an added liveliness. He read Martianus Capella on the Nuptials of Philology and Mercury, and Nigel Wireker's diverting Mirror of Fools, with the adventures of Dan Burnel the ass; and a scrap of the Eclogue of Theodulus once leaped back to his memory, endowed with an exquisite humour which he did not find in his original. He knew, as a student of his art who did not 'pipe but as the linnets sing,' the *Nova Poetria* of Geoffrey of Vinsauf, whom he calls his 'dere mayster soverayn,' and he made irresistible mock-heroic use, in the Nun's Priest's Tale, of one of his master's *exempla*. He at least dipped into the vast encyclopedic reaches of Vincent of Beauvais, and he read with obvious gusto and astounding results Saint Jerome's tractate against Jovinian on the subject of virginity. He was thoroughly familiar (to shift the key) with the Vulgate, and with the service and especially the great hymns of the Church, which inspired—in each case interwoven with lines from the crowning vision of the *Paradiso*—at least two of his loftiest passages. Whether he saw as he read the rich potentialities of his documents, or whether his stores came pouring back to memory as he composed, or whether both processes went on together, we can never know. But if anyone ever read (in the current phrase) 'creatively,' it was he.

And to all this evidence of abounding vitality and energy must be added the almost incredible list of his translations. The refrain of the *Balade* which Eustache Deschamps addressed to Chaucer and sent by the hand of Sir Lewis Clifford, is the line: 'Grant translateur, noble Geffroy Chaucier.' It was as a translator only, it would seem, that his fame had reached Deschamps. And the *Balade* itself makes it clear that Deschamps had in mind that translation of the *Roman de la Rose* which, in the Prologue to the *Legend*, gave such offence to the God of Love. And the God of Love's anger makes it further clear that Jean de Meun's huge continuation was included. As if this great task were not enough, he translated Jean de Meun's French version of Albertano of Brescia's *Liber Consolationis*, and also (for his tastes were richly catholic) the fierce misanthropy of Pope Innocent's *De Contemptu Mundi*, at which gloomy treatise Deschamps too had tried his hand. And there were besides the now lost translations of a work of Origen on Mary Magdalene, and of Machaut's *Dit dou Lyon*. But above all the rest stands Boethius' *On the Consolation of Philosophy*. He translated it, as Alfred the Great and Jean de Meun had done before him, and with the aid of Jean de Meun's French version, and he drew upon it, as in another fashion he levied tribute on the *Roman de la Rose*, until he ceased to write.

His reading in the science of his day is in some respects, I am inclined to think, the most remarkable of all. His singularly broad yet minute knowledge of medieval medicine, in which he anticipated Burton, I have elsewhere had occasion to discuss. But far more than his acquaintance with 'the loveres maladye of Hereos' is in point. Fourteenth-century medicine, like its twentieth-century descendant, was half psychology, and in its emphasis on dreams as a means of diagnosis anticipated Freud. And Madame Pertelote's diagnosis, by means of his dream, of Chauntecleer's malady, as well as her inimitable discourse on dreams as symptoms, is scientifically accurate. So is her *materia medica*. The herbs which she prescribes—'Pekke hem up right as they growe, and ete hem in'—are the medically proper herbs. And the quintessential touch is her inclusion in Chauntecleer's dietary of 'wormes' for 'a day or two.' For worms—you may read a learned and matter-of-fact chapter on *Vermes terrenae* in the *Medica Materia* of Dioscorides—were among the recognized correctives. It is easy enough to slip into one's narrative as evidence of erudition an excerpt from some learned document. But such casual exactness, imbued with delicious humour to boot, is not something which one gets up over night. In alchemy—witness the Canon's Yeoman's Tale—Chaucer was no less deeply grounded than in medicine. He had read enough in the alchemical treatises of Arnoldus de Villanova, for example, his 'Arnold of the Newe Toun,' to ascribe to one of Arnold's treatises a highly picturesque and abstruse dictum which he quotes, when he had actually read it in another. As for physics, one of the very best pieces of exposition, as exposition, which I know in English is the erudite Eagle's discourse in the House of Fame on the transmission of sound, and that again is founded on accepted authority. So is Chaucer's astrology, and in astronomy proper he could point with just pride to that Treatise on the Astrolabe which he wrote, with its charming Preface, for his 'litel son Lowis,' using freely a Latin translation of the Arabian astronomer Messahala. These are the barest shreds and patches only. The scope and thoroughness of Chaucer's scientific reading would still be remarkable, had he read nothing else.

There, then, are the raw materials of his art—men and their doings, and books—God's plenty of each, in all conscience. And since he began with books (with which, to be sure, he never ended) it is much to the point to consider how he read. Did he have the books on our list, for example, in his own possession, and therefore ready at hand for pleasure or need?

Without question a large, perhaps a very large proportion of them were his own. He declared, fairly late in his life—or rather, the God of Love asserted for him—that he had in his chest 'sixty bokes, olde and newe,' and there is no reason to doubt the statement. But that number may easily have represented three or four times sixty 'books,' in the sense in which we use the word. For book, as Chaucer employs the term, must be thought of in the light of medieval manuscripts, and a single manuscript was often a small library in itself. The 'boke' which Chaucer was reading when he fell asleep over the tale of Ceyx and Alcyone was an omnium gatherum of verse, and lives of queens and kings, and 'many othere thinges smale.' The 'book' (and again the word is the same) which the Wife of Bath's fifth husband revelled in contained, she declared, Valerius *ad Rufinum*, Theophrastus, Jerome against Jovinian, Tertullian, the mysterious Crisippus, Trotula, the Epistles of Eloise, the Parables of Solomon, and the *Ars Amatoria*—'And alle thise were bounden in o volume.' And one need only recall, among extant examples, the Auchinleck MS., with its more than forty separate pieces, or, for that matter, Harley 7333 among the manuscripts of the Canterbury Tales. Chaucer's library was a rich one for his day, and like his own clerk of Oxford who had 'at his beddes heed' his 'Twenty bokes, clad in blak or reed,' and like that clerk of another kidney, 'hende Nicholas,' who likewise kept in his lodgings 'his Almageste, and bokes grete and smale . . . On shelves couched at his beddes heed,' one may be fairly sure that Chaucer's sixty books were not far from his hand.

But is there any way of knowing, aside from these more or less material considerations, how he actually read? There are two subjects, and two only, on which Chaucer vouchsafes us personal information about himself—his love of books, and his imperviousness, real or assumed, to love. On those two topics he is, in William Wordsworth's phrase but with a difference, 'right voluble.' And two passages are especially in point. In one, that preternaturally intelligent bird, the Eagle of the House of Fame, gently chides him for his habits. He knows nothing now, says the Eagle, of what is going on about him; even 'of thy verray neyghebores That dwellen almost at thy dores, Thou herest neither that ne this.' And then follows, under cover of the Eagle's irresponsible loquacity, the most precious autobiographical touch that Chaucer left:

> For whan thy labour doon al is,
> And hast y-maad thy rekeninges,
> In stede of reste and newe thinges,
> Thou gost hoom to thy hous anoon;
> And, also domb as any stoon,
> Thou sittest at another boke,
> Til fully daswed is thy loke,
> And livest thus as an hermyte,
> Although thyn abstinence is lyte.

That picture—the account books of the customs exchanged after hours for vastly different books (the Eagle's 'another' is pregnant), and Chaucer reading on, oblivious of all else, until his eyes dazzle in his head—that picture tells more than pages, not merely of the intimate relation in which his books stood to his business, but also of the absorbed intentness with which he read. And there is another passage which illuminates yet another quality of his reading. 'Not yore agon,' he writes in the Parlement of Foules,

> . . . hit happed me for to beholde
> Upon a boke, was write with lettres olde;
> And ther-upon, *a certeyn thing to lerne,*
> The longe day *ful faste I radde and yerne.*

I do not know which is the more characteristic of Chaucer—the fact that he was reading with the definite purpose of learning a certain thing, or the fact that he was reading fast and eagerly. The two belong together. You cannot divide his invincible zest from his incorrigibly inquiring spirit—that 'besy gost' of his, as he called it once, 'that thrusteth alwey newe.' And because he brought both to his books, his reading became a live and plastic thing for his art to seize on.

He was gifted, finally, with another quality of mind which is peculiarly bound up with his art. He possessed, in a word, like Virgil and Milton and Coleridge, a powerfully associative memory, which played, as he read, over the multitude of impressions from previous reading, with which his mind was stored. And the zest with which he read gave freshness to his recollections, and one can sometimes almost see the hovering associations precipitate themselves as he reads. A single phrase in Boccaccio (and I am speaking by the book) calls up the lines of a famous passage in Dante in which the same phrase occurs, and the result is a *tertium quid* of his own, enriched from the spoils of both. He finds in Boccaccio's *Filostrato*, as he works it over into his own Troilus, the lovely Virgilian simile of the lily cut by the plough and withering. But Dante, in a canto of the *Inferno*, the opening lines of which Chaucer elsewhere quotes, has a simile of falling, withering leaves. And again, through a common element, Boccaccio's lines recall the lines of Dante, and the falling leaves replace the fading lily in Chaucer's simile. And Boccaccio and Dante in turn had each in like fashion recalled his simile from Virgil. It would be easy to rehearse such instances by the score—instances, too, in which with his reminiscences of books are interwoven his recollections of experience. For that continuity of poetry of which I spoke consists in the perpetual enrichment, through just such incremental transformations, of the present through the past. And one of the happiest gifts of the gods to English poetry, at the strategic moment of its history, was that prehensile, amalgamating memory of Chaucer's which had for its playground the prodigious array of promiscuous writings which a moment ago I ruthlessly catalogued.

What now of his art in its larger relations? For everything that I have so far said has been said with that definitely in view. It is perilous, in the first place, to divide Chaucer's poetic biography mechanically into periods. There was nothing cataclysmic about his development. He was not a new creature, as Professor Kittredge once observed, when he came back to London from his first visit to Italy, nor does the poet of the Canterbury Tales startle us by a 'leap of buds into ripe flowers.' Rather—if I too may yield to an association—'Morn into noon did pass, noon into eve.' Transitions there were, of course, but they were gradual. French poetry yielded first place to Italian, and both to an absorption in human life, in which books and men were fused as in a crucible. But even after his momentous discovery of Boccaccio and Dante, the influence of French poetry went on, though its character changed—changed (to put it briefly) from the mood of Guillaume de Lorris and Machaut to the mood of Jean de Meun and Deschamps and the *fabliaux*. And *pari passu*, as his powers developed, there came a significant shift of values, and his reading of books played a lesser and his reading of life a larger rôle in his art. But throughout his career, that art kept curiously even pace with his active life. It was dominantly French while he was in personal attendance on a court where French was still the more familiar language. His so-called Italian period, which was never Italian in the sense in which the earlier period had been French, coincided roughly with those activities—his missions and the customs—which brought him into various relations with Italy, Italians, and Italian letters. And when his broadening affairs afforded wider opportunities for observation, his art, keeping all that it had won from France and Italy, became at once English and universal.

Everybody knows that Chaucer began as a follower of the contemporary French school of poetry, and that the most powerful influence upon that school was the thirteenth-century *Roman de la Rose*. But the *Roman de la Rose* was influential in two entirely different ways. Guillaume de Lorris, who began it, was a dreamer of dreams and a poet of exquisite grace and charm. Jean de Meun, who continued it and multiplied its length by five, was a caustic and disillusioned satirist, trenchant, arrogant, and absolute master of a mordant pen. If Pope had taken it into his head to complete the *Faerie Queene*, or if Swift had been seized by the fancy of carrying on the *Rape of the Lock* in the mood of Gulliver's fierce misanthropy, we might have had an adequate parallel. And the fourteenth-century French poets, as a consequence of this strange duplex authorship, fall roughly into two schools—the sons of Guillaume de Lorris and the sons of Jean de Meun. But common to them all, and giving the framework to half their verse, was the allegorical love vision.

The contemporary Frenchmen whose influence on Chaucer was farthest reaching were three: Guillaume de Machaut, an elder contemporary; Jean Froissart, his coeval; and Eustache Deschamps, who was younger. Machaut, who like Chaucer was courtier and man of affairs as well as poet, and who with his master, John of Bohemia, had 'reysed,' like the Knight, against the 'mescreans' in Prussia and the Tartars in the snows of Lithuania, was the most influential French poet of his day. And he was so chiefly by virtue of a highly sophisticated, artificial, exquisitely elaborated technique. Froissart, whom Chaucer probably knew at Court as the protégé of Queen Philippa, was an incomparably less finished craftsman than Machaut, to whose school he belongs. When he tells a story, like that in the *Dit dou Florin*, of his reading aloud to Gaston Phebus, Count of Foix, night after night for weeks, his interminable *Méliador*, the tale becomes, through the art of the chronicler, vivid with firelight and candles and flagons; and when he writes of his boyhood and young manhood—of the games that he played, and of the maiden whom he one day found reading the *Cléomadès*—his verse is suffused with personal charm. But when he falls into the vein of the school, he can be both long-winded and very dull. And finally Deschamps, who calls Machaut his master, but who was really of the tribe of Jean de Meun, was an inordinately prolific versifier, with the skill of a virtuoso, but without music, grace, or charm; could be as minutely circumstantial as Mistress Quickly over her silver-gilt goblet; and was possessed by a passion like that of Pepys for autobiographical memoranda. Of the three, Machaut was Chaucer's earliest master; from Froissart he effectively borrowed more than once; and Deschamps twice furnished him with subject matter to which, on the two occasions, each time with a technique already mastered, he gave consummate form. There were others, of course, but these three were the chief influences during the period when Chaucer was saturated with the later French poetry of courtly love, even while maintaining an amiable impermeability all his own to its inherent absurdities. And I am far from sure that it was not to these very absurdities that Chaucer's genius owed the turn which from the first it took.

For he found in his French models, and especially in Machaut, the framework of the vision, as that had come down, with growing elaboration on the way, from Guillaume de Lorris. And he used the machinery of the vision in the Book of the Duchess, the House of Fame, the Parliament of Fowls, and in the first version of the Prologue to the Legend of Good Women. It was the most popular and, in Machaut's expert hands, the most sophisticated device of his day, and Chaucer was then writing for a sophisticated audience. But the visions were allegorical love visions, and as such they were thick sown with artifices at which Chaucer balked. And the more thoroughly one is steeped in Chaucer, so that one sees in a measure with his eyes, the more readily one understands the impossibility of his acquiescence in the then current artificialities of the *genre*. The framework of the vision, to be sure, offered freedom in both choice and disposition of subject matter. But it was precisely in the character of the French subject matter, to judge from the cold shoulder which Chaucer turned to it, that one source of his disrelish lay. For it was obviously as barren of interest to Geoffrey Chaucer as interminable subtilizings about love—especially when nothing comes of them— have been and are to any normally constituted Anglo-Saxon. Moreover, the visions are thickly peopled with personified abstractions. Esperance, Attemprance, Mesure, Douce Pensée, Plaisance, Desirs, Franchise, Pité, Loyauté, Espoirs, Raison, Suffisance, Patience, Paour—those are the denizens of less than half of Machaut's *Remede de Fortune*. Like Criseyde listening under trying circumstances to the 'wommanisshe thinges' of her feminine callers, Chaucer must have 'felte almost [his] herte dye For wo, and wery of that companye.' Nor was it subject matter alone which he found alien. The phraseology, too, was remote alike from his tastes and his aptitudes. There is nothing I know which rivals in its tireless facility of recurrence the later vocabulary of courtly love. If one read long enough, one is obsessed by the uncanny feeling that the phraseology walks alone, without need of the poet's intervention, and carries the poet with it of its own momentum. Specific meaning disappears. Machaut's Peronne, in that amazing Goethe-and-Bettina correspondence, the *Voir-Dit*, is 'en douceur douce com coulombelle, En loyauté loyal com turturelle.' But the same columbine phrases slip from his pen, when, in *Prise d'Alexandrie*, he describes the Emperor Charles I of Luxembourg. He too, like Peronne, is 'humbles et piteus Plus que turtre ne colombele.' In that ineffably affected jargon discriminations vanish. 'Thought and affliction, passion, hell itself, [are turned] to favour and to prettiness.' And that was not Chaucer's way.

What he found, then, in the French vision poems, was a *frame*—a frame which possessed admirable potentialities, but which for him, to all intents and purposes, was empty. And Chaucer, who in his way was not unlike Nature herself, abhorred a vacuum. He proceeded, accordingly, to fill the frame, and incidentally to set one of the great traditions of English poetry. And into the vision framework, instead of consecrated phrases, wire-drawn subtleties, *ragionamente d'amore*, and the more fantastic elements of the courtly code, he poured the stores of that reading and observation on which we have dwelt so long. 'For out of olde feldes'— and this was his discovery, as 'the longe day ful faste [he] radde and yerne'—

> For out of olde feldes, as man seith,
> Cometh al this newe corn fro yeer to yere;
> And out of olde bokes, in good feith,
> Cometh al this newe science that men lere.

And into old bottles Chaucer poured with lavish hand a new and heady wine.

What happened may best be seen by a glance at his first three vision poems. His earliest essay, the Book of the Duchess, was made before he went to Italy, when his reading was almost wholly French, and when Machaut in particular was at his finger tips. It is a vision poem, with all the paraphernalia of the *genre*, and it is also an elegy—an elegy on the death of the Duchess Blanche, the first wife of his patron, John of Gaunt. But into the conventional frame he fits, with tact and feeling, and with considerable skill in adapting them to his ends, materials drawn from what was then his reading—to wit, in this instance, from no less than eight of Machaut's poems and one (at least) of Froissart's. Save for scattered reminiscences of the Bible, the *Roman de la Rose*, Boethius, and Benoit, there is little else. His instinct from the beginning was to enrich, and those were the stores which he then possessed. But his borrowings are interwoven with such art that for more than five hundred years nobody suspected that the poem was not all of a piece. And even when his appropriations are most unmistakable, they are still miraculously Chaucer and not Machaut. The little whelp that came creeping up, as if it knew him, to the Dreamer, and 'Hild doun his heed and joyned his eres, And leyde al smothe doun his heres'—that bewitching English puppy is Chaucer's metamorphosis of a fantastic lion, which Carpaccio would have revelled in, native to the bizarre landscape of the *Dit dou Lyon* of Machaut. And into his version of Machaut's catalogue of those remote regions to which the courtly lovers were dispatched to win their spurs, Chaucer has slipped that precious bit of hearsay about the Dry Sea and the Carrenar. The Book of the Duchess is not a masterpiece, but it is significant far beyond its intrinsic merit. For in it for the first time, with the still limited resources at his command, Chaucer loaded every rift with ore. And now the ore grew steadily richer.

For Chaucer went to Italy, and learned to read Boccaccio and Dante, and all the while that knowledge of books and men on which we have dwelt was broadening and deepening. The French influence waned as that of Italy waxed, but the shift of emphasis was gradual, and the vision poems still went on. And into the three that followed the Book of the Duchess poured those steadily growing stores. He begins the House of Fame—to follow what seems to me to be the true succession—a little dully, with a long résumé of the *Aeneid*, and an interlude from the *Metamorphoses*. And both the *Roman d'Eneas* and the *Ovide moralisé* were summoned, I feel certain, to his aid. Then all at once, into a desert recalled from Lucan sweeps an eagle which owed its sunlike brightness to the *Paradiso*, and the poem becomes vivid with new life. And the significant thing is not so much that the amazing eagle, throughout the flight through the air, shows himself equally at home in Ovid, and Boethius, and Theodulus, and Macrobius, and Dante's *Convito* and can even recognize Chaucer's unspoken thoughts of Martianus Capella and Alanus, as that he is a new and unique creation—as much a person as his creator, and utterly unthinkable in any vision which Machaut and his fellows ever dreamed. And only the keenest observer of men, endowed with the rarest humour, could have conceived the inimitable conversation which goes on, as the little earth recedes to a speck and the signs of the zodiac are left behind; and the poet of the Canterbury Tales is already present in that immortal dialogue. Then, into the third book, ushered in, like the second, by an invocation drawn from Dante, pours a phantasmagoria which Rabelais might have envied, and which defies all summary—reminiscences of books treading on the heels of recollections of experience, in bewildering profusion. Within the compass of thirty-five lines—to take a relatively simple passage only—Chaucer's memory, as the verse flows on without a ripple, has flashed to Boethius, and the *Roman de la Rose*, and a line from the *Metamorphoses*, and some account or other which he had read in the romances of those whirling houses which were a peculiarly captivating item in the romantic stock-in-trade, and Celtic wicker houses which he had either seen himself or heard of from his friends, and the noise of 'engynstones' remembered from his own campaign in France. Sketched as I am sketching it, the poem is a thing of shreds and patches. It is not so on the page. But I am putting asunder what Chaucer joined together, in order to give the barest inkling of the thronging recollections which, in his vision poems, his art curbed and concealed.

And now, in the Parlement of Foules, France slips gradually into the background and Italy assumes the major rôle. The cadre of the vision is still retained, but the familiar French couplet is discarded, and rime royal takes its place. In the last two books of the House of Fame Chaucer's crowding recollections are swept along as by a torrent; in the close-packed introductory sections of the Parlement there is a new serenity, and a sense of beauty which has been quickened and deepened alike. For the influence of Dante and Boccaccio upon Chaucer is to be sought not merely or even chiefly in his borrowings and imitations, but rather through the impregnation of his art with qualities which his earlier French masters never knew. And in the first half of the Parlement Chaucer's memory is busy with the Divine Comedy, and both his memory and his eyes with the *Teseide*. The Proem opens with a rendering, in a master's hand, of the first axiom of Hippocrates—

> The lyf so short, the craft so long to lerne,
> Th' assay so hard, so sharp the conquering.

It was a favourite with those elder medical authorities whom Chaucer read, and I suspect it came from them. Then, passing to the book which he had just been reading 'faste and yerne' all day long, he gives (I am sure for his own delight) a summary—compact and lucid and urbane—of the *Somnium Scipionis*. And night falls in the words with which Dante describes the first fall of evening in the *Inferno*. Then Chaucer's unrest before he sleeps recalls Boethius, and the thought of dreams brings back to mind the famous lines of Claudian, and because (as Chaucer shrewdly suggests) he has just been reading the dream of Scipio, Scipio himself becomes his guide. And the Proem ends with a flash of memory back to Jean de Meun.

Of the next one hundred lines or so, Boccaccio's *Teseide*, through a score of its most graphic and beautiful stanzas, has the lion's share. Twice at least, too, a phrase of Boccaccio recalls a passage of Dante, and the *Divina Commedia* and the *Teseide* flow together into a mould which is Chaucer's own. And *Inferno, Purgatorio*, and *Paradiso* are now all three at command. Then all at once the whole character of the vision changes. From the robe of the 'noble emperesse' Nature in Aleyn's 'Pleynt of Kinde,' Chaucer sweeps the birds of the air, which Alanus had depicted on it, adds others of his own, and sets them down before Nature, alive and gifted with the power of speech, in parliament assembled. And whatever, if any, the ulterior purpose of the poem, that assembly, with its unerring adjustment of sentiments and language to the ranks and classes of the fowls, was conceived and executed by a keen and detached observer of the foibles, not of worm-fowls, water-fowls and seed-fowls, but of his kind—even to such inter-changes of amenities as he had often heard along the Thames. And for the second time Chaucer's approach to human life has been through the medium of birds, as at the zenith of his powers he comes back to them again. For in that matchless trio of which the other members are Criseyde and the Wife of Bath, it is Madame Pertelote who makes the third.

The last, if not the greatest, of the visions poems, the Prologue to the Legend of Good Women, I must regretfully pass over, together with the Knight's Tale, which, like the Troilus and Criseyde, preceded it. It is Chaucer's dealings in the Troilus with the *Filostrato* to which I wish to come, for in the Troilus, never again to lose its ascendancy, life came, like a mighty river flowing in.

From Machaut and his French contemporaries Chaucer had taken over a form which for him was relatively empty of content. In Boccaccio and Dante he found for the first time among his moderns architectonic powers which in the case of Dante were supreme, and which Boccaccio in narrative exercised with a master's skill. Moreover, in Boccaccio, and superlatively in Dante, the greatness of the form was inseparable from the richness of the content, and that content was now no longer interminable lucubrations in a vacuum, but men and women, and their actions and their fates. And in the *Filostrato* he found a story richer in possibilities than any on which he had yet exercised his powers. Into none had so many strands been woven by ear-lier hands, from its far-off inception in the *Iliad*, down through a provocative catalogue of names in Dares, to three of which Benoit, through one of those inscrutable promptings of genius which set in motion incalculable trains of consequence, had attached a story of faithless love. And then Boccaccio, through his own *Filocolo*, poured into it the passion of his long eventful intrigue with Maria d'Aquino. And as the inevitable consequence, his Criseida and Troilo and Pandaro *live*, as his Palamon and Arcita and Emilia never do. In the *Filostrato* Chaucer at last had flesh and blood to deal with.

What the *Filostrato* did, accordingly, was to awaken as nothing else yet had done, his own creative powers. For the Troilus is a magnificently independent reworking of Boccaccio's narrative, bearing to its original, indeed, a relation not unlike that in which *King Lear*, for example, stands to the earlier play. For Chaucer had thought deeply through Boccaccio's story before he set pen to parchment for his own. Boccaccio's Criseida is a fair and fickle woman, conventional alike in her beauty and her faithlessness; Chaucer's Criseyde, in her baffling and complex femininity remains unrivalled, save in Shakespeare and one or two of the great novelists. And by a change as simple as it is consummate in its art, Chaucer opened the way for another transformation—the metamorphosis of a conventional young man-about-town into a masterpiece of characterization which he equalled only, if I may hazard my own opinion, in the Wife of Bath. For Boccaccio's Pandaro was Criseida's cousin; Chaucer's Pandarus is her uncle. And through that simple-seeming shift, not only is the irony of the situation deepened and the tragedy enhanced, but Pandarus also becomes what a younger man could never have been—the vehicle of Chaucer's own humour and urbanity and worldly wisdom, and of his inimitable raciness of speech. Somewhere, among his courtly friends in England or in Italy or both, he had come, one feels, to know the type to which he gave immortal individuality. It is in the Troilus, too, that one also feels, again for the first time, that detachment which is also the distinctive note of the greater Canterbury Tales—that wise and urbane detachment with which Chaucer came in the end to view the human comedy. And often when Pandare speaks, one is curiously aware of something in the background—like Meredith's Comic Spirit with its 'slim feasting smile'—which is playing the game with Pandare no less urbanely and ironically than he with Troilus and Criseyde. And those are but hints of what Chaucer's reading of life lent to his reading of Boccaccio.

Moreover, no sooner had he set out to write than his mind began to race beyond the text he was translating. In scores of stanzas, even in the first book, he will follow Boccaccio for three or four or five lines of his stanza, then go his own gate for the rest of it, as if his thought in its eagerness overleaped Boccaccio's. And often, before he returns to his text, he has carried on alone for three, four, or a score of stanzas. And when, in the great second and third books, he comes to the heart of the drama as he conceives it, he leaves Boccaccio almost wholly aside, and the great bulk of those two crucial books is Chaucer's own. And nowhere else, save in the plan of the Canterbury Tales, does he exercise such sovereign constructive powers. Life and his reading of the great Italians had made him master of his art.

✠ ✠ ✠

PROLOGUE TO HIS
TRANSLATION OF ENEYDOS (1490)

WILLIAM CAXTON

After dyuerse werkes made / translated and achieued / hauyng noo werke in
hande. I sittyng in my studye where as laye many dyuerse paunflettis and
bookys. happened that to my hande cam a lytyl booke in frenshe. which
late was translated oute of latyn by some noble clerke of fraunce whiche
booke is named Eneydos / made in latyn by that noble poete & grete clerke
vyrgle / whiche booke I sawe ouer and redde therin. How after the generall
destruccyon of the grete Troye. Eneas departed berynge his olde fader
anchises vpon his sholdres / his lityl son yolus on his honde. his wyfe wyth
moche other people folowynge / and how he shypped and departed wyth alle
thystorye of his aduentures that he had er he cam to the achieuement of his
conquest of ytalye as all a longe shall be shewed in this present boke. In
whiche booke I had grete playsyr. by cause of the fayr and honest termes &
wordes in frenshe / Whyche I neuer sawe to fore lyke. ne none so playsaunt
ne so wel ordred. whiche booke as me semed sholde be moche requysyte to
noble men to see as wel for the eloquence as the historyes / How wel that
many honderd yerys passed was the sayd booke of eneydos wyth other

Reprinted from *The Prologues and Epilogues of William Caxton,* edited by W. J. B. Crotch, by
permission of The Council of the Early English Text Society.

werkes made and lerned dayly in scolis specyally in ytalye & other places /
whiche historye the sayd vyrgyle made in metre / And whan I had aduysed me
in this sayd boke. I delybered and concluded to translate it in to englysshe
And forthwyth toke a penne & ynke and wrote a leef or tweyne / whyche I
ouersawe agayn to correcte it / And whan I sawe the fayr & straunge termes
therin / I doubted that it sholde not please some gentylmen which late blamed
me sayeng yᵗ in my translacyons I had ouer curyous termes whiche coude
not be vnderstande of comyn peple / and desired me to vse olde and homely
termes in my translacyons. and fayn wolde I satysfye euery many / and so
to doo toke an olde boke and redde therin / and certaynly the englysshe was
so rude and brood that I coude not wele vnderstande it. And also my lorde
abbot of westmynster ded do shewe to me late certayn euydences wryton in
olde englysshe for to reduce it in to our englysshe now vsid / And certaynly
it was wreton in suche wyse that it was more lyke to dutche than englysshe I
coude not reduce ne brynge it to be vnderstonden / And certaynly our langage
now vsed varyeth ferre from that. whiche was vsed and spoken whan I was
borne / For we englysshe men / ben borne vnder the domynacyon of the
mone. whiche in neuer stedfaste / but euer wauerynge / wexynge one season /
and waneth & dyscreaseth another season / And that comyn enyglsshe that is
spoken in one shyre varyeth from a nother. In so moche that in my dayes
happened that certayn marchauntes were in a shippe in tamyse for to haue
sayled ouer the see into selande / and for lacke of wynde thei taryed atte
forlond. and wente to lande for to refreshe them And one of theym named
sheffelde a mercer cam in to an hows and axed for mete. and specyally he
axed after eggys And the good wyf answerde. that she coude speke no
frenshe. And the marchaunt was angry. for he also coude speke no frenshe.
but wold haue hadde egges / and she vnderstode hym not / And thenne at
laste a nother sayd that he wolde haue eyren / then the good wyf sayd that she
vnderstod hym wel / Loo what sholde a man in thyse dayes now wryte. egges
or eyren / certaynly it is harde to playse euery man / by cause of dyuersite &
chaunge of langage. For in these dayes euery man that is in ony reputacyon
in his countre. wyll vtter his commynycacyon and maters in suche maners &
termes / that fewe men shall vnderstonde theym / And som honest and grete
clerkes haue ben wyth me and desired me to wryte the moste curyous termes
that I coude fynde / And thus beytwene playn rude / & curyous I stande
abasshed. but in my Iudgemente / the comyn termes that be dayli vsed ben
lyghter to be vnderstonde than the olde and auncyent englysshe / And for as
moche as this present booke is not for a rude vplondyssh man to laboure
therein / ne rede it / but onely for a clerke & a noble gentylman that feleth
and vnderstondeth in faytes of armes in loue & in noble chyualrye / Therfor
in a meane bytwene bothe I haue reduced & translated this sayd booke in to
our englysshe not ouer rude ne curyous but in suche termes as shall be
vnderstanden by goddys grace accordynge to my copye. And yf ony man
wyll entermete in redyng of hit and fyndeth suche termes that he can not
vnderstande late hym goo rede and lerne vyrgyll / or the pystles of ouyde /

and ther he shall see and vnderstonde lyghtly all / Yf he haue a good redar
& enformer / For this booke is not for euery rude and vnconnynge man to
see / but to clerkys and very gentylmen that vnderstande gentylnes and
scyence

Thenne I praye alle theym that shall rede in this lytyl treatys to holde me
for excused for the translatynge of hit. For I know-leche my selfe ignorant
of connynge to enpryse on me so hie and noble a werke / But I praye mayster
John Skelton late created poete laureate in the vnyuersite of oxenforde to
ouersee and correcte this sayd booke. And taddresse and expowne where as
shalle be founde faulte to theym that shall requyre it. For hym I knowe for
suffycyent to expowne and englysshe euery dyffyculte that is therein / For
he hath late translated the epystlys of Tulle / and the boke of dyodorus
syculus. and diuerse other werkes oute of latyn in to englysshe not in rude
and olde langage. but in polysshed and ornate termes craftely. as he hat hath
redde vyrgyle / ouyde. tyllye. and all the other noble poetes and oratours / to
me vnknowen: And also he hath redde the ix. muses and vnderstande theyr
musicalle scyences. and to whom of theym eche scyence is appropred. I suppose
he hath dronken of Elycons well. Then I praye hym & suche other to correcte
adde or mynysshe where as he or they shall fynde faulte / For I haue but
folowed my copye in frenshe as nygh as me is possyble / And yf ony worde
be sayd therin well / I am glad. and yf otherwyse I submytte my sayd boke
to theyr correctyon / Which boke I presente vnto the hye born. my tocomynge
naturell & souerayn lord Arthur by the grace of god Prynce of Walys Duc of
Cornewayll. & Erle of Chester fyrst bygoten sone and heyer vnto our most
dradde naturall & souerayn lorde & most crysten kynge / Henry the vij. by
the grace of god kynge of Englonde and of Fraunce & lord of Jrelonde /
byseching his noble grace to receyue it in thanke of me his moste humble
subget & seruaunt / And I shall praye vnto almyghty god for his prosperous
encresyng in vertue / wysedom / and humanyte that he may be egal wyth the
most renommed of alle his noble progenytours.

And so to lyue in this present lyf / that after this transitorye lyfe he and
we alle may come to euerlastynge luf in heuen / Amen:

PART FIVE

EARLY MODERN ENGLISH

✠

INTRODUCTION

Myers says, "An adjective often applied to Renaissance English is *luxuriant* —a term which suggests both the richness of the language and its freedom from the sort of restrictions that later came to be applied to it." His chapter describes not only that luxuriance and the richness of the language but its growth during this period and discusses the reasons for it: the spread of education, the weakening of class distinctions, the introduction of printing, traveling—among others.

The selection from Chute describes the education available to Shakespeare when he was a boy at Stratford. Schooling at the beginning of the last quarter of the sixteenth century seems to have been devoted largely to Latin rather than to English. As Highet shows, Shakespeare's knowledge of Latin and Latin authors, many of whom he read in later years in translation, "lead him . . . to love Greek and Roman myth, poetry and history" and to borrow heavily from them for plots, settings, and even particular passages in his plays. As Highet demonstrates, however, whatever Shakespeare took he clearly made his own; so Highet prefers to use the verb "transmuted" to describe the process rather than "borrowed."

The last two selections in this section demonstrate very clearly by their subject matter that when they were written the English language was becoming once again the language of primary importance in England. In his Preface to the *Abbreviation of the Statutes*, Rastell discusses the "Englishing" of the laws (i.e., translating them "out of French into English"). He explains that from the time of the conquest of England by William of Normandy (1066) until the reign of Henry VII (1485–1509) "the laws of this realme were indyted and written in the French tong," but that Henry VII caused them to be written in English and that Henry VIII continued that practice. As a result, Rastell was encouraged to undertake a translation into English of an abbreviation of the laws passed during the time of Henry VII and Henry VIII.

In the chapter from his *Elementarie*, Mulcaster argues staunchly for the competence of the English language on the basis of four arguments: "the antiquitie of our tung, the peples wit, their learning, and their experience." In anticipation of setting down his own plans for spelling reform, he takes to task those who, in his opinion, underestimate the strengths of English and explains why he is confident of the resources of the language.

By the sixteenth century, therefore, English is once again the language of such widely diversified fields as entertainment (drama) and the law and is important enough to the national life to be worthy of consideration (and reform) by some of the country's important educators and scholars.

✠ ✠ ✠

THE ENGLISH RENAISSANCE

L. M. MYERS

EARLY MODERN ENGLISH

The period from 1500 to 1650 is often called the English Renaissance, and the language of this period is known as Early Modern English. The dates are of course arbitrary, but they will do as well as any others to bound the era during which our language took on most of its present characteristics. Most modern students simply cannot read the language of 1450 without either special training or considerable editorial assistance, but before 1550 they can find a good deal of material which they can handle without difficulty. We cannot reasonably suppose that during the intervening century the language habits of the whole country changed quite so rapidly as the differences in the preserved writing seem to indicate, but a number of forces were working together to cause a rather decided break about this time. These include the rapid spread of education, a loosening in the class structure of society, the introduction of printing, and the growing belief that the development of the language could and should be controlled. The first three of these we can consider only very briefly, but we must examine the last more carefully, since it added a new dimension to the language. It is not much of an over-simplification to say that during the Old and Middle English periods the language just happened, while during the entire Modern period its development has been considerably modified by efforts (sometimes misguided) at conscious direction. From this time on it is necessary to consider attitudes toward the language as a part of its functioning machinery, along with the more obvious elements such as sounds and inflections.

During this period the changes in inflections were comparatively slight, but the changes in pronunciation were considerable, and the enlargement of the vocabulary was enormous. There were also some very important developments along what might be called the borderline between grammar and rhetoric. As English became a more responsible language the habit of using more sophisticated and better articulated sentences became fairly general. It is very difficult to decide how far changes of this sort should be attributed to the language itself, and how far simply to the skill of particular writers in using it; for habits of sentence construction are likely to vary more from person to person than any other element of a language. In order to communicate at all we have to stay pretty close together in our pronunciation, our vocabulary, and those inflections which have an actual signalling value; but the skill with which we fit our words together in order to convey the relations between ideas varies enormously—and of course depends at least as much on our ability to grasp complex relations as on our facility with words.

Another important development was the gradual emergence of a single, generally accepted system of spelling, which has remained in effect ever since with only a few slight modifications. It was a poor system at the time, and has become more and more unsatisfactory as our pronunciation has changed since; but it has had a very strong unifying effect on the language. The fact that we tend to think of the written form of a word as the real form has, as we have seen, some serious disadvantages; but it does make it easier for us to think of an unfamiliar pronunciation as a comprehensible variant rather than as something completely and arbitrarily different.

THE GREAT VOWEL SHIFT

The most important development in the sound system of English that took place during this period was a change in the values of all the long vowels, usually called "the great vowel shift." It is here described in a simplified form, with a footnote for those who want more details. For some reason people started pronouncing the long vowels with their tongues higher in their mouths. When the front part of the tongue was raised, / ɑ: / changed to / e: / and / e: / to / i: /; when the back part was raised, / ɔ: / changed to / o: / and / o: / changed to / u: /. The vowels / i: / and / u: / were already pronounced with the tongue so high that any further raising would have resulted in consonant rather than vowel sounds, so people backed up and made the diphthongs / ɑi / and / ɑu / instead.[1] The whole process sounds most unlikely, especially the last part. Nobody knows why it happened, so there is no use worrying about that. We have very convincing evidence that it somehow did, and at least it explains one of the main peculiarities in English spelling.

Exact dating of the shift is impossible, partly because of scanty and sometimes conflicting evidence, partly because some people were slower than others in following the new tendency. It apparently began in the fifteenth century, and is sometimes called the "fifteenth century vowel shift." The evidence of spelling suggests that the main development was rather later. There is some doubt that the modern diphthongs in such words as *bite* and *mouse* had been fully developed in Shakespeare's time, but they must have been well on their way. The evidence for the pronunciation at various times is of several kinds, of which the most obvious are English attempts at phonetic spelling of foreign words, and foreign attempts at phonetic spelling of English words. We also have some evidence from rhymes, some from nonstandard dialects which developed differently, and a few contemporary comments.

The following words indicate the changes:

Vowel	Word	Chaucerian pronunciation	Shakespearean pronunciation
/ ɑ: /	place	/ plɑsə /	/ ple:s /
/ e: /	feet	/ fe:t /	/ fi:t /
/ i: /	bite	/ bi:tə /	/ bait /
/ ɔ: /	stone	/ stɔ:n /	/ sto:n /
/ o: /	fool	/ fo:l /	/ fu:l /
/ u: /	mouse	/ mu:s /	/ mɑus /

... Chaucer's vowels had approximately the same values as those in modern Spanish and Italian, and each pair of short and long vowels had approximately the same quality. The difference between the short and long *e*, for instance, was simply in the length they were held, and not in a different placement of the tongue. If the shift had happened a century or two earlier our spelling would probably have reflected it; but since it occurred only after some of our spelling conventions had at least begun to solidify, it left us with our very curious habit of using the same letters to indicate phonetically unrelated vowel sounds. Our ancestors simply continued to spell with the letters they were used to, even when they had greatly changed their habits of pronunciation. The shift does not explain all our odd spellings of vowel sounds, since other factors are involved in many words; but it does account for the greatest single peculiarity.

THE SHORT VOWELS

There was no general shift in the short vowels, but / æ / was changed to / ɑ /, and in many words / u / was changed to / ə /. However, the later development of both these vowels has been so varied in different phonetic environments that it is not practicable to consider them thoroughly here.

CONSONANTS

The only general change in the consonant system during this period was that
/ χ / (spelled *gh*) either changed to·/ f / as in *cough* and *enough* or disappeared
entirely as in *thought* and *bough*. The tendency was for it to change to / f /
when final and disappear when followed by a *t*; but this tendency was often
disturbed by analogies too complicated to go into here.

Toward the end of the period / i / changed to / j / when it was preceded
by a consonant and followed by a lightly stressed vowel. This accounts for
our present pronunciation of words like *special* and *ambitious*, which often
(but not always, because the change was then under way) have an extra
syllable in Shakespeare.

The only other changes that need be mentioned are the shifts between
/ d / and / ð / in the neighborhood of / r /. Thus *fader* and *moder* changed
to *father* and *mother*, while *burthen* and *murther* changed to *burden* and
murder. Once again the full statement would be very complicated, and there
are a number of irregularities. For most purposes it will be sufficient to
remember that such changes were possible.

CHANGES IN INFLECTION

The changes in inflection during this period were comparatively slight, but
the following should be noticed:

Nouns   Constructions like "the King of England's crown," known as the
group genitive replaced the older "the King's crown of England."

The ordinary *-es* genitive ending was often written as *-is* or *-ys*, and probably usually pronounced / iz /, as it generally is today. "Charles's book"
therefore sounds exactly like "Charles his book" if both phrases are pronounced casually; and the idea that the second phrase is the original one
and the first a mere contraction, became widespread during this period.
(There are occasional examples of it even in Old English.) This idea has no
historical justification, and could hardly explain such combinations as "the
lady's dress," but it was held for centuries, and is taken for granted by many
people today, though the "correct" form now seldom appears except in
bookplates. The apostrophe which we still use in the genitive is due to this
misunderstanding.

Pronouns   In older English *his* had been the genitive form of *it* as well as
he; but in the neuter it was now supplanted, first by *it*, then by *its* (usually
written *it's* until about 1800). The use of the forms *ye* and *you* in the singular
when addressing superiors had begun in the thirteenth century. It later
became normal among equals unless they were particularly intimate, and
during the Renaissance the singular forms dropped out almost entirely in
the standard language. Moreover, the original distinction between the
nominative *ye* and the objective *you* became so blurred that either form
could be used for all purposes, with *you* gradually gaining.

The use of *who* and *which* as relative pronouns became common during this period, though there are occasional examples earlier. It is generally believed that this construction developed in three stages, something like this: First, the direct question, "Who was there?" Second, the reported question, "He asked who was there." Finally, the statement, "I know the man who was there."

Since there are some grammarians who seem to believe that the *wh-* relatives are the only fully legitimate ones, it is well to remember that "the man *that* I saw" was in use for centuries before "the man whom I saw." "The man I saw" is still earlier—and still good.

Adjectives Double comparatives and superlatives (*more nobler, most unkindest*) were used freely, but not by everybody. In other words, the permissible feeling that such expressions are redundant had not been put into a rule making them criminal. Also, long adjectives were often compared by *-er* and *-est*.

Verbs By far the most important changes in inflection took place among the verbs. The drift of the originally strong verbs into the weak class continued. Such verbs as *bide, crow,* and *dread*, among others, show the weak preterites *bided, crowed, dreaded* along with the older *bode, crew,* and *drad*. In fact the drift was so strong that a number of weak forms which have since been outlawed were in respectable use, such as *blowed, growed*, and *shrinked*.

In the third person singular the *-(e)s* ending, which in Middle English occurred only in the Northern dialect, began to compete with the *-(e)th* ending which had been in use throughout the rest of the country, and eventually drove it out. Shakespeare used both, frequently in the same sentence, and presumably chose whichever form he thought sounded better in a particular place. But in the first half of the seventeenth century the *-(e)s* ending apparently became universal in speech, though many writers continued to spell it as *-(e)th*. There are a number of comments on this inconsistency.

The Midland plural ending in *-(e)n* and the Southern one in *-(e)th* both dropped out of the standard language, leaving the uninflected form that we have today. But rather curiously, the *-(e)s* ending which had been used in the plural as well as the singular in the Northern dialect, now appeared for the first time in the plural in other areas. Though it is not nearly as common as the uninflected form, it appears so often in careful writing, and in verse where the extra syllable fits the meter, that it is generally accepted as a recognized variant rather than a mistake in agreement.

The *-(e)n* ending dropped out completely in the infinitive, and in most past participles except those in which it is still preserved.

We may summarize by saying that as far as inflections are concerned most verbs had reached the forms that they have now, except that the *-(e)th* third singular was still fairly common throughout most of the period, and the second singular *-(e)st* ending was still possible, though becoming infrequent. But our now rather rigid system of verb phrases had not fully developed. In questions Shakespeare could say "Goes he?" where we must use either "Does he go?" or "Is he going?" And in negative statements he could say either "He not goes" or "He goes not" where we have to use "He does not go" or "He is not going." On the other hand, he could say "I do go" without implying the special emphasis that such a sentence would now have.

On the whole the progressive forms (*is going,* etc.) were comparatively uncommon, partly because they were not needed in questions and negations, and partly because the simple forms could still be used to describe immediate action.

The most important difference in the "perfect tenses" is that *be* rather than *have* was used with verbs indicating change of condition or location—roughly the same kinds of verbs that require *être* rather than *avoir* in French or *sein* rather than *haben* in German. We have preserved this tendency only very erratically. Thus in the sixteenth century the regular expressions were *is come* and *is gone*, rather than *has come* and *has gone*. We can now say either *is* or *has gone*, but only *has come*.

THE SPREAD OF EDUCATION

So far we have considered only what might be called the automatic changes in the language. Before turning to those that owe at least something to theory we must consider some of the nonlinguistic developments which made efforts at deliberate improvement far more effective than they could have been in the Old and Middle English periods.

During most of the Middle Ages education had not only been completely controlled by the church but directed very largely toward ecclesiastical ends. The language taught was Latin, and one of the chief reasons for sending boys to school was to train them to sing in choirs. The connection between the two meanings of *clerical* now found in *clerical job* as opposed to *clerical collar* was so close that anybody who could read was entitled to "benefit of the clergy," which removed him from the jurisdiction of the secular courts, and was often very convenient if he didn't want to be hanged. Of course, not every student had a deep commitment to the church. Some education was obviously necessary for the law and certain other careers. But on the whole even bare literacy was comparatively rare, and not universally admired. Many of the noble class clearly regarded writing as a rather menial occupation, distinctly beneath their dignity; and most of their inferiors seem to have considered it as a mystery with which there was no reason for them to be concerned.

Both the spread and the secularization of education were gradual and complicated processes, but it is clear that they made considerable progress during the fifteenth century. A good many middle class people, including women, were now learning at least to read and write English as part of the natural order of things. One result of this was that when printing was introduced during the latter part of the century there was a much greater market for books, and especially for books in English, than there would have been even a hundred years earlier; and their effects on the language as well as the life of the times were consequently more widespread and very much faster. It has been estimated that by Shakespeare's time between a third and a half of the population of London could read—a situation which in Chaucer's age would have seemed absolutely incredible.

WEAKENING OF CLASS DISTINCTIONS

One important reason for the spread of education was that hereditary class distinctions were losing some of their rigidity, so that the chance of rising in the world (as distinct from the church) was a good deal more promising than it had been. We need not here go into the causes of this change, but we should notice two of the more obvious results. The first was simply that with the possibility of rising from one class to another a great many more people found it worth while to educate their children in order to prepare them for the new opportunities. The same situation is paralleled on a higher level today, when the concept of a "working class" has practically disappeared, and a college education is coming to be regarded as almost indispensable for a satisfactory life. The second was more complicated. When class lines are fixed, a man might as well behave naturally, because imitating his "betters" is more likely to bring him ridicule than rewards. But when it becomes possible to move from one class to another it is important for an ambitious man to learn to behave, linguistically and otherwise, like the members of the class into which he hopes to move. At the same time there is a tendency for those in the higher orders, no longer automatically protected from invasion, to become rather more careful in their own use of language as a sign of their continued superiority. The upshot is that class dialects are likely to become both more distinct and more important just at the time when a too simple analysis of the situation might suggest that they would break down.

It apparently took the schools of England a long time to adjust themselves to the problem of teaching "good English" to everybody who wanted to learn it; but ambitious people could read as well as listen, and there is no reasonable doubt that the written form of the language began to have a stronger effect on the spoken than it had ever had before.

INTRODUCTION OF PRINTING

William Caxton set up the first printing press in England about 1476, and others soon followed. Looking back, it would be hard for us to pick a more strategic date for the invention to have its maximum effect. Books could now be reproduced for a very small fraction of their former cost, and exact duplicates could be made in any numbers desired. The spread of education was therefore greatly accelerated, and the whole nature of the spread of knowledge—in and out of school—changed in many ways. It is easy for us to appreciate the effects of the economy brought about by printing, but it takes much more thought to realize how uniformity and immensely faster distribution affected the language.

Earlier we considered the extreme diversity of English manuscripts. An author might weep at the changes in his text made by a careless or independent copyist, but most people could not have had a very reliable idea of what the true text of even a single work was, to say nothing of an established set of conventions which should govern all works. Printing not only eliminated most of the diversity between copies but contributed greatly to the establishment of general conventions. It did not bring about any miraculously rapid change. A printer can make as many mistakes as a scribe, and it took some generations to develop the tools, the techniques, and the professional attitude which all seem so obvious once they have been achieved. But from the first, printers were forced by the very size of the audience at which they aimed to face some problems to which scribes had never had to pay much attention. And from the first the audience was presumably somewhat affected by the "authority of the printed page," which still has a powerful influence on most people—much in the way that a blueprint, which is merely an inexpensive reproduction of an architect's drawing, is likely to impress them with a feeling of inevitability that they never get from the drawing itself. The fact that London was the center of printing enormously reinforced the prestige of London English throughout the entire country. It no longer seemed reasonable for a northerner to translate a work from Southern English into his own dialect. Printed English was obviously for everybody.

Another effect of printing was to encourage writing as a way of making a living. Earlier authors were sometimes supported by patrons, but they could not possibly live on the sales of their work. Now printers and booksellers were willing to pay (in moderation) for copy, so that a career in letters was open to many more people than ever before. It is impossible to estimate how many books have been written primarily in the hope that they would be printed and sold, but at the most moderate guess the number is astronomical. Even if we consider only those both written and printed during the English Renaissance, the number is considerable, and many of these were either composed in or translated into English because writers and printers wanted to take advantage of the larger market in that language.

DEVELOPMENT OF SPELLING CONVENTIONS

Even today English spelling is notoriously confusing. Its general inconsistencies are so well known that there is no need to go into them here. Moreover, there are a number of characteristic differences between American and British practices, some of them affecting large classes of words (-or and -our, -er and -re, etc.), others only specific words (tire and tyre, curb and kerb, etc.). And finally, there are a fair number of words in which variant spellings are current and acceptable in each country. But at least the whole subject has been thoroughly surveyed, the results published, and for the vast majority of words a definite agreement has been reached. Most of us at least try to use the spellings authorized by the dictionaries; and if we get into print our publishers take a good deal of care to see that we do.

At the beginning of the Renaissance period there was not a single word with a definitely established spelling. Even the indefinite article *a* and the pronoun *I* might be spelled *o* and *y*. About the most that can be said is that the words taken directly from Latin (which did, of course, have a long orthographic tradition) were spelled with a much greater approach to uniformity than those from other sources.

A good many people, naturally enough, were fairly consistent in their own habits, and a number of them proposed reformed spelling systems for general use. Some of the proposals were for purely phonetic spelling. One Thomas Smith extended the alphabet to thirty-four letters, and in addition marked the long vowels. William Bullokar, objecting to the arbitrary new symbols, took only the familiar letters as his base, but he showed variations in sound with such a bewildering collection of accents, apostrophes, and what he called "hooks and strikes" that his material is extremely hard to read even after careful study. It is too bad, however, that we could not have adopted his Rule 17, which might be called the philosopher's stone of orthography. It is given here without the diacritical markings:

> And this stryk (ʼ) is excepcion general
> Too spel wordz truly when thœz rulz fail al.

I haven't the faintest idea how this result was to be obtained.

Fortunately or unfortunately, such radical systems received no general support. Richard Mulcaster, in his *Elementarie* (1582), took an entirely different approach. He did not consider that truly phonetic spelling was possible, since pronunciation was constantly changing. He even doubted that it was greatly to be desired, since the use of one letter to indicate more than one sound seemed to him no worse than the use of one word to indicate more than one meaning—a variation which is inevitable unless we are to insist on a vocabulary far too large for any human memory to master it. Moreover, he was convinced that any attempt at a wholesale revolution was so hopeless as to be a complete waste of time. He therefore wanted to start with whatever nucleus of general agreement he could find, make such minor improvements as might be accepted without too much resistance, and—above all—make the point that it is more important for everybody to spell in the same way than it is to find a theoretically perfect system.

His work was often quoted with approval and undoubtedly had some effect, though not all his specific recommendations were followed. By the end of the period most of our spellings had become pretty well standardized, and we have made few changes since except in some of the commonest endings. For instance, we now use *-y* instead of *-ie*, *-al* instead of *-all*, *-ess* instead of *-esse*, and *-ic* instead of *-ick*. Since the modern forms all remove silent letters, we may consider them improvements. At any rate, since the seventeenth century we have been spelling words borrowed (not too early) from Latin and Greek with fair consistency, though with some pedantic complications. For instance, we use the *-ant* ending for words derived from Latin verbs of the first conjugation, and the *-ent* ending for those from other conjugations. Such etymological precision probably seemed reasonable enough to a generation of Latinists; but most people today would certainly vote for the French practice of using *-ant* for them all.

A minor complication resulted from occasional efforts to bring words borrowed from French closer to the original Latin forms. Thus *debt, doubt,* and *fault* come from the French *dette, doute,* and *faute.* The restoration in the first two of the *b* from Latin *debitum* and *dubitum* did nothing but make them harder to spell, but for some reason the restored *l* in *fault* eventually came to be pronounced.

Doubtless[2] the printers had more to do with the development of uniform standards than the scholars did. As anybody who has ever had much to do with them knows, they are likely to have a passion for consistency in detail, though during the early years of printing they were tempted in the other direction. They had to "justify" their lines—that is, make them come out even at the right hand margins. They could do this by inserting little wedges to vary the spaces between letters, but it must have been a great convenience to use a variable spelling to gain the same end even more neatly. Eventually, however, it seemed even more convenient to spell everybody's writing the same way, and disregard the peculiar preferences of erratic authors. Nobody really knows who was responsible; but on the simple grounds that an approximate agreement was reached in only one hundred and seventy-five years, I am inclined to give most of the credit to the printers.

ENGLISH AND LATIN IN THE RENAISSANCE

We are now rather generally accustomed to thinking of English as a living language, and of Latin as not only a dead one, but one that has been dead since about the fifth century. Of course we have heard of medieval Latin, but most people seem to think of it as a comparatively small and decidedly gloomy appendix to classical Latin, consisting mostly of things like official charters and probably incomprehensible theology, all rather painfully and artificially translated from the languages in which it must have been originally conceived. It is in those languages that they expect to find all the really vivid impressions of medieval life and thought.

This evaluation would have seemed fantastic to the Middle Ages. To them Latin was, like Greek and Hebrew and a few others, a legitimate language going back to the Tower of Babel; and as the official language of Christendom it was ordained to last as long as the world. Though it was no longer the first language for anybody, educated people still spoke it as a matter of course —in casual conversation, not merely in set pieces; and much of the time they automatically thought in it. They were naturally inclined to write in it whenever they were addressing their peers, and their writing is amazingly varied, including fine drinking songs as well as magnificent hymns, and sophisticated satire along with sober history. English, on the other hand, was merely a "vernacular"—a corrupt form of speech with no particular future. A thirteenth century scholar (or even schoolboy) would have taken the idea that it could supplant Latin for all purposes about as seriously as a twentieth century scholar would take the suggestion that Pennsylvania Dutch would drive out Standard English as the future language of literature, learning, and government in this country.

There is some very fine Middle English poetry, but most of the prose and a great deal of pedestrian verse was written in a definitely missionary spirit, "for the common people to understand"—and to understand in a rather limited way. The laity were expected to *believe* the doctrine handed down to them rather than to analyze its structure. In other words, the audience was being talked down to—not contemptuously, but in a way that called for simplicity, and certainly discouraged any effort to "enrich and improve the language" in order to give them all the confusing details.

During the Renaissance translations and compilations from Latin sources were undertaken in a very different spirit. On one side, there was a much greater effort to give the full intellectual context; on the other, there was a growing respect for the capabilities of English, and a conscious and widespread effort to develop those capabilities. The result was an enormous increase in the vocabulary and a considerable development in the characteristic sentence structure. By the end of the period English was firmly established as adequate for all purposes.

THE DEBATABLE IMPORTANCE OF AUTHORS

Since some readers will feel that the preceding paragraph attributes far too much importance to the efforts of individual authors, it will be well to consider the question carefully. It used to be rather generally taken for granted (by such as had any opinion at all on the subject) that a language was formed by its great writers; and Chaucer, living at a critical time, was given especial importance. As late as 1932 G. K. Chesterton began a book on this poet with an almost casual assertion that he would be writing in French if Chaucer had not chosen to write in English. It is now more usual for linguists to hold the directly contrary opinion that language develops among the mass of the people, with writers simply using the medium as they find it, and affecting it very little. Both attitudes are exaggerated, but it is not very satisfactory to toss them aside with a sentence to the effect that "there is much to be said on both sides, and the truth no doubt lies somewhere between these two extremes." Conditions vary so much that any single operating formula is hopeless, but we can occasionally learn something by considering the evidence in specific cases.

There can be no doubt of Chaucer's influence on literature. All through the fifteenth century he was widely imitated and enthusiastically praised, and the following passage from Caxton's preface to his second edition of the *Canterbury Tales* (1484) will give some idea of the esteem in which he was held:

> Grete thankes, laude, and honour ought to be gyuen vnto the clerkes, poetes, and historiographs, that haue wreton many noble bokes of wysedom of the lyues, passions, and myracles of holy sayntes, of hystoryes, of noble and famous actes and faittes, and of the cronycles sith the begynnyng of the creacion of the world vnto thys present tyme, by whyche we ben dayly enformed and have knowleche of many thynges, of whom we shold not haue knowen, yf they had not left to vs theyr monumentis wreton. Emong whom and inespecial to-fore alle other we ought to gyue a synguler laude vnto that noble and grete philosopher Gefferey Chaucer, the whiche for his ornate wrytyng in our tongue may wel haue the name of a laureate poete.

> For to-fore that he by hys labour enbelysshyd, ornated, and made faire our Englisshe, in thys royame was had rude speche and incongrue, as yet it appiereth by olde bookes, whyche at thys day ought not to haue place ne be compared emong ne to hys beauteuous volumes and aournate writynges, of whom he made many bokes and treatyces of many a noble historye as wel in metre as in ryme and prose, and them so craftyly made, that he comprehended hys maters in short, quyck, and hye sentences, eschewing prolyxyte, castyng away the chaf of superfluyte, and shewyng the pyked grayn of sentence, utteryd by crafty and sugred eloquence. . . .[3]

We may cheerfully grant everything that Caxton says about the quality of Chaucer's writing; and for the sake of the argument we may even accept the contrast with all that had been written in English before as "rude speche and incongrue," though if Caxton had seen and been able to read all that is now available he might not have made his statement quite so strong. But the fact that Chaucer did wonderful things *with* the language does not in itself prove that he did anything *to* it. His influence does not, for instance, seem to have had the effect of making Caxton's own sentences particularly short and quick. It was not sufficient to keep the London dialect from changing markedly soon after his death, and losing most of the Southern forms in which his work abounds; and the best of his followers wrote in their own quite different Scottish dialect. We don't even know definitely that he added a single word to the vocabulary. He certainly contributed to the preservation of some that might otherwise have dropped from the language, but this was largely the result of later antiquarianism rather than of immediate contact. On the whole we must accept the belief that during the manuscript age the general drift of the language was not much influenced by literature.

But with the introduction of printing and wider education there was a much greater possibility of the language changing from the top down as well as from the bottom up. From Caxton's time on we find evidence of a growing desire to improve English, and to establish it as an adequate language for all purposes, on a par with Greek and Latin. Many of the workers had contradictory aims, and much of the effort may seem misdirected, but the total effect on the language was certainly considerable. Most of us can recognize that our own usage is heavily influenced by the books we have read and the instruction we have received, and even a complete illiterate today speaks differently from the way he would if Shakespeare had never written a play or Lowth a grammar.

INCREASE IN VOCABULARY

The most conspicuous change in the language during the Renaissance was the enormous growth of the vocabulary—a growth of which the literate public was well aware, and about which writers held strong though conflicting views. Some of them were simply against it. They saw no reason why the words already in the language should not be enough for anybody who took the trouble to use them effectively, and ridiculed all innovations. The borrowings from Latin they called "inkhorn terms"; those from the other modern languages "oversea language"; and the revivals of obsolete English words "Chaucerisms." Some of the innovators certainly gave them targets for legitimate ridicule, but the opposition to all changes now seems petty as well as absurd. Directly opposed to these conservatives was a group who believed in enriching the language by borrowing from all available sources; and in between was a third who were opposed to foreign borrowings, but believed the language could be improved not only by reviving old words but by making new compounds from native elements.

It is perhaps misleading to speak of the adherents of these three attitudes as groups. There was no movement in England with a unity or organization comparable to the school of poets known as the Pléiade, which at the same period was fighting a carefully planned campaign for the enrichment of the French language. But though the debate was less thoroughly organized, it was quite as vigorous, and even more interesting because there were no party lines to tone down individual differences of opinion.

THE CONSERVATIVES

A blow-by-blow account of the controversy would be long and confusing. Here we need only attempt to see the main issues in relation to their eventual effect on the language. We may begin by examining the position of a man who was quite satisfied with the language as it stood, and thought it only needed to be used more skilfully. In his *Arte of Rhetorique* (1553) Thomas Wilson has a famous passage on "Plainness what it is," which includes an imaginary "inkhorn letter" supposed to be written by a clergyman to a friend who might be able to help him get a position. It is here annotated rather thoroughly, partly because it illustrates some of the printing conventions of the times, and partly because many of the words differ from their

modern equivalents either in having been formed with different suffixes
from those that are now used, or in more closely preserving the literal meaning of their Latin originals. It will be noticed that the punctuation differs
from ours about as much as the spelling.

Emong al other lessons this should first be learned, y^t we neuer
affect any straũge ynkehorne termes, but so speake as is commonly
receiued: neither sekyng to be ouer fine, nor yet liuyng ouer care-
lesse, vsyng our speache as most men do & ordryng our wittes,
as the fewest haue doen. Some seke so farre for outlãdishe Eng-   5
lishe, that thei forget altogether their mothers lãguage. And I dare
swere this, if some of their mothers were aliue, thei were not able
to tell, what thei say, & yet these fine Englishe clerkes, wil saie
thei speake in their mother tongue, if a mã should charge thẽ for
coũterfeityng the kynges English. Some farre iorneid ientlemẽ at   10
their returne home, like as thei loue to go in forrein apparell, so
thei wil pouder their talke w^t ouersea lãguage. He that cometh
lately out of France, wil talke Frẽche English, & neuer blushe at
the matter. Another choppes in with Angleso Italiano: the lawyer
wil store his stomach with the pratyng of Pedlers. The Auditour in   15
makyng his accompt and rekenyng, cometh in with sise sould, and
cater denere, for vi. s. iiij d. The fine Courtier wil talke nothyng
but Chaucer. The misticall wise menne, and Poeticall Clerkes, will
speake nothyng but quaint prouerbes, and blynd allegories, de-
lityng much in their awne darkenesse, especially, when none can   20
tell what thei dooe saie. The vnlearned or foolishe phantasticall,
that smelles but of learnyng (suche felowes as haue seen learned
men in their daies) will so latine their tongues, that the simple
cannot but wonder at their talke, and thynke surely thei speake by
some Reuelacion. I know them that thynke Rhetorique, to stande   25
wholy vpon darke woordes, and he that can catche an ynke horne
terme by the taile, hym thei compt to bee a fine Englishe man,
and a good Rhetotician [sic] And the rather to set out this folie,
I will adde here suche a letter, as Willyam Sommer himself, could
not make a better for that purpose. Some will thinke and swere to,   30
that there was neuer any suche thyng writtẽ, well I wil not force
any man to beleue it, but I will saie thus muche, and abide by it to,
the like haue been made heretofore, and praised aboue the Moone.

An ynkehorne letter

Pondering, expẽding, and reuoluting with my self your ingent   35
affabilitie, and ingenious capacitee for mundane affairs: I cannot
but celebrate and extolle your magnificall dexteritee, aboue all
other. For how could you haue adepted suche illustrate prerogatiue,
and domenicall superioritee, if the fecunditee of your ingenie had
not been so fertile, & woũderfull pregnaunt. Now thefore beeyng   40
accersited, to suche splendent renoume, & dignitee splendidious:
I doubt not but you will adiuuate suche poore adnichilate
orphanes, as whilome ware cõdisciples with you, and of antique

familiaritie in Lincolne shire. Emong whom I beeyng a Scholas-
ticall panion, obtestate your sublimitee to extoll myne infirmitee.　　　*45*
There is a sacerdotall dignitee in my natiue countrey, contiguate
to me, where I now contemplate: whiche your worshipfull benigni-
tee, could sone impetrate for me, if it would like you to extend
your scedules, and collaude me in them to the right honorable
lorde Chauncellor, or rather Archigrãmacian of Englande. You　　　*50*
knowe my literature, you knowe the pastorall promocion, I obtestate your clemencie, to inuigilate thus muche for me, accordyng
to my confidence, and as you knowe my condigne merites, for
suche a compendious liuyng. But now I relinquishe to fatigate your
intelligence with any more friuolous verbositie, and therefore he　　　*55*
that rules the climates be euermore your beautreux, your fortresse,
and your bulwarke.
　　　Amen⁴

1. *yᵗ:* that. A carelessly made thorn (þ) looked rather like a *y,* and early printers
often abbreviated *the* as *yᵉ* and *that* as *yᵗ.* The pronunciation of this *yᵉ* as *ye* is a
purely modern error.

1. *neuer.* The letters *u* and *v* were orginally merely different forms of the same
letter, which could be used to indicate either the vowel or the consonant sound.
Printers generally adopted the practice found here, of using *v* for either sound
initially, and *u* for either sound in all other positions.

2. *straŭge.* In manuscripts a macron (ˉ) or tilde (˜) over a vowel indicated that a
following *m* or *n* had been omitted to save space. This practice is followed rather
erratically here, and in many other early books.

6. *mothers.* The convention of using an apostrophe to indicate the genitive had
not yet been developed.

10. *iorneid ientlemē:* journeyed gentlemen. The practice of using *i* for initial *j*
is very common. It is not so often used instead of *g,* as here.

12. *wᵗ:* with. This abbreviation is not nearly so common as *yᵗ.*

15. *pratyng of Pedlers.* Underworld slang.

17. *vi. s. iiij d. Six sous and four deniers* (French coins) for six shillings and six-
pence. The modern abbreviation for English money, £–s–d, are from the same source,
with £ standing for *livres* (pounds).

20. *awne:* own.

29. *Sommer.* Author of a Saxon-Latin-English dictionary, and thus well supplied
with all sorts of words if he wanted to use them.

35. *expēding:* weighing out. The modern meaning skips to the logical next step
of paying out.

35. *reuoluting.* Many Latin verbs had in the past participle an *-at-, -et-,* or *-ut-*
element which did not appear in the infinitive. French verbs are regularly taken from
the infinitive form, and many English verbs are taken from the French. But English
verbs borrowed directly from the Latin are regularly based on the past participle.
Thus we say *celebrate* and *contemplate* (both of which occur in this passage) where
the French have *célébrer* and *contempler. Revoluting* is thus as reasonable a form as
revolving, though it does not happen to have survived (except as a playful expression
for "making a revolution").

35. *ingent:* enormous. Probably dropped because it didn't sound big enough.

37. *magnificall.* After all, we say *beneficial* as well as *beneficent.*

38. *adepted: attained.* An *adept* has obtained a good deal of skill.

39. *domenicall: Lordly,* though we now use this word only in connection with the Lord's day (*dimanche* in French).

39. *ingenie:* intellect. From *ingenium,* and better etymology than our *ingenuity.*

41. *accersited:* brought.

42. *adiuuate: aid.* From the past participle *adiuvatus.*

42. *adnichilate:* reduced to nothing. A variant (on good authority) of *annihilate,* though here not quite as strong in meaning. Here, as in a few other words, the implication of the past participle is preserved without the addition of the *-d ending.* Compare *finite, destitute,* and so forth.

45. *panion.* From *panis,* meaning *bread.* We now say *companion,* or fellow bread-eater.

45. *obtestate:* call upon for testimony.

46. *sacerdotall dignitee:* priestly position.

46. *contiguate.* Change *-ate* to *-ous.*

48. *impetrate:* obtain by request.

49. *collaude.* The prefix which was omitted from *companion* is added here to *laud.*

52. *inuigilate:* look out for.

53. *condigne:* worthy.

54. *compendious.* Here, simply *convenient,* because so close at hand.

56. *beautreux:* buttress.

The gist of his argument is the sound Aristotelian advice that we should depend on our brains and skill rather than on our vocabularies for rhetorical effect; and it is presented so skilfully that unless we are very careful we may overlook its two serious defects. The first is that it simply assumes that the language is already completely adequate for all purposes; the second, that it considers only the practices of fools and a straw man set up to be conveniently demolished, and makes no attempt to consider what might be done by sensible men using the practices it opposes.

Obviously anybody who seriously wrote such a letter as the one presented would be an ass (unless he happened to know that the man he was addressing was one, and proceeded accordingly). But possibly he would have been an ass in any language, and a good many of the words that Wilson ridicules have not only passed into everyday use, but would be very hard to do without today. We may grant Wilson's principle that it is always bad to use a fancy word when a simple one will do the job as well; but we shall soon find evidence that some of the new words were being introduced because they could demonstrably do the job better. Wilson does go on to say that some borrowings are legitimate "either for lacke of store, or els because wee would enriche the language"; but since he excepts them from the charge of affectation only when "all other are agreed to folowe the same way," it is hard to see how anybody could legitimately introduce them.

Nearly forty years later (1592) Thomas Nash echoes Wilson, offering a "patheticall posie" of inkhorn words and phrases, including such (to him) obvious absurdities as *conscious mind, ingenuity, rascality, artificiality, addicted to theory, perfunctory discourses, amicable terms, extensively employed, notoriety,* and *negotiation.* But perhaps the most delightfully innocent summary of the conservative position is the following sentence from Samuel Daniel's *A Defence of Ryme* (1603):

And I cannot but wonder at the strange presumption of some men that dare so audaciously aduenture to introduce any whatsoeuer forraine wordes, bee they neuer so strange; and of themselues as it were, without a Parliament, without any consent, or allowance, stablish them as Free-denizens in our language.

It would be nice to know what *past Parliament* he thought had had the *strange presumption* to give *consent* or *allowance* to such *forraine* words as *stablish, audaciously,* and *aduenture,* and to *introduce* them as *denizens* in our *language.*

THE ENTHUSIASTS FOR NATIVE RESOURCES

Wilson's remark that "The fine Courtier will talke nothyng but Chaucer" is tantalizing. We don't know how much exaggeration it contained, nor how long the fad lasted. The movement to revive old terms, and to make new combinations of old elements, had a much slighter permanent effect on the language than borrowings from outside sources; but courtiers were not the only ones engaged in it. A number of poets, with Spenser as the most determined as well as the most distinguished example, were naturally enough delighted with Chaucer, and felt free to reintroduce any words that he had used—or that they thought he had or might have used. (It is quite unreasonable, but it is almost inevitable for a student of Middle English to wish that Spenser had been a better linguist. Obviously false antiques have a singular lack of charm for anybody who recognizes their synthetic quality.) And finally there were scholars like Sir John Cheke, interested not so much in the flavor of antiquity as in the theoretical purity of the language. In a letter to a friend (1557) he says:

I am of this opinion that our own tung shold be written cleane and pure, vnmixt and vnmangeled with borrowing of other tunges, wherein if we take not heed bi tijm, euer borrowing and neuer payeng, she shall be fain to keep her house as bankrupt. For then doth our tung naturallie and praisablie vtter her meaning, when she bouroweth no counterfeitnes of other tunges to attire her self withall, but vseth plainlie her own with such shift, as nature craft, experiens, and folowing of other excellent doth lead her vnto, and if she want at ani tijm (as being vnperfight she must) yet let her borrow with suche bashfulnes, that it mai appeer, that if either the mould of our own tung could serue vs to fascion a woord of our own, or if the old denisoned wordes could content and ease this neede we wold not boldly venture of vnknowen wordes. . . .[5]

Whatever we may think of the argument as a whole, the paragraph is a beautiful example of the difficulty of expressing a puristic attitude without doing violence to it in the very expression. We should write English clean and pure, unmixed and unmangled. Good enough. But while *cleane* and *vnmangeled* follow the precept in which they appear, *pure* is not pure in this sense, and *vnmixt* is decidedly mixed, since it contains a Latin root and an English prefix. In fact a sixth of all the words in the paragraph have foreign roots, which seems rather a high proportion for the "bashful" borrowing which Cheke condones since the language is "vnperfight." A great many later objections to borrowings, whether of Latin words, Americanisms, or slang terms, have been marked by the same kind of inconsistency.

Cheke did follow his expressed principles to the extent of coining such words as *hundreder* for *centurion* and *gainrising* for *resurrection*; but most of them failed to stick, and it seems likely that similar ones would fail in the same way today. It is a very curious fact that we seem to regard the roots and prefixes of Greek and Latin as the natural building blocks of new words, to be used with complete freedom, but are extremely conservative about making any combination with their English equivalents that are not already authorized by the dictionary. In this respect English is in strong contrast with German, which still compounds native elements so freely that no dictionary pretends to list all the legitimate combinations.

But curiously enough there was not in the Renaissance, and there is not now, any hesitation about the use of native suffixes, inflectional or otherwise, to shift borrowed words to new functions. As Richard Carew points out:

> For our owne partes, we imploye the borrowed ware soe far to our advantag that we raise a profitt of new woordes from the same stock, which yeat in their owne countrey are not merchantable; for example, wee deduce diuers wordes from the Latine which in the Latyne self cannot be yealded, as the verbes To *Aire, beard, cross, flame*, and their deriuations *ayring, ayred, bearder, bearding, bearded*, &c., as alsoe *closer, closely, closnes, glosingely, hourely, maiesticall, maiestically*. In like sort wee graffe vpon Frentch wordes those buddes to which that soyle affordeth noe growth, as *cheifly, faulty, slauish, precisenes*. Diuers wordes alsoe wee deriue out of the Latyne at second hand by the French and make good English, though both Latyne and French haue their handes closed in that behalfe, as verbes *Praye, Pointe, Paze, Prest, Rent*, &c., and also in the aduerbs *carpingly, currantly, actiuely, colourably*, &c.[6]

Half a century later Richard Verstegnan was carrying on Cheke's argument, and showing the same sort of inconsistency. He tells us that English is a branch of Teutonic, and traces Teutonic back to the Tower of Babel, thereby putting it on a par with Latin, Greek, and Hebrew. He even finds etymological evidence that Teutonic rather than Hebrew (as was generally believed) was the original, pre-Babelian language of all mankind. The argument is that the name *Adam* is cognate with the Teutonic word for breath (German *atem*), and *Eve* with *even*, as in "even the same"—Adam having been changed from clay to man by the Lord's breath, and Eve having been made even the same as her husband. Verstegnan does not insist on this theory, taking the stand that its originator's "opinion exceeded his proofs"; but he puts it in for whatever it may be worth. After several pages of demonstration that a language of such antiquity needs no help from strangers, he sums up his argument in the following words:

> For mine owne part, I hold them deceived that thinke our speech bettered by the aboundance of our daily borrowed words, for they being of an other nature, & not Orginally belonging to our language, do not neyther can they in our tongue, beare their naturall, and true derivation. . . .[7]

Counting the Scandinavian pronoun forms, exactly one-fourth of these words are of foreign origin.

THE TRAVELERS: OVERSEA LANGUAGE

Foreign travel was very fashionable, and apparently most of the travelers thought it was worth advertising. The young man who returned from the continent wearing strange clothes and filling his talk with foreign phrases is a popular object of Elizabethan ridicule. Borrowing from French, of course, was nothing new, and most of us would find it impossible to distinguish between the words taken in at this time and those imported earlier, though contemporaries could recognize their novelty. Italian and Spanish words had a much more exotic flavor, especially in their -a and -o endings (which the Elizabethans frequently confused). Many of these other words have now lost their endings, and their flavor with them. *Barricade, cavalier, duel,* and *grenade* have nothing like the exotic effect of *barricado, cavaliero, duello,* and *grenado.* Other words have retained their endings but become commonplace through everyday use—*banana, potato, tobacco,* for instance. But we still have many that retain some of their original tang, though we might disagree about just which these are. *Bastinado, bravado, cupola, desperado, embargo, peccadillo,* and *sombrero* are examples.

SCHOLARLY INNOVATORS: INKHORN TERMS—AND OTHERS

Much more important than either the Chaucerisms or the oversea language were the thousands of words taken from the classical languages. Some of these were taken directly from Greek; but since many Greek words had already been borrowed by Latin, and reached English through this language, they will here be lumped together as Latin borrowings. They differed from earlier ones from the same source in two important ways. In the first place, a much higher proportion of them were learned rather than popular, since learned borrowings now had a much better chance of becoming permanent. A word borrowed earlier in a manuscript might easily be replaced the first time that manuscript was copied, if the scribe happened to dislike it or fail to understand it; and in any case its spread into general use was necessarily slow—often a matter of generations. But a word borrowed in print could get to thousands of readers in a very short time, and therefore had an excellent chance of being used again and again until it was generally accepted, and used in speech as well as in other books. The delight in words, of which we find so much evidence in Elizabethan literature, made the chances of survival greater than they would have been somewhat earlier. This delight was not, as we have seen, shared by everybody; but the general climate was decidedly favorable to rapid growth. No impersonal way of evaluating this growth is possible. An inkhorn term might be defined as a newly imported polysyllable that you don't happen to like. There is therefore no reliable way of determining exactly which of the new words could legitimately be called inkhorn, but we should all now agree that at least a good many of the imports were valuable.

In the second place, many of the new additions were the result of a conscious and to some extent concerted, effort to improve the language. The Renaissance had made available a great many Latin works which had been unknown in England during the Middle Ages, and the spread of education had created a large new class of readers who knew no Latin, or at least not enough to allow them to use it with comfort. Both writers and publishers were tempted by this public. As a result there was great activity in both translation and the compilation of new works based largely on Latin sources. Translators and compilers almost inevitably borrowed freely. Often there were no English words in existence which could render a technical term or an unfamiliar shade of meaning. Even if such words existed, they might not occur to the writer who had the Latin words right before his eyes, or might not seem to him either sufficiently precise or sufficiently dignified. Intellectual snobbery, on the part of authors and readers alike, certainly played its part, but many of the new words were so useful that we can now hardly imagine being without them.

Perhaps the most interesting of these innovators was Sir Thomas Elyot. In the "proheme" to *The Knowledge that Maketh a Wise Man* (1533) he says:

His highnesse benignely receyuynge my boke which I named the Gouernour, in the redynge therof sone perceyued that I intended to augment our Englyshe tongue, whereby men shulde as well expresse more abundantly the thynge that they conceyued in theyr hartis (wherfore language was ordeyned) hauynge wordes apte for the pourpose: as also interprete out of greke, latyn or any other tonge into Englyshe, as sufficiently as out of any one of the said tongues into an other. His grace also perceyued that through out the boke there was no terme new made by me of a latine or frenche worde, but it was there declared so playnly by one mene or other to a diligent reder that no sentĕce is therby made derke or harde to be understande.[8]

Some examples of the ways in which he "declared" his new terms follow:

to *deuulgate* or sette fourth some part of my study
shulde *animate* or gyue courage to others

the beste fourme of *education* or bringing up of noble children
shall be *appoynted* or chosen by the soueraigne gouernour
without *adminiculation* or aid
made his exile to be more *facile* and easy
inclination and towardnes to vertue
agilitie and nymblenesse
Affabilitie . . . where a man is facile or aesy to be spoken unto
Metamorphosios, whiche is as moche to saye as, chaungynge of men in to
   other figure or fourme
Wherefore I am constrained to usurpe a latine worde, calling it *maturitie* . . .
   that word *maturitie* is translated to the actis of man . . . reseruyng the
   wordes rype and redy to frute and other thinges
   wisdome, in a more elegant worde called *Sapience*[9]

These examples have been chosen to illustrate the whole range from those like *devulgate* and *adminiculation*, which are likely to strike us as purest inkhorn, to ones like *appoint* and *education*, which we can hardly imagine doing without. It is just as well to bear in mind that our immediate reactions to strange words are not necessarily sound. *Devulgate*—to make common— has not stuck, possibly because *divulge*, with a somewhat different implica- ion has; but the word itself seems in no way inferior to *popularize*. *Admini- culation* for *aid* (presumably only a little of it) strikes me as ridiculously over- analytical; but no more so than thousands of words which are current today —and perhaps a few that I use myself.

Another comment in much the same spirit as Elyot's is this from Richard Eden (1562):

And whereas the Master of Savoye tolde me that your Honour sumwhat Doubted that the booke coulde not be translated into the Englysshe toonge, I assure you Honour that this I Dare saye without arrogancie, that to translate the variable historie of Plinie into our toonge, I wolde be ashamed to borowe so muche of the Latine as he Dothe of the Greke, althowgh the Latine toonge be accompted ryche, and the Englysshe indigent and barbarous, as it hathe byn in tyme past, muche more than it nowe is, before it was enriched and amplified by sundry bookes in manner of all artes translated owt of Latine and other toonges into Englysshe.[10]

COPIOUSNESS

One of the particular aims of the borrowers was to make English *copious*— that is, to provide it with a wealth of approximate synonyms which would serve to express exact shades of meaning. Elyot's *maturity* is an obvious example of this effort. He wants to use this word for a distinctly human quality, confining *ripeness* to things like fruit. There can be no doubt that a high degree of copiousness was obtained. It is often said that no other language is as rich as English in the ability to express fine distinctions; and it is sometimes added that there are no exact synonyms in the language.

The first of these statements is, to the best of my knowledge, true. The second is a half truth. There is probably no word which can satisfactorily be exchanged for any other in all positions; but it certainly cannot be proved that one of a set of synonyms is inevitably best in any position, and that the substitution of any other will necessarily take something from the sentence. Any word that we encounter often will build up a set of associations, and if we attempt to communicate above a very simple level we must gamble that our audience will have a fairly similar set. But, as in any gamble, we will sometimes lose. The distinction that Elyot makes between *ripe* and *mature*, and their corresponding nouns, is of course sometimes followed today. We are probably more likely to speak of *ripe fruit* and a *mature man* (or *plan*) than the other way around. But we can also speak of *mature fruit*; and (unless I am losing this gamble) we can speak only of a *mature tree*, not a *ripe* one. On the other hand, a man may be either *ripe* or *mature*, with or without an intended difference of meaning. If Shakespeare had said "maturity is all" the line would probably never have been quoted—except perhaps by psychologists.

COMPENDIOUSNESS

Another aim often expressed was to make English *compendious*—that is, compact and economical. If we tried to write English now without using any of our Latin borrowings, we would often have to use four or five words in place of one. To consider only a few of the words introduced at this time, take *absurdity, analogy, compatible, contradictory, democracy*, and *education*. If we tried to paraphrase a passage containing several of these words, using only native words to do so, the result would inevitably be much longer than the original, and would probably seem almost childish in its simplicity. (And if we tried to write that last sentence without using *paraphrase, native, result, inevitably, original, probably*, and *simplicity* we would have another—well, *task* is not quite as good as *problem* here, but it will have to do.)

We have all been advised so often to write simply and use concrete terms whenever we can that we may be tempted to think that all polysyllables are always inferior, but this is not so. It is a sound rule never to use a long and comparatively fancy word when it says no more than a short, everyday one (unless you are saying so little that you have to depend on sound rather than sense to make any impression at all). In most sentences, and to most people, *remuneration* means no more than *pay*. The language could spare it without much loss. But when a long word not only takes the place of several short ones, but sums up their relationship in a familiar arrangement that can be grasped as a unit, it can be very useful.

Such words, sensibly used, are abstractions in the best sense, because they abstract the particular features of a complicated situation which we want to consider at a given time. They have the same sort of value as the simple symbols which mathematicians use to sum up complicated equations when they want to move into still higher orders of complexity; or that the term *field army* has to a soldier, who knows that it means an organization composed of several corps, each composed of several divisions plus supporting artillery, and so on all the way down the line. The advice so often given to young writers to "avoid abstractions" would, if taken literally, reduce us all to a kindergarten level. What is actually meant is something like this: "Avoid using abstract terms unless you have a very clear idea of what they stand for, and can convey that idea to your intended audience."

The two preceding paragraphs may seem to belong to a freshman English text rather than a history of the language; but it is impossible to consider Renaissance borrowings intelligently without giving some thought to their possibilities, both good and bad. The translations and much of the new literature needed many new abstract terms unless they were to be intolerably wordy.

OTHER REASONS FOR BORROWING

The workmanlike and demonstrable qualities of copiousness and compendiousness were not the only ones sought in the development of the vocabulary. Such terms as *choice, sweet,* and *elegant* occur again and again in the discussions. It would be silly to deny the importance of the qualities indicated by these words; but it would be just as silly to pretend that we can examine them with impersonal accuracy. They did not mean the same thing to everybody, and we can never be sure that we know exactly what they meant to anybody. Our esthetic reactions to words are based on a mixture of immediate sense-impressions and past associations which it is simply impossible to separate. Even when we hear a word for the first time, the effect it has on us depends partly on the way we subconsciously associate it with other words we have known.

Of course many people have complete faith in the absolute validity of their own reactions, and we hear confident assertions that such and such words are "the most beautiful in the language." But beauty contests among words are no more conclusive than they are among women. I recall a student who was perfectly sure that she reacted simply to the sounds, not to the associations, but believed that it was a natural, if somewhat mysterious, process for us to give beautiful names to beautiful objects. For her prize example she chose *ermine*, a word as lovely as the fur it names. To prove that this was not an accident, she pointed out that the French word for the mysterious medieval fur, *vair*, was equally beautiful. She repeated both words aloud, several times, and they certainly sounded fine. But when it was suggested that an even more beautiful word, combining the qualities of the first two, was *vermin*, we had to change the subject.

It is natural that some of the words borrowed for esthetic reasons have not pleased enough people to remain in the language. Even when the aim was copiousness or compendiousness it often happened that competing words or competing forms of words were borrowed by different people to meet the same purpose. Sometimes these were later differentiated in meaning, to give a still more copious effect, as in the pairs *continuous-continual* and *beneficial-beneficent*, but naturally some of the words simply dropped out of use. Thus *obtestate* seems to have gone completely, *splendent* has given way to *splendid* (though we still have *resplendent*), *magnifical* to *magnificent*, and *contiguate* to *contiguous*. No principle of choice in such cases seems to be discoverable.

Many borrowings from Greek and Latin have lost much of their effectiveness with the general decrease in the knowledge of these languages. *Conflagration*, for instance, conveys to a ready Latinist the idea of a number of fires burning together and reinforcing each other. It is thus a fine term, significant as well as resounding, when used among Latinists. But to most people now it means simply "big fire"; and though it has the apparent advantage of being one word against two, it has the more important disadvantage of being four syllables against two, and those syllables less meaningful. Nobody ever seems to speak of the "San Francisco conflagration," or even "the great conflagration of London." It therefore seems to be approaching the end of its usefulness. Perhaps the moral is that we can afford to be compendious only about situations that arise again and again. It is easier to be a little diffuse now and then than to control too enormous a vocabulary.

Considered simply as a debate, the long argument about improving the language did not get anywhere in particular. At the end of the period we still find adherents of the three main theories—for enrichment, for purification, and for a more careful use of the language as it was—stating their positions as strongly as ever. As Edward Phillips wrote in *The New World of English Words* (1658): "Whether this innovation of words deprave, or enrich our English tongue is a consideration that admits of various censures, according to the different fancies of men." But when we turn from theoretical discussions to observable facts, there can be no doubt that the vocabulary was enormously increased during the period, and that the methods of addition were so well established that it has been increasing on the same lines ever since. It is also clear that much of the enlargement was due to conscious effort rather than passive absorption, and that far more people than ever before developed a lively interest in the quality of the language, and took pride in trying to use it well.

Men still have different fancies, but now that three centuries have passed since Phillips wrote, very few of them would argue that this particular issue "admits of various censures." Most of us would agree with what George Pettie wrote in the preface to a translation in 1581:

There are some others yet who will set light by my labours, because I write in English: and those are some nice Trauailors, who retourne home with such queasie stomachs, that nothing will downe with them but French, Italian, or Spanish, and though a worke bee but meanelie written in one of those tongues, and finelie translated into our Language, yet they will not sticke farre to preferre the Originall before the Translation:... For the barbarousnesse of our tongue, I must likewise saie that it is much the worse for them, and some such curious fellowes as they are: who if one chance to deriue anie word from the Latine, which is insolent to their eares (as perchance they will take that phrase to be) they forthwith make a iest at it, and tearme it an Inkhorne tearme. And though for my part I vse those wordes as little as anie, yet I know no reason why I should not vse them; for it is in deed the readie waie to inrich our tongue, and make it copious, and it is the waie which all tongues haue taken to inrich themselues; For take the Latine wordes from the Spanish tongue, and it shall bee as barren as most part of their Countrie; take them from the Italian, & you take away in a manner the whole tongue: take thẽ frõ the French, & you marre the grace of it: yea take from the Latine it selfe the wordes deriued from the Greeke, & it shall not be so flowing & flourishing as it is. Wherefore I meruaille how our English tõgue hath crackt it credit, that it may not borrow of the Latine as wel as other tongues: and if it haue broken, it is but of late, for it is not vnknowen to all men, how many wordes we haue fetcht from thence within these few yeeres, which if they should be all counted inkpot tearmes, I know not how we should speak anie thing without blacking our mouths with inke: for what word can be more plaine thã this word (plaine) & yet what can come more neere to the Latine? What more manifest than (manifest)? & yet in a manner Latine: What more com-mune than (rare), or less rare thã (commune) & yet both of them comminge of the Latine? But you will saie, long vse hath made these wordes currant: and why may not vse doe as much for these wordes which we shall now deriue? Why should not we doe as much for the posteritie, as we haue receiued of the antiquitie? and yet if a thing be of it selfe ill, I see not how the oldnesse of it can make it good, and if it be of it selfe good, I see not how the newnesse of it can make it naught: wherevpon I infer, that those wordes which your selues confesse by vse to be made good, are good the first time they are vttered, and therefore not to be iested at, nor to be misliked. But how hardlie so euer you deale with your tongue, how little so euer you esteeme it, I durste my selfe vndertake (if I were furnished with learning other-wise) to write in it as copiouslie for varietie, as compendiouslie for breuetie, as choicelie for words, as pithilie for sentences, as pleasantlie for figures, & euerie waie as eloquentlie, as anie writer should do in anie vulgar tongue whatsoeuer.[11]

RENAISSANCE NEGLECT OF GRAMMAR

In an age like ours, when "good grammar" and "good English" are generally regarded as synonymous terms, it may seem curious that grammar got so little attention during a period so greatly concerned with the language; but there seems to have been quite general agreement with the famous remark of Sir Philip Sidney which has convinced so many modern students that he was indeed the flower of his age:

Nay truly, it [English] hath that prayse, that it wanteth not Grammer; for Grammer it might haue, but it needs it not; being so easie of it self, and so voyd of those cumbersome differences of Cases, Genders, Moodes, and Tenses, which I thinke was a peece of the Tower of Babilons curse, that a man should be put to schoole to learne his mother-tongue.[12]

This of course is a naive statement. The fact that English is comparatively "voyd of those cumbersome differences" does not mean that English has less grammar than more highly inflected languages, but only that its structural patterns are of a different sort; and Sidney found it "easie of it self" simply because he had grown up with it. No Frenchman forced to learn the language would have agreed with him. Communication is possible only when a group of speakers have a similar reaction to patterns of arrangement as well as to individual words. Whether these patterns have been explicitly described and formally taught is a secondary, though not a trivial, matter.

Nevertheless, Sidney had a point that is worth emphasizing because it is hard for most people today to believe that the situation he took for granted could ever have existed. In matters of syntax and accidence the "don't do this" age had not yet arrived. Toward the end of the period we find a few attempts to explain the structure of English to foreigners, and a few others aimed at teaching children, in English, those principles of grammar which they would later need in studying Latin; but it is not until a century later that we find any serious efforts to teach native speakers the grammar of English for its own sake. Those critics who accuse Shakespeare of being ungrammatical are a trifle anticipatory, since the rules he broke had not yet been either formulated in books or arrived at by tacit agreement.

DEVELOPMENT OF SENTENCE STRUCTURE

But even without a formal theory there was a remarkable change in the standards of sentence construction. It seems to have come mostly from an increased respect for the language and a greater sense of responsibility about using it. Here again the influence of Latin was of great importance. It cannot be proved by any such definite evidence as we have for the borrowing of words, and the opinions expressed in this section are certainly open to argument. But since the matter is too important to be passed over, they are given for whatever they may be worth.

For centuries students had been trained in the exact analysis of Latin sentences, as some are still being trained today. They were required to identify the precise form in which each word appeared, explain why it was in that form, and exactly what function it performed. It was assumed that any sound sentence could meet the test of such analysis—that its total meaning was the inevitable result of all the detailed interrelations within it. The structure of most Classical Latin sentences can, in fact, be analyzed as definitely and finally as algebraic equations—though it is not unlikely that this is true of some of them only because they have been emended by centuries of scholarship. And students were sternly encouraged to compose sentences of their own that could meet the same tests.

It is only since the middle of the eighteenth century that any such analysis has been applied to English. Its value is open to question, and will not be debated here. The point we are concerned with is that though in Old and

Middle English comparatively short grammatical patterns were as definite and significant as ours, there were no strict and generally recognized standards for combining them. There was a tendency to join the clauses of a long sentence loosely by a series of *and*'s rather than precisely by the appropriate subordinating conjunctions. It was very common to change the construction in the middle—to start out in one person and finish in another, to shift from one number or tense to another, or to mix direct and reported statements. The result is that many sentences are ambiguous. And often even when we are quite sure, from the context or by intuition, that we know what an author meant by a sentence, we can't prove it—or anything else—by the most careful analysis. The sentence simply does not hang together as we have been taught that it should.

As we have already seen, one reason for the lack of discipline in English sentences was the fact that so many books were composed in an effort to meet uneducated people on their own ground. A writer was likely to take the attitude expressed in the explanation of why *The Castle of Love* (which is moralistic rather than romantic) is put in English for those who know no other language:

> Þauh hit on Englisch be dim and derk
> Ne nabbe no sauur bifore clerk
> ffor lewed men that luitel connen
> On English it is thus bigonnen.[13]

If this attitude seems curious, we must remember that in the Middle Ages the laity were often asked to believe rather than understand, and it may have seemed more important to address them in the comfortable rhythms of familiar speech than to confuse them with exact reasoning. But a Renaissance man, writing for his peers and taking pride in his language, was naturally inclined to attempt a higher standard of performance. Translators and compilers, for instance, were no longer content to make the English a loose equivalent of the Latin; they felt responsible for preserving the precise relations between ideas. There was a good deal of difference of opinion as to how far this was possible. Even at the beginning of the period we find some writers arguing that the language is already fit for the highest tasks. Even at the end we find others scorning its attempts to compete with its natural betters. But all the way through we find still others holding the view that it can be made better than it is, and working to make it so. Some would be content to put it on a par with the other modern or "common" languages; others saw no reason why it should not rival or even surpass the classical or "learned" languages. Among them, they established the English sentence as a solid and coherent unit.

This is not to argue that the basic structure of the language was changed because a few writers were handling it more carefully. The point is rather that the whole literate population was exposed to more carefully constructed

English than their ancestors could have encountered, and that this exposure had a very perceptible effect on their own use of it.

THE STATUS OF LOCAL DIALECTS

The spoken language of the uneducated classes still varied greatly in different parts of the country, as the following quotation from Richard Verstegnan will illustrate:

> ... in some severall parts of *England* it selfe, both the names of things, and pronountiations of words are somewhat different, and that among the Country people that never borrow any words out of the *Latin* or *French,* and of this different pronountiation one example in steed of many shall suffice, as this: for pronouncing according as one would say at London *I would eat more cheese if I had it,* the Northern man saith *Ay sud eat mare cheese gin ay hadet,* and the Westerne man saith, *Chud eat more cheese an chad it.*[14]

But although such departures from the London usage had once been perfectly respectable, they were now regarded as "uplandish" or countrified. Sir Walter Raleigh, in spite of his learning and position at the court is reported to have spoken broad Devonshire to his dying day. The interesting thing about this is not that it shows his independent spirit, but that it was considered worth mentioning as something remarkable.

In written, or at least in published English, all the local dialects practically disappeared except for the Scottish. This had once been simply a subvariety of the Northern dialect; but its use had gradually become a national rather than a geographical habit, and its distinct qualities were patriotically preserved.

THE QUALITY OF RENAISSANCE ENGLISH

An adjective often applied to Renaissance English is *luxuriant*—a term which suggests both the richness of the language and its freedom from the sort of restrictions that later came to be applied to it. Although Court English had become a national standard, it was in itself not nearly so rigid as it later became. Grammarians and schoolmasters had not yet begun the attempt to "ascertain" it—that is, to decide which of the various ways of saying anything was right, and to outlaw all the others. The general feeling of guilt about the language which has plagued most educated speakers for the past two hundred years had not yet been aroused. Some people had strong objections to borrowing words from other languages, but everybody seems to have felt free to use whatever words he regarded as English however he liked—with reasonable attention to their meaning, of course, but with no fear of misusing a part of speech, and little concern about which was the accepted idiom. Among the unsettled questions that are likely to strike us most forcefully were the forms of many verbs and the idiomatic uses of prepositions and the articles.

As for the richness of the language, we have been talking about it ever since; and in spite of those traveled show-offs who sneered, it seems to have been quite generally appreciated at the time. Choosing from the many glorifications of the state of the tongue, we may close the chapter with this from William L'Isle:

... our language is improued aboue all others now spoken by any nation, and became the fairest, the nimblest, the fullest; most apt to vary the phrase, most ready to receiue good composition, most adorned with sweet words and sentences, with witty quips and ouer-ruling Prouerbes: yea able to expresse any hard conceit whatsoeuer with great dexterity; waighty in weighty matters, merry in merry, braue in braue. Tell me not it is a mingle-mangle; for so are all: but the punishment of confusion we marke not so much in other tongues, because wee know not them, and their borrowing so well as our owne; and this is also delightfull to know.[15]

NOTES

1. Actually there were two long *e*'s in Middle English: the open *e*, [ɛ:], which is a prolongation of the vowel sound in *met*, and the close *e*, [e:], which is a prolongation of the first element of the diphthong in *bait*. The open *e* sound was often spelled *ea*, and the close *e* sound *ee*, though there is a good deal of inconsistency. During the great vowel shift [ɛ:] was raised to [e:], and [e:] to [i:]. Immediately after this *clean* rhymed with *plain* rather than *keen*, and *tea* with *day* rather than *see*. This explains some of Pope's rhymes, and also the conservative pronunciation of some proper names, such as *O'Dea*. However, early in the eighteenth century the new [e:] shifted further to [i:], so that the result indicated in the text was eventually attained. The difference between the two *e* sounds in Middle English has hitherto been disregarded in this book simply because Chaucer, who is the only Middle English writer that most people are likely to be concerned about pronouncing, often rhymes the two sounds. It could not be disregarded in a more searching study of the language.

2. In academic writing the word *doubtless* generally means that the writer is bringing forth an opinion for which he has no real evidence.

3. Rolf Kaiser, *Medieval English* (Berlin-Wilmersdorf, 1961), p. 566, lines 118–136.

4. J. L. Moore, *Tudor-Stuart Views on the Growth, Status, and Destiny of the English Language* (Halle, 1910), pp. 91–93.

5. Moore, p. 94.

6. *The Excellency of the English Tongue,* Moore, p. 114.

7. From a *Restitution of Decayed Intelligence,* Moore, p. 128.

8. Moore, p. 82.

9. Moore, pp. 83–86.

10. Letter to Sir W. Cecil, Moore, pp. 94–95.

11. Moore, pp. 103–104.

12. Moore, pp. 105–106.

13. Kaiser, p. 243.

14. Moore, p. 126.

15. Moore, p. 139.

✠ ✠ ✠

SHAKESPEARE'S EDUCATION

MARCHETTE CHUTE

As a Stratford boy grew older he found less time for roaming, for school was a serious business in his community. There had always been a free school in Stratford, financed before the Reformation by the Guild of the Holy Cross and since then by borough revenues. The Stratford charter stipulated that the town was to have a "free grammar school for the training and education of children" to be "continued forever," and the boys in Stratford were expected to enter it for a free education as soon as they knew how to read and write.

By the end of the century there was a man in Stratford who taught the children reading and writing while his wife taught needlework, and unless there was a similar arrangement when William Shakespeare was a small boy he probably learned his letters from the parish clerk. The Stratford grammar school was not supposed to handle elementary work of this kind, although it was apparently sometimes forced to assume what it called the "tedious trouble" of teaching the young to read. It was a trouble to the young also, and one weak-minded English uncle of the previous decade spent twenty times as much on sugar plums as on hornbooks before his nephew succeeded in learning his letters.

The hornbook was a slab of wood on which a page full of letters had been fastened and which was covered over with a thin, transparent sheet of horn to protect it from grubby small fingers. Countless generations of children had learned to read clutching the handle of a hornbook and William Shakespeare could hardly have been an exception. From that he probably graduated to *The ABC and Little Catechism*, which gave the youth of England their letters and their religious instruction simultaneously and sold in England at the rate of ten thousand copies in eight months.

Shakespeare learned to form his letters in the way all the little boys in rural districts formed them. The new Italian hand, which corresponds roughly to the modern way of writing, had made great headway in court and city circles, but the medieval way of writing, the one called the secretary hand, was still being used in the country. Some of Shakespeare's fellow-dramatists, like George Peele, used the new Italian way of writing; some of them, like Thomas Kyd and George Chapman, used both fashions interchangeably, and at least one of them, Ben Jonson, worked out an efficient compromise between the two. The few signatures which are all that remain of Shakespeare's writing are done in the old-fashioned secretary hand he was taught in Stratford, and it is probable that he did not bother to change it after he came to London.

As soon as he could read and write and knew his Catechism, young William Shakespeare was ready to enter Stratford grammar school. He was the son of one of the most prominent men in Stratford, but he received the same education that was democratically open to every boy in town and there was no charge for the instruction.

The curriculum of Stratford grammar school, like that of every other grammar school in England, was serious, thorough and dull. There was no attempt whatever to fit the boys for the ordinary life they were going to find when they graduated, for all school theory in England was based on the medieval system. The purpose of schools in the Middle Ages was to turn out learned clerks for church positions, and therefore what the little boys of Renaissance England learned was Latin, more Latin and still more Latin. About a decade after Shakespeare entered the classroom a London teacher urged that English should also be taught in the schools, but no one paid any attention to so radical a suggestion.

The chief difference between the education given Shakespeare and that given Geoffrey Chaucer two centuries earlier was that Chaucer's comparatively simple instruction book, called the Donat, had been replaced by an authorized Latin grammar written by William Lily. Lily was the first headmaster of the school at St. Paul's Cathedral, and his book must have made him more cordially hated by harassed seven-year olds than any man before or since. The whole of the English educational system united to pound Lily's Latin grammar into the heads of the young, and if a schoolboy was wise he resigned himself to having to memorize the whole book.

Not one boy in a hundred had any real use for Latin in his subsequent career, and it is sad to think how the young Quineys and Walkers and Shakespeares worked over their construing in the schoolroom, in what one

London teacher compassionately called an "unnatural stillness," while the whole of the sunlit world waited for them outside. One of their number was eventually to become an actor and no doubt the strict training in memory-work did him a certain amount of good, but it is hard to see how their work in the schoolroom really benefited most of them.

In the average grammar school the boys worked at their grammar about four years, although an earlier educationalist had urged a little more consideration of the boy's own point of view. "By the time he cometh to the sweet and pleasant reading of old authors, the sparks of fervent desire for learning is extinct with its burden of grammar." Another reformer agreed that it was "cold and uncomfortable" for both teacher and pupil, when grammar was taught without an allied course of reading, but he added gloomily that it was "the common way." It was much easier to teach rules than to give boys a real love of Latin literature, and the average teacher took the easier way.

Here and there an imaginative teacher who loved his work triumphed over Lily and kindled a love of Latin writers in the hearts of the young. William Camden, the great London teacher, lit such a fire in the heart of one of his students that Ben Jonson worshipped both Camden and the classics all his life. Somewhere at Cambridge Christopher Marlowe evidently found a teacher who did the same, but there is no indication that any schoolmaster set off a similar spark in young William Shakespeare. Like Geoffrey Chaucer before him, Shakespeare preferred to approach his Latin authors through a translation whenever he could.

Like Chaucer, Shakespeare's one real love among the schoolroom worthies was Ovid, but it was never difficult to arouse a schoolboy's interest in Ovid. The chief difficulty, rather, was to distract his mind from that amorous and delightful storyteller. Nearly all the mythology that Shakespeare knew came from Ovid's *Metamorphoses*, as did that of most of his fellow writers, but it is evident that Shakespeare was much more familiar with the first book or two than he was with the rest of it and even in the case of Ovid he was not above working with a translation.

Apart from learning to read Latin and write Latin, an English schoolboy was also expected to recite Latin, and here again was an aspect of the curriculum that might conceivably be of some use to a future actor. There was considerable emphasis on good public speaking and a controlled, intelligent use of the voice, and many schoolmasters let their boys act out Latin plays by Plautus and Terence to give them experience in handling the spoken word.

Richard Mulcaster, who was head for many years of the excellent school conducted by the Merchant Tailors in London, always kept the spoken word in the forefront of his mind when he taught Latin. When he expounded the mysteries of punctuation to his classes he did it as a singing teacher might, with the emphasis on "tunable uttering." A parenthesis meant the use of a lower and quicker voice, a comma was a place to catch the breath a little, and a period was a place where the breath could be caught completely. This sort of training would have been of great use to William Shakespeare when he started work as a professional actor and had to learn to translate the words written on a cue sheet into the sound of a living voice, and if he did not learn it from some imaginative teacher in the schoolroom it was one of the many things he had to pick up for himself after he reached London.

Apart from teaching him Latin, Stratford grammar school taught Shakespeare nothing at all. It did not teach him mathematics or any of the natural sciences. It did not teach him history, unless a few pieces of information about ancient events strayed in through Latin quotations. It did not teach him geography, for the first (and most inadequate) textbook on geography did not appear until the end of the century, and maps and atlases were rare even in university circles. It did not teach him modern languages, for when a second language was taught at a grammar school it was invariably Greek.

What Shakespeare learned about any of these subjects he learned for himself later, in London. London was the one great storehouse in England of living, contemporary knowledge and in that great city an alert and intelligent man could find out almost anything he wanted to know. It was in London, for instance, that Shakespeare learned French; and French was taught by Frenchmen who worked in competition with each other and used oral, conversational methods that were designed to get colloquial French into the student's head as quickly as possible.

When French was finally accepted into the grammar school curriculum it was subjected to the heavy emphasis on rules and grammar with which the Latin tongue was already burdened, and Shakespeare was probably very fortunate that no one tried to teach him English by the same system. All the rules, the ritual and the reverent embalming were focussed on Latin, and as a result the writers of the late sixteenth century had a lighthearted sense of freedom where their native tongue was concerned because it had never been laid out in the schoolroom and expounded. Much respect was given to the Latin language, but all the affection, the excited experimentation and the warm sense of personal ownership went into the English. If a writer needed an effective word he could not go to a dictionary for it. There were no English dictionaries, although Richard Mulcaster remarked it would be a praiseworthy deed to compile one. The writer could either reach back into his memory, a practice that forced every writer to be also an alert listener, or else he could invent a new word entirely.

There was still some doubt among thoughtful men whether it was quite respectful to the language to use it in so lighthearted a fashion. George Puttenham apologized for using such "strange and unaccustomed" new words as *idiom, method, impression, numerous, penetrate, savage* and *obscure*. Gabriel Harvey was scolded for using such abnormalities as *theory* and *jovial* and *negotiation*; and Ben Jonson, who could never forget his classical education, was horrified by a fellow playwright who used such outlandish words as *damp, clumsy, strenuous* and *puffy*.

This use of new words could degenerate into complete confusion in the hands of incompetent writers but it gave Shakespeare exactly the freedom he needed. He felt at complete liberty to pick up effective new words and combinations of words wherever he could find them, and a play like *Hamlet* is so full of them that it would have made a schoolmaster turn pale if he had had any responsibility for teaching his charges the English language. Fortunately he had no such responsibility, and young William Shakespeare was free to discover the great reaches of the English language as a freeborn and independent citizen.

Every weekday, summer and winter, from the time when he was about seven years old, young Shakespeare went to school. He walked down Henley Street, turned at the Market Cross and went the two long blocks to the guild buildings. During most of Shakespeare's boyhood the schoolroom was up-stairs over the Council room, except for a short period when it had to be repaired, and the same bell that called William to school every morning called his father about once a month to the Council meeting in one of the rooms downstairs.

No single schoolmaster can be assigned the honor of having given William Shakespeare his schooling, since there happened to be a succession of teachers in Stratford during Shakespeare's boyhood. When he entered school the master was Walter Roche, who left because he was given a rectory. Roche's successor was Simon Hunt, who left in 1575 to become a Jesuit. The teacher for the next four years was Thomas Jenkins, and when Jenkins left his post Shakespeare was fifteen and certainly no longer in school. All these men were university graduates, each of them holding a degree from Oxford, for the pay in Stratford was excellent and the twenty pounds a year that went to the schoolmaster was almost twice what he would have received in a large town like Warwick. All three men were presumably competent and well-trained, since there must have been many candidates for the post. It is to be hoped that at least one of them had a spark of Mulcaster's imagination, but they may have been merely the routine pedagogues that the educational system of the time encouraged.

When a boy had completed the curriculum of the grammar school in Stratford, he would have his head well stocked with the principles of Latin grammar and also with a miscellaneous collection of quotations from Latin authors, designed to illustrate the different parts of speech and supply him with a little moral education besides. He had probably been taught to keep a commonplace book, in which he was encouraged to write down any quotations that pleased him in his reading from ancient authors. He had learned how to make a pen neatly, cutting off the goose feathers with his penknife and softening the nib with his tongue. He had learned to sit upright when he was writing so that the humors of the brain would not fall down into his forehead and affect his eyesight, and he had learned how to endure the discipline of long hours of labor.

The school hours for the average English boy were long, usually extending from seven in the morning to five at night, with two hours off in the middle of the day to go home for dinner. The only difference made by the coming of summer was that the school hours were generally longer because there were more hours of daylight. Since curfew was at eight in the summertime, a well-brought-up little Stratfordian had comparatively few hours to play. For the rest, each small scholar was supposed to supply his own books and satchel with pens and ink, with candles extra in the winter; and, as William Lily opened his grammar by pointing out sternly, he was also supposed to come to school with his face washed and his hair combed, and on no account was he to loiter by the way.

SHAKESPEARE'S CLASSICS

GILBERT HIGHET

There is no doubt whatever that Shakespeare was deeply and valuably influenced by Greek and Latin culture. The problem is to define how that influence reached him, and how it affected his poetry.

Forty large works, including the two long narrative poems and the sonnet-sequence, are attributed to Shakespeare. Of these:

six deal with Roman history—four with the republic and two with the empire;[1]

six have a Greek background;[2]

twelve concern British history, chiefly the period of the dynastic struggles in the late Middle Ages and early Renaissance;

fourteen are played in Renaissance Europe. In these, even when the story is antique, the settings and the manner are quite contemporary. For instance, in *Hamlet*, the prince whose companions (in the original tale told by Saxo Grammaticus) carried 'runes carved in wood' now forges a diplomatic dispatch and its seal,[3] and in his own court discusses the stage of Elizabethan London.[4] Half of these plays are localized in Renaissance Italy,[5] while two are set more or less in France (*As You Like It* and *All's Well*). The other five are in vaguely defined places which are Italianate (*Measure for Measure, Twelfth Night*, and *The*

Tempest), Frenchified (*Love's Labour's Lost*), or northern European (*Hamlet*);

one play, *The Merry Wives of Windsor*, is laid in an England almost wholly contemporary in feeling; but its hero is Falstaff, who started life in the fourteenth century. Only the Sonnets can be said to deal directly with Shakespeare's own time and country.

Of course Shakespeare took little care to exclude geographical and historical incongruities, or to create a complete illusion of local and temporal colour. All his plays have touches, and many have complete scenes and characters, which could only be contemporary English. But from this broad classification of his themes it is evident that three great interests stimulated his imagination. The first was the Renaissance culture of western Europe. The second was England, and particularly her monarchy and nobility. The third, equal in importance to the second, was the history and legends of Greece and Rome.

From his characters and their speech we derive a similar impression. To begin with, most of Shakespeare's writing is English of the English. No poet has ever expressed England, its character, its folk-speech and song, its virtues and its follies and some of its vices, and even its physical appearance, so sensitively and memorably. Rosalind is the daughter of a banished duke (therefore not an English girl, but French or Italian); yet she goes into exile in the forest of Arden, which is near Stratford-on-Avon,[6] and her nature and her way of talking are English to the heart's core. Then, intertwined with the Englishness of Shakespeare's characters, there is a silken strand of Italian charm and subtlety. A number of his best plays are stories of the intricate villainy which flourished in Renaissance Italy: Iago is only one such villain; think of Sebastian and Antonio in *The Tempest* and the beastly Iachimo in *Cymbeline*. And much of the wit and fine manners (particularly in the early dramas) is of the type cultivated by Englishmen Italianate—for instance, Osric's ridiculous courtesies in *Hamlet*. Pandarus actually calls Cressida by an Italian pet-name, *capocchia*.[7] But lastly, there is an all-pervading use of Greek and Latin imagery and decorative reference, which is sometimes superficial but more often incomparably effective. Think of the aubade in *Cymbeline*.[8]

> Hark, hark, the lark at heaven's gate sings,
>   And Phoebus 'gins arise,
> His steeds to water at those springs
>   On chaliced flowers that lies.

Or of Perdita's garland:[9]

>   . . . violets dim,
> But sweeter than the lids of Juno's eyes
>   Or Cytherea's breath.

Or of Hamlet's godlike father:[10]

> See, what a grace was seated on this brow;
> Hyperion's curls, the front of Jove himself,
> An eye like Mars, to threaten and command,
> A station like the herald Mercury
> New lighted on a heaven-kissing hill.

Or of the idyllic love duet:[11]

> In such a night
> Stood Dido with a willow in her hand
> Upon the wild sea-banks, and waft her love
> To come again to Carthage.

The poet who wrote like that knew and loved the classics.

The power of the classical world on Shakespeare can also be proved negatively. We have seen how many of the writers of the Renaissance belonged spiritually to both worlds: that of the Middle Ages, with knights and ladies and enchanters and magical animals and strange quests and impossible beliefs, and that of Greco-Roman myth and art. Such, for example, were Ariosto, and Rabelais, and Spenser. But Shakespeare, like Milton, rejected and practically ignored the world of the Middle Ages. Even his historical dramas are contemporary in tone, far more than they are medieval: who could dream that Sir John Falstaff was supposed to be a contemporary of the Canterbury Pilgrims?

It is significant to observe Shakespeare's few allusions to medieval thought: they are pretty or quaint, but they show that he did not feel the Middle Ages vital and stimulating. Mistress Quickly, when describing the death of Falstaff, declares that he must be in heaven. The biblical phrase is 'in Abraham's bosom,' but the hostess says: 'He's in Arthur's bosom, if ever man went to Arthur's bosom,' for unconsciously she finds it easier to think of Sir John being received by the old symbol of immortal British chivalry than by a Hebrew patriarch.[12] Again, one of the men whom Shakespeare most despises, Mr. Justice Shallow, explains the technique of drill by recalling 'a little quiver fellow' whom he knew when he himself played 'Sir Dagonet in Arthur's show.'[13] And sometimes there are echoes of the Middle Ages in proverbs and in songs; Edgar as a madman sings snatches of old ballads, among them a beautiful anachronism which was to inspire another English poet to revive the medieval tradition: 'Child Rowland to the dark tower came.'[14] The only important element in Shakespeare's work which can really be called medieval is the supernatural: Oberon and his fairies, the witches and their spells. Even in that there are Hellenic touches, and the rest has been shrunk and softened by distance, the fairies have grown smaller and kinder, the gargoyles and fiends have vanished for ever.

Now we must analyse Shakespeare's classical knowledge in more detail. The first fact we observe is that he knows much more and feels much more sensitively about Rome than about Greece, with the single exception of the Greek myths which reached the modern world through Rome. The Roman plays—plus some anachronisms and some solidly English touches—are like Rome. The Greek plays are not like Greece. Although Shakespeare took several of his best plots from the Roman biographies of Plutarch, he almost entirely ignored the Greek statesmen whom Plutarch described as *parallel* to his Roman heroes, and used only Alcibiades and Timon. In *Timon of Athens* itself there are only two or three Greek names; all the rest are Latin —some of them, such as Varro and Isidore, ridiculously inappropriate; and the Athenian state is represented by senators, which shows that Shakespeare wrongly imagined it to be a republic like Rome. It is true that in *Troilus and Cressida* his warriors were not the anachronistic chevaliers who appear in the medieval romances of Troy; and that he has borrowed some things from the *Iliad*—the duel of Hector and Ajax, the speech of Ulysses in 1. 3. 78 f., the stupidity of Ajax, and certainly the character of Thersites, who does not appear in the romances.[15] (No doubt he had been reading Chapman's translation of *Iliad*, 1–2 and 7–11, which came out in 1598.) But even so, the whole play is not merely anti-heroic: it is a distant, ignorant, and unconvincing caricature of Greece.

The Roman plays are far more real and elaborate in detail than the Greek. Sometimes they are wrong in secondary matters like costume and furniture. But the touches of reality in the Greek dramas are fewer, and the anachronisms are far worse: Hector quotes Aristotle,[16] Pandarus talks of Friday and Sunday,[17] and the brothers Antipholus are the long-lost sons of an abbess.[18] In the Roman plays there are few large misrepresentations and much deep insight into character. The strong, law-abiding, patriotic plebeians of the early republic appear in *Coriolanus*, because of Shakespeare's contempt for the mob, as an excitable degenerate rabble like the idle creatures of *Julius Caesar*. Antony is made a much better man than he was; but there Shakespeare has exercised the dramatist's right to re-create character, and has made him a hero with a fault, like Leicester, like Essex, like Bacon, like so many great men of the Renaissance. For the rest, he has rendered better than anyone else, better even than the sources which he used, the essence of the Roman republic and its aristocracy. On the other hand, the Athenian noble Alcibiades, who appears in *Timon*, was a complex personality who would have much interested Shakespeare if he had known anything about him; but he never understood the Greeks enough to portray him properly.

Just as Shakespeare has more command over Roman than Greek themes, so the spirit of his tragic plays is much less Greek than Roman. Of course the Greeks founded and developed drama; without them, neither we nor the Romans could have written tragedies; and most of the essentials of Latin as of modern tragedy are borrowed from them. Nevertheless, the English Renaissance playwrights did not as a rule know Greek tragedy, and they did know Seneca, whose tragedies appeared severally in translation from 1559 onwards, and complete in 1581. Less than ten years later the sharp and satirical Nashe was sneering at the writers who from Seneca 'read by candlelight' copied 'whole *Hamlets*, I should say handfuls, of tragical speeches.'[19] Ghosts, and revenge, and the horrors of treachery, bloody cruelty, and kinsmen's murder, and a spirit of frenzied violence unlike the Hellenic loftiness—these Shakespeare found in Seneca, and he converted them into the sombre fury of his tragedies.

Shakespeare's free use of Greek and Latin imagery has already been mentioned. He is fluent and happy in his classical allusions. No writer who dislikes the classics, who receives no real stimulus from them, who brings in Greek and Roman decorations merely to parade his learning or to satisfy convention, can create so many apt and beautiful classical symbols as Shakespeare. Except the simplest fools and yokels, all his characters—from Hamlet to Pistol, from Rosalind to Portia—can command Greek and Latin reminiscences to enhance the grace and emotion of their speech. It is of course clear that Shakespeare was not a bookman. Miss Spurgeon's analysis of his similes and metaphors[20] shows that the fields from which he preferred to draw likenesses were, in order: *daily life* (social types, sport, trades, &c.), *nature* (in particular, growing things and weather), *domestic life* and *bodily actions* (which are surely both very closely connected with 'daily life'), *animals*, and then, after all these, *learning*. And even within the range of his learning Shakespeare's classical knowledge occupies a comparatively small space. He knew more about mythology than about ancient history—he knew the classical myths far better than the Bible. But he had far fewer classical symbols present to his mind than Marlowe. Learning meant little to him unless he could translate it into living human terms. It is mostly his pedants who quote the classics by book and author, and such quotations are either weak or ridiculous, and almost always inappropriate, as when Touchstone tells his poor virgin: 'I am here with thee and thy goats, as the most capricious poet, honest Ovid, was among the Goths.'[21] But the classical images which, for Shakespeare, emerge from books to become as real as animals, and colours, and stars—these images are used so strikingly as to show that classical culture was for him a spectacle not less vivid, though smaller, than the life around him. The loveliest, most loving girl in his plays, waiting for her wedding-night, gazes at the bright sky, sees the sun rushing on towards evening, and urges it to hurry, hurry, even at the risk of destroying the world. She does not say so: the direct wish would be too extravagant; but it is conveyed by the superb image:

> Gallop apace, you fiery-footed steeds,
> Towards Phoebus' lodging; such a waggoner
> As Phaethon would whip you to the west,
> And bring in cloudy night immediately.[22]

It would scarcely be possible to distinguish between Greek and Roman imagery in the plays; at most one might point to the predominance of Rome among his historical images. But in language it is clear that, as Ben Jonson said, Shakespeare had 'small Latin and less Greek.'[23] He uses only three or four Greek words.[24] He does bring in Latin words and phrases, but not so freely as many of his contemporaries, and with less sureness than he uses French and Italian. Latin is quoted most freely in the early plays. *Love's Labour's Lost* has a comic schoolmaster who talks Latin,[25] but, like the rest of Shakespeare's latinists, he is not a really learned pedant, on the same level as the Limousin student in Rabelais.[26] He can only string a few schoolbook Latin words together—and this in a play where Berowne's speech on love introduces some exquisite classical allusions, used with fine imaginative freedom:

> Subtle as Sphinx: as sweet and musical
> As bright Apollo's lute, strung with his hair.[27]

Few are the sentences in Shakespeare that seem to have been suggested by a direct memory of a Latin phrase, while in Milton, Tasso, Jonson, Ronsard, and other Renaissance poets they are myriad. But he often uses English words of Latin derivation in such a way as to show that he understands their origin and root-meaning. Occasionally he makes an eccentric attempt to 'despumate the Latial verbocination,' such as the word *juvenal* for *youngster*; and when he experiments with the importation of Latin into English he is as likely to fail (*exsufflicate* in *Othello*, 3.3.182) as to succeed (*impartial* in *Richard II*, 1.1.115). All this matters little. Shakespeare wrote the English language.

To quote phrases from Roman poetry, either in Latin or in translation, and to imitate striking passages, was not pedantry in the Renaissance poets. . . . it was one of their methods of adding beauty and authority to their work. The taste and learning of the individual poet determined how frequently he would use quotations, how far he would disguise or emphasize them, how carefully he would follow the original text or how freely he would adapt memorable words, images, and ideas. No great modern writer has ever surpassed Milton in his ability to embellish his work with jewels cut by other craftsmen. Of the Renaissance dramatists Ben Jonson, easily the best scholar, was much the busiest borrower and the most sedulous translator: some of his most important speeches are almost literal renderings of passages from the Roman historians who gave him his plots. Compared with Milton and

Jonson, Shakespeare quotes the classics seldom; but by other standards (for instance, in comparison with Racine) he quotes freely and often.

Ben Jonson's judgement of Shakespeare's classical knowledge has often been misquoted, and often teased into a comparative rather than an absolute judgement: that Shakespeare merely knew less Latin and much less Greek than Jonson—which would still allow him to be a fair scholar. But the way in which Shakespeare quotes the classics is, like his use of Latin words, proof that Jonson was literally correct. Shakespeare did not know much of the Latin language, he new virtually no Greek, and he was vague and unscholarly in using what he did know. But he used it nearly all with the flair of a great imaginative artist. What Jonson could have added, and what we must not forget, is that Shakespeare loved Latin and Greek literature. What he had been taught at school he remembered, he improved his knowledge afterwards by reading translations, and he used both what he remembered and what he got from translations as verbal embellishment, decorative imagery, and plot material throughout his career.

Beginning in 1767 with Richard Farmer's *Learning of Shakespeare*, there have been many, many discussions of Shakespeare's use of his classical sources—too many to treat here. It is a specialist field of considerable interest, still incompletely covered, since not many scholars who know enough about Shakespeare and his time have had the classical training which would enable them to make all the right connexions. Its chief value for the general reader is that it keeps him from conceiving Shakespeare as an Ariel warbling his native woodnotes wild. Shakespeare was indeed part Ariel; but he was more Prospero, with volumes that he prized above a dukedom.[28]

The most convenient way to assess Shakespeare's classical equipment and the use to which he put it is to distinguish the authors he knew well from those he knew imperfectly or at second hand. The difficulty of making this investigation accurate is the same difficulty that meets every student of the transmission of artistic and spiritual influence. It is seldom easy to decide whether a similarity between the thought or expression of two writers means that one has copied the other. It is particularly hard when one of those writers is as great as Shakespeare, whose soul was so copious, whose eloquence was so fluent. We can be sure, for instance, that he had not read Aeschylus. Yet what can we say when we find some of Aeschylus' thoughts appearing in Shakespeare's plays? The only explanation is that great poets in times and countries distant from each other often have similar thoughts and express them similarly. On the other hand, we are reluctant to believe that, given the opportunity, a great writer would borrow anything valuable from a lesser man. Yet some resemblances are too striking to be denied; and it is folly to imagine that Shakespeare could take his plot from one book and his names from another and yet balk at borrowing a fine image from a third.

This is perhaps a suitable place to suggest a simple set of rules by which parallel passages in two writers can be taken to establish the dependence of one on the other. First, it must be shown that one writer read, or probably read, the other's work. Then a close similarity of thought or imagery must be demonstrated. Thirdly, there should be a clear structural parallelism: in the sequence of the reasoning, in the structure of the sentences, in the position of the words within the lines of poetry, or in some or all of these together.

Sometimes it is impossible to prove that the later writer read the works of the earlier, but possible to conjecture that he heard them discussed. In periods of great intellectual activity a man with a lively imagination and a retentive memory often picks up great ideas not from the books which contain them (and which may be closed to him) but from the conversation of his friends and from adaptations of them in the work of his contemporaries. We know that Ben Jonson was a good scholar. We know that Shakespeare had long and lively discussions with him. Often Jonson must have tried to break the rapier of Shakespeare's imagination with the bludgeon of a learned quotation or an abstruse philosophical doctrine, only to find Shakespeare, in a later tournament or even in a play produced next season, using the weapon that had once been Jonson's, now lightened, remodelled, and apparently moulded to Shakespeare's own hand. The channels by which remote but valuable ideas reach imaginative writers are as complex and difficult to retrace as those by which they learn their psychology and subtilize their sense of words; but in estimating a various-minded man like Shakespeare we must make the widest possible allowance for his power of assimilating classical ideas from the classical atmosphere that surrounded him.

There is a good example of this in one of Shakespeare's most imaginative scenes. Plato made known to the modern world the noble idea that the physical universe is a group of eight concentric spheres, each of which, as it turns, sings one note; and that the notes of the eight blend into a divine harmony, which we can hear only after death when we have escaped from this prison of flesh. Somewhere Shakespeare had heard this. He had not read it in Plato: because he altered it—freely, and, for a student of Plato, wrongly, but, for all his readers, superbly. In a scene where two lovers have already recalled much beauty from classical legend and poetry, he made Lorenzo tell his mistress, not that the Ptolemaic spheres sang eight harmonious notes, but (with a reminiscence of the time when 'the morning stars sang together') that every single star in the sky sang while it moved, with the angels as the audience of the divine concert:

> There's not the smallest orb which thou behold'st
> But in his motion like an angel sings,
> Still quiring to the young-eyed cherubins;
> Such harmony is in immortal souls;
> But, whilst this muddy vesture of decay
> Doth grossly close us in, we cannot hear it.[29]

Shakespeare was therefore, directly and indirectly, a classically educated poet who loved the classics. They were his chief book-education. They were one of the greatest challenges to his creative power. His classical training was wholly successful, because it taught him their beauties at school, encouraged him to continue his reading of the classics in mature life, and helped to make him a complete poet, and a whole man.

He knew three classical authors well, a fourth partially, and a number of others fragmentarily. Ovid, Seneca, and Plutarch enriched his mind and his imagination. Plautus gave him material for one play and trained him for others. From Vergil and other authors he took stories, isolated thoughts, and similes, sometimes of great beauty. Because of his early training he was able to respond to the manifold stimuli which the reading of translations gave to his creative genius.

Shakespeare's favourite classical author was Ovid. Like other English schoolboys of the time, he very probably learnt some Ovid at school.[30] He read him later, both in the original Latin and in Golding's translation of the *Metamorphoses*. He often imitated him, from his first work to his last. His friends knew this. In a survey of contemporary literature published in 1598 Francis Meres said Shakespeare was a reincarnation of Ovid:

'As the soul of Euphorbus was thought to live in Pythagoras, so the sweet witty soul of Ovid lives in mellifluous and honey-tongued Shakespeare; witness his Venus and Adonis, his Lucrece, his sugared sonnets among his private friends.'[31]

The first book he published, and, according to him, the first he wrote,[32] was a sumptuous blending and elaboration of two Greek myths which he found in Ovid's *Metamorphoses*;[33] and he prefaced it with a couplet from Ovid's *Loves*.[34] The quotation throws a valuable light on his artistic ideals. It reads

> Vilia miretur vulgus; mihi flavus Apollo
> pocula Castalia plena ministret aqua;

which means

> Let cheap things please the mob; may bright Apollo
> serve me full draughts from the Castalian spring.

His other long poem, *The Rape of Lucrece*, is based partly on Livy, partly on Ovid's *Fasti*, with several close correspondences of language and thought.[35]

Several quotations of Ovid's own words are scattered through the plays. In *The Taming of the Shrew* Lucentio poses as a Latin tutor in order to make love to Bianca. He conveys his message to her through the device used by schoolboys in classroom repetition and convicts in hymn-singing:

BIANCA: Where left we last?
LUCENTIO: Here, madam:
> Hac ibat Simois; hic est Sigeia tellus;
> Hic steterat Priami regia celsa senis.

BIANCA: Construe them.

LUCENTIO: Hac ibat, as I told you before, Simois, I am Lucentio, hic est, son unto
Vincentio of Pisa, Sigeia tellus, disguised thus to get your love; Hic steterat,
and that Lucentio that comes a-wooing, Priami, is my man Tranio, regia,
bearing my port, celsa senis, that we might beguile the old pantaloon.[36]

(Of course the translation is not meant to make sense, but there is an allusion
to the original meaning in 'the old pantaloon.')

Direct quotations also occur in two of the doubtful plays.[37] And there is
one very famous echo which Shakespeare has made his own. The name of
the fairy queen in *A Midsummer-Night's Dream* is not taken from Celtic
legend like her husband's. It is a Greco-Latin word, Titania, which means
'Titan's daughter' or 'Titan's sister.' The name occurs only in Ovid, who
uses it five times, and, in the two best-known passages, of Diana and Circe.[38]
From these two queens of air and darkness and from their melodious title,
Shakespeare has created a new and not less enchanting spirit.

Golding's translation of Ovid's *Metamorphoses* was a coarse free version
in lumbering 'fourteeners,' very unlike the suave graceful original. But
Shakespeare could read the original, he had incomparable taste, and, as T. S.
Eliot has remarked,[39] he 'had that ability, which is not native to everyone, to
extract the utmost possible from translations.' Therefore several fine passages,
which we now regard as heirs of his own invention, were borrowed—no, not
borrowed, but transmuted from Ovid through the Golding translation.

> Like as the waves make towards the pebbled shore,
> So do our minutes hasten to their end;
> Each changing place with that which goes before,
> In sequent toil all forwards to contend.

This famous quatrain in Sonnet 60 is a transmutation of Ovid, as Englished
by Golding:

> As every wave drives others forth, and that which comes behind
> Both thrusteth and is thrust himself: even so the times by kind
> Do fly and follow both at once, and evermore renew.[40]

But that is only one aspect of a complex philosophical idea, the idea that
nature is constantly changing, so that nothing is permanent and yet nothing
is destroyed. This is expounded in the sermon of Pythagoras towards the
end of the *Metamorphoses*, and is the theme of several of Shakespeare's
finest sonnets.[41]

There is, however, not much philosophy in either Ovid or Shakespeare—
indeed, one of Shakespeare's characters explicitly distinguishes Ovid and
philosophy, implying that the former is far more delightful.[42] But most of the
Metamorphoses is concerned with sex and the supernatural, both of which
interested Shakespeare. His most sensual poem, *Venus and Adonis*, was

inspired, as we have seen, by episodes in the *Metamorphoses*. Again, when Juliet says:

> Thou may'st prove false; at lovers' perjuries,
> They say, Jove laughs,

she is quoting Ovid's *Art of Love*,[43] the book which Lucentio also says is his special subject.[44] In his other great love-drama Shakespeare based the character of Cleopatra on Dido as drawn by Ovid, and actually made her quote an angry line from Dido's reproaches.[45] As for magic, Prospero's incantation in *The Tempest*:

> Ye elves of hills, brooks, standing lakes, and groves;
> And ye, that on the sands with printless foot
> Do chase the ebbing Neptune and do fly him
> When he comes back; you demi-puppets, that
> By moonshine do the green sour ringlets make
> Whereof the ewe not bites; and you, whose pastime
> Is to make midnight mushrooms; that rejoice
> To hear the solemn curfew; by whose aid—
> Weak masters though ye be—I have bedimmed
> The noontide sun, called forth the mutinous winds,
> And 'twixt the green sea and the azured vault
> Set roaring war: to the dread-rattling thunder
> Have I given fire, and rifted Jove's stout oak
> With his own bolt; the strong-based promontory
> Have I made shake; and by the spurs plucked up
> The pine and cedar; graves at my command
> Have waked their sleepers, oped, and let them forth
> By my so potent art. . . .[46]

this splendid speech, apart from some light, inappropriate, and quite British fairy-lore, is based on Medea's invocation in Ovid, *Met.* 7. 197 f., as translated by Golding, thus:

Ye Ayres and Windes; ye Elves of Hilles, of Brookes, of Woods alone,
Of standing Lakes, and of the Night approche ye everychone.
Through helpe of whom (the crooked bankes much wondring at the thing)
I have compelled streames to run cleane backward to their spring.
By charmes I make the calme Seas rough, and make ye rough Seas plaine
And cover all the Skie with Cloudes, and chase them thence againe.
By charmes I rayse and lay the windes, and burst the Vipers jaw,
And from the bowels of the Earth both stones and trees doe drawe.
Whole Woods and Forestes I remove: I make the Mountains shake,
And even the Earth it selfe to grone and fearfully to quake.
I call up dead men from their graves; and thee O Lightsome Moone
I darken oft, though beaten brasse abate thy perill soone.
Our Sorcerie dimmes the Morning faire, and darkes ye Sun at Noone.

Some of the ingredients of the witches' cauldron in *Macbeth*[47] came from Medea's pharmacopoeia in Ovid,[48] which also provided the vaporous drop profound that hangs upon the corner of the moon.[49] In another field, it was Golding's rather Jorrocksy translation of Actaeon's kennel-book[50] that inspired the heroic hunting-conversation in *A Midsummer-Night's Dream*.[51] A number of passages contain explicit references to Ovid's own personality[52] and to his books.[53] But Shakespeare's greatest debt to Ovid is visible all through his plays. It was the world of fable which the *Metamorphoses* opened to him, and which he used as freely as he used the world of visible humanity around him, now making a tale of star-crossed lovers into a clownish farce,[54] and now exalting the myth of Pygmalion to symbolize a higher love.[55]

Shakespeare knew one other Latin author fairly well. This was that enigmatic and decadent figure Seneca, the Stoic millionaire, Nero's tutor, minister, and victim, the Spanish philosopher who taught serene fulfilment of duty and wrote nine dramas of revenge, cruelty, and madness. For the English playwrights of the Renaissance Seneca was the master of tragedy; and even although, at first glance, Stoicism would not appear to be a creed sympathetic to that stirring age, the pithy energetic thinking of his letters and treatises impressed many contemporary writers. He is never quoted in the original by Shakespeare, except in the doubtful *Titus Andronicus*.[56] But he deeply influenced Shakespeare's conception of tragedy, and added certain elements of importance to his dramatic technique, while several memorable Shakespearian speeches are inspired by his work.[57]

Shakespeare's great tragedies are dominated by a hopeless fatalism which is far more pessimistic than the purifying agonies of Greek tragedy, and almost utterly godless. None of them shows any belief in 'the righteous government of the world,' except in so far as successful evildoers are later punished for their own cruel schemes. Sometimes his tragic heroes speak of life as ruled by fate inhuman, unpredictable, and meaningless;[58] and sometimes, more bitterly, cry out against vicious mankind which is unfit to live,[59] and cruel gods who 'kill us for their sport.'[60] That much of this hopeless gloom came from Shakespeare's own heart, no one can doubt; but he found it expressed decisively and eloquently in the Stoical pessimism of Seneca.[61]

To the realization that life is directed by forces indifferent or hostile to man's hopes, there are several possible responses. One, which Seneca's philosophy teaches, is taciturn indifference: emotionless, or even proud, obedience to an irresistible fate. This philosophical disdain of external events occasionally appeared in the Renaissance, where it was strengthened by chivalrous (particularly Spanish) traditions. Shakespeare's heroes usually die in eloquence, but some of his villains withdraw into Stoical silence, and the Stoicism which challenges and even welcomes death appears in the death-scenes of later Elizabethan dramatists.[62] Another response is a furious protest, the yell of suffering given words, the raving self-assertion which grows close to madness. The two responses both appear in Seneca's own works. The Elizabethans, and Shakespeare in particular, preferred the second. We hear it in the ranting of Laertes and Hamlet in Ophelia's grave,[63] in Hotspur's boasts,[64] in Timon's curses.[65] Not so much single speeches as the general tone of tremendous emotional pressure in his tragedies, of a boiling energy which repression only increases and which threatens to erupt at every moment—that, however strengthened by the pains and ardours of his own life and increased by the excitements of the Renaissance, is Shakespeare's inheritance from Seneca.

In technique, the general Elizabethan use of stock Senecan characters— ghosts, witches, and others—has already been mentioned. It has also been suggested that Shakespeare's gloomy, introspective, self-dramatizing heroes are partly inspired by those of Seneca, so unlike the heroes of Greek tragedy.[66] There was moreover an interesting device of dramatic verse invented by the Greeks, which reached Shakespeare and his contemporaries through Seneca's plays. It was a series of repartees in single lines, or occasionally half-lines, in which two opponents strove to out-argue one another, often echoing each other's words and often putting their arguments in the form of competing philosophical maxims. Called stichomythia, it sounds in Euripides and Seneca like a philosophers' debate; in the Elizabethans it is more like the rapid thrust and counter-thrust of fencing. It is most noticeable in Shakespeare's early play, *Richard III*, where the hero and the plot are also shaped on Senecan models.[67]

A number of scenes in Shakespeare's histories and tragedies are closely parallel in thought or imagery to passages in Seneca; and in some of them there are structural similarities also. There are examples in early plays— *Richard III* and *King John*—and in *Titus Andronicus* and *Henry VI*;[68] but there are also several striking instances in that great tragedy of witchcraft, oracles, ghosts, murder, and madness, *Macbeth*. After his stepmother has polluted him by an attempted seduction, Seneca's Hippolytus cries out:

> What Tanais will wash me? what Maeotis,
> urging strange floods into the Pontic sea?
> No, not the mighty father with all his Ocean
> will wash away such sin.[69]

In a second tragedy Seneca elaborates the same idea, adding the dreadful half-line: 'deep the deed will cling.'[70] This is certainly the model for the great scenes in which Macbeth and Lady Macbeth, married in their sin like two parts of a guilty soul, vainly hope to clean the hands stained with their crime:

> Will all great Neptune's ocean wash this blood
> Clean from my hand? No, this my hand will rather
> The multitudinous seas incarnadine. . . .

and later, in the woman's words: 'All the perfumes of Arabia will not sweeten this little hand.'[71]

Again, after recovering from his murderous frenzy, Seneca's Hercules says:

> Why this my soul should linger in the world
> there's now no reason. Lost are all my goods—
> mind, weapons, glory, wife, children, strength,
> even my madness.[72]

Even so Macbeth, at the end of his crimes, mutters:

> I have lived long enough: my way of life
> Is fallen into the sear, the yellow leaf;
> And that which should accompany old age,
> As honour, love, obedience, troops of friends,
> I must not look to have.[73]

In the same passage[74] Hercules cries: 'A mind polluted / No one can cure.' And in the same scene[75] Macbeth asks: 'Canst thou not minister to a mind diseased?' Other Senecan parallels in *Macbeth* are no less powerful.[76]

The third of Shakespeare's favourite classical authors was Plutarch, the Greek moralist and historian who wrote *Parallel Lives* of Greek and Roman statesmen. Plutarch entered western culture in 1559 through the fine translation made by Jacques Amyot. (Montaigne was one of its most enthusiastic readers, and it continued to be part of French thought for centuries: we shall see it as one of the forces inspiring the French Revolution.) Sir Thomas North turned Amyot's version into English in 1579, and through him Plutarch became the author who made the greatest single new impression on Shakespeare. *Julius Ceasar, Coriolanus, Antony and Cleopatra*, and *Timon of Athens* all come from the *Lives*. Plutarch was not a great historian. North was not an accurate translator. Shakespeare was sometimes careless in adapting material from him,[77] sometimes almost echoic in versifying his prose. Yet the results were superb.

Once again we see how incalculably various, how unpredictably fertile, is the stimulus of classical culture. The tradesman's son who attended an unimportant provincial school, who was far from scholarly and went to no university, who toured and acted and collaborated and adapted and wrote plays from all sorts of material, who read Latin keenly but sketchily and Greek not at all, who was more moved by life than by any books, still was so moved in middle life by a second-hand English translation of a second-rate Greek historian that he wrought it into dramas far more tense and vigorous, far more delicate in psychical perception, far fuller in emotion than the biographical essays that introduced him to Roman history.[78] Long afterwards a young English student who wanted to be a poet was lent the translation of Homer made by one of Shakespeare's contemporaries. After reading and thinking all night, he wrote a poem saying it had been for him like a new planet for an astronomer, or, for an explorer, a new ocean. And so for Shakespeare the reading of Plutarch was an unimagined revelation. It showed him serious history instead of playful myth. And it showed him more. Listen.

> Since Cassius first did whet me against Caesar,
> I have not slept.
> Between the acting of a dreadful thing
> And the first motion, all the interim is
> Like a phantasma, or a hideous dream.[79]

That is a new voice. It is the voice of Brutus. But beyond it we can hear the sombre brooding voices of Macbeth; of Hamlet. *Julius Ceasar*, the first of Shakespeare's plays from Plutarch and one of his greatest dramas, marked a climax in his experience. It was his entrance into the realm of high tragedy.[80]

Analysis of Shakespeare's sources will not dull, but intensify, our admiration for his art. To read a chapter of North's plain prose, full of interesting but straightforward facts, and then to see the facts, in Shakespeare's hand, begin to glow with inward life and the words to move and chime in immortal music, is to realize once again that poets are not (as Plato said) copyists, but seers, or creators.[81] Take North's version of Plutarch's life of Caesar, chapters 62.4 to 63.3. The passage deals with the jealousies, hatreds, and omens threatening Caesar's life. Every single sentence in it is used by Shakespeare in *Julius Ceasar*, but the details, instead of being crowded together, are scattered over the first three acts. What Plutarch made flat narrative, Shakespeare makes energetic description or crescendo action. As a dramatist, he initiates at least one important change. Plutarch speaks of Caesar as suspecting and even fearing Cassius. Shakespeare could not make an heroic figure out of an apprehensive dictator: he felt that if Caesar had really feared Cassius he would have protected himself or eliminated the danger; doubtless he remembered the many anecdotes of Caesar's remarkable courage. Therefore he altered these incidents, to show Caesar not indeed as quite fearless, but as affecting the imperturbability of marble. Plutarch writes:

'Caesar also had Cassius in great jealousy and suspected him much: whereupon he said . . . to his friends, "What will Cassius do, think ye? I like not his pale looks." Another time, when Caesar's friends complained unto him of Antonius and Dolabella, . . . he answered them again, "As for those fat men and smooth-combed heads," quoth he, "I never reckon of them; but these pale-visaged and carrion lean people, I fear them most."'

In Shakespeare's mind, this changed into:

CAESAR: Let me have men about me that are fat;
    Sleek-headed men and such as sleep o' nights.
    Yond Cassius has a lean and hungry look;
    He thinks too much; such men are dangerous.

ANTONY: Fear him not, Caesar, he's not dangerous;
   He is a noble Roman, and well given.
CAESAR: Would he were fatter! but I fear him not;
   Yet if my name were liable to fear,
   I do not know the man I should avoid
   So soon as that spare Cassius.[82]

Again, Plutarch mentions the omen of the sacrificial victim which had no heart; but all he can add is the obvious comment 'and that was a strange thing in nature, how a beast could live without a heart.' Shakespeare cannot show the sacrifice on the stage. But he has the omen reported, and invents a lofty reply for Caesar:[83]

CAESAR: What say the augurers?
SERVANT: They would not have you to stir forth today.
   Plucking the entrails of an offering forth,
   They could not find a heart within the beast.
CAESAR: The gods do this in shame of cowardice;
   Caesar should be a beast without a heart
   If he should stay at home today for fear.

So indeed Caesar must, or should, have spoken.

One example is enough to show how Shakespeare turns Plutarch's prose descriptions into poetry—keeping the touches of beauty which were part of the original scene described, colouring it with fancies and images, and adding his own eloquence. In chapter 26 of his life of Marcus Antonius, Plutarch describes the first appearance of Cleopatra:

'Therefore, when she was sent unto by divers letters, both from Antonius himself, and also from his friends, she made so light of it and mocked Antonius so much, that she disdained to set forward otherwise, but to take her barge in the river of Cydnus, the poop whereof was of gold, the sails of purple, and the oars of silver, which kept stroke in rowing after the sound of the music of flutes, howboys, citherns, viols, and such other instruments as they played upon in the barge. And now for the person of herself: she was laid under a pavilion of cloth of gold of tissue, apparelled and attired like the goddess Venus commonly drawn in picture; and hard by her, on either hand of her, pretty fair boys apparelled as painters do set forth god Cupid, with little fans in their hands, with the which they fanned wind upon her. Her Ladies and gentlewomen also, the fairest of them, were apparelled like the nymphs Nereides (which are the mermaids of the waters) and like the Graces, some steering the helm, others tending the tackle and ropes of the barge, out of the which there came a wonderful passing sweet savour of perfumes, that perfumed the wharf's side, pestered with innumerable multitudes of people. Some of them followed the barge all alongst the river's side; others also ran out of the city to see her coming in. So that in th' end, there ran such multitudes of people one after another to see her, that Antonius was left post alone in the market place in his Imperial seat to give audience.'

In Shakespeare[84] this becomes:

ENOBARBUS: When she first met Mark Antony she pursed up his heart, upon the river of Cydnus.
AGRIPPA: There she appeared indeed, or my reporter devised well for her.
ENOBARBUS: I will tell you.
> The barge she sat in, like a burnished throne,
> Burned on the water; the poop was beaten gold,
> Purple the sails, and so perfumed, that
> The winds were love-sick with them, the oars were silver
> Which to the tune of flutes kept stroke, and made
> The water which they beat to follow faster,
> As amorous of their strokes. For her own person,
> It beggared all description; she did lie
> In her pavilion—cloth-of-gold of tissue—
> O'er-picturing that Venus where we see
> The fancy outwork nature; on each side her
> Stood pretty dimpled boys, like smiling Cupids,
> With divers-coloured fans, whose wind did seem
> To glow the delicate cheeks which they did cool,
> And what they undid did.
AGRIPPA: O! rare for Antony!
ENOBARBUS: Her gentlewomen, like the Nereides,
> So many mermaids, tended her i' the eyes,
> And made their bends adornings; at the helm
> A seeming mermaid steers; the silken tackle
> Swell with the touches of those flower-soft hands,
> That yarely frame the office. From the barge
> A strange invisible perfume hits the sense
> Of the adjacent wharfs. The city cast
> Her people out upon her, and Antony,
> Enthroned i' the market-place, did sit alone,
> Whistling to the air; which, but for vacancy,
> Had gone to gaze on Cleopatra too,
> And made a gap in nature.
AGRIPPA: Rare Egyptian!

Nearly every phrase in North contains something flat, or repetitious, or clumsy; 'and such other instruments as they played upon in the barge'; 'apparelled and attired'; 'commonly drawn in picture'; 'with the which they fanned wind upon her'; 'a wonderful passing sweet savour of perfumes that perfumed.' And consider the structure of the first sentence. It is still possible for the reader to understand that the scene was exquisitely beautiful; but the words dull it. Shakespeare omits or emends the infelicities, invents his own graces, and adds verbal harmonies, which, like the perfumes of Cleopatra's sails, draw the world after them.

Ovid, Seneca, Plutarch: these were Shakespeare's chief classical sources. A fourth author helped him early in his career, but did not stay long with him. This was the Roman comedian Plautus.

In *The Brothers Manaechmus* Plautus told (from the Greek) a merry tale of identical twins separated in childhood, grown to manhood ignorant of each other, and suddenly brought together in the city where one has a wife and a home while the other, his exact duplicate, is a stranger. The resulting confusions and the ultimate recognition made a good comedy. This was the basic plot Shakespeare used in *The Comedy of Errors*; but, by adding a great deal to it, he improved it. He altered the names of the characters, and changed the locale from a little-known port to a famous city. He made the twin brothers have identical twin servants—multiplying the confusion by eight, at least. He made the stranger brother fall in love with his twin's sister-in-law. He made the early separation more real by making it more pathetic: the father who has lost both sons appears in the first scene, under sentence of death as an enemy alien, and only in the last scene, where he meets his sons and his wife, supposed dead, is he reprieved.

Some of these enlargements Shakespeare himself invented. Some he took from sources outside the drama: the shipwreck, apparently, from the romance *Apollonius of Tyre*. But the grand complication, the creation of twin servants, he took from another of Plautus' comedies, *Amphitryon*. And a careful reading of *The Comedy of Errors* with Plautus' two plays will show that Shakespeare did not merely lift the idea from *Amphitryon* and insert it *en bloc* into the other play, but blended the two plays in an organic fusion to make a new and richer drama.

Amphitryon was not translated into English until long after Shakespeare was dead. The only known translation of *The Brothers Menaechmus* was printed in 1595, some years after the accepted date for Shakespeare's *Comedy of Errors*. The conclusion is virtually certain. Shakespeare read Plautus' comedies in the original Latin.[85] He used them just as he used the stories he took from all his other sources—as a basis of interwoven action which he made into poetry by adding deeply human characterization and the poetry of his own inimitable words. As a result *The Comedy of Errors* is more of a drama than most of Plautus' comedies: more carefully wrought, more finely characterized, more various, less funny but more moving, and, despite its naughtiness, nobler in moral tone.[86]

Still, the limitations of his classical knowledge came out clearly in his adaptation of Plautus. They are those we have noticed already. For a great imaginative poet, they were not defects but advantages. We must, however, recognize their existence. Shakespeare knew Latin enough to get the story of the plays when he read them, but not enough to appreciate the language as well as the dramatic art of the poet. Plautus is a very witty writer, full of puns and deft verbal twists and comic volubility. Anyone who can read his language fluently is bound to be infected by the rattling gaiety of his words. Shakespeare (who could not even get the name of Epidamnus right) failed, in *The Comedy of Errors*, to take over Plautus' verbal skill, although he mastered his plotting and surpassed his characterization. But we cannot be anything but grateful for this. A more intimate knowledge of the style of other comedians might well have hindered the development of Shakespeare's own incomparable eloquence. If he had stopped at *Lucrece* and *The Comedy of Errors*, we could regret that his classical learning was so much inferior to Marlowe's, to Spenser's, to Milton's. But even then, he was Ovid reincarnated; and now he became Plautus romanticized. He was still growing and learning. Plautus gave him another part of his education: the ability to build a long story out of coincidences and complications which, although credible, were always fresh and unexpected. What Plautus might have given him in verbal dexterity he later achieved for himself; and thereby made his language indistinguishably a part of his own characters, the very voice of his own thought.

Other authors he knew, but only in outline, or by quotations learnt in school and remembered afterwards, or by extracts published in the Reader's Digest type of collections which were so common in the Renaissance. Some of them gave him a beautiful line or a powerful description, but none deeply affected his thought. In an exhaustive work called *William Shakspere's Small Latine and Lesse Greeke*, Mr. T. W. Baldwin has analysed the educational system of England in Shakespeare's boyhood, inferring from that, and from echoes in the dramas, what were the books he probably read in school. To begin with, Shakespeare used the standard Latin grammar written by the two great Renaissance educators, John Colet and William Lily, for he quotes and parodies it several times.[87] It contained many illustrative quotations from classical authors. Even if Shakespeare did not read their works, he remembered the excerpts, and used them as they were given in the grammar.[88] This accounts for some otherwise inexplicable coincidences: they are due to Shakespeare's memory for good poetry. For instance, one of his first Latin texts was a collection of pastoral poems by the Italian humanist Baptista Spagnuoli, known as Baptista Mantuanus. The schoolmaster Holofernes in *Love's Labour's Lost* actually quotes a line from it and praises the poet.[89] Again, in *Hamlet*,[90] Laertes utters a beautiful epitaph over Ophelia:

> Lay her i' the earth,
> And from her fair and unpolluted flesh
> May violets spring!

It is impossible to escape the conclusion that this is a reminiscence of a sentence of the same shape, thought, and rhythm in the satirist Persius:[91]

> Now from his tomb and beatific ashes
> Won't violets grow?

Only it is equally impossible to believe that Shakespeare ever read that most difficult author. But Mr. Baldwin has pointed out that the passage from Persius is quoted in full in the explanatory notes on Mantuanus' elegies, where Shakespeare no doubt read and remembered it.[92]

Shakespeare also read some Vergil at school, but apparently only the early books, as elementary Latin pupils still do. The descriptions of the fall of Troy in *Lucrece*, 1366 f., and *Hamlet*, 2.2.481 f., are partly modelled on, partly exaggerated from Aeneas' account in *Aeneid*, 2; and the line with which Aeneas begins that famous history—'You bid me, queen, renew a grief unspeakable'—is echoed at the opening of *The Comedy of Errors*:

> A heavier task could not have been imposed
> Than I to speak my griefs unspeakable.[93]

That standard text-book, Caesar's *Gallic War*—or at least the part dealing with Britain (a suitable selection for English beginners)—was also known to Shakespeare. In *2 Henry VI*[94] old Lord Say, attempting to persuade Jack Cade and his Kultur-Bolsheviks that they should not lynch him, quotes it:

> Kent, in the Commentaries Caesar writ,
> Is termed the civil'st place of all this isle.

Of Livy, Shakespeare knew at least the first book, with the story of Tarquin and Lucrece.[95]

From other classical authors, he seems to have known only a few memorable passages. For instance, when Brutus is facing his doom, he cries

> O Julius Caesar, thou art mighty yet!
> Thy spirit walks abroad, and turns our swords
> In our own proper entrails.[96]

Apparently this is an echo of the opening lines of Lucan's poem on the civil war:[97]

> a might nation,
> its conquering hand against its vitals turned.

Like everyone in the Renaissance, Shakespeare brings in scientific and other information from Pliny's *Natural History*, but without naming its author. And when Polonius accosts Hamlet,[98] and asks him what he is reading, the bitter reply:

'Slanders, sir: for the satirical rogue says here that old men have grey beards, that their faces are wrinkled, their eyes purging thick amber and plum-tree gum, and that they have a plentiful lack of wit, together with most weak hams'—

points to only one satirical rogue known to us: the Roman Juvenal, whose tenth satire contains a terrible description of the ugliness and weakness of old age.[99] Slight as these and other such reminiscences are, they show Shakespeare's liking for the classics, his sensitive ear, his retentive memory, and the transforming magic of his eloquence. Others, like Jonson, stud their pages with quotation-marks, and talk in italics. When Shakespeare's characters speak, only the pedants quote: the rest speak from the fullness of their own heart, and of his.

Shakespeare was an Englishman of the Renaissance. It was a wonderful time—scarcely less wonderful than the world's great ages of Greece and Rome which returned again in it. One of the vital events which then gave vigour to men's minds and depth to their souls was the rebirth of classical culture. It was not the only such event. There were revolutions, explorations, and discoveries in many other regions distant, although not utterly alien, from it. But it was one of the most important: for it was a revolution of the mind. Like all sensitive and educated men, Shakespeare shared in its excitements. It was one of his great spiritual experiences. True, England was more important to him; and so was the social life of contemporary Europe, with its subtleties, its humours, and its villainies; and most important of all was humanity. But he was not the unschooled poet of nature. For him great books were an essential part of life.

He had a fair introduction to the Latin language, not enough to make him a scholar, not enough to allow him to read it fluently, but enough to lead him (like Chaucer and Keats) to love Greek and Roman myth, poetry, and history. He lived among men who knew and admired classical literature, and he learnt from them. His first books were adaptations of Greco-Roman originals, affectionately elaborated and sumptuously adorned by his superb imagination. Until late in his career he continued to read and use translations of Greek and Latin books; twelve of his forty works (and those among the greatest) dealt with themes from classical antiquity; and classical imagery was an organic part of his poetry from first to last. Greek and Roman literature provided not only the rhetorical and dramatic patterns which he and the other Renaissance poets used, not only rich material to feed his imagination, but the challenge of noble humanity and of consummate art. To that challenge many great souls in the Renaissance responded, none more greatly than the man who had small Latin and less Greek.

NOTES

There are many good books and articles on this subject. The following will be found particularly helpful:

P. Alexander, *Shakespeare's Life and Art* (London, 1939).

H. R. D. Anders, *Shakespeare's Books* (Schriften der deutschen Shakespeare-Gesellschaft, I, Berlin, 1904).

A. L. Attwater, 'Shakespeare's Sources,' in *A Companion to Shakespeare Studies*, ed. H. Granville-Barker and G. B. Harrison (New York, 1934).

T. W. Baldwin, *William Shakspere's Small Latine and Lesse Greeke* (Urbana, Ill., 1944).

D. Bush, *Mythology and the Renaissance Tradition in English Poetry* (Minneapolis and London, 1932).

J. W. Cunliffe, *The Influence of Seneca on Elizabethan Tragedy* (London, 1893).

T. S. Eliot, 'Shakespeare and the Stoicism of Seneca' and 'Seneca in Elizabethan Translation,' in *Selected Essays 1917–1932* (New York, 1932).

J. Engel, 'Die Spuren Senecas in Shakspores Dramen' (*Preussische Jahrbücher*, 112 (1903), 60–81).

E. I. Fripp, 'Shakespeare's Use of Ovid's *Metamorphoses*,' in his *Shakespeare Studies, Biographical and Literary* (London, 1930).

E. I. Fripp, *Shakespeare, Man and Artist* (London, 1938).

S. Lee, *A Life of William Shakespeare* (New York, 1925).

F. L. Lucas, *Seneca and Elizabethan Tragedy* (Cambridge, 1922).

M. W. MacCallum, *Shakespeare's Roman Plays and their Background* (London, 1910).

S. G. Owen, 'Ovid and Romance,' in *English Literature and the Classics* (ed. G. S. Gordon, Oxford, 1912).

L. Rick, 'Shakespeare und Ovid,' in *Jahrbuch der deutschen Shakespeare-Gesellschaft*, 55 (1919), 35–53.

R. K. Root, *Classical Mythology in Shakespeare* (New York, 1903).

W. W. Skeat, *Shakespeare's Plutarch* (London, 1875).

P. Stapfer, *Shakespeare and Classical Antiquity* (tr. E. J. Carey, London, 1880). Other works on the theme are mentioned in these notes.

1. *Lucrece, Coriolanus, Julius Caesar,* and *Antony and Cleopatra* concern the republic; *Cymbeline* the early empire, and *Titus Andronicus* the later empire at some time after the barbarian invasions had well begun. W. Dibelius, 'Zur Stoffgeschichte des *Titus Andronikus*' (*Jahrbuch der deutschen Shakespeare-Gesellschaft*, 48 (1912), 1–12), suggests that the scene is really Byzantium, that Titus Andronicus is the violent Byzantine emperor who reigned from 1183 to 1185, and that Tamora is Thamar of Georgia (1184–1220), the unidentifiable Demetrius being a Dmitri. See also 'The Story of Isaac and Andronicus' by E. H. McNeal, in *Speculum*, 9 (1934), 324–9. This tells how the emperor Andronicus was tortured to death with frightful barbarity, and explains how the story could have reached England via the army of Richard I: it appears in the chronicle of Benedict of Peterborough. The setting of *Cymbeline* is partly Roman, partly vague early-British; but the play really concerns Rome much less than the subject which long haunted Shakespeare's mind, the conflict between English honesty and Italian treachery: see 3. 2. 4. 5. 5. 197 f., 5. 5. 211.

2. One of these, *The Comedy of Errors,* is an adaptation of two Roman adaptations of Greek plays (see pp. 214, 624–5). One is from Athenian history (*Timon of Athens, c.* 407 B.C.). Three are set in the prehistoric past of myth (*Venus and Adonis, Troilus and Cressida, A Midsummer-Night's Dream*); and one, *Pericles,* is a retelling of a late Greek romance. [(On these romances see p. 163 f.)]

3. *Hamlet,* 5. 2. 29 f.

4. *Hamlet,* 2. 2. 350 f.

5. Two of the Italian plays take place in Venice and the Venetian empire (*Othello* and *The Merchant*); two in Verona (*Romeo and Juliet* and *The Two Gentlemen*); one in Messina (*Much Ado about Nothing*); one in Sicily (*The Winter's Tale*); and one in Padua (*The Taming of the Shrew*).

6. In Lodge's *Rosalynde,* from which Shakespeare took the basis of *As You Like It,* the setting was the forest of Ardenne in north-eastern France, pastoralized and

idyllized. By changing its name Shakespeare moved it to England near his own home: his mother's name was Mary Arden. H. Smith, 'Pastoral Influence in the English Drama' (*PMLA*, 12 (n.s. 5), 1897, 378 f.), shows how greatly Shakespeare reduced the conventional pastoral colouring in adapting Lodge's story, and how much more real and homely he made it.

7. *Troilus and Cressida*, 4. 2. 31.

8. *Cymbeline*, 2. 3. 21 f.

9. *The Winter's Tale*, 4. 3. 120 f.

10. *Hamlet*, 3. 4. 55 f.; and see p. 605.

11. *The Merchant of Venice*, 5. 1. 9 f.

12. *Henry V*, 2. 3. 9.

13. *2 Henry IV*, 3. 2. 300 f.

14. *King Lear*, 3. 4. 185; cf. Browning's *Childe Roland to the Dark Tower came*.

15. See Stapfer, *Shakespeare and Classical Antiquity* (cited in introductory note), 223, and Attwater (introductory note), 233–5. Ajax in *Troilus and Cressida* is made not only stupid, but vain—'covetous of praise, self-affected.' Homer's Ajax is not at all like that. R. K. Root (cited in introductory note) shows on p. 36 f. that this part of Ajax's character comes from Ovid (*Met* 13), where Ajax competes with Ulysses for the weapons of Achilles, and is presented, both in his own speech and in that of his rival, as ridiculously conceited.

16. *Troilus and Cressida*, 2. 2. 166.

17. *Troilus and Cressida*, 1. 1. 81. The seven-day week did not exist in Greece.

18. *The Comedy of Errors*, 5. 1.

19. Nashe, preface to Greene's *Menaphon*.

20. C. Spurgeon, *Shakespeare's Imagery* (New York, 1935). See especially pp. 13, 19–20, 44–5, and Chart V.

21. *As You Like It*, 3. 3. 7 f.

22. *Romeo and Juliet*, 3. 2. 1 f. The myth of Phaethon is in Ovid, *Metamorphoses*, 1. 748–2. 332; 'waggoner' is the Elizabethan translator Golding's word for the young charioteer, and no doubt Shakespeare remembered it. (See Root—cited in the introductory note—97).

23. The phrase comes from Jonson's commendatory verses in the First Folio. J. E. Spingarn, *Literary Criticism in the Renaissance* (New York, 1899), 89 n., suggests that Jonson was quoting a phrase from Minturno, *Arte poetica*, 158: *poco del latino e pochissimo del greco*. On the entire subject of Shakespeare's education see Mr. T. W. Baldwin's valuable book cited in the introductory note.

24. There are only a few striking nouns, like *cacodemon* (*Richard III*, 1. 3. 144), *anthropophagi* (*Othello*, also 1. 3. 144), and *misanthropos* (*Timon of Athens*, 4. 3. 53), which last comes from a footnote in North's Plutarch, is mispronounced, and is carefully explained.

25. The Welsh-spoken schoolmaster in *The Merry Wives* is apparently modelled on Thomas Jenkins, Shakespeare's own Latin master at Stratford (see Baldwin and Fripp, cited in the introductory note). John Aubrey reports a tradition from William Beeston's mouth that Shakespeare himself was 'in his younger years a schoolmaster in the country.'

26. See *Pantagruel*, 2. 6. and p. 108.

27. *Love's Labour's Lost*, 4. 3. 342 f.

28. *The Tempest*, 1. 2. 167.

29. *The Merchant of Venice*, 5. 1. 60 f.; cf. Plato, *Rep.* 10. 617 *b*.

30. Baldwin (cited in introductory note), 2. 418 f. R. K. Root (introductory note) has shown that the overwhelming majority of Shakespeare's mythological allusions come directly from Ovid, and the remainder, with few exceptions, from Vergil. 'In other words, a man familiar with these two authors, and with no others, would be able to make all the mythological allusions contained in the undisputed works of Shakespeare, barring some few exceptions.' Mr. Root also points out that, as Shakespeare matured, he almost gave up using mythology, and that he returned to it in later life, giving it much deeper meanings.

31. Meres, *Palladis Tamia: Wits Treasury,* 280.

32. 'The first heir of my invention' (Dedication to *Venus and Adonis*).

33. In Ovid's tale of Venus and Adonis (*Met.* 10. 519–59 and 705–39), Adonis is not cold and reluctant as Shakespeare makes him. Shakespeare took his froward resistance to love from Ovid's story of Hermaphroditus and Salmacis in *Met.* 4. 285–388. The two stories coalesce completely in *The Passionate Pilgrim,* 6, where Adonis bounces into a brook, and Venus cries 'O Jove, why was not I a flood?'— for Salmacis bounced in after her beloved, the two joined, and both became a flood. See D. Bush (cited in introductory note), 139 f., for a detailed analysis of the treatment of Adonis; and R. K. Root (introductory note), 31–3, for the proof that Shakespeare's description of the raging boar *(Venus and Adonis)* comes from a different passage of Ovid, *Met.* 8. 284–6, probably in Golding's version.

34. Ov. *Am.* 1. 15. 35–6.

35. The story of Lucretia is in Livy, 1. 57–9, and Ovid, *Fasti,* 2. 721–852. Since no English translation of the *Fasti* appeared until 1640, and since Shakespeare adapts phrases from the poem, he apparently knew the original. (See Owen—cited in the introductory note—Fripp (ditto), 1. 363 f., and Bush (ditto), 149 f.)

36. *The Taming of the Shrew,* 3. 1. 26 f. The quotation is from Ovid, *Heroides,* 1. 33–4. Penelope writes to Ulysses that the other heroes have all returned home, and are now telling their battles over again, sketching the terrain on the table, and saying

> Here flowed the Simois; here is Sigeum;
> here was old Priam's lofty citadel.

37. *Titus Andronicus,* 4. 3. 4 = Ov. *Met.* 1. 150; *3 Henry VI,* 1. 3. 48 = Ov. *Her.* 2. 66.

38. Ov. *Met.* 1. 395 (Pyrrha), 3. 173 (Diana), 6. 346 (Latona), 14. 382 and 438 (Circe). Anders (see introductory note), 22, points out that the name Titania is not in Golding's version of the *Metamorphoses,* so that Shakespeare, with his delicate ear, must have remembered it from the original Latin.

39. T. S. Eliot, *The Classics and the Man of Letters* (London and New York, 1943). Mr. Eliot's whole discussion of the classical tradition in Shakespeare's and Milton's education is well worth reading.

40. The original is Ov. *Met.* 15. 181 f.:

> ut unda impellitur unda
> urgeturque prior ueniente urgetque priorem,
> tempora sic fugiunt pariter pariterque sequuntur
> et noua sunt semper.

Shakespeare's 'sequent' may be a sign that he had looked at the original. In Ovid the waves are the separate waves of a river, the Greek philosophers' image for permanence in change. Shakespeare makes them the waves of the sea on the shore, because British rivers seldom have waves, and because he is thinking of the sea-image in Sonnet 64. (See S. G. Owen, cited in introductory note.)

41. Ov. *Met.* 15. 75 f., especially 165 f.: ultimately from Heraclitus.

42. Tranio, in *The Taming of the Shrew,* 1. 1. 29 f.

43. *Romeo and Juliet,* 2. 2. 92 f. = Ovid, *A. A.* 1. 633; but see Root (cited in introductory note), 82, for the suggestion that this idea may have reached Shakespeare through Boiardo's *Orlando innamorato,* 1. 22. 45.

44. *The Taming of the Shrew,* 4. 2. 8.

45. Shakespeare's source here was Ovid, *Her.* 7, the letter of Dido: there is at least one straight quotation:

> What says the married woman? You may go?
> Would she had never given you leave to come!
> *(Antony and Cleopatra,* 1. 3. 20–1).
> Sed iubet ire deus. Vellem uetuisset adire!
> *(Her.* 7. 139).

And in 4. 12. 53 Shakespeare makes Antony explicitly compare himself and Cleopatra with Aeneas and Dido. For this and other interesting parallels see T. Zielinski, 'Marginalien' *(Philologus,* 64 (n.F. 18), 1905, 1 f.), who points out that Cleopatra, like Dido in *Her.* 7. 133 f., hints at being pregnant: see *Antony and Cleopatra,* 1. 3. 89–95.

46. *The Tempest,* 5. 1. 33–50. The tiny fairies of the seashore and the glade, brothers to Pease-blossom, Cobweb, and Mustard-seed, are here reminiscences of Ariel's gentler kinsman Puck rather than assistants in Prospero's prodigious magic. Doubtless they were suggested to Shakespeare, not by the content of the invocation, but by Golding's word *elves.*

47. *Macbeth,* 4. 1. 4 f.

48. Ov. *Met.* 7. 262 f.

49. *Macbeth,* 3. 5. 23–4.

50. Ov. *Met.* 3. 206 f.

51. *M.N.D.* 4. 1. 118 f. See also *The Merry Wives,* 2. 1. 120: "Like Sir Actaeon he, with Ringwood at thy heels"—where Ringwood is the dog-name Golding substituted for Ovid's Hylactor, Barker. (See Root, cited in introductory note, 30.) The following passages also are worth comparing:

A Midsummer-Night's Dream, 1. 1. 170, and Ov. *Met.* 1. 470, a parallel which suggests that the difficult line 172 in Hermia's speech refers to the arrow, and ought to be placed before 171;

As You Like It, 3. 3. 10 f., and Ov. *Met.* 8. 626–30;

The Winter's Tale, 4. 3. 116 f., and Ov. *Met.* 5. 391 f.

52. e. g. *As You Like It,* 3. 3. 7 f., and *L.L.L.* 4. 2. 128, both containing Latin puns.

53. e.g. *Cymbeline,* 2. 2. 44 f., and *Titus Andronicus,* 4. 1. 42 f.

54. *A Midsummer-Night's Dream,* 5. 1. 129 f.

55. *The Winter's Tale,* 5. 3. 21 f. Fripp, *Shakespeare, Man and Artist* (London, 1938), 1. 102–14, has a detailed and sensitive discussion of Shakespeare's love for

Ovid. He also points out (1. 597, n. 4) that Shakespeare, who sympathized with Montaigne in so much, resembled him in his early admiration of the *Metamorphoses*. [(See p. 186.)]

56. *Titus Andronicus*, 2. 1. 133 f. = Sen. *Phaedra*, 1180, garbled; 4. 1. 81–2 = Sen. *Phaedra*, 671–2, with a textual variation that would occur only to a latinist. The latter passage is directly imitated in Jonson's *Catiline*, 3. 4. 1–2, and adapted in Tourneur's *The Revenger's Tragedy*, 4. 2.

57. This subject has been treated in detail by J. W. Cunliffe and F. L. Lucas, whose books are cited in the introductory note.

58. *Hamlet*, 5. 4. 232 f.; *Macbeth*, 5. 5. 19 f.

59. *Timon of Athens*, 4. 1, 4. 3.

60. *King Lear*, 4. 1. 36 f.

61. See Cunliffe (quoted in introductory note), 25 f., who refers to Seneca, *Phaedra*, 978 f.:

> Res humanas ordine nullo
> Fortuna regit sparsitque manu
> munera caeca, peiora fouens;
> uincit sanctos dira libido,
> fraus sublimi regnat in aula.

62. e.g. in Webster's *The Duchess of Malfi* (5. 3. fin., 5. 5 fin.).

63. *Hamlet*, 5. 1. 245 f.

64. *1 Henry IV*, 1. 3. 130 f.

65. *Timon of Athens*, 4. 3. 178 f.

66. So Cunliffe (cited in introductory note), 16–17, and T. S. Eliot, in his essay 'Seneca in Elizabethan Translation' (*Selected Essays 1917–1932*, New York, 1932).

67. See *Richard III*, 1. 2. 68 f., 4. 4. 344 f., and compare Eliot (cited in n. 69), 72 f., and Lucas (introductory note), 119 f.

68. Cunliffe (cited in introductory note) gives details on 68 f.

69. Sen. *Phaedra*, 715 f., in the same scene which contains Hippolytus' cry to heaven for vengeance, cited in note 56:

> Quis eluet me Tanais aut quae barbaris
> Maeotis undis Pontico incumbens mari?
> non ipse toto magnus Oceano pater
> tantum expiarit scelus.

70. Sen. *Herc. Fur.* 1323 f., ending 'haerebit altum facinus.'

71. *Macbeth*, 2. 2. 61 f., 5. 1. 56. Murder is constantly imaged as a blood-stain in this play: see 2. 2. 47 f., 2. 3. 118–23, 5. 1 throughout, and hints such as 4. 1. 123 and 4. 3. 40–1.

72. Sen. *Herc. Fur.* 1258–61.

73. *Macbeth*, 5. 3. 22 f.

74. Sen. *Herc. Fur.* 1261–2.

75. *Macbeth*, 5. 3. 40.

76. *Macbeth*, 1. 7. 7 f. = Sen. *Herc. Fur.* 735–6:

> quod quisque fecit patitur: auctorem scelus
> repetit suoque premitur exemplo nocens.

Macbeth, 4. 3. 209 f. = Sen. *Phaedra,* 607, a favourite line with the Elizabethans: 'curae leues loquuntur, ingentes stupent.' A parallel between the invocations of Lady Macbeth (*Macbeth,* 1. 5. 41 f.) and Medea (Sen. *Medea,* 1–55, especially 9–15 and 40–50) has been noticed, but is less convincing. But it seems clear that the long series of phrases in praise of sleep (*Macbeth,* 2. 2. 37 f.) was suggested by Seneca, *Herc. Fur.* 1065 f.; and still more reminiscences are given by Engel [whose essay is quoted in the introductory note to this chapter].

77. In the final scene of *Timon of Athens* (5. 4. 70 f.) Alcibiades reads out what is supposed to be an epitaph written for Timon by himself and engraved on his tomb:

> Here lies a wretched corse, of wretched soul bereft:
> Seek not my name; a plague consume you wicked caitiffs left!
> Here lie I, Timon; who, alive, all living men did hate:
> Pass by, and curse thy fill; but pass, and stay not here thy gait.

Obviously this is not one poem but two. A glance at Plutarch shows that he gives two different epitaphs written at different times (one by Callimachus, one attributed to Timon himself) and mutually incompatible. But Shakespeare, careless of the incongruity, runs the two together.

78. Shakespeare's father was a whittawer, who processed leather for the manufacture of gloves, purses, parchment, &c. As trades went, this was doubtless dignified and lucrative; but in its social opportunities it was far below the professions and the landed gentry. As for the school at Stratford, it was efficient enough, but it was not St. Paul's, or Winchester, or Eton.

79. *Julius Caesar,* 2. 1. 61–5.

80. Before this, Shakespeare knew Seneca, had copied him in *Richard III,* and, if *Titus Andronicus* be his or partly his, had tried his prentice hand at writing Senecan tragedy; but it was only after he married the manner of Seneca to the matter of Plutarch that he created great tragedy.

81. Shakespeare's use of North's Plutarch has been treated eloquently and in detail by M. W. MacCallum, whose book is cited in the introductory note. See also Skeat's reprint of the text, mentioned there. Skeat points out that many of the names of secondary characters in Shakespeare's other dramas come from Plutarch— Marcellus, Lysander, and perhaps Demetrius (but see note 1). W. Warde Fowler has a useful essay on *Julius Caesar* in his *Roman Essays and Interpretations* (Oxford, 1920).

82. *Julius Caesar,* 1. 2. 191 f.

83. *Julius Caesar,* 2. 2. 37 f. H. M. Ayres, in 'Shakespeare's *Julius Caesar* in the Light of some other Versions' (*PMLA,* n.s. 18 (1910), 183–227), points out that during the Renaissance the dramatic conception of Caesar's character had, in default of a model in classical tragedy, been distorted to resemble that of the braggart Hercules in Seneca (e.g. in Marc-Antoine Muret's Latin tragedy on Caesar), and that the passages in Shakespeare's play where Caesar struts and brags are affected by the hybristic heroes of Seneca and their copies in contemporary drama.

84. *Antony and Cleopatra,* 2. 2. 194 f.

85. The question whether Shakespeare used a translation of Plautus when writing *The Comedy of Errors* has been much vexed. It seems to me to have been given more importance than it deserves: for if Shakespeare could read *Amphitruo* in Latin, he

could surely read *Menaechmi,* and no one has undertaken to show that a translation of *Amphitruo* was available. However, these are some of the main facts:

(*a*) *The Comedy of Errors* was written and produced between 1589 and 1593, when France was 'making war against her heir,' Henri IV (see 3. 2. 127–8). The joke would be obscure before August 1589 and out of date after 1593.

(*b*) The only known Elizabethan translation of Plautus' *Menaechmi* was published by Creede in 1595 and attributed to W. W., who may have been William Warner. The publisher in his foreword says that W. W. had translated several plays of Plautus 'for the use and delight of his private friends, who in Plautus owne words are not able to understand them,' and that he himself had prevailed on W. W. to publish this one. If this is true, the translation had been circulating in manuscript. If Shakespeare was one of W. W.'s friends, he could have seen it. But it seems more probable that (as has been suggested) the success of *The Comedy of Errors* prompted W. W. to publish his version.

(*c*) A comparison of *The Comedy of Errors* with W. W.'s translation shows that the two do not coincide. Several important characters and dramatic roles are different, and although people in similar situations say similar things in both plays, Shakespeare's characters do not echo W. W.'s words. The presumption is therefore heavily against Shakespeare's use of W. W. (See the detailed comparison by H. Isaac, 'Shakespeares Comedy of Errors und die Menächmen des Plautus,' *Archiv für das Studium der neueren Sprachen und Litteraturen,* 70 (1883), 1–28.)

(*d*) On New Year's Day 1576–7, the 'children of Powles' produced something called *The Historie of Error* at Hampton Court. The boys of St. Paul's School were good latinists (as they still are) and this could have been an adaptation of *Menaechmi,* just as *Ralph Roister Doister* was an adaptation of themes from *Miles gloriosus.* If it was, Shakespeare could have seen and used it. But we do not know that it was, or that he ever saw it.

(*e*) M. Labinski, *Shakespeares Komödie der Irrungen* (Breslau, 1934), suggests that Shakespeare might have used an Italian adaptation of Plautus: for the names of Dromio and Adriana and Luciana, and the characters of the goldsmith Angelo and the merchant Balthazar, are contemporary Italian. But no adaptation very like his play has been found.

To the fact that Shakespeare read *Amphitruo* in the original should be added the fact that he also knew a third comedy by Plautus, the *Mostellaria.* In *The Taming of the Shrew* the names of the servants Tranio and Grumio come from the *Mostellaria*; and so also do some incidents, and the character of Tranio—who, as in Plautus, is made his young master's guardian, but instead turns him into merry ways (see his speech in 1. 1. 29 f.).

86. Several studies of Shakespeare's technique in *The Comedy of Errors* have shown that, in taking over the stories of Plautus' *Menaechmi* and *Amphitruo,* he was not hindered by any difficulty in understanding Latin, but felt quite free to alter and transform, as one feels free only when one has a firm grip on one's material. These articles emphasize, among others, the fact that he purified and ennobled the play by making the courtesan less prominent and the loving wife Adriana more real and human. See, in particular, E. Gill's 'A Comparison of the Characters in *The Comedy of Errors* with those in the *Menaechmi*' (*Texas University Studies in English,* 5 (1925), 79–95), the same author's very careful essay 'The Plot-structure of *The Comedy of Errors* in Relation to its Sources' (*Texas University Studies in English,* 10 (1930), 13–65), and M. Labinski's *Shakespeares Komödie der Irrungen* (Breslau,

1934). There are some suggestive remarks in V. G. Whitaker's 'Shakespeare's Use of his Sources' (*Philological Quarterly,* 20 (1941), esp. 380 f.). G. B. Parks, in 'Shakespeare's Map for "The Comedy of Errors"' (*Journal of English and Germanic Philology,* 39 (1940), 93–7), shows that, when Shakespeare wanted to find some other locale than the relatively unknown Epidamnus (where Plautus put the *Menaechmi*), he looked up the index of the great atlas of Ortelius of Antwerp, and there, beside Epidamnus, found Ephesus. He then moved the locale to Ephesus, which every modern reader knows from the sensational episode in the Acts of the Apostles; and he rearranged the journey of the chief characters very intelligently to fit the change. He also brought in Epidaurus, which appears in the index just after Epidamnus: see 1. 1. 93. Only one verbal reminiscence of Plautus' plays seems to have been pointed out in *The Comedy of Errors*—a small one at that: *The Comedy of Errors,* 3. 1. 80 = *Amphitruo,* 1048.

87. *1 Henry IV,* 2. 1. 104; *Much Ado About Nothing,* 4. 1. 21–2; and especially *The Merry Wives of Windsor,* 4. 1.

88. For instance, a servant in Terence (*Eun.* 1. 1. 29) tells his master that, since he has been captured by love, his only resort is to ransom himself as cheaply as possible: 'quid agas? nisi ut te redimas captum quam queas minumo.' Colet and Lily abbreviated this into one line, no doubt to illustrate the idiom of *quam* with the superlative (— 'as . . . as possible'); and in that form Tranio quotes it to his master (*The Taming of the Shrew,* 1. 1. 166):

> If love have touched you, nought remains but so:
> Redime te captum, quam queas minimo.

And although *Titus Andronicus* is shaky evidence for Shakespeare's practice, there is a most amusing illustration of this method of quotation in it. The villains are sent certain weapons bearing the inscription:

> Integer vitae scelerisque purus
> Non eget Mauri iaculis neque arcu
>   (Horace, *Carm.* 1. 22).
> An innocent unstained with crime
> will need no Moorish spears nor bow.

When Demetrius reads this out, Chiron observes:

> O! 'tis a verse in Horace; I know it well;
> I read it in the grammar long ago.
>   (*Titus Andronicus,* 4. 2. 20).

89. *L.L.L.* 4. 2. 96 f.
90. *Hamlet,* 5. 1. 260 f.
91. Persius, 1. 38–9:

> Nunc non e tumulo fortunataque fauilla
> nascentur uiolae?

92. Baldwin, *William Shakspere's Small Latine and Lesse Greeke*, 1. 649.

93. *The Comedy of Errors*, 1. 1. 31 = Verg. *Aen.* 2. 3: 'Infandum, regina, iubes renouare dolorem.' Other Vergilian reminiscences include:

The Tempest, 4. 1. 101–2 = Verg. *Aen.* 1. 46 blended with 1. 405;

the stage direction in *The Tempest*, 3. 3. 53 = Verg. *Aen.* 3. 219 f.: 'claps his wings' being a translation of *magnis quatiunt clangoribus alas*, 3. 226;

the saffron wings of Iris in *The Tempest*, 4. 1. 78 = Verg. *Aen.* 4. 700–2 (perhaps through Phaer's translation: see Root, *Classical Mythology in Shakespeare*, 77);

the herald Mercury in *Hamlet*, 3. 4. 58 = Verg. *Aen.* 4. 246–53 (Root, 85);

and a neat pun in *2 Henry VI*, 2. 1. 24 = Verg. *Aen.* 1. 11, where *caelestibus*, 'heavenly,' is taken as though it meant 'clerical.'

94. *2 Hen. VI*, 4. 7. 65 = Caesar, *B. G.* 5. 14. 1:

'ex eis omnibus longe sunt humanissimi qui Cantium incolunt'; of these (the southern British) the inhabitants of Kent are far the most civilized.

95. See E. I. Fripp, *Shakespeare, Man and Artist*, 96 f.

96. *Julius Caesar*, 5. 3. 94 f.

97. Lucan, *Bell. Ciu.* 1. 2–3. The probability that Shakespeare is echoing Lucan is strengthened by the oddity of the phrase 'turns our swords *in* our own proper entrails,' which looks like a remembered mistranslation of the Latin:

populumque potentem
in sua uictrici conuersum uiscera dextra.

98. *Hamlet*, 2. 2. 200 f.

99. Nevertheless, Shakespeare's knowledge of Juvenal's satire is obviously very vague: if he had read it, he would certainly have remembered it vividly. The brilliant detail 'thick amber and plum-tree gum' is not in Juvenal (who would have admired it), and the rest of Hamlet's speech is only a faint reflection of the poem. The satire is sometimes called *The Vanity of Human Wishes*, and was adapted in English by Johnson under that title. Theobald and others have detected a reminiscence of its powerful opening lines in Menecrates' warning to the ambitious Pompey (*Antony and Cleopatra*, 2. 1. 5–8):

We, ignorant of ourselves,
Beg often our own harms, which the wise powers
Deny us for our good; so find we profit
By losing of our prayers.

For a larger treatment of Shakespeare's satirical purposes and methods, see O. J. Campbell, *Comicall Satyre and Shakespeare's 'Troilus and Cressida'* (San Marino, Cal., 1938), and his *Shakespeare's Satire* (New York and London, 1943).

✠ ✠ ✠

PREFACE TO THE ABBREVIATION
OF THE STATUTES (1520)

JOHN RASTELL

Because that ye lawys of this realme of Englond as well the statutes as other iugmentes & decrees, be made & wryten moost comenly in the frenche tonge: dyuers men thereof muse & haue oftimis communycacion and argument: consyderyng that in reason euery law wherto any people shuld be boundyn, ought and shulde be wryttyn insuch manere and so opynly publisshyd and declaryd that the people myght sone wythout gret dyffyculte haue the knoulege of the seyd laws. But the verey cause why the seyd laws of Englond were writin in the French tongue shuld seme to be this—furst yt ys not vnknowyn that when Wyllyam duke of Normandy came in to thys land and slew kyng Herrold and conqueryd the hole realme: there was a grete nomber of people as well gentylmen as other that cam wyth hym whych vnderstode not the vulgar tong that was at that tyme vsyd in this realme, but onely the French tong. and also because the seyd kyng and other grete wyse men of hys counsel perseyuyd and suposeyd that the vulgar tong which was then vsed in thys realme was in a manere but homely and rude, nor had not so grete copy and haboundaunce of wordys as the Frenche tong than had, nor that vulgare thong was not of yt selff suffycyent to expown and to

Reprinted from *Typographical Antiquities*, Volume III, by Thomas Frognall Dibdin, 1816.

declare the matter of such lawys and ordenauncis as they had determynid to be made for the good gouernaunce of the people so effectually and so sybstancyally as they cowd indyte them in the French tong: therfore they orderid wrot and indytyd the seyd lawys that they made in the French tong. And forthermore long affter the commyng off king Wylyam conquerour be cause that the vse of the French tong in this realme began to mynyssh and be cause that dyuers people than inhabityd wythin this realme wich coud nother speke the vulgare tonge of thys realme nother the French tong: thefore the wys men of thys realme causyd to be ordyryd that the matters of the law and accions between partes shuld be pledyd, shewyd and defendyd, answerd, debatyd and iuggyd in the English vulgar tong: and more over that wryttyn and enteryd of record in the rollys in the latyn tong because that euery man generally and indifferently myght haue the knolege thereof as apperyth by a statute made in the xxxvi. yere of E. iii. ca. vitimo. wherfore as J suppose for these causis before rehersyd the laws of this realme were indytyd and wryttyn in the French tong which was intendyd for a ryght good purpose.

But yet besyde thys now of late days the most noble prynce our late soverayne lord kyng Henry the. vii. worthi to be callid the second Salomon (which excellyd in polytyk wysdome all other princes that reinid in thys realme before hys time) concydering and wel parceyvyng that our vulgare Englysh tong was maruellously amended and augmentyd by reason that dyuers famous clerkis and lernyd men had translate and made many noble workis into our Englysh tong wherby there was mych more plenty and haboundaunce off Englysh vsyd than ther was in tymys past and by reason therof our vulgar tong so amplyfyed and suffycyent of hyt self to expown any lawys or ordynancys whych was nedeful to be made for the order of thys realme, and also the same wise prince consideryng that the vniuersal people of this realme had gret plesur and gaue themself greatly to the redyng of the vulgare Englysh tong: ordeynyd and causyd that all the statutys and ordynauncis whych were made for the commyn welth of thys realme in hys days, shuld be endytyd and wrytyn in the vulgare Englysh tong, and to be publyshyd declaryd and ymprinted, so that then vniuersally the people of the realme myght sone haue the knolege of the seyd statutes and ordynauncys which they were bounde to observe, and so by reason of that knolege to auoyd the dangere and penaltes of the same statutys, and also the better to lyff in tranquylyte and peace. whych dyscrete charytable and reasonable order our most dred sovereyne lorde that now ys kyng Henry the. viii. hath continuyd and followyd, and causyd all the statutys that haue be made in his dayes to be also indytyde and wryttyn in our Englysh tong, to the intente that all hys lege people myght haue the knoleg thereof. All whych goodly purposys and intentys in my mynde ofte tymys reuoluyde: hath causyd me to take thys lytyll payne to translate out of Frenche into Englisshe the abbreuiacyon of the statutys which conteyn forfeytours and penaltes made before the fyrst yere of the reyn of our late souerein lorde kyng Henry the. vii. And also though the statutys made as wel in the tyme of the seyd kyng Henry the. vii. as in the tyme of our souerein lorde that now ys be sufficyently indytid and writyn in our Englysh tong: yet to them that be desirous shortly to knowe the effect of them they be now more tedyouse to rede than though the mater and effect of them were compendyously abbreuiat: wherfore now as farr as my symple wytt and small lernynge wyll extende, J haue here takyn vpon me to abregg the effect of them more shortly in this lyttyl book: besechyng all them to whome the syght here of shall come to accept hyt in gree. and though they shall fortune to fynde any thynge misreportyd or omytted by my neglygens elis by neglygens of the prynters that yt wolde lyke them to pardon me and to consider my good wyl which haue intendid yt for a comyn welth for the causis and consideracyons before rehersyde. and also that yt fortune them to be in dout in any poynt thereof: yet yf it pleas them they may resorte to the hole statute whereof thys book is but a bregement and in manere but a kalender. And forther more J wyll aduertyse euery man that shall fortune to haue any matter in vre to resorte to some man that ys lernyd in the laws of thys realme, to haue his councel in such poyntis which he thinkith doubtfull concernyng these seid statutis: by the knolege wherof and by the dylygent obseruyng of the same, he may the better do hys dewte to hys prynce and souerine, and also lyf in tranquilitie and pease wyth his neyghbour, accordyng to the pleasure and commandment of all mighti God to whom be eternal laud and glori. Amen.

✠ ✠ ✠

'THAT THE ENGLISH TUNG HATH IN IT SELF SUFFICIENT MATTER TO WORK HER OWN ARTIFICIALL DIRECTION, FOR THE RIGHT WRITING THEREOF'

RICHARD MULCASTER

It must nedes be that our English tung hath matter enough in hir own writing, which maie direct her own right, if it be reduced to certain precept, and rule of Art, tho it haue not as yet bene thoroughlie perceaued.

The causes why it hath not as yet bene thoroughlie perceaued, ar, the hope & despare of such, as haue either thought vpon it, and not dealt in it, or that haue delt in it, but not rightlie thought vpon it.

For som considering the great difficultie, which theie found to be in the writing thereof, euerie letter almost being deputed to manie, and seuerall, naie to manie and wellnigh contrarie sounds and vses, euerie word almost either wanting letters, for his necessarie sound, or hauing some more than

Reprinted from *The First Part of the Elementarie*, Chapter XIII, by Richard Mulcaster, 1582.

necessitie requireth, began to despare in the midst of such a confusion, euer
to find out anie sure direction, whereon to ground Art, and to set it certain.
And what if either theie did not seke, or did not know how to seke, in right
form of Art, and the compòsing method? But whe*f*her difficultie in the thing,
or infirmitie in the searchers, gaue cause thereunto, the parties them selues
gaue ouer the thing, as in a desperat case, and by not medling thorough
despare, theie helped not the right.

Again som others bearing a good affection to their naturall tung, and
resolued to burst thorough the midst of all these difficulties, which offered
such resistence, as theie misliked the confusion, wherewith the other were
afraid, so theie deuised a new mean, wherein theie laid their hope, to bring
the thing about. Wherevpon som of them being of great place and good
learning, set furth in print particular treatises of that argument, with these
their new conceaused means, how we ought to write, and so to write right.
But their good hope by reason of their strange mean, had the same euent,
that the others despare had, by their either misconceauing the thing at first,
or their diffidence at the last. Wherein the parties them selues no dout deserue
some praise, and thanks to, of vs and our cuntrie in both these extremities of
hope and despare, tho theie helped not the thing, which theie went about,
but in common apparence, did somwhat hinder it rather. For both he, that
despared in the end, took great pains, before diffidence caused him giue
ouer to despare: and he that did hope by his own deuise to supply the generall
want, was not verie idle both in brain, to deuise, and in hand to deliuer the
thing, which he deuised. Which their trauell in the thing, and desire to do
good, deserue great thanks, tho that waie which their took, did not take
effect.

The causes why theie took not effect, and thereby in part did hinder the
thing, by making of manie think the case more desperat then it was in dede,
bycause such fellowes did so faill, were these. Their despare, which thought,
that the tung was vncapable of anie direction, came of a wrong cause, the
falt rising in dede not of the thing, which theie did condemn, as altogether
rude and vnrulie, but of the parties them selues, who mistook their waie.
For the thing it self will soon be ordered (our custom is grown so orderable)
tho it require som diligence, and good consideration, in him that must find it
out. But when a writer taketh a wrong principle, quite contrarie to common
practis, where triall must be tuch, and practis must confirm the mean, which
he conceaueth, is it anie maruell if the vse of a tung ouerthwart such a mean,
which is not conformable vnto it? Herevpon proceded the despare to hit
right, bycause theie missed of their minde, whereas in dede theie should haue
changed their minde, to haue hit vpon that right, which as it is in the thing,
so will it soon be found out, if it be rightlie sought for.

Again the others hope deceiued them to as much. For theie considered
not, that whereas common reason, and common custom haue bene long
dealers in seking out of their own currant, themselues wilbe councellers, and
will neuer yeild to anie priuat conceit, which shall seme euidentlie either to

force them or to crosse them, as theie themselues do, neuer giuing anie
precept, how to write right, till theie haue rated at custom, as a most perni-
cious enemie to truth and right, euen in that thing, where custom hath most
right, if it haue right in anie. Wherefor when theie proceded on in a customarie
argument, with the enemitie of him, which is Lord of the soill, was it anie
wonder if theie failed of their purpos, & hindered the finding out of our
right writing, which must nedes be compased by customs consent, and reasons
frindship? So in the mean time, while despare deceiues the one, and hope
begiles the other, the one missing his waie, the other making a fo, and
both going astraie, theie both lease their labor, and let the finding out of our
right in writing, by their ill led, and worse laid labor, bycause the artificiall
course, in finding out such a thing, hath another currant, as I haue shewed
before in the last title.

Yet notwithstanding all this, it is verie manifest, that the tung it self hath
matter enough in it self, to furnish out an art, & that the same mean, which
hath bene vsed in the reducing of other tungs to their right, will serue this
of ours, both for generalitie of precept, and certaintie of ground, as maie be
easilie proued by these four arguments, the antiquitie of our tung, the peples
wit, their learning, and their experience. For how can it be, but that a tung,
which hath continewed manie hundred years, not onelie a tung, but one of
good account, both in speche, and pen, hath growen in all that time to som
finesse, and assurance of it self, by so long and so generall an vse, tho it be
not as yet founded, the peple that haue vsed it, being none of the dullest,
and trauelling continuallie in all exercises that concern learning, in all
practises that procure experience, either in peace or war, either in publike,
or priuat, either at home or abrode?

As for the antiquitie of our speche, whether it be measured by the ancient
Almane, whence it cummeth originallie, or euen but by the latest terms which
it boroweth daielie from foren tungs, either of pure necessitie in new matters,
or of mere brauerie, to garnish it self withall, it cannot be young. Onelesse
the *Germane* himself be young, which claimeth a prerogatiue for the age of his
speche, of an infinit prescription: Onelesse the *Latin* and *Greke* be young,
whose words we enfranchise to our own vse, tho not allwaie immediatlie
from them selues, but mostwhat thorough the *Italian, French*, and *Spanish*:
Onelesse other tungs, which be neither *Greke* nor *Latin*, nor anie of the
forenamed, from whom we haue somwhat, as theie haue from ours, will for
companie sake be content to be young, that ours maie not be old. But I am
well assured, that euerie one of these, will striue for antiquitie, and rather
grant it to vs, then forgo it themselues. So that if the verie newest words,
which we vse do sauor of great antiquitie, and the ground of our speche be
most ancient, it must nedes then folow, that our hole tung was weined long
ago, as hauing all her tethe.

For the account of our tung, both in pen and speche, no man will dout
thereof, who is able to iudge what those thinges be, which make anie tung
to be of account, which things I take to be thré, the autoritie of the peple

which speak it, the matter & argument, wherein the speche dealeth, the manifold vse, for which the speche serueth. For all which thré, our tung nedeth not to giue place, to anie of her peres.

First to saie somwhat for the peple, that vse the tung, the *English* nation hath allwaie bene of good credit, and great estimation, euer since credit and estimation by historie came on this side the *Alps*, which appeareth to be trew, euen by foren cronicles (not to vse our own in a case of our own) which would neuer haue said so much of the peple, if it had bene obscure, and not for an historie, or not but well worthie of a perpetuall historie.

Next, for the argument, wherein it dealeth, whether priuat or publik, it maie compare with som other, that think verie well of their own selues. For not to tuch ordinarie affairs in comon life, will matters of learning in anie kind of argument, make a tung of account? Our nation then, I think, will hardlie be proued to haue bene vnlearned at anie time, in anie kind of learning, not to vse anie bigger speche. Wherefor hauing learning by confession of all men, & vttering that learning in their own tung, for their own vse, of verie pure necessitie (bycause we learn to vse, and the vse is in our own) theie could not but enrich the tung, and purchace it account.

Will matters of war, whether ciuill or foren, make a tung of account? Our neighbor nations will not deny our peple to be verie warrious, and our own cuntrie will confesse it, tho loth to fele it, both by remembring the smart, & comparing with som other, neither to vaunt our selues, nor to gall our frinds, with anie mo words.

Now in offring matter to speche, war is such a bréder, as tho it be opposit to learning, bycause it is enemie to the Muses, yet it dare compare with anie point in learning, for multitude of discourses, tho not commonlie so certain, ne yet of so good vse, as learned arguments be. For war (besides all graue and sad considerations about it, which be manie and wise) as somtime it sendeth vs trew reports, either priuatelie in proiects and deuises, that be entended, or publikelie in euents, which be blased abrode, bycause theie be don, so mostwhat it giueth out infinit and extreme, I dare not saie lies, but verie incredible newes, bycause it maie hatch them at will, being in no danger of controllment, and comonlie in such practises and places, as haue not manie witnesses, while euerie man seketh as well to saue him self, as to harm his enemie, besides som curteous entertainment, which a deuising referendarie hath euen by telling that, which is not trew, to such as loue to hear, and either like or will like. All which occasions, and infinit mo, about stratagemes & engins, giue matter to speche, and cause of new words, and by making it so redie, do make it of renoun.

With all kindes of trade, and all sorts of traffik, make a tung of account? If the spreading sea, and the spacious land could vse anie speche, theie would both shew you, where, and in how manie strange places, theie haue sene our peple, and also giue you to wit, that theie deall in as much, and as great varietie of matters, as anie other peple do, whether at home or abrode. Which is the reason why our tung doth serue to so manie vses, bycause it is conuersant with so manie peple, and so well acquainted with so manie matters, in so sundrie kindes of dealing. Now all this varietie of matter, and diuersitie of trade, make both matter for our speche, & mean to enlarge it. For he that is so practised, will vtter that, which he practiseth in his naturall tung, and if the strangenesse of the matter do so require, he that is to vtter, rather then he will stik in his vtterance, will vse the foren term, by waie of premunition, that the cuntrie peple do call it so, and by that mean make a foren word, an English denison.

All which reasons concerning but the tung, and the account thereof, being put together, as of themselues, theie proue the nations exercise in learning, and their practis in other dealings: so theie seme to infer no base witted peple, not to amplify it with more, bycause it is not for foulls to be so well learned, to be so warrious, to be so well practised. I shall not nede to proue anie of these my positions, either by foren or home historie: seing my reader stranger, will not striue with me for them, and mine own nation, will not gainsaie me in them, I think, which knoweth them to be trew, and maie vse them for their honor.

Wherefor I maie well conclude my first position: that if *vse* and *custom* hauing the help of so long time, and continuance, wherein to fine our tung: of so great learning and experience, which furnish matter for the fining: of so good wits and iudgements, which can tell how to fine, haue griped at nothing in all that time with all that cunning, by all those wits, which theie will not let go, but hold for most certaine, in the right of our writing: that then our tung hath no certaintie to trust to, but writeth all at randon. But the antecedent in my opinion, is alltogether vnpossible, wherefor the conse-quent, is a great deall more then probable, which is, that our tung hath in hir own possession, and writing verie good euidence to proue hir own right writing: Which tho no man as yet, by anie publik writing of his, semeth to haue sene, yet the tung it self is redie to shew them, to anie whosoeuer, which is able to read them, and withall to iudge, what euidence is right in the right of writing. Wherefor seing I haue proued sufficientlie in mine own opinion, that there is great cause, why our tung should haue som good right, in her own writing, and take my self to haue had the sight of that euidence, whereby that same right appeareth most iustifiable, and am not alltogither ignorant, how to giue sentence thereof, I will do my best, according to that course, which I said was kept in the first, and generall fining of anie speche, which also hath bene translated to euerie secondarie, and particular tung, to set furth som certaintie for the English writing, by those notes, which I haue obserued in the tung it self, the pure best and finest therein, offering mean by comparison with them selues, both to correct, and to direct the worse and more grosse, without either innouating anie thing, as theie do, which set furth new deuises, or by mistaking my waie, as theie do, which despare, that our tung can be brought to anie certaintie, without som maruellous foren help. Thus much for the artificiall stuf in our tung, now to the obiec-tions which charge it with infirmities.

PART SIX

CONCERNS ABOUT THE
DEVELOPING LANGUAGE

✠

INTRODUCTION

Three of the selections in section IV and V of this book and the three which follow in this section provide a series of examples of the English language at intervals of from thirty to eighty years from the earliest days of the English Renaissance to the time of the American Revolution, a period of over two hundred and sixty years:*

   1490 Caxton, Prologue to *Eneydos*
   1520 Rastell, Preface to *Abbreviation of the Statutes*
   1582 Mulcaster, "That the English tung . . ."
   1651 Hobbes, "Of Speech"
   1733 Franklin, "Essay on Literary Style"
   1773 Johnson, Preface to *A Dictionary*

The three selections in this section, however, are also interesting in their own right, for they show the reader the growing interest of the intellectuals of the seventeenth and eighteenth centuries in the capabilities of language in general and of English in particular for ordering the universe and for communicating.

In "Of Speech," Hobbes discusses a variety of concepts with which semanticists are still concerned: the relation of thought and language, misuse of language, abstraction, categorization, generalization, definition, signification. Franklin, arguing in his "Essay on Literary Style" that writing should be smooth, clear, and short, provides admonitions still offered by modern rhetorics: "If [a Writer] would *inform*, he must advance regularly from Things known to things unknown, distinctly without confusion, and the lower he begins the better"; "if the Author does not intend his Piece for general Reading, he must exactly suit his Stile and Manner to the particular Taste

*The Myers selection, which introduces section V, contains several additional examples, mostly from the sixteenth century: 1484, Caxton; 1533 Elyot; 1553, Wilson; 1557, Cheke; 1562, Eden; 1581, Pettie. The exercises contain still further examples: 1482, Caxton; 1526, Tyndale; 1593, Elizabeth; 1623, Shakespeare; 1715, Burnet. And the two chapters from Scott's *Ivanhoe* (1819) in section IV and the passage from Shelley in Exercise 12 (1822) provide examples of writing from the early part of the nineteenth century. Taken together, these complete selections and shorter passages provide an excellent picture of how Modern English developed over a period of three and a half centuries. Various other selections in the book carry this picture into the present century and up to the present day. Passages from Old and Middle English in sections III and IV and in the exercises similarly provide a good picture of the earlier development of the language.

of those he proposes for his readers"; "Pieces meerly humorous, are of all Sorts the hardest to succeed in."

Johnson, too, in his "Preface" to his *Dictionary* frequently sounds very modern in his explanation of the procedures he used as a lexicographer. Like the modern lexicographers, he developed his definitions after "perusal of our writers." Like modern linguists, he affirms that "As language was at its beginning merely oral, all words of necessary or common use were spoken before they were written." Unlike most contemporary lexicographers and grammarians, however, he insists that he knows the difference between those irregularities and anomalies in the language which must be tolerated and those "improprieties and absurdities" which must be corrected or proscribed. He continues to exhibit this self-confidence throughout the essay as he describes what he has done and how language functions.

Each of the three essayists shows a keen understanding of language and a concern for its effective use. In doing so, each also projects a different personality and demonstrates the wide range of expression available to speakers and writers of Modern English.

✠ ✠ ✠

OF SPEECH

THOMAS HOBBES

The Invention of *Printing*, though ingenious, compared with the invention
of *Letters*, is no great matter. But who was the first that found the use of
Letters, is not known. He that first brought them into *Greece*, men say was
Cadmus, the sonne of *Agenor*, King of Phaenicia. A profitable Invention for
continuing the memory of time past, and the conjunction of mankind, dis-
persed into so many, and distant regions of the Earth; and with all difficult,
as proceeding from a watchful observation of the divers motions of the
Tongue, Palat, Lips, and other organs of Speech; whereby to make as many
differences of characters, to remember them. But the most noble and profitable invention of all other, was that of SPEECH, consisting of *Names* or
Appellations, and their Connextion; whereby men register their Thoughts;
recall them when they are past; and also declare them one to another for
mutuall utility and conversation; without which, there had been amongst
men, neither Common-wealth, nor Society, nor Contract, nor Peace, no
more than amongst Lyons, Bears, and Wolves. The first author of Speech
was *God* himself, that instructed *Adam* how to name such creatures as he
presented to his sight; For the Scripture goeth no further in this matter. But
this was sufficient to direct him to adde more names, as the experience and
use of the creatures should give him occasion; and to joyn them in such

Reprinted from *Leviathan*, Volume I, Chapter IV, by Thomas Hobbes, 1651.

manner by degrees, as to make himself understood; and so by succession of time, so much language might be gotten, as he had found use for; though not so copious, as an Orator or Philosopher has need of. For I do not find any thing in the Scripture, out of which, directly or by consequence can be gathered, that *Adam* was taught the names of all Figures, Numbers, Measures, Colours, Sounds, Fancies, Relations; much less the names of Words and Speech, as *Generall, Speciall, Affirmative, Negative, Interrogative, Optative, Infinitive,* all which are usefull; and least of all, of *Entity, Intentionality, Quiddity,* and other insignificant words of the School.

But all this language gotten, and augmented by *Adam* and his posterity, was again lost at the tower of *Babel,* when by the hand of God, every man was stricken for his rebellion, with an oblivion of his former language. And being hereby forced to disperse themselves into severall parts of the world, it must needs be, that the diversity of Tongues that now is, proceeded by degrees from them, in such manner, as need (the mother of all inventions) taught them; and in tract of time grew every where more copious.

The generall use of Speech, is to transferre our Mentall Discourse, into Verbal; or the Trayne of our Thoughts, into a Trayne of Words; and that for two commodities; whereof one is, the Registring of the Consequences of our Thoughts; which being apt to slip out of our memory, and put us to a new labour, may again be recalled, by such words as they were marked by. So that the first use of names, is to serve for *Markes,* or *Notes* of remembrance. Another is, when many use the same words, to signifie (by their connexion and order,) one to another, what they conceive, or think of each matter; and also what they desire, feare, or have any other passion for. And for this use they are called *Signes.* Speciall uses of Speech are these; First, to Register, what by cogitation, wee find to be the cause of any thing, present or past; and what we find things present or past may produce, or effect: which in summe, is acquiring of Arts. Secondly, to shew to others that knowledge which we have attained; which is, to Counsell, and Teach one another. Thirdly, to make known to others our wills, and purposes, that we may have the mutuall help of one another. Fourthly, to please and delight our selves, and others, by playing with our words, for pleasure or ornament, innocently.

To these Uses, there are also foure correspondent Abuses. First, when men register their thoughts wrong, by the inconstancy of the signification of their words; by which they register for their conceptions, that which they never conceived; and so deceive themselves. Secondly, when they use words metaphorically; that is, in other sense than that they are ordained for; and thereby deceive others. Thirdly, when by words they declare that to be their will, which is not. Fourthly, when they use them to grieve one another; for seeing nature hath armed living creatures, some with teeth, some with horns, and some with hands, to grieve an enemy, it is but an abuse of Speech, to grieve him with the tongue, unlesse it be one whom wee are obliged to govern; and then it is not to grieve, but to correct and amend.

The manner how Speech serveth to the remembrance of the consequence of causes and effects, consisteth in the imposing of *Names*, and the *Connexion* of them.

Of Names, some are *Proper*, and singular to one onely thing; as *Peter, Iohn, This man, this Tree*: and some are *Common* to many things; as *Man, Horse, Tree*; every of which though but one Name, is nevertheless the name of divers particular things; in respect of all which together, it is called an *Universall*; there being nothing in the world Universall but Names; for the things named, are every one of them Individuall and Singular.

One Universall name is imposed on many things, for their similitude in some quality, or other accident: And wheras a Proper Name bringeth to mind one thing onely; Universals recall any one of those many.

And of Names Universall, some are of more, and some of lesse extent; the larger comprehending the lesse large: and some again of equall extent, comprehending each other reciprocally. As for example, the Name *Body* is of larger signification than the word *Man*, and comprehendeth it; and the names *Man* and *Rationall*, are of equall extent, comprehending mutually one another. But here wee must take notice, that by a Name is not always understood, as in Grammar, one onely Word; but sometimes by circumlocution many words together. For all these words, *Hee that in his actions observeth the Lawes of his Country*, make but one Name, equivalent to this one word, *Just*.

By this imposition of Names, some of larger, some of stricter signification, we turn the reckoning of the consequences of things imagined in the mind, into a reckoning of the consequences of Appellations. For example, a man that hath no use of Speech at all, (such, as is born and remains perfectly deafe and dumb,) if he set before his eyes a triangle, and by it two right angles, (such as are the corners of a square figure,) he may by meditation compare and find, that the three angles of that triangle, are equall to those two right angles that stand by it. But if another triangle be shewn him different in shape from the former, he cannot know without a new labour, whether the three angles of that also be equall to the same. But he that hath the use of words, when he observes, that such equality was consequent, not to the length of the sides, nor to any other particular thing in his triangle; but onely to this, that the sides were straight, and the angles three; and that that was all, for which he named it a Triangle; will boldly conclude Universally, that such equality of angles is in all triangles whatsoever; and register his invention in these generall termes, *Every triangle hath its three angles equall to two right angles*. And thus the consequence found in one particular, comes to be registred and remembred, as an Universall rule; and discharges our mentall reckoning, of time and place; and delivers us from all labour of the mind, saving the first; and makes that which was found true *here*, and *now*, to be true in *all times* and *places*.

But the use of words in registring our thoughts, is in nothing so evident as in Numbring. A naturall foole that could never learn by heart the order of numerall words, as *one*, *two*, and *three*, may observe every stroak of the Clock, and nod to it, or say one, one, one; but can never know what houre it strikes. And it seems, there was a time when those names of number were not in use; and men were fayn to apply their fingers of one or both hands, to those things they desired to keep account of; and that thence it proceeded, that now our numerall words are but ten, in any Nation, and in some but five, and then they begin again. And he that can tell ten, if he recite them out of order, will lose himselfe, and not know when he has done: Much lesse will he be able to adde, and subtract, and performe all other operations of Arithmetique. So that without words, there is no possibility of reckoning of Numbers; much lesse of Magnitudes, of Swiftnesse, of Force, and other things, the reckonings whereof are necessary to the being, or well-being of man-kind.

When two Names are joyned together into a Consequence, or Affirmation; as thus, *A man is a living creature*; or this, *if he be a man, he is a living creature*, If the later name *Living creature*, signifie all that the former name *Man* signifieth, then the affirmation, or consequence is *true*; otherwise *false*. For *True* and *False* are attributes of Speech, not of Things. And where Speech is not, there is neither *Truth* nor *Falshood*. *Errour* there may be, as when wee expect that which shall not be; or suspect what has not been; but in neither case can a man be charged with Untruth.

Seeing then that *truth* consisteth in the right ordering of names in our affirmations, a man that seeketh precise *truth*, had need to remember what every name he uses stands for; and to place it accordingly or else he will find himselfe entangled in words, as a bird in lime-twiggs; the more he struggles, the more belimed. And therefore in Geometry, (which is the onely Science that it hath pleased God hitherto to bestow on mankind,) men begin at settling the significations of their words; which settling of significations, they call *Definitions*; and place them in the beginning of their reckoning.

By this it appears how necessary it is for any man that aspires to true Knowledge, to examine the Definitions of former Authors; and either to correct them, where they are negligently set down; or to make them himselfe. For the errours of Definitions multiply themselves, according as the reckoning proceeds; and lead men into absurdities, which at last they see, but cannot avoyd, without reckoning anew from the beginning; in which lyes the foundation of their errours. From whence it happens, that they which trust to books, do as they that cast up many little summs into a greater, without considering whether those little summes were rightly cast up or not; and at last finding the errour visible, and not mistrusting their first grounds, know not which way to cleere themselves; but spend time in fluttering over their books; as birds that entring by the chimney, and finding themselves inclosed in a chamber, flutter at the false light of a glasse window, for want of wit to consider which way they came in. So that is the right Definition of Names, lyes the first use of Speech; which is the Acquisition of Science: And in wrong, or no Definitions, lyes the first abuse; from which proceed all false and senselesse Tenets; which make those men that take their instruction from the authority of books, and not from their own mediation, to be as much below the condition of ignorant men, as men endued with true Science are above it. For between true Science, and erroneous Doctrines, Ignorance is in the middle. Naturall sense and imagination, are not subject to absurdity. Nature it selfe cannot erre: and as men abound in copiousnesse of language; so they become more wise, or more mad than ordinary. Nor is it possible without Letters for any man to become either excellently wise, or (unless his memory be hurt by disease, or ill constitution of organs) excellently foolish. For words are wise mens counters, they do but reckon by them: but they are the mony of fooles, that value them by the authority of an *Aristotle*, a *Cicero*, or a *Thomas*, or any other Doctor whatsoever, if but a man.

Subject to Names, is whatsoever can enter into, or be considered in an account; and be added one to another to make a summe; or subtracted one from another, and leave a remainder. The Latines called Accounts of mony *Rationes*, and accounting, *Ratiocinatio*; and that which we in bills or books of account call *Items*, they called *Nomina*; that is, *Names*: and thence it seems to proceed, that they extended the word *Ratio*, to the faculty of Reckoning in all other things. The Greeks have but one word λόγος, for both *Speech* and *Reason*; not that they thought there was no Speech without Reason; but no Reasoning without Speech: And the act of reasoning they called *Syllogisme*; which signifieth summing up of the consequences of one saying to another. And because the same things may enter into account for divers accidents; their names are (to shew that diversity) diversly wrested, and diversified. This diversity of names may be reduced to foure generall heads.

First, a thing may enter into account for *Matter*, or *Body*; as *living, sensible, rationall, hot, cold, moved, quiet*; with all which names the word *Matter*, or *Body* is understood; all such, being names of Matter.

Secondly, it may enter into account, or be considered, for some accident or quality, which we conceive to be in it; as for *being moved*, for *being so long*, for *being hot*, &c; and then, of the name of the thing it selfe, by a little change or wresting, wee make a name for that accident, which we consider; and for living put into the account life; for *moved, motion*; for *hot, heat*; for *long, length*, and the like: And all such Names, are the names of the accidents and properties, by which one Matter, and Body is distinguished from another. These are called *names Abstract*; because severed (not from Matter, but) from the account of Matter.

Thirdly, we bring into account, the Properties of our own bodies, whereby we make such distinction: as when any thing is *Seen* by us, we reckon not the thing it selfe; but the *sight*, the *Colour*, the *Idea* of it in the fancy: and when any thing is *heard*, wee reckon it not; but the *hearing*, or *sound* onely, which is our fancy or conception of it by the Eare: and such are names of fancies.

Fourthly, we bring into account, consider, and give names, to *Names* themselves, and to *Speeches*: For, *generall, universall, speciall, equivocall*, are names of Names. And *Affirmation, Interrogation, Commandment, Narration, Syllogisme, Sermon, Oration*, and many other such, are names of Speeches. And this is all the variety of Names *Positive*; which are put to mark somewhat which is in Nature, or may be feigned by the mind of man, as Bodies that are, or may be feigned to be; or Words and Speech.

There be also other Names, called *Negative*; which are notes to signifie that a word is not the name of the thing in question; as these words *Nothing, no man, infinite, indocible, three want foure*, and the like; which are nevertheless of use in reckoning, or in correcting of reckoning; and call to mind our past cogitations, though they be not names of any thing; because they make us refuse to admit of Names not rightly used.

All other Names, are but insignificant sounds; and those of two sorts. One, when they are new, and yet their meaning not explained by Definition; whereof there have been aboundance coyned by Schoole-men, and pusled Philosophers.

Another, when men make a name of two Names, whose significations are contradictory and inconsistent; as this name, an *incorporeall body*, or (which is all one) an *incorporeall substance*, and a great number more. For whensoever any affirmation is false, the two names of which it is composed, put together and made one, signifie nothing at all. For example, if it be a false affirmation to say a *quadrangle is round*, the word *round quadrangle* signifies nothing; but is a meere sound. So likewise if it be false, to say that vertue can be powred, or blown up and down; the words *In-powred vertue, In-blown vertue*, are as absurd and insignificant, as a *round quadrangle*. And therefore you shall hardly meet with a senslesse and insignificant word, that is not made up of some Latin or Greek names. A Frenchman seldome hears our Saviour called by the name of *Parole*, but by the name of *Verbe* often; yet *Verbe* and *Parole* differ no more, but that one is Latin, the other French.

When a man upon the hearing of any Speech, hath those thoughts which the words of that Speech, and their connexion were ordained and constituted to signifie; Then he is said to understand it: *Understanding* being nothing else, but conception caused by Speech. And therefore if Speech be peculiar to man (as for ought I know it is,) then is Understanding peculiar to him also. And therefore of absurd and false affirmations, in case they be universall, there can be no Understanding; though many think they understand, then, when they do but repeat the words softly, or con them in their mind.

What kinds of Speeches signifie the Appetites, Aversions, and Passions of mans mind; and of their use and abuse, I shall speak when I have spoken of the Passions.

The names of such things as affect us, that is, which please, and displease us, because all men be not alike affected with the same thing, nor the same man at all times, are in the common discourses of men, of *inconstant* signification. For seeing all names are imposed to signifie our conceptions; and all our affections are but conceptions; when we conceive the same things differently, we can hardly avoyd different naming of them. For though the nature of that we conceive, be the same; yet the diversity of our reception of it, in respect of different constitutions of body, and prejudices of opinion, gives every thing a tincture of our different passions. And therefore in reasoning, a man must take heed of words; which besides the signification of what we imagine of their nature, have a signification also of the nature, disposition, and interest of the speaker; such as are the names of Vertues, and Vices; For one man calleth *Wisdome*, what another calleth *feare*; and one *cruelty*, what another *justice*; one *prodigality*, what another *magnanimity*; and one *gravity*, what another *stupidicy*, &c. And therefore such names can never be true grounds of any ratiocination. No more can Metaphors, and Tropes of speech: but these are less dangerous, because they profess their inconstancy; which the other do not.

✠ ✠ ✠

ESSAY ON LITERARY STYLE

BENJAMIN FRANKLIN

There are few Men, of Capacity for making any considerable Figure in Life, who have not frequent Occasion to communicate their Thoughts to others in *Writing*; if not sometimes publickly as Authors, yet continually in the Management of their private Affairs, both of Business and Friendship: and since, when ill-express'd, the most proper Sentiments and justest Reasoning lose much of their native Force and Beauty, it seems to me that there is scarce any Accomplishment more necessary to a Man of Sense, than that of *Writing well* in his Mother Tongue: But as most other polite Acquirements, make a greater Appearance in a Man's Character, this however useful, is generally neglected or forgotten.

I believe there is no better Means of learning to write well, than this of attempting to entertain the Publick now and then in one of your Papers. When the Writer conceals himself, he has the Advantage of hearing the Censure both of Friends and Enemies, express'd with more Impartiality. And since, in some degree, it concerns the Credit of the Province, that such Things as are printed be performed tolerably well, mutual Improvement seems to be the Duty of all Lovers of Writing: I shall therefore frankly communicate the Observations I have made or collected on this Subject, and request those of others in Return.

Reprinted from *The Pennsylvania Gazette,* August 2, 1733.

I have thought in general, that whoever would write so as not to displease good Judges, should have particular Regard to these three Things, *viz.* That his Performance be *smooth, clear*, and *short*: for the contrary Qualities are apt to offend, either the Ear, the Understanding, or the Patience.

'Tis an Observation of Dr. *Swift*, that modern Writers injure the Smoothness of our Tongue, by omitting Vowels wherever it is possible, and joining the harshest Consonants together with only an Apostrophe between; thus for *judged*, in it self not the smoothest of Words, they say *judg'd*; for *disturbed, disturb'd*, &c. It may be added to this, says another, that by changing *eth* into *s*, they have shortened one Syllable in a multitude of Words, and have thereby encreased, not only the *Hissing*, too offensive before, but also the great Number of Monosyllables, of which, without great Difficulty, a smooth Sentence cannot be composed. The Smoothness of a Period is also often Hurt by Parentheses, and therefore the best Writers endeavour to avoid them.

To write *clearly*, not only the most expressive, but the plainest Words should be chosen. In this, as well as in every other Particular requisite to Clearness, Dr. *Tillotson* is an excellent Example. The Fondness of some Writers for such Words as carry with them an Air of Learning, renders them unintelligible to more than half their Countrymen. If a Man would that his Writings have an Effect on the Generality of Readers, he had better imitate that Gentleman, who would use no Word in his Works that was not well understood by his Cook-maid.

A too frequent Use of Phrases ought likewise to be avoided by him that would write clearly. They trouble the Language, not only rendring it extreamly difficult to Foreigners, but make the Meaning obscure to a great number of English Readers. Phrases, like learned Words, are seldom used without Affectation; when, with all true Judges, the simplest Stile is the most beautiful.

But supposing the most proper Words and Expressions chosen, the Performance may yet be weak and obscure, if it has not *Method*. If a Writer would *persuade*, he should proceed gradually from Things already allow'd, to those from which Assent is yet with-held, and make their Connection manifest. If he would *inform*, he must advance regularly from Things known to things unknown, distinctly without Confusion, and the lower he begins the better. It is a common Fault in Writers, to allow their Readers too much Knowledge: They begin with that which should be in the Middle, and skipping backwards and forwards, 'tis impossible for any one but he who is perfect in the Subject before, to understand their Work, and such an one has no Occasion to read it. Perhaps a Habit of using good Method, cannot be better acquired, than by learning a little Geometry or Algebra.

Amplification, or the Art of saying Little in Much, should only be allowed to Speakers. If they preach, a Discourse of considerable Length is expected from them, upon every Subject they undertake, and perhaps they are not stock'd with naked Thoughts sufficient to furnish it out. If they plead in the Courts, it is of Use to speak abundance, tho' they reason little; for the

Ignorant in a Jury, can scarcely believe it possible that a Man can talk so much and long without being in the Right. Let them have the Liberty then, of repeating the same Sentences in other Words; let them put an Adjective to every Substantive, and double every Substantive with a Synonima; for this is more agreeable than hauking, spitting, taking Snuff, or any other Means of concealing Hesitation. Let them multiply Definitions, Comparisons, Similitudes and Examples. Permit them to make a Detail of Causes and Effects, enumerate all the Consequences, and express one Half by Metaphor and Circumlocution: Nay, allow the Preacher to tell us whatever a Thing is negatively, before he begins to tell us what it is affirmatively; and suffer him to divide and subdivide as far as *Two and fiftiethly.* All this is not intolerable while it is not written. But when a Discourse is to be bound down upon Paper, and subjected to the calm leisurely Examination of nice Judgment, every Thing that is needless gives Offence; and therefore all should be re-trenched, that does not directly conduce to the End design'd. Had this been always done, many large and tiresome Folio's would have shrunk into Pamphlets, and many a Pamphlet into a single Period. However, tho' a multitude of Words obscure the Sense, and 'tis necessary to abridge a verbose Author in order to understand him; yet a Writer should take especial Care on the other Hand, that his Brevity doth not hurt his Perspicuity.

After all, if the Author does not intend his Piece for general Reading, he must exactly suit his Stile and Manner to the particular Taste of those he proposes for his Readers. Every one observes, the different Ways of Writing and Expression used by the different Sects of Religion; and can readily enough pronounce, that it is improper to use some of these Stiles in common, or to use the common Stile, when we address some of these Sects in particular.

To conclude, I shall venture to lay it down as a Maxim, *That no Piece can be properly called good, and well written, which is void of any Tendency to benefit the Reader, either by improving his Virtue or his Knowledge.* This Principle every Writer would do well to have in View, whenever he undertakes to write. All Performances done for meer Ostentation of Parts, are really contemptible; and withal far more subject to the Severity of Criticism, than those more meanly written, wherein the Author appears to have aimed at the Good of others. For when 'tis visible to every one, that a Man writes to show his Wit only, all his Expressions are sifted, and his Sense examined, in the nicest and most ill-natur'd manner; and every one is glad of an Opportunity to mortify him. —But, what a vast Destruction would there be of Books, if they were to be saved or condemned on a Tryal by this Rule!

Besides, Pieces meerly humorous, are of all Sorts the hardest to succeed in. If they are not natural, they are stark naught; and there can be no real Humour in an Affectation of Humour.

Perhaps it may be said, that an ill Man is able to write an ill Thing well; that is, having an ill Design, and considering who are to be his Readers, he may use the properest Stile and Arguments to attain his Point. In this Sense, that is best wrote, which is best adapted to the Purpose of the Writer.

I am apprehensive, dear Readers, lest in this Piece, I should be guilty of every Fault I condemn, and deficient in every Thing I recommend; so much easier it is to offer Rules than to practise them. I am sure, however, of this, that I am

Your very sincere Friend and Servant.

✠ ✠ ✠

PREFACE TO A DICTIONARY OF THE ENGLISH LANGUAGE (1773 EDITION)

SAMUEL JOHNSON

It is the fate of those who toil at the lower employments of life, to be rather driven by the fear of evil, than attracted by the prospect of good; to be exposed to censure, without hope of praise; to be disgraced by miscarriage, or punished for neglect, where success would have been without applause, and diligence without reward.

Among these unhappy mortals is the writer of dictionaries; whom mankind have considered, not as the pupil, but the slave of science, the pionier of literature, doomed only to remove rubbish and clear obstructions from the paths through which Learning and Genius press forward to conquest and glory, without bestowing a smile on the humble drudge that facilitates their progress. Every other authour may aspire to praise; the lexicographer can only hope to escape reproach, and even this negative recompense has been yet granted to very few.

I have, notwithstanding this discouragement, attempted a dictionary of the *English* language, which, while it was employed in the cultivation of every species of literature, has itself been hitherto neglected; suffered to spread, under the direction of chance, into wild exuberance; resigned to the tyranny of time and fashion; and exposed to the corruptions of ignorance, and caprices of innovation.

When I took the first survey of my undertaking, I found our speech copious without order, and energetick without rules: wherever I turned my view, there was perplexity to be disentangled, and confusion to be regulated; choice was to be made out of boundless variety, without any established principle of selection; adulterations were to be detected, without a settled test of purity; and modes of expression to be rejected or received, without the suffrages of any writers of classical reputation or acknowledged authority.

Having therefore no assistance but from general grammar, I applied myself to the perusal of our writers; and noting whatever might be of use to ascertain or illustrate any word or phrase, accumulated in time the materials of a dictionary, which, by degrees, I reduced to method, establishing to myself, in the progress of the work, such rules as experience and analogy suggested to me; experience, which practice and observation were continually increasing; and analogy, which, though in some words obscure, was evident in others.

In adjusting the ORTHOGRAPHY, which has been to this time unsettled and fortuitous, I found it necessary to distinguish those irregularities that are inherent in our tongue, and perhaps coeval with it, from others which the ignorance or negligence of later writers has produced. Every language has its anomalies, which, though inconvenient, and in themselves once unnecessary, must be tolerated among the imperfections of human things, and which require only to be registered, that they may not be increased, and ascertained, that they may not be confounded: but every language has likewise its improprieties and absurdities, which it is the duty of the lexicographer to correct or proscribe.

As language was at its beginning merely oral, all words of necessary or common use were spoken before they were written; and while they were unfixed by any visible signs, must have been spoken with great diversity, as we now observe those who cannot read to catch sounds imperfectly, and utter them negligently. When this wild and barbarous jargon was first reduced to an alphabet, every penman endeavoured to express, as he could, the sounds which he was accustomed to pronounce or to receive, and vitiated in writing such words as were already vitiated in speech. The powers of the letters, when they were applied to a new language, must have been vague and unsettled, and therefore different hands would exhibit the same sound by different combinations.

From this uncertain pronunciation arise in a great part the various dialects of the same country, which will always be observed to grow fewer, and less different, as books are multiplied; and from this arbitrary representation of sounds by letters, proceeds that diversity of spelling observable in the *Saxon* remains, and I suppose in the first books of every nation, which perplexes or destroys analogy, and produces anomalous formations, that, being once incorporated, can never be afterward dismissed or reformed.

Of this kind are the derivatives *length* from *long, strength* from *strong, darling* from *dear, breadth* from *broad,* from *dry, drought,* and from *high, height,* which *Milton,* in zeal for analogy, writes *highth; Quid te exempta juvat spinis de pluribus una;* to change all would be too much, and to change one is nothing.

This uncertainty is most frequent in the vowels, which are so capriciously pronounced, and so differently modified, by accident or affectation, not only in every province, but in every mouth, that to them, as is well known to etymologists, little regard is to be shewn in the deduction of one language from another.

Such defects are not errours in orthography, but spots of barbarity impressed so deep in the *English* language, that criticism can never wash them away: these, therefore, must be permitted to remain untouched; but many words have likewise been altered by accident, or depraved by ignorance, as the pronunciation of the vulgar has been weakly followed; and some still continue to be variously written, as authours differ in their care or skill: of these it was proper to enquire the true orthography, which I have always considered as depending on their derivation, and have therefore referred them to their original languages: thus I write *enchant, enchantment, enchanter,* after the *French,* and *incantation* after the *Latin;* thus *entire* is chosen rather than *intire,* because it passed to us not from the *Latin integer,* but from the *French entier.*

Of many words it is difficult to say whether they were immediately received from the *Latin* or the *French,* since at the time when we had dominions in *France,* we had *Latin* service in our churches. It is, however, my opinion, that the *French* generally supplied us; for we have few *Latin* words, among the terms of domestick use, which are not *French;* but many *French,* which are very remote from *Latin.*

Even in words of which the derivation is apparent, I have been often obliged to sacrifice uniformity to custom; thus I write, in compliance with a numberless majority, *convey* and *inveigh, deceit* and *receipt, fancy* and *phantom;* sometimes the derivative varies from the primitive, as *explain* and *explanation, repeat* and *repetition.*

Some combinations of letters having the same power are used indifferently without any discoverable reason of choice, as in *choak, choke; soap, sope; fewel, fuel,* and many others; which I have sometimes inserted twice, that those who search for them under either form, may not search in vain.

In examining the orthography of any doubtful word, the mode of spelling by which it is inserted in the series of the dictionary, is to be considered as that to which I give, perhaps not often rashly, the preference. I have left, in the examples, to every authour his own practice unmolested, that the reader may balance suffrages, and judge between us: but this question is not always to be determined by reputed or by real learning; some men, intent upon greater things, have thought little on sounds and derivations; some, knowing in the ancient tongues, have neglected those in which our words are commonly to be sought. Thus *Hammond* writes *fecibleness* for *feasibleness*, because I suppose he imagined it derived immediately from the *Latin*; and some words, such as *dependant, dependent; dependance, dependence*, vary their final syllable, as one or another language is present to the writer.

In this part of the work, where caprice has long wantoned without controul, and vanity sought praise by petty reformation, I have endeavoured to proceed with a scholar's reverence for antiquity, and a grammarian's regard to the genius of our tongue. I have attempted few alterations, and among those few, perhaps the greater part is from the modern to the ancient practice; and I hope I may be allowed to recommend to those, whose thoughts have been perhaps employed too anxiously on verbal singularities, not to disturb, upon narrow views, or for minute propriety, the orthography of their fathers. It has been asserted, that for the law to be *known*, is of more importance than to be *right*. Change, says *Hooker*, is not made without inconvenience, even from worse to better. There is in constancy and stability a general and lasting advantage, which will always overbalance the slow improvements of gradual correction. Much less ought our written language to comply with the corruptions of oral utterance, or copy that which every variation of time or place makes different from itself, and imitate those changes, which will again be changed, while imitation is employed in observing them.

This recommendation of steadiness and uniformity does not proceed from an opinion, that particular combinations of letters have much influence on human happiness; or that truth may not be successfully taught by modes of spelling fanciful and erroneous: I am not yet so lost in lexicography, as to forget that *words are the daughters of earth, and that things are the sons of heaven*. Language is only the instrument of science, and words are but the signs of ideas: I wish, however, that the instrument might be less apt to decay, and that signs might be permanent, like the things which they denote.

In settling the orthography, I have not wholly neglected the pronunciation, which I have directed, by printing an accent upon the acute or elevated syllable. It will sometimes be found, that the accent is placed by the authour quoted, on a different syllable from that marked in the alphabetical series; it is then to be understood, that custom has varied, or that the authour has, in my opinion, pronounced wrong. Short directions are sometimes given where the sound of letters is irregular; and if they are sometimes omitted, defect in such minute observations will be more easily excused, than superfluity.

In the investigation both of the orthography and signification of words, their ETYMOLOGY was necessarily to be considered, and they were therefore to be divided into primitives and derivatives. A primitive word, is that which can be traced no further to any *English* root; thus *circumspect, circumvent, circumstance, delude, concave*, and *complicate*, though compounds in the *Latin*, are to us primitives. Derivatives, are all those that can be referred to any word in *English* of greater simplicity.

The derivatives I have referred to their primitives, with an accuracy some-times needless; for who does not see that *remoteness* comes from *remote, lovely* from *love, concavity* from *concave*, and *demonstrative* from *demon-strate*? but this grammatical exuberance the scheme of my work did not allow me to repress. It is of great importance in examining the general fabrick of a language, to trace one word from another, by noting the usual modes of derivation and inflection; and uniformity must be preserved in systematical works, though sometimes at the expence of particular propriety.

Among other derivatives I have been careful to insert and elucidate the anomalous plurals of nouns and preterites of verbs, which in the *Teutonick* dialects are very frequent, and though familiar to those who have always used them, interrupt and embarrass the learners of our language.

The two languages from which our primitives have been derived are the *Roman* and *Teutonick*: under the *Roman* I comprehend the *French* and pro-vincial tongues; and under the *Teutonick* range the *Saxon, German*, and all their kindred dialects. Most of our polysyllables are *Roman*, and our words of one syllable are very often *Teutonick*.

In assigning the *Roman* original, it has perhaps sometimes happened that I have mentioned only the *Latin*, when the word was borrowed from the *French*; and considering myself as employed only in the illustration of my own language, I have not been very careful to observe whether the *Latin* word be pure or barbarous, or the *French* elegant or obsolete.

For the *Teutonick* etymologies I am commonly indebted to *Junius* and *Skinner*, the only names which I have forborn to quote when I copied their books; not that I might appropriate their labours or usurp their honours, but that I might spare a perpetual repetition by one general acknowledgment. Of these, whom I ought not to mention but with the reverence due to instruc-tors and benefactors, *Junius* appears to have excelled in extent of learning, and *Skinner* in rectitude of understanding. *Junius* was accurately skilled in all the northern languages, *Skinner* probably examined the ancient and remoter dialects only by occasional inspection into dictionaries; but the learning of *Junius* is often of no other use than to show him a track by which he may deviate from his purpose, to which *Skinner* always presses forward by the shortest way. *Skinner* is often ignorant, but never ridiculous: *Junius* is always full of knowledge; but his variety distracts his judgment, and his learning is very frequently disgraced by his absurdities.

The votaries of the northern muses will not perhaps easily restrain their indignation, when they find the name of *Junius* thus degraded by a dis-advantageous comparison; but whatever reverence is due to his diligence, or his attainments, it can be no criminal degree of censoriousness to charge that etymologist with want of judgment, who can seriously derive *dream* from *drama*, because *life is a drama, and a drama is a dream*; and who declares with a tone of defiance, that no man can fail to derive *moan* from μόνος, *monos, single* or *solitary*, who considers that grief naturally loves to be *alone*.

Our knowledge of the northern literature is so scanty, that of words undoubtedly *Teutonick* the original is not always to be found in any ancient language; and I have therefore inserted *Dutch* or *German* substitutes, which I consider not as radical but parallel, not as the parents, but sisters of the *English*.

The words which are represented as thus related by descent or cognation, do not always agree in sense; for it is incident to words, as to their authours, to degenerate from their ancestors, and to change their manners when they change their country. It is sufficient, in etymological enquiries, if the senses of kindred words be found such as may easily pass into each other, or such as may both be referred to one general idea.

The etymology, so far as it is yet known, was easily found in the volumes where it is particularly and professedly delivered; and, by proper attention to the rules of derivation, the orthography was soon adjusted. But to COLLECT the WORDS of our language was a task of greater difficulty: the deficiency of dictionaries was immediately apparent; and when they were exhausted, what was yet wanting must be sought by fortuitous and unguided excursions into books, and gleaned as industry should find, or chance should offer it, in the boundless chaos of a living speech. My search, however, has been either skilful or lucky; for I have much augmented the vocabulary.

As my design was a dictionary, common or appellative, I have omitted all words which have relation to proper names; such as *Arian, Socinian, Calvinist, Benedictine, Mahometan*; but have retained those of a more general nature, as *Heathen, Pagan*.

Of the terms of art I have received such as could be found either in books of science or technical dictionaries; and have often inserted, from philosophical writers, words which are supported perhaps only by a single authority, and which being not admitted into general use, stand yet as candidates or probationers, and must depend for their adoption on the suffrage of futurity.

The words which our authours have introduced by their knowledge of foreign languages, or ignorance of their own, by vanity or wantonness, by compliance with fashion or lust of innovation, I have registered as they occurred, though commonly only to censure them, and warn others against the folly of naturalizing useless foreigners to the injury of the natives.

I have not rejected any by design, merely because they were unnecessary or exuberant; but have received those which by different writers have been differently formed, as *viscid*, and *viscidity*, *viscous*, and *viscosity*.

Compounded or double words I have seldom noted, except when they obtain a signification different from that which the components have in their simple state. Thus *highwayman, woodman,* and *horsecourser*, require an explication; but of *thieflike* or *coachdriver* no notice was needed, because the primitives contain the meaning of the compounds.

Words arbitrarily formed by a constant and settled analogy, like diminutive adjectives in *ish*, as *greenish, bluish*, adverbs in *ly*, as *dully, openly*, substantives in *ness,* as *vileness, faultiness,* were less diligently sought, and sometimes have been omitted, when I had no authority that invited me to insert them; not that they are not genuine and regular offsprings of *English* roots, but because their relation to the primitive being always the same, their signification cannot be mistaken.

The verbal nouns in *ing,* such as the *keeping* of the *castle,* the *leading* of the *army,* are always neglected, or placed only to illustrate the sense of the verb, except when they signify things as well as actions, and have therefore a plural number, as *dwelling, living;* or have an absolute and abstract signification, as *colouring, painting, learning.*

The participles are likewise omitted, unless, by signifying rather habit or quality than action, they take the nature of adjectives; as a *thinking* man, a man of prudence; a *pacing* horse, a horse that can pace: these I have ventured to call *participial adjectives.* But neither are these always inserted, because they are commonly to be understood, without any danger of mistake, by consulting the verb.

Obsolete words are admitted, when they are found in authours not obsolete, or when they have any force or beauty that may deserve revival.

As composition is one of the chief characteristicks of a language, I have endeavoured to make some reparation for the universal negligence of my predecessors, by inserting great numbers of compounded words, as may be found under *after, fore, new, night, fair,* and many more. These, numerous as they are, might be multiplied, but that use and curiosity are here satisfied, and the frame of our language and modes of our combination amply discovered.

Of some forms of composition, such as that by which *re* is prefixed to note *repetition,* and *un* to signify *contrariety* or *privation,* all the examples cannot be accumulated, because the use of these particles, if not wholly arbitrary, is so little limited, that they are hourly affixed to new words as occasion requires, or is imagined to require them.

There is another kind of composition more frequent in our language than perhaps in any other, from which arises to foreigners the greatest difficulty. We modify the signification of many words by a particle subjoined; as to *come off,* to escape by a fetch; to *fall on,* to attack; to *fall off,* to apostatize; to *break off,* to stop abruptly; to *bear out,* to justify; to *fall in,* to comply; to *give over,* to cease; to *set off,* to embellish; to *set in,* to begin a continual tenour; to *set out,* to begin a course or journey; to *take off,* to copy; with innumerable expressions of the same kind, of which some appear wildly irregular, being so far distant from the sense of the simple words, that no sagacity will be able to trace the steps by which they arrived at the present use. These I have noted with great care; and though I cannot flatter myself that the collection is complete, I believe I have so far assisted the students of our language, that this kind of phraseology will be no longer insuperable; and the combinations of verbs and particles, by chance omitted, will be easily explained by comparison with those that may be found.

Many words yet stand supported only by the name of *Bailey, Ainsworth, Philips,* or the contracted *Dict.* for *Dictionaries* subjoined; of these I am not always certain that they are read in any book but the works of lexicographers. Of such I have omitted many, because I had never read them; and many I have inserted, because they may perhaps exist, though they have escaped my notice: they are, however, to be yet considered as resting only upon the credit of former dictionaries. Others, which I considered as useful, or know to be proper, though I could not at present support them by authorities, I have suffered to stand upon my own attestation, claiming the same privilege with my predecessors of being sometimes credited without proof.

The words, thus selected and disposed, are grammatically considered; they are referred to the different parts of speech; traced, when they are irregularly inflected, through their various terminations; and illustrated by observations, not indeed of great or striking importance, separately considered, but necessary to the elucidation of our language, and hitherto neglected or forgotten by *English* grammarians.

That part of my work on which I expect malignity most frequently to fasten, is the *Explanation*; in which I cannot hope to satisfy those, who are perhaps not inclined to be pleased, since I have not always been able to satisfy myself. To interpret a language by itself is very difficult; many words cannot be explained by synonimes, because the idea signified by them has not more than one appellation; nor by paraphrase, because simple ideas cannot be described. When the nature of things is unknown, or the notion unsettled and indefinite, and various in various minds, the words by which such notions are conveyed, or such things denoted, will be ambiguous and perplexed. And such is the fate of hapless lexicography, that not only darkness, but light, impedes and distresses it; things may be not only too little, but too much known, to be happily illustrated. To explain, requires the use of terms less abstruse than that which is to be explained, and such terms cannot always be found; for as nothing can be proved but by supposing something intuitively known, and evident without proof, so nothing can be defined but by the use of words too plain to admit a definition.

Other words there are, of which the sense is too subtle and evanescent to be fixed in a paraphrase; such are all those which are by the grammarians termed *expletives*, and, in dead languages, are suffered to pass for empty sounds, of no other use than to fill a verse, or to modulate a period, but which are easily perceived in living tongues to have power and emphasis, though it be sometimes such as no other form of expression can convey.

My labour has likewise been much increased by a class of verbs too frequent in the *English* language, of which the signification is so loose and general, the use so vague and indeterminate, and the senses detorted so widely from the first idea, that it is hard to trace them through the maze of variation, to catch them on the brink of utter inanity, to circumscribe them by any limitations, or interpret them by any words of distinct and settled meaning; such are *bear, break, come, cast, fall, get, give, do, put, set, go, run, make, take, turn, throw*. If of these the whole power is not accurately delivered, it must be remembered, that while our language is yet living, and variable by the caprice of every one that speaks it, these words are hourly shifting their relations, and can no more be ascertained in a dictionary, than a grove, in the agitation of a storm, can be accurately delineated from its picture in the water.

The particles are among all nations applied with so great latitude, that they are not easily reducible under any regular scheme of explication: this difficulty is not less, nor perhaps greater, in *English*, than in other languages. I have laboured them with diligence, I hope with success; such at least as can be expected in a task, which no man, however learned or sagacious, has yet been able to perform.

Some words there are which I cannot explain, because I do not understand them; these might have been omitted very often with little inconvenience, but I would not so far indulge my vanity as to decline this confession: for when *Tully* owns himself ignorant whether *lessus*, in the twelve tables, means a *funeral song*, or *mourning garment*; and *Aristotle* doubts whether οὔρευς, in the Iliad, signifies a *mule*, or *muleteer*, I may surely, without shame, leave some obscurities to happier industry, or future information.

The rigour of interpretative lexicography requires that *the explanation, and the word explained, should be always reciprocal*; this I have always endeavoured, but could not always attain. Words are seldom exactly synonimous; a new term was not introduced, but because the former was thought inadequate: names, therefore, have often many ideas, but few ideas have many names. It was then necessary to use the proximate word, for the deficiency of single terms can very seldom be supplied by circumlocution; nor is the inconvenience great of such mutilated interpretations, because the sense may easily be collected entire from the examples.

In every word of extensive use, it was requisite to mark the progress of its meaning, and show by what gradations of intermediate sense it has passed from its primitive to its remote and accidental signification; so that every foregoing explanation should tend to that which follows, and the series be regularly concatenated from the first notion to the last.

This is specious, but not always practicable; kindred senses may be so interwoven, that the perplexity cannot be disentangled, nor any reason be assigned why one should be ranged before the other. When the radical idea branches out into parallel ramifications, how can a consecutive series be formed of senses in their nature collateral? The shades of meaning sometimes pass imperceptibly into each other; so that though on one side they apparently differ, yet it is impossible to mark the point of contact. Ideas of the same race, though not exactly alike, are sometimes so little different, that no words can express the dissimilitude, though the mind easily perceives it, when they are exhibited together; and sometimes there is such a confusion of acceptations, that discernment is wearied, and distinction puzzled, and perseverance herself hurries to an end, by crouding together what she cannot separate.

These complaints of difficulty will, by those that have never considered words beyond their popular use, be thought only the jargon of a man willing to magnify his labours, and procure veneration to his studies by involution and obscurity. But every art is obscure to those that have not learned it: this uncertainty of terms, and commixture of ideas, is well known to those who have joined philosophy with grammar; and if I have not expressed them very clearly, it must be remembered that I am speaking of that which words are insufficient to explain.

The original sense of words is often driven out of use by their metaphorical acceptations, yet must be inserted for the sake of a regular origination. Thus I know not whether *ardour* is used for *material heat*, or whether *flagrant*, in *English*, ever signifies the same with *burning*; yet such are the primitive ideas of these words, which are therefore set first, though without examples, that the figurative senses may be commodiously deduced.

Such is the exuberance of signification which many words have obtained, that it was scarcely possible to collect all their senses; sometimes the meaning of derivatives must be sought in the mother term, and sometimes deficient explanations of the primitive may be supplied in the train of derivation. In any case of doubt or difficulty, it will be always proper to examine all the words of the same race; for some words are slightly passed over to avoid repetition, some admitted easier and clearer explanation than others, and all will be better understood, as they are considered in greater variety of structures and relations.

All the interpretations of words are not written with the same skill, or the same happiness: things equally easy in themselves, are not all equally easy to any single mind. Every writer of a long work commits errours, where there appears neither ambiguity to mislead, nor obscurity to confound him; and in a search like this, many felicities of expression will be casually overlooked, many convenient parallels will be forgotten, and many particulars will admit improvement from a mind utterly unequal to the whole performance.

But many seeming faults are to be imputed rather to the nature of the undertaking, than the negligence of the performer. Thus some explanations are unavoidably reciprocal or circular, as *hind, the female of the stag*; *stag, the male of the hind*: sometimes easier words are changed into harder, as *burial* into *sepulture* or *interment, drier* into *desiccative, dryness* into *siccity* or *aridity, fit* into *paroxysm*; for the easiest word, whatever it be, can never be translated into one more easy. But easiness and difficulty are merely relative, and if the present prevalence of our language should invite foreigners to this dictionary, many will be assisted by those words which now seem only to increase or produce obscurity. For this reason I have endeavoured frequently to join a *Teutonick* and *Roman* interpretation, as to CHEER, to *gladden*, or *exhilarate*, that every learner of *English* may be assisted by his own tongue.

The solution of all difficulties, and the supply of all defects, must be sought in the examples, subjoined to the various senses of each word, and ranged according to the time of their authours.

When first I collected these authorities, I was desirous that every quotation should be useful to some other end than the illustration of a word; I therefore extracted from philosophers principles of science; from historians remarkable facts; from chymists complete processes; from divines striking exhortations; and from poets beautiful descriptions. Such is design, while it is yet at a distance from execution. When the time called upon me to range this accumulation of elegance and wisdom into an alphabetical series, I soon discovered that the bulk of my volumes would fright away the student, and was forced to depart from my scheme of including all that was pleasing or useful in *English* literature, and reduce my transcripts very often to clusters of words, in which scarcely any meaning is retained; thus to the weariness of copying, I was condemned to add the vexation of expunging. Some passages I have yet spared, which may relieve the labour of verbal searches, and intersperse with verdure and flowers the dusty desarts of barren philology.

The examples, thus mutilated, are no longer to be considered as conveying the sentiments or doctrine of their authours; the word for the sake of which they are inserted, with all its appendant clauses, has been carefully preserved; but it may somtimes happen, by hasty detruncation, that the general tendency of the sentence may be changed: the divine may desert his tenets, or the philosopher his system.

Some of the examples have been taken from writers who were never mentioned as masters of elegance or models of stile; but words must be sought where they are used; and in what pages, eminent for purity, can terms of manufacture or agriculture be found? Many quotations serve no other purpose, than that of proving the bare existence of words, and are therefore selected with less scrupulousness than those which are to teach their structures and relations.

My purpose was to admit no testimony of living authours, that I might not be misled by partiality, and that none of my contemporaries might have reason to complain; nor have I departed from this resolution, but when some performance of uncommon excellence excited my veneration, when my memory supplied me, from late books, with an example that was wanting, or when my heart, in the tenderness of friendship, solicited admission for a favourite name.

So far have I been from any care to grace my pages with modern decorations, that I have studiously endeavoured to collect examples and authorities from the writers before the restoration, whose works I regard as *the wells of English undefiled*, as the pure sources of genuine diction. Our language, for almost a century, has, by the concurrence of many causes, been gradually departing from its original *Teutonick* character, and deviating towards a *Gallick* structure and phraseology, from which it ought to be our endeavour to recal it, by making our ancient volumes the groundwork of stile, admitting among the additions of later times, only such as may supply real deficiencies, such as are readily adopted by the genius of our tongue, and incorporate easily with our native idioms.

But as every language has a time of rudeness antecedent to perfection, as well as of false refinement and declension, I have been cautious lest my zeal for antiquity might drive me into times too remote, and croud my book with words now no longer understood. I have fixed *Sidney's* work for the boundary, beyond which I make few excursions. From the authours which rose in the time of *Elizabeth*, a speech might be formed adequate to all the purposes of use and elegance. If the language of theology were extracted from *Hooker* and the translation of the Bible; the terms of natural knowledge from *Bacon*; the phrases of policy, war, and navigation from *Raleigh*; the dialect of poetry and fiction from *Spenser* and *Sidney*; and the diction of common life from *Shakespeare*, few ideas would be lost to mankind, for want of *English* words, in which they might be expressed.

It is not sufficient that a word is found, unless it be so combined as that its meaning is apparently determined by the tract and tenour of the sentence; such passages I have therefore chosen, and when it happened that any authour gave a definition of a term, or such an explanation as is equivalent to a definition, I have placed his authority as a supplement to my own, without regard to the chronological order, that is otherwise observed.

Some words, indeed, stand unsupported by any authority, but they are commonly derivative nouns or adverbs, formed from their primitives by regular and constant analogy, or names of things seldom occurring in books, or words of which I have reason to doubt the existence.

There is more danger of censure from the multiplicity than paucity of examples; authorities will sometimes seem to have been accumulated without necessity or use, and perhaps some will be found, which might, without loss, have been omitted. But a work of this kind is not hastily to be charged with superfluities: those quotations, which to careless or unskilful perusers appear only to repeat the same sense, will often exhibit, to a more accurate examiner, diversities of signification, or, at least, afford different shades of the same meaning: one will shew the word applied to persons, another to things; one will express an ill, another a good, and a third a neutral sense; one will prove the expression genuine from an ancient authour; another will shew it elegant from a modern: a doubtful authority is corroborated by another of more credit; an ambiguous sentence is ascertained by a passage clear and determinate; the word, how often soever repeated, appears with new associates and in different combinations, and every quotation contributes something to the stability or enlargement of the language.

When words are used equivocally, I receive them in either sense; when they are metaphorical, I adopt them in their primitive acceptation.

I have sometimes, though rarely, yielded to the temptation of exhibiting a genealogy of sentiments, by shewing how one authour copied the thoughts and diction of another: such quotations are indeed little more than repetitions, which might justly be censured, did they not gratify the mind, by affording a kind of intellectual history.

The various syntactical structures occurring in the examples have been carefully noted; the licence or negligence with which many words have been hitherto used, has made our stile capricious and indeterminate; when the different combinations of the same word are exhibited together, the preference is readily given to propriety, and I have often endeavoured to direct the choice.

Thus have I laboured by settling the orthography, displaying the analogy, regulating the structures, and ascertaining the signification of *English* words, to perform all the parts of a faithful lexicographer: but I have not always executed my own scheme, or satisfied my own expectations. The work, whatever proofs of diligence and attention it may exhibit, is yet capable of many improvements: the orthography which I recommend is still controvertible, the etymology which I adopt is uncertain, and perhaps frequently erroneous; the explanations are sometimes too much contracted, and sometimes too much diffused, the significations are distinguished rather with subtilty than skill, and the attention is harassed with unnecessary minuteness.

The examples are too often injudiciously truncated, and perhaps sometimes, I hope very rarely, alleged in a mistaken sense; for in making this collection I trusted more to memory, than, in a state of disquiet and embarrassment, memory can contain, and purposed to supply at the review what was left incomplete in the first transcription.

Many terms appropriated to particular occupations, though necessary and significant, are undoubtedly omitted; and of the words most studiously considered and exemplified, many senses have escaped observation.

Yet these failures, however frequent, may admit extenuation and apology. To have attempted much is always laudable, even when the enterprize is above the strength that undertakes it: To rest below his own aim is incident to every one whose fancy is active, and whose views are comprehensive; nor is any man satisfied with himself because he has done much, but because he can conceive little. When first I engaged in this work, I resolved to leave neither words nor things unexamined, and pleased myself with a prospect of the hours which I should revel away in feasts of literature, with the obscure recesses of northern learning, which I should enter and ransack; the treasures with which I expected every search into those neglected mines to reward my labour, and the triumph with which I should display my acquisitions to mankind. When I had thus enquired into the original of words, I resolved to show likewise my attention to things; to pierce deep into every science, to enquire the nature of every substance of which I inserted the name, to limit every idea by a definition strictly logical, and exhibit every production of art or nature in an accurate description, that my book might be in place of all other dictionaries whether appellative or technical. But these were the dreams of a poet doomed at last to wake a lexicographer. I soon found that it is too late to look for instruments, when the work calls for execution, and that whatever abilities I had brought to my task, with those I must finally perform it. To deliberate whenever I doubted, to enquire whenever I was ignorant, would have protracted the undertaking without end, and, perhaps, without much improvement; for I did not find by my first experiments, that what I had not of my own was easily to be obtained: I saw that one enquiry only gave occasion to another, that book referred to book, that to search was not always to find, and to find was not always to be informed; and that thus to persue perfection, was, like the first inhabitants of Arcadia, to chace the sun, which, when they had reached the hill where he seemed to rest, was still beheld at the same distance from them.

I then contracted my design, determining to confide in myself, and no longer to solicit auxiliaries, which produced more incumbrance than assistance: by this I obtained at least one advantage, that I set limits to my work, which would in time be ended, though not completed.

Despondency has never so far prevailed as to depress me to negligence; some faults will at last appear to be the effects of anxious diligence and persevering activity. The nice and subtle ramifications of meaning were not easily avoided by a mind intent upon accuracy, and convinced of the necessity of disentangling combinations, and separating similitudes. Many of the distinctions which to common readers appear useless and idle, will be found real and important by men versed in the school philosophy, without which no dictionary shall ever by accurately compiled, or skilfully examined.

Some sense however there are, which, though not the same, are yet so nearly allied, that they are often confounded. Most men think indistinctly, and therefore cannot speak with exactness; and consequently some examples might be indifferently put to either signification: this uncertainty is not to be imputed to me, who do not form, but register the language; who do not teach men how they should think, but relate how they have hitherto expressed their thoughts.

The imperfect sense of some examples I lamented, but could not remedy, and hope they will be compensated by innumerable passages selected with propriety, and preserved with exactness; some shining with sparks of imagination, and some replete with treasures of wisdom.

The orthography and etymology, though imperfect, are not imperfect for want of care, but because care will not always be successful, and recollection or information come too late for use.

That many terms of art and manufacture are omitted, must be frankly acknowledged; but for this defect I may boldly allege that it was unavoidable: I could not visit caverns to learn the miner's language, nor take a voyage to perfect my skill in the dialect of navigation, nor visit the warehouses of merchants, and shops of artificers, to gain the names of wares, tools and operations, of which no mention is found in books; what favourable accident, or easy enquiry brought within my reach, has not been neglected; but it had been a hopeless labour to glean up words, by courting living information, and contesting with the sullenness of one, and the roughness of another.

To furnish the academicians *della Crusca* with words of this kind, a series of comedies called *la Fiera*, or *the Fair*, was professedly written by *Buonaroti*; but I had no such assistant, and therefore was content to want what they must have wanted likewise, had they not luckily been so supplied.

Nor are all words which are not found in the vocabulary, to be lamented as omissions. Of the laborious and mercantile part of the people, the diction is in a great measure casual and mutable; many of their terms are formed for some temporary or local convenience, and though current at certain times and places, are in others utterly unknown. This fugitive cant, which is always in a state of increase or decay, cannot be regarded as any part of the durable materials of a language, and therefore must be suffered to perish with other things unworthy of preservation.

Care will sometimes betray to the appearance of negligence. He that is catching opportunities which seldom occur, will suffer those to pass by unregarded, which he expects hourly to return; he that is searching for rare and remote things, will neglect those that are obvious and familiar: thus many of the most common and cursory words have been inserted with little illustration, because in gathering the authorities, I forbore to copy those which I thought likely to occur whenever they were wanted. It is remarkable that, in reviewing my collection, I found the word SEA unexemplified.

Thus it happens, that in things difficult there is danger from ignorance, and in things easy from confidence; the mind, afraid of greatness, and disdainful of littleness, hastily withdraws herself from painful searches, and passes with scornful rapidity over tasks not adequate to her powers, sometimes too secure for caution, and again too anxious for vigorous effort; sometimes idle in a plain path, and sometimes distracted in labyrinths, and dissipated by different intentions.

A large work is difficult because it is large, even though all its parts might singly be performed with facility; where there are many things to be done, each must be allowed its share of time and labour, in the proportion only which it bears to the whole; nor can it be expected, that the stones which form the dome of a temple, should be squared and polished like the diamond of a ring.

Of the event of this work, for which, having laboured it with so much application, I cannot but have some degree of parental fondness, it is natural to form conjectures. Those who have been persuaded to think well of my design, will require that it should fix our language, and put a stop to those alterations which time and chance have hitherto been suffered to make in it without opposition. With this consequence I will confess that I flattered myself for a while; but now begin to fear that I have indulged expectation which neither reason nor experience can justify. When we see men grow old and die at a certain time one after another, from century to century, we laugh at the elixir that promises to prolong life to a thousand years; and with equal justice may the lexicographer be derided, who being able to produce no example of a nation that has preserved their words and phrases from mutability, shall imagine that his dictionary can embalm his language, and secure it from corruption and decay, that it is in his power to change sublunary nature, and clear the world at once from folly, vanity, and affectation.

With this hope, however, academies have been instituted, to guard the avenues of their languages, to retain fugitives, and repulse intruders; but their vigilance and activity have hitherto been vain; sounds are too volatile and subtile for legal restraints; to enchain syllables, and to lash the wind, are equally the undertakings of pride, unwilling to measure its desires by its strength. The *French* language has visibly changed under the inspection of the academy; the stile of *Amelot*'s translation of father *Paul* is observed by *Le Courayer* to be *un peu passé*; and no *Italian* will maintain, that the diction of any modern writer is not perceptibly different from that of *Boccace*, *Machiavel*, or *Caro*.

Total and sudden transformations of a language seldom happen; conquests and migrations are now very rare: but there are other causes of change, which, though slow in their operation, and invisible in their progress, are perhaps as much superiour to human resistance, as the revolutions of the sky, or intumescence of the tide. Commerce, however necessary, however lucrative, as it depraves the manners, corrupts the language; they that have frequent intercourse with strangers, to whom they endeavour to accommodate themselves, must in time learn a mingled dialect, like the jargon which serves the traffickers on the *Mediterranean* and *Indian* coasts. This will not always be confined to the exchange, the warehouse, or the port, but will be communicated by degrees to other ranks of the people, and be at last incorporated with the current speech.

There are likewise internal causes equally forcible. The language most likely to continue long without alteration, would be that of a nation raised a little, and but a little above barbarity, secluded from strangers, and totally employed in procuring the conveniencies of life; either without books, or, like some of the *Mahometan* countries, with very few: men thus busied and unlearned, having only such words as common use requires, would perhaps long continue to express the same notions by the same signs. But no such constancy can be expected in a people polished by arts, and classed by subordination, where one part of the community is sustained and accommodated by the labour of the other. Those who have much leisure to think, will always be enlarging the stock of ideas, and every increase of knowledge, whether real or fancied, will produce new words, or combinations of words. When the mind is unchained from necessity, it will range after convenience; when it is left at large in the fields of speculation, it will shift opinions; as any custom is disused, the words that expressed it must perish with it; as any opinion grows popular, it will innovate speech in the same proportion as it alters practice.

As by the cultivation of various sciences, a language is amplified, it will be more furnished with words deflected from their original sense; the geometrician will talk of a courtier's zenith, or the excentrick virtue of a wild hero, and the physician of sanguine expectations and phlegmatick delays. Copiousness of speech will give opportunities to capricious choice, by which some words will be preferred, and others degraded; vicissitudes of fashion will enforce the use of new, or extend the signification of known terms. The tropes of poetry will make hourly encroachments, and the metaphorical will become the current sense: pronunciation will be varied by levity or ignorance, and the pen must at length comply with the tongue; illiterate writers will at one time or other, by publick infatuation, rise into renown, who, not knowing the original import of words, will use them with colloquial licentiousness, confound distinction, and forget propriety. As politeness increases, some expressions will be considered as too gross and vulgar for the delicate, others as too formal and ceremonious for the gay and airy; new phrases are therefore adopted, which must, for the same reasons, be in time dismissed. *Swift*, in his petty treatise on the *English* language, allows that new words must sometimes be introduced, but proposes that none should be suffered to become obsolete. But what makes a word obsolete, more than general agreement to forbear it? and how shall it be continued, when it conveys an offensive idea, or recalled again into the mouths of mankind, when it has once become unfamiliar by disuse, and unpleasing by unfamiliarity.

There is another cause of alteration more prevalent than any other, which yet in the present state of the world cannot be obviated. A mixture of two languages will produce a third distinct from both, and they will always be mixed, where the chief part of education, and the most conspicuous accomplishment, is skill in ancient or in foreign tongues. He that has long cultivated another language, will find its words and combinations croud upon his memory; and haste and negligence, refinement and affectation, will obtrude borrowed terms and exotick expressions.

The great pest of speech is frequency of translation. No book was ever turned from one language into another, without imparting something of its native idiom; this is the most mischievous and comprehensive innovation; single words may enter by thousands, and the fabrick of the tongue continue the same, but new phraseology changes much at once; it alters not the single stones of the building, but the order of the columns. If an academy should be established for the cultivation of our stile, which I, who can never wish to see dependance multiplied, hope the spirit of *English* liberty will hinder or destroy, let them, instead of compiling grammars and dictionaries, endeavour, with all their influence, to stop the licence of translatours, whose idleness and ignorance, if it be suffered to proceed, will reduce us to babble a dialect of *France*.

If the changes that we fear be thus irresistible, what remains but to acquiesce with silence, as in the other insurmountable distresses of humanity? It remains that we retard what we cannot repel, that we palliate what we cannot cure. Life may be lengthened by care, though death cannot be ultimately defeated: tongues, like governments, have a natural tendency to degeneration;

we have long preserved our constitution, let us make some struggles for our language.

In hope of giving longevity to that which its own nature forbids to be immortal, I have devoted this book, the labour of years, to the honour of my country, that we may no longer yield the palm of philology, without a contest, to the nations of the continent. The chief glory of every people arises from its authours: whether I shall add any thing by my own writings to the reputation of *English* literature, must be left to time: much of my life has been lost under the pressures of disease; much has been trifled away; and much has always been spent in provision for the day that was passing over me; but I shall not think my employment useless or ignoble, if by my assistance foreign nations, and distant ages, gain access to the propagators of knowledge, and understand the teachers of truth; if my labours afford light to the repositories of science, and add celebrity to *Bacon*, to *Hooker*, to *Milton*, and to *Boyle*.

When I am animated by this wish, I look with pleasure on my book, however defective, and deliver it to the world with the spirit of a man that has endeavoured well. That it will immediately become popular I have not promised to myself: a few wild blunders, and risible absurdities, from which no work of such multiplicity was ever free, may for a time furnish folly with laughter, and harden ignorance in contempt; but useful diligence will at last prevail, and there never can be wanting some who distinguish desert; who will consider that no dictionary of a living tongue ever can be perfect, since while it is hastening to publication, some words are budding, and some falling away; that a whole life cannot be spent upon syntax and etymology, and that even a whole life would not be sufficient; that he, whose design includes whatever language can express, must often speak of what he does not understand; that a writer will sometimes be hurried by eagerness to the end, and sometimes faint with weariness under a task, which *Scaliger* compares to the labours of the anvil and the mine; that what is obvious is not always known, and what is known is not always present; that sudden fits of inadvertency will surprize vigilance, slight avocations will seduce attention, and casual eclipses of the mind will darken learning; and that the writer shall often in vain trace his memory at the moment of need, for that which yesterday he knew with intuitive readiness, and which will come uncalled into his thoughts to-morrow.

In this work, when it shall be found that much is omitted, let it not be forgotten that much likewise is performed; and though no book was ever spared out of tenderness to the authour, and the world is little solicitous to know whence proceeded the faults of that which it condemns; yet it may gratify curiosity to inform it, that the *English Dictionary* was written with little assistance of the learned, and without any patronage of the great; not in the soft obscurities of retirement, or under the shelter of academick bowers, but amidst inconvenience and distraction, in sickness and in sorrow. It may repress the triumph of malignant criticism to observe, that if our language is not here fully displayed, I have only failed in an attempt which no human powers have hitherto completed. If the lexicons of ancient tongues, now immutably fixed, and comprised in a few volumes, be yet, after the toil of successive ages, inadequate and delusive; if the aggregated knowledge, and co-operating diligence of the *Italian* academicians, did not secure them from the censure of *Beni*; if the embodied criticks of *France*, when fifty years had been spent upon their work, were obliged to change its oeconomy, and give their second edition another form, I may surely be contented without the praise of perfection, which, if I could obtain, in this gloom of solitude, what would it avail me? I have protracted my work till most of those whom I wished to please have sunk into the grave, and success and miscarriage are empty sounds: I therefore dismiss it with frigid tranquillity, having little to fear or hope from censure or from praise.

PART SEVEN

MODERN ENGLISH
AND THE FUTURE

✠

INTRODUCTION

The three selections in this final section of the book examine twentieth-century English, particularly its mechanisms of change and the direction it is likely to take in the future. Pyles discusses the differences between British and American English and concludes that they are greatest in the specialized languages (jargon) of particular interest groups or professions and in slang. He feels strongly, however, that British and American English are essentially one language.

Mencken celebrates the difference between British and American slang and sees American slang as an expression of the vitality of this country. "Slang," he says, "originates in the effort of ingenious individuals to make the language more pungent and picturesque—to increase the store of terse and striking words, to widen the boundaries of metaphor, and to provide a vocabulary for new shades of difference in meaning." Quite clearly, he feels that the United States has more than its share of such ingenious individuals.

In discussing "The Future of English," Marckwardt touches on many matters discussed in earlier selections: inflections, word order, borrowing, word formation, sound shifts, drift, strong and weak verbs, the difference between British and American English, among others. On the basis of trends now visible in the language, he speculates about changes which may occur in the future and considers two major—and diametrically opposed—possibilities: that as a result of the freedom of the forces operating within it, the English language will lose its unity; and that highly restrictive attitudes will so confine the language that it will lose its flexibility and thus its opportunity to realize completely its potential. Healthy linguistic attitudes, he feels, will insure "that some individuals can and will attain greatness in the use of the language, which in turn will make of it a more flexible and sensitive medium for the rest of us." A promising note on which to end!

✠ ✠ ✠

AMERICAN AND BRITISH
WORD USAGES

THOMAS PYLES

Except for the somewhat exaggerated subservience of American speech to
the normative influence of the schools, a factor which has given rise to a good
many artificialities in pronunciation and syntax in the usage of the self-
consciously educated part of the American community, the most notable
development of the English language in this country has been in vocabulary.
Despite undeniable present differences in all phases of British and American
linguistic usage, it is unlikely that there are very many characteristics of
American pronunciation and syntax which can be shown to be of American
origin or development; there are unquestionably some, but we remain largely
in the dark about them for lack of a linguistic atlas of the British Isles.

It is, however, unlikely that there are many features of normal, unaffected
American speech which are not traceable to earlier usages in one part or another
of Great Britain, a phenomenon clearly demonstrable in the case of a good
many American local and regional word usages in the speech of the folk. It is
hardly surprising that American developments should be more or less restricted to the rather superficial level of vocabulary when we consider the

relatively short time that we have been separated—though never completely isolated—from the mother country. Even Mr. Mencken modified considerably in the fourth (1936) edition of *The American Language*, the somewhat extreme views which he held in regard to the extent of these differences at the time of the first publication of that work (1919). By the time of the fourth edition he no longer believed that the English of America was diverging so markedly from the English of England as to become a distinct language, though the Anglophobia which is to some extent a humorous literary device with him led him to declare that British English was becoming so much like American English that in time the Englishman might find himself speaking "a kind of dialect of American."

There is, however, no very convincing evidence for such a belief. It is quite true, of course, that many Americanisms have entered the speech of England, some imperceptibly, some over a great deal of opposition. The transfer, as a matter of fact, began quite early, long before talking films and radio were even thought of. Sir William Craigie states in *The Study of American English* (Oxford, 1927) that although, "for some two centuries, roughly down to 1820, the passage of new words or senses across the Atlantic was regularly westwards," practically the only exceptions being words denoting things peculiar to America, "with the nineteenth century . . . the contrary current begins to set in . . . bearing with it many a piece of drift-wood to the shores of Britain." He cites as evidence such importations from America as *backwoods, beeline, blizzard, bluff, logrolling, lumber* "timber," *prairie, shanty, snag, squatter, swamp, bunkum, carpetbagger, caucus, gerrymander, governmental, lynch-law, wire-pulling, bowie knife, cross-cut saw, to strike oil, to make one's pile, ahead of* (in the figurative sense), *at that, to take a back seat, to boom, boss, to catch on, to appreciate* "to rise in value," *balance* "remainder," *to belittle, cloudburst, doughnut, graveyard, loafer, law-abiding*, and *whole-souled*. Even the incomplete material furnished by Thornton's *American Glossary* indicates more than two hundred such borrowings. *To antagonize, to placate, to advocate, lengthy*, and *reliable* all finally found a place in the British word stock despite the terrific lambasting which they had to take from British commentators. It will be noted that many of these words, as well as later borrowings from America like *cafeteria, phonograph*, and *radio* (now about as well known in England as *wireless*) and some of those cited by Craigie, are by no means slangy or colloquial; *whole-souled, law-abiding*, and *to demoralize*, for instance, would occur as a rule only in formal contexts.

There can be no doubt that the enrichment of British English by way of America has been considerably accelerated by such agencies as the movies and radio. Many a Cockney moppet is now able to hiss "Stick 'em up, you mug!" out of the side of his mouth, like Mr. George Raft, or without any perceptible lip-movement, like Mr. Alan Ladd. The *Times* has officially deplored this baleful assault of Hollywood upon the purity of British English, which from a frequently encountered British point of view is "pure" English, all deviations therefrom partaking of the nature of barbarisms. A more liberal English attitude is that of Ernest Weekley, who in his *Adjectives— And Other Words* (New York, 1930) finds it remarkable that his country- men should have got on so long without *stunt, dope fiend, highbrow*, and *sob stuff*, which last somewhat out-of-date compound, it must be said, most Americans have got on very well without for a number of years. Elsewhere, in his *The English Language* (New York, 1929), Weekley refers to the "eager adoption" by the English of *brass tacks, to cut no ice, live wire* (in the figura- tive slang sense "alert person"), *to butt in, snag, to pan out, bedrock, to sidetrack, washout, third degree, frame-up*, and *gunman*. H. W. Seaman, another English writer, observed in the *American Mercury* for September, 1933, that *high-hat, hokum, getaway, panties, water-wagon*, and *hangover* are all used in British English. To these might be added the following, according to H. W. Horwill's *Modern American Usage: filling station, float* "moving platform bearing a display," *to get away with* "to succeed in doing," *fudge* "candy," *to make good* "to succeed," *happening* "event," *jaywalker, layer cake, highbrow, lowbrow, to get a move on, to put over* and *to get over* "to accomplish by shrewdness," *to park, publicity* "advertising," *mass meeting, to rattle* "to unnerve," *to register* (in a hotel), *to round up* and *roundup* (extensions of cowboy lingo), *to shut down* "to close" and *shutdown* "closing (of a factory)," *to turn down* "to refuse," *up against* "confronted with," *up to* "incumbent upon," *wear* in such combinations as *footwear* and *neckwear, to fill the bill, hot air* "windy talk," *to blow in* "to appear," *to feature, fan* "devotee of some game or other form of entertainment," *to cut* "to reduce," *cut* "reduction," and, of course, *O.K.* Somewhat less familiar but still widely known and in fairly wide use in England are *to bank on* "to count on," *bargain counter, bromide* in the senses "platitude" and "plati- tudinous person," *begin to* with a negative as in "It does not begin to do justice to . . . ," *to contact, to cover* "to report (journalistic)," *cub* "novice," *to doll up, to step on the gas* "to depress the accelerator" and figuratively "to hurry up," *good and* "thoroughly" (as in "good and hard"), *hardboiled* "tough," *to hold down* "keep" (as in "to hold down a job"), *to hold up* in the sense[3] "to rob" and "to delay" along with *holdup* as a noun, *hookup* (radio), *horse sense, hot dog, to hustle* "to hurry" (the usual English meaning is "to jostle"), *joy ride, key man, to see the light* "to become convinced," *logrolling* (as a political term), *machine* "party organization," *to soft-pedal, proposition* "affair" (as in "a tough proposition"), *pull* "influence," *punch* "energy," *pep, roughhouse, showdown, to stay put, stung* "cheated," *uplift* "moral exaltation," *to have no use for* "to dislike," and *yes man*.

Horwill furnishes interesting evidence of what Mencken has called the "infiltration of English by Americanisms." During a residence in this country in the early years of the present century, he jotted down a good many Ameri- can linguistic usages that were unfamiliar to him as an Englishman. Many of these expressions were subsequently to become so familiar in England that in 1935 Horwill expressed doubt whether he would have thought of them as originally American had he trusted to his memory alone.

But facts like these—and a good many more might be cited—still do not justify the slightest suspicion that American English will ever supersede British English in England. They simply mean that the British have found a good many American expressions too colorful, useful, or economical to be rejected and have adopted them, frequently with no awareness of their American origin. In far more fundamental respects, such as phonology, intonation, and morphology, it is safe to say that there has been no influence of American on British. It would be difficult to find an Englishman affecting an American accent; there are, on the other hand, a fair number of Americans (they would, of course, constitute only a very insignificant portion of our total population) who try with varying degrees of success to use what they conceive to be a British accent.

In the matter of recent vocabulary, there has indeed been an exchange back and forth, though there can be no question that England has gained more than we have. Obviously, any circumstance that makes for increased communication between the two peoples brings about a wider familiarity with the differentiae of their respective vocabularies. Thus, in the course of two world wars, many of our soldiers found out that *petrol* was the British term for what they had been all their lives calling *gas* (less frequently *gasoline*), and became for the time being almost as familiar with *lorry* as with *truck*, although there was no tendency to adopt the terms. On the other side of the ledger, as reported by *Yank*, the service man's magazine, in its issue of October 7, 1942, "the average Englishman today can tell you without hesitation where the nearest subway station is, where you can find a movie house, whether you can park an automobile here, or how many blocks away the nearest Army gasoline pumps are located." There was a time when the American in England, if he expected to be understood immediately and without condescension, would have had to refer to such things as an *underground station, a cinema, a motorcar*, and a *petrol station. Blocks* would probably have been interpreted to mean *blocks of flats* (in America, *apartment houses*). According to *Yank*, it was no longer necessary in 1942 to ask the telephone operator for "Directory enquiry, please": "Information, please" was readily understood, and "Exchange nine-four hundred" did just as well as "Exchange nine-four-double 0." "Some quick-witted hello girls even go so far now as to tell a Yank 'Here's your party,' rather than 'You're through, sir.' " The author speculates that "Hi-Yo Silver! Away!" may in time supplant "Tallyho!" in British English, but this seems to be going rather too far.

On the other hand, the American levy upon the British vocabulary has been considerably less extensive. H. W. Seaman, in the *American Mercury* article already alluded to cites *swank, spoof, to click* "to be successful," *to tell off*, and *to tick off* as Briticisms in American use. There are others, of course, such as *shop, dressing gown*, and *dinner jacket*, if they can indeed be called Briticisms. When we come to a listing of differentiae, we shall see that a good many supposed Briticisms are actually in fairly wide use in the United States.

It is likely that many of them have been used as variants in American English for so long and to such an extent that they should not be regarded as Briticisms at all, if indeed they ever were so regarded by their users. Expressions thought of as characteristically British—for instance, *jolly* and *bloody* as intensifiers, *cheerio*, and *righto*—have certainly had no vogue at any time in American English, and Mencken is fully correct when he declares in *The American Language* that such words would strike "most members of the American Legion as almost as unmanly as *tummy* or *pee-pee*" (p. 265). There are, of course, a good many borderline cases.

The differences in vocabulary and idiom are none the less sufficiently great that few English writers (P. G. Wodehouse is a notable exception) are able to reproduce American speech with any degree of accuracy. These differences usually occur, however, on a comparatively simple level of communication and for the most part consist of names of concrete objects. The more abstract or philosophical the subject matter of speech, the fewer the differences in word choice are likely to be. It is, as a matter of fact, principally in slang and in specialized vocabularies that we notice very striking differences. In the specialized language of motoring, for instance, the folding top of a car is in England called the *hood*; what Americans call the *hood* is in England the *bonnet*. Similarly, British *gear lever* corresponds to American *gearshift, first speed* to *low gear, dynamo* to *generator, accumulator* to *battery, sparking plug* to *spark plug, windscreen* to *windshield, wing* (or *mudguard*) to *fender, silencer* to *muffler, dickey* to *rumble seat, saloon car* (or simply *saloon*) to *sedan*, and *two-seater* to *roadster. Carburettor* is so spelled by the British, who pronounce the *e* as in *get*. American spelling usually employs only a single *t*, the last two syllables of the word practically always riming with *freighter*. Although *automobile* (with its abbreviation *auto*) is perfectly well known to the English, the word seems to have made little headway among them in actual use. The usual British term is *motorcar*, or simply *car. Motorcar* is quite familiar in America, though seldom used; *car*, however, is very common, perhaps even more usual nowadays than *automobile*, which remains the formal term. Horwill is surely in error when he cites *autoist* as the usual American equivalent of British *motorist*, for *motorist* is by far the commoner term in America; *autoist* is rarely if ever heard. Similar differences occur in the vocabulary of sports, of the various trades and professions, of shopping, and of transportation. The two last-named activities, common to American and British travelers, have perhaps given many an exaggerated notion of vocabulary differences in British and American English.

Regrettable as the fact may be to sturdy linguistic patriots in our midst, a group of Briticisms which have connotations of swank for Americans have gained a firm footing in this country. *Dressing gown*, for instance, must be almost as frequent by now as *bathrobe*, particularly since the writers of "slick" advertising copy, aided and abetted by Hollywood, have made of the garment a glamorous appurtenance of masculine attire; the thick, fuzzy, blanket-like "bathrobes" worn for warmth in the days before American women demanded that "their" houses should always be overheated have given way to silk, rayon, or lightweight flannel "dressing gowns." *Tuxedo*, which has, ironically enough, been adopted to some extent in England, has given ground in America to *dinner jacket*. Perhaps the awful vulgarity of *tux* (or even *tuck*), which was current among the seedier class of collegians in the 1920s and 1930s to designate the cheap, satin-lapelled, ready-made, frequently rented suit has played some part in the change to *dinner jacket*, now felt by many Americans (or at any rate by their wives) to be more refined. *Esquire* has for a long time carried notices of *braces* (suspenders), and in a single advertisement in the *New Yorker* (March 11, 1950) a "master cravatier" offers *cravats* (probably a genteelism rather than a Briticism), *braces*, and *sock suspenders* (men's garters) for sale at impressively high prices. A change in fashion has made the widely publicized distinction between British *boot* and American *shoe* practically obsolete, inasmuch as only policemen, firemen, soldiers, and elderly gentlemen with wobbly ankles wear what the English used to call *boots*, that is, footwear fastening over the ankle. As this type of footwear has gone out of fashion, so has the word denoting it; *shoe*, the ordinary British as well as American term for a low-cut boot, is thus the word used for the footwear now ordinarily worn in towns and cities by men in both countries. With the obsolescence of the foot covering which laced or buttoned above the ankle, if only a little above, the Englishman has few occasions to use *boot* except in the sense in which it is also used by Americans, that is, to designate an article of footwear which reaches at least to within a few inches of the knee, such as a riding boot.

Other differences in word use have received a great deal of attention from British and American commentators, some of them far more than their actual importance seems to justify, so that by now most of us are perfectly well aware that what in America is called an *elevator* is in England called a *lift*, and that, whereas an American, when not using a belt for the purpose, holds up his *pants* with *suspenders*, or even with *galluses* if he is a very old-fashioned man of rural upbringing, an Englishman holds his *trousers* up with *braces* and uses *suspenders* for his socks.

Comparative lists, with British words usages on one side of the page and their American equivalents on the other, are interesting to read, but sometimes misleading in the impression which they give. Such lists can be very impressive, nevertheless, because of their sheer bulk. Sometimes, however, their items may not actually represent general use, though there is a great deal of disagreement among commentators on both sides of the Atlantic as to what constitutes general use. Certainly some of the entries on the American side of most such lists are widely known in England (some are even in fairly wide use there), just as a good many of the expressions labeled *British* are known and used in America. Frequently it is simply a matter of degree— a question of a word or a phrase being somewhat more familiar in one country than in the other. As we have seen, American English has preserved a number of older British usages which have never quite gone out of use in

England; some of these have indeed reëntered British English by way of America, to be much more widely used in England than the compilers of differential word lists lead one to suspect. Likewise, regional and local usages vary a good deal in this country, and a good many supposed Briticisms are in wide use in particular sections of the United States, even though they may not be known in Chicago, Omaha, or Los Angeles; as has been pointed out earlier, *sidewalk* is the usual term in most parts of America for that part of a street reserved for pedestrians; yet in the large and culturally important Philadelphia trade area *pavement* is practically the only term used, precisely as in British English. To cite another instance, one must not infer from such a list that *mailman* is always used in America for what the English call a *postman*, for the fact is that many Americans use *postman*. What is true is that *mailman* is more widely used in America than *postman*, not that *postman* is British and *mailman* (or *letter carrier*) American. Many American speakers, however, including the present writer, never use *mailman*, though it is safe to say that no American uses *post* for *mail*, as in British English "Has the post arrived yet?" or as a verb, as in "to post a letter." It should be noted that *postman* is at least sufficiently common in American use that Hollywood did not find it necessary to change the title of James M. Cain's novel *The Postman Always Rings Twice* when it was filmed. Some of the national differences in vocabulary are, indeed, no more striking than local and regional differences existing within the United States.

Lists of equivalents invariably include (the British or supposed British equivalent is given first in the pairs to be cited) *boot/shoe, shop/store*, and *flat/apartment*. The status of the first two pairs has been discussed elsewhere; it might be added, however, that *flat*, which is in fairly wide use in American English, frequently denotes living quarters somewhat less spacious than does *apartment*, which usually denotes a suite of rooms among other suites in the same building. Equally questionable as national variants, despite the fact that some of them appear in the Army's *Short Guide to Great Britain* (1942), are *return ticket/round-trip ticket, bath/bathtub, wallet/billfold, funny bone/ crazy bone, snack/lunch, chest of drawers/bureau* (the commercial term *dresser*, though offensive to many Americans, is also used), *lounge suit/business suit, cupboard/closet, Christian name/given name, nursing home/hospital* (private), *whiskey and soda/highball, rubbish/junk, life belt/life preserver, timber/lumber, letter box/mailbox, perhaps/maybe, parcel/package, tie/ necktie, flat/puncture, lodger/roomer, timetable/schedule, shoelace/shoestring, kipper/smoked herring, tap/spigot* (or *faucet*, depending upon the region), *neat* (of drink)*/straight*, and *wastepaper basket/wastebasket*. In every one of these pairs, the first term, usually labeled British, is perfectly well known to Americans; the second term in many, though not in all, is perfectly well known to the British, though it may not be much used by them. In actual fact, some of the supposedly British terms are in fairly wide use in this country. *Wallet* is now about as common as *billfold*; the same is true of *snack, cupboard, whiskey and soda, funny bone, rubbish, perhaps, tie*, and *kipper*. The others occur perhaps only in the usage of a cultivated minority, but they are all understood. Only one calls for comment, *closet*, which is avoided by the English in the sense "cupboard" because it suggests to them *water closet*—a term practically archaic in America, having been supplanted by *toilet* and, on the colloquial level, a good many less polite terms.

There are, of course, a great many expressions used in British English which are never used in America. Some of them, in fact, would not even be generally understood in this country. *Perambulator* with its contracted form *pram*, is well known to us through our reading of English books, though an American would no more use it for *baby carriage* than he would call a *billboard* a *hoarding* or a *water heater* a *geyser* (pronounced *geezer* by the English when used in this sense). *Beetroot* would probably not be understood in America to denote *beets*, once in common use in England but surviving only in this country. *Chemist's shop* as the British equivalent of *drug store* is a stock Briticism, widely known in America as a "curiosity" but never used even by the most egregious Anglophiles.

Also little known in America, and certainly never used here, are *draughts* (checkers), *leader* and *leading article* (editorial), *cotton wool* (absorbent cotton), *wood wool* (excelsior), *flex* (extension cord), *dustbin* (ash can, garbage can), *dustman* (garbage man), *trunk call* (long-distance call), *treacle* (molasses, syrup for human consumption; the English use *molasses* to designate a syrup used in animal feeds), *white wax* (paraffin), *paraffin* (kerosene, also called *coal oil* in America), *ticket-of-leave* (parole), *kiosk* (newsstand), *potato crisp* (potato chip), *public house* or *pub* (drinking place), *char-à-banc* (sight-seeing bus), *ladder* (run in a stocking), *bowler* (derby or derby hat), *boater* (straw hat with hard, flat crown and brim), *sleeping partner* (silent partner), *reel* (spool of thread), *vegetable marrow* (squash), *call box* (telephone booth), and *drawing pin* (thumbtack).

The fact that the same word or phrase may have different senses in America and England may sometimes be attended with embarrassing consequences, as when a demure English girl traveling in this country replied, in answer to a polite query whether she had slept well the night before, that she would have done so had she not been knocked up so early in the morning by one of the young men in her party. *To knock up*, which means "to get with child" in American low colloquial use (the phrase is also well known to most educated males), means simply "to arouse from sleep" in British English. (Jos Sedley's declaration in *Vanity Fair* that he would marry Becky Sharp even if he had to "knock up the Archbishop of Canterbury at Lambeth" to do so is always bound to give rise to prurient undergraduate sniggers in American classrooms.) Similarly, the British colloquial use of *screw* "wages" (as in "a poor screw," "a weekly screw") and of *to screw* "to stint" (as in Wyld's illustrative example in the *Universal Dictionary*, "the old curmudgeon had screwed all his life") might meet with a somewhat less than cordial reception in the chaster circles of American society. For reasons which are doubtless equally obvious to the American reader, colloquial *pecker* "courage," frequent in British English, as in "to keep one's pecker up," is not used in most types of American English. The British metaphorical use of *ass* "silly fellow," although well known in this country, has ribald suggestions for most Americans, since in American English *arse* "buttocks" is homophonous with it.

Equally unhappy, from the British point of view, is the American familiar use of *bum* for "tramp" or in any of its derivative senses, inasmuch as the word means "backside" in British English and is hence somewhat inappropriate to the drawing room. To say that a person has "plenty of spunk" or is "full of spunk" would cause some degree of consternation in present-day English society, though the Scots use *spunk* in the same sense which it has in America. No American ever uses *bloody* in the shocking English sense—or rather lack of sense, for no one seems to know precisely what it means: the *Universal Dictionary* defines it as a "low, vulgar, blasphemous epithet; also meaningless adjective much used among very low persons." But for an American in England to refer to an automobile accident which he had witnessed as a "bloody mess" would show a regrettable lack of social and linguistic tact. *Bug*, which in American popular use may name practically any insect, sometimes extending its meaning to include bacilli as well, is defined in a representative dictionary of British usage (Wyld's *Universal*) as "a nasty, flat, ill-smelling, verminous, wingless insect, genus *Cimex*, found in dirty houses and furniture," that is, what is called a *bedbug* in America. The American guest in an English house would therefore be well advised not to refer to flies, gnats, midges, and other comparatively decorous flying creatures as *bugs*, but rather as *insects*, which is also used in American English, but only on a rather stiffly formal level. But it is obvious that *bug*, long a shibboleth word, has lost much of its disgusting connotation in British English, if we may judge by the headline *The Bug Is Boss* which recently appeared in the *London Daily Express* (quoted by *Time*, February 12, 1951), referring to the "influenza bug."

Practically all literate Americans are quite well aware that the English *public school* corresponds roughly to the American private boarding school, usually called in America a *preparatory* (or *prep*) *school*; thus, Eton, Rugby, Winchester, and Harrow are public schools, though all are expensive and to a large extent exclusive. The American *public school* corresponds to the English *council school* or *board school*. The English use *preparatory school* to designate what in America is called the *elementary school*; it prepares pupils for the public school (in the British sense), not for the university. Other scholastic terminology differs considerably in the two countries. The term *grade* as used in American elementary schools is an Americanism corresponding roughly in meaning to British *form*, used also in many of our private preparatory schools. Horwill points out that a class (first, second, or third) in Oxford or Cambridge is a division in which one is placed after successfully passing an "honours" examination. To say that two university men were in the same class means to an Englishman not merely that they graduated in the same year, but that they were placed in the same status (or class) in the same "honours" examination in the same year. Incidentally, *sophomore, junior*, and *senior* are not in use in England to denote respectively students in the second, third, and fourth year of their university career as in America, where the words have extended their scope to include even high-school pupils. The complicated academic hierarchy of the American college or university, with its assistants, instructors, assistant professors, adjunct professors, associate professors, and full professors, is little known and less understood by the English, to whom *professor* indicates a somewhat more rarefied personage than many American teachers bearing the title either by courtesy or legitimately with one modification or another. The American use of *professor* as a title preceding the name of the principal of a high school (though it was likely to be conferred upon any male pedagogue of mature years) is practically obsolete nowadays save in the more remote sections. It was formerly also a courtesy title of male teachers of music, piano players in the tonier New Orleans bordellos (the late, great "Jelly Roll" Morton was once a "professor" in this sense), orchestra leaders, conjurers, and acrobats. The aeronaut who all during the years of my boyhood made a parachute jump from a balloon at the country fair held in my native town was always billed as Professor Mike Jacobson.

It would be possible to pile up many more examples of vocabulary differentiae, but the reader, if he is interested in pursuing the matter further, will find plenty of examples in the books by Mencken and Horwill, though these valuable works must be used with some exercise of judgment based on his own observation. He will most probably conclude that many of the differentiae are quite insignificant, like American *bakery*/British *baker's shop*, Am. *toilet*/Br. *lavatory*, Am. *living room*/Br. *sitting room*, and Am. *stairway*/Br. *staircase*; it is also likely that he will be quite aware of the fact that the second term in the last three of these pairs is indeed in fairly wide use in America, even though the first may be the more common.

To summarize, it is in specialized languages such as those of travel, sports, trades, and professions that we notice the most striking differences in word choice in the two countries. On the level of slang the differences are likewise considerable. But a great deal of current slang of American teenagers is incomprehensible to their own elders; and among teen-agers themselves there is considerable variation from section to section, and even from social class to social class. It is thus not particularly surprising that much American slang is incomprehensible to the Englishman, and that the British slang is at least equally mystifying to the American. Misunderstanding, real or pretended, of an American interviewer's reference to him as "a regular guy," which would mean in British English "a thoroughly grotesque person," furnished the late G. K. Chesterton with a good anecdote; in educated use, however, genuine occurrences of this type of international ambiguity must be rather rare.

It is on such levels, however, that the "quaint" usages beloved of the lay linguist are most likely to occur, and it is easy to give an exaggerated impression of their importance. There is considerable temptation for writers to play down the essential oneness of American and British English. As a matter of fact, in the intellectual reaches of language the differences are practically nonexistent. It should be obvious that a great deal depends upon who is doing the talking (or writing), what the occasion is, and what is being talked (or written) about.

✠ ✠ ✠

ON SLANG

H. L. MENCKEN

Slang is defined by the Oxford Dictionary as "language of a highly colloquial type, considered as below the level of standard educated speech, and consisting either of new words or of current words employed in some special sense." The origin of the word is unknown. Ernest Weekley, in his "Etymological Dictionary of Modern English," 1921, suggests that it may have some relation to the verb *to sling*, and cites two Norwegian dialect words, based upon the cognate verb *slenge* or *slengje*, that appear to be its brothers: *slengjeord*, a neologism, and *slengjenamm*, a nickname. But he is not sure, so he adds the note that "some regard it as an argotic perversion of the French *langue*, language." A German philologian, O. Ritter, believes that it may be derived, not from *langue*, but from *language* itself, most probably by a combination of blending and shortening, as in *thieve(s' lang)uage, beggar(s' lang)uage*, and so on. Webster's New International, 1934, follows somewhat haltingly after Weekley. The Oxford Dictionary, 1919, evades the question by dismissing *slang* as "a word of cant origin, the ultimate source of which is not apparent." When it first appeared in English, about the middle of the eighteenth century, it was employed as a synonym of *cant*, and so designated "the special vocabulary used by any set of persons of a low or disreputable character"; and half a century later it began to be used interchangeably with *argot*, which means the vocabulary special to any group, trade, or profession. But during the past fifty years the three terms have tended to be more or less clearly distinguished. The jargon of criminals is both a kind of slang and a kind of argot, but it is best described as *cant*, a word derived from the Latin *cantus*, and going back, in its present sense, to *c.* 1540. One of the principal aims of cant is to make what is said unintelligible to persons outside the group, a purpose that is absent from most forms of argot and slang. Argot often includes slang, as when a circus man calls his patrons *suckers* and speaks of refunding money to one full of complaints as *squaring the beef,* but when he calls the circus grounds the *lot* and the manager's quarters the *white wagon,* he is simply using the special language of his trade, and it is quite as respectable as the argot of lawyers or diplomats. The essence of slang is that it is of general dispersion, but still stands outside the accepted canon of the language. It is, says George H. McKnight, "a form of colloquial speech created in a spirit of defiance and aiming at freshness and novelty. . . . Its figures are consciously farfetched and are intentionally drawn from the most ignoble of sources. Closely akin to profanity in its spirit, its aim is to shock." Among the impulses leading to its invention, adds Henry Bradley, "the two more important seem to be the desire to secure increased vivacity and the desire to secure increased sense of intimacy in the use of language." "It seldom attempts," says the London *Times,* "to supply deficiencies in conventional language; its object is nearly always to provide a new and different way of saying what can be perfectly well said without it." What chiefly lies behind it is simply a kind of linguistic exuberance, and excess of word-making energy. It relates itself to the standard language a great deal as dancing relates itself to music. But there is also something else. The best slang is not only ingenious and amusing; it also embodies a kind of social criticism. It not only provides new names for a series of everyday concepts, some new and some old; it also says something about them. "Words which produce the slang effect," observes Frank K. Sechrist, "arouse associations which are incongruous or incompatible with those of customary thinking."

Everyone, including even the metaphysician in his study and the eremite in his cell, has a large vocabulary of slang, but the vocabulary of the vulgar is likely to be larger than that of the cultured, and it is harder worked. Its content may be divided into two categories: (a) old words, whether used singly or in combination, that have been put to new uses, usually metaphorical, and (b) new words that have not yet been admitted to the standard vocabulary. Examples of the first type are *rubberneck,* for a gaping and prying person, and *iceberg,* for a cold woman; examples of the second are *hoosegow, flimflam, blurb, bazoo,* and *blah.* There is a constant movement of slang terms into accepted usage. *Nice,* as an adjective of all work, signifying anything satisfactory, was once in slang use only, and the purists denounced it, but today no one would question "a *nice* day," "a *nice* time," or "a *nice* hotel."

The French word *tête* has been a sound name for the human head for many centuries, but its origin was in *testa*, meaning a pot, a favorite slang word of the soldiers of the decaying Roman Empire, exactly analogous to our *block, nut*, and *bean*. The verb-phrase *to hold up* is now perfectly American, but so recently as 1901 the late Brander Matthews was sneering at it as slang. In the same way many other verb-phrases, e.g. *to cave in, to fill the bill*, and *to fly off the handle*, once viewed askance, have gradually worked their way to a relatively high level of the standard speech. On some indeterminate tomorrow *to stick up* and *to take for a ride* may follow them. "Even the greatest purist," says Robert Lynd, "does not object today to the inclusion of the word *bogus* in a literary English vocabulary, though a hundred years ago *bogus* was an American slang word meaning an apparatus for coining false money. *Carpetbagger* and *bunkum* are other American slang words that have naturalized themselves in English speech, and *mob* is an example of English slang that was once as vulgar as *incog* or *photo*." Sometimes a word comes in below the salt, gradually wins respectability, and then drops to the level of slang, and is worked to death. An example is offered by *strenuous*. It was first used by John Marston, the dramatist, in 1599, and apparently he invented it, as he invented *puffy, chilblained, spurious*, and *clumsy*. As strange as it may seem to us today, all these words were frowned on by the purists of the time as uncouth and vulgar, and Ben Jonson attacked them with violence in his *Poetaster*, written in 1601. In particular, Ben was upset by *strenuous*. But it made its way despite him, and during the next three centuries it was used by a multitude of impeccable authors, including Milton, Swift, Burke, Hazlitt, and Macaulay. And then Theodore Roosevelt invented and announced the Strenuous Life, the adjective struck the American fancy and passed into slang, and in a little while it was so horribly threadbare that all persons of careful speech sickened of it, and to this day it bears the ridiculous connotation that hangs about most slang, and is seldom used seriously.

All neologisms, of course, are not slang. At about the time the word *hoosegow*, derived from the Spanish, came into American slang use, the word *rodeo*, also Spanish, came into the standard vocabulary. The distinction between the two is not hard to make out. *Hoosegow* was really not needed. We had plenty of words to designate a jail, and they were old and good words. *Hoosegow* came in simply because there was something arresting and outlandish about it—and the users of slang have a great liking for pungent novelties. *Rodeo*, on the other hand, designated something for which there was no other word in American—something, indeed, of which the generality of Americans had just become aware—and so it was accepted at once. Many neologisms have been the deliberate inventions of quite serious men, e.g., *gas, kodak, vaseline*. *Scientist* was concocted in 1840 by William Whewell, professor of moral theology and casuistical divinity at Cambridge. *Ampere* was proposed solemnly by the Electric Congress which met in Paris in 1881, and was taken into all civilized languages instantly. *Radio* was suggested for wireless telegrams by an international convention held in Berlin in 1906, and was extended to wireless broadcasts in the United States about 1920, though the English prefer *wireless* in the latter sense. But such words as these were never slang; they came into general and respectable use at once, along with *argon, x-ray, carburetor, stratosphere, bacillus,* and many another of the sort. These words were all sorely needed; it was impossible to convey the ideas behind them without them, save by clumsy circumlocutions. It is one of the functions of slang, also, to serve a short cut, but it is seldom if ever really necessary. Instead, as W. D. Whitney once said, it is only a wanton product of "the exuberance of mental activity, and the natural delight of language-making." This mental activity, of course, is the function of a relatively small class. "The unconscious genius of the people," said Paul Shorey, "no more invents slang than it invents epics. It is coined in the sweat of their brow by smart writers who, as they would say, are *out for the coin.*" Or, if not out for the coin, then at least out for notice, *kudos,* admiration, or maybe simply for satisfaction of the "natural delight of language-making." Some of the best slang emerges from the argot of college students, but everyone who has observed the process of its gestation knows that the general run of students have nothing to do with the matter, save maybe to provide an eager welcome for the novelties set before them. College slang is actually made by the campus wits, just as general slang is made by the wits of the newspapers and theaters. The idea of calling an engagement ring a *handcuff* did not occur to the young gentlemen of Harvard by mass inspiration; it occurred to a certain definite one of them, probably after long and deliberate cogitation, and he gave it to the rest and to his country.

Toward the end of 1933, W. J. Funk and Wagnalls Company, publishers of the Standard Dictionary and the *Literary Digest,* undertook to supply the newspapers with the names of the ten most fecund makers of the American slang then current. He nominated T. A. (Tad) Dorgan, the cartoonist; Sime Silverman, editor of the theatrical weekly, *Variety;* Gene Buck, the song writer; Damon Runyan, the sports writer; Walter Winchell and Arthur (Bugs) Baer, newspaper columnists; George Ade, Ring Lardner, and Gelett Burgess.* He should have added Jack Conway and Johnny O'Connor of the staff of *Variety;* James Gleason, author of "Is Zat So?"; Rube Goldberg, the cartoonist; Johnny Stanley and Johnny Lyman, Broadway figures; Wilson Mizner and Milt Gross. Conway, who died in 1928, is credited with the invention of *palooka* (a third-rater), *belly-laugh, Arab* (for Jew), *S.A.* (sex appeal), *high-hat, pushover, boloney* (for buncombe, later adopted by Alfred E. Smith), *headache* (wife), and the verbs *to scram, to click* (meaning to succeed), and *to laugh that off.* Winchell, if he did not actually invent *whoopee,* at least gave it the popularity it enjoyed, *c.* 1930. He is also the father of *Chicagorilla, Joosh* (for Jewish), *pash* (for passion), and *shafts* (for legs), and he has devised a great many nonce words and phrases, some of

---

*The tenth man named by Mr. Funk was Mr. Mencken, who, in a footnote, modestly dismisses the nomination as "only a fraternal courtesy."

them euphemistic and others far from it, e.g., for married: *welded, sealed, lohengrined, merged,* and *middle-aisled*; for divorced: *Reno-vated*; for contemplating divorce: *telling it to a judge, soured, curdled, in husband trouble, this-and-that-way,* and *on the verge*; for in love: *on the merge, on fire, uh-huh, that way, cupiding, Adam-and-Eveing,* and *man-and-womaning it*; for expecting young: *infanticipating, baby-bound,* and *storked.* I add a few other characteristic specimens of his art: *go-ghetto, debutramp, phffft, foofff* (a pest), *Wildeman* (a homosexual), *heheheh* (a mocking laugh), *Hard-Times Square* (Times Square), *blessed-event* (the birth of young), *the Hardened Artery* (Broadway), *radiodor* (a radio announcer), *moom-pitcher* (movie), *Park Rowgue* (a newspaper reporter), *girl-mad,* and *intelligentlemen.* Most of these, of course, had only their brief days, but a few promise to survive. Dorgan, who died in 1929, was the begetter of *applesauce, twenty-three skiddoo, ball-and-chain* (for wife), *cake-eater, dumb Dora, dumbbell* (for stupid person), *nobody home,* and *you said it.* He also gave the world "Yes, we have no bananas," though he did not write the song, and he seems to have originated *the cat's pajamas,* which was followed by a long series of similar superlatives. The sports writers, of course, are all assiduous makers of slang, and many of their inventions are taken into the general vocabulary. Thus, those who specialize in boxing have contributed, in recent years, *kayo, cauliflower-ear, prelim, shadow-boxing, slugfest, title-holder, punch-drunk, brother-act, punk, to side-step,* and *to go the limit*; those who cover baseball have made many additions to the list of baseball terms and those who follow the golf tournaments have given currency to *birdie, fore, par, bunker, divot, fairway, to tee off, stance,* and *onesome, twosome, threesome,* and so on—some of them received into the standard speech, but the majority lingering in the twilight of slang.

George Philip Krapp attempts to distinguish between slang and sound idiom by setting up the doctrine that the former is "more expressive than the situation demands." "It is," he says, "a kind of hyperesthesia in the use of language. *To laugh in your sleeve* is idiom because it arises out of a natural situation; it is a metaphor derived from the picture of one raising his sleeve to his face to hide a smile, a metaphor which arose naturally enough in early periods when sleeves were long and flowing; but *to talk through your hat* is slang, not only because it is new, but also because it is a grotesque exaggeration of the truth." The theory, unluckily, is combated by many plain facts. *To hand it to him, to get away with it,* and even *to hand him a lemon* are certainly not metaphors that transcend the practicable and probable, and yet all are undoubtedly slang. On the other hand, there is palpable exaggeration in such phrases as "he is not worth the powder it would take to kill him," in such adjectives as *breakbone* (fever), and in such compounds as *fire-eater,* and yet it would be absurd to dismiss them as slang. Between *blockhead* and *bonehead* there is little to choose, but the former is sound English, whereas the latter is American slang. So with many familiar similes, e.g., *like greased lightning, as scarce as hen's teeth*: they are grotesque hyperboles, but hardly slang.

The true distinction, in so far as any distinction exists at all, is that indicated by Whitney, Bradley, Sechrist, and McKnight. Slang originates in the effort of ingenious individuals to make the language more pungent and picturesque—to increase the store of terse and striking words, to widen the boundaries of metaphor, and to provide a vocabulary for new shades of difference in meaning. As Dr. Otto Jespersen has pointed out, this is also the aim of poets (as, indeed, it is of prose writers), but they are restrained by consideration of taste and decorum, and also, not infrequently, by historical or logical considerations. The maker of slang is under no such limitations: he is free to confect his neologism by any process that can be grasped by his customers, and out of any materials available, whether native or foreign. He may adopt any of the traditional devices of metaphor. Making an attribute do duty for the whole gives him *stiff* for corpse, *flat-foot* for policeman, *smoke-eater* for fireman, *skirt* for woman, *lunger* for consumptive, and *yes-man* for sycophant. Hidden resemblances give him *morgue* for newspaper's file of clippings, *bean* for head, and *sinker* for doughnut. The substitution of far-fetched figures for literal description gives him *glad-rags* for fine clothing, *bonehead* for ignoramus, *booze-foundry* for saloon, and *cart-wheel* for dollar, and the contrary resort to a brutal literalness gives him *kill-joy, low-life*, and *hand-out*. He makes abbreviations with a free hand—*beaut* for beauty, *gas* for gasoline, and so on. He makes bold avail of composition, as in *attaboy*, and *whatdyecallem*, and of onomatopoeia, as in *biff, zowie, honky-tonk*, and *wow*. He enriches the ancient counters of speech with picturesque synonyms, as in *guy, gink, duck, bird*, and *bozo* for fellow. He transfers proper names to common usage, as in *ostermoor* for mattress, and then sometimes gives them remote figurative significance, as in *ostermoors* for whiskers. Above all, he enriches the vocabulary of action with many new verbs and verb-phrases, e.g., *to burp, to neck, to gang, to frame up, to hit the pipe, to give him the works*, and so on. If, by the fortunes that condition language-making, his neologism acquires a special and limited meaning, not served by any existing locution, it enters into sound idiom and is presently wholly legitimatized; if, on the contrary, it is adopted by the populace as a counter-word and employed with such banal imitativeness that it soon loses any definite significance whatever, then it remains slang and is avoided by the finical. An example of the former process is afforded by *tommy-rot*. It first appeared as English schoolboy slang, but its obvious utility soon brought it into good usage. In one of Jerome K. Jerome's books, *Paul Kelver*, there is the following dialogue:

"The wonderful songs that nobody ever sings, the wonderful pictures that nobody ever paints, and all the rest of it. It's *tommy-rot!*"

"I wish you wouldn't use slang."

"Well, you know what I mean. What is the proper word? Give it to me."

"I suppose you mean *cant*."

"No, I don't. *Cant* is something that you don't believe in yourself. It's tommy-rot; there isn't any other word."

Nor were there any other words for *hubbub, fireworks, foppish, fretful, sportive, dog-weary, to bump,* and *to dwindle* in Shakespeare's time; he adopted and dignified them because they met genuine needs. Nor was there any other satisfactory word for *graft* when it came in, nor for *rowdy,* nor for *boom,* nor for *joy-ride,* nor for *slacker,* nor for *trustbuster.* Such words often retain a humorous quality; they are used satirically and hence appear but seldom in wholly serious discourse. But they have standing in the language nevertheless, and only a prig would hesitate to use them as George Saintsbury used *the best of the bunch* and *joke-smith.* So recently as 1929 the Encyclopaedia Britannica listed *boot-legger, speakeasy, dry, wet, crook, fake, fizzle, hike, hobo, poppycock, racketeer,* and *O.K.* as American slang terms, but today most of them are in perfectly good usage. What would one call a racketeer if *racketeer* were actually forbidden? It would take a phrase of four or five words at least, and they would certainly not express the idea clearly.

On the other hand, many an apt and ingenious neologism, by falling too quickly into the gaping maw of the proletariat is spoiled forthwith and forever. Once it becomes, in Oliver Wendell Holmes's phrase, "a cheap generic term, a substitute for differentiated specific expressions," it quickly acquires such flatness that the fastidious flee it as a plague. The case of *strenuous* I have already mentioned. One recalls, too, many capital verb-phrases thus ruined by unintelligent appreciation, e.g., *to freeze on to, to have the goods, to cut no ice, to fall for,* and *to get by*; and some excellent substantives, e.g., *dope* and *dub,* and compounds, e.g., *come-on* and *easy-mark,* and simple verbs, e.g., *to neck* and *to vamp.* These are all quite as sound in structure as the great majority of our most familiar words and phrases—*to cut no ice,* for example, is certainly as good as *to butter no parsnips*—but their adoption by the ignorant and their endless use and misuse in all sorts of situations have left them tattered and obnoxious, and soon or late they will probably go the way, as Brander Matthews once said, of all the other "temporary phrases which spring up, one scarcely knows how, and flourish unaccountably for a few months, and then disappear forever, leaving no sign." Matthews was wrong in two particulars here. They do not arrive by any mysterious parthenogenesis, but come from sources which, in many cases, may be determined. And they last, alas, a good deal more than a month. *Shoo-fly* afflicted the American people for four or five years, and "*I don't think,*" *aber nit, over the left, good night,* and *oh yeah* were scarcely less long-lived. There are, indeed, slang terms that have survived for centuries never dropping quite out of use and yet never attaining to good usage. Among verbs, *to do* for to cheat has been traced to 1847, *jug* for prison to 1834, *lip* for insolence to 1821, *sap* for fool to 1815, *murphy* for potato to 1811, *racket* to 1785, *breadbasket* for stomach to 1753, *hush-money* to 1709, *hick* to 1690, *gold-mine* for profitable venture to 1664, *grub* for food to 1659, *rot-gut* to 1597, and *bones* for dice to c. 1386. Among the adjectives, *lousy* in the sense of inferior goes back to 1690; when it burst into American slang in 1910 or thereabout it was already more than two centuries old. *Booze* has never got into Standard English, but it was known to slang in the first years of the fourteenth century. When *nuts* in the sense revealed by "Chicago was *nuts* for the Giants" came into popularity in the United States *c.* 1920, it was treated by most of the newspaper commentators on current slang as a neologism, but in truth it had been used in precisely the same sense by R. H. Dana, Jr., in *Two Years Before the Mast*, 1840, and by Mark Twain in *Following the Equator*, 1897. Sometimes an old slang word suddenly acquires a new meaning. An example is offered by *to chisel*. In the sense of to cheat, as in "He *chiseled* me out of $3," it goes back to the first years of the nineteenth century, but with the advent of the N.R.A., in the late summer of 1933, it took on the new meaning of to evade compliance with the law by concealment or stealth. It has been credited to Franklin D. Roosevelt, but I believe that its true father was General Hugh S. Johnson, J.D.

With the possible exception of the French, the Americans now produce more slang than any other people, and put it to heavier use in their daily affairs. But they entered upon its concoction relatively late, and down to the second decade of the nineteenth century they were content to take their supply from England. American slang, says George Philip Krapp, "is the child of the new nationalism, the new spirit of joyous adventure that entered American life after the close of the War of 1812." There was, during the colonial and early republican periods, a great production of neologisms, but very little of it was properly describable as slang. I find *to boost*, defined as to raise up, to lift up, to exalt, in the glossary appended to David Humphrey's *The Yankey in England*, 1815, but all other slang terms listed, e.g., *duds* for clothes, *spunk* for courage, and *uppish*, are in Francis Grose's Classical Dictionary of the Vulgar Tongue, published in London thirty years before. The Rev. John Witherspoon's denunciation of slang in *The Druid*, 1781, is a denunciation of English slang, though he is discussing the speech habits of Americans. But with the great movement into the West, following the War of 1812, the American vulgate came into its own, and soon the men of the ever-receding frontier were pouring out a copious stream of neologisms, many of them showing the audacious fancy of true slang. When these novelties penetrated to the East they produced a sort of linguistic shock, and the finicky were as much upset by the "tall talk" in which they were embodied as English pedants are today by the slang of Hollywood. That some of them were extremely extravagant is a fact: I need only point to *blustiferous, clamjamphrie, conbobberation, helliferocious, mollagausauger, peedoodles, ripsniptiously, slangwhanger, sockdolager, to exflunctify, to flummuck, to giraffe, to hornswoggle, to obflisticate*, and *to puckerstopple*. Most of these, of course, had their brief days and then disappeared, but there were others that got into the common vocabulary and still survive, e.g., *blizzard, to hornswoggle, sockdolager*, and *rambunctious*, the last-named the final step in a process which began with *robustious* and ran through *rumbustious* and *rambustious* in England before Americans took a hand in it. With them came many verb-phrases, e.g., *to pick a crow with, to cut one's eye-teeth, to go the whole hog*. This "tall talk," despite the horror of the delicate, was a great success in the East, and its salient practitioners—for example, David Crockett—were popular heroes. Its example encouraged the production of like neologisms everywhere, and by 1840, the use of slang was very widespread. It is to those days before the Civil War that we owe many of the colorful American terms for strong drink, still current, e.g., *panther-sweat, nose-paint, red-eye, corn-juice, forty-rod, mountain-dew, coffin-varnish, bust-head, stagger-soup, tonsil-paint, squirrel-whiskey*, and so on, and for drunk, e.g., *boiled, canned, cock-eyed, frazzled, fried, oiled, ossified, pifflicated, pie-eyed, plastered, snozzled, stewed, stuccoed, tanked, woozy*. "Perhaps the most striking difference be-tween British and American slang," says Krapp, "is that the former is more largely merely a matter of the use of queer-sounding words, like *bally* and *swank*, whereas American slang suggests vivid images and pictures." This was hardly true in the heyday of "tall talk," but that it is true now is revealed by a comparison of current English and American college slang. The vocabu-lary of Oxford and Cambridge seems inordinately obvious and banal to an American undergraduate. At Oxford it is made up in large part of a series of childish perversions of common and proper nouns, effected by adding *-er* or inserting *gg*. Thus, breakfast becomes *brekker*, collection becomes *collecker*, the Queen Street Cinema becomes the *Queener*, St. John's becomes *Jaggers*, and the Prince of Wales becomes the *Pragger-Wagger*. The rest of the vocabu-lary is equally feeble. To match the magnificent American *lounge-lizard* the best the Oxonians can achieve is *a bit of a lad*, and in place of the multitudi-nous American synonyms for *girl* there are only *bint* (Arabic for *woman*) and a few other such flabby terms. All college slang, of course, borrows heavily from the general slang vocabulary. For example, *chicken*, which designated a young girl on most American campuses until 1921 or there-about, was used by Steele in 1711, and, in the form of *no chicken*, by Swift in 1720. It had acquired a disparaging significance in the United States by 1788, as the following lines show:

> From visiting bagnios, those seats of despair,
> Where chickens will call you *my duck* and *my dear*
> In hopes that your purse may fall to their share,
>   Deliver me!

Like the vulgar language in general, popular American slang has got very little sober study from the professional philologians. The only existing glossary of it by a native scholar—"A Dictionary of American Slang," by Maurice H. Weseen, associate professor of English at the University of Nebraska—is an extremely slipshod and even ridiculous work. There are several collections by laymen, but most of them are still worse. The best, and by far, is "Slang Today and Yesterday," by Eric Partridge, which deals prin-cipally with English slang, but also has a valuable section on American slang.

All the dictionaries of Americanisms, of course, include words reasonably describable as slang, but they appear only incidentally, and not in large numbers. Thornton, for example, bars out a great deal of interesting and amusing material by confining his researches to written records. In England the literature of the subject is far more extensive. It began in the sixteenth century with the publication of several vocabularies of thieves' argot, and has been enriched in recent years by a number of valuable works, notably the Partridge volume just cited, "Slang, Phrase and Idiom in Colloquial English and Their Use," by Thomas R. G. Lyell, and the monumental "Slang and Its Analogues," by John S. Farmer and W. E. Henley. Before the completion of the last-named, the chief authorities on English slang were "A Dictionary of Slang, Jargon and Cant," by Albert Barrere and Charles G. Leland, and "A Dictionary of Modern Cant, Slang and Vulgar Words," by J. C. Hotten. Relatively little attention is paid to slang in the philological journals, but it is frequently discussed in the magazines of general circulation and in the newspapers. When the English papers denounce Americanisms, which is very often, it is commonly slang that arouses their most violent dudgeon. This dudgeon, of course, is grounded upon its very success: the American movies and talkies have implanted American slang in England even more copiously than they have implanted more decorous American neologisms. As the *Spectator* was saying lately, its influence "on the British Empire continues, ever more rapidly, to increase—a portent frequently mentioned and almost as frequently deplored." Sometimes it is belabored as intolerably vulgar, indecent and against God, as when the *Christian World* blamed it for the prevalence of "dishonest and debased thought" and ascribed its use to "a sneaking fear and dislike of calling beautiful things by their beautiful names and of calling ugly things by their ugly names"; sometimes it is sneered at as empty and puerile, signifying nothing, as when Allan Monkhouse demanded piously "What is the good of all this?" and answered "Such words are the ghosts of old facetiousness, and the world would be better without them"; and sometimes efforts are made to dispose of it by proving that it is all stolen from England, as when Dr. C. T. Onions, one of the editors of the Oxford Dictionary, offered to show a London reporter that the dictionary listed any American slang term he could name. Alas, for Dr. Onions, after making good with *to grill, fresh, to figure* (in the sense of to conclude), *bunkum* (he apparently forgot its clearly American origin) and *rake-off* (he had to fall back upon an American example), he came to grief with *boloney* and *nerts*. One of the favorite forms of this latter enterprise is a letter to the editor announcing the discovery that this or that locution, lately come into popularity by way of the talkies, is to be found in Shakespeare, or the Authorized Version of the Bible, or maybe even in Piers Plowman. There are also the specialists who devote themselves to demonstrating that American slang is simply a series of borrowings from the Continental languages, particularly French—for example, that *and how* is a translation of *et comment*, that *you're telling me* is from *à qui le dites-vous*, and that *to get one's goat* is from *prendre sa chèvre*. But not all Englishmen, of course, oppose and deride the American invasion, whether of slang or of novelties on high levels. Not a few agree with Horace Annesley Vachell that "American slanguage is not a tyranny, but a beneficent autocracy. *Lounge-lizard*, for example, is excellent. . . . It is humiliating to reflect that English slang at its best has to curtsey to American slang." To which "Jackdaw" adds in *John O'London's Weekly*: "We do but pick up the crumbs that fall from Jonathan's table."

During the World War there was some compensatory borrowing of English army slang and argot by the American troops, but it did not go very far. Indeed, the list of loan-words that came into anything approaching general use in the A.E.F. was about limited to *ace, blimp, cootie, Frog, Jack Johnson, Jerry, blotto, over the top* and *whizz-bang*. Some of the favorites of the English soldiers, e.g., *fag, blighty, cheerio, to strafe, funk-hole* and *righto*, were seldom if ever used by the Americans. The greater part of the American vocabulary came from the Regular Army, and some of it was of very respectable antiquity, e.g., *hand-shaker, Holy Joe* (for chaplain), *slum* (stew), *corned willie* (corned beef hash), *outfit, belly-robber, dog-robber* (an officer's servant or orderly), *doughboy, jawbone* (meaning credit, or anything spurious or dubious), *mud-splasher* (artilleryman), *buck-private, top-kick, gold-fish* (canned salmon), *gob, leatherneck, padre, chow* and *punk* (bread). A few novelties came in, e.g., *tin-hat* and *a.w.o.l.*, and there was some fashioning of counter-words and phrases from French materials, e.g., *boocoo* or *boocoop* (beaucoup), *toot sweet* (tout de suite) and *trez beans* (très bien), but neither class was numerous. Naturally enough, a large part of the daily conversation of the troops was obscene, or, at all events, excessively vulgar. Their common name for cavalryman, for example, could hardly be printed here. The English called the military police *red-caps*, but the American name was *M.P.'s*. The British used *O.C.* for Officer Commanding; the Americans used *C.O.* for Commanding Officer. The British were fond of a number of Americanisms, e.g., *cold-feet, kibosh, nix, pal*, and *to chew the rag*, but whether they were borrowed from the A.E.F. or acquired by some less direct route I do not know. About *gob, leatherneck* and *doughboy* there have been bitter etymological wrangles. *Gob* has been traced variously to a Chinese word (*gobshite*), of unknown meaning and probably mythical; to *gobble*, an allusion to the somewhat earnest methods of feeding prevailing among sailors; and to *gob*, an archaic English dialect word signifying expectoration. The English coast-guardsmen, who are said to be free spitters, are often called *gobbies*. In May, 1928, Admiral H. A. Wiley, then commander-in-chief of the United States Fleet, forbade the use of *gob* in ship's newspapers, calling it "undignified and unworthy." But the gobs continue to cherish it. *Leatherneck*, I have been told, originated in the fact that the collar of the Marines used to be lined with leather. But the Navy prefers to believe that it has something to do with the fact that a sailor, when he washes, strips to the waist and renovates his whole upper works, whereas a Marine simply rolls up his sleeves and washes in the scantier manner of a civilian. It is the theory of all gobs that all Marines are dirty fellows. But the step from unwashed necks to leather seems to me to be somewhat long and perilous. The term *devil-dogs*, often applied to the Marines during the World War, was supposed to be a translation of the German *teufelhunde*. During the fighting around Château Thierry, in June and July, 1918, the Marines were heavily engaged, and the story went at the time that the Germans, finding them very formidable, called them *teufelhunde*. But I have been told by German officers who were in that fighting that no such word was known in the German army. *Doughboy* is an old English navy term for dumpling. It was formerly applied to the infantry only, and its use is said to have originated in the fact that the infantrymen once pipe-clayed parts of their uniforms, with the result that they became covered with a doughy mess when it rained.

✠ ✠ ✠

THE FUTURE OF ENGLISH

ALBERT H. MARCKWARDT

The analysis of the development of American English [shows] the relationship of this development to the most salient features in the cultural life and history of the American people. It would be equally interesting for someone to make a complementary study of the particular facets of British English, and indeed of the English spoken in the various dominions of the Empire, indicating the relationships between language and culture which exist there as well.

But when all is said and done, English, despite the vast numbers who speak it and its widespread dissemination over the globe, is still but a single language, and to paraphrase an earlier commentator, the differences between its widest extremes, though extensive in certain features of the language, are still remarkably few. As a language it is highly unified; more so than many tongues spoken by a far smaller number of people.

This raises the question of the probable future of English. We have already noted that 230 million speakers of English as a first language are spread over four continents. We have noted too that this represents more than a forty-fold, almost a fiftyfold, increase over the number of speakers who used the language in 1600. At that time it was fifth among the languages of the Western world, surpassed in numbers by speakers of French, German, Spanish, and Italian. In 1750 it was still fifth, Russian having replaced Italian as a fourth. A century later English had gone ahead of the others, the sudden addition of twenty-three million speakers of the language in the United States apparently sufficing to put it into first place.

With this as a background, it might be argued that if the fiftyfold multiplication of the last four centuries were to be cut to merely a fivefold increase over the next four, we might expect one billion speakers of English by 2350 —nearly one-half of the present world population. Or the recent rate of increase of from fifteen to twenty million per decade would give us very nearly the same result. The probability of such an increment may be questioned on the ground that the nineteenth-century aggrandizement of English was largely dependent upon the opening up of the North American continent to settlers who eventually adopted the language. With the twentieth century more than half over, it does not seem likely that any single English-speaking country will repeat the feat of the United States in the nineteenth century. Yet Australia, South Africa, and Canada will unquestionably show pronounced gains, and a total of 300 million speakers of English as a first language some time in the twenty-first century is by no means inconceivable. It could reach 350 million. At any rate no other European language, not even Russian, is currently in a position to compete with it.

It is, however, in its development as a second language that the real opportunities for the future development of English seem to lie. It is probably fair to say that after some tinkering with international languages, we can only conclude that no one of them has yet been sufficiently successful to justify much confidence in its future. Consequently, if we are to look forward to any single language which might serve as an international auxiliary—and the increase in rapidity and extent of travel and communication somehow leads us to expect this—such a language will undoubtedly be one of those in use at the present time. The English language would seem to be the best candidate for a number of reasons.

In the first place it is the native language of *two* of the most powerful and influential nations of the world. This is not true of French, German, Russian, Spanish, or Chinese. Moreover, it is used today both in speech and in writing to an extent unsurpassed by any other. It has been estimated that three-fifths of the world's radio stations broadcast in English and that three-fourths of the world's mail is written in the language.

There are in particular certain features of English which make for its convenience as an international auxiliary. Its vocabulary is composed of vast numbers of words both of Teutonic and of Latin origin, making large portions of its word stock readily comprehensible to millions of speakers of other languages. The words are short; the language is free from a complicated inflectional system, giving at least the illusion of ease of mastery. At the same time we must not fail to observe that our wretched spelling system, which so successfully obscures any consistent relationship between the spoken and written forms of the language, will undoubtedly act as a deterrent to some degree, but probably not enough to counterbalance the other factors which have been cited.

It is extremely difficult to estimate the number of speakers of English as a second language: some authorities place the number at fifty million, others at 125 million. Whatever the facts may be, there can be no doubt that it is on the increase. It is replacing French as a second language in the schools of Latin America and in some of the European countries. It has always been important as an auxiliary language in Holland and the Scandinavian countries. Until very recently Russia placed considerable emphasis upon the teaching of English in her schools. Various types of pidgin English serve as a trade language in the Far East. If, within the next century, a more highly interdependent world will have to depend upon bilingualism to conduct its affairs, a doubling of the numbers who now speak English as a second language is not inconceivable. At the end of that time we may assume that probably 500 million people will be speaking some form of English, either as a first or a second language.

This leads to a further question—what kind of English will these half a billion speakers use? What will the language be like? In attempting to answer this, we must remember that English has never been anything like a uniform language. No academy has ever attempted to rule upon its vocabulary and grammar. In America, at least, this lack of uniformity has been due in part to a constant increase in the number of speakers. If the increase should continue at anything like its present rate, it is not likely that a greater uniformity will be established, despite the leveling influence of improved means of communication. This may not be a bad thing; undoubtedly the English language owes much of its vigor to the variety existing within it.

We have seen that a language may be considered from the point of view of its words, its sounds, its inflectional endings, and its patterns of word order. We know also that for the last several centuries the vocabulary of English has been very large, and some words have been borrowed from languages in almost every part of the world. Certain languages, principally Latin, French, and the Scandinavian tongues, have contributed heavily to our present lexicon. Moreover, the dictionaries of the English language at various periods of its history seem to reflect a consistent present lexicon. Moreover, the dictionaries of the English language as it was used approximately 1000 years ago, contain about 37,000 words. A fairly complete dictionary of Middle English—that is, of the language of 500 years ago—would have between 50,000 and 70,000 entries. It is likely that a dictionary of Early Modern English, the period of Shakespeare and his contemporaries, would contain at least 140,000 words, and it is a wellknown fact that unabridged dictionaries of present-day English have approximately half a million entries.

Even if we consider the probability that the early records of our language are so fragmentary that the numbers just cited for Old and Middle English fall far short of what the language actually contained, yet the apparent quad-rupling of our stock of words during the last three and a half centuries is significant evidence of a strong tendency toward vocabulary increase. There is no reason to suppose that this will not continue.

We have noticed, in addition, that the recent extensions of our vocabulary have come not so much through word borrowing as from the manipulation of elements which are already in the language. Such processes as compound-ing, the addition of derivative prefixes and suffixes, and change in grammatical function account for considerably more than half of our new words today. Without question we shall continue to borrow some words from foreign languages in the future. We did so during both world wars, and as the lan-guage spreads over areas of the Far East, for example, it is reasonable to look forward to new words coming from Malay, as well as from Russian, possibly even from Swahili and Bantu, but the principal growth in the English vocabulary will undoubtedly come as the result of the processes which have just been mentioned—up to what point is hard to guess. A doubling of the vocabulary in the next two centuries is not difficult to conceive in the light of what has happened since 1600.

If the area over which English is spoken and the number of speakers of English increase, as we expect them to, it is highly probable that a consider-able number of words will be used in one regional form of English but not in another. It is likely, too, that the increasing complexities of modern life and modern technology will demand a larger vocabulary of the individual, as has been evidenced by the replacement of the horse by the automobile, of the town crier by the newspaper, of the candle by electric lighting. But there has always been a large gap between the vocabulary of the individual and the total word count of the language, and this will very likely increase as time goes on.

We may ask next, 'How will the English of the future sound?' To most of us the language of Chaucer sounds somewhat more like the present-day speech of one of the Low Countries than like Modern English, and ... Shakespeare's lines, uttered as we think he and his contemporaries pro-nounced them, ring somewhat strangely in our ears. Will the speech of our descendants 300 years hence sound equally strange? Or has the English language attained a phonetic stability? There is really no reason to believe that it has. Present differences in the way in which English is pronounced throughout the world may, and in fact do reflect certain differences in the rate at which sound changes have operated in the past.

We shall probably make more progress in attempting to answer this ques-tion if we consider it in the light of the various kinds of sounds: consonants, long and short vowels. On the whole our consonants have changed relatively little since the period from the twelfth to the fourteenth centuries, when such pairs as s and z, f and v became meaningfully distinct instead of mere variants of the same sound. Prior to that time such contrasts as those of *feel* and *veal* or *ice* and *eyes* could not have occurred in English. It was just about the same time that the *ng* in *sing* and *long* emerged as a sound in its own right. Since that time English has acquired but one new consonant, the *zh* sound of *vision* or *measure*. Other changes have been confined either to individual words or at most to particular phonetic situations: the development of the *sh* sound in *sugar* and of *j* in *soldier*. There may be more changes of this nature ahead of us, but any basic alteration of the whole consonant system would be surprising.

At the other extreme, the popularly called 'long' vowels have always changed considerably, particularly within the last 500 years. At the beginning of the Christian era, the stressed vowel of the word *home* was pronounced with the sound of *i*, as it still is in the cognate German word *Heim*. By the time of King Alfred the vowel in this word had acquired the sound of *ah*, which then developed to *aw* at approximately 1200. The word attained its present *o*-like quality probably by 1500, as did most others with the same stressed vowel sound. Nor is this a rare or exceptional instance. In the 200 years separating the period of Chaucer from that of Shakespeare, virtually every long vowel in English underwent some sort of change, not only in its own quality but very often in respect to its relationship to other vowel sounds in the language. It is only since the time of Shakespeare, or slightly before, that words such as *read* and *reed, caught* and *bought, pain* and *pane* have come to be pronounced with the same vowel sound, and conversely words such as *coat* and *cot* or *made* and *mad*, then having the same quality of sound, have become differentiated.

Despite the extent and variety of this change, much of it does fit into a pattern. What seems to be involved here is a gradual raising of the tongue and jaw position for making the sounds in question until they reach a point where they cannot be raised any more, after which they develop into diphthongs. Thus the word which Chaucer and his contemporaries pronounced as *moos* is now given the diphthongal pronunciation *mouse*. Conversely, most diphthongs in the earlier periods of the language are now simple vowels —*law* was pronounced earlier with an *ow* sound; today, despite its spelling, it has but a single vowel. Developments as striking as these may easily continue. In fact we may have the beginnings of something like it in the *eh-oo* one encounters in the British pronunciation of words like *know* and *home*.

In comparison, the so-called 'short' vowels have changed very little in the course of the last 1000 years. Words like *bed, this, ox*, and *full* have been pronounced with the same vowels for the last ten centuries and even more. It would seem reasonable, then, to conclude that they will undergo no major changes in the immediate future.

Another kind of pronunciation change is confined particularly to foreign words taken into the language: a shift of stress or accent toward the front. This is occurring today with such words as *cigarette, Detroit, inquiry*, and *robust*, all of which are heard from time to time with the stress on the first syllable. This happened centuries ago to words like *liquor, pleasant*, and *nation*, originally pronounced with principal stress on the final syllable.

From one point of view, the disappearance of secondary stress in the British pronunciation of words like *secretary* and *circumstance* could be considered as a part of the same general development. Without question this tendency will continue to operate, although it is impossible to know which particular words will be affected.

The comparative freedom of English from inflectional or grammatical endings—at least as compared with Latin or German—has often been considered one of its strongest claims as a potential international language. What has happened is that through the years certain other devices have come to take the place of inflections. First, though, let us look at those inflectional suffixes which are indispensable to the structure and operation of English today. The two most important of these are the *-s* plural of nouns and the *-ed* which forms the past tense and past participle of the vast majority of English verbs.

The first of these, originally only one of eight or nine ways of indicating the plural, has expanded to a point where today there are relatively few native nouns which form their plural in any way other than the addition of *-s*. A small number of foreign words, such as *antenna, nucleus*, and *phenomenon*, at times retain the plural inflection of their language of origin. It is possible that the *-s* plural will be extended to some of these, particularly when they pass, as *antenna* has already done, from the learned into everyday language.

In much the same manner the regular *-ed* verb inflection has encroached upon all others during the last ten centuries. Verbs newly admitted into the language have adopted this inflection. Such old verbs as *help* and *climb* have lost their irregular past forms *holp* and *clomb*, which have been replaced in the standard language by *helped* and *climbed*. Even now the very uncertainty which many speakers and writers feel with respect to *strive* and *wake* indicates that a change is under way. The 360 verbs in Old English which indicated changes in tense through alterations of their principal vowel (e.g. *sing, sang, sung*) have been reduced to a mere sixty. The language as a whole now has only about 125 irregular verbs of any kind. It seems safe to predict that this number will become smaller as time goes on.

A few other inflections are now in the process of being replaced by constructions involving what are often called function words. For example, the inflected genitive, or possessive, often alternates with a construction employing the preposition of: *the horse's head, the head of the horse*. Throughout the last several centuries the sphere of *of* has been steadily increasing at the expense of the inflectional ending. We can no longer say *water's glass* for *glass of water*, or *ours one* for *one of ours*. We may well ask whether in time it will seem equally awkward to say *year's vacation, world's fair*, or *St. Joseph's Hospital*. Likewise, the comparative and superlative adjective endings *-er* and *-est* have slowly given way to constructions with *more* and *most*. We are no longer able to employ such formations as *interestinger* and *honestest*. Could this taboo ultimately extend to *prettier* and *hottest*? Finally, it would not seem unreasonable to expect that the few situations where the inflected subjunctive of the verb still remains intact will eventually give way to formations with such auxiliaries as *may, might*, and *should*.

There are also situations in English where the few remaining forms specifically indicative of case, e.g. *me, who, him*, conflict with the normal word-order patterns of the language. In general, an object form such as *me* will follow the verb, whereas a subject form such as *who* will precede it. This tendency toward the fixation of word order accounts for such apparent solecisms as *It is me, Who are you looking for?* Even more important is the general principle behind such developments. When the choice of a form based upon word order conflicts with the choice of a form based upon an inflectional paradigm or pattern, word order generally turns out to be the determining factor. No matter how we feel about these particular constructions, they are undoubtedly here to stay, but because of the scarcity of case-distinctive forms, it is not likely that many more changes of this type will occur.

Word order is, however, one aspect of the larger problem of syntax. In general, largely to compensate for the loss of inflectional endings, English word order has become more rigid. Shakespeare had more freedom than we have now. Will our great-grandchildren have less?

For example, when the modifying elements of place, manner, and time are all included within a single sentence, we are able to say:

He wrote the exercise carefully at home this afternoon.
This afternoon he wrote the exercise carefully at home.
He carefully wrote the exercise at home this afternoon.

Certainly the following constructions seem somewhat more awkward and would occur less frequently:

He wrote the exercise at home carefully this afternoon.
He wrote the exercise carefully this afternoon at home.

We would be even less likely to say:

He wrote the exercise at home this afternoon carefully.
He wrote the exercise this afternoon at home carefully.

Moreover, although we may begin the sentence with the time element, we may place neither the modifier of place nor of manner in initial position. Consequently we cannot say:

Carefully he wrote the exercise this afternoon at home.
At home he wrote the exercise this afternoon carefully.

It is not unreasonable to expect a further fixation and limitation of such patterns as time goes on.

Another kind of syntactical development concerns the shift in the function of inflection and auxiliary verbs. In the language of King Alfred, even in that of Chaucer, the auxiliary *can* literally and specifically meant 'to know' or 'to know how.' At that time the verb *may* was employed to indicate ability, whereas the inflected subjunctive denoted possibility. At present, *can* indicates ability, *may* indicates possibility and upon occasion permission, and the inflected subjunctive has all but disappeared. In fact, *can* now often usurps the function of possibility and permission: *It could rain. Can I go?* Is the next step the disappearance of *may* and the replacement of *can* by some other construction?

Our present use of the verb *got* raises a series of similar questions. *Have got*, indicating possession, at times replaces *have,* which in turn, displaced an earlier *owe, ought. Have got to*, meaning necessity or obligation, is likewise taking the place of *ought* and *must.* Will these latter auxiliaries disappear altogether, as certain others, notably *thearf*, 'to need' and *dow*, 'to avail, befit,' have done in the past? It is already evident that *going to* is encroaching upon the domain of *shall* and *will* to indicate future time.

Speculations of this nature might go on indefinitely, but at least some of the possible lines of development the English language may follow in the future have been suggested. To sum up: as possible developments in the English language of the next few centuries, we may expect that it will be spoken by more people, that it will include more words, that the pronunciations of its stressed vowels may change, that the noun plural and regular past tense inflections will be strengthened and that certain other inflections will gradually disappear, and that there will be a continued fixation of word-order patterns, and a shift in some verb auxiliaries.

In considering the future of English one inevitably comes up against the question which has been one of the concerns of the present work, the differences between the language as spoken in England and in America. Will these become greater as time goes on, or will they tend to disappear?

This question can best be answered in terms of the particular facets of American culture which the preceding chapters have shown to be reflected in the English language as it is spoken here. We have seen that American English reflects, among other things, the melting pot aspect of American culture chiefly through its verbal borrowings. By preserving some of the words, meanings, and features of the pronunciation of sixteenth- and seventeenth-century English, it mirrors the cultural lag so often reflected in a colony separated from the mother country by some distance. The sinewy vigor of the frontiersman, his ingenuity born of necessity, and his disregard of convention find their counterpart in the bold creation of new compounds and derivatives, the free employment of functional changes, and the bizarre blended forms; even his lusty humor is matched by his playfully hyperbolical tall talk. On the other hand, the glorification of the commonplace and an accompanying tendency toward euphemism betokens the squeamishness of a somewhat culturally insecure middle-class and a mid-nineteenth-century deference to feminine taste. To the extent that these culture traits are likely to persist and be strengthened, it may be presumed that the language will continue to reflect them. When or as they become less prominent their influence will diminish.

The verbal borrowings from immigrant nations have clearly become less numerous. Many of our early loan words are now obsolete, and the languages spoken by the bulk of our late nineteenth- and early twentieth-century immigrant peoples have left little trace upon English. With immigration during the last three decades reduced to a mere trickle, any further influx of borrowings beyond an occasional adoption here and there seems unlikely. The retention of features of sixteenth- and seventeenth-century English is not likely to be influenced greatly over the years. There are few, if any, indications that our drugstore will become a chemist's shop, or that the *r* coloring of our vowels will grow less prominent. Though the gap between American and British English in this respect is not likely to close, there are certainly no indications that it will widen.

We shall undoubtedly continue to develop new compound and derivative formations; word blending and functional change will continue as active processes, but it must be remembered that these are confined to certain quite definitely circumscribed areas of the vocabulary. Many of our most ludicrous euphemisms have already disappeared from current use, and on the question of cultural insecurity we shall have something to say a little later. All in all, there would seem to be little reason for anticipating a further divergence between British and American English.

There is also the question of the extent to which British English is being influenced by Americanisms, a question which can best be answered accurately and scientifically by one who speaks British English. There is no question that the availability of American books, newspapers, and films has served to acquaint millions of Englishmen with American features of the language which, however, they do not normally employ. Recognition or passing acquaintance does not necessarily mean adoption, and while it is possible here and there to point to English acceptance and use of an American term, there is no more reason for expecting that American cooking and food terminology, political jargon, or the lexicon of the automobile is going to be taken over bodily than there is to suppose that the English are going to cook like Americans or to alter their political organizations and practices.

One must remember, however, that no matter how striking the differences between British and American English may be, the similarities far outweigh them, for it is in grammatical structure and syntax—essentially the operational machinery of the language—that the difference is negligible. It is neither exaggeration nor idle chauvinism to say that the English language, with an exceptional past behind it, appears to be on the threshold of a still greater future. Moreover, this future is to a considerable extent in the hands of those who regularly speak and write the language. What can they do to insure and even to further the development which lies ahead?

This basic question may best be answered by considering the dangers which may conceivably beset a language in the particular situation in which English finds itself today. There would seem to be two such perils, diametrically opposed to each other. On the one hand there are some who have seen, even in certain of the developments which have been mentioned earlier in this chapter—for example, the disappearance of the inflected subjunctive, the establishment of *who* in pre-verbal position, the use of *have got* to indicate possession—indications of a too great liberty, if not license. The unchecked development of tendencies such as these, it is argued, could lead to developments so divergent that the English language would lose its unity, and consequently its utility as a medium of communication. Opposed to this is the view that highly restrictive rules and conservative attitudes springing from a fear of solecism and leading to a denial of what is actual usage will exert such a confining influence upon the language that its flexibility will be lost and its ultimate potentialities remain unrealized.

Although there may be some danger from the first of these, the present social and cultural situation, in the United States especially, would seem to indicate that the greater of the two perils is the second. A number of factors enter into this situation. We have seen that from the beginning until late in the nineteenth century there was always a frontier, an area where unlettered pioneers toiled to secure cultural advantages for their children— including the mastery of Standard English. Moreover, the children of foreign-speaking immigrants felt the sting of social disapproval if their language betrayed their origin. The spread of higher education to social groups who in Europe would have remained comfortably within the confines of a regional or class dialect, also brought with it an emphasis upon correctness of speech and writing.

In learning a language, whether it be a different form of our native tongue or a totally foreign idiom, we operate inductively. We learn specific facts and usages first. When we have absorbed enough of these, we begin to synthesize —we form patterns, general behavior traits, upon which we then rely when a new situation faces us. The more uncertain we are of ourselves, culturally or in any other way, the more insistent we are upon guidance in specific facts and instances, and the more reluctant we are to rely upon an instinctive grasp of these general patterns. As far as raising the level of English is concerned, American textbooks and teaching practices have too seldom taken the students beyond the level of instruction in specific matters. As a consequence, most people in the United States carry about with them a strange assortment of linguistic taboos. The feeling against *ain't*, even as a first person interrogative, is very widespread. Some react against *like* for *as*. For many the pronunciation *ice cream* with primary stress on the first syllable is taboo; for others the taboo against *John and me* is so powerful that it prompts them to use *John and I* even when it is structurally objective and *me* would normally be demanded.

It may be reasonably argued that these taboos, which are after all the results of a primarily negative approach to language, or to expression, have performed their function and outlived their usefulness. They should be replaced with something positive. We are at a point where the doctrine of original sin, linguistically speaking, must be replaced by a faith in intuition, by dependence upon the established, unconsciously known patterns of the language. Such an instinct can be developed only by giving attention to the broader aspects of structure and the evolving tendencies of the language.

The history of English during the last two centuries demonstrates that highly restrictive and unrealistic rules of grammar do not have a lasting effect upon the language as a whole. The more incredible portions of the body of rules developed by Nathaniel Ward, Dr. Johnson, Lindley Murray, and their followers have generally disappeared. In the present situation, however, the attitude behind the creation of a mass of non-pertinent and unscientific linguistic legislation can still do positive harm. It can create and preserve taboos, which ought never to have been created, against certain expressions and constructions. It can develop anxiety neuroses in many of the people who employ the language. Both of these are undesirable conditions for the future development of the English language. We cannot expect a medium of communication to develop in advance of the courage and resourcefulness of the people who employ it.

It is our responsibility to realize whither the language is tending, and the duty of our schools and teachers to promulgate healthy linguistic attitudes. If this is done, we may be certain that some individuals can and will attain greatness in the use of the language, which in turn will make of it a more flexible and sensitive medium for the rest of us. In this sense, a new era lies before all the English-speaking peoples.

PART EIGHT

EXERCISES IN
THE HISTORY OF ENGLISH

✠

INTRODUCTION

Millions of speakers of English today know nothing of the origin of their language, its relation to other languages, or its development over the course of some twelve hundred years. Yet, for the most part, they are fluent speakers; they carry out their day to day activities with apparent ease. Many of them write as well and about as comfortably as they speak. Most of our contemporary writers have had no formal training in, and little private inquiry into, the English language. It cannot be said, therefore, that a knowledge of the history and the development of one's native language will lead to practical results, will make one a better speaker or writer or reader or listener of contemporary English. On the contrary, we know perfectly well that competence and performance in language depend on continuous activity in those four linguistic skills, on engaging vigorously, from day to day, with or without formal training, in the most fundamental of all human and social activities, using language. If, therefore, it cannot be claimed that knowledge of the history and development of English will have any appreciable effect upon performance in that language, why, then, should one bother with it?

The easiest thing to say, of course, is that no one could read a text written in older English if some knowledge of the phonology, the morphology, and the syntax of English, at whatever date one chose to read it, were not available, if a grammar of that language were not constructed. Chaucer's Squire, who hoped "to stonden in his lady grace," would be totally irretrievable; Guinevere, speaking thus to Launcelot, "therefor, wyt thou wel I am sette in such a plyte to gete my soule hele," might be misunderstood by us; the *Authorized Version* rendering in Isaiah xiv:9–12, "O Lucifer, sonne of the morning? How art thou cut downe to the ground, which didst weaken the nations?" would strike us as non-English; Falstaff's curt order to Quickly to "wash thy face, and draw thy Action" might seem absurd; John Locke's judgment of the Greeks and their language ("On the Teaching of English") that "it is plain [they] were yet more nice in theirs" would be incomprehensible. Hundreds of examples, both earlier and later, could be strung out here, but there is little need for that. The point is clear: without instruction we could not read the texts our ancestors produced, we could not have access to the record and literature of the past. Since much of the glory and wisdom of humanity would on that account be lost to posterity, many of us would be inclined to say that the study of the history of our language, if it prevents that calamity, is indeed justified. But there is not likely to be an overwhelming majority of that persuasion among those for whom these exercises are intended.

If we set immediately practical considerations aside, however, we will be able to recognize the appeal of historical study of the type represented in these exercises. During the past few decades, because of the necessity for isolating what one "needs to know," many of us have altogether lost sight of the exciting area of human activity called "the nice to know." In our hurry to accomplish some limited goals we have come close to rushing right out of the world without ever having sampled the largest portion of experience in it. A major justification for studies in historical grammar—or grammar of any sort, for that matter—is the opportunity they afford for putting intellectual curiosity and a general power of analysis to work. One might then regard a problem in, say, Old English syntax, as a proper sphere of study in its own right, worthy of the most concentrated mental effort.

The qualities of mind exercised by engaging in research in historical linguistics are, among others, curiosity, analysis, and patience, all directed to a quest for knowledge for its own sake, its own (often private) reward. That is what the study of historical grammar has to offer—knowledge. What is asked for here is careful observation, collection, and classification of language data, plus the ability to draw out, at the end of that activity, sound inferences, or conclusions, which are supported rigorously by that data.

The purpose of the following exercises is to provide an introduction to the historical study of our language. While the information which can be accumulated as a result of working through these exercises is sound and valuable in itself, it is elementary and partial. Only one short drill in phonology, for example, has been included. And the syntactical elements, although, once again, quite sound, in no way constitute a thorough history of English syntax. But this book is not a text for an advanced course in the history of English; rather, it was designed as a set of readings and exercises to satisfy the initial curiosity of students in English language and literature classes who might be expected to have some interest in the history and development of their language.

PLAN OF THE EXERCISES

The pursuit of knowledge about the English language is best carried on by employing an inductive methodology. Only after a reasonably wide assortment of language data has been observed, assembled, and analyzed can we make valid generalizations about language. Those are the assumptions that inform the texts and questions constituting these exercises. In the best sense of it, these exercises are a "do-it-yourself" course in The History and Development of the English Language. Although a good deal of information has been supplied, each of you will arrive at a number of answers on your own; the collective force of your own answers will become your basic knowledge of the history of your language.

The arrangement of texts is chronological, from earliest to latest. While this ordering of material does impose difficulties at first, the sense of progression to be gained by following this order will, we think, more than offset any initial hardships you may encounter. Also, the greatest help is provided in the early exercises. By examining passages chosen to represent the four stages in the development of English (Old English = OE, Middle English = ME, Early Modern English = EMnE, and Modern English = MnE), one can gain a reasonably well informed opinion about the course of his language.

In each of the exercises there are texts and questions for you to answer. Frequently there is also a translation or some explanatory material (a glossary or notes—or both). The order in which these materials appear varies from exercise to exercise, depending upon what you are asked to do with them. When you undertake an exercise, therefore, you should first skim it from beginning to end so that you will know what help has been provided for you and what is being asked of you. You will then be able to proceed through the exercise with confidence.

A FEW FINAL WORDS

Although each set of texts and exercises constitutes a reasonably good self-contained unit of information, it would be prudent to consult from time to time a few of the many reference books and texts which contain information relevant to the development of the English language. Here is a very short list of useful books; the bibliographies and notes found in them can lead the curious even further.

1. *OED. The Oxford English Dictionary.* 13 vols. The original title of this work was *A New English Dictionary on Historical Principles (NED),* but it is now universally called the *OED.* First on any list, this is the single most important book for the study of the development of English. It is also the best dictionary of its kind in the world. Abridged editions are available and may have to be used, but one should become familiar with the whole set and, especially, its prefatory material.

2. John Algeo and Thomas Pyles. *Problems in the Origins and Development of the English Language.* New York: Harcourt, Brace, and World, 1966. The very best workbook available, it is keyed to Pyles' book, q.v., below.

3. Albert C. Baugh. *A History of the English Language.* 2nd ed. New York: Appleton, Century, Croft 1957.

4. Morton W. Bloomfield and Leonard Newmark. *A Linguistic Introduction to the History of English.* New York: Random House, 1963.

5. W. Nelson Francis. *The English Language: An Introduction–Background for Writing.* New York: W. W. Norton Co., 1965.

6. H. A. Gleason, Jr. *Linguistics and English Grammar.* New York: Holt, Rinehart, Winston, 1965.

7. Albert H. Marckwardt. *Introduction to the English Language.* New York: Oxford University Press, 1942.

8. L. M. Meyers. *The Roots of Modern English.* Boston: Little, Brown & Co., 1966.

9. John Nist. *A Structural History of English.* New York: St. Martin's Press, 1966.

10. Thomas Pyles. *The Origins and Development of the English Language.* New York: Harcourt, Brace, & World, 1964.

11. Stuart Robertson and Frederic G. Cassidy. *The Development of Modern English.* 2nd ed. New York: Prentice-Hall, Inc., 1954.

Before letting you go off on your own, a bit of cautionary advice seems appropriate. It would be wise to keep that eighteenth-century dictum about 'a little knowledge' in mind. Do not expect to know everything about the development of English when you have finished these exercises. No one knows 'everything' about language. Large areas of study have not even been suggested here. Think, for example, of the condition of English at the present time, of the varieties of English spoken by native English speakers in Britain, in the United States, in Canada, in Australia, in New Zealand, and in many other countries in the world, and of the type of English being spoken and written by native speakers of other languages who have learned English as a second language in every country of the world, and of the opportunities for research and study regarding the future of English this situation presents. Much, therefore, is left to be examined. For further study, however, these exercises will furnish a decent foundation; and that is a sufficient beginning.

To make the following exercises more meaningful and informative, and to render meaningful the list of abbreviations and the glossary that appear in Exercise 1, we suggest examining this preliminary exercise and answering the questions in it.

PRELIMINARY EXERCISE

A sound view of the parts of speech and grammatical properties is essential in making accurate translations. Old English, as you will discover, is an inflected language, much closer, in this respect, to modern German than it is to Modern English. In MnE 'he did not say' is a grammatical sentence, but none of the following sentences is grammatical:

he not did say
not say he did
he not say did
not said he

and 'did he not say' is not equivalent. We test grammaticalness, in these instances, by relating each utterance to word order models we have learned. In OE, however, *ne sǣgde hē* (literally, word for word, equivalent to MnE '*not said he')* is grammatical and equivalent, in translation, to 'he did not say.' We are able to construct this equivalence in our translation by drawing on our knowledge of grammar, by realizing that OE word order is different from, and based on principles of organization which are different from, that of MnE. In this instance we need to know this much (at least) of OE grammar:

1. the negative particle *ne* (not) often appears initially in a negative sentence

2. as is the case in OE with an initial *þa* (*þa fērde hē*, then he travelled), after *ne* the verb almost always appears next, the subject appearing after the verb

3. the conjugation of the verb *secgan* (say) shows that *sǣgde* is third person singular preterite indicative (i.e., 'said,' with 'he,' 'she,' or 'it' as possible subjects)

4. as we contruct 'said' from 'say' we observe that we can place 'I,' 'you,' 'he,' or 'she,' and 'they' before it, but in OE, in an equivalent situation, 'I' and 'he' or 'she' would require *sǣgde*, 'you' would require *sǣgdest*, and 'they' would require *sǣgdon*. Thus the final -*e* of *sǣgde* carries with it a certain type of grammatical information not contained in its MnE equivalent, 'said.'

QUESTIONS

It might be helpful, in answering these questions, to consult a handbook or traditional description of MnE.

1. What is a grammatical property?
2. What is a part of speech? How many of them are there?
3. What does *gender* signify? How is it determined and recognized?
4. What does *number* signify? How is it determined and recognized?
5. What does *case* signify? How is it determined and recognized?
6. How many *cases* are there, in MnE, for nouns?
7. In verb constructions what does *number* signify? How is it determined and recognized? Wherein does it reside?
8. To what natural phenomenon does *tense* relate? How is it determined and recognized?
9. What is *mood*? How is it determined and recognized?
10. What is *concord* (or agreement)? Under what grammatical circumstances is it required? Why?

*Asterisk in front of a structure signifies that the structure is nongrammatical, not permitted in MnE.

11. What is a *declension*? a *conjugation*? a *paradigm*?

12. What is a *pro*-noun? What other *pro*-forms do you recognize in MnE? Under what grammatical circumstances can they occur?

13. Do you understand each of the definitions cited for the abbreviations listed in the glossary for Exercise 1 on pages 377–381?

14. After you complete this exercise, read "The Legend of St. Andrew," which follows. Answer the first twelve questions above as if they were directed to that OE text, and compare your answers with the responses you have just made. What differences show up?

✠ ✠ ✠

OLD ENGLISH
450–1154

It is not possible to fix the exact date of the earliest surviving Old English text. Perhaps the poem *Widsiþ*, which is dated sometime in the seventh century, is the earliest English writing we possess. There no doubt were other works, and of course a flourishing oral language, in what is now modern England, long before that. It is convenient, therefore, to give the date 450, a time when Teutonic adventurers, having initiated what was over the course of several centuries to become a major invasion, conquest, and settlement of Britain, had arrived in the island in sufficient numbers to found a linguistic community. We can call these people Anglo-Saxons and their language Old English. It is not as difficult to fix the end of the Old English period. The year of the last entry in *The Anglo-Saxon Chronicle*, 1154, closing out as it does a major literary document in the period, has become the traditional date to mark this event.

During this period of seven centuries the Anglo-Saxons evolved a language which sustained a major literature of the world. We can represent just a small portion of their production. Three texts, dated at about the year 1000, written in the Late West-Saxon dialect, the form of Old English used by King Alfred the Great (849–899), have been chosen. These are the texts:

1. *The Legend of St. Andrew. Anon.* The first forty-nine lines of this homiletic treatise—in this case a lively adventure designed to demonstrate the true wonder and glory of Christ as well as to teach the virtue of persever-

ance—constitute a representative passage of Old English prose. A complete glossary has been included.

2. *The Legend of St. Andrew.* The next thirty-two lines are given, with a literal inter-linear translation, to permit an observation of continuous development of a subject.

3. *The Assumption of St. John the Apostle.* Ælfric (955–1020). These first fifty lines represent the peak of Old English prose. They are followed by a partial glossary, some grammatical hints, and another translation.

THE LEGEND OF ST. ANDREW
lines 1–49, Ca. 975

Hēr segð þæt æfter þām þe Drihten Hǣlend Crīst tō
heofonum āstāh, þæt þā apostolī wǣron ætsomne; and
hīe sendon hlot him betwēonum, hwider hyra gehwylc
faran scolde tō lǣranne. Segþ þæt sē ēadiga Mathēus
gehlēat tō Marmadonia þǣre ceastre; segð þonne þæt þā   *5*
men þe on þǣre ceastre wǣron þæt hī hlāf ne ǣton, nē
wæter ne druncon, ac ǣton mana līchaman and heora
blōd druncon; and ǣghwylc man þe on þǣre ceastre cōm
ælþēodisc, segð þæt hīe hine sōna genāmon and his ēagan
ūt āstungon, and hīe him sealdon āttor drincan þæt mid   *10*
myclum lybcræfte wæs geblanden, and mid þȳ þe hīe
þone drenc druncon, hraþe heora heorte wæs tōlēsed and
heora mōd onwended. Sē ēadiga Mathēus þā in ēode on
þā ceastre, and hraðe hīe hine genāmon and his ēagan
ūt āstungon, and hīe him sealdon āttor drincan, and hine   *15*
sendon on carcerne, and hīe hine hēton þæt āttor etan,
and hē hit etan nolde; for þon his heorte næs tōlēsed,
nē his mōd onwended; ac hē wæs simle tō Drihtne biddende mid myclum wōpe, and cwæð tō him, 'Mīn Drihten
Hǣlend Crīst, for þon wē ealle forlēton ūre cnēorisse,   *20*
and wǣron þē fylgende, and þū eart ūre ealra fultum, þā
þe on þē gelȳfaþ, beheald nū and geseoh hū þās men
þīnum þēowe dōð. And ic þē bidde, Drihten, þæt þū mē
forgife mīnra ēagna lēoht, þæt ic gesēo þā þe mē onginnað
dōn on þisse ceastre þā weorstan tintrego; and ne for-   *25*
lǣt mē, mīn Drihten Hǣlend Crīst, nē mē ne sele on
þone bitterestan dēaþ.'
    Mid þȳ þe hē þis gebed sē ēadiga Mathēus gecweden
hæfde, mycel lēoht and beorht onlēohte þæt carcern,
and Drihtnes stefn wæs geworden tō him on þǣm   *30*
lēohte cweþende, 'Mathēus, mīn sē lēofa, beheald on mē.'
Mathēus þā lōciende hē geseah Drihten Crīst, and
eft Drihtnes stefn wæs geworden tō him cweþende,
'Mathēus, wes þū gestrangod, and ne ondrǣd þū þē, for
þon ne forlǣte ic þē ǣfre, ac ic þē gefrēolsige of ealre   *35*
frēcennesse, and nālæs þæt ān, ac simle ealle þīne brō-
ðor, and ealle þā þe on mē gelȳfað on eallum tīdum oþ

Reprinted from *Bright's Anglo-Saxon Reader,* revised and enlarged, by J. R. Hulbert, by permission
of Holt, Rinehart and Winston, Inc.

ēcnesse. Ac onbīd hēr seofon and twēntig nihta, and
æfter þon ic sende tō þē Andrēas, þīnne brōþor, and hē
þē ūt ālǣdeþ of þissum carcerne, and ealle þā þe mid þē   *40*
syndon.' Mid þȳ þe þis gecweden wæs, Drihten him
eft tō cwæð, 'Sib sī mid þē, Mathēus.' Hē þā þurhwuniende mid gebedum wæs Drihtnes lof singende on þām
carcerne. And þā unrihtan men in ēodon on þæt carcern þæt hīe þā men ūt lǣdan woldon and him tō mete   *45*
dōn. Sē ēadiga Mathēus þā betȳnde his ēagan þȳ lǣs þā
cwelleras gesāwan þæt his ēagan geopenede wǣron; and
hīe cwǣdon him betwȳnum, 'Þrȳ dagas nū tō lāfe syndon
þæt wē hine willað ācwellan and ūs tō mete gedōn.'

ABBREVIATIONS USED

acc.–accusative	*pers.*–person
(*adv.*)–adverb	*persl.*–personal
art.–article	*pl.*–plural
comb.–in combination with	(*poss. adj.*)–possessive adjective
comp.–comparative	(*poss. pron.*)–possessive pronoun
(*conj.*)–conjunction	*p. ptc.*–past participle
dat.–dative	(*prep.*)–preposition
demons.–demonstrative	*pres.*–present
f.–feminine	*pret.*–preterite
gen.–genitive	(*pron.*)–pronoun
ger.–gerund	(*prop. n.*)–proper noun
imp.–imperative	*pr. ptc.*–present participle
ind.–indicative	*rel. part.*–relative particle
inf.–infinitive	*sg.*–singular
m.–masculine	*subj.*–subjunctive
n.–neuter	*supl.*-superlative
(*n.*)–noun	*v.*–vide
neg. part.–negative particle	(*v.*)–verb
nom.–nominative	*w.*–with
(*num.*)–numeral	

GLOSSARY

The order is alphabetic, *æ* occurring between *ad* and *af*, and *ð* or *þ* occurring after *t*.

Each word in the text (with the line in the text where it occurs) is cited here, although in many instances an instruction will be given to look elsewhere. For example, the entry for ælþēodisc, in line 9, reads: **ælþēodisc,** v. *elþēodisc.* Under *elþēodisc* the definition of *ælþēodisc* will be found. Where several Modern English (MnE) equivalents for Old English (OE) words are cited, choose the word which makes for the most appropriate translation.

Since the object of this exercise is to enable you to construct a reliable comparison of OE syntax with MnE syntax, a certain amount of grammatical information is also cited with each word: part of speech, gender, case, and number, where applicable, and tense, person, number, and mood, where applicable. Some unusual constructions, or combinations of words, are also explained.

ac (*conj.*), but, unless: 7, 18, 35, 36, 38.

ācwellan (*v.*), kill: *inf.*, 49.

æfre (*adv.*), ever: 35.

æfter (*prep. w. dat., adv.*), after [a time or place]: *comb.*, æfter þām þe, at a time after, 1; æfter þon, after that time, 39.

æghwilc (*adj., pron.*), each, every: *nom. sg.*, 8.

æghwylc, *v.* æghwilc.

ælþēodisc, *v.* elþēodisc.

ǣton, *v.* etan.

ætsomne (*adv.*), together: 2.

ālǣdan (*v.*), lead, conduct: *3 sg. pres. ind.*, 40.

ālǣdeþ, *v.* ālǣdan.

ān (*adj., num.*), one, a certain one, alone: *comb.* þæt ān, only that, 36.

and (*conj.*), and: 2, 7, etc. (total of 34 occurrences).

Andrēas (*prop. n.*), St. Andrew: 39.

apostol (*n.*), apostle: *m. nom. pl.*, 2.

apostoli, *v.* apostol.

āstāh, *v.* āstīgan.

āstīgan (*v.*), ascend, mount: *3 sg. pret. ind.*, 2.

āstingan (*v.*), pierce, pluck: *3 pl. preṫ. ind.*, 10, 15.

āstungon, *v.* āstingan.

āttor (*n.*), poison: *n. acc. sg.*, 10, 15, 16.

beheald, *v.* behealdan.

behealdan (*v.*), hold, guard, protect, behold, look: *imp. 2 sg.*, 22, 31.

bēon (*v.*), be: (eart: are) *2 sg. pres. ind.*, 21; (næs = ne + wæs: was not) *3 sg. pret. ind.*, 17; (sī: be) *2 sg. imp.*, 42; (syndon: are) *pl. pres. ind.*, 41, 48; (wǣron: were) *pl. pret. ind.*, 2, 6, 21, 47; (wæs: was) *3 sg. pret. ind.*, 11, 12, 18, 30, 33, 41, 43; (wes: be) *2 sg. imp.*, 34.

beorht (*adj.*), bright, shining, glorious: *nom. sg.*, 29.

betwēonum (*prep. w. dat.*), among, between: 3, 48.

betwȳnum, *v.* betwēonum.

betȳnan (*v.*), close, finish, enclose, imprison: *3 sg. pret. ind.*, 46.

betȳnde, *v.* betȳnan.

biddan (*v.*), ask, entreat, request (*used w. acc. of pers. and gen. of things*): *1 sg. pres. ind.*, 23; *pr. ptc.*, 18.

bidde, *v.* biddan.

biddende, *v.* biddan.

biter (*adj.*), bitter, disastrous, fierce, severe: *supl. acc. sg.*, 27.

bitterestan, *v.* biter.

blōd (*n.*), blood: *n. acc. sg.*, 8.

brōþor (*n.*), brother: *m. acc. pl.*, 36; *m. acc. sg.*, 39.

carcern (*n.*), prison: *n. acc. sg.*, 29, 44; *n. dat. sg.*, 16, 40, 44.

carcerne, *v.* carcern.

ceaster (*n.*), city, fort, town: *f. dat. sg.*, 5, 6, 8, 25; *f. acc. sg.*, 14.

ceastre, *v.* ceaster.

cnēoriss (*n.*), family, generation, people, tribe: *f. acc. sg.*, 20.

cnēorisse, *v.* cnēoriss.

cōm, *v.* cuman.

Crist (*prop. n.*), Christ: *comb.* Drihten Hǣlend Crīst, Lord Saviour Christ, 1, 20, 26; *comb.* Drihten Crīst, Lord Christ, 32.

cuman (*v.*), come: *3 sg. pret. ind.*, 8.

cwǣdon, *v.* cweðan.

cwæð, *v.* cweðan.

cwelleras, *v.* cwellere.

cwellere (*n.*), executioner: *m. nom. pl.*, 47.

cweðan (*v.*), say, speak: *3 pl. pret. ind.*, 48; *3 sg. pret. ind.*, 19, 42; *pr. ptc.*, 31, 33.

cweþende, *v.* cweðan.

dæg (*n.*), day: *m. nom. pl.*, 48.

dagas, *v.* dæg.

dēaþ (*n.*), death; *m. acc. sg.*, 27.

dōn (*v.*), act, cause, do, place, put: *inf.*, 25, 46; *3 pl. pres. ind.*, 23.

dōð, *v.* dōn.

drenc (*n.*), drink: *m. acc. sg.*, 12.

drihten (*n.*), Lord, prince, ruler: *m. acc. sg.*, 23; *m. nom. sg.*, 41; *m. dat. sg.*, 18; *m. gen. sg.*, 30, 33, 43; *comb.* Crīst, Hǣlend, *v.* Crīst.

drihtne, *v.* drihten.

drihtnes, *v.* drihten.

drincan (*v.*), drink: *inf.*, 10. 15; *3 pl. pret. ind.*, 7, 8, 12.

druncon, *v.* drincan.

ēadig (*adj.*), blessed, happy, rich: *nom. sg.*, 4, 13, 28, 46.

ēadiga, *v.* ēadig.

ēagan, *v.* ēage.

ēage (*n.*), eye: *n. gen. pl.*, 24, 46, 47; *n. acc. pl.*, 9, 14.

ēagna, *v.* ēage.

eall (*adj.*), all; *nom. pl.*, 36, 37, 40; *gen. pl.*, 21, 35; *dat. pl.*, 37; (*adv.*), totally, completely: 20.

ealle, *v.* eall.

ealra, *v.* eall.

ealre, *v.* eall.

eallum, *v.* eall.

eart, *v.* bēon.

ēcnes (*n.*), eternity: *f. acc. sg.*, 38.

ēcnesse, *v.* ēcnes.

eft (*adv.*), again, afterwards, back: 33, 42.

elþēodisc (*adj.*), foreign, strange: *nom. sg.*, 9.

ēode, *v.* gān.

ēodon, *v.* gān.

etan (*v.*), eat: *inf.*, 16, 17; *3 pl. pret. ind.*, 6, 7.

faran (*v.*), go, march, travel: *inf.*, 4.

folgian (*v.*), follow, serve, obey: *pr. ptc.*, 21.

for (*prep. w. dat. & acc., conj.*), for, on account of: 20; *comb.* for þon, therefore, 17; *comb.* for þon, because, 34.

forgiefan (*v.*), give, grant, forgive: *2 sg. pres. subj.*, 24.

forgife, *v.* forgiefan.

forlǣt, *v.* forlǣtan.

forlǣtan (*v.*), leave, abandon, neglect: *1 sg. pres. ind.*, 35; *3 sg. pres. ind.*, 25; *3 pl. pret. ind.*, 20.

forlǣte, *v.* forlǣtan.

forlēton, *v.* forlǣtan.

frēcennes (*n.*), danger, harm: *f. dat. sg.*, 36.

frēcennesse, *v.* frēcennes.

fultum (*n.*), army, help: *m. nom. sg.*, 21.

fylgende, *v.* folgian.

gān (*v.*), go, walk, come: *3 sg. pret. ind.*, 13; *3 pl. pret. ind.*, 44.

gebed (*n.*), prayer: *n. acc. sg.*, 28; *n. dat. pl.*, 43.

gebedum, *v.* gebed.

geblandan (*v.*), blend, mix: *p. ptc.*, 11.

geblanden, *v.* geblandan.

gecweden, *v.* gecweðan.

gecweðan (*v.*), say, speak: *p. ptc.*, 28, 41.

gedōn (*v.*), do, cause to be, put into a certain condition: *inf.*, 49.

gefrēolsian (*v.*), deliver, set free: *1 sg. pres. ind.*, 35.

gefrēolsige, *v.* gefrēolsian.

gehlēat, *v.* gehlēotan.

gehlēotan (*v.*), cast or draw lots: *3 sg. pret. ind.*, 5.

gehwylc, gehwilc (*adj., pron.*), each, each one: 3.

gelīefan (*v.*), believe: *3 pl. pres. ind.*, 22, 37.

gelȳfað, *v.* gelīefan.

gelȳfaþ, *v.* gelīefan.

genāmon, *v.* geniman.

geniman (*v.*), take, seize; *3 pl. pret. ind.*, 9, 14.

geopenede, *v.* geopenian.

geopenian (*v.*), open: *pl. p. ptc.*, 47.

gesāwan, *v.* gesēon.

geseah, *v.* gesēon.

gesēo, *v.* gesēon.

geseoh, *v.* gesēon.

gesēon (*v.*), see, observe, consider: *3 pl. pret. ind.*, 47; *3 sg. pret. ind.*, 32; *1 sg. subj.*, 24; *2 sg. imp.*, 22.

gestrangian (*v.*), strengthen: *p. ptc.*, 34.

gestrangod, *v.* gestrangian.

geworden, *v.* geweorþan.

geweorþan (*v.*), happen, become, come to pass, make known: *p. ptc.*, 30, 33.

habban (*v.*), have: *3 sg. pret. ind.*, 29.
hæfde, *v.* habban.
Hǣlend (*n.*), Saviour: *v.* Crīst.
hātan (*v.*), command, order: *3 pl. pret. ind.*, 16.
hē, hēo, hit (*3 persl. pron.*), he, she, it: (hē: he), *m. nom. sg.*, 17, 18, 28, 32, 39, 42; (heora: their), *gen. pl.*, 7, 12, 13; (hī: they), *nom. pl.*, 6; (hīe: they), *nom. pl.*, 3, 9, 10, 11, 14, 15, 16, 45, 48; (him: to him), *m. dat. sg.*, 3, 10, 15, 19, 30, 33, 41, 45, 48; (hine: him), *m. acc. sg.*, 9, 14, 15, 16, 49; (his: his), *m. gen. sg.*, 9, 14, 17, 18, 46, 47; (hit: it), *m. acc. sg.*, 17; (hyra: their), *gen. pl.*, 3.
heofon (*n.*), heaven: *m. dat. pl.*, 2.
hoefonum, *v.* heofon.
heora, *v.* hē,
heorte (*n.*), heart: *f. gen. pl.*, 12; *f. gen. sg.*, 17.
hēr (*adv.*), here: 1, 38.
hēton, *v.* hātan.
hi, *v.* hē.
hie, *v.* hē.
him, *v.* hē.
hine, *v.* hē.
his, *v.* hē.
hit, *v.* hē.
hlāf (*n.*), bread, loaf: *m. acc. sg.*, 6.
hlot (*n.*), lot: *n. acc. sg.*, 3; *comb.* sendon hlot, cast lots, 3.
hraðe, *v.* hraþe.
hraþe (*adv.*), quickly, soon: 12, 14.
hū (*adv.*), how: 22.
hwider (*adv.*), whither, to what place: 3.
hyra, *v.* hē.

ic (*1st persl. pron.*), I: (ic: I), *nom. sg.*, 23, 24, 35, 39; (mē: to or on me), *dat. sg.*, 23, 24, 31, 37; (mē: me), *acc. sg.*, 26; (mīn: my), *gen. sg.*, 19, 26, 31; (ūre: our), *gen. pl.*, 20, 21; (ūs: to or for us), *dat. pl.*, 49; (wē: we), *nom. pl.*, 20, 49.
in (*prep. w. dat. & acc.*), in, into: 13, 44.

lǣdan (*v.*), bring, conduct, lead: *inf.*, 45.
lǣran (*v.*), teach, advise: *ger.* (tō lǣranne), 4.

lǣs (*comp. adv.*), less: *comb.* þy lǣs (*conj.*), lest, 46.
lāf (*n.*), remainder: *f. dat. sg. comb.* tō lāfe, remaining, 48.
lāfe, *v.* lāf.
lēof (*adj.*), beloved, dear: *nom. sg.*, 31.
lēofa, *v.* lēof.
lēoht (*n.*), brightness, light: *n. acc. sg.*, 24; *n. nom. sg.*, 29; *n. dat. sg.*, 31.
lēohte, *v.* leoht.
lichaman, *v.* līchoma.
lichoma (*n.*), body: *m. gen. sg.*, 7.
lōcian (*v.*), look: *pres. ptc.*, 32.
lōciende, *v.* lōcian.
lof (*n.*), praise, glory, song of praise: *m. acc. sg.*, 43.
lybcræft (*n.*), skillful use of drugs or poison: *m. dat. sg.*, 11.
lybcræfte, *v.* lybcræft.

man, *v.* monn.
manna, *v.* monn.
Marmadonia (*prop. n.*), said to be a city among the anthropophagi: 5.
Mathēus (*prop. n.*), St. Matthew: 4, 13, 28, 31, 32, 34, 42, 46.
mē, *v.* ic.
men, *v.* monn.
mete (*n.*), meat, food: *m. dat. sg.*, 45, 49.
micel (*adj.*), much, great, large: *nom. sg.*, 29; *dat. sing.*, 11, 19.
mid (*prep. w. dat. & acc.*), with: 10, 19, 40, 42, 43; *comb.* mid þȳ þe, when, 11, 28, 41.
min, *v.* ic.
minra (*poss. adj.*), my, mine; *gen. pl.*, 24.
mōd (*n.*), mind, mood, courage: *n. nom. sg.*, 13, 18.
monn (*n.*), man: *m. nom. sg.*, 8; *m. gen. pl.*, 7; *m. nom. pl.*, 6, 22, 44; *m. acc. pl.*, 45.
mycel, *v.* micel.
myclum, *v.* micel.

næs, *v.* bēon.
nālæs (*adv.*), not at all: 36.
ne (*neg. part.*), not: 6, 7, 25, 26, 34, 35.
nē (*adj., conj.*), and not, nor: 6, 18, 26.

niht (*n.*), night: *f. gen. pl.*, 38. (Literally 'of nights;' i.e., a number of days.)
nihta, *v.* niht.
nolde, *v.* willan.
nū (*adv.*), now: 22, 48.

of (*prep. w. dat.*), of, from, concerning, among: 35, 40.
on (*prep. w. dat. & acc.*), on, at, in, during, into, among, against: 6, 8, 13, 16, 22, 25, 26, 30, 31, 37, 43, 44.
onbid, *v.* onbīdan.
onbīdan (*v.*), abide, wait, tarry: *2 sg. imp.*, 38.
ondrǣd, *v.* ondrǣdan.
ondrǣdan (*v.*), fear: *2 sg. imp.*, 34.
onginnan (*v.*), begin, attempt: *3 pl. pres. ind.*, 24.
onginnaᚦ, *v.* onginnan.
onlēohte, *v.* onlȳhtan.
onlȳhtan (*v.*), enlighten, illuminate: *3 sg. pret. ind.*, 29.
onwendan (*v.*), turn, change, overturn, amend: *p. ptc.*, 13, 18.
onwended, *v.* onwendan.
oþ (*prep. w. acc.*), up to, as far as, until: 37.

scolde, *v.* sculan.
sculan (*v.*), shall, ought, be necessary: *3 sg. pret. ind.*, 4.
sē (*art. & demons. pron.*), the, that: (sē: the, that), *m. nom. sg.*, 4, 13, 28, 31, 46; (þā: the, that, those), *f. acc. sg.*, 14; *nom. pl.*, 2, 5, 21, 24, 37, 46, 48; *acc. pl.*, 25, 45; (*comb.* þā þe, *v.* þe.); (þām: the, that, those), *n. dat. sg.*, 43; (þǣm: the, that, those), *n. dat. sg.*, 30; (þǣre: the, that), *f. dat. sg.*, 5, 6, 8; (þæt: the, that), *n. acc. sg.*, 16, 29, 44; (*comb.* þæt an, *v.* an); (þon: whom), *rel. pron.*, 20; (þon, *comb.* æfter þon, *v.* æfter); (þone: the, that), *m. acc. sg.*, 12, 27.
sealdon, *v.* sellan.
secgan (*v.*), say, tell: *3 sg., pres. ind.*, 1, 4, 5, 9.
segᚦ, *v.* secgan.
segþ, *v.* secgan.
sele, *v.* sellan.

sellan (*v.*), give, sell: *2 sg. pres. ind.*, 26; *3 pl. pret. ind.*, 10, 15.
sendan (*v.*), send: *1 sg. pres. ind.*, 39; *3 pl. pret. ind.*, 16; sendon hlot, 3, *v.* hlot.
sende, *v.* sendan.
sendon, *v.* sendan.
seofon (*num.*), seven: 38
si, *v.* bēon.
sib (*n.*), friendship, peace: *f. nom. sg.*, 42.
simle, *v.* symble.
singan (*v.*), sing, compose poetry: *pres. ptc.*, 43.
singende, *v.* singan.
sona (*adv.*), at once, immediately: 9.
stefn (*n.*), voice, sound: *f. nom. sg.*, 30, 33.
symble (*adv.*), ever, always: 18, 36.
syndon, *v.* bēon.

tid (*n.*), time, hour, tide: *f. dat. pl.*, 37.
tidum, *v.* tīd.
tintreg (*n.*), torment, torture: *n. acc. pl.*, 25.
tintrego, *v.* tintreg.
tō (*prep. w. dat.*), to, at, for: 1, 5, 18, 19, 30, 33, 39, 42, 45, 49; tō lāfe, *v.* lāf; *signal of gerund,* tō lǣranne, *v.* lǣran.
tōlēsed, *v.* tōlȳsan.
tōlȳsan (*v.*), unhinge, loosen, relax: *p. ptc.*, 12, 17.
twēntig (*num.*), twenty: 38.

þā (*adv., conj.*), then, when: 13, 32, 42, 44, 46.
þā, *v.* sē.
þǣm, *v.* sē.
þǣre, *v.* sē.
þæt (*conj.*), that, so that: 1, 2, 4, 5, 6, 9, 10, 23, 24, 45, 47, 49; *comb.* þæt ān, *v.* ān.
þæt, *v.* sē.
þām, *comb.* after þām þe, *v.* æfter.
þām, *v.* sē.
þās, *v.* þēs.
þe (*rel. part.*), who: 6, 8, 22, 24, 37, 40; *comb.* æfter þām þe, *v.* æfter; *comb.* mid þȳ þe, *v.* mid; *comb.* þā þe, those: 37.
þē, *v.* þū.
þēow (*n.*), servant: *m. dat. sg.*, 23.

þēowe, v. þēow.

þēs (*demons. pron.*), this: (þās: these), *nom. pl.*, 22; (þis: this), *n. acc. sg.*, 28; *n. nom. sg.*, 41; (þisse: this), *f. dat. sg.*, 25; (þissum: this), *m. dat. sg.*, 40.

þin (*poss. pron.*), thine, your: þīne, *acc. pl.*, 36; þīnne, *acc. sg.*, 39; þīnum, *dat. sg.*, 23.

þon, v. æfter, for, sē; *comb.* for þon, because, 34; *comb.* for þon, therefore, 17.

þone, v. sē.

þonne (*adv.*), then: 5.

þri (*num.*), three: 48.

þrȳ, v. þrī.

þū (*2 persl. pron.*), you: (þū: you), *nom. sg.*, 21, 23, 34; (þē: you, thee), *acc. sg.*, 21, 23, 34, 35, 40; (þē: you, thee), *dat. sg.*, 22, 39, 40, 42.

þurhwunian (*v.*), continue, be steadfast: *pr. ptc.*, 42.

þurhwuniende, v. þurhwunian.

þȳ, v. læs, mid.

unriht (*adj.*), wicked, wrong: *nom. pl.*, 44.

unrihtan, v. unriht.

ūre, v. ic.

ūs, v. ic.

ūt (*adv.*), out: 10, 15, 40, 45.

wǣron, v. bēon.

wæs, v. bēon.

wæter (*n.*), water: *n. acc. sg.*, 7.

wē, v. ic.

weorstan, v. yfel.

wes, v. bēon.

willan (*v.*), will, wish, be about to: *1 pl. pres. ind.*, 49; *3 pl. pret. ind.*, 45; nolde (*comb.* ne *plus* willan), *3 sg. pret. ind.*, 17.

willað, v. willan.

woldon, v. willan.

wōp (*n.*), weeping, lamentation: *m. dat. sg.*, 19.

wōpe, v. wōp.

yfel (*adj.*), evil, bad: *supl. acc. pl.* (weorstan), 25.

QUESTIONS

The first thing you might notice about the text is that a good many of the letters have a dash printed above them; e.g., *þām* and *tō*, in line 1. It is a macron, a diacritical mark over a vowel or diphthong to indicate that it is 'long.' At this time ignore it; it will be of use when you turn to the exercise on phonology. Modern editions of Old English texts contain this marking; it is not used in editions of Middle English or Early Modern English texts.

1. Translate the passage into Modern English. First make a literal, word-for-word rendering; then transcribe into your normal composition. At first glance this might seem a formidable task, but by using the glossary wisely you will find it less frightening. The first two lines are worked out in this manner:

a. List all the words	b. List grammatical information and equivalents	
hēr	adv.	here
segð	3 sg. pres. ind.	says, tells
þæt	conj. or v. sē	that or the, that
after ⎫		
þām ⎬	adverbial	at a time after
þe ⎭		
Drihten ⎫		
Hǣlend ⎬	prop. n.	Lord Saviour Christ
Crīst ⎭		

tō	prep. or signal for ger.	to, at, for (or ger.)
heofonum	n., masc. dat. pl.	heavens
āstāh	3 sg. pret. ind.	ascended, mounted
þæt	conj. or v. sē	that or the, that
þā	adv., conj. or v. sē	then, when, or the
apostolī	n., masc. nom. pl.	apostles
wǣron	pl. pret. ind, bēon	were
ætsomne	adv.	together

c. Construct the first string—same word order as original—here (says, tells) (that, the) at a time after Lord Saviour Christ (to, at, for) heavens (ascended, mounted) (that, the) (then, when, the) apostles were together

d. Find each verb and its subject; we know the nominative case is the case for the subject
says, tells—?
ascended, mounted—Lord Saviour Christ
were—apostles

e. Eliminate, making use of your sense of context, what appear to be unlikely lexical choices
says—tells: either will do, choose one
that—the: 'the' cannot precede 'at a time after'; retain *that*
to—at—for: which fits best with the next verb? probably *to*
ascended—mounted: either will do, but *ascended* feels better
that—the: consider the next group; 'the' cannot precede 'any'; retain *that*
then—when—the: all can precede 'apostles,' but if 'when' or 'then' is selected, we should expect something to occur after 'together'; retain *the*

f. Construct the second string
here says that at a time after Lord Saviour Christ to heavens ascended that the apostles were together

g. We have not yet found a subject for 'says'; *here* cannot be the subject; supply *it*; such a construction is not unusual in OE

h. Articles do not always occur in OE where, in a similar MnE construction, we expect them to occur. Is there a noun here without an article where we would expect it? We would insert *the* before *heavens*. (Note: if it were 'heaven,' i.e., singular, MnE would not require an article; but it is plural, *heavens,* and therefore the article is required.) We may or may not choose to insert an article before *Lord Saviour Christ*. These, too, are not unusual constructions in OE

i. Construct the third string
here it says that at a time after the Lord Saviour Christ to the heavens ascended that the apostles were together

j. Rearrange the word order where you think MnE usage would suggest reordering and insert punctuation
It says here that at a time after the Lord Saviour Christ ascended to the heavens, that the apostles were together;

k. Do not worry about the antecedent of *it*. The translation is correct. The writer apparently is following the habit set by many writers of chronicles, who often begin with "It says here" or something like this: *Hēr gefeaht Ecgbryht cyning,* In this year (here) King Ecgbryht fought. The *it* may refer to some other document, real or imagined, or the writer may, as we have said, just be falling back on the habit of chroniclers

There is no real need to set down the results of your work in this eleven step format. The format is a representation of what actually must be done in order to translate the passage. You must consult the glossary, you must observe the grammatical information given there, and you must arrive at an accurate MnE rendering of the original text. Whatever short cuts you find, take them. Translate the rest of the passage. (Do not be discouraged if it takes you a few hours to do it. It is not unwise, either, for several persons to work together, so long as it is understood that each comes away from such an exercise with a comprehension, and some knowledge, of OE directly proportionate to the effort he expended. This next remark has nothing whatsoever to do with either this exercise or anything you do with this book; it is simply a corollary pronouncement. Nobody can *teach* anybody a second language, or how to read a second language: teachers can set out models and guides, but anyone who wishes to *learn* to *use* a second language has to *learn* it himself.)

2. Make a list showing each verb with its subject. Supply *hit* for *segð*. What does the verb inflectional ending -*on* signify? What does the verb inflectional ending -*an* signify? What do you make of the form *gesawan* in 1. 47? How do you explain it? Consult the glossary where necessary.

3. The personal endings for strong and weak verbs in the present and preterite indicative are shown in the following list:

Strong (and Weak, Class I)   *Weak, Class II*

Pres. Ind.

Sg. 1	-e	-ie
Sg. 2	-est	-ast
Sg. 3	-eþ	-aþ
Pl. 1, 2, 3	-aþ	-iaþ

Pret. Ind.

Sg. 1	-	-e
Sg. 2	-e	-est
Sg. 3	-	-e
Pl. 1, 2, 3	-on	-on

Find as many examples from the text to match the slots in this paradigm. Which slots are vacant? Do you find any occurrences of verbs which you cannot fit in any slot? What is the construction of *forgife* in 1. 24? What conclusion does this occurrence suggest? Consult the glossary where necessary.

4. Compare the constructions observed in questions 2 and 3 with their corresponding forms in MnE: write out several complete conjugations of MnE verbs, fitting the paradigm used in question 3. What differences do you observe between

the MnE and the OE paradigms? What can you conclude about the development of these verb forms from the OE period to the MnE period?

5. Set out all the forms of *bēon* which occur in the text in paradigmatic form and place their MnE equivalent forms next to them. What has been the development of 'be'? Would you say 'be' has been more or less stable than the strong and weak verbs?

6. Make a list of all verbal negation and interrogatory constructions and compare each with its MnE construction. What differences do you observe? Formulate a general statement about the function of the MnE 'carrier' (or auxilliary) 'do' in negative and interrogatory constructions. Would you say English has become more or less efficient in this regard?

7. The concept of substitution of linguistic forms is easily demonstrated by the occurrence of pronouns in MnE. For example, a) 'When John fell *he* hurt his knee' and b) 'When John fell *John* hurt his knee' have equivalent meaning. We can also say that pro-*verbs* occur in MnE; for example, a) 'I often run and so does John' and b) 'I often run and so does John run' have equivalent meaning, c) 'I don't run but John does' and d) 'I don't run but John runs' have equivalent meaning, and e) 'I have never run but John has' and f) 'I have never run but John has run' have equivalent meaning. These are occurrences of pro-verbs. Are there any occurrences of the pro-verb in OE?

8. Which nouns occur with articles? which without? Compare those occurrences with MnE practise.

9. Observe the occurrence of adjectives and adverbs. Are the modification patterns (the position of the modifier with respect to the word or element modified) similar or dissimilar to corresponding MnE practise?

10. How are relative patterns constructed in OE? Do you find any occurrence here of the practise in MnE of omitting the relative marker? (E.g., 'This is the man I saw' is equivalent in meaning to 'This is the man *whom* I saw.')

11. In the original text the word *and* occurs 34 times. In an accurate MnE translation of the passage, what might be the minimum occurrence of 'and'? What does this suggest about OE syntax?

12. In Exercise 14, "Phonological Change," you will see the text of "The Legend of St. Andrew" again. There the text is 'normalized,' i.e., the editor put the text into the form of Late West Saxon used by Alfred. Compare the two texts. What differences in spelling occur? What do those differences suggest? (What is a dialect? How may one dialect differ from another? If you were an editor, would you choose to normalize a text? Why?)

13. Consult your 'final' translation of this passage and compare it with the original text. If this were the only sample of OE you could examine, if there were no other data to consult, what would you say constitutes the most significant differences between OE and MnE? (There is a suggestion here, of course, for an essay or a class discussion—only to be followed at great risk, however, before the first twelve questions are answered.)

THE LEGEND OF ST. ANDREW
lines 50–96

Se eadiga Matheus þa gefelde xx   daga. Þa Drihten Hælend Crist
the blessed Matthew then filled   twenty days then Lord   Savior   Christ

cwæð to Andrea his apostole, mid þi þe he wæs in Achaia þam lande and
said   to Andrew his apostle   when he was in Achaia the land   and

þær lærde his discipuli, he cwæð, 'Gang on Marmadonia ceastre, and alæd
there taught his disciples he said   go   to Marmadonia city   and lead

þanon Matheum þinne broþor of   þæm carcerne, for þon þe nu git þry
thence Matthew your brother from the   prison   because   now still three

dagas to lafe   syndon, þæt hie   hine willað acwellan and him to mete
days remaining are   that they him will   kill   and him to meat   5

gedon.' Se haliga Andreas him andswarode, and he cwæð, 'Min Drihten
do   the holy   Andrew him answered   and he said   my Lord

Hælend Crist, hu mæg ic hit on þrim dagum gefaran? Ac ma   wen is
Savior   Christ how might I it in three days   travel   but better hope is

þæt þu onsende þinne engel se   hit mæg hrædlicor   gefaran, for þon,
that you will send your   angel who it   might more readily travel   because

min Drihten, þu wast þæt ic eam flæsclic man, and ic hit ne mæg hrædlice
my Lord   you know that I am fleshly man and I it   not might readily

gefaran, for þon þe, min Drihten, se siðfæt is þider to lang, and ic
travel   because   my Lord   the journey is thither too long and I   10

þone weg ne can.' Drihten him to cwæð, 'Andreas, geher me for þon þe ic þe
the   way not know Lord   him to said   Andrew   hear me because   I you

geworhte, and ic þinne sið   gestaþelode and getrymede. Gang nu to þæs sæs
made   and I your journey established   and prepared   go   now to the sea's

waroðe mid þinum discipulum, and þu þær gemetest scip on þam waroðe;
shore with your   disciples   and you there will meet ship on the   shore

and astig on þæt mid þinum discipulum.' And mid þy þe he þis cwæð,
and mount on that with your   disciples   and when   he this said

Drihten Hælend ða git wæs sprecende and cwæð, 'Sib   mid þe and mid
Lord   Savior   then still was speaking   and said   peace [be] with you and   15

Reprinted from *Bright's Anglo-Saxon Reader*, revised and enlarged by J. R. Hulbert, by permission of Holt, Rinehart and Winston, Inc.

eallum þinum discipulum.' And he astag   on   heofonas.
with   all your disciples   and he ascended to [the] heavens

  Se haliga Andreas þa   aras on mergen, and he eode to þære sæ mid
  the holy   Andrew then arose next morning and he went to the   sea with

his discipulum, and he geseah scip on þam waroðe and þry weras on þam
his disciples   and he saw   ship on the   shore   and three men   in it

sittende; and he wæs gefeonde mid mycle gefean, and him to cwæð, 'Broðor,
sitting   and he was rejoicing with great delight and them to said   brothers

hwider wille ge   faran mid þis medmiclum scipe?' Drihten Hælend wæs
whither will   you travel with this small   ship   Lord   Savior   was   20

on þam scipe swa se steorreðra, and his twegen englas mid him, þa
on the   ship as   the helmsman and his two   angels   with him who

wæron gehwyrfede   on manna onsyne. Drihten Crist him þa   to cwæð, 'On
were   transformed   in men's shape   Lord   Christ him then to said   to

Marmadonia ceastre.' Se haliga Andreas him andswarode, and he cwæð,
Marmadonia city   the holy   Andrew him answered   and he said

'Broðor, onfoh us mid eow on þæt scip and gelædað us on þa ceastre.'
brothers take   us with you in that ship and lead   us to the city

Drihten him to cwæð, 'Ealle men fleoð of   þære ceastre; to hwæm wille
Lord   him to said   all   men flee from the city   why   will   25

ge þider faran?' Se haliga Andreas him andswarode, he cwæð, 'Medmycel
you thither travel   the holy   Andrew him answered   he said   small

ærende we þider habbað, and us   is þearf þæt we hit þeh   gefyllon.'
errand we thither have   and [to] us is need that we it   nonetheless fullfil

Drihten Hælend him to cwæð, 'Astigað on þis scip to   us, and sellað us
Lord   Savior him to said   mount in this ship with us and give   us

eowerne færsceat.' Se haliga Andreas him andswarode, 'Gehyrað
your   fare   the holy   Andrew him answered   hear

gebroðor, nabbað we færsceat, ac we syndon discupli Drihtnes Hælendes
brother   not have we fare   but we are   disciples [of] Lord Savior   30

Cristes, þa   he geceas; and þis bebod   he us sealde, and he cwæð, "þonne
Christ whom he chose and this command he us gave   and he said   when

ge   faren godspel to lærenne, þonne   nabbe ge mid eow hlaf ne feoh,   ne
you travel gospel teaching   then not have you with you bread nor property nor

twifeald hrægl." Gif þu þonne wille mildheortnesse mid us don, saga us
twofold garments if you then   will gentleness with us do tell us

þæt hrædlice; gif þu þonne nelle, gecyð   us swa þeah þone weg.' Drihten
that quickly; if you then   no   will show us nonetheless the   way   Lord

Hælend him to cwæð, 'Gif þis gebod   eow   wære geseald fram eowrum
Savior   them to said   if   this command [to] you were   given   by   our   *35*

Drihtene, astigað hider mid gefean on min scip.'
Lord   climb   hither with joy   in my ship

QUESTIONS

You will notice that in this selection the macron has not been printed to mark the length of vowels and diphthongs.

 1. Rewrite the interlinear translation in your normal composition style.
 2. We may use this passage to illustrate how the grammatical devices of OE differ from the grammatical devices of MnE. A grammatical device is a structural signal inherent in the system of a language which is employed (in oral as well as written communication) by users of the language to indicate relationships which exist between various elements of the language. Syntax is, from this point of view, the study and perception of the grammatical signals, or devices, which a language employs. OE relied heavily on inflection to provide signals of grammatical, or structural meaning. Lexical (referential), or 'dictionary,' meaning of words does not indicate these relationships: structural (differential), or grammatical, meaning is signaled by various devices. In 1. 5, for example, we read *hie hine willað acwellan*. Because we know that *hie* is nom. pl. (and accords with the -*að* of the verb) and that *hine* is acc. sg., we know which is the subject and which is the object, and we know therefore that we must read 'they will kill him.' *Inflections,* then, are a signal. To an extent larger than we often realize, they are also a signal in MnE. For example, 'they' and 'him' in MnE are distinguished by their form. But observe, too, that we cannot say '*they him will kill,' because in this pattern we expect the verb to precede its object, and we therefore say 'they will kill him,' even though, it might be argued, the formal difference between 'they' and 'him' should be a sufficient signal to make sure that we know which is subject and which is object. In this case, as in so many others (fortunately for ease of communication), MnE shows its tendency to display redundant signals. Thus the pattern itself, *word order,* is a grammatical signal. The occurrence, in 1. 12, of *sæs waroðe* (sea's shore), and, in 1. 20, of *manna onsyne* (the shape of men), suggests that the genitive case (and the function that it performs) in OE, signalled by inflection, may, in MnE, be signalled by either word order or by the use of a *function word,* 'of.' In OE the genitive relationship desired between 'sea' and 'shore' could be signaled only by inflection, but in MnE we may signal that same relationship by making use of all three devices:
    inflection—sea's shore
    word order—sea shore ('shore sea' is not equivalent)
    function word—shore of the sea
The very existence of these three devices—inflection, word order, and function word—constitutes an excellent base for a comparison of OE syntax with MnE syntax. (Two other signals familiar to speakers of MnE—*derivational contrast* and *intonation contour*—the differences, that is, between *good* and *goodness,* where -*ness* signals a noun, and between the two occurrences of *suspect* in 'we suspéct the súspect,' that sort of thing, are not taken up in this exercise.)

Examine this passage, and those of Exercises 1 and 3, to determine where MnE usage, in the same compositional situation, would (1) *require* a different signalling system from what you find in the original and (2) where it would *permit* a different signalling system. To make use of contemporary syntactical terms, make a comparison (and write a report setting out your conclusions) of the *obligatory* and *optional* constructions available in OE and MnE composition.

3. Would you say, having completed that study, that the grammar of English has been 'simplified' during the years which separate us from the OE period? Consult Sidney's *Apology for Poetry,* published in 1595, especially where he writes that English 'wanteth (i.e., lacks) grammar.' What do you suppose he might have meant? Was he right?

(Having got you through the first 96 lines of this text—as it is printed in *Bright's Anglo-Saxon Reader*—it is only fair to point out to some of you, who might want to learn what happened to Andrew in Marmadonia—and things get rather interesting for Matthew and Andrew—that you can find translations of the rest of the story; but, give it a thought, some of you could now read the whole text in Old English, and the text is contained in many of the Old English anthologies.)

THE ASSUMPTION OF ST. JOHN THE APOSTLE
Ælfric, ca. 990, lines 1–52

Iōhannes sē godspellere, Crīstes dȳrling, wearð on ðysum
dæge tō heofenan rīces myrhðe þurh Godes nēosunge ge-
numen. Hē wæs Crīstes mōddrian sunu, and hē hine lufode
synderlīce, nā swā micclum for ðære mæglican sibbe swā for
ðære clænnysse his ansundan mægðhādes. Hē wæs on mægð-   5
hāde Gode gecoren, and hē on ēcnysse on ungewemmedum
mægðhāde þurhwunode. Hit is geræd on gewyrdelicum
racum þæt hē wolde wīfian, and Crīst wearð tō his gyftum
gelaðod. Þā gelamp hit þæt æt ðām gyftum wīn wearð
ātēorod. Sē Hælend ðā hēt þā ðēningmen āfyllan six   10
stænene fatu mid hlūttrum wætere, and hē mid his bletsunge
þæt wæter tō æðelum wīne āwende. Þis is þæt forme tācn
ðe hē on his menniscnysse openlīce geworhte. Þā wearð
Iōhannes swā onbryrd þurh þæt tācn, þæt hē ðærrihte his
brȳde on mægðhāde forlēt, and symle syððan Drihtne   15
folgode, and wearð ðā him inweardlīce gelufod, for ðan ðe
hē hine ætbræd þām flæsclicum lustum. Witodlīce ðisum
lēofan leorningcnihte befæste sē Hælend his mōdor, þā þā hē
on rōdehengene manncynn ālȳsde, þæt his clæne līf ðæs
clænan mædenes Marīan gȳmde; and hēo ðā on hyre   20
swyster suna þēnungum wunode.

   Eft on fyrste, æfter Crīstes ūpstige tō heofonum, rīxode
sum wælhrēow cāsere on Rōmāna rīce, æfter Nerōne, sē
wæs Domiciānus gehāten, crīstenra manna ēhtere: sē hēt
āfyllan āne cȳfe mid weallendum ele, and þone mæran   25
godspellere þæron hēt bescūfan; ac hē ðurh Godes gescyldnysse ungewemmed of ðām hātum bæðe ēode. Eft, ðā ðā
sē wælhrēowa ne mihte ðæs ēadigan apostoles bodunge
ālecgan, þā āsende hē hine on wræcsīð tō ānum īgeoðe þe
is Paðmas gecīged, þæt hē ðær þurh hungres scearpnysse   30
ācwæle. Ac sē ælmihtiga Hælend ne forlēt tō gȳmelēaste
his gelufedan apostol, ac geswutelode him on ðām wræcsīðe
þā tōweardan onwrigennysse, be ðære hē āwrāt ðā bōc ðe is
gehāten 'Apocalipsis': and sē wælhrēowa Domiciānus on
ðām ylcan gēare wearð ācweald æt his witena handum;   35
and hī ealle ānmōdlīce ræddon þæt ealle his gesetnyssa
āȳdlode wæron. Þā wearð Nerua, swīðe ārfæst man, tō
cāsere gecoren. Be his geþafunge gecyrde sē apostol

Reprinted from Sweet's *Anglo-Saxon Reader*, revised by C. T. Onions, 14th ed. (Oxford: The
Clarendon Press, 1959), by permission of The Clarendon Press, Oxford.

ongēan mid micclum wurðmynte, sē ðe mid hospe tō
wræcsīðe āsend wæs. Him urnon ongēan weras and wīf   40
fægnigende and cweðende: 'Gebletsod is sē ðe cōm on
Godes naman.'

Mid þām ðe sē apostol Iōhannes stōp intō ðǣre byrig
Ephesum, þā bær man him tōgēanes ānre wydewan līc
tō byrigenne; hire nama wæs Drūsiāna. Hēo wæs swīðe   45
gelȳfed and ælmesgeorn, and þā ðearfan, ðe hēo mid cystigum mōde eallunga āfēdde, drēorige mid wōpe ðām līce
folgodon. Þā hēt sē apostol ðā bǣre settan, and cwæð: 'Mīn
Drihten, Hǣlend Crīst, ārǣre ðē, Drūsiāna; ārīs, and gecyrr
hām, and gearca ūs gereordunge on þīnum hūse.' Drūsiāna   50
þā ārās swilce of slǣpe āwreht, and carfull be ðæs apostoles
hǣse hām gewende.

GLOSSARY

In this glossary words not found in the glossary for "The Legend of St. Andrew"
will be defined *in the order in which they occur,* cited by the line number from the
text. Since only the grammatical information not found in the first glossary is given
here, *both* glossaries may have to be consulted during the course of this exercise.
You should note, by examining the texts closely, that some letters are used interchangeably; e.g., 'i and y' and 'þ and ð' are frequently interchanged. It is
also expected that you will know, in line two, that 'Godes' is the genitive singular
of God, that, in line fifteen, 'forlēt' is certainly the same verb as 'forlǣtan' in the
first glossary, that sort of thing. In other words, you will have learned some OE
by the time you reach this exercise. And, of course, you also have the translations
to help you over rough spots.

1 **Iōhannes** (*prop. n.*), St. John;
godspellere (*n.*), evangelist: *m. nom.
sg.*;**dȳrling** (*n.*), favorite: *m. nom.
sg.*; **wearð**, *3 sg. pret. ind. of* weorþan,
become, be, made, happen, *fre-
quently used as passive auxilliary.*

2 **rices** (*n.*), kingdom: *n. gen. sg.*;
myrhðe (*n.*), mirth, joy: *f. dat. sg.*;
nēosunge (*n.*), visitation: *f. dat.
sg.*

3 **mōddrian** (*n.*), aunt: *f. gen. sg.*; **sunu**
(*n.*), son: *m. acc. sg.*

4 **synderlice** (*adv.*), especially; **mǣglican
sibbe**: relationship of kin.

5 **clǣnnysse** (*n.*), cleanness, purity,
chastity: *f. dat. sg.*; **ansundan** (*adj.*),
sound, uninjured; **mægðhādes** (*n.*),
virginity: *m. gen. sg.*

6 **gecoren**, *p. ptc. of* cēosan, choose;
ungewemmedum (*ptc. as adj.*), undefiled.

7 **gerǣd**, *p. ptc. of* rǣdan, read, advise,
discuss; **gewyrdelicum** (*adj.*),
historical: *dat. pl.*

8 **racum** (*n.*), narrative, account,
reckoning: *f. dat. pl.*; **wifian**, *inf.*, to
marry; **gyftum** (*n.*), dowry, *in pl.*,
marriage, wedding: *f. dat. pl.*

9 **gelaðod**, *p. ptc. of* laðian, invite,
summon; **gelamp**, *3 sg. pret. ind. of*
limpan, happen; **win** (*n.*), wine: *n.
nom. sg.*

10 **āteorod**, *p. ptc. of* āteorian, fail,
become exhausted; **ðēningmen** (*n.*),
servant: *m. acc. pl.*; **āfyllan**, *inf.*, to
fill; **six** (*num.*), six.

11 **stǣnene** (*cf.* stān: stone), of stone;
fatu (*n.*), vessel, jar: *n. acc. pl.*;
hlūttrum (*adj.*), clear: *dat. sg.*;
bletsunge (*n.*), blessing: *f. gen. sg.*

12 **æðelum** (*adj.*), noble, excellent: *dat. sg.*; **āwende**, *3 sg. pret. ind. of* āwendan, turn, change; **forme** (*ordinal num.*), first; **tācn** (*n.*), sign, token, miracle; *n. nom. sg.*

13 **menniscnysse** (*n.*), incarnation: *f. dat. sg.*; **openlice** (*adv.*), publicly, openly; **geworhte**, *3 sg. pret. ind. of* gewyrcan, work, perform.

14 **onbryrd**, *p. ptc. of* onbryrdan, inspire, exhalt; **þǣrrihte** (*adv.*), forthwith, at once.

15 **brȳde** (*n.*), bride: *f. acc. sg.*; **syððan** (*adv., conj.*), since, after that, afterwards.

16 **inweardlice** (*adv.*), inwardly, deeply; **gelufod**, *p. ptc. of* lufian, love.

17 **ætbrǣd**, *3 sg. pret. ind. of* ætbregdan, take away, deprive, release; **flǣsclicum** (*adj.*), fleshly, carnal: *dat. pl.*; **lustum** (*n.*), lust, desire, pleasure: *m. dat. pl.*; **witodlice** (*adv.*), truly, indeed.

18 **leorningcnihte** (*n.*), disciple, pupil: *m. dat. sg.*; **befæste**, *3 sg. pret. ind. of* befæstan, fasten, fix, entrust, put in safe keeping; **mōdor** (*n.*), mother: *f. acc. sg.*

19 **rōdehengene** (*n.*), crucifixion: *f. dat. sg.*; **manncynn** (*n.*), mankind: *n. acc. sg.*; **ālȳsde**, *3 sg. pret. ind. of* ālȳsan, loosen, release, redeem, ransom; **clǣne** (*adj.*), clean, pure: *nom. sg.*; **lif** (*n.*), life: *n. nom. sg.*

20 **mǣdenes** (*n.*), maiden, virgin: *n. gen. sg.*; **Marian** (*prop. n.*), Mary; **gȳmde**, *3 sg. pret. subj. of* gīeman, care for, regard.

21 **swyster** (*n.*), sister: *f. gen. sg.*; **þēnungum** (*n.*), service, ministration: *f. dat. pl.*; **wunode**, *3 sg. pret. ind. of* wunian, dwell, remain, live.

22 **eft on fyrste** (*adverbial*), later on; **upstige** (*n.*), ascension: *m. dat. sg.*;

rixode, *3 sg. pret. ind. of* rīcsian, rule, reign.

23 **sum** (*pron., adj.*), some, some one, certain, certain one: *nom. sg.*; **wælhrēow** (*adj.*), murderous, cruel: *nom. sg.*; **cāsere** (*n.*), emperor: *m. nom. sg.*; **Rōmāna** (*prop. n.*), Roman: *gen. pl.*; **Nerōne** (*prop. n.*), Nero.

24 **Domiciānus** (*prop. n.*), Domitian; **gehāten**, *p. ptc. of* gehātan, name; **cristenra** (*adj.*), Christian: *gen. pl.*; **ēhtere** (*n.*), persecutor: *m. nom. sg.*

25 **āfyllan**, *inf.*, to fill; **cȳfe** (*n.*), tub, vessel: *f. acc. sg.*; **weallendum**, *pres. ptc.* (*used as adj.*) *of* weallan, boil; **ele** (*n.*), oil: *m. dat. sg.*

26 **bescūfan**, *inf.*, to shove, thrust; **gescyldnysse** (*n.*), care, protection: *f. acc. sg.*

27 **ungewemmed** (*p. ptc. as adj.*), undefiled, pure, sound: *dat. pl.*; **hātum** (*adj.*), hot: *dat. sg.*; **bæðe** (*n.*), bath: *n. dat. sg.*

28 **mihte**, *3 sg. pret. subj. of* magan, may, be able; **bodunge** (*n.*), preaching: *f. acc. sg.*

29 **ālecgan**, *inf.*, to refute; **āsende**, *3 sg. pret. ind. of* āsendan, send; **wrǣcsið** (*n.*), exile: *m. dat. sg.*; **igeoðe** (*n.*), small island: *m. dat. sg.*

30 **Paðmas** (*prop. n.*), Patmos: **geciged**, *p. ptc. of* gecīegan, call, name; **hungres** (*n.*), hunger: *m. gen. sg.*; **scearpnysse** (*n.*), sharpness: *f. acc. sg.*

31 **ælmihtiga** (*adj.*), almighty: *nom. sg.*; **gȳmelēaste** (*n.*), neglect: *f. dat. sg.*

32 **geswutelode**, *3 sg. pret. ind. of* geswutelian, show, make manifest.

33 **tōweardan** (*adj.*), future: *acc. sg.*; **onwrigennysse** (*n.*), revelation: *f. acc. sg.*; **be ðære** (*prep.*), on account of which; **āwrāt**, *3 sg. pret. ind. of* āwrītan, write, compose; **bōc** (*n.*), book: *f. acc. sg.*

35 **ylcan** (*pron.*), the same: *dat. sg.*; **gēare** (*n.*), year: *n. dat. sg.*; **witena** (*n.*), councilor: *m. gen. pl.*; **handum** (*n.*), hand: *f. dat. pl.*

36 ānmōdlice (*adv.*), unanimously; **rǣd-don**, *3 pl. pret. ind. of* rǣdan, advise, counsel; **gesetnyssa** (*n.*), decree: *f. acc. pl.*

37 **āȳdlode**, *pl. p. ptc. of* āȳdlian, annul; **Nerua** (*prop. n.*), Nerva; **swiðe** (*adv.*), very, exceedingly; **ārfæst** (*adj.*), honorable, virtuous, merciful: *nom. sg.*

38 **gecoren**, *p. ptc. of* gecēosan, choose, elect; **geþafunge** (*n.*), assent, permission: *f. dat. sg.*; **gecyrde**, *3 sg. pret. ind. of* geciernan, return.

39 **wurðmynte** (*n.*), honor, glory, reverence: *f. dat. sg.*; **hospe** (*n.*), contempt, insult: *m. dat. sg.*

40 **urnon**, *3 pl. pret. ind. of* yrnan, run; **weras** (*n.*), man: *m. nom. pl.*; **wif** (*n.*), woman, wife: *f. nom. pl.*

41 **fægnigende**, *pres. ptc. of* fægnian, rejoice; **gebletsod**, *p. ptc. of* geblētsian, bless.

42 **naman** (*n.*), name: *m. acc. sg.*

43 **stōp**, *3 sg. pret. ind. of* steppan, step, advance, go; **byrig** (*n.*), fort, borough, town, city: *f. dat. sg.*

44 **Ephesum**, (*prop. n.*), Ephesus, ancient city in Ionia, near present city of Selsuk; **bær**, *3 sg. pret. ind. of* beran, bear; **wydewan** (*n.*), widow: *f. gen. sg.*; **lic** (*n.*), corpse, body: *n. acc. sg.*

45 **tō byrigenne**, *ger. of* byrgan, bury; **Drūsiana** (*prop. n.*).

46 **gelȳfed**, *p. ptc. of* gelīefan, believe (filled with belief); **ælmesgeorn** (*adj.*), generous, liberal of alms; **ðearfan** (*n.*), poor man: *m. nom. pl.*; **cystigum** (*adj.*), virtuous, charitable: *d. sg.*

47 **āfēdde**, *3 sg. pret. ind. of* āfēdan, feed, sustain; **drēorige** (*adj.*), sad, dreary: *nom. pl.*

48 **settan**, *inf.*, to set, place.

49 **ārǣre**, *3 sg. pres. subj. of* ārǣran, raise, erect; **āris**, *2 sg. imp. of* ārīsan, arise.

50. **hām** (*n.*), home: *m. acc. sg.*; **gearca**, *2 sg. imp. of* gearcian, prepare; **gereordunge** (*n.*), refection, meal: *f. acc. sg.*; **hūse** (*n.*), house: *n. dat. sg.*

51 **swilce** (*adv., conj.*), in such manner, thus; **slǣpe** (*n.*), sleep: *m. dat. sg.*; **āwreht**, *p. ptc. of* āweccan, awake, arouse; **carfull** (*adj.*), careful: *dat. sg.*

52 **hǣse** (*n.*), behest, command: *f. dat. sg.*; **gewende**, *3 sg. pret. ind. of* gewendan, return, go.

A LITTLE MORE GRAMMAR

Some significant differences between OE and MnE, which will shed some light on the shape of OE syntax, can be illustrated rather quickly. Some account of them must be taken in our consideration of the development of the English Language. What is set out here, of course, is in no way intended as a complete description: on the contrary, the examples are to be taken as hints in arriving at decent translations and, as well, a better view of the course of our language.

Negation

1. The verb in OE is transformed to the negative by placing *ne* immediately before it; *ne bād ðæt sweord*; the sword did not bite. Sometimes, when the idea of negation is stressed, *nā* or *nō* may occur, instead of *ne*.

2. *Ne* contracts with a following word beginning with a vowel or *h* or *w nis*, from *ne is*; *næfde*, from *ne hæfde*; *nillan*, from *ne willan*; etc.

3. *Ne* occurring before other than a finite verb is a conjunction; *ne bān ne limu*; neither bones nor limbs; *ne singan ne sprecan*; neither (to) sing nor (to) say.

4. *Nā* and *nō* are used to negate words which are not finite verbs; *sēo wæs þǣre cwēne þēow ond nā cwēn*; she was the queens' servant and no (not a) queen.

5. The use of multiple negatives in a structure is not unusual and is not an indication of sub-standard usage, as it might be in MnE; *ond Apollonius nān ðing ne æt*; and Apollonius did not eat a thing (lit., and A. no thing not ate; cf. MnE sub-s., didn't eat nothing).

Prepositions

Here is a list of some important OE prepositions, with MnE equivalents, and the cases they govern.

æfter	dat.	after, along, according to
ǣr	dat.	before
æt	dat.	at, from, by
be	dat.	by, along, about
ēac	dat.	besides, in addition to
for	dat.	before (a place), in front of, because of
fram	dat.	from, by
geond	acc.	throughout, during
in	acc., dat.	in, into
mid	acc., dat.	among, with, by means of
of	dat.	from, of
on	acc., dat.	in, into, on
ongēan	acc., dat.	against, towards
oþ	acc., dat.	up to, until
tō	gen.	at, for, so
tō	dat.	to, towards, at, near
þurh	acc., dat.	through, throughout, by means of
wiþ	acc., dat., gen.	against, opposite, alongside of, by, towards, upon, in the presence of, from, with

The OE *wiþ* suggests the necessity of relating all these words to the context in which they occur; e.g., *hēr gefeat Ecgbryht cyning wiþ fīf and twēntig sciphlæsta æt Carrum*; what did King Ecgbryht do? Did he fight at Carhampton with twenty-five shiploads of men [i.e., on their side], or did he fight against them?

When it is said that prepositions 'govern a case' it is meant that the preposition determines the case of the noun, in most instances appearing after the preposition, with which (syntactically) it is associated: *tō mīn hūses*; at (for) my house: gen.; *far tō þam lande*; travel to (towards, at, near) the land: dat.

Agreement

The grammatical property of concord (agreement) is observed in OE, as it is for all inflected languages. In MnE we must observe the property of agreement between subjects and verbs; 'he runs—they run.' We say the subject and verb must agree in number (sg. or pl.) and person (1, 2, 3). OE observes the same rule. But in addition, in OE (1) nouns, pronouns, and their modifiers must agree in number, gender, and case and (2) pronouns and their antecedents must agree in number and gender. While MnE displays some of this agreement (e.g., 'thirty white horses'; 'each of his wishes is granted'), the situation in OE is further complicated by the requirement for agreement in gender, where, not infrequently, a conflict exists between grammatical gender and natural gender.

MnE has dispensed (largely) with grammatical 'gender. The tendency is to relate gender with sex, and thus, for animate objects, to assign male, female, or common gender on natural grounds, and for inanimate objects, to assign neuter gender (no sex implied) universally. But in no instance does MnE, except in the case of personal pronouns, display any formal characteristic to signal gender. Occasionally, to be sure, we might speak of a sports car, or a boat, say, as 'she' or 'her,' but that is exceptional. In OE, however, objects were assigned an arbitrary gender, and the structure of the language provides formal characteristics (inflectional endings) to signal gender. Thus, for example, *sunne*; sun: f.; *mōna*; moon: m.; *ēage*; eye: n.; *fōt*; foot: m.; *hand*; hand, f. While some exceptions occur, usually because of a conflict between grammatical and natural gender (e.g., Alfred writes in his transla- tion of Boethius, while relating the story of Orpheus and Eurydice, *hē hæfde ān swīðe ænlic wif, sīo wæs hāten Eurydice*; he had a wife without peer, who was called Eurydice, where the antecedent of the f. pron., *sīo*, is the n. noun, *wif*.), in OE nouns, pronouns, and their modifiers or antecedents most frequently agree in number, gender, and, where applicable, case.

Occasionally, too, a subject and verb will not agree in number; look for collective nouns, or indefinite pronouns, to cause about the same difficulty as they do today. For example, Alfred, once again, in describing a curious custom which the voyager, Wulfstan, related to him, writes *and þonne rīdeð ælc hys weges mid ðǣm fēo, and hyt motan habban eall*; and then each rides his way towards the property, and (they) might have it all, where the singular forms *rīdeð ælc* do not appear to agree with the plural implication of *mōtan habban*. In these situations, obviously, Alfred was giving way to 'the feeling of the moment,' and the requirement for grammatical agreement was, happily, forgotten.

Articles

Since OE does not possess a distinctive, formal article, the demonstrative pro- nouns, *sē* and *þēs,* are used for 'the, that,' and 'this.' It should be observed, too, that OE will or will not display the demonstrative, so used, where, in MnE, we would not or would expect an article to occur. *Sē,* it should be recalled (examples occur in the texts given for these exercises), is also used as a relative pronoun.

Pronoun Reference

The third person pronoun frequently is used ambiguously; often it is difficult to determine to whom it refers. The well-known entry in *The Anglo-Saxon Chronicle* for the year 755 displays a bewildering array of loose third person pronoun ref- erences. We ourselves are sometimes guilty of similar lapses and should, therefore, impute this celebrated example of careless writing to its author, not to any flaw in the structure of OE.

Verbs

1. Since there is, with the single exception of *bēon*; be, no inflected form for the future tense in OE, the present tense forms are also used to signal the future; *ic ārīse and ic fare tō mīnum fæder and ic secge him*; I will arise and I will go to my father and I will say to him. *Ārīse, fare,* and *secge* are all 1 sg. pres. ind. forms, but the context in which they occur suggests future meaning. This situation, by the way, has not changed in MnE, which also has no formal future tense; the future is

formed by combining an auxilliary with an infinitive. We are able, too, to suggest future meaning by use of the simple present tense alone; 'I go to New York next week.' We permit 'I go today' and 'I go tomorrow,' but not '*I go yesterday.'

2. *Bēon* is conjugated in the present indicative as follows:

sg.	1	ic eom	I am	ic bēo
	2	ðū eart	you are	ðū bist
	3	hē is	he is	hē biþ
pl.	1	wē sindon	we are	wē bēoþ
	2	gē sindon	you are	gē bēoþ
	3	hīe sindon	they are	gē bēoþ

The *bēo* forms frequently are used for the future. The distinction between *ðū eart—ðū bist* and *gē sindon—gē bēoþ,* that is, the distinction between *ðū* and *gē,* has disappeared in MnE, where we make no formal distinction between second person singular and second person plural forms of the personal pronoun. We may translate the OE singular forms as 'thou art' and the plural forms as 'you are.'

3. The simple past tense (preterite) is used to signal a single action completed in the past or a continuing action in the past; *Sōþlīce þā þā menn slēpon, þā cōm his feonda sum*; Truly, when men slept (were sleeping), one of his enemies came.

4. Only one verb in OE, *hātan,* had an inflected passive voice form; *þæt wīf hatte Wealhþēo*; the woman was called Wealhtheow. In all other instances, compound forms made by combining the past participle of the main verb with forms of *bēon, wesan,* or *weorþan* were used to construct the passive voice: with *bēon—bēon ðā oferhȳdegan ealle gescende*; may the proud be confounded; with *wesan—þæs gēares wǣrun ofslagen nigon eorlas*; nine earls were killed that year; with *weorþan —þæs gēares wurdon nigon folcgefeoht gefohton*; nine battles were fought that year.

A Few Constructions

The following constructions occur very frequently; their MnE equivalents, often governed by context, should be committed to memory.

æt niehstan, in the next place, thereupon
for hwon, why
for þǣm, for þām, therefore, because
for þǣm þe, for þām þe, because
for þan þe, therefore, because, for
for þon, forðon, therefore, because, for
for þon þe, for, because, therefore
for þȳ, for þȳ þe, therefore, because, for
mid þām þe, when, after, because
mid þȳ, mid þe, when, after, because
oððe . . . oððe, either . . . or
tō hwām, why
tō þæs þe, until
to þon þæt, in order that
þā . . . þā, when . . . then
þæs þe, since, afterwards, after, of which
þēah þe . . . þēah, although . . . nevertheless
þurh þæt þe, because

The grammatical information contained in the exercises on the selections from the earliest stage of our language, the Old English period (once again, from *ca.* 449, the traditional date for the advent of the Saxons in England to 1154, the date of the last entry in the Peterborough recension of *The Anglo-Saxon Chronicle*—although we represent it here as English of the year 1000), together with the grammatical hints given in various places in this section devoted to OE, is not, of course, all the information one needs to have to read Old English well. You might think of it as a slight, but firm, foundation. At some time in the future some of you will study Old English in greater depth, either with or without a teacher. If with a teacher, he will prescribe the text(s) to be used. For those who wish to carry out their own study many excellent texts are available. The short list here contains those texts which are both easily obtained and eminently helpful for the study of OE.

1. S. Moore and T. A. Knott. *The Elements of Old English.* 9th ed. Ann Arbor, Michigan: George Wahr, 1942.
2. J. R. Hulbert. *Bright's Anglo-Saxon Reader.* Latest ed. New York: Holt, 1947.
3. C. T. Onions. *Sweet's Anglo-Saxon Reader.* 14th ed. Oxford: The Clarendon Press, 1959.
4. A. J. Wyatt. *An Anglo-Saxon Reader.* Cambridge: Cambridge University Press, 1925.
5. R. C. Alston. *An Introduction to Old English.* Evanston, Ill.: Row, Peterson, 1962.
6. B. Mitchell. *A Guide to Old English.* Oxford: Basil Blackwell, 1965.
7. R. Quirk and C. L. Wrenn. *An Old English Grammar.* New York: Holt, Rinehart & Winston, 1957.
8. A. Campbell. *Old English Grammar.* Oxford: The Clarendon Press, 1959.

Number 1 is the easiest text to begin on; 2, 3, and 4 are anthologies, but 2 contains a useful 'Outline of Anglo-Saxon Grammar' and 'Sketch of Anglo-Saxon Literature'; 5 makes a good choice for a start because, in addition to the outline of grammar, it contains excellent exercises and a good description of syntax; 6 and 7 contain no reading selections but do contain admirable treatments of syntax—these two small books should be in the hands of all students of OE; 8, the most comprehensive grammar of OE, is the indispensible item on this list.

QUESTIONS

1. Without consulting the translation which follows these questions, translate the passage. Follow the same procedure established for the first two exercises.
2. Now study the translation which follows. You have two translations of this passage at hand; your own and the one which follows. Drawing on your own experience in writing translations, and making whatever use you can of the grammatical hints provided in these three exercises and in the glossaries, write a paper evaluating the Magoun-Walker translation. Your essay should take into consideration these points:

   a. the purpose of translation

   b. accurate reflection of the original text in balance with the style of the translation

c. conflicts caused, if any, by the translator having to choose (as King Alfred said about his own translations) between translating 'word by word' and translating 'sense to sense'

d. your opinion about the use of archaisms (attempt by translator to lend 'flavor of the past' to his work) in either structure or vocabulary in writing translations

e. the validity of 'supplying' what might appear to be missing in the original text

f. any other criteria you might add to help you to judge—to decide if a translation is good or bad

ÆLFRIC'S HOMILY ON THE ASSUMPTION
OF ST. JOHN THE EVANGELIST

Translated by F. P. Magoun, Jr., and J. A. Walker

John the Evangelist, favorite of Christ, was on this day (December 27th) through the visitation of God taken to the joy of the Kingdom of Heaven. He was the son of the sister of Christ's mother and the Latter loved him particularly (John 13: 23; 21: 7, 20), not so much because of the tie of kinship as for the purity of his perfect virginity. In (a state of) chastity he was chosen to God and to Eternity he remained in immaculate purity. One reads (lit. it is read) in authentic accounts that he was about to take a wife, and Christ was invited to his nuptials. Then it happened that at the nuptials (the) wine gave out. The Savior ordered the serving men to fill up six earthen-ware vessels with pure water and with His blessing He turned the water into very fine wine. This is the first miracle that He publicly performed during His Incarnation (John 2). Then John was so inspired by that miracle that then and there he left his bride in (a state of) virginity and ever after followed the Lord and was intensely loved by Him because he had snatched himself away from the lusts of the flesh. Indeed, to this beloved disciple the Savior entrusted His Mother when He redeemed mankind through the Crucifixion (lit. hanging on the Cross), so that the former's pure person might look after Mary the pure Virgin (cp. John 19: 27). And she then remained in the household of her sister's son.

In turn in time, after Christ's Ascension into Heaven, there ruled in the Roman Empire after Nero a certain blood-thirsty emperor. He was called Domitian (regn. 81–96 A.D.), a persecutor of all Christian persons; he ordered a tub to be filled with boiling oil and the illustrious evangelist to be thrust into it. However, through the protection of God he came out of that hot bath unharmed. Again, when that blood-thirsty man was unable to suppress the Blessed Apostle's preaching, then he sent him into exile to an island that is called Patmos, so that there he might die through the pangs (lit. sharpness) of hunger. But the Almighty Savior did not in too neglectful fashion abandon His beloved Apostle but revealed to him in that exile the revelation of the future, according to which he wrote that book which is called Apocalypse (cp. Rev. 1: 9). And the blood-thirsty Domitian in that same year (A.D. 96) was slain at the hands of his senators (historically by a freedman Stephanus), and they all unanimously advised that all the latter's decrees be invalidated. Then Nerva (regn. 96–98 A.D.), a most virtuous man, was chosen emperor. By his permission the Apostle returned again (to Rome) with great honor, he who had in insulting fashion been sent into exile. Men and women ran to meet him, rejoicing and saying, "Blessed is he who has come in the name of the Lord."

As the Apostle John was entering the city of Ephesus (mod. Ayasuluk), then people were carrying in his direction the body of a widow to be buried; her name was Drusiana. She was a staunch believer and charitable, and the needy whom she

Reprinted from *An Old-English Anthology*, by F. P. Magoun and J. A. Walker, Wm. C. Brown Company, 1950, by permission of F. P. Magoun.

with generous spirit had entirely supported, sad followed the corpse weeping (lit. with weeping). Then the Apostle ordered the beir to be set down and said, "May My Lord Savior raise you up, Drusiana; arise and go home and prepare a meal for us in your house." Then Drusiana arose as if awakened from sleep and, mindful of the Apostle's command, went home.

✠ ✠ ✠

TRANSITION

One passage has been selected to illustrate the quality of prose produced at about the year 1200, midway between the best of Old English prose and the mature compositions of the Middle English period. This is the text:

4. *Ancrene Wisse.* Written probably in the last quarter of the twelfth century, this "Rule for Anchoresses" clearly shows that its author possessed an extremely sensitive insight and depth of human sympathy, and, what is more, that he was master of an elegant, forceful prose style. The entire work was first published by James Morton (*The Ancren Riwle,* Camden Society No. LVII, London, 1853).

THE LOVE OF CHRIST

Ancrene Wisse, ca. 1170–1200

lines 1–68

3. THE LOVE OF CHRIST

A leafdi wes mid hire fan biset al abuten, hire lond al
destruet ant heo al povre, inwið an eorðene castel. A mihti
kinges luve wes þah biturnd upon hire, swa unimete swiðe
þet he for wohlech sende hire his sonden, an efter oðer, ofte
somet monie, sende hire beawbelex baðe feole and feire,   5
sucurs of liveneð, help of his hehe hird to halden hire castel.
Heo underfeng al as on unrecheles ant swa wes heard
i-heortet þet hire luve ne mahte he neaver beo þe neorre.
Hwet wult tu mare? He com himseolf on ende, schawde
hire his feire neb, as þe þe wes of alle men fehrest to bihal-   10
den, spec se swiðe swoteliche ant wordes se murie þet ha
mahten deade arearen to live, wrahte feole wundres ant dude
muchele meistries bivoren hire ehsihðe, schawde hire his
mihte, talde hire of his kinedom, bead to makien hire cwen
of al þet he ahte. Al þis ne heold nawt. Nes þis hoker   15
wunder? For heo nes neaver wurðe for to beon his þuften.
Ah swa, þurh his deboneirte, luve hefde overcumen him þet
he seide on ende: 'Dame, þu art i-weorret, ant þine van
beoð se stronge þet tu ne maht nanes-weis, wiðute mi sucurs
edfleon hare honden, þet ha ne don þe to scheome deað efter   20
al þi weane. Ich chulle, for þe luve of þe, neome þet feht upo
me, ant arudde þe of ham þe þi deað secheð. Ich wat þah
to soðe þet ich schal bituhen ham neomen deaðes wunde:
ant ich hit wulle heorteliche for te ofgan þin heorte. Nu
þenne, biseche ich þe, for þe luve þet ich cuðe þe, þet tu   25
luvie me lanhure efter þe ilke deað, hwen þu naldest lives!'
Þes king dude al þus, arudde hire of alle hire van, ant wes
himseolf to wundre i-tuket, ant i-slein on ende. Þurh miracle
aras þah from deaðe to live. Nere þeos ilke leafdi of uveles
cunnes cunde, ȝef ha over alle þing ne luvede him herefter?   30
   Þes king is Jesu, Godes sune, þet al o þisse wise wohede
ure sawle þe deoflen hefden bihest. Ant he, as noble wohere
efter monie messagers ant feole god deden, com to pruvien

Reprinted from F. Mossé, *A Handbook of Middle English*, J. A. Walker (tr.) (Baltimore: The
Johns Hopkins Press, 1952), pp. 142–147, by permission of the publisher. The translation to
Modern English which follows is Alan M. Markman's.

his luve, and schawde þurh cnihtschipe þet he was luve-
wurðe, as weren sumhwile cnihtes i-wunet to donne, dude   35
him i turneiment ant hefde for his leoves luve his scheld i
feht, as kene cniht, on euche half i-þurlet. His scheld þe
wreah his Goddhead wes his leove licome þet wes i-spread o
rode, brad as scheld buven in his i-strahte earmes, nearow
bineoðen, as þe an fot, efter monies wene, set upo þe oðer.   40
Þet þis scheld naveð siden is for bitacnunge þet his deciples,
þe schulden stonden bu him ant habben i-beon his siden,
fluhen alle from him ant leafden him as fremede as þe
godspel seið: *Relicto eo, omnes fugerunt.* Þis scheld is
i-ȝeven us aȝein alle temptatiuns, as Jeremie witneð: *Dabis*   45
scutum cordis laborem tuum. Nawt ane þis scheld ne schilt
us from alle uveles ah deð ȝet mare, cruneð us in heovene:
Scuto bonae voluntatis. 'Laverd,' he seið, Davið, 'wið þe
scheld of þi gode wil þu havest us i-crunet.' Scheld, he seið,
of god wil; for willes he þolede al þet he þolede. Ysaias: 50
Oblatus est quia voluit. 'Me, Laverd,' þu seist, 'hwerto? Ne
mahte he wið leasse gref habben arud us?' ȝeoi, i-wis, ful
lihtlice; ah he nalde. For-hwi? For to bineomen us euch
bitellunge aȝein him of ure luve, þet he se deore bohte. Me
buð lihtliche þing þet me luveð lutel. He bohte us wið his   55
heorte blod, deorre pris nes neaver, for te ofdrahen of us ure
luve toward him þet costnede him se sare. I scheld beoð
þreo þinges, þe treo ant te leðer ant te litunge. Alswa wes i
þis scheld þe treo of þe rode, þet leðer of Godes licome, þe
litunge of þe reade blod þet heowede hire se feire. Eft, þe   60
þridde reisun: Efter kene cnihtes deað, me hongeð hehe i
chirche his scheld on his mungunge. Alswa is þis scheld, þet
is þe crucifix, i chirche i-set i swuch stude þer me hit sonest
seo, for te þenchen þerbi o Jesu Cristes cnihtschipe þet he
dude o rode. His leofmon bihalde þron hu he bohte hire   65
luve, lette þurlin his scheld, openin his side, to schawin hire
his heorte, to schawin hire openliche hu inwardliche he
luvede hire ant to ofdrahen hire heorte.

    This text is translated, quite literally, word for word in this way:

A lady was with her enemies beset all about, her land all
destroyed and she all poor, within an earthen castle. A mighty
king's love was however turned towards her, so immeasurably very
that he for courting sent her his messengers, one after other, often
together many, sent her baubles both many and fair,   5
help of living, help of his high court to hold her castle.
She received all as one careless and so was hard
hearted that her love not might he never be the nearer.
What wilt thou more? He came himself on end, showed
her his fair face, as he who was of all men fairest to behold,   10
spoke so exceedingly sweetly and words so merry that they

might the dead raise to life, wrought many wonders and did
great marvels before her eyesight, showed her his
might, told her of his kingdom, bade to make her queen
of all that he owned. All this not held naught. Not was this scorn   15
marvelous? For she not was never worthy for to be his slave.
But so, through his debonairness, love had overcome him that
he said on end: "Madam, you are attacked, and thy foes
be so strong that you not might not at all, without my help
escape their hands, that they not do thee to ashamed death after   20
all thy misery. I shall, for the love of thee, take that fight upon
me, and save thee from them who thy death seek. I know though
in truth that I shall between them take death's wound:
and I it wish heartily for to obtain thine heart. Now
then, beseech I thee, for the love that I made known to thee, that you   25
love me at least after the same death when you would not while alive!"
This king did all thus, saved her from all her enemies, and was
himself terribly mistreated, and slain at the end. Through a miracle
arose though from death to life. Not were this same lady of evils
kinds nature, if she over all matters not loved him hereafter?   30
This king is Jesus, God's son, who completely in this manner courted
our souls which devils had besieged. And he, as a great wooer
after many messengers and many good deeds, came to prove
his love, and showed through knightship that he was worthy of love
as were sometime knights accustomed to do, did   35
him in tournament and had for his beloved's love his shield in
a combat, as a bold knight, on each side pierced. His shield which
covered his Godhead was his dear body that was stretched out on
the cross, broad as a shield above in his stretched out arms, narrow
below, as the one foot, for the hopes of many, was placed over the other. 40
That this shield not has sides is for betokening that his disciples,
who should stand by him and have been his sides,
fled all from him and left him as foreign as the
gospel says: *Relicto eo, omnes fugerunt.* This shield is
given us against all temptations, as Jeremiah witnesses: *Dabis*   45
scutum cordis laborem tuum. Not only this shield not shields
us from all evils but does yet more, crowns us in heaven:
scuto bonæ voluntatis. "Lord," he says, David, "with the
shield of thy goodness will you have us crowned." Shield, he says,
of good will; for of will he suffered all that he suffered. Isaiah: 50
Oblatus est quia voluit. 'Me,' Lord, you say, 'why?' Not
might he with less grief have saved us? Yes, certainly, for sure, very
easily, but he not would. Why? For to deprive us each
excuse against him of our love, that he so dearly purchased. It
purchases to me lightly thing that to me loves little. He bought us with his 55
heart's blood, dearer prize not was never, for to draw from us our
love toward him that cost him so sorely. In the shield are
three things, the tree and the leather and the color. At the same time was in
this shield the tree of the cross, the leather of God's body, the
color of the red blood that colored her so fairly. Finally, the   60

third reason: After bold knight's death, men hang high in
church his shield in his memory. At the same time is this shield, that
is the crucifix, in church placed in such place there where men it soonest
see, for to think thereby on Jesus Christ's knightship that he
did on cross. Let his dearly beloved behold thereon how he bought her   65
love, permitted to pierce his shield, open his side, to show her
his heart, to show her openly how inwardly he
loved her and to draw off her heart.

QUESTIONS

Roughly two centuries separate this text from the OE texts you have read. To perceive the nature of the changes in the language during that time, you might well begin by considering the phenomenon of *levelling*. When the full inflectional system of OE started to give way to the system of grammatical signals employed in MnE, certain inflectional endings weakened, eventually to be replaced by word order signals or function words. One development to be observed is the loss of final *-n*. In OE the infinitive of the verb ended in *-an* or *-ian*. In this passage, however, the usual infinitive ending is *-en,* and for weak verbs *-in* (*openin,* 1. 66, *þurlin,* 1. 66, *schawin,* 1. 67) or *-ien* (*makien,* 1. 14). In OE the vowel of the infinitive ending had the sound of the vowel in MnE 'hot' or 'box' and was stressed. What probably occurred is that as stress weakened on the vowel of the infinitive ending it came to be sounded as the first vowel in MnE 'about' is sounded, and as stress weakened further the vowel, in its written representation, came to be spelled as it is in this text with *e,* and the final *-n* was also subjected to weakened stress. Eventually the final *-n* disappeared (as even earlier final *-m* changed to *-n*) and the final *-e* thus left also, in time, disappeared. In this text, however, only the first step can be observed; the change of the vowel of the inflectional ending has occurred, but the final *-n* is still retained. But we can project this process:

900	1200	MnE
behealdan	bihalden	behold

Something of this identical feature can be observed in prepositions in this text, where, with weakened or no stress, *in* and *on* are printed as *i* and *o*. MnE, of course, has retained 'in' and 'on.' There also are numerous noun plurals in this text which end in *-en,* all of which will, in the next few centuries, lose that inflection and adopt the final *-s* as the signal of the plural. (A few exceptions to that general development remain in MnE; 'ox' and 'child,' for example.) Your later texts, from the late ME and the EMnE periods will show further stages of levelling. While examining this passage it will prove helpful, as you consider in what ways the English of 1200 differs from the English of 1000, to look for evidence of early levelling and the consequent appearance of other grammatical signals replacing the inflectional functions.

1. Rewrite the passage in your own compositional style.

2. Here is a series of questions designed to illustrate some of the distinctive features of this text.

a. *deade,* 1. 12, is a pl. adj.; how is it used here?

b. *leoves,* 1. 36, is an adj. in the gen. case; how is it used here?

c. what is the number of *þing* in 1. 30?

d. what is the construction of *deaðes* in 1. 23?

e. what is the construction and function of *hire* in 1. 60?

f. *me,* in 1. 54 and 55, is dat.; what is its function?

g. *fremede,* 1. 43, is an adj.; what is its function?

h. forms of *do* occur in 1. 12, 20, 27, 35, and 65; what are their functions?

i. does *to* ever occur (in front of the verb) as the signal of the infinitive? If so, what does that suggest?

j. are there any superfluous negative particles in the text?

k. *þe* can mean 'the' or 'thee'; how are its meanings distinguished?

3. Summarize your findings regarding the changes which took place in the English language between 900 and 1200.

✠ ✠ ✠

MIDDLE ENGLISH
1150–1471

Here too it is not possible to assign exact dates for the beginning and end of this stage in the development of our language. Indeed, as it will become obvious once all the texts have been examined, clearly defined limits, or boundaries, marking off one level of the development of language from another do not exist. Changes in language occur slowly, over the spread of generations, as a result of various pressures and forces exerted upon the speakers. A vast, complex matrix of political, economic, and social mobilities erodes, most often as scarcely noticeable sorties, sometimes as radical upheavals, those conservative popular barriers which resist change. In this period, of course, the victory which William the Conqueror long ago gained over Harold Godwinson at the Battle of Hastings in 1066 was the most significant cause for change, because, as a result, in the generations that followed, thousands upon thousands of speakers of Anglo-Norman French spread over the lands of Britain, eventually to mingle with the Saxons and to produce, in time, speakers of a new, more resourceful English. In the fourteenth century—the height of the period— English writers produced a world famous literature, still widely read, its authors, some anonymous, some known to us, still admired. Again, for the sake of convenience, we choose the middle of the twelfth century to mark the start of the Middle English period and the death of Malory, 1471 (roughly equivalent, too, with Caxton and the introduction of printing into Britain), to signal its close.

To represent Middle English we have selected three texts which illustrate English of the year 1400, the year in which Chaucer died. Two of the selections are the work of Chaucer; the third, while not clearly established as his, might be from his hand. These are the texts:

5. *The Canterbury Tales*. Geoffrey Chaucer, 1385. From the *General Prologue*, the 'portrait' of the Prioress constitutes a sample of superior composition, in verse, in Middle English.

6. *The Romaunt of the Rose*. Chaucer (?), 1370. This passage, in verse, is a translation into Middle English of a great twelfth century Old French poem.

7. *A Treatise on the Astrolabe*. Geoffrey Chaucer, 1385. The opening paragraphs of this work (as arranged by modern editors) illustrate the achievement of Middle English prose.

EXERCISE 5
THE CANTERBURY TALES
Chaucer, ca. 1385
A, 118–162

GENERAL PROLOGUE, PORTRAIT OF THE PRIORESS

Ther was also a Nonne, a Prioresse,
That of hir smyling was ful simple and coy;
Hir gretteste ooth was but by seynte Loy;   *120*
And she was cleped madame Eglentyne.
Ful wel she song the service divyne,
Entuned in hir nose ful semely;
And Frensh she spak ful faire and fetisly,
After the scole of Stratford atte Bowe,   *125*
For Frensh of Paris was to hir unknowe.
At mete wel y-taught was she with-alle;
She leet no morsel from hir lippes falle,
Ne wette hir fingres in hir sauce depe.
Wel coude she carie a morsel, and wel kepe,   *130*
That no drope ne fille up-on hir brest.
In curteisye was set ful muche hir lest.
Hir over lippe wyped she so clene,
That in hir coppe was no ferthing sene
Of grece, whan she dronken hadde hir draughte.   *135*
Ful semely after hir mete she raughte,
And sikerly she was of greet disport,
And ful plesaunt, and amiable of port,
And peyned hir to countrefete chere
Of court, and been estatlich of manere,   *140*
And to ben holden digne of reverence.
But, for to speken of hir conscience,
She was so charitable and so pitous,
She wolde wepe, if that she sawe a mous
Caught in a trappe, if it were deed or bledde.   *145*
Of smale houndes had she, that she fedde
With rosted flesh, or milk and wastel-breed.
But sore weep she if oon of hem were deed,
Or if men smoot it with a yerde smerte:
And al was conscience and tendre herte.   *150*
Ful semely hir wimpel pinched was;
Hir nose tretys; hir eyen greye as glas;

Hir mouth ful smal, and ther-to softe and reed;
But sikerly she hadde a fair forheed;
It was almost a spanne brood, I trowe;   155
For, hardily, she was nat undergrowe.
Ful fetis was hir cloke, as I was war.
Of smal coral aboute hir arm she bar
A peire of bedes, gauded al with grene;
And ther-on heng a broche of gold ful shene,   160
On which ther was first write a crowned A,
And after, *Amor vincit omnia.*

GLOSSARY

In this listing will be found only words which are unfamiliar in contemporary English; they are cited in alphabetical order with the line number from this text.

cleped, called: 121.
countrefete, imitate: 139.
digne, worthy: 141.
estatlich, stately, royal: 140.
ferthing, bit, small piece: 134.
fetis, skilfull: 157.
fetisly, skilfully: 124.
flesh, meat: 147.
gauded, dyed, enameled: 159.
lest, desire, wish: 132.
mete, meat, the dining table: 127.

peyned, took pains: 139.
pinched, pleated: 151.
raughte, reached: 136.
scole, school: 125.
semely, fashionably: 123, 151.
shene, beautiful, glittering: 160.
sikerly, truly, indeed: 137, 154.
smerte, smartly: 149.
tretys, straight, well made: 152.
yerde, stick: 149.

QUESTIONS

1. Translate the passage. The glossary provides meanings for all words which have not retained their same meaning in MnE or which, in their ME spelling, look in some way odd to us. Make a comparison of Chaucer's syntax with MnE practise, allowing, of course, for the fact that this is a passage of poetry. In your remarks include a statement about the use of adjectives, i.e., the position of the adj. (in ll. 121, 129, 146, 147, 152, 154) with regard to the noun it modifies. Is the use of *tretys,* l. 152, of the same order as the others?

2. In the language of 1400 we should expect a certain number of French loan words to occur. A *loan word* is one appearing in one language, which is not a native word but which has been borrowed from another language. English has been a good borrower. Make a chart on the model shown below in which you place each word (in its MnE form) from the text (only of the classes indicated, the four principal parts of speech). Consult the *OED,* or an unabridged dictionary, to determine which are French loan words.

Noun	Verb	Adj.	Adv.
118	nun	was		also
	prioress			
119	smiling	was	simple	full
			coy	
120	oath	was	greatest	
	saint			

Complete your chart. What is the percentage of French loan words in the text? In what part of speech was borrowing heaviest? How can you determine if a word had been borrowed by French from Latin and then from French by English? Would you call such an example an English borrowing from French?

3. Inflectional levelling has proceeded further than it had by the year 1200. Make a list of all plural nouns which occur in the text. What is the normal inflection? How do you account for the form of the plural noun in 1. 152? What is the MnE form for each of these words? Can you explain how the MnE form developed?

4. You will have observed that a good many of the words in this text end in a final -e. The final -e in the English of 1400 has in the past been the subject of much inquiry and concern. Was it pronounced? If it was not pronounced we can state that it had no significance, i.e., if in normal conversation it was not heard, then no signal was uttered. If pronounced, was it a grammatical signal? We can determine if the final -e in this text is to be pronounced by scanning the lines of verse. We assume that Chaucer's metrical skill is superior and that, intending to write iambic pentameter in this passage, he was not likely to make errors. Confine the inquiry now to singular nouns ending in final -e. There are two in the first line. The line may be scanned in this way:

thĕr wás ăl só ă Nónne ă Prí ŏr ésse

Since no marker appears over the final -e's, it is evident that neither was pronounced. Make a similar test for each singular noun in the text and place all the nouns which show a pronounced final -e in a list. (*Mete,* 1. 127, for example, has a pronounced final -e: ăt mé tĕ wél ў taúght . . .) Consult the *OED* for the origin of each word on your list. If you find a loan word, how would you regard the pronounced final -e? If a native English word, how would you regard it? What has happened in MnE to each of these words? (Try to establish a distinction between a derivational, or etymological, ending and an inflectional ending.) Can you, finally, make a general statement, using just this text as evidence, about the final -e in Chaucer's poetry: when is it pronounced and when is it not? (When pronounced, it has the sound of the first vowel in MnE 'about.')

EXERCISE 6

THE ROMAUNT OF THE ROSE

Chaucer, lines 1–40, ca. 1370

Many men sayn that in sweveninges
Ther nys but fables and lesynges;
But men may some swevenes sene
Whiche hardely that false ne bene,
But afterwarde ben apparaunt.   *5*
This maye I drawe to warraunt
An authour that hight Macrobes,
That halte nat dremes false ne lees,
But undothe us the avysioun
That whilom mette kyng Cipioun.   *10*
And who-so saith, or weneth it be
A jape, or elles nycete,
To wene that dremes after falle,
Lette who so lyste a fole me calle.
For this trowe I, and say for me,   *15*
That dremes signifiaunce be
Of good and harme to many wightes,
That dremen in her slepe a nyghtes
Ful many thynges covertly,
That fallen after al openly.   *20*
Within my twenty yere of age,
Whan that Love taketh his cariage
Of yonge folke, I wente soone
To bedde, as I was wont to done,
And faste I slepte; and in slepyng   *25*
Me mette suche a swevenyng
That lyked me wonder wele.
But in that sweven is never a dele
That it nys afterwarde befalle,
Ryght as this dreme wol tel us alle.   *30*
Nowe this dreme wol I ryme a-right,
To make your hertes gaye and lyght,
For Love it prayeth and also
Commaundeth me that it be so.
And if there any aske me,   *35*
Whether that it be he or she,
Howe this booke whiche is here
Shal hatte, that I rede you here;
It is the Romance of the Rose,
In whiche al the Arte of Love I close.   *40*

GLOSSARY

Here is a list of all words which might prove troublesome.

close, disclose: 40.
dele, part, bit: 28.
hatte, be called: 38.
hight, is called: 7.
jape, joke: 12.
lesynges, lies: 2.
lyste, please, like: 14.

mette, dreamed: 26.
nycete, a foolishness: 12.
rede, advise: 38.
sweveninges, dreams: 1.
trowe, believe: 15.
undothe, discloses: 9.
wightes, persons: 17.

QUESTIONS

1. Translate this passage.

2. From this text and the text for Exercise 5 make a list of all the personal pronouns which occur. What is the form of the 3d sg. fem. gen.? Its MnE equivalent is 'her.' The corresponding form in OE was *hire*; can you account for the evolution of 'her'? In 1. 148, Exercise 5, *hem* occurs and in this text, 1. 18, *her* occurs; what is the construction of each? Consult the *OED* to determine the source of the MnE equivalents. What does this suggest about English lexical borrowing habits?

3. From this text and the text for Exercise 5 make a list of all verbal constructions. Place your examples into a paradigmatic format. Compare each inflectional form with its OE and MnE counterparts. What has been the development of these forms since the end of the OE period? In Exercise 5, 1. 127, the form *y-taught* occurs. Consult the *OED* for the orgin of the prefix *y-*. What was the normal signal for the past participle in OE? in these ME texts?

EXERCISE 7
A TREATISE ON THE ASTROLABE
Chaucer, ca. 1385, lines 1–39

Lyte Lowys my sone, I aperceyve wel by certeyne evydences thyn abilite to lerne
sciences touching nombres and proporciouns; and as wel considre I thy bisy
praier in special to lerne the Tretys of the Astrelabie. Than for as mochel as a
philosofre saith, 'he wrappith him in his frende, that condescendith to the
rightful praiers of his frende,' therefore have I yeven the a suffisant Astrolabie   5
as for oure orizonte compowned after the latitude of Oxenford; upon which, by
mediacioun of this litel tretys, I propose to teche the a certein nombre of
conclusions perteynyng to the same instrument. I seie a certein of conclusions
for thre causes. The first cause is this: truste wel that alle the conclusions that
han be founde, or ellys possibly might be founde in so noble an instrument as   10
is an Astrelabie ben unknowe parfitly to eny mortal man in this regioun, as I
suppose. Another cause is this, that sothly in any tretis of the Astrelabie that I
have sene there be somme conclusions that wol not in alle thinges parformen
her bihestes; and somme of hem ben to harde to thy tendir age of x yere to
conceyve.   15
   This tretis, divided in 5 parties, wol I shewe the under full light reules and
naked wordes in Englisshe, for Latyn canst thou yit but small, my litel sone.
But natheles suffise to the these trewe conclusions in Englisshe as wel as
sufficith to these noble clerkes Grekes these same conclusions in Greke; and to
Arabiens in Arabike, and to Iewes in Ebrewe, and to the Latyn folk in Latyn;   20
whiche Latyn folke had hem first oute of othere dyverse langages, and writen
hem in her owne tunge, that is to seyn in Latyn. And God woot that in alle these
langages and in many moo han these conclusions ben suffisantly lerned and
taught, and yit by diveres reules; right as diverse pathes leden diverse folke the
right way to Rome. Now wol I preie mekely every discret persone that redith or   25
herith this litel tretys to have my rude endityng for excused, and my superfluite
of wordes, for two causes. The first cause is for that curiouse endityng and harde
sentence is ful hevy at onys for such a childe to lerne. And the secunde cause is
this, that sothly me semith better to writen unto a childe twyes a gode sentence,
than he forgete it onys.   30
   And Lowys, yf so be that I shewe the in my light Englisshe as trewe conclusions touching this mater, and not oonly as trewe but as many and as subtile
conclusiouns, as ben shewid in Latyn in eny commune tretys of the Astrelabie,
konne me the more thanke. And preie God save the King, that is lorde of this
langage, and alle that him feithe berith and obeieth, everiche in his degre, the   35
more and the lasse. But considre wel that I ne usurpe not to have founden this
werke of my labour or of myn engyn. I nam but a lewde compilator of the
labour of olde astrologiens, and have it translatid in myn Englisshe oonly for
thy doctrine. And with this swerde shal I sleen envie.

GLOSSARY

endityng, writing: 27.
engyn, ingenuity: 37.
founden, invented: 36.
sentence, meaning: 28 (in 29 read MnE
'sentence').

QUESTIONS

1. Translate the passage.
2. Employing all the techniques encountered so far in previous exercises, write a paper comparing Chaucer's prose with Aelfric's.
3. Read further in an edition of Chaucer's complete works from "The Parson's Tale" and "The Tale of Melibeus" for a larger sampling of Chaucer's prose. In what respect might you say that Chaucer is or is not a more "modern" writer than Aelfric?

✠ ✠ ✠

TRANSITION

One passage has been selected to illustrate the quality of prose produced midway between the end of the thirteenth century and the close of the fifteenth. Caxton's modernization of Trevisa's translation of *Polychronicon Ranulphi Higden,* which he printed in 1482, serves this purpose and one other too: it provides, as well, a contemporary observation on the English language. But it must be remembered, Higden died in 1364, and John of Trevisa's translation was finished in 1387. Therefore, while the style of this text is Caxton's, and the language in which it is written is the English of 1482, the content reflects the condition of English in 1387, in the period, that is, of Chaucer's mature expression. This is the text:

  8. *Polychronicon.* Caxton, 1482. Fifty lines and a partial glossary are provided.

MODERNIZATION AND PRINTING OF JOHN OF TREVISA'S TRANSLATION OF HIGDEN'S

POLYCHRONICON

William Caxton, lines 1–49, 1482

As it is knowen how many maner peple ben in this Ilond ther ben also many
langages and tonges. Netheles walshmen and scottes that ben not medled with
other nacions kepe neygh yet theyr first langage and speche/ But yet tho scottes
that were sometyme confederate and dwellyd with pyctes drawe somwhat after
theyr speche/ But the Flemynges that dwelle in the westside of wales have lefte   5
her straunge speche & speken lyke to saxons/ also englysshmen though they had
fro the begynnyng thre maner speches Southern northern and myddel speche in
the middel of the londe as they come of thre maner of people of Germania.
Netheles by commyxtion and medlyng with danes and afterward with normans
In many thynges the countreye langage is appayred/ffor somme use straunge   10
wlaffyng/chyteryng harryng garryng and grisbytyng/ this appayryng of the
langage cometh of two thynges/One is by cause that children that gon to scole
lerne to speke first englysshe/& than ben compellid to constrewe her lessons in
Frenssh and that have ben used syn the normans come in to Englond/Also
gentilmens childeren ben lerned and taught from theyr yongthe to speke   15
frenssh.

And uplondish men will counterfete and likene hem self to gentilmen and arn
besy to speke frensshe for to be more sette by. Wherfor it is sayd by a comyn
proverbe Jack wold be a gentilman if he coude speke frensshe. This manner
was moche used to fore the grete deth. But syth it is somdele chaunged For sir   20
Johan cornuayl a mayster of gramer chaunged the techyng in gramer scole and
construction of Frenssh in to englysshe. and other Schoolmaysters use the same
way now in the yere of oure lord/M.iij/C.lx.v. the /IX yere of kyng Rychard the
secund and leve all frenssh in scoles and use al construction in englisshe. wherein
they have avantage one way. that is that they lerne the sonner theyr gramer And   25
in another disavauntage/For nowe they lerne no ffrenssh ne can none/whiche is
hurte for them that shal passe the see/And also gentilmen have moche lefte to
teche theyr children to speke frenssh Hit semeth a grete wonder that Englyssmen
have so grete dyversyte in theyr owne langage in sowne and in spekyng of it/
whiche is all in one ylond. And the langage of Normandye is comen oute of   30
another lond/and hath one manner soune among al men that speketh it in
englond For a man of Kente Southern/ western and northern men speken
Frensshe al lyke in sowne & speche. But they can not speke theyr englyssh so
Netheles ther is as many dyverse manere of Frensshe in the Royamme of
Fraunce as is dyverse englysshe in the Royamme of Engelond Also of the   35

Reprinted from F. Mossé, *A Handbook of Middle English*, J. A. Walker (tr.) (Baltimore: The
Johns Hopkins Press, 1952), pp. 286–289, by permission of the publisher.

forsayd tong whiche is departed in thre is grete wonder/For men of the este
with the men of the west acorde better in sownyng of theyr speche than men of
the north with men of the south/

Therfor it is that men of mercij that ben of myddel englond as it were
partyners with the endes understande better the side langages northern & 40
sothern than northern & southern understande eyther other. Alle the langages
of the northumbres & specially at york is so sharp slytyng frotyng and unshape
that we sothern men may unneth understande that langage I suppose the cause
be that they be nygh to the alyens that speke straungely. And also by cause that
the kynges of englond abyde and dwelle more in the south countreye than in 45
the north countrey.

The cause why they abyde more in the south countrey than in the north
countrey. is by cause that ther is better corne londe more peple moo noble
cytees. & moo prouffytable havenes in the south contrey than in the north.

GLOSSARY

alyens, aliens: 44.
appayred, deteriorated: 10.
appayryng, deterioration: 11.
can, know: 26: are able: 33.
chyteryng, chattering: 11.
corne, wheat, grain: 48.
frotyng, grinding: 42.
garryng, grating: 11.

grete deth, the mid-fourteenth-century
plague: 20.
grisbytyng, grinding the teeth: 11.
harryng, snarling: 11.
havenes, harbors: 49.
mercij, Mercia: 39.
slytyng, piercing: 42.
unneth, not easily: 43.
wlaffyng, stammering: 11.

QUESTIONS

This passage was written at a time roughly half way between the productions of
Chaucer and those of Shakespeare. The fifteenth century frequently has been called
'the century of transition.' We should expect the English of 1482 to display some
traces of its ME heritage and, at the same time, to show some resemblance to what,
yet, lies ahead.

1. List all the verb, noun, and pronoun constructions. Has levelling proceeded
further than it had at 1400? What percentage (roughly) of final -*n* forms occur?

2. What is the form of the future tense here?

3. The *virgule* (a short oblique stroke, /, which we today sometimes use between
two words to suggest that either interpretation may be used, as in 'and/or') was,
on occasion, used by early printers to mark the end of word groups. What is its
relationship to modern punctuation marks? Does it suggest anything about pronunciation or pauses?

4. If you were to prepare a modernized edition of this passage, what changes
would you make?

5. Do you regard this passage in any way to be an advance over Chaucer's
prose?

✠ ✠ ✠

EARLY MODERN ENGLISH
1500–1700

By the beginning of the sixteenth century, owing to the increased production of books made possible by the activities of the printers and their presses, and to a marked rise in volume of written communication in general, it is evident that a new stage in the development of English had been reached. While the English language of 1500 does not yet look, in its written form, like ours, nor in its oral production could it yet have sounded like ours, it is clear, nevertheless, that English was embarking upon a new series of changes, which, over the course of two centuries, were destined to leave an indelible trace upon it. It is in this period, of course, that two of the greatest poets England has produced, Shakespeare and Milton, lived and wrote their works. It was a period of great bustle, intense social activity, and a general expansion of man's inquiry and action everywhere. And the English language, borrowing here, adapting there, became a flexible medium of expression, sufficiently versatile to sustain all the needs of communication which attended the largest burst of human energy the world had up to that time witnessed. While the limits are, once again, hard to fix, we are safe enough in choosing 1500 as the start and 1700, the year of the death of Dryden, a writer whose works display most of the features of Modern English, as the close of the most vigorous period in the history of our language.

We have selected three passages from Shakespeare, two in verse and one (partially) in prose, to represent the Early Modern English period. These are the texts:

9. *As You Like It*. This passage is reproduced as it was printed in the 1623 Folio Edition.

10. *Romeo and Juliet*. The printing of the 1623 Folio Edition is used.

11. *Hamlet*. This text is taken from a modern edition.

EXERCISE 9
AS YOU LIKE IT
I. iii. 43–111, Shakespeare, 1623 Folio

DUK. Mistris, dispatch you with your fastest haste,
  And get you from our Court.
ROS. Me Vncle?
DUK. You Cosen,
  Within these ten daies if that thou beest found   *45*
  So neere our publike Court as twentie miles,
  Thou diest for it.
ROS. I doe beseech your Grace
  Let me the knowledge of my fault beare with me:
  If with my selfe I hold intelligence,   *50*
  Or haue acquaintance with mine owne desires,
  If that I doe not dreame, or be not franticke,
  (As I doe trust I am not) then deere Vncle,
  Neuer so much as in a thought vnborne,
  Did I offend your highnesse.   *55*
DUK. Thus doe all Traitors,
  If their purgation did consist in words,
  They are as innocent as grace itselfe;
  Let it suffice thee that I trust thee not.
ROS. Yet your mistrust cannot make me a Traitor;   *60*
  Tell me whereon the likelihoods depends?
DUK. Thou art thy Fathers daughter, there's enough.
ROS. So was I when your highness took his Dukedom,
  So was I when your highness banisht him;
  Treason is not inherited my Lord,   *65*
  Or if we did deriue it from our friends,
  What's that to me, my Father was no Traitor,
  Then good my Leige, mistake me not so much,
  To thinke my pouertie is treacherous.
CEL. Deere Soueraigne heare me speake.   *70*
DUK. I Celia, we staid her for your sake,
  Else had she with her Father rang'd along.
CEL. I did not then entreat to haue her stay,
  It was your pleasure, and your owne remorse,
  I was too yong that time to value her,   *75*
  But now I know her: if she be a Traitor,
  Why so am I: we still haue slept together
  Rose at an instant, learn'd, plaid, eate together,

Reprinted from Albert H. Marckwardt, *Introduction to the English Language* (New York: Oxford University Press, 1942), by permission of the publisher.

And wheresoere we went, like *Iunos* Swans,
Still we went coupled and inseperable.   *80*
DUK.   She is too subtile for thee, and her smoothness;
Her verie silence, and (h)er patience,
Speake to the people, and they pittie her:
Thou art a foole, she robs thee of thy name,
And thou wilt show more bright, & seem more vertuous
When she is gone: then open not thy lips   *85*
Firme, and irreuocable is my doombe,
Which I haue past vpon her, she is banish'd.
CEL.   Pronounce that sentence then on me my Leige,
I cannot liue out of her companie.
DUK.   You are a foole: you Neice prouide your selfe,   *90*
If you out-stay the time, vpon mine honor,
And in the greatnesse of my word you die.

                                                    Exit Duke, etc.
CEL.   O my poore *Rosaline,* whether wilt thou goe?
Wilt thou change Fathers? I will giue thee mine: *95*
I charge thee be not thou more grieu'd then I am.
ROS.   I haue more cause.
CEL.   Thou hast not Cosen,
Prethee be cheereful; know'st thou not the Duke
Hath banish'd me his daughter?   *100*
ROS.   That he hath not.
CEL.   No, hath not? Rosaline lacks then the loue
Which teacheth thee that thou and I am one,
Shall we be sundred? shall we part sweete girle?
No, let my Father seeke another heire: *105*
Therefore deuise with me how we may flie
Whether to goe, and what to beare with vs,
And doe not seeke to take your change vpon you,
To beare your griefes your selfe, and leaue me out:
For by this heauen, now at our sorrowes pale;   *110*
Say what thou canst, Ile goe along with thee.

QUESTIONS

1. Write the forms for the plural of these MnE nouns: 'cat,' 'dog,' 'brush,' 'ox,' 'deer.' Make a list of all the plural nouns in this text. Is the practise for forming the plural in EMnE more like that of ME or that of MnE?

2. What is the practise here for forming the genitive case?

3. List all the verbal constructions. Is *do* used as it is in MnE? Are questions and negatives formed as they are in MnE? Is the spelling of the verbal constructions consistent? (The EMnE form of MnE 'banished' occurs in ll. 64, 87, and 100. Which probably best represents the actual pronunciation?) Does 'to' occur as the sign of the infinitive? How is the apostrophe used? All in all, do Shakespeare's verbal constructions seem to be closer to ME practise or to MnE practise?

4. What do you observe about the grammatical property of *concord* in l. 61? Are there other instances of this kind?

ROMEO AND JULIET
I. i. 35–71, Shakespeare, 1623 Folio

SAMP.   Me they shall feele while I am able to stand: *35*
  And 'tis knowne I am a pretty peece of flesh.
GREG.   'Tis well thou art not Fish: If thou hadst thou
  had'st beene poore Iohn. Draw thy Toole,
  here comes (two) of the House of the *Mountagues.*

Enter two other Seruingmen.

SAM.   My naked weapon is out: quarrel, I will back thee.   *40*
GRE.   How? Turne thy backe, and run.
SAM.   Feare me not.
GRE.   No marry: I feare thee.
SAM.   Let vs take the Law of our sides: let them begin.
GRE.   I wil frown as I passe by, & let the(m) take it as they list.   *45*
SAM.   Nay, as they dare. I wil bite my Thumb at them,
  which is a disgrace to them, if they beare it.
ABRA.   Do you bite your Thumbe at vs sir?
SAMP.   I do bite my Thumbe, sir.
ABRA.   Do you bite your Thumbe at vs, sir?   *50*
SAM.   Is the law of our side, if I say I?   GRE.   No.
SAM.   No sir, I do not bite my Thumbe at you sir: but
  I bite my Thumbe sir.
GREG.   Do you quarrell sir?
ABRA.   Quarrell sir? no sir.   *55*
SAM.   If you do sir, I am for you, I serue as good a man as you.
ABRA.   No better?   SAMP.   Well sir.

Enter Benuolio.

GR.   Say better: here comes one of my masters kinsmen.
SAMP.   Yes, better.
ABRA.   You Lye.   *60*
SAM.   Draw if you be men.   GREGORY,   remember thy
  (s)washing blow.   *They fight.*
BEN.   Part Fooles, put vp your swords, you know not
  what you do.

Enter Tibalt.

TYB.   What are thou drawne, among these heartlesse   *65*
  Hindes? Turne thee Benuolio, looke vpon thy death.
BEN.   I do but keepe the peace, put vp thy Sword,
  Or manage it to part these men with me.

Reprinted from Albert H. Marckwardt, *Introduction to the English Language* (New York: Oxford University Press, 1942), by permission of the publisher.

TYB.   What draw, and talke of peace? I hate the word
    As I hate hell, all *Mountagues,* and thee: *70*
    Haue at thee Coward.   *Fight.*

QUESTIONS

In answering these questions use the texts for both Exercise 9 and Exercise 10.

1. List all the pronouns. In general, is the practise here similar to that of MnE? What are the forms of genitive pronouns? Under what circumstances are *my* and *mine* used? What is the practise for forming reflexive pronouns?

2. Observe the context in which the second person pronouns are used. When are the *y*-forms (*you,* etc.) used and when are the *th*-forms (*thou,* etc.) used? Prepare a general statement about Shakespeare's practise in maintaining a distinction between these two forms of the second person pronoun. Do you think MnE has gained or lost in its practise in this regard?

3. Read further in any edition of Shakespeare and in the Bible (Authorized Version, 1611) for examples of EMnE use of *it.* How does the practise here compare with MnE usage? Do you find any occurrence of the MnE practise exemplified in these two sentences:

    a. *It* rained yesterday.

    b. I found out that my car had lost *its* shine.

Consult the *OED* for its treatment of 'its.'

4. Are there any occurrences of prepositions which contrast with MnE usage? (In the text for Exercise 9, what do you make of l. 89?)

5. Is Shakespeare's use of adjectives and adverbs similar to MnE usage? (Extend your examination beyond the limit of these two texts; consider, too, the occurrence of comparative and superlative forms.)

EXERCISE 11
HAMLET
III. i. 1–92, Shakespeare, first printed 1603

A hall in the castle.
Enter HAMLET *and two or three of the*
PLAYERS.

HAMLET.

Speak the speech, I pray you, as I pronounced it to you, trippingly on the tongue;
but if you mouth it, as many of your players do, I
had as lief the town-crier spoke my lines. Nor do
not saw the air too much with your hand, thus;   *5*
but use all gently: for in the very torrent, tempest,
and, as I may say, the whirlwind of passion, you
must acquire and beget a temperance that may
give it smoothness. O, it offends me to the soul to
hear a robostious periwig-pated fellow tear a   *10*
passion to tatters, to very rags, to split the ears of
the groundlings, who, for the most part, are
capable of nothing but inexplicable dumb-shows
and noise: I would have such a fellow whipt for
o'erdoing Termagant; it out-herods Herod: pray   *15*
you, avoid it.

FIRST PLAYER.

I warrant your honour.

HAMLET.

But not too tame neither, but let your own discretion be your tutor: suit the action to the word,
the word to the action; with this special observ-   *20*
ance, that you o'erstep not the modesty of nature:
for anything so overdone is from the purpose of
playing, whose end, both at the first and now,
was and is, to hold, as 'twere, the mirror up to
nature; to show virtue her own feature, scorn her   *25*
own image, and the very age and body of the time
his form and pressure. Now, this overdone, or

Reprinted from *Hamlet,* Shakespeare Head Press Edition (New York: Oxford University Press).

come tardy off, though it make the unskilful
laugh, cannot but make the judicious grieve; the
censure of the which one must, in your allowance,   30
o'erweigh a whole theatre of others. O there be
players that I have seen play,—and heard others
praise, and that highly,—not to speak it pro-
fanely, that, neither having the accent of Chris-
tians, nor the gait of Christian, pagan, nor man,   35
have so strutted and bellowed, that I have thought
some of nature's journeymen had made them,
and not made them well, they imitated humanity
so abominably.

FIRST PLAYER.

I hope we have reform'd that indifferently with   40
us, sir.

HAMLET.

O, reform it altogether. And let those that play
your clowns speak no more than is set down for
them: for there be of them that will themselves
laugh, to set on some quantity of barren specta-   45
tors to laugh too; though, in the mean time, some
necessary question of the play be then to be consider'd; that's villainous, and shows a most pitiful
ambition in the fool that uses it. Go, make you
ready.   [*Exeunt* PLAYERS.   50

Enter POLONIUS, ROSENCRANTZ, *and*
GUILDENSTERN.

How now, my lord! will the king hear this piece
of work?

POLONIUS.

And the queen, too, and that presently.

HAMLET.

Bid the players make haste.   [*Exeunt* POLONIUS.
Will you two help to hasten them?   55

ROSENCRANTZ *and* GUILDENSTERN.

We will, my lord.
                                    [*Exeunt* ROSENCRANTZ *and* GUILDENSTERN.

HAMLET.

What, ho, Horatio!

Enter HORATIO.

HORATIO.

Here, sweet lord, at your service.

HAMLET.

Horatio, thou art e'en as just a man
As e'er my conversation coped withal.   60

HORATIO.

O, my dear lord, —

HAMLET.

        Nay, do not think I flatter;
For what advancement may I hope from thee,
That no revenue hast, but thy good spirits,
To feed and clothe thee? Why should the poor be flatter'd?
No, let the candied tongue lick absurd pomp;   65
And crook the pregnant hinges of the knee
Where thrift may follow fawning. Dost thou hear?
Since my dear soul was mistress of her choice,
And could of men distinguish, her election
Hath seal'd thee for herself: for thou hast been   70
As one, in suffering all, that suffers nothing;
A man that fortune's buffets and rewards
Hast ta'en with equal thanks: and blest are those
Whose blood and judgement are so well commingled,
That they are not a pipe for fortune's finger   75
To sound what stop she please. Give me that man
That is not passion's slave, and I will wear him
In my heart's core, ay, in my heart of heart,
As I do thee. — Something too much of this. —
There is a play to-night before the king;   80
One scene of it comes near the circumstance
Which I have told thee of my father's death:
I prithee, when thou seest that act a-foot,
Even with the very comment of thy soul
Observe my uncle: if his occulted guilt   85
Do not itself unkennel in one speech,
It is a damned ghost that we have seen;
And my imaginations are as foul
As Vulcan's stithy. Give him heedful note:
For I mine eyes will rivet to his face;   90
And, after, we will both our judgements join
In censure of his seeming.

QUESTION

Rewrite the prose section of this text as you would speak it in your normal conversation. Do the same thing for the first twenty lines of *As You Like It,* I. i. Do not fuss too much about changing Shakespeare's vocabulary (but by all means notice the difference between his and yours). Give first attention to syntactical changes. What modifications (word order, function words, etc.) did you have to make? Compare Shakespeare's prose with OE and ME prose. What changes must still occur before English prose becomes modern?

⊹ ✠ ⊹

TRANSITION

Although most of the significant linguistic features of Modern English are present, fixed in the language of 1700, by no means can we conclude that all writers from that time forward display a style and set of language habits which are totally similar to the average usage represented in contemporary English. To suggest the nature of language change still possible, and, what is more, to invite a consideration of the stability of grammatical features and the flexibility of rhetoric—to suggest, that is, that one should ask if the language is changing or if it is only the habits of usage, of style, which are changing—we have included two passages produced after 1600, one dated roughly at 1700, the other at 1800. These are the texts:

12. *The Battle of Dunbar.* Gilbert Burnet, d. 1715.
13. *A Defence of Poetry.* Percy Bysshe Shelley, d. 1822.

EXERCISE 12
THE BATTLE OF DUNBAR
Gilbert Burnet, Bishop of Salisbury (d. 1715)
lines 1–37

The army was indeed one of the best that ever *Scotland* had brought together, but it was ill commanded: for all that had made defection from their cause, or that were thought indifferent as to either side, which they called detestable neutrality, were put out of commission. The preachers thought it an army of saints, and seemed well assured of success. They drew near *Cromwell,* who being 5 pressed by them retired towards *Dunbar,* where his ships and provisions lay. The *Scots* followed him, and were posted on a hill about a mile from thence, where there was no attacking them. *Cromwell* was then in great distress, and looked on himself as undone. There was no marching towards *Berwick,* the ground was too narrow: Nor could he come back into the country without 10 being separated from his ships, and starving his army. The least evil seemed to be to kill his horses, and put his army on board, and sail back to *Newcastle;* which, in the disposition that *England* was in at that time, would have been all their destruction, for it would have occasioned an universal insurrection for the King. They had not above three days' forage for their horses. So *Cromwell* 15 called his officers to a day of seeking the Lord, in their style. He loved to talk much of that matter all his life long afterwards: He said he felt such an enlargement of heart in prayer, and such quiet upon it, that he bade all about him take heart, for God had certainly heard them, and would appear for them. After prayer they walked in the Earl of Roxburgh's gardens, that lie under the hill: 20 And by prospective glasses they discerned a great motion in the *Scotish* Camp: upon which *Cromwell* said, 'God is delivering them into our hands, they are coming down to us.' *Leslie* was in the chief command: but he had a committee of the States with him to give him his orders, among whom *Warriston* was one. These were weary of lying in the fields, and thought that *Leslie* made not haste 25 enough to destroy those Sectaries; for so they loved to call them. He told them, by lying there all was sure, but that by engaging into action with gallant and desperate men all might be lost: Yet they still called on him to fall on. Many have thought that all this was treachery, done on design to deliver up our army to *Cromwell*; some laying it upon *Leslie,* and others upon my uncle. I am 30 persuaded there was no treachery in it: only *Warriston* was too hot and *Leslie* was too cold, and yielded too easily to their humours, which he ought not to have done. They were all night employed in coming down the hill: And in the morning, before they were put in order, *Cromwell* fell upon them. Two regiments stood their ground, and were almost all killed in their ranks: The rest did run 35 in a most shameful manner: So that both their artillery and baggage, and with these a great many prisoners, were taken, some thousands in all.

Reprinted from *The Oxford Book of English Prose*, edited by Sir Arthur Thomas Quiller-Couch (New York: The Oxford University Press, 1925).

QUESTIONS

This text, like that for Exercise 13, is a modern edition. Both texts will show, however, the general condition of English within two centuries of Shakespeare's death.

1. Are there any instances here of punctuation usage which does not yet quite accord with contemporary usage?

2. Can you, from observation of the punctuation, come to any conclusion about sentence rhythm? Do these sentences sound like contemporary sentences?

3. If you were to rewrite this passage, would you feel obliged to make any changes in vocabulary or structure? Is *do* used the same way you would use it?

4. If there were no date for this text, and you were to find it, would you regard it as 'fairly recent,' 'old fashioned,' good or bad writing? Why?

EXERCISE 13
A DEFENCE OF POETRY
Percy Bysshe Shelley (d. 1822)
lines 1–51

Poetry is indeed something divine. It is at once the centre and circumference
of knowledge; it is that which comprehends all science, and that to which all
science must be referred. It is at the same time the root and blossom of all other
systems of thought; it is that from which all spring, and that which adorns all;
and that which, if blighted, denies the fruit and seed, and withholds from the   5
barren world the nourishment and the succession of the scions of the tree of
life. It is the perfect and consummate surface and bloom of all things; it is as the
odour and the colour of the rose to the texture of the elements which compose
it, as the form and splendour of unfaded beauty to the secrets of anatomy and
corruption. What were virtue, love, patriotism, friendship—what were the   10
scenery of this beautiful universe which we inhabit; what were our consolations
on this side of the grave—and what were our aspirations beyond it, if poetry
did not ascend to bring light and fire from those eternal regions where the owl-
winged faculty of calculation dare not ever soar? Poetry is not like reasoning,
a power to be exerted according to the determination of the will. A man cannot   15
say, 'I will compose poetry.' The greatest poet even cannot say it; for the mind
in creation is as a fading coal, which some invisible influence, like an inconstant
wind, awakens to transitory brightness; this power arises from within, like the
colour of a flower which fades and changes as it is developed, and the conscious
portions of our natures are unprophetic either of its approach or its departure.   20
Could this influence be durable in its original purity and force, it is impossible
to predict the greatness of the results; but when composition begins, inspiration
is already on the decline, and the most glorious poetry that has ever been
communicated to the world is probably a feeble shadow of the original conceptions of the poet.   25
Poetry is the record of the best and happiest moments of the happiest and
best minds. We are aware of evanescent visitations of thought and feeling
sometimes associated with place or person, sometimes regarding our own mind
alone, and always arising unforeseen and departing unbidden, but elevating
and delightful beyond all expression: so that even in the desire and regret they   30
leave, there cannot but be pleasure, participating as it does in the nature of its
object. It is as it were the interpenetration of a diviner nature through our
own; but its footsteps are like those of a wind over the sea, which the coming
calm erases, and whose traces remain only, as on the wrinkled sand which paves
it. These and corresponding conditions of being are experienced principally by   35
those of the most delicate sensibility and the most enlarged imagination; and
the state of mind produced by them is at war with every base desire. The

Reprinted from *The Oxford Book of English Prose*, edited by Sir Arthur Thomas Quiller-Couch
(New York: University of Oxford Press), by permission of The Clarendon Press.

enthusiasm of virtue, love, patriotism, and friendship, is essentially linked with such emotions; and whilst they last, self appears as what it is, an atom to a universe. Poets are not only subject to these experiences as spirits of the most *40* refined organization, but they can colour all that they combine with the evanescent hues of this ethereal world; a word, a trait in the representation of a scene or a passion, will touch the enchanted chord, and reanimate, in those who have ever experienced these emotions, the sleeping, the cold, the buried image of the past. Poetry thus makes immortal all that is best and most beautiful in *45* the world; it arrests the vanishing apparitions which haunt the interlunations of life, and veiling them, or in language or in form, sends them forth among mankind, bearing sweet news of kindred joy to those with whom their sisters abide—abide, because there is no portal of expression from the caverns of the spirit which they inhabit into the universe of things. Poetry redeems from decay *50* the visitations of the divinity in man.

QUESTIONS

By the beginning of the nineteenth century the grammatical features of English have, for the most part, assumed the look and sound of contemporary English. This passage presents no structural difficulties to the contemporary reader.

    1. Would you call it, however, ordinary, contemporary English?

    2. What would you say about its diction (vocabulary)?

    3. What would you say about its style—formal, stilted, concise, what? How would you rate it, good or bad?

    4. Consult other first editions of early nineteenth-century English prose, both American and British, and prepare a paper describing what you feel to be the principal differences between early nineteenth-century and twentieth-century English.

is today pronounced with the diphthong used in MnE 'mean.' Such regularity suggests a phonological law. Not all the changes which have occurred are that orderly, although, when you have seen more evidence, you will be able to conclude that the directions of phonological change have not been altogether arbitrary and that some of them can be explained quite reasonably.

Because thorough competence in phonology (the study of the sounds employed in a language) requires a great deal of work—and lies beyond the scope of this exercise—you will observe here a set of restricted texts. Therefore not every phonological change which has occurred in English can be demonstrated, although the principal ones will be. We must start by considering the need for a neutral alphabet to represent the sounds of English. Conventional spelling, although more so now than it used to be, is not altogether logical or consistent. We use the same set of spelling characters to represent more than one sound. For example, the actual value (sound) of the stressed diphthong in 'say' is identical with that of 'weigh,' 'main,' and 'pale'; 'ay,' 'ei,' 'ai,' and 'a–e' all represent the same sound. A careful analysis of the relationship between sound and spelling will reveal many more examples of mismatching of sound and spelling. The problem arises because our alphabet of twenty-six characters is used to represent at least thirty-one to thirty-three sounds, the actual sounds used in contemporary English. A phonemic notation, using one character to represent only one sound, will suit our present need. We say, when we use such a system, that we transcribe speech, or a written text, into phonemic notation, or that we make a phonemic transcription. Awareness of the distinction between a phonetic and a phonemic transcription is not important for this exercise. Neither will it be necessary to annotate stress, pitch, or juncture. For the purpose of this exercise we will establish these guides:

a. a phoneme is a set of sounds, so restricted that a single sound must belong to only *one* set; no sound can belong to more than one set; therefore, the sets are mutually exclusive and contrast with each other, e.g., of 'see' and 'say' we can state that the initial consonant of both belongs to the same set, but the stressed diphthongs of each belong to different sets

b. the following equivalencies are established between the symbol used and the sound it represents:

Consonants

b	*b*ait	s	*s*in
d	*d*ate	š	*sh*in
f	*f*ate	t	*t*in
g	*g*ate	θ	*th*igh
k	*c*ake	ð	*th*y
h	*h*ate	v	*v*an
m	*m*ate	z	*z*est
n	*n*o	ž	vi*s*ion, *Zh*ivago
ŋ	sa*ng*	č	*ch*ur*ch*
p	*p*ark	ǰ	*j*oke, *G*eor*g*e

Semi-Vowels

l	*l*ay
r	*r*ay
y	*y*ell
w	*w*ay

Vowels

	FRONT	CENTRAL	BACK
High	i b<u>i</u>t	ɨ start<u>e</u>d	u b<u>oo</u>k
Mid	e b<u>e</u>t	ə b<u>u</u>t	ɔ b<u>ou</u>ght
Low	æ b<u>a</u>t	a b<u>o</u>x	

The vowels are placed in this chart, labelled as indicated, to show the relative point of articulation of the vowel. Think of the left as close to the lips of the mouth, the right side as close to the back of the mouth, the top close to the roof of the mouth, and the bottom as lower down. The tongue mass moves into approximately one of the nine available positions when the vowel is uttered. Front vowels are articulated with the lips unrounded, back vowels with the lips rounded. The jaw also drops lower as the vowel uttered is lower. (Why does the physician ask you to utter /a/ when he wishes to examine your throat?)

Diphthongs (combine a vowel with a semi-vowel)

Those diphthongs made with a vowel and the semi-vowel /y/ are articulated closer to the front of the mouth than the ones made with the semi-vowel /w/ are.

iy	b*ea*t	uw	b*oo*t
ey	b*ai*t	ow	b*oa*t
oy	b*oy*	aw	(a)b*ou*t
ay	b*i*te		

We will add two other combinations of sound:

yuw, 'b*eau*ty,' to distinguish a transcription of that combination of sounds from the sound of the stressed diphthong in 'boot.' It is also the difference between 'feud' and 'food.'

-ər, the sound of the last syllable in 'sing*er*.'

Some sample phonemic transcriptions, using the equivalencies from the table, follow; study them and then transcribe the words and passages listed below. Remember, transcription represents sounds, as used in normal conversation, *not* spellings. Transcriptions are placed within slant lines: /—/.

packed /pækt/	sink /siŋk/	food /fuwd/
rise /rayz/	mother /məðər/	feud /fyuwd/
rice /rays/	table /teybəl/	witty /witiy/
vision /vižən/	floor /flɔr/	believe /bəliyv/
elevator /eləveytər/	singer /siŋər/	baited /beytid/
shining /šayniŋ/	finger /fiŋgər/	shop /šap/
hangar /hæŋər/	church /čərč/	shopped /šapt/
hunger /həŋgər/	Charlie /čarliy/	jabbed /jæbd/

Friday and Saturday afternoon /fraydiy ən sætərdiy æftərnuwn/

I'll take sugar and spice /ayl teyk šugər ən spays/

TRANSCRIBE

1. Sunday, Monday, and Tuesday
2. April, May, June, and July
3. see saw Marjorie Daw
4. Sue sells sea shells
5. Four score and twenty years ago our forefathers brought forth upon this nation
6. application
7. penny
8. pen knife
9. weigh
10. wail
11. whale
12. who's in a hurry
13. where's the fire
14. pumpkin pie and ice cream
15. cheese and crackers got all muddy

So far in this exercise we have conducted a preliminary discussion necessary for a consideration of historical phonological change. We may now move to that consideration. Printed below are three short passages. Those in OE and ME you have already seen in earlier exercises. But you will notice that the passage in OE, the opening lines, once again, of "The Legend of St. Andrew," does not correspond precisely with the same lines as they are printed in Exercise 1. Here the text has been normalized and altered to fit the orthographical practise current in the Late West Saxon dialect. There are several reasons for using now a normalized text. You can, to begin with, compare the two versions to see how the spellings differ, and that type of experience in making a contrastive analysis should provide for you an insight into a technique which has proved most useful to the historical linguist, although, to be quite honest, the texts are too short to enable you to make more than a superficial analysis. More important, using the Late West Saxon dialect assures us of tracing the development of sound changes from the widest base of OE—most of the OE documents are preserved in this dialect. Should you continue your study of OE you would discover the importance, in the development of English, of other OE dialects. For the present it is sufficient to restrict the data to the evidence of this one dialect.

Accompanying each passage is a transcription employing the notation you have just learned. Where sounds occur (and are transcribed) which are different from sounds found in MnE, they are explained. Study the passages carefully and read the transcriptions aloud. It is a good idea to read each aloud as many times as you need to until you feel you can read each passage easily, reproducing, as the transcription indicates, the sounds (so far as we are able to reconstruct them) which would have been heard at the time the original was produced. Then answer the questions which follow. The same passages which you have already studied in OE and ME are used here again because, to complete this exercise, you need to know the MnE equivalent of the words in the text; there are no unfamiliar words in the EMnE text.

I. OE

Hēr sæġþ þæt *æfter* þām þe Drihten Hǣlend *Crist* tō heo-
heyr sæyθ θæt æfter θa:m θe drixten hæ:lend kriy:st tow: heo

fenum āstāh, *þæt* þā apostoli *wæron* ætsomne. And hīe *sendon*
vənum a:sta:x θæt θa: apɔstəliy wæ:rɔn ætsɔmne and hiy:ə sendɔn

hlot him betwēonum,   hwider hira ġehwelċ faran *sceolde*   *tō*
hlɔt him betwey:ownum hwider hira yehwelč faran šeowlde tow:

lǣrenne. Sæġþ þæt sē   ēadiga   Matheus ġehlēat   *tō*   Marmadonia
læ:ren:e sæyθ θæt sey: æ:ədigə maθeus yehlæ:ət tow: marmədowniə

þǣre ċeastre. Sæġþ þonne *þæt* þā *men* þe on þǣre ċeastre   5
θæ:rə čæəstre sæyθ θɔn:e θæt θa: men θe ɔn θæ:rə čæəstre

wǣron, þæt hīe   *hlāf* ne ǣton, nē   *wæter* ne *druncon;* ac hīe
wæ:rɔn θæt hiy:ə xla:f ne æ:tɔn ney: wæter ne drunkɔn ak hiy:ə

ǣton manna līċhaman and hiera *blōd*   *druncon.* And ǣġhwelċ
æ:tɔn man:a liy:čaman and hiəra blow:d drunkɔn and   æ:yhwelč

man þe on þǣre ċeastre cōm   elþēodisc,   sæġþ þæt hīe   *hine sōna*
man θe ɔn θæ:re čæəstre kow:m elθey:owdiš sæyθ θæt hiy:ə hine sow:na

ġenōmon   and *his* ēagan   *ūt*   āstungon, and hīe   *him* sealdon āttor
yenow:man and his æ:əgan uw:t a:stungɔn and hiy:ə him sæəldɔn a:t:ɔr

drincan þæt mid miclum lybcræfte *wæs ġeblanden,* and mid   10
drinkan θæt mid miklum lybkræfte wæs yeblanden and mid

þām þe hīe   þone *drenċ druncon,* hraþe hiera heorte   *wæs* tōlīesed
θam θey hiy:ə θɔne drenč drunkɔn xraθe hiəra heowrte wæs tow:liy:əsed

and hiere mōd   onwended.
and hiəra mow:d ɔnwended

NOTES

1. The notation /:/ after a character indicates that the sound is long; not different but longer; i.e., more time is consumed in saying it. It is very important to observe the short–long distinction.

2. The character /x/ represents the sound of the spelling *ch* in the German word *ach.*

3. The character /Y/ represents a high-front-rounded vowel which has the sound of the spelling *ü* in the German word *müssen.*

4. You will also need the words in the following list for this exercise:

OE Spelling	Transcription	MnE Spelling
nama	nama	name
sǣ	sæ:	sea
dæġ	dæy	day
healfe	hæəlfe	half
wē	wey:	we
crabba	krab:a	crab
ðynnum	θYn:um	thin
lǣdan	læ:dan	lead (v.)
yfele	Yfelə	evil
æcer	æker	acre

II. ME

Ther was also   a *Nonne*, a *Prioresse*,
θær was alsow: ə nun   ə priy:ɔres:ə

That of *hir smyling* was *ful simple and coy;*
θat ɔf ir smiy:ling was ful simpl and koy

Hir gretteste *ooth* was *but* by *seynte* Loy;
ir   gret:əst ɔ:θ   was but bi sæintə loy

And *she* was cleped   *madame* Eglentyne.
and šey: was kley:pəd madam egləntiy:nə

Ful wel she song the *service divyne,*   5
ful wel šey: sɔng θə servisə diviy:nə

Entuned   in hir *nose* ful *semely;*
entyuwnəd in ir   nɔ:z ful sey:məli

And Frensh she spak ful faire and *fetisly,*
and frenš šey: spak ful fæir and fetisli

After the *scole* of Stratford atte Bowe,
æftər θə skow:l of stratfɔrd at:ə bɔ:wə

For Frensh of Paris was *to*   hir unknowe.
fɔr frenš ɔf paris was tow: ir   unknɔ:wə

At *mete* *wel* *y-taught* was she *with-alle;*   10
at mæ:tə wel itawxt   was šey: wiθal:ə

She leet *no morsel* from hir *lippes* falle,
šey: ley:t nɔ: mɔrsəl frɔm ir lip:əs fal:ə

Ne *wette* hir *fingres* in hir *sauce depe.*
nə wet: ir fingrəs in ir   sawsə dey:pə

Wel coude she carie a *morsel,* and *wel kepe,*
wel kuw,d šey: kari ə mɔrsəl and wel key:pə

That *no* *drope* ne fille up-on hir *brest.*
θæt nɔ: drɔp nə fil: upɔn ir brest

In curteisye was *set* ful *muche* hir lest.   15
in kuwrtæisi was set ful mutš ir lest

NOTES

1. You will need two more words for this exercise:

ME Spelling	Transcription	MnE Spelling
mous	muw:s	mouse
houndes	huw:ndəs	hounds

2. You will observe that the final -e occurring at the end of a line of verse has been transcribed /ə/, indicating that it was pronounced. In Exercise 5, however, the first line of this passage, which ends in a final -e, was scanned, and there it was suggested that the final -e at the end of the line of verse was *not* pronounced. The older view is that every final -e occurring at the end of a line of verse *was* pronounced. Today all authorities do not agree; there are some who believe that the rhythm of the line is the best guide in this matter, and that if the line does not *demand* it, to fit the basic iambic meter, it should not be pronounced. Unfortunately, we cannot reconstitute a fourteenth century Londoner to settle the issue.

III. EMnE

Oh that this too too   solid Flesh, would   melt,
ow: ðæt ðis tuw: tuw: sɔlid fleš   wuw:ld melt

Thaw, and resolue it selfe into   a Dew:
θɔ: ænd rizɔlv itself   intuw: ə duw

Or that the Eurlasting had not fixt
ɔr ðæt ði evərlæstiŋ hæd nɔt fikst

His Cannon 'gainst Selfe-slaughter. O   God, O   God!
hiz kænən gæinst self slɔ:tr   ow: gɔd ow: gɔd

How weary, stale, flat, and vnprofitable   5
həw wey:ri stæ:l flæt ənd unprɔfitæ:bl

Seemes to me   all the vses   of this world?
siy:mz tə miy: ɔ:l ðə yuwsiz əv ðis wɔrld

Fie on't? Oh fie, fie, 'tis an vnweeded   Garden
fəy ɔnt   ow: fəy fəy tiz ən unwiy:did gærdn

That growes to Seed: Things rank, and   grosse in Nature
ðæt grow:z tə siy:d θiŋz   ræŋk ənd grow:s in næ:tyər

Possesse it meerely. That it should come to this:
pəzes   it miy:rli ðæt it šuw:ld kum tə ðis

But two monthes dead: Nay, not so   much; not two,   10
but tuw: munθs ded   næi nɔt sow: muč   nɔt tuw:

So   excellent a King, that was to this
sow: eksələnt ə kiŋ   ðæt wæz tə ðis

Hiperion   to a Satyre: so   louing to my Mother
həypey:ryən tuw: a sæ:tir   sow: luviŋ tə məy muðr

That he might not beteeme the windes of heauen
ðæt i məyt nɔt bitiy:m ðə windz əv hevn

Visit her face too   roughly. Heauen and Earth
vizit ər fæ:s tuw: rufli   hevn   ənd erθ

Must I remember: why she would hang on him,   15
must əy rimembr   wəy šiy wuw:ld hæŋ on im

As if encrease of Appetite had growne
əz if inkrey:z əv æpətəyt həd grow:n

By what it fed on;
bəy wæt it fed ɔn

NOTES

Also use these words for this exercise:

EMnE Spelling	Transcription	MnE Spelling
teares	tey:rz	tears
reason	rey:zn	reason
toy	toy	toy
vnrighteous	unrəytyəs	unrighteous
doubt	dəwt	doubt

After you have read these passages and have made yourself familiar with the transcriptions, you are in a position to commence a preliminary investigation of the development of English sounds. But you do not have sufficient information to make a thorough study, because, for one thing, nothing has been indicated about the occurrence of stress (relative loudness in pronunciation) in the earlier stages of the language or how, in some instances, it shifted. But you can make a good many observations with the limited data you have. Begin by preparing charts, one for each transcription shown above. Draw sixteen columns on a piece of paper, one for each of the MnE stressed vowels and diphthongs displayed earlier in this exercise; omit the high central vowel /i/ but add /ər/. Your chart, at the beginning, will look like this:

OE CHART

MnE	bit	bet	bat	but	box	book	bought
	i	e	æ	ə	a	u	ɔ
			æfter				

beat	bait	boy	bite	boot	boat	bout	– er	feud
iy	ey	oy	ay	uw	ow	zw	ər	yuw
			kriy:st	tow:				

Make three charts, one for OE, one for ME, and one for EMnE. For each transcription (and using all words from each list of transcriptions added after a text), place the *transcription* of each word which is italicized in the text (from the EMnE text place each word) in the column headed by the stressed vowel or diphthong which represents the contemporary pronunciation of its stressed vowel or diphthong. The three *italicized* words in the first line of the OE text would be placed on your OE chart as follows:

æfter (stressed vowel in OE is *æ*): in the *æ* column, because the stressed vowel in MnE 'after' is also *æ*; place /æfter/ there

Crist (stressed vowel in OE is *iy:*): in the *ay* column, because the stressed diphthong in MnE 'Christ' is *ay*; place /kriy:st/ there

tō (stressed vowel in OE is *ow:*): in the *uw* column, because the stressed diphthong in MnE 'to' is *uw*; place /tow:/ there

Complete these charts.

QUESTIONS

With the preceding charts as your evidence, answer the following questions.

1. What would have been the missing forms in this chart? The entries are transcriptions, not spellings.

OE	ME	MnE
nama	_____	neym
_____	giltəs	gilts
sun:e	sun:ə	_____
muw:s	_____	maws
fey:dan	fey:d	_____
_____	stɔ:n	stown
man	_____	mæn
_____	koy	koy
sendan	sendə	_____
_____	riy:də	rayd

(Note: a shortcoming in the transcription system we have used shows up here. The fourth entry in the OE column (muw:s) accurately represents the OE spelling *mūs*, but the symbol used to represent the OE long vowel *ū* is a diphthong symbol. You must look to the *spellings* of the OE text to identify an OE diphthong. Double vowel spellings in OE are diphthongs. There are eight of them: ea, ēa; eo, ēo; io, īo; ic, īe. Therefore *ē* in OE is a long vowel, pronounced /ey:/; although we have to use the symbol of a MnE diphthong to represent it, *ē*, in OE, was a vowel. When you consider the development of the OE vowels and diphthongs, look to the OE spellings—the transcriptions represent their quality, or equivalent sound value.)

2. For this question we shall agree that MnE has seven vowels: /i, e, æ, ə, a, u, ɔ/.

    a. What OE vowels are not present in MnE?

    b. What MnE vowels were present in OE?

    c. Are there any MnE vowels not present in OE?

    d. Which OE vowels were most stable (i.e., exhibit the least change from OE to MnE)?

3. For this question we shall agree that MnE has seven diphthongs, (iy, ey, oy, ay, uw, ow, aw/, and the combinations /yuw, ər/.

    a. What are the OE sources of the MnE diphthongs?

    b. Are any unaccounted for by OE sources? If so, can you account for that fact?

4. Repeat questions 2 and 3 for ME.

5. In their transition from OE to ME were the vowels and dipthongs stable, very stable, or not very stable?

6. Repeat questions 2, 3, and 5 for EMnE.

7. Do you observe any instance, in any of the three stages, of a change in sound in a short vowel or diphthong where the same change did not occur in the long version of the same sound? ME *drope* (1. 14, p. 438) and ME *ooth* (1. 3, p. 438) became what MnE words? Are there other similar occurrences? Are the long or the short sounds the most stable?

8. With your response to question 7 in mind, can you formulate a statement about the ME *spellings* of vowels and diphthongs?

9. Sometime before the beginning of the ME period and ending sometime after the beginning of the EMnE period all the vowels of English went through a change which has been called 'The Great Vowel Shift.' Consult any of the textbooks which have been mentioned in these exercises for a description of that shift. Does the evidence which you have assembled here confirm the general description you read?

10. Are there any consonants in MnE which were not present in any of the three earlier stages of English?

11. Are there any consonants in any of the three earlier stages which are not present in MnE? If so, have they been replaced by other sounds? What has been the history of what in MnE we spell '-ing'? Consult the *OED* for earlier pronunciations of 'doubt,' 'dumb,' 'doom'; what do you find? What appears to be the source of the MnE spelling 'gh'?

12. What appears to be the effect of the occurrence of one of the semi-vowels next to a vowel?

13. Some consonant changes can be explained by observing the movements of the tongue as sounds are articulated (pronounced) and by knowing what changes a shift in stress can cause. For example, MnE 'feature' was at one time trisyllabic and was pronounced with heavy stress on the first and last syllables: /fíy ti ùr/. It lost its heavy final stress, changed its final vowel to /ə/, and became disyllabic: /fíy tiər/. It can be shown that /i/ before a lightly stressed vowel tends to become a semi-vowel: thus, /fíy tyər/. It can also be shown that the occurrence of /ty/ causes an assimilation to take place. The tongue positions for /t/ and /y/ are quite close, and in the movement from the first to the second it fell into the position for /č/: thus, /fíy čər/. See if

you now can explain how the MnE pronunciation of *nature* developed from the pronunciation of it indicated in 1. 8, p. 439.

14. Although a good deal has been skipped in this exercise, you are, nonetheless, in a position now to prepare a first paper, or class discussion, on the development of English sounds. Do that.

EXERCISE 15
SEMANTIC CHANGE

Just as the structure (and therefore the grammar) and the sounds of English have changed over the years of its history and use, so too has its vocabulary changed. We have observed already one manifestation of vocabulary change, the appearance of loan words in the language. Other changes also took place, resulting, in addition to gains in the word stock, to some losses, as words formerly in the lexicon of English have dropped out. The *OED,* for example, lists many forms which are labelled 'obsolete,' no longer in use. Perhaps more striking has been the fate of words, both native English words and loan words, during the centuries of their existence in our language. It can be stated with almost the authority of a general law that *not all* words retain, in general usage, the meanings which they originally had. A *deer* for Shakespeare was not what we would call a 'deer'; 'knave' would not have meant to Chaucer what it means to us; a 'nice girl' (for us) would have implied something quite different to Samuel Johnson: hundreds of examples could be cited to show that changes in meaning, often drastic, have occurred.

It is not always possible to demonstrate why these changes took place. Perhaps a simplified explanation of the *semantic process* will help to identify some of the difficulties involved in trying to account for changes in meaning. Linguistic Semantics (not to be confused with General Semantics, an altogether different matter) is the study of meaning. The semanticist regards what we call *word* as an arbitrary symbol, which, as is true of all symbols, has no (contains no) meaning in itself, but points to, or stands for, something outside of itself where meaning may be said to reside. From this diagram we infer that an *observer* (or communicator) perceives a *sign* (symbol or word), follows its signal (direction) to an area of the *referent* (all contextual experience), selects the *meaning* equivalent (corresponding) to the *sign* for that contextual situation, and receives *comprehension*. Thus in each linguistic community speakers have agreed upon a large number of arbitrary signs as carriers

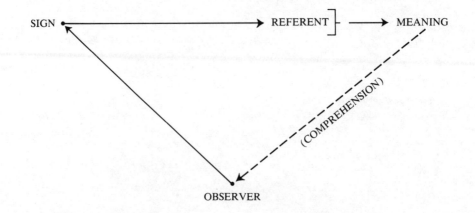

(when combined into the *code* by structural signals) of their *messages*. It is possible that conditions conducive to change may exist at any of the five stages represented in the diagram. The sign may change in form, the referent may narrow or enlarge, meaning may add or substract elements, comprehension may shift, and the attitude of the observer, towards all four of the other stages, may change. In actual usage, over the centuries, any or all of those forces may exert pressures on "word meanings" as the speakers of the language, constantly mobile in social situations, engage in the process of communication. When we do inquire into meaning, however, at least three other conditions, semantic environments, must be accounted for:

1. *Regional Variants.* A 'pail' to one speaker of English is a 'bucket' to another speaker. A 'dope' in one region is a 'coke' or 'coca-cola' in another, and may at the same time in both regions be a "dull, foolish person."

2. *Context.* If we ask for a 'pipe' in one store we will not receive the same object someone else will receive when he asks for a pipe in a different store.

3. *Time.* In the eighteenth century, when one traveled, he might have ridden in a 'coach.' If he traveled in the nineteenth century, the coach he rode in would have been quite different from the vehicle used by the traveler a century before, although called the same. And the twentieth century traveler, going 'coach fare,' could ride in a bus, a train, or an airplane.

Why do words change their meanings, and what must be considered when meaning is investigated are, as it should now be clear, vexing questions. It is much easier to observe *what* has happened.

Words change their meanings in one of four ways. They may generalize, specialize, pejorate, or ameliorate. An example of each type of change is illustrated by the development of the meaning of 'dedicate,' 'wife,' 'churl,' and 'steward.' Consult the *OED* for the history of the meanings attached, at different times, to those words. In general, this is what you will find:

1. 'Dedicate' has *generalized*. At first it was restricted in usage to indicating that one offered his person, service, or work to God. Now one may dedicate his person, service, or work to anyone or anything, and buildings or memorials can be dedicated. Obviously the area of the referent has enlarged. Note, too, that all the earlier meanings are still in general use.

2. 'Wife' has *specialized*. At first a wife was any adult female, but now she is a married female. In time, 'woman' took over the earlier meaning of wife. Obviously the area of the referent has restricted. Note that the earlier meaning is *not* now in general use.

3. 'Churl' has *pejorated*. At first 'churl' meant any country fellow, a rustic, but now the implication of unsavory moral behaviour is attached to it. In 900 "a good churl" was a permitted utterance; today, unless used ironically, it would not be understood. Obviously the attitude taken by speakers towards the referent has changed. The earlier meaning is no longer in general use.

4. 'Steward' has *ameliorated*. At first a keeper or guardian of a hall or sty (perhaps a pig sty), a steward now may be a respected public official or officer of a club. Its development has been just the opposite of that of 'churl.' The earlier meaning has been obscured.

It is convenient to divide these four types of semantic change into two sets of two changes, to show further the permissible changes a word may experience.

REFERENTIAL CHANGES	ATTITUDE CHANGES
(*Denotation*)	(*Connotation*)
Generalization	Pejoration
Specialization	Amelioration

At the same time, change is permitted in the direction of one member of each set and one member of the other set. Thus, a word cannot, for example, generalize and specialize at the same time, nor can it pejorate and ameliorate at the same time, but it could generalize and pejorate, or generalize and ameliorate, or specialize and pejorate, or specialize and ameliorate at the same time. And some words, having taken one direction, have, at a later time, reversed that direction.

QUESTIONS

1. Consult the *OED* to discover the semantic development of each word in the following list. In each instance, state

    a. what type of semantic change is illustrated
    b. whether the older meanings still survive in contemporary usage
    c. what periods of over-lapping of meanings occurred, if any
    d. what word has replaced it, if it did not survive

article	disease	lewd	pretty
bard	drive	libel	proposition
butcher	enthusiasm	lust	ring (n.)
chest	flesh	marshall	sail (v.)
chivalry	fond	martyr	smirk
circumstance	governor	meat	starve
coast (n.)	harlot	nice	thing
corn	hussy	pen	undertaker
counterfeiter	injury	picture	villain
crafty	knight	pirate	virtue

    2. Do semantic changes appear to occur more readily in words belonging to one part of speech class than to words in another class?
    3. Do loan words appear to be subjected to change to the same degree as native English words?

AN ADDED NOTE

Some attention to word borrowing and semantic change is an antidote to the 'etymological fallacy.' Etymology, as you have now determined, is not always a safe guide for determining the *present* meaning of a word. A distinguished American poet once deplored such phrases as 'Crime Crusade' and 'Cancer Crusade' because he believed 'crusade' should be restricted to mean the activities of religiously motivated men in the Middle Ages who 'took up the cross' to defend Christianity against attacks by 'heathens.' Not only did he ignore the historical fact that those medieval gentlemen had to travel thousands of miles from their homes to wage that defense, committing quite as many atrocities along the way as performing noble deeds, but he also failed to comprehend that 'Crime Crusade' and 'Cancer Crusade' are utterly sanctioned by contemporary usage. One might not like to hear 'crusade' used in that way, but it is useless to deplore, and not particularly honest to suggest to others, that it is wrong, or in bad taste, to use it that way.

It may not be unnecessary to add, also, that this one exercise does not exhaust the subject of semantic change. Still to be investigated would be such phenomena as euphemism, genteelism, hyperbole, understatement (litotes), folk-etymology, slang, British-American differences in usage, word coinage, and ironic use of language. All are interesting topics. This has been a restricted exercise. Additional information about semantic change and loan words, moreover, may prove rewarding. Seek it in these two excellent books:

1. Mary S. Serjeanston. *A History of Foreign Words in English*. New York: Dutton, 1936.

2. Gustav Stern. *Meaning and Change of Meaning*. Gothenburg: Wettergren and Kerber, 1931.

✠ ✠ ✠

SUMMARY

Two sets of parallel passages have been placed at the end of these exercises to provide data for a discussion of the development of English from its earliest period to the present time. These are the texts:

16. *De Consolatione Philosophiæ,* Boethius
    . a. the Latin text, 524
    b. Alfred's translation, 900
    c. Chaucer's translation, 1400
    d. the translation of Queen Elizabeth I, 1593
    e. a modern translation, 1962

17. *The New Testament,* Matthew vi. 9–21
    a. Gothic Text, 360
    b. Old English Text, 1000
    c. Middle English, Wycliffe, 1389
    d. Early Modern English, Tyndale, 1526
    e. Modern English, Monsignor Knox, 1944
    f. Modern English, Revised Standard Version, 1952

EXERCISE 16
PARALLEL TEXTS OF
DE CONSOLATIONE PHILOSOPHIÆ
III, vii, 1–58

The Latin Text
BOETHIUS,
524

Felix qui potuit boni
Fontem uisere lucidum,
Felix qui potuit grauis
Terræ soluere uincula.
Quondam funera coniugis   5
Vates threicius gemens,
Postquam flebilibus modis
Siluas currere mobiles,
Amnes stare coegerat,
Iunxitque intrepidum latus   10
Sæuis cerua leonibus,
Nec uisum timuit lepos
Iam cantu placidum canem.
Cum flagrantior intima
Feruor pectoris ureret   15
Nec qui cuncta subegerant
Mulcerent dominum modi,
Inmites superos querens
Infernas adiit domos.
Illic blanda sonantibus   20
Chordis carmina temperans
Quidquid præcipuis deæ
Matris fontibus hauserat,
Quod luctus dabat impotens,
Quod luctum geminans amor,   25
Deflet Tænara commouens,
El dulci ueniam prece
Vmbrarum dominos rogat.
Stupet tergeminus nouo

Captus carmine ianitor,   30
Quæ sontes agitant metu
Vltrices scelerum deæ
Iam mastæ lacrimis madent.
Non ixionium caput
Velox præcipitat rota,   35
Et longa site perditus
Spernit flumina Tantalus.
Vultur dum satur est modis,
Non traxit Tityi iecur.
Tandem "uincimur" arbiter   40
Vmbrarum miserans ait:
"Donamus comitem uiro
Emptam carmine coniugem.
Sed lex dona coerceat,
Ne, dum Tartara liqueret,   45
Fas sit lumina flectere."
Quis legem det amantibus?
Maior lex amor est sibi.
Heu noctis prope terminos
Orpheus Eurydicen suam   50
Vidit perdidit occidit.
Vos hæc fabula respicit
Quicumque in superum diem
Mentem ducere quæritis.
Nam qui tartareum in specus   55
Victus lumina flexerit,
Quidquid præcipuum trahit,
Perdit, dum uidet inferos.

Reprinted from Early English Text Society, original series, vol. 113 (London: K. Paul, Trench, Trübner & Co., 1899; Revised, 1931), by permission of the publisher.

Old English
ALFRED'S TRANSLATION,
Orpheus and Eurydice, 900

Hit gelamp gīo ðætte ān hearpere wæs on ðǣre ðīode ðe Ðrācia hātte, sīo wæs
on Grēca rīce; sē hearpere wæs swīðe ungefrǣglīce good, ðæs nama wæs Orfeus;
hē hæfde ān swīðe ǣnlīc wīf, sīo wæs hāten Eurudice. Ðā ongon mon secgan be
ðām hearpere, þæt hē meahte hearpian þæt sē wudu wagode, ond þā stānas hī
styredon for ðȳ swēge, ond wildu dīor ðǣr woldon tō irnan ond stondan swilce   5
hī tamu wǣren, swā stille, ðēah him men oððe hundas wið ēodon, ðæt hī hī nā ne
onscunedon. Ðā sǣdon hī þæt ðæs hearperes wīf sceolde ācwelan, ond hire sāule
mon sceolde lǣdan tō helle. Ða sceolde sē hearpere weorðan swā sārig, þæt hē
ne meahte ongemong ōðrum monnum bīon, ac tēah tō wuda, ond sæt on ðǣm
muntum, ǣgðer ge dæges ge nihtes, wēop ond hearpode, ðæt ðā wudas bifedon,   10
ond ðā ēa stōdon, ond nān heort ne onscunede nǣnne lēon, nē nān hara nǣnne
hund, nē nān nēat nyste nǣnne andan nē nǣnne ege tō ōðrum, for ðǣre mergðe
ðæs sōnes. Ða ðǣm hearpere ðā ðūhte ðæt hine nānes ðinges ne lyste on ðisse
worulde, ðā ðōhte hē ðæt hē wolde gesēcan helle godu, ond onginnan him
ōleccan mid his hearpan, ond biddan þæt hī him āgēafen eft his wif. Ðā hē ðā   15
ðider cōm, ðā sceolde cuman ðǣre helle hund ongēan hine, þæs nama wæs
Ceruerus, sē sceolde habban þrīo hēafdu, ond onfægnian mid his steorte, ond
plegian wið hine for his hearpunga. Ðā wæs ðǣr ēac swīðe egeslīc geatweard,
ðæs nama sceolde bīon Caron, sē hæfde ēac þrīo hēafdu, ond wæs swīðe
oreald. Ðā ongon sē hearpere hine biddan þæt hē hine gemundbyrde ðā hwīle   20
þe hē ðǣr wǣre, ond hine gesundne eft ðonan brōhte. Ðā gehēt hē him ðæt,
for ðǣm hē wæs oflyst ðæs seldcūðan sōnes. Ðā ēode hē furður oð hē gemētte
ðā graman gydena ðe folcise men hātað Parcas, ðā hī secgað ðæt on nānum men
nyten nāne āre, ac ǣlcum men wrecen be his gewyrhtum; þā hī secgað ðæt
wealden ǣlces mannes wyrde. Ða ongon hē biddan heora miltse; ða ongunnon   25
hī wēpan mid him. Ðā ēode hē furður, ond him urnon ealle hellwaran ongēan,
ond lǣddon hine tō hiora cyninge, ond ongunnon ealle sprecan mid him, ond
biddan ðæs ðe hē bæd. Ond þæt unstille hwēol ðe Ixīon wæs tō gebunden, Leuita
cyning, for his scylde, ðæt oðstōd for his hearpunga; ond Tantulus sē cyning,
ðe on ðisse worulde ungemetlīce gīfre wæs, ond him ðǣr ðæt ilce yfel filgde   30
ðǣre gifernesse, hē gestilde. Ond sē vultor sceolde forlǣtan ðæt hē ne slāt
ðā lifre Tyties ðæs cyninges, ðe hine ǣr mid ðȳ wītnode; ond eall hellwara wītu
gestildon, ðā hwīle þe hē beforan ðam cyninge hearpode. Ðā hē ðā longe ond
longe hearpode, ðā cleopode sē hellwara cyning, ond cwæð: 'Wutun āgifan
ðǣm esne his wīf, for ðǣm hē hī hæfð geearnad mid his hearpunga.' Bebēad him   35

Reprinted from Sweet's *Anglo-Saxon Reader,* 14th ed., revised by C. T. Onions (Oxford: The
Clarendon Press, 1959), by permission of The Clarendon Press, Oxford.

ðā ðæt hē geare wisse, ðæt hē hine næfre under bæc ne besāwe, siððan hē
ðonanweard wǣre; ond sǣde, gif hē hine under bæc besāwe, ðæt hē sceolde
forlǣtan ðæt wīf. Ac ðā lufe mon mæg swīðe unēaðe oððe nā forbēodan: wēi
lā wēi! hwæt, Orpheus ðā lǣdde his wīf mid him, oð ðe hē cōm on þæt gemǣre
lēohtes ond ðīostro; ðā ēode þæt wīf æfter him. Ðā hē forð on ðæt lēoht cōm,   40
ðā beseah hē hine under bæc wið ðæs wīfes: ðā losade hīo him sōna. Ðās
lēasan spell lǣrað gehwylcne mon ðāra ðe wilnað helle ðīostro tō flīonne, ond tō
ðæs sōðan Godes līohte tō cumanne, ðæt hē hine ne besīo tō his ealdum yflum,
swā ðæt hē hī eft swā fullīce fullfremme swā hē hī ǣr dyde; for ðǣm swā hwā
swā mid fulle willan his mōd went tō ðǣm yflum ðe hē ǣr forlēt, ond hī ðonne   45
fullfremeð, ond hī him ðonne fullīce līciað, and hē hī næfre forlǣtan ne
þenceð, ðonne forlȳst hē eall his ǣrran good, būton hē hit eft gebēte.

Middle English
CHAUCER'S TRANSLATION,
Liber Tertius, Metrum 12, 1400

"Felix qui potuit." Blisful is that man that may seen the clere welle of good!
Blisful is he that mai unbynden hym fro the boondes of the hevy erthe! The
poete of Trace (Orpheus), that whilom hadde ryght greet sorwe for the deth of
his wyf, aftir that he hadde makid by his weeply songes the wodes moevable to
renne, and hadde makid the ryveris to stonden stille, and hadde maked the   5
hertes and the hyndes to joynen dreedles here sydes to cruel lyouns (for to
herknen his song), and hadde maked that the hare was nat agast of the hound,
which was plesed by his song; so, whanne the moste ardaunt love of his wif
brende the entrayles of his breest, ne the songes that hadden overcomen alle
thinges ne mighten nat asswagen hir lord (orpheus), he pleynid hym of the   10
hevene goddis that weren cruel to hym. He wente hym to the houses of helle, and
ther he tempride his blaundysschinge songes by resounynge strenges, and spak
and song in wepynge al that evere he hadde resceyved and lavyd out of the
noble welles of his modir (Callyope), the goddesse. And he sang, with as mochel
as he myghte of wepynge, and with as moche as love, that doublide his sorwe, 15
myghte yeve hym and teche hym, and he commoevede the helle, and requyred
and bysoughte by swete preyere the lordes of soules in helle of relessynge (that
is to seyn, to yelden hym his wyf). Cerberus, the porter of helle, with his thre
hevedes was caught and al abasschid of the newe song. And the thre goddesses,
furiis and vengeresses of felonyes, that tormenten and agasten the soules by   20
anoy, woxen sorweful and sory, and wepyn teeris for pite. Tho was nat the heved
of Ixion ytormented by the overthrowynge wheel. And Tantalus, that was
destroied by the woodnesse of long thurst, despyseth the floodes to drynken.
The foul that highte voltor, that etith the stomak or the gyser of Tycius, is so
fulfild of his song that it nil eten ne tiren no more. At the laste the lord and juge 25
of soules was moevid to misericordes, and cryede: 'We ben overcomen,' quod
he; 'yyve we to Orpheus his wif to beren hym compaignye; he hath wel
ybought hire by his faire song and his ditee. But we wolen putten a lawe in this
and covenaunt in the yifte; that is to seyn that, til he be out of helle, yif he loke
byhynde hym, that his wyf schal comen ageyn unto us.' But what is he that may 30
yeven a lawe to loverys? Love is a grettere lawe and a strengere to hymself
(thanne any lawe that men mai yyeven). Allas! whanne Orpheus and his wyf
weren almost at the termes of the nyght (that is to seyn, at the laste boundes of
helle), Orpheus lokede abakward on Erudyce his wif, and lost hire, and was
deed. This fable apertenith to yow alle, whosoevere desireth or seketh to lede his 35

thought into the sovereyn day (that is to seyn, into cleernesse of sovereyn good). For whoso that evere be so overcomen that he ficche his eien into the put of helle (that is to seyn, whoso sette his thoughtes in erthly thinges), al that evere he hath drawen of the noble good celestial he lesith it, whanne he looketh the helles (that is to seyn, into lowe thinges of the erthe)." *40*

Early Modern English
ELIZABETH I's TRANSLATION,
The Third Booke, XII, Myter, 1593

Blist, that may of Good
The fontaine Clire behold,
happy that Can Of waighty
Erthe the bondes to breake.
The Tracian profit wons   5
his wives funeralz wailing
Whan with sorows note
The wauering trees he moued,
And stedy rivers made,
And hind caused Join   10
Unfearing Sides to Lion fierce.
Nor hare did feare the Looke
Of Cruel dog so plised with Song,
Whan ferventar desir the inward
brest more burnt,   15
Nor Could the notes that al subdued
Pacefie ther Lord,
Of Ireful Godz Complaining
The helly house went to.
Ther faining verse   20
Tuning to Sounding Stringe
What he drew from springes
The greatest of Mother Godz,
What feable mone could Giue,
What doubled Love afourd,   25
by Wailes and hel doth stur
And with dulce suite pardon
Of darkenes Lorde besiche.
Wondar doth the thre hedded
Jailor amasid with unwonted verse,   30

Revenging Goddes of faultes
That wontid Gilty feare
Sorowing with teares bedewed thé were.
not Ixiones hed
The whirling while did turne   35
And lost with longue thirst
Tantalus riuers skornes.
The Vultur fild with notes,
Tityus livor tared not.
At last wailing Said the Juge   40
Of Shady place "we yeld;
To man we giue his wife for feere,
Won by his Song.
With this Law bound be the gift,
While in the Tartar thou bidest,   45
turne back thy looke thou must not."
but who to Loue giues Law?
for greatest Law his Love he made.
So night drawing to her ende,
Eurydicen his Oreus   50
Sawe, Lost, and killed.
this fable toucheth you
Who so doth seak to gide
To hiest day his mynd.
for who in helly Shade   55
Won man his yees doth bend,
What so he chifest held
In vewing hel hathe lost.
     Et Sic bene.[1]

Reprinted from Early English Text Society, original series, vol. 113 (London: K. Paul, Trench, Trübner & Co., 1899; Revised, 1931).
[1]This line is added by the Queen.

Modern English
RICHARD H. GREEN'S TRANSLATION,
Book Three, Poem 12, 1962

'Happy is he who can look into the shining spring of good; happy is he who can break the heavy chains of earth.

'Long ago the Thracian poet, Orpheus, mourned for his dead wife. With his sorrowful music he made the woodland dance and the rivers stand still. He made the fearful deer lie down bravely with the fierce lions; the rabbit no longer   *5*
feared the dog quieted by his song.

'But as the sorrow within his breast burned more fiercely, that music which calmed all nature could not console its maker. Finding the gods unbending, he went to the regions of hell. There he sang sweet songs to the music of his harp, songs drawn from the noble fountains of his goddess mother, songs inspired by   *10*
his powerless grief and the love which doubled his grief.

'Hell is moved to pity when, with his melodious prayer, he begs the favor of those shades. The three-headed guardian of the gate is paralyzed by that new song; and the Furies, avengers of crimes who torture guilty souls with fear, are touched and weep in pity. Ixion's head is not tormented by the swift wheel, and   *15*
Tantalus, long maddened by his thirst, ignores the waters he now might drink. The vulture is filled by the melody and ignores the liver of Tityus.

'At last, the judge of souls, moved by pity, declares, "we are conquered. We return to this man his wife, his companion, purchased by his song. But our gift is bound by the condition that he must not look back until he has left hell." But   *20*
who can give lovers a law? Love is a stronger law unto itself. As they approached the edge of night, Orpheus looked back at Eurydice, lost her, and died.

'This fable applies to all of you who seek to raise your minds to sovereign day. For whoever is conquered and turns his eyes to the pit of hell, looking into the inferno, loses all the excellence he has gained.'   *25*

Gothic Text (translated by Bishop Ulfilas)
Ca., 360

9. Swa nu bidyaiþ yus, Atta unsar þu in himinam, weihnai namo þein;
10. Qimai þiudinassus þeins; wairþai wilya þeins swe in himina yah ana airþai;
11. Hlaif unsarana þana sinteinan gif uns himma daga;
12. Yah aflet una þatei skulans siyaima, swaswe yah weis afletam skulam unsaraim;
13. Yah ni briggais uns in fraistubnyai, ak lausei uns af þamma ubilin; unte þeina ist þiudangardi, yah mahts, yah wulþus in aiwins, Amen.
14. Unte yabai afletiþ mannam missadedins ize, afletiþ yah izwis atta izwar sa ufar himinam.
15. Iþyabai ni afletiþ mannam missadedins ize, ni þau atta izwar afletiþ missadedins izwaros.
16. Aþþan biþe fastaiþ, ni wairþaiþ swaswe þai liutans gaurain, frawardyand auk andwairþya seina, eigasaiwhaindau mannam fastandans; amen qiþa izwis, þatei andnemun mizdon seina.
17. Iþ þu fastands, salbo haubiþ þein, yah ludya þeina þwah,
18. Ei ni gasaiwhaizau mannam fastands, ak attin þeinamma þamma in fulhsnya, yah atta þeins saei saiwhiþ in fulhsnya, usgibiþ þus.
19. Ni huzdyaiþ izwis huzda ana airþai, þarei malo yah nidwa frawardieþ, yah þarei þiubos ufgraband yah hlifand;
20. Iþ huzdyaiþ izwis huzda in himina, þarei nih malo nih nidwa frawardeiþ, yah þarei þiubos ni ufgraband, nih stiland.
21. þarei auk ist huzd izwar, þaruh ist yah hairto izwar.

9. Eornostlīce gebiddaþ ēow þus Fæder ūre þū þe eart on heofonum, sīe þīn nama gehālgod.
10. Tōcume þīn rīce. Gewurþe þīn willa on eorþan swā swā on heofonum.
11. Ūrne daeghwǣmlīcan hlāf syle ūs tōdæg.
12. And forgyf ūs ūre gyltas swā swā we forgyfaþ ūrum gyltendum.
13. And ne gelǣd þū ūs on costnunge ac ālȳs ūs of yfele.
14. Witodlīce gyf gē forgyfaþ mannum hyra synna, þonne forgyfþ ēower sē heofonlīca fæder ēow ēowre gyltas.
15. Gyf gē sōþlīce ne forgyfaþ mannum, ne ēower fæder ne forgyfþ ēow ēowre synna.
16. Sōþlīce þonne gē fæston, nellon gē wesan swylce lēase-licceteras, hīg fornymaþ hyra ansyna, þæt hīg æteowun mannum fæstende; sōþlīce ic secge ēow, þæt hīg onfēngon hyra mede.
17. Ðū sōþlīce þonne þū fæste, smȳra þīn heafod, and þweah þīne ansȳne,
18. Ðæt þū ne sȳ gesewen fram mannum fæstende, ac þīnum fæder þē ys on dȳglum, and þīn fæder þē gesyhþ on dȳglum, hyt āgylt þē.
19. Nellen gē gold-hordian ēow gold-hordas on eorþan, þær ōm and moþþe hit fornimþ, and þær þeofas hit delfaþ and forstelaþ;
20. Gold-hordiaþ ēow sōþlīce gold-hordas on heofenan, þær nador ōm ne moþþe hit ne fornimþ, and þær þeofas hit ne delfaþ, ne ne forstelaþ.
21. Wītodlīce þær þīn gold-hord is, þær is þīn heorte.

9. Forsothe thus ȝe shulen preyen, Oure fadir that art in heuenes, halwid be thi name;
10. Thy kyngdom cumme to; be thi wille don as in heuen and in erthe;
11. Ȝif to vs this day oure breed ouer other substaunce;
12. And forȝeue to vs oure dettis, as we forȝeue to oure dettours;
13. And leede vs nat in to temptacioun, but delyuere vs fro yuel. Amen.
14. Forsothe ȝif ȝee shulen forȝeuue to men her synnys, and ȝoure heuenly fadir shal forȝeue to ȝou ȝoure trespassis.
15. Sothely ȝif ȝee shulen forȝeue not to men, neither ȝoure fadir shal forȝeue to ȝou ȝoure synnes.
16. But when ȝee fasten, nyl ȝe be maad as ypocritis sorweful, for thei putten her facis out of kyndly termys, that their seme fastynge to men; trewly Y say to ȝou, thei han resseyued her meede.
17. But whan thou fastist, anoynte thin hede, and washe thi face,
18. That thou be nat seen fastynge to men, but to thi fadir that is in hidlis, and thi fadir seeth in hidlis, shal ȝeelde to thee.
19. Nyle ȝe tresoure to ȝou tresours in erthe, wher rust and mouȝthe distruyeth, and wher theeues deluen out and stelen;
20. But tresoure ȝee to ȝou tresouris in heuene, wher neither rust ne mouȝthe distruyeth, and wher theues deluen nat out, ne stelen.
21. Forsothe wher thi tresour is, there and thin herte is.

9. After thys maner there fore praye ye, O oure father which arte in heven, halowed be thy name;
10. Let thy kingdom come; thy wyll be fulfilled as well in erth as hit ys in heven;
11. Geve vs this daye oure dayly breade;
12. And forgeve vs oure treaspases, even as we forgeve them which trespas vs;
13. Leede vs not into temptacion, but delyvre vs ffrom yvell. Amen.
14. For and yff ye shall forgeve other men there trespases, youre father in heven shal also forgeve you.
15. But and ye wyll not forgeve men there trespases, no more shall youre father forgeve youre trespases.
16. Moreovre when ye faste, be not sad as the yporcrites are, for they disfigure there faces, that hit myght apere vnto men that they faste; verely Y say vnto you, they have there rewarde.
17. But thou when thou fastest, annoynte thyne heed, and washe thy face,
18. That it appere nott vnto men howe that thou fastest, but vnto thy father which is in secrete, and thy father which seith in secret, shall rewarde the openly.
19. Gaddre not treasure together on erth, where rust and mothes corrupte, and where theves breake through and steale;
20. But gaddre ye treasure togedder in heven, where nether rust nor mothes corrupte, and wher theves nether breake vp, nor yet steale.
21. For whearesoever youre treasure ys, ther are youre hertes also.

MONSIGNOR KNOX, 1944

This, then, is to be your prayer, Our Father, who art in heaven, hallowed be thy name; thy kingdom come; thy will be done, on earth as it is in heaven; give us this day our daily bread;[1] and forgive us our trespasses, as we forgive them that trespass against us; and lead us not into temptation, but deliver us from evil. Amen. Your heavenly Father will forgive you your transgressions, if you   *5* forgive your fellow-men theirs; if you do not forgive them, your heavenly Father will not forgive your transgressions either. (vv. 9–15)

Again, when you fast, do not shew it by gloomy looks, as the hypocrites do. They make their faces unsightly, so that men can see they are fasting; believe me, they have their reward already. But do thou, at thy times of fasting, anoint thy   *10* head and wash thy face, so that thy fast may not be known to men, but to thy Father who dwells in secret; and then thy Father, who sees what is done in secret, will reward thee. (vv. 16–18)

Do not lay up treasures for yourselves on earth, where there is moth and rust to consume it, where there are thieves to break in and steal it; lay up   *15* treasures for yourselves in heaven, where there is no moth or rust to consume it, no thieves to break in and steal. Where your treasure-house is, there your heart is too. (vv. 19–21)

The scripture quotations are in the translation of Monsignor Ronald Knox, copyright 1944, 1948, and 1950, Sheed & Ward, Inc., New York, with the kind permission of his Eminence the Cardinal Archbishop of Westminster.

[1]'Daily': the Latin here (but not in Lk. II. 3) coins the word *supersubstantialis*, which has sometimes been understood as a direct reference to the Holy Eucharist.

Modern English
REVISED STANDARD VERSION, 1952

9. Pray then like this:
   Our Father who art in heaven,
   Hallowed by thy name.
10. Thy kingdom come,
    Thy will be done,
        On Earth as it is in heaven.
11. Give us this day our daily bread;[1]
12. And forgive us our debts,
        As we also have forgiven our debtors;
13. And lead us not into temptation,
        But deliver us from evil.[2]
14. For if you forgive men their trespasses, your heavenly Father also will forgive you;
15. but if you do not forgive men their trespasses, neither will your Father forgive your trespasses.
16. And when you fast, do not look dismal, like the hypocrites, for they disfigure their faces that their fasting may be seen by men. Truly, I say to you, they have their reward.
17. But when you fast, anoint your head and wash your face,
18. that your fasting may not be seen by men but by your Father who is in secret; and your Father who sees in secret will reward you.
19. Do not lay up for yourselves treasures on earth, where moths and rust[3] consume and where thieves break in and steal,
20. but lay up for yourselves treasures in heaven, where neither moth nor rust[4] consumes and where thieves do not break in and steal.
21. For where your treasure is, there will your heart be also.

QUESTION

In Exercise 7, using a sample of Chaucer's prose to represent the English language of 1400, you prepared a paper evaluating prose writing. That exercise might now be regarded as a type of "mid-way" demonstration, where you brought together your

    [1]Or—our bread for the morrow
    [2]Or—the evil one. Other authorities, some ancient, add, in some form—For thine is the kingdom and the power and the glory, for ever. Amen.
    [3]Or—worm
    [4]Or—worm

observations about the changes in the language from its beginning to a point roughly half way through its development until now. Now you can pick up those earlier conclusions and complete your general survey of the history of English. These texts show how writers at different times, from earliest to contemporary, have dealt with the same material, have used the resources of their language—the English of their time—to prepare translations adequate for their age, sufficient to the needs of audiences of their generation. These texts are, in short, an actual display, in brief compass, of the history and development of the English language. They constitute a restricted, manageable body of material which may serve as the base for either written reports or class discussions to draw out, as you employ all the techniques you have learned, statements about the development of your language.